ECONOMIC GOVERNANCE IN THE
AGE OF GLOBALIZATION

ECONOMIC GOVERNANCE IN THE AGE OF

Globalization

WILLIAM K. TABB

Columbia University Press   New York

Columbia University Press

Publishers Since 1893

New York, Chichester, West Sussex

Copyright © 2004 Columbia University Press

All rights Reserved

Library of Congress Cataloging-in-Publication Data

Tabb, William K.

Economic governance in the age of globalization /
William K. Tabb.

p. cm.

Includes bibliographical references and index.

ISBN 0–231–13154–2 (cloth)

ISBN 0–231–13155–0 (pbk.)

1. International economic relations.

2. Globalization—Economic aspects.

3. Globalization—Political aspects.

4. Globalization—Moral and ethical aspects.

I. Title.

HF1359.T3322   2004

337—dc22   2003067479

References to Internet Web Sites (URLs) were
accurate at the time of writing. Neither the author
nor Columbia University Press is responsible for
Web sites that may have expired or changed since
the articles were prepared

Columbia University Press books are printed on
permanent and durable acid-free paper

Printed in the United States of America

Designed by Audrey Smith

c 10 9 8 7 6 5 4 3 2 1

p 10 9 8 7 6 5 4 3 2 1

CONTENTS

Chapter One
Introduction
I

Chapter Two
The Verb and the Noun
15

Chapter Three
Debating Globalization
39

Chapter Four
The Nature and Scope of International Political Economy
69

Chapter Five
The Postwar Economic Order and Global State
Economic Governance Institutions
102

Chapter Six
Clubs, Soft Law and International Financial Institutions
141

Chapter Seven
The Bretton Woods Institutions in Operation
184

Chapter Eight
Finance: Orthodox and Heterodox
220

Chapter Nine
Transnational Corporations and Trade Theory
259

Chapter Ten
From International Trade Organization to
World Trade Organization
289

Chapter Eleven
Market Efficiency Versus Labor Rights and
Environmental Protection
331

Chapter Twelve
Redecorating and New Architecture
373

Chapter Thirteen
The Evolving Political Economy
417

References
431

Index
489

ECONOMIC GOVERNANCE IN THE
AGE OF GLOBALIZATION

CHAPTER ONE

Introduction

"Four years ago, journalist Richard Swift arrived in the fields of western Ghana, where cheap cocoa is harvested to be shipped to Switzerland. The journalist carried some chocolate bars in his backpack. The native harvesters had never tasted chocolate before. They loved it."
—*Eduardo Galeano* (2003)

"Without social equity, economic growth cannot be sustained. Without enlarging the real opportunities available to all citizens, the markets will work only for the elites. This means providing everyone with access to education, health care, decent work, and—as the new Brazilian president Lula has pointed out—with at least three meals a day.
—*James D. Wolfensohn* (2003)

A reading of globalization at the start of the twenty-first century needs to reconsider such concepts as stateness, sovereignty, governance, efficiency, and social justice. I undertake this task here within a framework combining elements of critical theory drawn from mainline political economy, Gramscian and materialist understandings of the international political economy (throughout ipe will be used for the international political economy which is "out there" and IPE to denote the academic study of the ipe) drawing on classical institutionalism and other strands of heterodox political economy. It is about the disjuncture between understandings of the world political economy among elites, social movements of global civil society, mainstream social scientists, and critical realists. The project is motivated by concerns for improved income distribution, an inclusive pattern of sustainable development, good governance, financial stability, fair treatment of less powerful countries currently discriminated against by the most powerful ones, labor and democratic rights, appropriate reform and regulation of the global financial system, increased and properly targeted foreign aid and debt relief, and a host of other goals which are widely shared.

I examine conflicting approaches to economic and financial rule making and enforcement mechanisms and at the key actors: transnational corporations, nongovernmental organizations (NGOs), and global state economic governance institutions. I also look at the literatures which have been produced in recent years concerning what we know and think we know about these issues. Where there is disagreement, I examine why they occur and persist. Throughout this undertaking we need to bear in mind that the pre-analytic vision with which IPE theorists approach their work matters. So too does the sympathy each has for the project of the hegemonic power of the post World War II era, and so the generosity or suspicion with which they approach the U.S. agenda, and the way they valiance negotiator's rhetoric and intentions. Everyone pretty much agrees that the United States as the global hegemon exerts preponderant influence over the structuring of the accepted rules and expectations other governments bring to any conversation. The question is what are the consequences of American intentions, especially in the post-September 11 world.

What is unquestioned is American dominance. This supremacy is not only military (although it is also true that by 2004 the United States was spending amost as much on defense as the rest of the world put together and doing so at a cost of only four percent of its gross domestic product, a low figure compared to America's post-World War II spending. The U.S. economy is larger than the next three members of the G-8—Japan, Germany, and Great Britain—put together). With a mere five percent of the world's population the United States accounts for 43 percent of the world's total production and half of global research and development. Because of its importance to everyone else what the United States does and what its leaders say is parsed carefully, continuously, perhaps obsessively. This reality of the United States as the 800 pound gorilla of the ipe is not central at all to a U.S.-centric IPE. U.S.-based students of globalization inevitably "see" through the lens of national identity and loyalty. Those observing events from other locations often see matters differently. They typically do not lean to appreciation of reasonableness of hegemonic policies, nor to an automatic assumption of essentially benign intentions of U.S. policymakers. What in America is seen as leadership can appear as domination or imperialism to others (who may also be overly generous in attributing their own problems to the actions of the United States).

My own view is that the United States exerts its power not all that differently than many other governments would if they were in a hegemonic position. Indeed, in many ways Americans have been more generous and responsible than any number of other governments might be if the distribution of power were rearranged in their favor to the same extent. This, however, is hardly to offer anything approaching blanket endorsement of American policies and the demands it has made on others and in its design of global state economic governance institutions. Nor, on another level, is it to accept an autonomy of the state, any state, from the sources of power emanating from the political economy. The strength of the economy and the resources at the disposal of those who control these resources influence state action in two profoundly important ways. Structurally states depend on economic actors to provide tax revenues, to contribute to the growth and stability the society enjoys, employment, and the production of goods and services. Governments must be supportive in return of those so important to the well being of the state. Instrumentally it is the case that the leadership of the state and its key technocratic policymakers is drawn from and overlaps with those who hold power and exercise managerial control in the economic sphere. There are differences within this class based on sectoral and regional locations and ideological dispositions of various kinds which may be determining. The connection between economic and political elites tends to be a close one.

Economic growth is co-constituted by the political and especially the regulatory framing of markets. The social embeddedness of rules and norms guides and constrains economic possibilities in ways theories based on pure exchange in free markets ignore. Such negotiation is never innocent of power. Contestation among politically well connected corporate interests in the richer economies, their governments, the governments of the poorer countries, NGOs, and the social justice movements of global civil society has many fronts and multiple agendas. The ideologically hegemonic position has been the neoliberal agenda (widely called the Washington Consensus). It calls for trade and financial liberalization, privatization, deregulation, openness to foreign direct investment, a competitive exchange rate, fiscal discipline, lower taxes, and smaller government (Williamson, 1990).

Neoliberalism is widely understood by even many mainstream economists and policy wonks to have failed in terms of its announced goals. It has not brought more rapid economic growth, reduced poverty, or made economies more stable. In fact over the years of neoliberal hegemony growth has slowed, poverty has increased, and economic and financial crises have plagued most countries of the world economy. The data on all of this are overwhelming. Neoliberalism has, however, succeeded as the project of the most internationalized fractions of capital. In its unannounced goal it has increased the dominance of transnational corporations, international financiers, and sectors of local elites. The admission that neoliberalism has failed in terms of its announced goals led to an Augmented Washington Consensus (Rodrik, 2002) which blames client states and not the global state economic governance institutions or transnational capital for these failures. If the countries involved can be convinced to "take ownership" the program can work, it is said. To the original Washington Consensus policymakers add "prudent" capital account opening in deference to the failures financial market liberalization produced on such a large scale in the past. It is to be up to the local governments to do a better job of carrying out the program. Central banks are told they must put in place a "proper" regulatory framework, financial standards, and enforcement capabilities. There is recognition that corporate governance matters. There need to be anti-corruption rules, even social safety nets and targeted poverty reduction strategies, as part of the conditionalities imposed by the overseers. These obvious steps were absent for the last decades during which lower income countries forced to remove the protections they had so imperfectly tried to build against foreign control and spreading instability from the fluctuations in the global economy. The corruption they point to has long been recognized as the way things work. Banks continue to arrange crony loans, currency speculation, and capital flight but the problem of such excesses now threatens faith in the system itself, and not just in the poorer countries. Enron, Worldcom, and the collusion and participation of accountants, lawyers, Wall Street analysts and investment banks, as well as high government officials in the United States, Japan, and throughout Europe are now better understood (Baker, 2002).

Global state economic governance institutions (hereafter GSEGIs, an admittedly awkward acronym) , like governments and state agencies at the national and local levels, are used to channel resources through constraining and enabling regulations. GSEGIs such as the International Monetary Fund (IMF) and the World Trade Organization (WTO), and their operations raise questions for economists and theorists of democratic governance concerning what is meant or should be meant by not only efficiency on a world scale, but also global equity and the relation of both to growth and development. Discussed publicly in idealist terms, they are too often manipulated for economic gain by interests capable of influencing their decisions in the same way that other organs of governments or agencies of governance are so utilized. The question of who can influence their policies and activities, who chooses their leaders and key staff people, are political questions with economic impact. In debate over rights—property rights, human rights, labor rights, the rights of investors and so on—which rights are acknowledged and secured reflect power relations in political processes.

Among the most important governance institutions are the Bretton

Woods institutions (BWIs), the IMF and the World Bank Group. The WTO and its predecessor the General Agreement on Tariffs and Trade (GATT), which for half a century filled in for the aborted International Trade Organization (ITO) is the third leg of the postwar finance and trade regimes proposed in the Bretton Woods era. There are many other GSEGIs. Some of these are associated with finance and related issues such as the Bank for International Settlements (BIS). But it is these three, the two BWIs, the Fund and the Bank, and the WTO which are of dominant importance. In the absence of world government, elements of stateness adhere to such global governance institutions. We describe them as global state economic governance institutions to convey that they are the organized form of a nascent international state which will not necessarily look like, or operate like, nation states were presumed to do under the Westphalian order (to be discussed in the next chapter). GSEGIs take on qualities of stateness overriding to some extent the sovereignty of national economies presumed even in the closing decades of the twentieth century.

GSEGIs are instrumentalities of an evolving global governance system and are projections of power by the strongest states, most especially the United States. To the extent that these countries have shaped multilateral trade, investment, and finance, negotiations of the agenda have reflected not so much an unproblematic national interests but favor their most internationalized corporations and financiers, the most dominant sectors of contemporary world capitalism. The GSEGIs are called upon to provide international collective goods which market participants are unable to provide as well, or at all, for themselves. Those forces which are most active in constructing GSEGIs have been highly selective. They choose areas which substantially impact their interests and avoid consideration of the connection of these economic and financial regimes with policy concerns for which they prefer responsibility not be taken. While realists are not surprised that GSEGIs reinforce the hegemonic practices, liberal institutionalists and constructivists stress their capacity to expand the policy arena to include concerns for market access, more aid demanded by developing economies, and such issues as the environment, and labor rights—concerns which have been central to social mobilization and mass protest. If we understand the state in terms of governance rather than simply government, we can accept both the emergence of GSEGIs as powerful norm setting frameworks and see their task as supplementing and in some areas superseding governments. They provide an alternative mechanism for rule making and consensus formation by using a soft law approach rather than the formal treaty making of classic diplomacy (as will be discussed in chapter 6).

Our focus is in areas of trade, finance, and investment regime formation, which international relations (hereafter IR) scholars have considered "low" politics as opposed to the "high" politics of war and peace; although, in the present era, such a conceptual separation may be less useful than in the past as U.S. military dominance finds new purpose. Indeed, the tradition of IR scholarship which maintains a firm distinction between the two is brought into question by International Political Economy which theorizes international politics and international economic issues within a single optic. The IPE framing allows an escape from state-centric mental maps of the world and the domination of the strict dichotomous public-private distinction. Such a frame allows the theorization of powerful supra-national actors from transnational corporations to the bond market, as well as international governance institutions and NGOs. It promises an appreciation of the importance of nonstate actors and of deterritorialized communities and economically connected spaces whose boundaries do not coincide with national jurisdictions. As GSEGIs gain greater purchase on everyday life they impact understandings of citizenship and nationalism in a host of important ways beyond the scope of this study (but see Hall, 1999; Rosenau, 1997).

As to governance, Robert Cox is not alone in seeing the particular form globalization is taking as the product of a conscious political project with its ideological justifications, including the claim of inevitability for a project knowingly undertaken by these actors. To him the term global governance

> suggests control and orientation in the absence of formally legitimated coercive power. There is something that could be called a nascent global historic bloc consisting of the most powerful corporate and economic forces, their allies in government, and the variety of networks that evolve policy guidelines and propagate the ideology of globalization. States now by and large play the role of agencies of the global economy, with the task of adjusting national economic policies and practices to the perceived exigencies of global economic liberalism.   (Cox, 1999: 12)

The success of these policies has been widely questioned. For example, the IMF accepts in the findings of a technical report co-authored by its U.S.-appointed chief economist Kenneth Rogoff, that "The empirical evidence has not established a definitive proof that financial integration has enhanced growth for developing countries. Furthermore, it may be associated with higher consumption volatility," (Prasad, et al., 2003: 58).

As Jagdish Bhagwati and Daniel Tarullo (2003: 13) wrote at that key moment, the free flow of capital "can bring panic and crashing markets and currencies, particularly in developing countries." This recognition, widely shared as shall be shown, that liberalization could put poor countries at greater risk of crisis, has not at all stopped the United States from continuing to insist on just such policies. In 2003 the United States demanded over the opposition of Chile and Singapore that in new trade agreements between those countries and the U.S. there be the inclusion of restrictions on the use of capital controls. The evidence rehearsed in later chapters supports the benefits such controls can bring for developing countries whose currency is exposed to wide destabilizing swings. It is expected that the Bush Administration plans to use these agreements as prototypes for future negotiations. It may persist despite the evidence of the harm such an insistence can cause because it sees such freedom from controls as in the interest of U.S. financial institutions and the dollar. "American unilateralism has become a pressing global concern even when the White House purports to act in pursuit of universal values," Bhagwati and Tarullo write, "So the use of US muscle to advance the administration's narrow, ideologically driven aims is hardly in the interests of America, let alone the rest of the world." It is an instance of a troubling unilateralism which is evident in the role the U.S. plays in the GSEGIs.

None of this should be terribly surprising. A hegemonic power often takes advantage of its strength to get what it wants and dresses its own interests as the general interest. Sometimes they even are. But the war on terrorism framed all issues for the Bush Administration in a single optic. Supachai Panitchpakdi, the head of the WTO, expressed a similar concern, although more diplomatically. Worried that the Bush Administration's go-it-alone approach was threatening international trade, respect for international rules, and would lead to serious economic consequences with devastating practical impact in a world in which trade was contracting for the first time in twenty years, oil prices were worrisome, and even the cost of property insurance rose dramatically as U.S. invasion of Iraq approached, he said: "I can feel a sense of trepidation. Whatever happens, if the U.S. will maintain the way we use multilateral solutions, it will be highly appreciated" (Becker, 2003: A8). Similar worries were expressed that the world had turned some kind of corner. War making policy impacted profoundly on attitude toward economic negotiations. As the U.S. Trade Representative Robert Zoellick said, "The long-term war against terrorism has to include trade, openness and development." "Trade is more than about economic efficiency. It's about America's role in the world." (Becker and

Andrews, 2003: C1) A widespread perception outside of America was that by putting these issues into the unilateralist context of the U.S. war on terrorism Zoellick sought negotiating leverage by instilling fear.

It is obvious, when one considers the establishment of international economic and financial governance regimes since the Second World War, that coming out of that great conflict the dominance by the United States had unrivaled mastery over how the postwar economy was to be structured and how the then new international institutions like the World Bank and the United Nations were to work. The way America managed its place in the world then and through the years of the Cold War is widely accepted to have been to project as the guiding principle of its democracy the elevation of law over arbitrary power onto the world stage. To Philip Stephens (2003: 15) "The deal Washington made with its allies was an honest one. They acknowledged US leadership. In return they got a say in writing the rules. The system thus legitimated US power." This bargain, he added writing in the winter of 2003, "is disintegrating as George W. Bush prepares for war against Iraq." The audacity of the Bush Doctrine, signally different than the pragmatic realism of his father and the Bush II White House, as well as to the liberal institutionalism of the Clinton Administration is not our topic. The impact a determined unilateralist approach by American policymakers would have on the issues with which we are concerned, international economic and financial regimes, is important however. Before the Bush II approach was tested, the world understood the choice of the United States to operate in a multilateral framework was a self-imposed restraint, one which was in the hegemon's interest as well as that of most of the rest of the world. Opinion differs on whether the American preference for a rule of law (which to some extent surely bound it to regime rules that in specific instances could go against its own short-term interests) was the result of an American commitment to democratic ideals, a calculation that such a system allowed it to get what it wanted at lower cost by leaving others their dignity, or whether Cold War rivalry pushed it to be concerned with the hearts and minds of others more than it might otherwise have been. The dominant IPE view is that U.S. proposals are constructive, and yes, what is good for America is good for the world.

The postwar order, based on recognition of U.S. power allowed for true negotiation and sometimes significant concessions by Washington— often to better preserve the alliance under U.S. leadership. Yet the failure of most poor countries to increase their rate of growth or make a serious dent into the numbers living in poverty has brought the agenda of U.S. led institutions such as the IMF and the WTO into question. The desperate need poor countries have for foreign aid and access to the markets of rich countries adds to the imbalance of the negotiating process. On the other hand, as these countries recognize that the noble sentiments expressed in preambles to international agreements are not matched by specific measures which might actually help them, asymmetric bargaining power and forced compliance breed resentments. The perception of unfairness promotes mobilization of support from movements of global civil society and is inherent to the critique of global governance prominent among heterodox thinkers.

Mainstream economists tend to be optimistic about the gains from an open trading system, the prospects of reform, and so the benefits of the Augmented Washington Consensus. They stress the harm done by rent seeking state bureaucrats and politicians who extort bribes, governments which free ride by not contributing to the upkeep of international collective goods, do not obey the rules of international regimes, and whose protectionist and opportunist policies decrease global well being. Liberal institutionalists among IR theorists (as will be discussed in chapter 4) contemplate the extent to which the anarchy of the world system can be addressed and overcome through interstate cooperation to create a peaceful and prosperous international political economy. Despite the turn after September 11 toward a national security orientation, mainstream globalization discussion reflects, and is reflected in, American policymakers' emphasis on their country's essentially benign intentions, the benefits of cooperation among nations, and a certain careless backgrounding of just why it is America has the right to organize and dominate such proceedings. The easily worn ethnocentrism which has gone and goes largely unexamined among most scholars in the U.S., if not everywhere globalization's impacts are felt, comes under question and this has not changed in the post-September 11 period. Despite the initial outpouring of support for the United States from around the world in the wake of the terrorist attacks of September 11, 2001, on the World Trade Center and the Pentagon, discontent over many aspects of U.S. responses to those events has since then grown in all types of nations, among long-time NATO allies, in developing countries, and most dramatically in Muslim societies as the Pew Global Attitude surveys, which have interviewed tens of thousands of people in dozens of countries, since that tragic day have shown. These surveys, perhaps the most complete and representative of such studies, demonstrate that people around the world both embrace things American and at the same time decry many U.S. government policies and what appears to be bullying behavior by the planetary hyperpower.

Still, at the dawn of the twenty-first century the United States economy was the unchallenged global hegemon, although an undertone of doubt could be heard as the longest expansion in U.S. history came to an end with the collapse of the technology boom in 1999 followed by years of decline in the stock market, unfolding broad corporate corruption scandals, loss of faith in the basic accounting on which profits were reported. Still, the American government dominated global politics as only an only superpower can. U.S.-based transnationals were the most successful competitors. Not surprisingly American academics were the dominant interpreters of these developments. Criticism of U.S. regency came from some other advanced economies and newly industrializing ones that saw themselves as competitors being treated unfairly by the one remaining global superpower, from governments of the poorer countries who believed they were trapped, coerced into accepting policies which favor foreign investors yet did not bring the sort of economic growth they had been promised, and from people everywhere who believed they were victims or those whom they viewed as victims rather than beneficiaries of existing globalization patterns. Aspects of competitive jealousies born of unequal influence on the rules of the game, fear of continued marginalization, and anger at perceived injustices all combined to produce complaints, especially given the Bush Administration's preemptive war doctrine and its demand that nations were either "with us or with the terrorists" despite the perceived penalties of opposing U.S. policies in the economic sphere had come to be linked issues of loyalty in the security sphere. The Bush Administration's unilateralism and focus on the projection of military force raised the question of whether the bipartisan strategies of multilateralism through which the country's leaders had long framed hegemonic leadership had come to an end and been replaced by a new more muscular stance toward the world.

The task of scholars is to step back from the givens to evaluate, assess, and consider better alternatives. This involves evaluation of options pertaining to emergent forms of international law and global governance. As in all such projects there are clashing interests and values. Outcome will, as always, be historically contingent yet can appear in retrospect as inevitable, natural, and reasonable. The particular institutional forms which are brought into being at the global level provide a model of governance claiming legitimacy, be accorded constitutionality, and its aspects of stateness accepted as logical and justified. These institutions will function as rule making and enforcement bodies. This is not to say that GSEGIs in their official evaluations and judgments are not on important occasions critical of their most powerful members (as the IMF was of the Bush II outsized deficits for example or the decisions by WTO panels which went repeatedly against the U.S. on its export subsidies). Indeed the GSEGIs, despite being creatures of the most powerful states, represent the interests of capital as against the system-weakening actions of particular corporate and government interests. At the same time, often the establishment of particular regulatory frameworks and agreements can be traced to particular concept entrepreneurs such as Edmund Pratt, CEO of Pfizer who in the 1980s influentially argued for linking an expanded conception of intellectual property with trade negotiations, chaired key industry and trade association committees, and was a close adviser to government TRIPs (the Agreement on Trade Related Aspects of Intellectual Property Rights) negotiators.

Organizationally the Coalition of Service Industries was formed in 1982 to ensure that U.S. trade in services, which had never been considered as part of trade negotiations, became a central goal for future liberalization. The CSI played a major role in shaping the WTO's General Agreement on Trade in Services (GATS) and was a forceful advocate of other agreements on telecommunications and financial services which will be discussed in subsequent chapters, advising the U.S. government agencies and lobbying Congress. Such private-public interactions are central and ongoing in the construction and modification of economic and financial regimes.

Problems at the level of theory result in part from the separation of the disciplines which study globalization phenomena. It is not simply that economists tend to leave politics out and political scientists generally prefer to consign economics to the economists—after all there are gains from specialization and the division of intellectual labors—but that when such contributions are not integrated the totality can get lost along with the critical moment in the analysis of what is a too limited appreciation of what might be. Subdisciplines and cross disciplinary studies try to overcome these problems but they too carry baggage. Within political science, IPE devolves from IR and bearing the legacy of its birth can be overtly state centric, focusing on diplomatic strategy games, and can give inadequate attention to the agency of transnational capital and to the constraints economic forces impose on statesmen.

CONTENT AND PRESENTATION

This book proceeds on two parallel tracks. The first presents an anatomy of IPE which develops an understanding of the functioning and evolution of global state economic governance institutions concentrating on the period since the closing days of World War II and examining their future prospects. This first track develops the conceptual frame of concentric club formation and the processes through which the most internationalized sectors of capital guide this process and clash with both nationalist interests of various kinds and the social justice movements of an emergent global civil society. The second track considers the critique of hegemonic power associated with unequal exchange, ideological domination, and corporate globalization which suggests the costs associated with the present pattern of globalization are undesirable and unsustainable. Chapter 2 considers the dual meaning of "rules" as both verb and noun and the significance of ways of looking at the problematic revealed in this fashion. To say that "globalization rules," that it is inevitable and driven by unstoppable forces (rule as the verb) clashes with the notion that there must be rules for globalization (rule as the noun), that like any social phenomena conscious human intervention can make an important difference in shaping our common future.

Chapter 3 explores a variety of conceptions of globalization and how they impact understandings of basic constructs such as sovereignty and regime. The fourth chapter reviews the IPE field and the tensions between two very different understandings of economics and political economy which underpins the distinctive approaches to IPE. The postwar economic order, as chapter 5 investigates, is built on a compromise between a perceived need for social control of capital movements and of other market forces which the experience of the Great Depression had convinced most policymakers was essential, and the desire of the strongest economic power, the United States, for a liberalized international regime of free movement of capital and goods. Chapter 6 lays out the evolution of the legal personality of GSEGIs and demonstrates the transformation from a primarily diplomatic model for negotiation by international economic and financial institutions to a legal regime imposing limitations based on economic criteria through a process of the development of soft law and then the formalization of regimes in a process of concentric club formation. Later chapters examine changes in the ipe, the GSEGI responses, and criticisms of institutions from both free market libertarian right and social movement perspectives.

Chapter 7 tells the story for the financial regime with a focus on the Bretton Woods institutions, the international Monetary Fund, and the World Bank, and considers criticism of these GSEGIs. Chapter 8 discusses the character and meaning of financial crises from a Keynes-Minsky perspective. It may seem unobjectionable, even obvious to say that uncontrolled financial markets can, and do, produce crises. Yet many mainstream economists widely believe there is are self-equilibrating mechanisms at play and that financial crises are made worse for government interference and that real business cycles reflect necessary and unavoidable natural adjustment processes. (The post World War II economic order reflected, as chapter 5 demonstrates, a very different balance of understandings of the relation of state to market.) The efficiency assumption at the heart of the classical model of international trade, chapter 9 suggests, needs to be subject to a more political analysis and challenged from other traditions of political economy. The institutional development of the trade regime is the subject of chapter 10, which considers the aborted International Trade Organization, the General Agreement on Tariffs and Trade which substituted for it, and its successor, the World Trade Organization, drawing together considerations coming from economics and legal theory as well as IPE analytical concepts to understand how a global trade regime has evolved over the last half century or so. Chapter 11 continues this discussion with emphasis on the trade and issues of labor rights and environmental protection. Chapter 12 discusses the calls in the late 1990s for a new financial architecture with consideration of matters of debt forgiveness and proposals ranging from a multilateral agreement on investment to development oriented strategies aimed at a more inclusive growth model for the global political economy in the early twenty-first century. The final chapter looks at a murky present and an unknowable future suggesting some of the structural weaknesses found in earlier chapters in the developing countries may be present in the United States political economy and that should such fragility persist there may be consequences not only for the U.S. but the world economy as well. These last chapters and indeed much of the book raise the issue that as technology allows greater freedom from local regulation the basic question arises whether nations need to move to greater deregulation or collectively agree on a common type and global level of (re)regulation. They reinforce key themes of this book—that the United States for better and worse is the principal architect of global governance regimes and that the interests of transnational capital and international finance guide the terms under which GSEGIs are constructed, modified, over time and used to define and enforce property rights.

In the past the United States has generally sought to exercise leadership in ways which both forwarded U.S. interests and, at the same time, by favoring multinational negotiations, privileged a more inclusive style, even as it structured decisionmaking to slant the playing field in a manner conducive to outcomes this country favored. As a result of such behavior, from the end of World War II, when many students of U.S. foreign policy—most especially those located in the United States—considered the U.S. role as the world's hegemon it was, and remains typically, in the context of how America generously, even selflessly, provides international public goods helping the system function more smoothly. There tends to be neglect, again especially among U.S.-based scholars, of why others might find grounds to object to U.S. designs. The debate, over the cost the United States assumes in doing the right thing for the rest of the world, is whether the U.S. can afford to continue to be so generous and the possible limits of such largesse. While considerations of self-interest and differentials in power are not absent from the discourse (realists are more cynical, or perhaps realistic, about cooperation with the world's one superpower which is in a far stronger position than others to shape a new international order), the emphasis among liberal institutionalists and constructivists is on mutual gain to be achieved through cooperation among sovereign governments and free trade in a more competitive globalized economy, on new and better designs coming out of conversations about how best to govern the international political economy. In this they do not so much deny U.S. hegemonic power as they lobby U.S. decisionmakers to take the broader view which these theorists argue is ultimately in the best interests of not only the world community but the U.S. as well.

The next chapter examines meanings of globalization in preparation of examining theorization of the ipe and then applying them to consider the GSEGIs and the IPE fault line which separates those who see the forces of technology and the market as natural forces driving globalization, and those who see globalization as socially constructed and would impose rules to guide and constrain its trajectory.

CHAPTER TWO

The Verb and the Noun

"Any doubt I might have had about the globalization of economic thinking was shattered when I met with Chinese Premier Zhu Rhongi in early 1997 in the same pavilion where Chairman Mao had received foreign visitors. After being offered a Diet Coke I was asked a variety of searching questions about the possible use of put options in defending a currency, and how they might be structured."

—*Lawrence H. Summers* (1999: 4)

"'Miracle economies' one month turn into incompetent bastions of 'crony capitalism' the next, and the commentators don't skip a beat"

—*Lance Taylor* (2001: 255)

To many IPE scholars as well as policymakers and political pundits "globalization rules." It is the technological imperative of our time. It demands an open global economy and an end to statist interference on pain of slowing growth and depriving the world of its fullest benefits. Politics in this view should not be allowed to "interfere." Intervention would slow the process of transformation. It might avoid some pain in the short run but encourages resistance by interest groups attempting to protect their status quo privileges and so allocates resources inefficiently, allowing appropriation through rent seeking in distributional aspects of state functioning. For the general good, it is said, far better to get out of the way and let the forces of globalization rule. Such an approach ignores that globalization is a political project of the most internationalized sectors of capital and not surprisingly is guided by their perception of self-interest and so its coercion of state policies can itself be seen as a form of rent seeking.

It is unremarkable that the media and political leaders tend to present the interests of elites as the general interest. They typically do this in every society. This does not mean that in any particular case the interests of elites and the masses do not coincide, but objective social scientists would do well to be cautious about too easy an acceptance of conventional wisdom.

It may be that it is the weakest and most vulnerable who gain "the most," as is so often asserted, but again some skepticism may be in order. Those who have little or no protection against the destructiveness that accompanies rapid changes in the international political economy in a social order which has incentive to compensate losers or to internalize social and environmental costs in private calculations are unlikely to be among the most powerful voices in the marketplace. A democratic polity might want to consider non-market rights as part of any new international regime through a more comprehensive set of globalization rules. The noun formulation invites questions of what kind of rules and who shall make them. Thus the conflict between verb and noun. The global justice movements (Tabb,2002) denies the desirability and the inevitability of the verb form which privileges the freedom of market forces implied in the slogan "Globalization Rules." Instead it proposes rules for globalization. Because of the power imbalances in inter-state negotiations and the penalties and incentives at the disposal of the hegemonic power it is often the non governmental organizations and movements of global civil society which are more effective in challenging the regimes being put in place. Political scientists with their state-centric focus often miss the significance of these actors even as many constructivists both within the academy and on the streets who propose new rules and potentially governing norms did not in pre-September 11 days perhaps give adequate attention to violence capacities in the modern world political economy.

However while there are surely important and intense negotiations which go on with regard to such issues as tariffs on steel or agriculture or what type of investments will receive national treatment, these are struggles over what is to be allowed within the established rules. The more radical issue raised in massive demonstrations and in the advocacy research of NGOs is: what sort of rules are appropriate in the world political economy in an era of globalization? From this perspective it is not a matter of resisting globalization, of being anti-globalization, but rather of what type of globalization we shall have. Will the rules be those preferred by those who say there is no choice, that "globalization rules," or will the concerns of the global justice movement contribute to and perhaps guide the terms of rule making for globalization in the twenty-first century? Terrorism and war on terrorism not withstanding these questions remain central.

The verb and the noun do not belong to completely different discourses. Even those who prefer the verb form and think that "globalization rules" advocate some rules. They suggest protection of property and so must be involved in defining the limits of particular property rights, the border separating ownership of intellectual property monopolies and the division of social knowledge from the public's claims to reasonably priced goods and services. Generally they favor rules which speed and smooth the path of globalization, although it is not always clear which these are in particular cases. In doing so they frequently reveal an analytic internal contradiction. On the one hand the "globalization rules" (verb) perspective declares that we are witnessing the unrelenting unfolding of a technology driven new globalized economy which is bringing benefits that suggest an unstoppable and propitious new industrial or postindustrial revolution. However even though inevitable and beneficial, government must play a key role. The government, while it just needs to get out of the way, needs to do so by becoming active in deregulating, privatizing, and downsizing the social functions of government as part of a broad activist neoliberal agenda. Technology inexorably drives globalization yet the wrong politics can stop or at least seriously impede its progress. And because, although this part is reluctantly offered, there are losers in the process and these losers, potential losers, and those perceived as victims, seem so large in number, governments must as quickly and as completely as possible cede power to the market so that it will not be possible for a democracy to later reject or reverse this coerced globalization. This process of negotiating regime construction is often presented as nonantagonistic, more concerned with technical matters best left to experts to negotiate. It is however a highly political process and reflects the deep contradictions of the global order which are decentered in mainstream Anglo-American IPE. It is important, if our task is to analyze what is actually occurring, to take such status quo bias more centrally into account.

While the context of U.S. unipolar power is historically specific to the contemporary conjuncture, how actors, governments, NGOs and corporations, are affected by flows of money, goods, people, and messages across international boundaries, and what they choose to do about it, are always the core issues of International Political Economy. These are the concerns today as they were a century and two centuries ago even if the forms they take seem new. Globalization as a continuing process raises questions about the way economists treat "international" trade and the way political scientists, especially International Relations scholars, theorize the state and sovereignty today as the world seems to be becoming a smaller place at a faster rate. It opens new discourses on ipe continuities, cultural penetration, and the connections among civil society, the state, transnational capital, and democratic possibilities because of the ways territorial and cultural distance is more easily overcome. The international arena which is its theater is fraught with a tension between the principle of sovereignty and the principle of openness. This core problematic of IPE is in a fundamental sense a meditation on the two concepts: globalization and sovereignty. The complexities of each theoretical construct, evolving definitions of what they mean, and how it is best to deploy understandings of globalization and sovereignty, differ. The competing frames set the terms for much discussion of IPE and for concrete investigation of the ipe.

THE CASUAL HEGEMON

Consider the first quotation which announces this chapter. It may be read as containing an implicit message to non-economists to the effect that it is technical proficiency in arcane, yet practical economics which will save the world, or that the design of market wise competence is what counts in an era of global integration. Summers' story can also be read as a comment on the tendency of economists to reduce uncertainty to risk. Put options are a method of buying one's way out of risk for a price in the hope of doing away with the consequences of uncertainty (a lack of knowledge of what will be) by transforming it into risk (a mathematically weighted distribution of all relevant possible outcomes which can be priced). It is confidence that uncertainty can be reduced to risk which has produced many a nasty surprise. (Of course a cultural studies reading might see the passage as an instance of a product placement, the kind of subtly crafted almost subliminal advertising which goes unnoticed in its obvious ubiquity. The central image is not the leader of the next superpower, of the technocratic mandarin, or an amulet of the high risk society, but something beyond these lesser tokens of power, the can of Coke.) Globalization invites multiple readings.

There is no doubt that economics has contributed a great deal to the discussion, and has increasingly influenced the way others, particularly political scientists, theorize the international political economy. Yet serious problems have been created by the wide acceptance of mainstream economic thinking. Economists tend to think of politics as interference with markets by those seeking unearned advantage. While Summers has been around Washington and world capitals long enough to know that "politics matters," one suspects that he wished it didn't, and that technically optimal, most efficient policies could be crafted by competent economists without interference from the economic illiterate. The view (the hope?) is perhaps that Mao's successors have accepted the system, embrace it, and strive to learn it more effectively. More complexly Chinese market-Leninism may be straining to adopt whatever works in the pursuit of nationalist power and that rather than simply becoming part of the Western system is seeking tools to challenge its dominance.

Lance Taylor's comment, which serves as a second epigraph to this chapter, captures another aspect of this self-centered outlook on the world political economy. When the East Asian economies were growing dramatically it was said it was because they were open to the global economy and their success showed that all countries could prosper if they followed sound market principles and were outwardly oriented. When there is failure it is the fault of the bad practices of the countries involved and never of the larger regime rules of the world system. Booms and busts are explained in terms of market distortions, excessive fiscal expansion, or too cozy a relationship between corrupt politicians and their cronies rather than the lack of effective regulation of financial markets or awareness that premeditated laxity on the part of these governments was pushed on countries by what some see as the market fundamentalism of the International Monetary Fund and the United States. In this view, which I share, the structures of free markets in finance had produced strong incentives for destabilizing financial behavior. The thought that there are technical fixes, financial innovations which can finally control risk, and that any failures result from a lack of transparency, or an unwillingness to allow markets to work their magic, is in this view part of the ideology of globalism of our time. I shall argue that transparency alone doesn't solve financial sector problems because interpretation of information is subjective and markets over react. Unless speculation is brought under social control it can wreck economies, as it has at intervals since the dawn of capitalism, and as it has done with increased frequency since the model of global neoliberalism became dominant in the last decades of the twentieth century. It has been the case that with each crisis, that of Latin America from the early 1980s, East Asia in the late 1990s, and in the other instances which will be discussed, the financial sector of the U.S. economy grew stronger as a result of the crises elsewhere and the way they were solved at the promptings of the American government and the global state economic governance institutions over which it holds dominant influence.

In the United States there is a tendency to explain its own success not as the result of a projection of power but a triumph of a more market friendly set of institutions and a more dynamic entrepreneurial spirit. It is American willingness to take risks, to abandon old ways for the possibility of better ones which has been rewarded. Since capital's value represents discounted future earnings, successful innovation revalues assets. Technical and organizational change devalues the old and outdated. The present value of the new and better is rewarded in proportion to risk adjusted expected profitability. From such a perspective, globalization can be seen to have "shaken up" economies everywhere, increasing the value of assets which in the new circumstances promise higher returns. As it becomes more comfortable for market participants to buy and sell assets offshore and over the Internet, competitive deregulation resulted from the fact that national borders less easily constrain economic activities. That the less regulated market frequently grows at the expense of the more regulated can be seen, although this is not the view which will be taken here, as a competitive outcome and so "efficient." Deregulation has been an especially American project consistent with the particular character of the American version of capitalism, a more laissez faire regime as opposed to the European corporatist or Japanese state capitalisms which are favored by other modes of international regulation.

An unreflected acceptance of the benign role of the U.S. as the world's only superpower and the generous valancing of its globalist agenda pervades the American literature which claims "our way is the best way" but is questioned in periods when the American model looks shakier. Because of its size, position, and distinct modes of regulation, the imposition of American definitions and rules imposes costs on other national capitals and social formations. Samuel Huntington, addressing the image of the benign hegemon, has written that the United States has attempted, or been perceived as attempting, to unilaterally "promote American corporate interests under the slogans of free trade and open markets; shape World Bank and International Monetary Fund policies to serve those same corporate interests . . . bludgeon other countries to adopt economic and social policies that will benefit American economic interests; promote American arms sales abroad while attempting to prevent comparable sales by other countries; force out one UN secretary-general and dictate the appointment of his successor . . . and categorize certain countries as 'rogue states,' excluding them from global institutions because they refuse to kowtow to American wishes" (Huntington,1999: 37- 38). Other observers have been even more critical of U.S. imperialism and unilateralism.

While all nations may partially and potentially gain from policy coordination the point that not all benefit equally tends to receive short shrift. It is the case, as Michael Webb (1991: 249), summarizing an investigation of international coordination, concludes, that "In the 1980s, the United States was uniquely able to evade the costs of imprudent macro-economic policies and uniquely able to win coordination on its own terms." It is quite likely that a similar inquiry for the 1990s and into the twenty-first century would show that the United States did even better as other economies stumbled and their relative weakness enhanced the ability of the United States to set the terms for coordination and harmonization it favored. Adjustment costs were overwhelmingly born by others in the way financial crises were resolved and standards for international regulation decided. The relation of the U.S. state and the financial institutions and other leading transnational corporations which are domiciled in the country interact in ways which are to be expected under either structural or instrumentalist state theories. Why wouldn't the government negotiators work to pursue the interests of these important constituencies? This close symbiotic association is not, however, analytically central to the analyses of most international political economists writing in liberal institutionalist and constructivist traditions. One of the tasks of this essay is to explore this relationship. Of course from the dawn of capitalist development when merchants set up rules and regulations to structure relations among themselves and then turned to rulers to allow such practices to have the sanction of law, business interests have looked to the state to accept and enforce where necessary regimes of their own design.

What is contested is why so many countries and people are left behind or harmed in a process which is presented as benefitting all. Polar positions ask: Is this because they have not yet opened themselves to market forces and so stay mired in backwardness? Is it because structured inequality within these societies is nurtured and reinforced by imperialism? Related discourses concern the nature of the global economy in the early twenty-first century and range from highlighting the knowledge economy to stressing financial fragility. These too must be incorporated. Central to economic developments is this broader sectoral growth of information technology embracing a revolution in telephone service, computer software and hardware, and the development of the Internet which brings these technologies powerfully together. Could it all just be the power of technology and the intentions of the United States whether benign or self interested are beside the point? That what drives globalization is not politics but technology? And that the gains, after some initial disruption of old ways, will be unambiguously beneficial?

TECHNOLOGY, SPACES OF PRODUCTION, AND FINANCIALIZATION

The cost of a three minute telephone call from New York City to London in 1930 was more than $300 (in year 2000 prices) making instant contact expensive. Today the charge is trivial. The result has been the slashing of the cost of processing orders for business by 90 percent or more. Banking on the Internet costs pennies a transaction instead of dollars by traditional methods. Such supply side changes have increased consumption and raised living standards dramatically. Add the growth of media and its capacity to power global brands and deliver cultural products to a world-wide audience and one can understand the celebration of a new economy. Over the last third of the twentieth century the real price of computer processing power fell by 35 percent on average *each year*. Such changes are surely impressive and explain why in discussing what is new about contemporary globalization attention has focused on the role of new technologies in economic integration and the growing importance of international links thanks to real time capital markets, 24-hour trading, transacting by high speed computers and telecommunications networks, the Internet, and the Web. Trends toward convergence of telephone, computer, and broadcast industries as a result of a continuing flow of breakthrough innovation should continue to further globalize an information intensive economy which reorganizes production on a world scale.

Such developments affect old-economy industries as well. Some of the products which symbolize the New Economy—Palm Pilots, Sony Web TV, Hewlett-Packard printers and less familiar items such as Johnson & Johnson blood-glucose monitors—it turns out are all manufactured by Flextronics International in its Guadalajara factory. Such contract manufacturing in Third World countries is another side of the New Economy's relation to globalization. New communications capacities, digital design, and quality norms allow companies like Flextronics, which like to be called electronic-manufacturing service providers, to work closely with transnationals with factories around the world to ramp up production on short notice, moving production lines when they need to and working for many brand name producers to put out a diverse product mix. This allows high value added activities to stay with the brand name company. Cisco Systems for example can be one of the world's largest companies as measured by market capitalization and yet be a virtual company with a mere three plants of its own which do only high end equipment and prototypes. Its

Internet routers are made by contractors who interface with the Cisco web site in real time bidding. The New Economy's thirst for up to date information has created huge companies able to meet its needs and niche players which can be quite successful as Bloomberg has been providing its financial information service. With Fed Ex and United Parcel Service, Apple I-Books arrive in the United States or Europe from Taiwan a few days after they are ordered. Worth Global Style Network allows subscribers to browse photos of fashion shows held around the world in the last few days or view window displays in twenty or more cities, and candid photos of "cool kids" in LA with next trend fashions as captured by freelance "cool hunters" who hang out in the right bars and discos with digital cameras. The company's 300,000 pages of current trends with constant updates has won its web site a following among the global fashion houses and marketers (Agins, 2000: B1).

Gains to small economies from global integration can be substantial. Integration allows producers with modest domestic markets to achieve real economies of scale by selling to the world. Niche producers can be viable and grow large and successful this way. The market capitalization of Nokia, the Finish-based telecommunications firm, is greater than Finland's gross domestic product. Other small economies such as Taiwan's have also done remarkably well by becoming even more reliant on global markets. High levels of regulation in the Scandinavian countries and tight state control in Taiwan have not prevented their transnationals from achieving impressive growth in the global economy, suggesting that the sort of simple-minded liberalization of investment, trade, and finance urged in the orthodoxy of the Washington Consensus (to be discussed in some detail below) is not the key to successfully taking advantage of possibilities offered by the world economy.

As global integration proceeds, international trade becomes relatively less important while foreign direct investment becomes more crucial. The stock of foreign direct investment (FDI) as a proportion of GDP quadrupled in the second half of the twentieth century. By century's end two-thirds of it was still going to the developed economies, only for a dozen newly industrializing economies was direct foreign investment the source of a fifth or more of gross domestic capital formation. At the same time, while concentrated in this relatively small number of countries, investment outside the core was no longer dominated by raw material production but by manufactures and high value added services. International outsourcing has grown more important as more products come from foreign affiliates and subcontractors, a process which does not involve equity stakes. Sales of foreign affiliates, which equaled $3 trillion in 1980, amounted to $14 trillion in 1999. By the latter date such sales were nearly twice as large as global exports. Combining production at all locations, UNCTAD put multinational corporation output at a quarter of world gross domestic product in 1999 (United Nations Conference on Trade and Development, 2001: xv). As low wage countries increase their share of exports to the core economies and absorb more of their FDI, a single global labor market comes into being for both production of goods and services.

The developing countries complain that while they are told that they cannot subsidize crops or protect their markets, the rich countries subsidize their agricultural sector and impose significant tariffs to protect their own labor intensive industries from more competitive exports from the developing economies. The United States government has long used military contracts to fund technology development and the way governments treat capital gains, business expenditures, and other tax-write-offs. Subsidies to transportation, energy generation, and other products all effect prices, profits, and competitiveness. To only attribute rent seeking behavior to actors in developing countries would seem on empirical grounds an incorrect supposition. To take existing prices as correct prices when confronted with pervasive government intervention and corporate financing of political campaigns and extensive market power in the core economies would seem questionable methodology.

If small countries can gain from the ability to trade goods and services internationally (although certainly many have been hurt by dependence on world markets with inelastic demand for their commodities and a lack of bargaining power vis-à-vis trading partners), and the gains to most industrializers it will be argued are far less than the more celebratory accounts claim, the experience of small economies with liberalization of finance has been generally disastrous. Joseph Stiglitz has described the impact of liberalized capital markets with a simple yet effective simile. Small countries, he says, are like small boats. Liberalizing capital markets is like sending them out on a rough sea. Even if the boats are sound, the captains capable, they are likely to be capsized by a big wave. That the IMF urged, indeed demanded, boats set forth "into the roughest parts of the sea before they were seaworthy, with untrained captains and crews, and without life vests" (Stiglitz, 2002: A18) may account for the almost universally disappointing if not disastrous results of IMF policy advice being followed.

The financialization of the global economy draws on information processing capacities of new technologies and has led to the explosion of financial sector growth, but also as shall be explored in subsequent chapters, to greater instability. The tension between greater efficiency as national capital markets merge into a single world financial order and the instabilities such freedom produces leads to a questioning of the theoretical models which explain how markets work. My position is that evidence supporting the strong version of the efficient market hypothesis as a real world phenomenon was never very strong and most of the arguments have been basically a rehearing of presumptions rather than anything that might be viewed as proof of the model in any rigorous meaning of the word (Findlay and Williams, 2000–2001). As a matter of historical record, markets repeatedly and systematically produce mistakenly overly optimistic valuations of future earnings potential. Speculative bubbles have a long and recurring history.

As a result there is widespread demand for new forms of international regulation even as there is disagreement on the details and even the nature of the reforms that are needed. In chapter 6 the costs of the widespread financial crises of recent decades will be discussed. It should be made clear at the outset however that evidence suggests financial liberalization delivers little (Gilbert, Irwin and Vines, 2001), leaves poor countries especially vulnerable (Anand and Sen, 2000), and that on balance privatization and deregulation have tended to increase inequality within countries and globally (Stewart and Berry, 1999). Lance Taylor and his associates (Taylor, 2000) tell us evidence for the post liberalization years shows few if any of the countries they studied found sustained growth paths. Summarizing the general findings Joseph Stiglitz (2001: 14) writes "There is now overwhelming support for the hypothesis that premature capital and financial market liberalization throughout the developing world, a central part of IMF reforms over the past two decades, was a central factor not only behind the most recent set of crises but also behind the instability that has characterized the global market over the past quarter century."

When developing countries ask for a review of the impact of the particular rules the WTO has adopted the United States maintains that liberalizing trade is a one way process and there can be no reversal of past decisions and so no purpose to an unbiased study of the impact of past decisions. The developing countries which maintain they did not understand what they were signing and have been hurt as a result of being had by the rich-country negotiators say they are simply asking for evaluation before more policies of a similar nature demanded by the rich countries are discussed and imposed. It can certainly be argued that comparing outcomes under alternative institutional arrangements should not be "banned." Nor should "efficiency" be the only acceptable criteria allowed in such investigations. Income distribution and wealth effects, employment, and a host of other quality of life indicators are thought germane by many, perhaps most people. Yet these criteria are not part of the assessments allowed to count under the neoliberal agenda. Such alternative perspectives being made by prominent economists, political scientists, and others, and a wider popular suspicion of emergent international regimes by activists and a broader public, has led to discussion of alternatives to neoliberalism.

GOVERNANCE, STATENESS, SOVEREIGNTY AND THE GSEGIS

The exercise of the defining instrumentalities of hegemony take new forms in an era of globalization and the manner in which GSEGIs are mediating instrumentalities of core state power and the interests which dominate domestic economies. It is perhaps for this reason the word "governance" has come into prominence to capture the activities of "stateness" exercised by the GSEGIs. Our effort here is to move from an understanding of globalization as an automatic and inexorable process to issues of emergent governance structures consciously created to embed the global market in a form of governance congenial to dominant transnational corporate actors and to consider the wide ranging debates over how the GSEGIs are, and should be, structured, and what sort of reforms are needed to better meet the needs of the twenty-first century.

The mainstream IPE discussion places the GSEGIs within a global public goods paradigm. In this model, the GSEGIs are seen as freely entered into out of mutual need. While there may be awareness that unequal power influences outcomes, the central focus is nevertheless that each state does better acting through collective agencies than standing apart. In the global public goods paradigm the decisionmakers in GSEGIs are technical experts specializing in, and government figures with responsibilities for, areas of economics and finance. They include treasury officials and central bankers and their advisers. The presumption is that better international organizations provide a public good in the very function of serving as a preferable forum for settlement of disputes and enforcement of agreements. In the mainstream regime theory litera-

ture this appears as a noncontroversial arrangement. International relations theorists and international political economists see their research on
strengthening such international organizations in positive and unproblematic terms.

That the GSEGIs are treaty based decisionmaking fora is significant
from a legal point of view since courts have been loathe to intervene in
what have traditionally been interpreted as matters of foreign policy. Certainly in the United States the courts have removed themselves, denying
jurisdiction even when these treaties can have profound impact on citizen
rights presumably protected under domestic legislation (which the courts
do review). Thus implicitly a trade agreement can move decisions on labor
and the environment regulation beyond the capacity of citizens groups to
raise challenges in the courts. The very procedures of these organizations,
which may not be transparent to outsiders, deny those affected information relevant to their own evaluation of the justice of procedures which
have occurred outside the purview of non-state parties who lack standing.
The presumption of equality before the law is subverted by regimes which
put rulings beyond the reach of citizens whose interests are not represented in specific international negotiations by their own governments.
(There are important exceptions in some cases in which agreements give
those companies who claim to have suffered economic loss rights to a
hearing as a result of which states may have to pay such private parties
compensation for losses or income foregone because of state actions
which violate trade and investment agreements.) That the specialized
agencies of governments which are involved represent financial, commercial, and manufacturing interests at the GSEGIs, not the departments in
which environmental and labor responsibilities are lodged, means that the
state representatives who negotiate on trade, investment and finance are
not knowledgeable on these issues and may not be sympathetic to such
interests.

To speak of government policymaking without awareness of the distinction and conflict between what Pierre Bordieu (1998: 2) has called the
left hand of the state (those agencies responsible for education, health,
and welfare programs), and the right hand of the state,(those dealing with
finance, trade, and investment), is to miss the central contradiction built
into the political system of capitalist governance. The issues with which
GSEGIs deal have consequences for the broader public and directly and
indirectly affect such areas as employment and the environment (which
domestically are the responsibility of the left hand of the state) which generate, use and influence patterns of resource allocation that are inade-

quately addressed in international fora which preclude such "left" side of state functioning from their self-defined design. GSEGIs increasingly impact domestic economic areas and political relations within countries. "Left hand" institutions globally are designed to be talk shops. "Right hand" institutions can function as mailed fists. They include as well the military and spy agencies of the state. Today the traditional realists' focus on the role of force and the threat of the use of force to coerce behavior on weaker governments is all too evident in the way Washington uses economic rewards and threats to solicit cooperation from other countries in its war on terrorism. After a decade or more in which the Cold War context of economic policy had given way to a more economistic framing of national interests the new U.S. crusade changed the focus back to a security oriented Manichean view of the world complicating discussion of the role of global state economic governance institutions.

It is a given that the policies GSEGIs project are good for the creditors in the countries of the core and for economic interests wishing more security in penetrating these economies by having their rights, as they understand them, respected. Given the expected return from lobbying and participation in such regime formation it is clearly those corporate and financial interests with the most at stake which will try to influence outcomes in such arenas. What has come to be known as the global social justice movement has called attention to such self-seeking behavior and denies that the rules or the overall strategy of the GSEGIs are in the interests of the majority of citizens of these countries. They suggest the adjustment costs to the local population are often high, that there are losses to service recipient citizens, taxpayers, workers, and businesses not allied with transnational capital. They claim that GSEGIs often produce lower real incomes, rising unemployment, bankruptcies, diminution in public services, and other costs to those not enjoying political favor. Whether they will be able to focus attention on such concerns in the present climate is an open question. There can however be no doubt that for most of the world's people the issue of social justice and meeting basic needs will remain the central concern and that the rich countries will have to continue to respond no matter how reluctantly and be part of this conversation.

In examining the merits of the positions it is not enough to say that foreign investors are seeking to impose conditions which will benefit them, although this is no doubt a valid observation. If such changes were harmful to the interests of transnational economic elites the governments which represent their interests would be unlikely to be so active in working to achieve them. The question remains, even if transnational capital gains, do ordinary people in the effected countries also gain? The answer may be a conditional yes. They may gain, but only if the reforms which diminish the rent appropriations of local elites are not replaced by rent seeking by transnational capital, which invests some of its not inconsiderable resources in obtaining labor, taxation and other governance regimes that use the state power inherent in such institutions to appropriate income and wealth at the expense of others. In a world in which all citizens do not equally influence the results of such negotiations those who already have disproportionate power tend to find the outcome of such regime negotiations congenial to their interests. If interpersonal and class inequalities are reinforced or worsened by liberalization the majority of people in the effected countries will not be better off even if per capita income rises. It is not that trade per se is good or bad or a question of accepting or rejecting globalization. The question at issue is of the terms under which globalization is constructed.

The dominant historical current of the ipe at the start of the twenty-first century is the assertion of the power of capital to reshape the world system not so much in new ways, but by using instrumentalities which, while not totally unfamiliar to students of the economic history of earlier eras, take different form at the start of the new millennium. It is not, as some have claimed, that capital has escaped state control, but rather that governments have accommodated the historically specific desires of transnational capital to shape new international regimes. With growing interdependence and cross-border spillovers, there emerge problems of collective action requiring new mechanisms for conflict resolution in economic and financial realms. There has been extensive discussion about "outsourcing" the tasks of national government by placing some services in the hands of the private sector, but the outsourcing of other functions to GSEGIs is evident in the arenas of growing GSEGI influence. While in the nineteenth and the first half of the twentieth century the naval and other military presences projected by the great powers were perceived as doing the dictating, today, while force and the threat of force are still actively used, of course, they are heavily supplemented by IMF and WTO coercion. An international state enforcement system is under construction based on a redefinition of property rights. These GSEGIs demand open economies, deregulation, and privatization. The globalized economic regimes they sponsor are evident in the newer institutional forms, which are being negotiated and which are changing rules of international economic governance.

THE STUDY OF INTERNATIONAL
POLITICAL ECONOMY

Many academics who study globalization see their role as offering policy advice to decisionmakers concerning the best way governments can address problems associated with the growing global interconnectedness. Foremost to most of them is the task of institution building, creating the organizational infrastructure capable of expediting fruitful dialogue and overcoming collective action problems so that countries can work better with each other rather than being divided by unnecessary antagonisms due to parochial, mutually counterproductive understandings of self-interest. While appreciating the idealism and good intentions which motivates such scholarship, my approach is somewhat different, in that I separate the analytical moment from that of the policy adviser, to allow some distance from the interests and presumptions of power. The frustration for such well-intentioned advisers can come from making seemingly helpful suggestions for positive sum solutions and finding those with power operating from positions of far narrower conceptions of self-interest, defending prerogatives and status quo distributional formations. This suggests that as social scientists the idealistic moment should be balanced by a realism concerning such anchoring concerns as wealth, its sources and distribution, power, and the ways it is mobilized and projected in the ipe, and divisions by identity communities, classes, and class fractions. Finally, there should be a place for those who would give advice to the nonpowerful in the epistemic communities of those whose work concerns globalization. The perspective with regard to the boundaries of relevant discourse of the fraternity is narrower than necessary or desirable for a community of free inquiry.

Such distortions can be compounded by the state-centric focus of such discussions, which obscure to a damaging extent the possibility of a balanced understanding of the crucial importance of non-state actors, especially market participants such as transnational corporations and international banks and other financial players in shaping the choices diplomats and international bureaucracies make. Differentials in state power come from economic disparities in a structural sense. State theory needs to pay attention to the instrumental power of capital. Corporate lawyers and executives from leading firms bring with them to government service a certain training and acculturation which influences those responsible for crafting the detailed institutional arrangements and regimes that shape the ipe. States are structurally dependent on their leading corporations for prosperity including employment and tax revenues.

Politicians in a narrow and direct sense also depend on the wealthiest two percent of the population who contribute 80 percent or so of the monies raised by those seeking public office. I shall discuss the impact of these phenomena in several instances in this study. The power of what in an earlier time was called, without necessarily any pejorative connotation, the capitalist class remains the absent center of much political economy discourse. Part of the task here is to unpack positions by questioning from a political economy standpoint, the workings of markets and modes of governance which rely on simple models of maximizing behavior. There is increased recognition of the inherent weaknesses of the unitary state actor model and mainline political economy offers useful insights for an alternative framing of issues. In doing so the expansion of relevant actors, and the way costs and benefits are measured for each, allows for a reformulating of other mainstream IPE norms which tend to reflect the genetic makeup of political science itself from its public administration parentage in nineteenth-century Germany and early twentieth-century America. Mainstream IPE bears the birthmarks of its lineage.

To summarize, international relations whether in its realist (and neorealist), liberal institutionalist (and its neo permutations), and in most of its constructivist forms is overwhelmingly state centric. It can accord an autonomy to states inherited from its IR origins which frames negotiating international regimes in a misleading context of Westphalian norms and in understanding states as autonomous, unitary actors. This ignores the power of capital to shape state identity, motivation, and activity. Its research in significant part is justified in terms of usefulness to state policymakers and so consciously or unconsciously assumes, or at least more reasonably takes centrally into account, their values and purposes. Both normatively and as a matter of positive analysis such an approach is too narrow. It pays insufficient attention to parts of the puzzle which do not fit the traditional state centric diplomatic frame. It has been slow to embrace the injunctions of critics who have long maintained the need to accord other actors participant status.

Normatively the approach here is to refocus and expand the remit of IPE to include a capacity to advise non-system actors, especially the sectors of global civil society critical of the efficiently-economistic model that has been labeled corporate globalization (Tabb, 2002). It is the strategy of transnational corporations, large international financial institutions, and of elite state decisionmakers associated with these interests. While the corporate vision that globalization is good for all has been assimilated by the media, the public remains skeptical. The alternative model of social justice globalization includes a critique of liberal institutionalist optimism in framing interstate negotiations as designed to overcome collective action problems. It stresses redistribution issues not merely among states but among classes, ethic groups, and gender categories, it challenges as well the realist presumption of the ultimate dominance of hegemonic power to script outcomes. Social activists falsely labeled antiglobalist in many accounts advocate an alternative internationalization from below based on the centrality of social justice concerns.

Critics of corporate globalization believe democratic polities have the right to override free markets, replacing free trade with fair trade because of harmful impacts of trade on others. In doing so they validate the centrality of what are externalities in the pure theory of international trade, nonmarket values with regard to environmental and labor rights for example. If one understands property rights to be socially defined and nonexistent until embedded in larger social institutions and morality, then the claims of social efficiency over private market efficiency legitimately questions mainstream theory's claim that its imperative of market efficiency trumps all others objectives. In the consideration of trade theory in chapter 8 such critique by global social activists will be explored. The legal studies literature is especially helpful in this regard because of its openness to adversarial formulations. It offers a counterpoint to mainstream economics with its perfect competition starting point to modeling and consideration of social costs as secondary issues treated, if at all, as externalities or as redistribution questions best left to others. In drawing on international legal theory we not only acknowledge the obvious and growing importance of formal adjudication where states have conflicting definition of property rights but also recognize that legal theorists from at least the time of Grotius have been active in structuring arguments which become part of core political theory and which are usefully applied in the contemporary period to issues central to IPE.

We draw as well on the mainline tradition of political economy, the "other" great tradition in economics which is ignored in mainstream neoclassical theorizing to achieve this wider conceptualization of IPE. The distinction between mainstream economics and mainline political economy is explained in chapter 4 (and in Tabb, 1999). In making the mainline side of political economy integral to this project we also privilege the realities of uncertainty and collective agency denied in mainstream finance's acceptance of strong versions of rational expectations theory. It is simply not possible to effectively grasp the financial crises of recent decades any more than it is to understand the centuries of recurring financial overextensions, defaults, and restructurings which have been part and parcel of the capitalist world system for centuries by relying on models of perfect competition and strong rational expectations. We spend some time therefore in chapter 8 developing the alternative Keynes-Minsky framework. This allows critique of the IMF and other issues and organizations from a competing economic model's framing of the problematic.

FAIRNESS AND EQUAL TREATMENT

The original blueprint for the postwar international order was drawn up in the 1940s by American policymakers who at that time had projected the philosophy and as much as possible the form of the New Deal regulatory state onto the world. This New Deal perspective, which came to be decisively rejected in the wake of the Thatcher-Reagan ideological and policy revolution, was based on a market failure view of economic policy making expressed by John Maynard Keynes (1963: 312) when he famously wrote in 1926 on "The End of Laissez Faire" that "It is *not* a correct deduction from the Principles of Economics that enlightened self-interest always operates in the public interest. Nor is it true that self-interest generally *is* enlightened; more often individuals acting separately to promote their own ends are too ignorant or to weak to attain even these." In terms of international capital flows and trade relations, there had emerged a consensus as enunciated by Keynes's counterpart at Bretton Woods, Harry Dexter White, in 1942, "The theoretical basis for the belief still so widely held, that interference with trade and with capital and gold movements, etc., are harmful, are hangovers from a nineteenth century creed, which held that international economic adjustments, if left alone, would work themselves out toward an 'equilibrium" with a minimum of harm to world trade and prosperity. It is doubtful whether that belief was ever sound." (Ikenberry,1993: 162).

Since the late 1960s there has been movement away from National Keynesianism to Global Neoliberalism (Tabb, 2000: 51-56), which involved dramatic realignment of domestic coalitions based on a different relation between the nation state and the world system. The growth of multinational corporations marketing to the world and producing outside the home country jurisdiction was decisive. In the European countries which had adopted national champion strategies, protected and subsidized domestic industry, and accommodated organized workers' wage aspirations in corporatist fashion the growth model involved control of capital flows, investment, exports and imports to varying degrees. As companies no longer looked primarily to the national context, industry-wide bargaining came under pressure along with the Welfare State, and monetarism came to be seen "as a necessary evil for social democracy" (Iversen, 1998: 73). EU competition policy reflects the priority of competition integration and processes of liberalization, deregulation, privatization. Such neoliberal pressures did not however mean an eclipse of the state. Indeed, it would be useful to consider the development of stateness in the European Union which, as James March and Johan Olsen (1998: 327) have noted, "has become the most highly institutionalized international organization in history." It is surely the case that the Europeanization of law and the increased significance of norms in international politics which derive from European unity efforts and experience have compromised the identity of territorial authority and redefined stateness in ways relevant to the present study. Examining the EU more closely would allow for a particularly fruitful examination of the power of the "status quo bias" (Strange,1983) found in international organizations and the processes through which they are challenged. But these and other extensions would threaten an unmanageably broad canvas in what is already an overly ambitious undertaking although much of what we have to say here is relevant to discussions of regional formations such as the EU and the FTAA, the Free Trade Area of the Americas under negotiation.

The richer nations speaking for their transnational corporations wish to streamline international regulation making it easier for those who do business globally by establishing one set of rules and procedures. I will argue in chapter 4 that this approach can be understood as a contemporary version of what is known as the *lex mercatoria* ("merchants' law"). The new constitutionalism is, in modern guise, this practice of powerful market participants developing a set of preferred regulations for their dealings, avoiding political interference as much as possible and then gaining state endorsement to allow enforcement of their preferred understanding of property rights. It has been called "entrepreneurial diplomacy" by Paula Stern, a former chair of the United States Trade Commission under presidents Carter and Reagan, a diplomacy in which the corporations involved work out accommodations among themselves to then be approved by the GSEGIs. Negotiators and lobbyists representing those corporate interests bring their viewpoints and clout to the bargaining process. Negotiations are based on these proposals which are then put forward by policymakers of the hegemonic state, perhaps in conjunction with key allies. They put forward the private consensus of fractions of capital whose interests are effected. The individuals leading government-to-government negotiations typically come from the world of transnational corporations and global financial institutions and the law firms which represent them and act as the interface with state decisionmakers and regulators. Once the new rules are worked out other nations are invited to adopt them. It is through this process which we will call concentric club formation, and describe further in chapter 5, that private law is constructed and then ratified by international agreement. The GSEGIs are structured and administered by such a process. Official decisions typically follow consensus worked out in pre-meeting gatherings by the major players who control the agenda typically in a process of concentric club rule making in which a detailed agenda and set of proposals is proffered by the most powerful participant(s) and agreements forged in a limited gathering of key players before the agreed rules are presented at a broader gathering where only the most modest modifications are likely to be approved.

There is support more broadly for the suspicion that great powers do not make great multilateralists (Holloway, 2000). As Hurrell and Woods (1995: 461) remind us, "Although international institutions ostensibly arise amongst states concerned with solving common problems and promoting overall welfare, in fact they reflect a pattern of structural power which is central to the management of interdependence." Such a negotiating stance by the richer nations is understandable from their perspective, but is not satisfactory to other more vulnerable participants in the interstate system. The opposition to corporate globalization agenda comes from dependent states to the extent they are willing to risk the displeasure of the most powerful actors of the world system and from NGOs and other elements of global civil society which have been increasingly active in world politics. Academic scholarship at the turn of the twenty-first century experienced a certain democratization in subject matter and approach, and a broadening of actors allowed onto the canvas of conflict analysis and its applications to global governance issues.

The civil society approach to globalization to a substantial degree replaced Marxism as the pole of left critique. The decentralized, participatory nature of the movements for social justice contrast with the top down organization of industrial era working-class movements of the socialist and communist lefts. The critique of democratic capitalism's triumph and the end of history celebration is that real democracy is not possible in a world dominated by elites who control (to use the banished language of Marxism) the means of production and which buy elections and politicians, and make it exceedingly difficult for ordinary people to have much say except by going into the streets in front of the places elites meet to run the world. One of the most fascinating aspects of the popular politics of our time is the construction of such a civil society oppositional politics.

RESPONDING TO GLOBALIZATION

Globalization trends and the impact of technological breakthroughs undercut a host of nation-state autonomy strategies from the possibility of autocentric development and import substitution industrialization in what is anachronistically called the Third World, to the defeat of the national champion strategy of European corporatists. Local elites have found it in their self-interest to abandon nationalism and the pursuit of import substitution strategies, to drop alliances with national labor, and to accommodate to foreign capital. With the fall of the Soviet Union and the general increase in global openness the proportion of the workers of the world shielded from the international economy dropped from an estimated two-thirds in the late 1970s to a tenth or so by the late 1990s, according to World Bank estimates. The Bank concludes that despite distortions the process is beneficial and efforts to impede continued flexibility and openness are, and would be, counterproductive (World Bank, 1995). Others are less sure. They remind us that the consequences of the rules and procedures followed by GSEGIs are to bifurcate the arena of international relations between an economic realm and human rights and environmental concerns. Discussion of property rights takes place in one set of venues. Discussion of human rights and environmental protection in another (and the right hand of the state has no concern with what the left hand's priorities may be). This division is artificial and what we typically have is a clash of values concerning pieces of a holistic pattern of globalist development, of resource generation and allocation.

The core of an IPE relevant to these debates is the clash between the argument that economic efficiency is a public good and that only through freeing the market to do its magic can the poor of the world be incorporated into a global prosperity, and the view that sees the way the poor are incorporated into the global economy as the problem. From the latter perspective the idea that economic efficiency is a means to increasing the general welfare ignores the nature of capitalism as a process of redistributional growth which generates exploitation and exclusion and sees existing patterns of "growth" as socially and environmentally irresponsible. Private accumulation is understood to be in conflict with other legitimate goals which should take precedence. Because such a critique has been so widely embraced there needs to be mechanisms to bring oppositional voices to the table where currently elites discuss economic and financial governance regimes without such participation. Because preferences about preferences are involved it is not quite right to say that markets are about self-interest and politics about aggregating given individual preferences. If politics is a process through which individual preferences may change, political institutions should not be modeled in microeconomic terms as aggregating devices for atomistic exogenously given preferences. For those who believe democracy should be more participatory, and that politics has an inescapably deliberative dimension which should not be reduced to calculation of monetary costs and benefits, an expansion of the agenda and the participants is in order. Political institutions are understood by some theorists as capable of changing individual and group attitudes and redefining self-interest as understood by participants in the process. The presumption that communication increases agents' cooperative and solidaristic behavior is made in liberal institutionalist understandings of the logic of collective action and negotiations among nations within such fora. Repeated "games" promote cooperation and collegiality and reduce the confrontational stance of those with whom trust relations are strengthened.

In the closing decades of the twentieth century critique of the strategy and tactics of the GSEGIs came with increasing frequency from prominent academics, government officials, and former officials, and from politicians of the core and the periphery of the world system. These included internal critiques from a perspective accepting the logic of free markets as efficient allocators of resources and promoters of economic growth who saw the GSEGIs as acting counterproductively. Contemporary discomfort concerning the meaning, import, and future of globalization and governance and related confusions as to the nature and scope of the academic discipline or subdiscipline of IPE are the occasion for this book. The creation and evolution of the ipe and of GSEGIs are explored. The international trade and finance regimes are distinguished and discussed. However as globalization has proceeded distinction among such regimes has become less useful, the contrast between trade and investment conceptually less clear. Problems have arisen particularly with regard to the extension of free trade arguments to the movement of capital, especially of short-term speculative capital flows. The financial sector has grown in relative importance and trade in financial and other business services have become much more important. A trade regime designed for the international exchange of goods has been revised to include intellectual property, investment and services, raising a host of complex issues. This book addresses these issues from a critical realist position.

CHAPTER THREE

Debating Globalization

"The nation state has become an unnatural, even dysfunctional, unit for organizing human activity and managing economic endeavor in a borderless world. It represents no genuine, shared, community of economic interests; it defines no meaningful flows of economic activity. In fact, it overlooks the true linkages and synergies among often disparate populations by combining important measures of human activity at the wrong level of analysis."

—*Kenichi Ohmae* (1993: 78)

"[F]earsome dislocations are bound to accompany the weakening of the central institutions of society. The prophets of an internetted world in which national identities gradually fade, proclaim its revolutionary nature and yet believe the changes will be wholly benign. They won't be. The shift from national to some other political allegiance, if it comes, will be an emotional, cultural, and political earthquake."

—*Jessica Matthews* (1997: 65)

Awareness of globalization grew in the last decades of the twentieth century as indices of interconnectedness all shot upward. The ratio of exports to gross domestic product doubled between 1960 and 1990 for the OECD countries. Foreign direct investment rose three times faster than trade. By the mid-1980s, on a world scale, a third of employment and of sales of the sixty-eight largest manufacturing corporations was accounted for by their foreign subsidiaries. All multinationals together controlled a third of the world's private sector's productive assets. The global stock of foreign direct investment jumped more than tenfold between 1980 and 2002, to more than $7 trillion as transnationals increased their global reach (United Nations Conference on Trade and Development, 2003). Over these decades wealth and power became more concentrated. Cross border mergers, acquisitions, and relational contracting remade the map of the world political economy. The growing dominance of transnational corporations and global financial interests in controlling the choices of governments everywhere was especially evident. By the start of the new millennium globalization was one of the most frequent of terms bandied about in policy circles and among the academic interpreters of world events although even after a decade or two of incessant employment the continuous effort to obtain purchase on the meaning(s) of the term revealed a moving target of uncertain scope and dimension.

This chapter first reviews a number of definitions of the phenomenon. It is an indication both of perceived newness and complexity of globalization that so many scholars feel compelled to offer their own definitions as prologue to contributions to the debate. That the concept's meaning remained so uncertain indicates in part awareness that it remains a contested term, its various aspects assuming different shape and significance over time. Following review of these understandings the concepts of "sovereignty" and "regime" are interrogated to better understand the manner in which globalization has effected states in the world system and the emergence of economic governance structures. The chapter concludes with a comparison between liberal market economies and coordinated market economies among the advanced countries and the struggle between the approaches historically taken by each in negotiating harmonization of standards in the global economy.

DEFINING GLOBALIZATION

Gerald Helleiner suggests that the very term globalization "has now become so slippery, so ambiguous, so subject to misunderstanding and political manipulation, that it should be banned from further use, at least until there is precise agreement as to its meaning." (Helleiner, 2001: 242) But of course if this is to be to the criteria, the term could never be used. The very conflict over its meaning reflect the contested nature of the reality the term is employed to identify. The variations in usage have not prevented globalization from becoming "the most over used and under specified term in the international policy sciences since the end of the Cold War." (Devetak and Higgott, 1999: 483). Indeed, it has replaced the Cold War as the unifying theme of a new era. A survey taken of the opinions of economists reports that globalization emerges as the phenomenon most likely to have a major impact on the economic system and its institutions in the twenty-first century (Pryor, 2000).

The term globalization has been centrallly used to describe the growing economic and financial linkages that integrate territorial formations more extensively over time. Common to most definitions is the idea that globalization refers to the linkages and interconnections between states and societies of the world system. It describes the process by which events, decisions, and activities in one part of the world come to have significant consequences for individuals and communities in physically distant places. It is widely understood to define a set of processes which embrace most of the globe and operate world-wide. It implies intensification of interactions, interconnectedness and interdependence between states and societies and suggests the emergence for the first time in human history of a truly global society. Particular inquiries may stress, depending on specialist interest, aspects of media or culture more broadly, population movements, or concerns over cross border pollution (Held, et al., 1999).

Matthew Patterson (1999: 140) suggests that both discursively and materially "globalization" is largely just an extension and reorganization of "development," understood as "a set of goals, techniques and practices designed to incorporate those parts of the world only loosely connected to the global economy more fully into it." To that should be added that while globalization is merely the most recent stage in such efforts to integrate the world economy, it represents as well a deepening or thickening of existing connectedness. It is the increased density and immediacy of interaction which is characteristic of globalization today compared to earlier periods. Globalization is seen as the growing, and in some versions the unprecedented, international integration of economic life involving a major increase in trade and foreign direct investment relative to production, a surge in international financial transactions, and the growth of global economic institutions such as the multinational corporation and international organizations. Discussions of globalization tend to deny the classic dichotomies of domestic and global, public and private, projecting a new mixture of private and public power which transcends individual governments. The global is now everywhere. It is part of the local. The definition of local now must have global dimensions. Global is not "out there" but transforms and redefines the meanings of domestic and international.

From my own perspective, while technological possibilities are enabling of contemporary forms of globalization, the particular social relations, rules, and other constraints which guide the process are the outcome of contested political struggles among national capitals, groups of citizens, governments, and other players. The investigation undertaken here suggests currently existing globalization has been overwhelmingly the result of a political project, an agenda of the most internationalized fractions of capital in the leading states of the world carried on in significant measure through both private consultations by peak organizations of the business community in the most powerful economies and through the agency of their governments, actualized above all through the leadership of the executive branch of the American government. This does not imply a conspiracy, unless one wishes to characterize the normal working of government and the economy in capitalist society this way. The regimes and their rules of the contemporary international political economy are not inevitable, predetermined. They are human constructs open to contestation and change.

From a not totally dissimilar position liberal institutionalists see the globalization of the world economy and the expanding role of international institutions as creating a powerful form of global regulation in which major international institutions are increasingly laying down rules and guidelines that governments must follow to attract foreign investment and generate growth. Here the "partnership" between governments and transnational capital takes on a more coerced nature. From a functionalist perspective the most fundamental question scholars can ask about these international institutions concerns their effectiveness: "What structures, processes, and practices make international institutions more or less capable of affecting policies and outcomes in desired ways?" (Keohane, 1998a: 89) It would seem however that prior questions are as relevant: how do these institutions in fact impact diverse locations? to what ends? For while one can appreciate the international administration focuses mainly on the concern that the agencies do a good job, there may be less agreement on what policies and outcomes are desirable. Here is one of the great divisions among IPE scholars. Some, while they recognize the nature of goals and the powerful hand of superordinate power in the way they are pursued, see these negotiating fora primarily as a place where all participants benefit from a mutually satisfactory agreement on procedure and rule of law. Others highlight the manner in which capitalist industrialism has always rested on inequalities in power and that transnational corporations today basically call the shots with critical implications for the people and the planet.

POLITICAL VOICES AND ECONOMIC RESTRUCTURING

Globalization increases a sense of connectedness in ways which make it more difficult to define territorial "us" in distinction to an over there somewhere else "them." We are connected through a sense of residency in McLuhan's global village, if not yet citizenship of a global society. Alexander Wendt (1999: 129) is not alone in the realization that to the extent that a perception of transnational community is being born, it is much more a community of capital and states than of people. The idea of interdependence which comes from such interpenetration destabilizes understandings of national autonomy. At the same time it strengthens more local and immediate individualities based on religion, ethnicity, race, and other identity communities. There is a cause-effect relation involved. The pressure for continued privatization and the expansion of the market at the expense of the public sector is a process in which citizenship for individuals is restricted to nations at the same time that world citizenship is granted corporations. With citizenship for individuals limited to nations, corporations become the only citizens with full rights of mobility and political representation. The economic base to globalization, driven as it is by market forces and new types of scale and scope economies comes from internetted access to arm's length suppliers and customers, as well as to relational contracting alliances. The corresponding governance discussion has been of the norms and standards appropriate in the new circumstances, and the policies and institutions conducive to a more open political economy. The wider menu of investments open to asset-holders increases their influence on government policymaking and the possibilities of their citizens. The fault line of globalization exposes the divide between groups who have the skills and mobility to flourish in global markets and those who don't have these advantages or who perceive the expansion of unregulated markets as "inimical to social stability and deeply held norms." (Rodrik, 1997a: 2)

Richard Higgott (1999b) as part of remarks on the seventy-fifth anniversary of the journal *International Affairs* suggested that perhaps the most important issue in international affairs in this century will revolve around the relationship between the impact of globalization and the unbundling of territorial boundaries and the traditional sense of justice tied to "Westphalian coordinates" which have come unmoored. Reweaving the social bond in a post-Westphalian order under conditions of globalization is more than a normative task, if indeed the normative issue can be separate from a positive analysis of globalization whose interpretative subjectivities are integral to its definition.

On the one hand there have been the deliberations of the GSEGIs where the business of business gets conducted, and on the other, the various agencies and world conclaves sponsored by the UN and its agencies described as talk shops by the practical men of affairs and other hard headed realists. This characterization is a measure of the difficulty changing the *status quo* given the power relations of the ipe. Nonetheless, the message of the anti-hegemonic forces expressed in many of the UN conferences and documents is receiving a wider hearing: "The opportunities and rewards of globalization are spread unequally and inequitably—concentrating power and wealth in a select group of people, nations and corporations, marginalizing others." (United Nations Development Programme, 1999: 2). In what has been for some time an intra-elite discussion carried out in technocratic language by a management class, the social justice focus once marginal to GSEGI deliberations is now never far from view given concern that the markets have gone too far, unacceptably dominating social and political outcomes.

The two conversations, of market rationality and social justice, cannot be kept separate not only because the popular movements have made themselves heard and can no longer be ignored, but also because the negative impacts of globalization adversely affect the broader public and the interests of the powerful. As the nontraditional threats to national security become increasingly evident, such front-page issues as terrorism, organized crime, drug trafficking, environmental catastrophe, rapid population growth and massive migrations of economic refugees, civilians displaced by civil wars, the stagnation and collapse of failed states, "soft concerns" challenge the bottom line and high politics views of the world. The threats of globalization in the twenty-first century come from social and economic instability and the gap between the capacities of different regions will feed xenophobia, intolerant religious fundamentalism and aggressive nationalism that will exacerbate the other problems. As Andrei Kozyrev, Foreign Minister of the Russian Federation, told a 1995 meeting of the Trilateral Commission, "The threat of a Soviet tank strike has long since been replaced by dangers and risks of "civilian" origin. . . . These are: uncontrolled migration, ethnic conflict, international crime and money laundering, and the ecological crisis." (Kozyrev, 1995: 8) The meanings and limits of sovereignty shift. It is in the context of these cross cutting complexities that the Bush Administration's single minded pursuit of terrorists threatens to lose sight of the other perils to stability which have emerged as front burner concerns and are now pushed once again to the margins of policymaker interest.

Consider the way AIDS had come to be perceived as an issue of national security by U.S. military planners. It is in an odd way characteristic of globalization's unexpected dangers. A White House interagency working group has been convened to develop expanded international initiatives to combat this disease based on a National Intelligence Estimate and National Security Council involvement has resulted from fears that governments will collapse causing disastrous instability as a result of the scale of the disease's devastations not only in sub-Saharan Africa but also over the next twenty years in, for example South Asia and the countries of the former Soviet Union. What is obvious in sub-Saharan Africa, where tens of million people are infected or have died, is a developing trend elsewhere. The number of people who are dying, the impact on elites, the army, teachers, and others is already severe and the Pentagon fears the undermining of its military-to-military programs with a number of countries. The relation of individual safety and the U.S. sense of national security are being redefined in American policymaking circles as the impacts of conditions of daily life around the globe effect countries foreign relations and military strength (Matthews, 1997).

Communities of identity grow in search of security from the destabilizing force of globalization but also as a resource to better engage with the global economy. At the local level normative consensus is reflected in networks of relationships, common values, norms, and expectations which can empower small producers (as in what is known as the Third Italy where localized but small scale modern export production complexes that are based on unique cultural attributes survive and thrive between transnationals and state champions). Other localisms close off from the forces of globalism to seek isolation, often violently enforced. Sustaining separatist localisms can require repressive measures because of the porousness of borders under the pressures of global commodification of social life, the power of media, and the seductive lifestyle goods and services which once encountered become desired. Traditionalists would keep away from such temptations. One thinks of the Taliban for example. But to focus on the violence of responses without coming to grips with the insecurities and destabilized societal moorings which have resulted from the commodification of seemingly every aspect of life, the robbing of traditional certainties and alienated emotions in a world ruled invaded by foreign cultures and the sales effort would be to miss the context in which a variety of reactions, not only terrorism, inevitably result in reaction.

Sovereignty thus has both devolved to identity forms of politics, to micronationalisms and cultural nationalisms, which do not necessarily involve recognizable state form but nonetheless are demands for individual and group space and for territorial autonomy. The economic reorganization of distance and the cultural manifestations of localisms are entangled. The new nationalisms arise from the disintegration of the state formation no longer able to command allegiance because it could effectively claim something approaching sovereignty in the older Westphalian sense. That construction of sovereignty as incontestable control of within-border activities has eroded even for core states of the interstate system. Contract law involving cross border transactions has increasingly restrained domestic practices and state autonomy. The emergence of international governance procedures and enforcement mechanisms undermine exclusivist views of sovereignty in much the same manner as economic and social regulation do to simple notions of property. At all levels, that of the firm, the state, and the world system, categories once understood in simpler terms are being destabilized by the globalization processes.

WHAT IS NEW ABOUT GLOBALIZATION?

Many scholars maintain that none of this is really unique. Janet Abu-Lougod (1989) reminds us that pre-fourteenth-century Europe was intimately tied to developments in the Far East and across Central Asia. The transnational challenge to the state is old hat (Krasner, 1999). With regard to the processes of trade, some analysts make the distinction between internationalization and globalization, suggesting that in earlier periods it was best to think of trade as occurring internationally, between independent nation states which exchanged goods to mutual advantage, but that in recent years globalization has brought an interdependence so that intracorporate trade, commodity webs, and other forms of relational contracting have made borders less relevant. But for most parts of the world colonialism and imperialism long ago reorganized local economies which from that rosy dawn of capitalist social relations produced the dependence (or interdependence) which is now seen by some as a new phenomenon. For the world system there has always been a degree of functional integration between dispersed locations. Production has not typically been organized within national economies, nor have most states had the sort of autonomy trade theory suggests (a point discussed at greater length in chapter 6).

It is certainly true that at the end of the fourteenth century Italian bankers had developed multinational financial organizations of great sophistication. The Medici bank, the largest business enterprise in the fifteenth century had branches in Rome, Venice, Geneva, Basel, Lyons, and London among other places. It was organized as a holding company in

Florence. For the banks, the nature of the problems and possible disasters facing international finance have not really changed since the days of the Medici. Nor are matters so different for governments. Montesquieu saw the foreign exchange constraint as a limit to the actions of the sovereign. The Bardi and Peruzzi were the largest business enterprises in Europe before the default of Edward II in the 1340s forced them into bankruptcy. There is nothing new in the ability of an unaccountable sovereign actor to destroy major banks and to create economic dislocations through irresponsible economic policies.

Before Adam Smith celebrated the invisible hand the Muscovy Company and the Dutch East India Company were among the multinational corporate entities investing on the peripheries of the New as well as the Old Worlds (Curtin, 1984). Globalization outcomes involve an interplay of technology, the state, the transnational corporation, self-awareness by elites of their interests and in different ways and to different effects in different eras the popular consciousness of ordinary people. All have been important to the evolution of the political economy at least since the nation state emerged, and the East India Company (if not the Levant Corporation), and the other historically prominent chartered corporate entities explored the world, reorganizing the sales and production of commodities for the global market. It can also be argued that the emergence of a cosmopolitan bourgeoisie and class of *haute financiers* emerged in the second half of the nineteenth century (Jones, 1987). At the same time it may be true, as world-systems analysts tell us, that the period 1945-90 "was the moment of the most massive expansion the world-economy has experienced in the whole of the 500-year existence of the modern world-system." (Hopkins and Wallerstein, 1996: 1)

Globalization in world system terms is the universalization of capitalist social relations and it is possible to stress both the essential continuity of the capitalist world system's expansionist logic and its intensification. It is a process which has gone on for hundreds of years but can be seen as having been interrupted in the twentieth century by two world wars and postwar disruptions (a Great Depression after the first, a Cold War and recovery of capitalist dynamism after the second) and a major structural transformation based on what some have called a third industrial revolution of information technology which seriously diminished the importance of second industrial revolution–based Fordist manufacturing industries and forms of organization. What some analysts have understood as a decisive historical rupture, a shift from a modern age to a postmodern one for example can also be seen as a reassertion of globalization or universalization which had only been interrupted during what Hobsbawm (1994) has describes as the short twentieth century (lasting from 1914 to 1989).

From such a vantage point economic historians who discount talk of uniquely transformative globalization in the late twentieth century suggest the really big events integrating capital markets (such as the opening of the trans-Atlantic cable) were long ago innovations. Bringing communication by ship from three weeks to the ability to execute trades overnight and obtaining immediate market information were far more substantial changes than recent innovations which reduced delay from hours to minutes (Garbade and Silber, 1978). It may well be that the discussion of whether the telegraph, telephone, the railroad, iron hulled steamships, and the opening of the Suez and Panama canals did more to globalize capital and shifted flows of goods, investment, and people than commercial jets, containerized superfreighters, computers, satellites, and the Internet is probably unresolvable, yet if globalization theorists mean that today's economy is one in which each part of the world is linked by markets sharing close to real-time information, then that can be said to have began "not in the 1970s but in the 1870s." (Hirst and Thompson, 1996: 10)

Creating a world market has been a long and continuous process punctuated by technological breakthroughs to be sure but the global market was not born yesterday. On the issue of openness we may rely on Keynes's description of the great financial openness in the years before World War I (Keynes, 1920: 11). A substantial literature exists suggesting that neither inflation, risk, nor interest rates are as closely coordinated globally in the postwar period as under the gold standard (Grassman and Lundberg eds., 1981). Robert Zevin (1992) provocatively has declared that it is doubtful if the computer has created a class of transactions and orders that are conceptually more complex than those invented by the Dutch in the seventeenth century. The larger point is that the time-space compression is nothing new. Capitalism has continuously revolutionized the means of production and created disorder and substantial disruptions in the process. Economists from Marx to Schumpeter have understood the evolution of the system in just such terms. It is the equilibrium, nature-makes-no-jumps school of neoclassical economics which has no place for such awareness. At the same time we can agree with those who see late twentieth-century integration as fundamentally "thicker" than that of the late nineteenth century, that the earlier version amounted to a "low bandwidth globalization" as compared to late twentieth-century high bandwidth integration. In the latter customers can ask and receive precise product specifications and investors exercise supervisory more exacting control from a distance. Modern communication and transportation offer a level of close contact which qualitatively enhances a more intimate global integration.

Trying to distinguish between continuity and change in some decisive way is an exercise in diminishing intellectual returns, even if we can expect renewed episodes of "Is today's globalization new?" being replayed in each new conjuncture as issues which have been debated repeatedly seem novel once again in their historically unique clothing. In 1977 Keohane and Nye addressed the globalization debate between those who saw "a world without borders" and the traditionalists who called these assertions unfounded "globaloney." They pointed out, as other commentators have done in the contemporary go-round, that "our era is marked by both continuity and change" and argue that one extreme or the other "would be fruitless." It still would be. What needed, and needs, to be understood was, and is, the specificity of the asymmetries of power and dependence which are the sources of bargaining strength in the international political economy that shape each conjuncture and its social structure of accumulation. While as noted this debate is often presented in the form of a stark dichotomy of whether globalization is "good" or "bad," matters are more complicated. It will take much of the book to sort through the intricacies of who globalization as it unfolds is good and bad for, and how it might be made better for those who are considered to be paying unacceptably high costs.

The operation of the globalization process takes place within, and is mediated by, a set of governance frameworks stretching from the global to the local. It is the nature of these institutions, their operation, and the ways they could be reformed which are of interest. Accepting the free market outcome is not really a possibility because markets are always embedded in a larger societal framework. Markets need rules for contracting, standards for judging what is permissible behavior by participants, and enforcement of contracts. When market outcomes are experienced as favoring a smaller minority and seriously discommode majorities there are political ramifications, resistance, and organizational efforts which eventually change the rules. This has historically been the case. One presumes it will continue to be so.

It is well to remember that capitalism is always a process of redistributive growth. Its innovations are normally efficiency enhancing as this term is used by economists. They raise living standards on average and over time. But they do so in ways which typically sacrifice the interests of much of a generation of workers who are made obsolete and to whom little or no compensation is offered. While other workers get jobs in the emergent industries, it is rare that displaced workers, especially older ones, do as well in the new conjuncture. A generation of such workers and whole communities which depend on their custom for livelihood may wither. It is not enough to say that the general gain to society would be enough to offer adequate compensation. Such compensation may be possible in theory but is rarely paid in practice. Indeed, if such compensation were mandatory, the pace and form of change would be very different.

As global neoliberalism has gained momentum, the growth of real output has slowed. In the so-called Golden Age (1950 through 1973) real world GDP growth averaged 4.9 percent. It was only 3.3 percent a year in the 1980s and 2.3 percent for the 1990s leading some economists to ask whether the structures and practices of neoliberalism generated dilatory global growth. The pressure to cut costs and increase profit, while always present in our economic system, was mediated in the postwar period by policies protecting national economies through tripartite agreements and fiscal stimulus. The former has gone by the boards as corporations have raised their sights to global horizons. The latter is ineffective, or surely less effective given the leakages created by the greater mobility of capital. Simultaneous expansions by competing transnationals seeking to position themselves to seize global markets have produced overinvestment relative to demand. Demand itself is repressed by the redistributions, fiscal priorities, and labor market policies of national governments designed to attract investment. The rise of inequality globally is linked both to GSEGI disciplinary measures and the restructuring of economies in ways which have produced uneven patterns of economic development and periodic crises resulting from cycles of too rapid capital inflows, speculative excesses, and collapse of bubble economies.

SOVEREIGNTY'S IMPERIAL PAST

Globalization trends in recent decades redefined economic territoriality which impacts governmental functioning and makes analysts aware that "Sovereignty is alienable, states cede power to supra-state agencies, but it is not a fixed quantum. Sovereignty is alienable and divisible, but states acquire new roles even as they cede power: in particular, they come to have the function of legitimating and supporting the authorizes they have created by such grants of authority." (Hirst and Thompson, 1996: 190) With such state functional recomposition comes a basic redefinition of the state within political discourse. The state as representative of communities of fate whose members prosper or suffer with the prospects of the country as a whole has always been a fiction to the extent that juridical egalitarianism in practice is compatible with extreme divergence in opportunity. That the many might lose out to produce gains for dominant elites who control the state, always a possibility if not a likelihood, becomes the widespread pattern in an era of globalization as inequalities grow between and within nations. Yet even so the ability of the state to enforce dominance on complaining members preserves its power within its borders. This ability to define and carry out collectively binding decisions on members of a society in the name of the common interest is exercised in the service of advocating the inevitability and desirability of globalization. The state is urged by corporate globalization's advocates to use its authority to dismantle social insurance schemes and other forms of citizen protection in the name of staying competitive in a global economy.

While this seems a new role for the state, a willful surrender of key elements of sovereignty as traditionally understood, there is historical continuity in such a stance. For one thing the Westphalian system, with which Western theorists are so taken, never included the territories of the periphery. As noted, the rule of transnational corporations is not a new phenomenon for those whose history includes time under the control of the British East India Company, the Dutch West India Company, and the other great trading companies and their "mother" countries, which administered dependent territories. As observers from Immanuel Wallerstein to Stephen Krasner have observed, there never was some golden period in the past when the Westphalian System was universally honored. Enough has been written to suggesting that sovereignty is an institution characterized by organized hypocrisy. International relations discussions have too often accepted a Westphalian system uncritically in rather ahistoric fashion.

Before the age of colonialism the naturalist international law of the sixteenth and seventeenth centuries asserted a universal international law "derived from human reason" and applied to all peoples, non-European as well as Europeans. The positivist international law which replaced this naturalist law was complicitous with colonialism. The character of sovereignty in the non-European world was profoundly different from its character in the European world. Sovereignty represents at the most basic level an assertion of power and authority, a means by which a people may preserve and assert their distinctive culture. However for the non-European world sovereignty was "the complete negation of independent power, authority, and authenticity. This was not only because European sovereignty was used as a mechanism of suppression and management but," as Anghie (1999: 71) writes describing the age of colonialism, "also because acquiring sovereignty was equated with adopting European civilization. In effect, for the non-European society, personhood as recognized internationally was achieved precisely when the society ceased to have an independent existence, when it was absorbed into European colonial empires or when it profoundly altered its own cultural practices and political organizations." It might be said that global state economic governance institutions in the twenty-first century do not depart markedly from these criteria for the granting of sovereignty to peripheral social formations. The already sovereign states of the world adopt Western, and above all U.S., standards of governance of the political and economic spheres, remain under the close tutelage, and are subject to the continuous pressures by U.S. policymakers and the GSEGIs.

The effective management of the colonial scramble of the nineteenth-century imperial powers was a topic of deliberation in which, while it determined the future of hundreds of millions, the people affected played no part in the deliberations. Their governments were, if not directly controlled, then indirectly ruled and required to bring their legal, political, and economic regimes in line with standards set by the colonizing powers. They had to guarantee property rights, investment openness, and contract enforcement. When Prince Bismarck expressed the view that all the governments invited to the Berlin Conference of 1884–85 (devoted to rationalizing the imperialist project) "share the wish to bring natives of Africa within the pale of civilization by opening up the interior of the continent to commerce," and the British representative concurred that "trade would confer the advantages of civilization on the natives," it is possible that they were not insincere. As one hears similar generous offers from officials of the GSEGIs today, I do not myself hear a trace of disingenuous justification or awareness of self-interested behavior, but many in Asia, Africa, and Latin America do. It is not too much of a stretch for people with historical memories of such times to see the demands of the GSEGIs in a context suggesting such imperialist motives. The Chinese, who when negotiating admission to the WTO faced American and European insistence that they give up sovereignty in various economic and financial areas, may be perhaps excused for believing they had been there before in the treaties of Nanking which forced them to surrender to Western demands in an earlier episode of globalization.

If the 1840s are not so long ago to the Chinese, Muslims in the Middle East hearing President George W. Bush's call for a "crusade" of "good against evil" can be forgiven for reading his remarks from a perspective going back to the early Middle Ages and stretching through the modern conquest of Islamic territories by the imperialist West as well as the many interventions, bombings of civilian populations, and general contempt shown for the intelligence and character of the peoples of the region. In Western usage the word "crusade" has long lost its original meaning of "a war of the cross," but in the Middle East, where the extreme violence and cruelty of the crusaders is believed to have an echo in the United States, the prewar sanctions against Iraq, which people in the region blamed for the death of a half million people, half of them children under five, engendered intense hatred. Similarly, the bombings in Afghanistan in the wake of the September 11 attacks (which resulted in the deaths of more civilians than were killed in the attacks themselves) caused a massive flow of refugees, while the UN was rendered unable to deliver food to millions of starving Afghans—all this as part of what the White House had initially called "Operation Infinite Justice." In the West Bank and Jerusalem, the destruction of Palestinian homes and villages by Israel, using American weapons and presumed to be a U.S. surrogate, fanned similar hatred. The inability of the United States to understand why it is seen as an imperial power, and the resentment toward the GSEGIs, which are viewed as its tools, occur in this wider context whose existence can only be noted in passing.

Analytically the discourse of diplomatic negotiation among sovereign states was supplemented and to some extent replaced in the 1980s and 1990s with a very different focus. International relations theorists became enamored of two level game analyses (with application to the advanced economies) that introduced the relation of domestic policy contestations as a secondary arena along with diplomatic negotiations between states. The need to simultaneously negotiate among domestic constituency players and with foreign governments moved discussion away from assuming unitary state actors and the insistence of the state centric frame evident in most earlier game theory models. In such games governments are generally portrayed as equal players with different interests. In modeling of collective action in an anarchic world, prisoners dilemma and other games stress incentives to defect, problems of monitoring compliance, and of enforcing agreements in which rational actor nations as unitary agents with divergent interests attempt to find binding solutions to reach the Pareto frontier.

Some of the more benign models stress information concerns, such as how the two sides learn about each other and signal intentions. Others are distribution models, based on the role of a consumer model of democracy in which institutions are embraced as a result of individual participants with given preferences making rational choices for their intended effect. Constructivist approaches allow goals and even player perception of their own interest to change in the process of dialogue and positive sum outcomes negotiated (Martin and Simmons, 1998) but still do not put differences in the participants' material situation and unequal options at the core of the negotiations. Introducing as reaching agreement among domestic interests able to influence outcomes as an equally important "game" was a back door way to bring in economic interests and thus a more economistic framing of the rational choice preferences of players.

Such approaches, when they most closely mimic mainstream economics in modeling rigor, miss many of the elements which are crucial from a mainline political economy perspective. The economy constrains choices and orders politics even as it is susceptible to political influences. Rational institutionalists are yet to face the challenge of retheorizing anarchy in market terms rather than a strictly political sovereignty frame. By admitting domestic conflicts on international policy matters and considering transnational corporations, international governance, and NGOs as actors, the rationalist institutionalist research agenda catches up with popular understanding of globalization. But since formalization is primary there is a problem. Introducing so many relevant elements complicates model building substantially and promotes indeterminacies. There is greater realism in such models when it is recognized that weak actors as well as more powerful ones make choices, "even if they make them within more severe constraints" (Keohane, 1989: 154), but such power disparities are not easily modeled formally or in empirically realistic terms. As models reflect thick depictions which are descriptive of the international political economy the prized parsimony and determinism of models are compromised. The trade-off is, or should be, clear. The cost of the emphases of rational choice models for those interested in studying the reality of sovereignty has been substantial.

REGIME THEORY

Much of the discussion of regime theory in the context of a liberal institutionalist outlook is more promising. From such a perspective the task is to explain the possibility, condition, and consequences of international governance beyond anarchy and short of supranational government. In this light the formation and evolution of international regimes represents a concrete manifestation of the internationalization of political authority and of development toward the international state. The use of the term "state" for the regime exercising cross border authority may seem problematic (given the definition of a state in an interstate system which is the inheritance of the Westphalian understanding of sovereignty), but the growing jurisdiction of international institutions at the expense of "sovereign" states should be clear. That all governments are not equal participants in the creation of such regimes is also obvious. What is more controversial is the contention that such regimes represent the embryonic form of an international state. What has been under theorized is the importance instrumentally of corporate actors and what German Marxist literature calls capital logic.

Arguing the importance of nonstate actors over the single minded state centric optic of much IR theorizing is not to dismiss the role of governments and especially exercise of power by the world's only superpower. The New World Order proclaimed by the first President Bush was very much an exercise in U.S. contrivance. A framing of terms of the New World Order after September 11 and George W. Bush team's focus on terrorism and, in the family tradition, concentration on oil producing states, creates an intermingling of state politics and capital logic which interact in complex ways. Contingency plays a significant role as well, considering the way September 11 was thought to "change everything" and employed to change much. Nonetheless structurally we can continue to speak of the importance of the GSEGIs, transnational corporations, and international financial actors as playing a continued key role, even if at times they seemed overshadowed and subservient to military activism.

Robert Cox (1994) reconceptualized international regimes in terms of institutionalized hegemony giving theoretical form to the widespread observations that the United States was instrumental in the design and operation of the global state economic governance institutions. From such a perspective the ideal of neoliberalism corresponds to U.S. interests and the power exercised as a result of the U.S. hegemonic position in the international political economy. Cox's framework goes further, asserting that the basic norms of such institutionalized hegemony seen from the perspective of the "others" of the world system need to be challenged. From the economics of globalization side the politics of competition requires attention to the important nonstate players. These include the major international banks, law firms, consultancies, and accountants. Government must negotiate with foreign firms which control intellectual property, capital, and access to markets necessary to an economy's growth and to a satisfactory payments position.

Whatever the designs of transnational capital—a construction broader than U.S.-based corporate interests and its liberalization project, aided and abetted by the U.S. and other core governments—the process is hardly uncontested. The demand by developing nations in the 1970s for a New International Economic Order, for a debtors' cartel in the 1980s, for alternatives to IMF one size fits all austerity-structural adjustment in the 1990s, are examples of conflict which fit the neo-Gramscian IR theory and which will be discussed in some detail in the next chapter. Here we note that neo-Gramscians see beneath the formal structure of international regimes a struggle between global social forces representing corporations, the interests of state elites, and social justice movements over the legitimacy of parties qualified to participate, the decision procedures to be followed, and the operation of compliance mechanisms.

It is this perspective rather than game theoretic rational choice theory which informs the approach taken here. The underside of globalization, the resistance to local identity forces and the disorder which comes from contested claims for exclusive territorial control, are another part of globalization, as has been noted. As the forces of identity politics in their most violent representations, the impacts of failed states and excluded groupings, and the phenomena associated with disorganized capitalism and the stagnation forces and instabilities of global capitalism take their toll, the terms of the discussion change. For one thing imperialism resurfaces with its original positive Hobsonian connotations as the necessary task which must be undertaken by the Western powers for the good of the people of today's failed states and to transform rogue states through a process of subjugation and then nation building.

If we take as the central feature of the contemporary world system that relations of power and dependence characterize the context in which choices are made, much of the game theory modeling becomes of secondary applicability for the typical country within this system in its international diplomacy. The most important characterization of the international system is for them not that it is characterized by anarchy, but by profound inequality. It is the tight constraints that surround choice which are generally determining. The preferences of the most powerful actors, and today we can say that the most powerful actor is the United States, counts for more than the preferences of the majority of putatively sovereign states. This is best kept in mind when we consider liberal institutionalist approaches to the positive sum game of regime construction. We need to be continually sensitive to the structural context within which agreements are made.

Theorists of statist development whether in its Western European corporatist form, from the perspective of the decentralized regional industrial district politico-social complex, or the East Asian state-technocratic version, see the struggle as one among and between competing capitalist forms and the political institutional governance structures of which they are a part. The central contradiction is between, on the one hand, those who accept the desirability and inevitability of deregulation of economic spaces in a world system characterized by a basic anarchy not simply because of a lack of a global government structure but also as a result of the efficiency producing anarchy of the market forces of capitalism as a mode of production, and on the other hand theorists who ask whether it is possible to extend arrangements which have been developed at the level of the nation-state to create mechanisms capable of containing the destabilizing potential of transnational financial flows and the deflationary pressures of overinvestment which have global depression producing capacities, and promote through conscious redistributive arrangements a more equitable division of wealth, income, and political influence.

Recognition of U.S. hegemony and the political nature of the globalization project is a needed corrective to analyses which interpret nations as unable to stand up to globalization's demands said to be technologically determined. It is useful to focus on the U.S. role as an active participant in the structuring of globalization to clarify that if the United States has lost power to the international market, the loss has been largely self-inflicted. As Susan Strange (1994b: 213) argued in order to "make the rest of the world safe and welcoming to American capitalism," successive U.S. governments have broken down barriers to foreign investment and promoted capital mobility. These changes increase the asymmetries of power between states to the advantage of the more economically powerful. Delinking from the world economy is no longer a real possibility. That, as Strange wrote (1994b: 215), "is what dependency means today." Instead, as Robert Cox (1994: 49) asserts, the state is forced to become "a transmission belt from the global to the national economy, where hither to fore it had acted as the bulwark defending the domestic welfare from external disturbances." From such perspective, since opting out is not possible, the question is what kind of relationship nation-state formations will have to global capital and how they will use the power they individually and collectively retain in order to shape their own institutions and those of global governance.

To say that we expect states to join a regime in which they estimate the benefits of membership to outweigh the costs is not a very deep explanation of why governments become members of such organizations as the IMF and the WTO. They are made offers they cannot refuse by the Godfather, or god uncle who sees himself as a generous and paternalistic figure whose client states should show proper deference to his requests. There is little choice when the hegemon offers lesser nations the chance to join a club the god uncle thinks important to establish. They have little real choice about joining or not. In this basic sense the GSEGIs can be seen as imposed regimes, using the term as Keohane suggests (1999: 152) to mean "a regime agreed upon within constraints that are mandated by powerful actors." The structured inequality of the world system foreshadows outcomes which sovereign nations have inadequate power to escape. They make the best deals they can from the choices which confront them.

POWER AND THE MARKET

Formal models have been for the most part cooperation games in which the struggle is for relative advantage in a mutual accommodation within players' acceptable parameters and in which the issues at stake are clearly specified as payoff matrices. In most story telling approaches, on the other hand, power enters the decisionmaking process by influencing the choice of issues to be considered in international fora and of which organizations are deemed appropriate places for their negotiation. Rationality is always contextual and the constraints imposed on negotiators crucial. Coercion may be administered by circumstances and by those powerful enough to set the agendas and enforce preferred understanding of the issues and givens of the situation. Bounded rationality needs to be understood in ideologically constrained as well as informational absorption terms. Thus in the 1970s the Third World wanted discussion of trade issues at UNCTAD, the United Nations Commission on Trade and Development, the more open forum in which theirs was the majority voice. Most nations of the core preferred GATT, the General Agreement on Tariffs and Trade, tightly under the control of the leading industrial nations.

Such awareness of power relations and negotiating settings need to inform considerations of calls for the replacement of the modern state system with universal governance mechanisms that advocates claim would minimize conflict. Such proposals have been around for a long time. They go back at least to 1310 and Dante's *Monarchia*, to say nothing of the message of the great religions of the world with their explicit Golden Rule governance imperatives. The good intentions are clear. Yet power is never absent from such idealist enterprises and the weak resist the embrace of global governance mechanisms they consider agencies of domination. Part of the problem is the inequality of political and military power among states, as IR theorists have always known, but importantly, economic power, which IPE brought to the discussion more forcefully in the last decades of the twentieth century, grew more central.

The openness of the international political economy to unrestrained market forces, if granted by state authority, dissolves much of the pretense of what may remain of the Westphalian system. The international institutions of economic governance from the IMF to the WTO in enforcing liberalization of markets produce political as well as economic tensions. In this basic regard theirs is a political agenda. They are the agencies of the emergent contender for universal government, the international state, guided primarily by or responding in dependent fashion to, capital rather than monarchical or religious universalism or to a democratic polity. Contemporary globalization's universalism claims the right to reorganize the state system in market terms. The existing state formations are the midwives to the transformation. The American state's foremost role is complemented by the cooperation of subservient state formations. Globalization happens within each social formation. While it enters from outside, it is at the same time created through countless local adaptations to its dominance.

Modes of market governance redefine property rights as well as nation state sovereignty. Property rights, like sovereignty, are best not seen as an embracing claim to exclusive exercise of power. (In the case of sovereignty that of state power as a single governing authority within a territory with no external authority over it. In the case of property rights, exclusive possession, and control which allows unilateral usage and disposal of assets owned.) Property rights are a bundle of prerogatives which can be separated and redefined in social terms extending collective ownership over aspects of what had been considered private (as in earlier times an emergent capitalism had claimed the private right to redefine what had once been collective). For example, at the local level agencies decide what responsibilities forms of ownership entail with regard to permissible building materials, setbacks, and who owns air rights. Markets are institutions that rely upon states, how they are organized, regulated, embedded, and influenced by contingent events.

Markets are not naturally free. They are socially constructed. If the state mediates relations between the territory it governs and such forces of the world system, and if the initiating factors for the most part originate beyond national borders in forces not controlled by individual states, sovereignty needs to be understood as a much diminished construct. The state has far less autonomy than IR theorists have generally admitted. On the other hand, given common globalization pressures how states respond to constraints and opportunities can be seen as making states more, not less, important actors in the globalization process. The presumption that they either resist or accept globalization simplifies what is a more complex relation. Different sectors of the state, competing interest groups, and class fractions have different attitudes toward globalization as a project and to particular agendas which are part of this larger project.

It is thus to simplify when the questions are asked: Can states choose from a range of alternative ways to respond to globalization pressures? How much agency do they and should they have? The constraints of the international financial system surely must be seen as limiting both sovereignty and the maneuvering space of agency. A nation's capacity to pursue effective development strategies is conditioned not only by its access to external capital, foreign aid, international market opportunities, and economic location in the division of labor, but also by divisions within a social formation itself. From such a perspective state institutions need to be viewed as intervening variables rather than as the appropriate point of theoretical departure. At the same time there is reason to believe that some state formations over substantial periods of time are more successful in the promoting of if not autonomous development, than development which retains more of the surplus it can potentially produce for internal owners and allow higher standards of living for its citizens. It may also be noted that unique forms of capitalist development pursued by particular states do not bring continued success. Their success typically does not last. The questions of what accounts for economic miracles and developmental crises, how the domestic and the international are conjoined, and how the social relations of particular production systems allow for distribution and appropriation of benefits to be theorized are crucial ones for IPE.

HARMONIZATION

As global trade expands there is obvious need to harmonize standards. It would be nice for example if one's mobile phones worked without problems throughout the world. The problem is that since different countries and companies have developed competing specifications each has had interest in theirs being adopted as the universal norm. Generally in the high tech area the United States has had the market clout to have its standards adopted as the universal one. Everyone else has had to go along. This has not always meant the adoption of the best system. Sometimes the competitive process has not resulted in a clear winner as in the case of the mobile telephone standard which because of conflict among powerful participants and U.S. preference for leaving such things to the market there has been a prolonged period of incompatibility. The Americans have allowed domestic competitors to use their own proprietary systems. In Europe there has been agreement on a common system (GSM, global system for mobiles). This unity has helped make it the global standard in which two non-American firm's Nokia (Finland) and Ericsson (Sweden) led as the *de facto* standard for second generation digital telephony becoming the mobile system of choice for most subscribers since it works not only in Europe but the Middle East, India and the Pacific Rim.

In the United States, which did not back the GSM standard, first generation analog phones continued to dominate. The European equipment producers benefitted from the economies of scale and efficiencies associated with developing a stable technology platform. The European lead if maintained through third generation mobile phones gave these producers a significant advantage as new personal digital appliances become the principal wireless signal for watching video, receiving data, and carrying out transactions, as well as making phone calls. These achievements have propelled the European information technology industry to success in telecommunications equipment and services. The Japanese learned when they stuck to a domestic standard for second generation phones that such a strategy leads to isolation and defeat. In the third generation contest the Japanese joined with the Europeans against the Americans. It appears at this point in the hard fought negotiations that although three "modes," each corresponding to a standard put forward by combatants has been accepted, the U.S. companies will not have their usual predominant influence on the standard, but it remains to be seen how the issue is played out with so many billions of dollars at stake and technologies developing in unpredictable ways.

Traditionally, countries accepted that when their firms did business in other countries of relatively equal standing they would abide by the rules of that jurisdiction. However with globalization there has been pressure from TNCs for a single set of rules applicable everywhere to level the playing field and reduce the transaction costs involved in overlapping and contradictory requirements. Harmonization can be achieved in different ways. Reciprocity can be replaced by acceptance of externally imposed conditionality. For example, unless less powerful countries agree to rules favored by economically more important ones, they may be barred from their markets. The United States has used this tactic to great effect. Short of such threat diplomacy milder incentives can be structured to induce conformity on the assumption that all participants gain when transaction costs fall and differences fade with time, GSEGIs offer a single set of norms and procedures which may be accepted as preferable to an anarchic lack of formal structure in which might prevails. Issues related to harmonization and standardization underlie how the information economy understood to characterize early twenty-first century globalization are played out. It is useful to say something more about each of these topics, the information economy and standardization, and to remember that easy generalization about and celebration of the triumph of a particular national economic model typically do not long endure.

It was not too long ago that the literature was aflutter with dire pronouncements bemoaning the United States' fate as a declining hegemon. In the summer of 1992 when a distinguished group of economists and policymakers met at the Federal Reserve Board of Kansas City's annual Jackson Hole Wyoming Symposium, N. Gregory Mankiw (1992: 87) speaking on the search for growth, told the assemblage "Over the past 30 years, income per capita rose by 5.1 percent per year in Japan and 2.5 percent in Germany, but by only 2.1 percent in the United States. Of the 24 countries in the Organization for Economic Cooperation and Development (OECD) only three grew more slowly than the United States." Another prominent speaker, C. Fred Bergsten, devoted his remarks to what he said the Japanese call "the America problem" which was not just our slow growth but our long term problems and trajectory: "the fact that our productivity has expanded less than 1% per year for about 20 years and our real wages are flat or down over that twenty year period" among other seemingly intractable structural problems. Since Great Britain's performance was also poor there was consensus that the superior Germano-Japanese model of organization did a better job of monitoring corporate management and managing asymmetric information problems than the Anglo-American system of arm's length financing.

Within two decades the tables had turned and *Financial Times* columnist Martin Wolf (1999a: 12) summed up a new consensus when he wrote that good Anglo-Saxon growth performance "is no flash in the pan." He noted that between 1982 (the starting point of the previous economic cycle for the G7 as a whole) and the end of 1998, the last available data as he wrote, U.S. GDP rose 66% while the GDPs of both the UK and Canada increased by 54%, well above the growth rates in other advanced economies. Unemployment rates in the Anglo-Saxon economies were well below continental Europe. "Ah bliss . . . " he declared touting the "intrinsically extremely attractive" Anglo-Saxon model. Dramatic changes in perception can occur in so little time. Similarly, reevaluation of the East Asian miracle growth and state-led development regimes quickly turned to denunciation of "crony capitalism" said to have caused the region's deep crisis of the late 1990s. Such turnabouts should caution those who confidently make sweeping statements about the likely trajectory of the ipe.

Indeed, I would argue that such enthusiasm does not accurately measure the achievement of the U.S. economy in the second half of the 1990s. First America's lead is in part a matter of preferred measure of what to do with the fruits of increased productivity. Americans choose to work longer hours and take less leisure. The substantial lead the United States is supposed to enjoy over France for example, that exemplar of the "Old Europe," is explained almost entirely by the fact that Americans work twenty percent more hours than the French, who prefer a shorter work week, far longer summer vacations, and to retire earlier. The United States might be getting richer as a result but this is hardly an unambiguous victory. Similarly, making adjustments for the entire euro zone, while it is the case that for the 1980–2001 period real annual growth is nearly half again as fast in the United States, if growth is measured on a per capita basis nearly all of the difference disappears. The U.S. lead is mostly caused by population growth (Turner, 2003).

A second factor is that the figures for growth in productivity for the American miracle economy are highly suspect following widespread revelations of accounting fraud and the collapse of the high tech New Economy stock market bubble followed by years of poor performance. Between 1997 and the peaking of the U.S. stock market in 2000 profits for the U.S. nonfinancial corporate sector fell by 20 percent. One indication of these profit figures being inflated is the increasing number of firms which had to restate their profits as fraudulent accounting came to light. But even taking the profit figures at face value, as they were falling the stock market, which is supposed to reveal expected profitability continued to register an unfounded optimism. The broadest measure of U.S. corporate performance, the Wilshire 5000 Index rose between 1997 and 2000 by 65 percent while profits (after taxes and net of interest) fell by 23 percent. The 4200 companies listed on the Nasdaq made $145 billion in profits over the five years of the boom, 1995–2000. In the twelve months following July 1, 2000 they reported losses of $148 billion. The hype of the New Economy turned out to be just that hype. Robert Brenner (2003: 8), after rehearsing the relevant numbers offers the term "stock market Keynesianism" to describe the U.S. economic "miracle of the second half of the 1990s to suggest a smoke and mirrors market self levitation which through the wealth effect (the impact of higher asset values on consumer spending) led to the consumer driven expansion of these years.

This was also a period of growing consumer debt as people leveraged their expectations to support a lifestyle most of them would not be able to maintain. Considering the entire cycle of the 1990s the annual growth rate per capita was in any case an anemic 1.6 percent compared to a long term 2.2 percent for the country over the prior 100 years, 1889–1989. The average worker's real wage was lower at the end of the boom than it had been in 1973, a date which can serve as the start of the neoliberal era. Moreover the unhealthy relation between America's dependence on capital inflows amounted to 4 percent of GDP to cover its annual current account deficit, an imbalance which was producing increased fragility and danger for the world economy.

The presumption of overwhelming success for the American model of free market capitalism allowed critical attention to focus on the laggard economies of Europe, Japan, and the developing world, which were all criticized in rather pompous and patronizing terms by U.S. policymakers based on America's presumed brilliant performance and told they had to become "more like us." That the advice was for the most part bad and self-serving is obscured by the triumphalism which may prove even more misplaced with the passage of time. Indeed, as will be suggested in the final chapter, a next stage IPE may be focused less on the failings of the poor countries and more on the problems of the rich ones and more fundamentally of the neoliberal order.

With such a warning in mind the characteristics of the leading sectors of the globalized economy at the start of the twenty-first century nonetheless suggested to policymakers at the Treasury and at the GSEGIs that the liberal market economies, led by the United States—with their more flexible labor markets, price led contracting, and efficient capital markets—are institutionally more competitive than the less flexible coordinated market economies such as those of Japan and Germany, the second and third largest economies. The latter group's greater prevalence of non-market modes of collaboration as opposed to spot market forms of organization proved advantageous in the postwar period, allowing for longer term planning, a focus on constant improvement of process and quality of products, and inclusive deliberation modes which promoted stable growth and incremental innovation. The thicker common knowledge and more stable institutional learning created a culture in which cooperation produced superior results. The institutional complementarities increased returns by linking education, labor markets, government policy, and firm developments which succeeded in market terms while generating more egalitarian income distribution, provision of quality public goods, and other benefits.

By the 1990s liberal market economies with their mean and lean structure more readily jettisoned redundant workers, declining sectors, and redeployed capital driven by investors set on short-term profits. They were more successful in generating profits than the coordinated market economies. Workers without job guarantees meant not only that layoffs were not impeded by convention or contract but that short-term job tenure was accepted. Fluid labor markets from the point of view of employers meant that new technologies and new organizations could quickly be adopted by hiring workers with the marketable skills while laying off others. Venture capital's availability, payment with stock instead of cash, and willingness for major risk taking on the part of startups and even established firms moved new ideas and product strategies through to rapid implementation. Whether this model will continue to promote more rapid growth than the coordinated market approach cannot be known with the certainty its boosters claim. It is however the case that the shaping of GSEGIs is biased to considerable extent to policies reflecting the interests of countries and corporations committed to the liberal market model.

The information technology and telecommunications revolution brings with it challenges for the harmonization of standards across national systems of regulation. Questions of interoperability, open access versus proprietary control, and a host of other standard issues involve clashes among coercion, cooperation, and competition with different interest groups favoring more liberal or more regulationist modes based on perceptions of self-interest. In some countries there are state run standard-setting associations or industrial confederation negotiated agreements. In more liberal economies competition in the marketplace is the preferred way to establish standards through market testing of consumer preferences. Standard coordination in Japan was important to that country's economic miracle as research consortia and cooperation by leading firms within industrial associations allowed an interoperability and network effects subsidized and otherwise encouraged by the state with protection from foreign alternatives allowed domestic firms to compete in marketing, special features, and complementary products. By the 1990s the U.S. market oriented approach of little regulation and firms competing with their own proprietary standards against each other struggling for supremacy, which would bring with it dominance of their standard in a winner take all pattern, seemed the more effective route to greater innovation and more rapid growth. U.S. firms, sometimes in strategic alliance with foreign as well as domestic partners, compete against other such alliances under intense pressure. Competitors place high stakes bets on initiatives. Successful standard setting by a single dominant firm or team can be richly rewarded.

As the single global market emerges competition among national models for the management of standards and governance regimes more broadly become the central battlefield for national capitals where home companies function within a matrix of national institutional supports and constraints. While we talk of transnational corporations because this has now become standard practice, the term multinational more accurately reflects a reality in which most firms remain anchored in a specific national business culture even as they engage in activities around the globe. Few can claim to have become truly transnational in the sense of not being tied to a particular home economy and its business culture. National differences remain important. The French method, relying on state and professional associations which mediate among firms in the development of national standards, suggests a different global state economic governance institutional framing than the Anglo-American one or the German private industrial association pattern. British industrial companies, by supporting and as a result being trapped within a lowest common denominator approach to standardization, have been unable to provide the range and quality of process and product standards of other leading industrial economies. It has even been suggested that the rigidities in the British standardization system may be a proximate cause of Britain's long-standing relative industrial decline (Tate, 2001: 446). Britain has struggled with a low-skill, low-wage pattern because a deregulated labor market has produced an industrial relations system that discourages manufacturing firms from making long-term investments in their employees (Fioretos, 2001: 221).

In contrast German producers' ability to hold to high standards of quality and ongoing product and process improvement allowed them to pay high wages to their skilled workforce thanks in part to the binding standardization regulation which is so thoroughly part of the German variety of capitalism. This is not the product of state decrees. Standardization in Germany is the result of private-sector coordination by business led standards organizations. German trade associations create standards contractual structures or industrial frameworks which spread technologies and lower information costs for all participants and lead to widespread adoption of best practice techniques. German courts can effectively employ regulatory contract law doctrines based on social market norms that cannot be used in the United States where they are routinely dismissed by legal experts as untenable (Casper, 2001). The reason is that the non-market forms of coordination of Germany's standardized but sophisticated contractual structures facilitate forms of industrial organization which do not exist in the United States. However, as has been noted, while the German system's performance was superior in the postwar period, by the 1980s and 1990s U.S.-based companies have shown their less regulated model to create highly innovative forms of industrial organization allowing many of its firms to dominate in a range of high technology industries characterized by innovative strategies which the Germans, Japanese, and other coordinated market systems have been unable to match. U.S. firms with fewer regulations and maximum freedom to contract have a governance structure which has been superior in developing intellectual property across a spectrum of new industries.

Liberal market economy negotiators, whose companies' competitive strategies depend on maintaining deregulated product and labor markets and maximizing flexibility in contractual relations, are guided by such concerns in their international negotiating. The question of whose competitiveness rules will dominate the world trade regime is still unsettled although the U.S. has made significant progress in forcing the adaption of its conceptual frame and preferred regulations. If businesses obtain legal standing to bring complaints before the WTO, something they do not have, but that the U.S. is striving to achieve, one can expect a U.S.-style rationale and litigation processes to dominate. In a related area, a number of cases have come up where mergers approved in one jurisdiction are challenged in another where they are seen to be anti-competitive. While Europe has an antitrust authority which is at work harmonizing EU rules there is no global authority on antitrust leading to European regulators' rejections of some high-profile acquisitions by U.S. giants. There are efforts to move such discussions to the OECD, where the major industrial countries could work out a policy and then other nations could be encouraged to adopt these rules. In the meantime different national judiciaries have come to conflicting decisions as to whose law governs cases involving their own and foreign corporations operating within and outside of their jurisdiction.

The logic of globalization argues for a greater role for GSEGIs in setting norms and enforcing them. We can expect a harmonizing of bankruptcy laws and legal recourse more generally. Loss of sovereignty is inevitable for countries which want to join the various regime clubs. The incentive for membership is a powerful one—the ability to attract capital. Nonetheless for the largest of the transitional economies, China and Russia, and for India, the process is proving a lengthy one. Such large countries have a great deal of bargaining power and local elites have their own interests and strategies. The stakes are high and countries have major concerns they want addressed stemming both from unique national circumstance and preference for a liberal or a market coordinated model of capitalism. Developmental state models also continue to exist even if they like others have been modified under globalization pressures. These coercions are not the natural force of the invisible hand but rather the insistent enforcement of hegemonic preferences imposed upon them. The effort to paint these forced adaptations as the result of impersonal market forces is a political tactic and an ideological explanation which will require further attention. The trajectory of China alone will shape the world in ways now impossible to predict.

What sometimes appears to be the result of market forces overriding governmental preferences, past procedures, and laws can in fact be changes resulting from informal governance agreements outside traditional state-based fora. These agreements are effectively binding even when non-legal in character. They empower certain market practices and restrict the ability of state regulatory authorities to find alternative ways to regulate regime areas. Harmonization of rules, policies, and enforcement procedures advance through informal discussion among major market participants and then intergovernmental accords which leave states with the option of opting out of particular harmonization agreements. Global state economic governance institutions, individual rules, and broad regimes can be created by soft law, informal agreements typically reached as a process of concentric club formation (as will be discussed in chapter 4) and then made into hard law through formal diplomatic treaties. They then take the form of supranational laws and institutions which are able to bind states. Before we examine these procedures at work, we shall take a look at the IPE literatures as a source of theoretical guidance.

CHAPTER FOUR

The Nature and Scope of International Political Economy

"International political economy is a subject without clear boundaries. It is as old as trade and theft between societies—hence older than written history. It is spatially extensive: today, no spot on the globe is untouched by distant markets or their manipulation by powerful states, and if intergalactic trade were ever to become a reality, international political economy would surely study it. The actual agents number in the billions: they are firms and individuals, from parochial peasants to jet-setting tycoons and office-bound state bureaucrats. Unlike stylized versions of "international" (that is, interstate) politics, political economy cannot be encompassed solely by the interactions of states.

"This absence of boundaries implies an abundance of confusion."

—*Robert O. Keohane* (1997: 150)

"Questions of theory and method are inseparable from purpose. . . . [C]ritical theorists seek to transcend the milieu they are located in by uncovering its historically contingent origins, and the ideas and power relationships that sustain it, and inquiring as to how it may be changed. Problem solving theorists, on the other hand, see problems as isolated from complex wholes. The particular context is taken as given. The purpose of theory then becomes to solve the particular problem to restore the *status quo ante*."

—*Mitchell Bernard* (1997: 77)

In the 1970s, President Nixon's decision to end American commitment to the fixed gold parity for the dollar and the irreversible damage done to the Bretton Woods system of fixed exchange rates, followed eighteen months later by the OPEC (Organization of Petroleum Exporting Countries) dramatic price increase, ushered in an era dominated by issues that, as Susan Strange (1995a: 151) argued, "were superficially economic—but also fundamentally political in the sense that outcomes were the product of changing policies as well as of changing markets." It came to be widely understood that elections were won and lost on the basis of the condition of domestic economies, and the condition of domestic economies even in the largest countries were more and more conditioned by developments in the international political economy. Questions related to the global economy loomed larger in the domestic consciousness. Economics grew more important than traditional Cold War "hot button" issues. In 1978 Peter Gourevitch was asking: "Is the traditional distinction between international relations and domestic politics dead?" and was answering with a definite "Perhaps." At the start of the decade Susan Strange had seen the pace of developments in the international system accelerating "Outdistancing and out-growing the rather more static and rigid international political system" (Strange, 1970: 405) In an essay published in 1981 Richard Blackhurst proposed that more and more matters once considered domestic would be reclassified as international. He suggested: "the reclassification will continue into the foreseeable future, aiming toward an end point where few economic policies of any consequence will be considered primarily domestic." (Blackhurst, 1981: 363) In a 1993 article Ruggie could go a step further and conclude "Now that border barriers have been reduced to insignificant levels, domestic economic structures *ipso facto* are taking center stage in international trade disputes. If they diverge systematically and have 'important" effects on international transaction flows, then an international policy problem potentially exists" (Ruggie, 1993: 511).

Surely by the end of the twentieth century it was evident to U.S. policymakers that international economic policy problems needed to be dealt with not as afterthoughts to the high politics of diplomatic concerns, but systematically and not on an *ad hoc* basis, each somehow a surprise when it surfaced. Rather many were patterned and predictable in nature if not in the specific (who would have thought up a banana war between the U.S. and the EU as occurred in the late 1990s?). In such instances the businesses involved enlisted the assistance of their home governments as they fought each other for market advantage. Diplomacy had become triangular, as Strange noted (1995a: 167). It occurred between states and states, but also states and firms and firms and firms.

In this triangular perspective, if we accept that actors engage in politics whenever they needed the assistance of others to get what they want, then politics is everywhere in the economy. The economy is by nature a political economy. Running a business involved political relations between a firm and its suppliers and creditors. It turned out to be only sometimes about spot exchange in atomistic markets as mainstream theory teaches. It is more importantly about relational contracting and the management of transaction costs which are "political," or have important political elements, and many are inevitably international as well. What is remarkable is how little the leading journals in the field have themselves become globalized. U.S.-based authors thoroughly dominate. As Ole Wæver (1998: 689) remarks in a celebration of the first fifty years of the journal *International Organization*, the field bears "the strange combination of American insularity and hegemony," underlining the often unacknowledged but obviously undeniable point that International Relations and International Political Economy are American social science.

This chapter considers the boundary issues and mapping of IPE. Central is the comparison of theoretic treatments, especially between the two programs in economics/political economy which I describe as the mainstream and the mainline approaches (Tabb, 1999). The first is the parsimonious, abstract logic of pure theory most closely identified with neoclassical economics. The second is the heterodox method with its inductive generalization of historical and institutional data. There is innate tension between the two. The first is a theoretical framework which seeks to explain events and relationships in all times and places and so follows what is understood as the hard science model, seeing the social world as subject to laws whose regularity is similar to classical physics and mathematics. The latter focuses on contingency, historical specificity, and agency. The tension, as Joan Robinson put it, is between equilibrium and history. Mainstream economic models are overwhelmingly based on a comparative statics which compares states of rest in which everything else is held constant while one variable changes. The system is then shown to move in a deterministic fashion from one situation of equilibrium to another. Exogenous shocks quickly set in motion offsetting reactions and a new balance is efficiently produced. There is no tendency for the equilibrium to be disturbed except when external interferences occur. Resources are optimally allocated because individuals in the context of free markets will act whenever there are unrealized opportunities for mutual gain. Markets are efficient. Adjustment is unproblematic, modeled as instantaneous. Systems are internally stable.

To many of those concerned with the dramatic and radical changes in the international political economy such a methodology has severe limitations. The very things which need explaining are held constant. For example basic patterns of communication and transportation which are mediated by national boundaries and the institutional regulation of exchange reorganize production and distribution not along some given production frontier. It is, as shall be discussed more fully later in this chapter, the introduction of new possibilities which were not part of the given choice set which puts in motion Schumpeterian creative destruction and dynamic growth. After an examination of how IPE emerged out of IR within the discipline of political science this chapter considers ways of doing political economy in the face of the gathering force of globalization which transforms the terrain of world politics and the relationship between economics and politics.

THE EMERGENCE OF IPE

IPE, as any relatively new and evolving discourse, comes into being and matures in reaction to the perceived failures and omissions in other approaches to the subject matter with which it is concerned. The separate field of IPE has grown in part because of the tight grasp the pure theory of international trade had on the thinking of economists. Proud of its rigor based on parsimonious assumptions and tight deductive priors, trade theorists into the 1980s seemed to be missing the nature of changes in the ipe. It was among sociologists, geographers, political scientists, and heterodox economists that historical specificity, observance of intra-industry trade in which similar products were cross shipped (something the classical theory did not predict or easily accommodate), the development of commodity chains, complex subcontracting patterns, and the dominant role of direct foreign investment to service local markets were most usefully studied. Conventional trade based on resource endowment was inadequate. It required supplementation from new models to fill the huge vacuum left by simpler reductionist, and ahistorical understandings of comparative advantage. In the last decade the research of neighboring disciplines has stimulated a defensive catchup by trade economists some of whom have been quite creative in finding explanations for these trends and moving beyond the givens that previously confined their thinking.

While IPE as an intellectual project needs an economics foundation, the idea of joining the economic and the political is difficult if politics is centrally about power and economists categorically reject power as a valid category in their work, as most do, and if economics in its mainstream version presumes isolated individual actors with given preference orderings while much of politics is about how opinions are formed and how they can be molded. It is not without interest that the generation of economists that inspired attention by political scientists and other non-economist social scientists in the politics of the international economy were of a generation which had been involved or influenced by policy work in the New Deal and postwar recovery periods. Many in that earlier generation were sensitive to, even prescient about, new developments in the international political economy. In a 1968 book Richard Cooper wrote on *The Economics of Interdependence*. In a 1972 journal article Cooper put forward what became the position of a generation of liberal institutionalists rooting a new conception of the world economic order, one which privileged political economy, often dismissed by others as "low politics." Cooper argued that the fixed exchange regime, competitive markets, and occasional treaties were not viable as stabilizers in the long run. Charles Kindleberger's 1969 *American Business Abroad*, and Raymond Vernon's 1971 *Sovereignty at Bay* are too important to those who pioneered what became IPE. Robert Keohane and Joseph Nye's 1972 landmark *Transnational Relations and World Politics* was a response to such concerns. The next generation of economists brought up with a more abstract, theoretical and mathematical model of what a good economist does, did not follow up on these grounded policy interests.

There is widespread agreement among non-economists that "In reality, the recent history of the social sciences shows that enormous areas of scientific knowledge have been abandoned by the science of economics. These areas have been taken over by neighboring disciplines," as Mattei Dogan writes in *The Handbook of Political Science* (1996: 114). "At one particular moment, economics reached a fork in the path: it could have chosen intellectual expansion, the penetration of other disciplines, at the cost of diversification, and at the risk of dispersal (a risk taken by political science);" he writes but "instead it chose to remain unflinchingly pure, true to itself, thereby forfeiting vast territories. Yet many economists consider that the choice of purity, methodological rigor and hermetic terminology was the right choice."

Such a generalization needs qualification and perhaps is better rejected on a number of grounds. Economists through this period engaged in a spirited project of imperializing onto the ground of the other social sciences by applying their micro analysis to such areas as crime, racial discrimination, the family (Becker, 1976), and by the late 1990s were routinely writing on such matters as electoral politics, theorizing the role of interest groups (Grossman and Helpman, 1999) and analyzing voter turnout (Schachar and Nalebuff, 1999). Moreover, as noted, it is the seminal work of economists which political scientists took up and made the core of work in IPE. Kenneth Waltz's *Theory of International Politics* (1979) launched a neorealist school based on a micro model of the formation of markets transported to the international political realm and game theoretic models developed by among others Thomas Schelling. Robert Keohane's neoliberal institutionalism builds on transaction theories of the firm and the broader industrial organization literature developed by Oliver Williamson and other economists. The practitioners of constructivism (perspective which has become central to the IPE discourse to be discussed later in this chapter) would do well to (re)read Douglass North's 1993 Nobel Address for an appreciation of the complexities of the learning process of organizations and individual negotiators. Regime theory is premised on Ronald Coase's transaction costs and so on. The economist's concept of market failure becomes political market failure. The convergence of neorealism and neoliberalism evident in recent years is in significant measure the result of their shared commitment to analytic foundations in hypothetico-deductive theorizing by rational actors maximizing expected utility directly borrowed from economists.

I think the reason for the widely held presumption that economics has abandoned so much of the terrain of political economy (rather than being the theoretical center for so much of the theorizing in related social sciences) is that economics is so theory driven that it appears (and often is) so abstracted from real world specificities as to seem (and again many would say in fact is) lacking in usefulness. IR and IPE are still essentially problem driven, while hardly devoid of theory. (Indeed, the road to progress, and certainly to career advancement in political science as well as economics, is in advancing theory.) Theory needs to be continually reframed in terms of current problem solving and tied to formulating policy solutions in preference to privileging the logical consistency of abstract models. Nonetheless many political scientists and others consider the conceptual apparatuses (typically drawn from economics)—among them game theoretic models, collective good problems, free riding, and market failure—to be exceedingly valuable. How useful they have been in practice in solving immanent pressing problems is hotly contested.

The dramatic inroads rational choice modeling has made is interesting in this regard. Its progress is driven by the conceptual power of neoclassical economics and so is valued for its theoretical rigor and parsimonious elegance. It is thus possible to see the development of Nash equilibrium noncooperative games based on intelligent rational actor behavior as comparable to "the discovery of the DNA double helix in the biological sciences" (Myerson, 1999: 1067). Both political scientists and economists press ahead developing evolutionary rational choice models of how individual strategies produce social structures and such modeling techniques as we shall have occasion to note have not been without influence in IPE. The jury remains out with regard to claims to usefulness in policymaking. Some do not think the theory has gotten beyond the level of tautology. The "rigorous theory envy" does introduce an abstract quality to much writing in mainstream political science.

The complexity of discourse communities arises because scholars hold what, as we have noted, Joseph Schumpeter called different pre-analytic visions. To continue with the salient example of rational choice, political scientists doing IPE are drawn to neoclassical economists using similar methodologies and accepting the same behavioral assumptions because an atomistic social physics view of human interactions seems to them to best explain the deeper logic of social reality. Rationalists share a commitment to positivist social science and the assumption in IR and IPE that states are rational, unitary actors pursuing exogenously given preferences in an anarchic world. Institutionalists see preferences conditioned by norms and habits, influenced by social forces and interactions, and activities constrained through incentive structures imposed by and negotiated through institutions. Neo-Gramscians find heterodox political economists more congenial to their modes of thinking because of a competing understanding of the way material forces and ideology interact. This is not a matter of theory versus no theory but of very different ways of doing theory.

At another level while IPE from a political science perspective is undertaken as a project in designing better rules and decisionmaking processes, neoclassical economists see politics as basically inefficient, as the effort by interest groups to gain purchase on assets they are not entitled to as compensation for their marginal contributions to well being by using the coercive power of the state. The mainstream economist is inclined to favor the minimal state these days with maximal reliance on market incentives. For political scientists, even those sympathetic to the implicit priors of such a view, politics is still a valid category. They are after all *political* scientists. Thus, generally IPE from the political science side makes more fulsome background assumptions and starts with a pre-analytical vision in which socialization and constraints of institutions on individual and group choice are more central. Robert Gilpin (1987: 9) provides an influential description of IPE as a field which studied how "the state and its associated political processes affect the production and distribution of wealth and, in particular, how political decisions and interests influence the location of economic activities and the distribution of the costs and benefits of these activities" would seem capacious enough to encompass most perspectives in the ongoing debates. Gilpin's emphasis from a realist starting point on how economic forces alter the international distribution of political and military power ties IPE to its IR origins while his inquiry into the role of markets and economic agency in the political process gave IPE more autonomous grounding.

Within this broad terrain, the focus here is in line with Murphy and Tooze's understanding (1991: 24) that "in a fairly straightforward way, the construction of the universe of IPE reflects the policy concerns of the government of the United States throughout the era of U.S. global supremacy and, especially, contemporary concerns about various challenges to that supremacy." While the difficulty for U.S.-based students of IPE to meaningfully internalize such a project is acknowledged, it is necessary that we question a too easy acceptance of the assumptions of American policymakers and the subtle substitution of U.S. decisionmaking elites' interests for the general interest, a shift which seems to characterize much writing on the topic in the United States. If IPE is to deal with what after all is contestation over interpretations of the way the world economy is organized, and can be reorganized, then the longstanding conflict between liberal political economy (liberal in the European usage) of the Anglo-American orthodoxy needs to be compared and contrasted with German, Japanese, and other statist capitalisms in a more evenhanded manner, and the challenges offered by the social movements of global civil society taken more seriously at both the intellectual level and in terms of a social analysis of where these movements come from and what they represent in a context of mass democratic intrusion into what has been a more exclusively elite policymaking. The same consideration will have to be given in the coming period to the perspective of rising powers such as China, India, Brazil, and other countries with large populations whose economies are becoming more important within the world system. These governments will need to be listened to more seriously than their lesser relative power commanded in the past.

Neoclassical growth models have been effectively questioned by the theoretical frame built on the study of those Gershenkron has called the late industrializers as well as those Amsden has labeled as "late, late industrializers." From the postwar period on, these models have challenged the Anglo-American model of how markets can work and development can take place. Analysts in the Anglo-American intellectual milieu often deprecate such development strategies, painting them as rent seeking impediments rather than possibly legitimate and effective alternatives. Recent awareness on the part of the World Bank among others, that simply diminishing the role of the state is not a satisfactory precondition for more rapid economic growth has led to a reconsideration about the basic perquisites for capitalist development. It has not led to a very wide consideration of alternative state roles to those enshrined in what is called the Washington Consensus neoliberal view of how development takes place (a perspective which will be extensively discussed). Part of the contemporary anti-state bias which adheres to much contemporary policy analysis is rooted ideologically in mainstream economics and the general equilibrium theorizing which undergirds such analysis. It is useful to review these foundations.

INTERNATIONAL RELATIONS

IR as a field can be said to have emerged in the post World War I period as a reaction to what was seen as the misguided idealism of the prewar political theorists. It is a house that realists built in that very specific context. Realism proved convincing in the post–World War II years as the early hopefulness of the period after fascism's defeat gave way to the bipolarity of the Cold War. Earlier reflections by E. E. Carr and others on the naïveté of internationalist idealism found a receptive audience. In the waning years of communism IPE's appeal became stronger as questions of comparative capitalism within a single world system came to the fore. The U.S.-centric realist-institutionalist condominium seemed to lack space for students of the German economic miracle, French indicative planning, Sweden's Third Way, and other versions of national capitalisms, especially corporatist versions so influentially discussed by Andrew Shonfield (1965). Interest in comparative political economy laid the groundwork for the IPE specialization that was further encouraged by the newly industrializing economies which seemed to have successfully challenged a hard center-periphery dichotomous world view.

Such an integration of politics and economics had not been prominent in academia since the 1880s when the first graduate programs in political science were started at Columbia and Johns Hopkins. The programs fell under the influence of the German theorists of the state, who had lost the great *Methodenstreit*, the Battle of the Methods, out of which economics emerged in its mainstream neoclassical form and economic science was freed of concern for the social. These issues were spun off to sociologists and the political became the domain of political scientists. IPE developed a century later as a community of inquiry in the context of the post–World War II university's penchant for developing subfields, new combinations and problematics reflecting developments in the social world. This was in a sense the logical evolution resulting from the disunity dating from that long forgotten late nineteenth-century epistemological and ontological debate on method in the social sciences and the disciplinary boundaries the outcome of these vituperative battles engendered. IPE is only one of the subdisciplines which in the late twentieth century brought together specialists from different fields who had interests in common. As in the case of area studies, those interested in globalization typically have more to discuss with scholars doing similar work in related academic fields than with most of their own department colleagues. Globalization has produced a redeployment of intellectual energies, a back to the future of a more holistic approach.

Within the IR field, which had been about diplomacy and military power, alliances and statesmanlike maneuverings, the isolation from political economy has proven costly. This was especially the case for realists. As Geoffrey Underhill (1994: 25) writes: "For traditional realists, international politics is largely about the struggle for power and the skill of statesmen at reaching a workable balance that provided for systematic stability and the successful management of inevitable conflicts of national interest. International politics became for realists a world apart, divorced from day-to-day interaction of socio-economic groups and institutions common to domestic politics." The problem with such a political science was that it avoided important issues which drive politics for "If politics is not about what goes on in people's pockets or purses, then it is difficult to imagine the content of political conflict in a domestic or international context."

It was this double distortion—the exclusive emphasis on high politics over the politics of commerce (most importantly economic conflict) and the tight separation between the international and the domestic—that invited the creation of, or rediscovery of, international political economy as a field of study. Its origin left a mark on much of the literature. Since the intellectual roots of so many IPE writers have been in international relations, they continue to focus on power relations of states while ignoring "exogenous" factors central to an understanding of the evolving ipe: technology and market structure. The issue of what should concern IPE as a field of study is as well the question of the perspective from which the ipe is investigated, theorized, and policy decisions formulated. One of the reasons for studying international political economy rather than international relations is that IPE extends "the conventional limits of the study of politics, and the conventional concepts of who engages in politics, and of how and by whom power is exercised to influence outcomes" (Strange,

1994b: 218). We have noted how IPE developed from the 1970s as a response to a host of concerns associated with an emergent globalism: negotiations over currency and trade issues, OPEC, the rise of Japan, and development state success in the East Asian export economies. As the international organizations responding to global interdependence multiplied and problems from financial contagion to environmental commons drew attention to the importance of institutions beyond the nation state and to greater concern over economics as opposed to traditional diplomacy, IPE emerged as a major subfield.

The dissonance between the two approaches to economics/political economy was evident in the way IPE scholars drew on different elements and understandings of economics and political economy. One emphasis, rooted in the free market efficiency naturalism of David Ricardo (Murphy, 1996 is particularly helpful on the relation between Ricardian economics and rational choice theory in political science application), stresses the power of competitive forces to reshape the world by making better use of resources and to produce mutual gain through voluntary exchange. In the second approach, societal choices formulated through a dialogical political process, not laissez faire, is responsible for crucial beneficial outcomes involving public and merit goods. For many Europeans, Social Democrats and Christian Democrats, a corporatist understanding of society as a social organism made central the role of collective processes in place of the individualism of classic British and American economic presumptions. The East Asians also saw a major role for an activist state in promoting economic development. For a time it looked as though such systems were the better performers. The Anglo-American model has shown the better growth record only since the mid-1990s, although the costs of creative destruction, the high tech bubble, and declines registered in the U.S. stock market at the end of the decade give serious pause to accepting any clear permanent conclusions about competing national systems.

ECONOMICS AS A SOCIAL SCIENCE

Classical liberalism made a comeback in the last two decades of the twentieth century. The familiar view of a self-regulating economic system, the basis of classical liberalism, starts with the autonomous reasoning self-interested individual. Government is established to protect individual rights. Persons can do what they will so long as they do not hurt others.

The best government is that government which governs least, which provides equal protection under the law, and grants equal opportunity but not equal outcomes. Freedom is the absence of coercion. Within economics such ideas of classic liberalism are evident and central to public choice theory, real business cycle and rational expectations theories, and new classical economics.

Classical liberalism has a long history that traces back at least to the seventeenth century, with Hobbes's famous remark about lives being "nasty, brutish, and short." That pre–social contract world gave incentive for self-interested persons to offer government authority to define and protect individual rights. This story was an alternative to the divine rights doctrine as the source of royal power. This version, that society is constructed by individual consensus of isolated persons living in a state of nature, who realize that without government life is likely to be unpleasant and so the state is artificially created for mutual protection of individual rights, is the creation story of the state and of politics referred to in the last chapter.

Economists if they are philosophically inclined are more likely to start with John Locke and his ideas of individuals as basically self-interested and acquisitive and of government power as limited to the protection of private property. Such a state origin myth fits Adam Smith's invisible hand-magic of the marketplace economics. Since Smith's ethereal digits caught the wider imagination, the idea that the unintended consequences of a host of actions independently taken combine in unexpected ways for the best has held an important place in thinking about economics and politics. Selfish acts yield social betterment. Politicians can never have the information nor could they process it if they did as well as a decentralized market can. Global private maximizing produces social efficiency. "Errors"—too much or too little being produced—are quickly corrected through the working of the price mechanism. Those who read the signs best, or are just lucky in their choices, are rewarded correspondingly. Those who don't, or who aren't, aren't. Incentives assure full capacity utilization combining resources in the lowest cost manner to meet preferences. So long as economic agents are free to exchange for mutual gain the profit motive will create wealth for individuals and the society. Markets are self-regulating. There is little more need for government than its night watchman functions. The state is limited to protecting property rights, enforcing contracts, providing national defense and civil order, furnishing a stable currency, and providing public goods such as education which the private market will not produce adequately or at all. Or so the oft told tale tells.

The scientific core of modernist economics, general equilibrium and analysis of marginal costs and benefits justify the competitive market economy as the best possible allocator of resources. Agency is reduced to a passive reading of prices and selecting combinations of inputs from given resource combinations which minimize the cost of meeting market demand. Since this allocation problem is solved for known quantities and there is no uncertainty when making choices, solutions are straight forward. The price theory of mainstream economics tells us that the value of a good or service is the sum of the contribution of factor inputs, the marginal product of each when totaled exhausts the revenue from its sale. For this reason, as Paul Samuelson famously wrote in his introductory textbook, it did not matter whether labor hired capital or capital hired labor, the outcome would be the same.

Many economists have long been unhappy with this deterministic story in which real world choices are absent, movement is from one equilibrium state to another, and there is an automatic channeling of saving to productive investment by market magic. This way of thinking about what is economic, the orientation of individualistic rational maximizing and of cost minimization among given and known resources, has a static quality that follows from the notion of limited resources and given ends. It is frequently noted that economizing is a way of adapting to the way things are, not a process of change and development. Neoclassical price theory's framework permits a precision and mathematical formulation of relations which has allowed economics to be far more like "science" (mathematics, statistics, physics) than the softer social sciences which lack deterministic methodology. Indeed one of the great attractions of rational choice models to many political scientists is just this set of characteristics. The question has been: is the model of perfect competition the best first approximation which allows for rigorous analysis, or must a useful economics begin with such observable features as actual institutions, entrepreneurial capacities, technological change, monopoly power, collusion, increasing returns, and uncertainty?

Economists, even those who investigate institutions and concrete historical processes, are inclined to do so by modifying and extending neoclassical economics rather than beginning from other premises. New neoclassical economics makes use of incomplete, imperfect, or absent markets where there is lack of information, greater risk, and high transaction costs. People are rational, but information is an expense and so they operate within a context of bounded rationality in which information is costly, often incomplete, and institutions can change information costs to participants. Such modifications allow economists to start with simple models and add dimensions as they learn to model them deterministically or even stochastically. With such innovations the logic of the model is preserved and can still be specified in mathematically rigorous ways. More descriptive reality can be incorporated, although far less of course than most historians, political scientists, sociologists, anthropologists, and others prefer. Many of those who see the truth in accurate close observation of uniquenesses, and how these can be analyzed to form patterns of meaning, reject the new institutionalism's version of neoclassical economics as inadequate and misleading.

The context in which choice is presumed to be made is central to mainline political economy and distinguishes it from mainstream economics. Rational choice theory or what neoclassical economists call new political economy (creating some confusion since contemporary political economists who embrace the mainline tradition also call what they do political economy) is about how individuals make choices and in so doing collectively create and modify institutions. A rational choice perspective begins with methodological individualism. The microfoundation for all further analysis is the choosing/acting agent. But whether such persons are socialized individuals or economic man individuals makes all the difference. Often analysts are not clear on their view of human nature and agency/structure. Because the concept of rational choice "is slippery," Foss writes (1995: xvi) "the details of the rational choice approach are constantly questioned, criticized, defended and reformulated."

The mainstream's New Political Economy extends neoclassical economics by assuming elected officials and state functionaries are profit maximizers and act to further their own interests in a rather straight forward way. Politicians maximize their chance of election and reelection and of personally benefitting from government service. The state can be seen as paying excessively to fund the perks of office, to hire more employees than necessary, and to provide benefits for friends and collaborators of those in positions of power. Graft and waste are the product of a predatory state incapable of pursuing the public interest. Theories of rent seeking suggest that government officials attempt to redistribute rights and entitlements so as to maximize their own welfare, acting as brokers for wealth transfer, a redistribution which takes place at the public expense and reduces overall efficiency by taking resources from those who would use them more productively and paying more than necessary for inferior goods and services. Government distorts markets. The task of those who would advise on public policy is to help get prices right while providing reliable incentives so that resources will be allocated efficiently in this view.

PUBLIC CHOICE THEORY AND MAINLINE POLITICAL ECONOMY

In the essay "Politics without Romance" James Buchanan (1984: 11) writes: "Public choice theory has been the avenue through which a romantic and illusory set of notions about the workings of governments and the behavior of persons who govern have been replaced by a set of notions that embody more skepticism about what governments can do, notions that are severely more consistent with the political reality that we may observe about us." Public choice theory is the theory of government failure the same way that liberal (in the American usage of the term) or social democratic theory of government is a theory of market failure. Just as theories of market failure compared actual failures of the market to idealized service provision by the public sector, public choice theory contrasts the inadequacies of real world actual government to an idealized allocation through perfectly functioning markets.

Public choice theory is generated as critique of claims that the state through the political process somehow works its way toward transcendent "public good." There is an alleged Big Brother Knows Best caste to the theorizing of political institutions which is targeted by the public choice approach. Public choice theorists assert that government tends to overstep the bounds of the contract which properly gives the state legitimacy in the eyes of citizens. A close parallel between political exchange and market exchange is at the heart of the framework. Orderly trade in private goods and services can take place only within a legal structure that establishes individuals' rights of ownership and control of resources, enforces private contracts, and places limits on the exercise of governmental powers. The constitutional questions are how government should be constrained, what it should be allowed to do, and what is constitutionally authorized. Mutually advantageous political exchange takes place under a constitutional contract of a minimalist or night watchman state; for it is only such a state which promotes efficiency enhancing complex private exchanges. Such laissez faire thinking is a political rather than strictly a scientific position. There are arrangements which may strike economists as inefficient but seem fairer to voters. These are, or in a democracy should be, matters for debate and not to be determined solely by economistic calculation.

Less extreme in this methodological individualist tradition, the new institutionalism (or neo-institutionalism) stresses the idea as March and Olson put it of "history encoded in rules" (1984: 741). Randall Calvert

tells us that institutions include "informal norms, complex formal organizations, and processes and rules designed for the channeling of political
and economic activity—in short, any of the rules of the game by which
individuals in society find themselves confronted when contemplating
action" (1995: 217). But beyond this broad understanding there is a major
difference of opinion over the relative strength of structure versus agency
in institutional formation and reformation. On one side is the methodological individualism and rational choice bias in which rules consist of "a
pattern of individual actions and expectations" (Schotter, 1981: 217–18) and
in which an institution is understood as a long-lived equilibrium pattern
of rational behavior in some underlying game that society plays. Such a
neoclassical rational choice perspective requires a completely deregulated
market regime so that institutional obligations cease to be constraints,
"just as the order that generates them ceases to be one that exists outside
of the shifting volitions of its members." Structure on this account dissolves into agency. Of course whenever enough time is allowed all variables in a neoclassical model result from individual choice.

"Historically," as James March and Johan Olsen wrote in evaluating the
New Institutionalism, "political theory has treated political institutions as
determining, ordering, or modifying individual motives, and as acting
autonomously in terms of institutional needs." The institutions are presumed and structure individual choices and actions. "In contrast," they
write (1984: 735) "substantial elements of modern theoretical work in
political science assume that political phenomena are best understood as
the aggregate consequences of behavior comprehensible at the individual
or group level." I think we would now want to omit "or group"; or else,
in the spirit of rational choice analysis, we might more fully specify the
group as a collection of individuals voluntarily combining only so long as
individual preferences are satisfied and so reducible to individual motivation, rather than "group" of the sort presumed in mobilization theories of
collective action in which ascriptive identity is determinative of group
cohesion. Rational choice theorizing as applied to GSEGIs would correspondingly see them as totally voluntary organizations which are established to meet the needs of their individual members. They would cease
to exist if they did not do so or somehow harmed their members. Governments in such models are autonomous actors.

The economic assumptions which are now coming into wider use
among political scientists reverse attention to collective behavior (as previously understood in a context of given social and economic power asymmetries, of habitual or rigid attitudes, consciously or unconsciously

reflecting collective interests and the distribution of power). In this frame Barry Weingast (1997) has developed a game theoretic approach to the problem of political officials' respect for political and economic rights of citizens. It models the policing of rights as a coordination problem among citizens, but one with asymmetries difficult to resolve in a decentralized manner. He shows, in this framework, that democratic stability depends on self-enforcing equilibrium: it must be in the interests of political officials to respect democracy's limits on their behavior.

A similar model could be developed for transnational actors in a globalized economy. Voluntary compliance involves incentives and a cooperative framework which suggests many regulatory requirements will be ineffective. The givens of such models make such conclusions follow logically from the assumptions. Individual choice produces collective institutions. Here again the same assumptions are considered unproblematic. We will observe that the economics which is being imported into political science is a very extreme invisible hand of cost minimization and under-socialized economics in which the dismal science is seen as studying institutions in a framework of individualism. It is a study of "how individual economic agents pursuing their own selfish ends evolve institutions as a means to satisfy them" (Schotter, 1981: 5). Our consideration of global state economic governance institutions rejects this rational choice framing.

The "new" political economy of utility maximization can also be criticized because "it requires intellectual contortions," as Robert Keohane (1989: 389) has put it, to view particular institutions as the product of a deterministic equilibrium process in which rational adaptation to the environment plays the key role. When we look around we see "variations in institutional arrangements in different political cultures and states for which the origins of particular institutions are often not the same and rationality often appears not to be the exclusive or dominant feature of existing arrangements." Even if state leaders constructed governance structures which they found rational (because these arrangements maximized their own well-being) this is a far cry from an institutional framework the majority of citizens would see as designed to promote justice and equal enforcement of universal rights. Desirable arrangements may not appear "efficient" in the economic sense since "Justice can be a slow, cumbersome, and inefficient process" (Caporaso and Levine, 1992: 98). The role of democracy, the extent of citizen participation versus the role of experts, and the difficult issue of the relation of experts, epistemic communities, and the courts to the political decision makers and influentials who impact decisions in less transparent ways, will be discussed in chapter

10 as part of a consideration of the relation of labor rights and environmental concerns to GSEGI decisionmaking processes. In general we can say that the reason the political process is important for most citizens is that markets need a regulatory context and citizens want to be able to override market forces to achieve other goals they value.

In general the approach taken in the chapters which follow will be more in line with the old institutionalism than with the new institutionalism. It will follow a social analysis informed by Bourdieu more than Buchanan. But because the leadership of the GSEGIs see themselves and are seen by most mainstream economists as working to get prices right and pursue efficiency goals it is useful to apply the same public choice assumptions to global state economic governance institutions that public choice political economists typically apply to rent seeking states. GSEGIs have followed policies that manifestly would seem to have failed to benefit from any learning from past failures. Could this be a rational response rather than lack of competence because those who control these institutions are involved in their own rent seeking activities? Their policies allow public funds to be appropriated by the international banks and bond holders of the same core countries which dominate their governance structures. Given the self-interest of the core states and the power especially of the United States to replace leadership, influence promotion and compensation of staff, it would seem that application of self-interest and the constraints beyond which it is impolitic to go, would explain GSEGI's continued failure to learn from past policy initiatives which have failed to achieve their announced goals.

Different specification of rights lead to different valuations and so solutions to maximization and minimization calculations. As Warren Samuels has written (1981: 154) "To argue that wealth maximization can determine rights serves only to mask a choice of which interests to protect as rights. Legal decisions or changes can be said to be efficient only from the point of view of the party whose interests are given effect through the identification and assignment of rights." Following Samuel's logic Mercurio and Medema (1997: 119) explain, "Each possible legal solution points to a different efficient outcome. . . . The determination of a particular efficient solution involves a normative and selective choice as to whose interests will be accommodated, who will realize gains and who will realize losses." It is the non-uniqueness of neoclassical economics efficiency which is central to the claim that other values can be democratically incorporated and that advocacy for other moral and ethical concerns as a legitimate part of political economy are justified. This appreciation of how a market economy operates within a moral society was central to classical political economy as a fuller reading of Adam Smith makes clear (Tabb, 1999: chapter 3). This broader understanding that "the concept of efficiency as separate from distribution is false" and that rights determination is a normative activity with both efficiency and equity consequences so that choice of rights is ultimately a distributional issue at the core of the Scottish tradition of moral philosophy which undergirds classical political economy and remains integral to the mainline tradition.

Discussion of the creation of international regimes raises these issues anew. The IMF and WTO were established to engineer the redefinition of rights in a context which of course presumes a given constellation of power and wealth among the negotiators. Transaction cost economics supposes opportunistic behavior, "a self-seeking with guile" in Oliver Williamson's famous phrase (1985: 30). If one looks at regime formation with the possibility or prospect of such self-interested behavior in mind, rather than a magnanimous liberal institutional overcoming of collective action problems, admitting self-seeking into the motivational frame of negotiators, perhaps giving such motivation pride of place, it is more easily possible to explain the poorer, less powerful countries' complaints concerning the structure of negotiations and the outcomes which typically result.

We may think of the lack of participation by most developed country governments in the multiple simultaneous negotiations as clearheaded self-interested behavior. Given their likelihood of prevailing and information and other transaction costs, their failure to insist on counter positions may be understood as rational ignorance in the bounded rationality sense. Failure to be involved in the contract negotiations given their limited resources, most are either unrepresented or grossly underrepresented in the ongoing numerous discussions compared to the size and specialized training of the negotiators fielded by the core countries, and especially the large and technically practiced team the United States fields in Geneva and, given the likely outcome of negotiations in any case, their lack of participation should be predictable. It is only when one theorizes choices in terms of perfect competition among equal state actors capable of comparable skills and resources in policing their own claims and property rights, monitoring the performance of other actors, and equally likely to prevail in disputes and equally capable of achieving satisfaction when rulings are made in their favor, that the WTO system can be seen as a fair one. Given the disparate incentives and constraints actually faced by state participants in the international political arena it is more accurate to say that the WTO functions about the way we should expect it to, to perpetuate inequalities in the distribution of costs and benefits in the way the trade system is designed to operate.

THE SOCIAL INTRUDES

The trend in political science has been to see institutions as created by, and responsive to, individual preferences and actions. With the growing influence of rational actor models the inclination is to reject collective identity consciousness and stable representation of group interest, which had been central to understanding of the political. It is an understanding, however, of socialized individuals acting on ideals more than self-interest, here narrowly defined as material interest, acting collectively. Such collective action is crucial to the study of global civil society, the growth of NGOs, and the social and environmental action groups which have become the third dimension of globalization policy debates. Collective actor theorizing also had a place for class interest, helpful in explaining the emergence of global state governance institutions and their relation to national elite policymakers. The contrast between this older traditional social science, which is embraced in this essay, and the rational choice theorizing and new institutionalism is sharp. The way history is approached in each of the frames is quite different as are the implications for how social choices are, and can be made.

The problem is that socially efficient institutions for overcoming suboptimal equilibria cannot be established by agents who act in the way rational choice actors are supposed to act. When asked to follow guidelines in circumstances where to do so would not be in their interests they may well renege. In our view these institutions work because of the asymmetrical power relations involved in the negotiations and in the institutional operation of international regimes with which we are concerned. They do not produce outcomes which can reasonably be described as voluntary. The debate centrally important to us, but which we theorize from a particular vantage point, is over the way the global hegemon (that is to say the United States) influences the international finance and trade institutions which are our concern, and secondly the way in which laissez faire economics and neoclassical models are used to advocate for positions the United States endorses and in which there is a challenge by other actors who see this theoretical approach and the uses to which it is put as ideological rather than scientific. The locational subjectivity of Anglo-American mainstream IPE leads to a trivial theorization of such core relationships. Weaker nations may "choose" to cooperate much against their will because the cost of noncooperation is prohibitively high. Only within a market theory of exchange, which assumes the absence of power in the market, can such compliance be considered voluntary cooperation and Pareto optimal. We prefer to see this, as they often do, as coerced compliance. Thus the construction of "reality" and of policy consensus is not simply a matter of overcoming ideational difference to reach mutual agreement.

Much of public administration oriented political science deals with how to make institutions function better and expends little energy on the forces which create and destroy institutions. State norms and functionings of long standing can be swept away by unexpected forces or wither with developments in the larger international political economy. The debate over market freedom is between those who see these costs as dominant and those who stress the higher standard of living that lower cost of living and greater choice afford as a result of such creative destruction processes. Changes which often matter most are likely to be destabilizing. They disrupt. But they also may, and in the powerful cases of entrepreneurial innovation have, eventually raised living standards, often dramatically. The displaced and discarded are naturally less inclined to appreciate the immediate impacts of such epochal shifts. The railroads created massive unemployment for stage coach drivers, relay station attendants, and others who were put to pasture with the horses. But the railroad carried more people and goods more efficiently, created employment, and allowed distribution (and so production) on a hither-to-fore unimagined scale. Such revolutionary change is not the result of incremental investments and gradual improvement to which adjustment comes easily. As Joseph Schumpeter famously wrote, we can add as many stage coaches as we like—we will not thereby get a railroad. In his classic *Capitalism, Socialism and Democracy* he explains how capitalists succeed by coping with the unknowable, and responding effectively to the "perennial gale of creative destruction" which sweeps aside business as usual along with those who cannot cope with these radical change. He influentially wrote "the problem that is usually being visualized is how capitalism administers existing structures, whereas the relevant problem is how it creates and destroys them" (Schumpeter, 1947: 84).

In the very different mainline tradition political economy is understood as the study of the mechanisms used or usable by society to operate the social economy. The social economy in this tradition is understood to comprise the tools, institutions, and human energies which produce goods and services. Political economy begins with social individuals facing contingent choices under bounded rationality and considers institutions and governance mechanisms which constrain and guide individual and larger group activity. Such a political economy considers as endogenous many of the parameters held constant in most mainstream economics— technology and state policy for example—and focuses on political-economic organization, a reconceptualization of what is the border area between politics and economics.

Political economy is historical, institutional, and comparative. It does not privilege "free" markets but sees all markets as embedded in larger social relations. Nor does it give primacy to individualism but rather to the historically specific societal and institutional context which shapes and constrains individual actions. Its alternative approach is to start with the social actor who has agency but also a place in the social order which constrains choices and modes of thinking. Such individuals have habits, are socialized, and are subject to social influences such as family, religion, and advertising. As well they are impacted by subconscious needs and fears which can make them seem fickle and even irrational since the complex inputs to their decisionmaking are for many purposes not reducible to obvious elements. Deterministic models are likely to leave out what in particular instances are crucial elements. Given such influences information-transaction-governance models include "the socio-economic and institutional environment which have a significant effect on the kind of information we receive, our cognition of it, our preferences, and thereby much of our behaviour" (Hodgson, 1988: 41).

Within such a framework of agency, structures, and contingency, societal decisionmaking (which is not the same thing as summing the preferences of isolated individuals) and conjunctural constraints are important. In such a political economy institutions rather than unsocialized individuals are the starting point. In the broad definition of institutions and regimes offered by Robert Keohane (1989: 383) and accepted here, they "involve persistent and connected sets of rules (formal or informal) that prescribe behavioral roles, constrain activity, and shape expectations." Under such a definition specific practices are associated with institutions. They are embedded and "highly institutionalized in the sociological sense of being taken for granted by participants as social facts that are not to be challenged although their implication for behavior can be explicated" (384). Institutions are the framework within which issues are considered and so their nature, rules, norms, and assumptions shape the understanding participants have about the character of situations and possible out-comes to be expected or that have normative priority.

APPLICATION TO GLOBALIZATION

In the post-postwar years, globalization gained momentum as transna-tional corporations outgrew national boundaries and the postwar strate-gies of promoting national champions proved a poor one in the face of the greater efficiency of the transnational corporation. Capital accumulation within state borders gave way to a more fully globalized structure of accumulation. Neoliberalism became the hegemonic political project. Among international political economists who wish to contest any inher-ent inevitability of this process Karl Polanyi has become popular. His state-ment: "There was nothing natural about *laissez faire*; free markets could never have come into being merely by allowing things to take their course. *Laissez faire* was itself enforced by the state" (1944: 139) is widely quoted in such circles.

In an era of globalization the same issue again becomes prominent. What processes should be understood as "natural" and "inevitable"? The view taken here accords with Polanyi's judgment (applicable to our own time as much as to the epoch of capitalism's emergence) that "the gearing of markets into a self-regulating system of tremendous power was not a result of the inherent tendency of markets toward excrescence, but rather the effect of highly artificial stimulants administered to the body social in order to meet a situation which was created by the no less artificial phe-nomenon of the machine" (Polanyi, 1944: 57). A parallel argument is per-tinent today. Whether one wants to consider globalization "artificial," it is surely constructed.

According to Polanyi, there are not one, but two basic principles at work in society. The first is the self-expansion of the market as the accu-mulation process proceeds. Economic liberalism, or today we would say neoliberalism, aims, Polanyi wrote, "at the establishment of a self-regulating market, relying on the support of the trading classes and using largely laissez faire and free trade as its method." But opposing such a process is a second, 'social protection aiming at the conservation of man and nature as well as productive organization, relying on the support of those most immediately affected by the deleterious action of the market" (Polanyi, 1944: 132). The realm of the market expands but is met by a counter movement checking the expansion (Polanyi, 1944: 130). Polanyi's treatment of the double movement in capitalist development, in which the creation of the market society was an "unprecedented and revolutionary development insofar as it implied the subordination of all other social and political processes to the creation and maintenance of the capitalist market system," required active state enforcement and its dislocations and social costs brought into being broad movements of resistance leading to a regulation of the market by the state. Many contemporary commentators see a similar process at work in the current period, (or perhaps hope that Polanyi is right that society inevitably reacts against the commodification of life which reaches limits in the inevitable self-protective impulses of society).

Polanyi's analysis of capitalism in the nineteenth and the first half of the twentieth century is used as a thesis concerning the future as well. In the first phase of the double movement he describes there was an attempt to impose "a utopia" called the self-regulating market. As its impact was felt, new social movements developed and political constraints came to be placed on the operation of markets. From factory legislation to state-enforced industrial relations regimes, and on to the Welfare State, social and political controls were successfully imposed so that the market came to be accepted as best embedded in a regulatory order. Our own reading is consistent with Polanyi's double movement theory. Globalization takes place not despite the state but through its agency, which forces society to become market conforming to an extent that creates severe social pain. In so doing it produces widespread resistance which generates social struggle and the eventual construction of a new regulatory structure although it is not without interest to recall Polanyi's consideration (1944: 226) of the mid-nineteenth-century Chartist movement in England: "The Chartists had fought for the right to stop the mill of the market which ground the lives of the people. But the people were granted rights only when the awful adjustment had been made. Inside and outside England from Macaulay to Mises, from Spenser to Sumner, there was not a militant liberal who did not express his conviction that popular democracy was a danger to capitalism." Today opponents of neoliberalism are denounced by opinion molders in similar fashion.

Globalization reawakens the free market utopian dream of an unregulated economy. But once again income polarization, social disintegration, and failed states unable to cope with anarchy of the global marketplace call out for new regulation, a new phase in the double movement—this time to address the neoclassical globalist utopian project. Corporate globalization's logic is supported by the formulation of free trade classical liberals who believe considerations such as labor rights and environmental protection should remain at the GSEGI policy level unrelated to trade and investment. Social protection is declared protectionism, redistributive justice rent seeking, environmental concerns anti-business, and democratic participation economically inefficient and in need of being precluded by international agreements. The conflict between unfettered capitalism and social democracy is once again sharp, even if unacknowledged in most mainstream discussion which frames the issues. Neoclassical versions of the story deny the state role in the establishment of corporate globalization. It pictures the creation of the capitalist market society as a free choice entered into for mutual advantage and whose historical evolution is theorized to be the result of individual efficiency enhancing activities.

The discussion of globalization is in part a debate over the meaning of artificial and natural in the social world. It is the mainstream economists' presumption that there is a natural order to which things tend to be guided by the invisible hand. In the mainline tradition's social analysis power, the ability to coerce choices made by others is crucial to the restructuring process. Existing institutions and role positions allow inequalities of influence and pattern outcomes. We shall have more to say about the form such intellectual and popular contestation is taking, and of course, cannot know their future dimensions and outcomes but would entertain the hypothesis that globalization has had its negative moment of sweeping away older accommodations and is entering a phase of building new institutions of global governance.

This positive moment of transformation is driven by recognition that efforts to reduce the state to a simple pro-market organization without considering the need for "institutional glue" is not a sustainable long-term accommodation. Without some degree of citizen loyalty, dominant powers are left only with coercion. Some level of identification is preferable. Loyalty or willingness to accede to "the rules" is dependent on belief in the legitimacy of the state which in turn, if it is not to rest solely on coercion depends, on a belief that government is concerned with citizen well being. A pure market society erodes such faith and reduces the trust level of shared commitment to the point of raising the cost of doing business and reducing profits rather than increasing them. Liberal institutionalism is the midway position between the social justice movement's activism and its calls for social controls and progressive redistributive arrangements and corporate globalization's neoliberalism, which re-creates the subordination of all other rights to property rights. It promises attention to the reforms demanded by the movements for social justice even as it isolates the more radical sectors of this movement and wins over public opinion for the type of changes to which the system can more easily accommodate. Liberal institutionalism's critique of corporate globalization's excesses is an internal one. Short sighted greed is not good for the system. Long-term profitability demands a stability best achieved, in the face of massive opposition, through strategic concessions. Such controlled accommodations can demobilize popular movements for change. It is the recalcitrance of a vulnerably appearing system that can spur greater activism and commitment.

LIBERAL INSTITUTIONALISTS

The goal of IPE from the dominant perspective within the profession is I think to contribute to building international governance organizations capable of containing the destabilizing potential of globalization. The Enlightenment view of many, perhaps most, international studies scholars is the "commitment to promote human progress, defined in terms of the welfare, liberty and security of individuals, with special attention to the principles of justice" (Keohane, 1989: 380) that typically produces a mind set in which international collaboration and cooperation are organizationally foremost and overcoming resistance to regime formation is politically uppermost. This does not mean that liberal institutionalists fail to understand that the preferences of the most powerful actors will be accorded the greatest weight. In applying rational choice theory to the formation and maintenance of international regimes, "Voluntary choice does not imply equality of situation; in explaining outcomes, prior constraints may be more important than the process of choice itself." (Keohane, 1984: 71–72) Cooperation can still be mutually beneficial, although difficult to achieve in a world of competing interests. "But our awareness of cooperation's fragility does not require us to accept dogmatic forms of realism, which see international relations as inherently doomed to persistent zero-sum conflict and warfare," writes Keohane (1988: 381) from a vantage point of liberal institutionalism which perceives economic interdependence as the key characteristic of the contemporary international political economy. The close linking of markets and large volume of cross border transactions means that nation level policies in one country impact broadly and there are gains to be realized through harmonization.

Different modes of harmonization favor particular interests and it is to the benefit of the various parties to present their preferred set of accommodations as the one which serves the general good most effectively as interdependence is negotiated. The liberal institutionalist position starts with the seemingly unexceptional judgment that there are "evidently" considerable benefits to be secured from mutual agreement (if an agreement is mutual how could this not be evident?) Trade treaties as well as rules for war fall under this generalization. Institutions make it easier to cooperate because they set up a framework for repeated rounds of negotiation—as game theorists tell us—even though in a one-off game noncooperation is likely to be a prisoners' dilemma situation, in a repeated game context cooperation is typically achieved. Successful cooperation is of course not automatic despite potential gains. But once locally dominant ruling coalitions or even dictators come to function as normal state actors, cooperation is more likely (hence constructive engagement and the use of sanctions to promote conformity to international regime rules). The pressure of institutional norms can be heavy.

The literature on the general difficulty of thinking about the relationship between agency and structure is huge of course. What constructivism contributes (as do a number of deconstructionist discourses) is the "denaturalizing" of the taken-for-grantedness of so much social science and policymaking discourse. By the end of the 1990s much work in IPE was framed within a meta-theoretical commitment to constructivism, a reaction against the rational choice approaches to state interest evident in much of the institutionalist writing influenced by neoclassical economics. And to the naturalism assumed in realist doctrine. It reflected the interlinguistic turn in the social sciences and was not unrelated to the interpretivisms which were for some time transforming discourse in the humanities. The wider frame within which constructivism falls is the understanding of knowledge and the manner in which the "real world" is perceived are social or intersubjective phenomena which help form interests and identities of actors and observers. The discussion of "meaning worlds" is itself beyond the scope of our project. Yet this work too in an applied manner is an investigation into the social construction of meaning, seeing regime formation as a matter of choices made concerning how relations are to be understood, what is taken as given, and so not open to proposals for alternate rules.

It is the acceptance of limits to the possibility in construction of knowledge which I would question. Too much of such idealist constructionism ignores ever present power inequalities. If, as constructionists suggest, structure must be understood as social practice and not as objective constraint, than the ideational components (and ideological premises) of structure are soft pedaled and the coerced component in the formulation of shared beliefs avoided at some cost to accurate and complete analysis of this process in many, if not most instances with which this book is concerned. It is one thing to say that ideas, identities, interests and structures are co-constituted as constructivists do, and another to stress and celebrate the openness of the process of change and the dynamism of role construction in a manner which fails to be specific about whose initial interests carry more weight in the structuring of how agendas are formulated, how the conversation process is allowed to proceed, and in weighing the structuring of final agreements. While the importance of subordinate and superordinate orderings is not denied by constructivists there is a backgrounding of such structured inequality. While applauding the possibilities flowing from conversation and wanting to endorse the possibility of epistomological breaks, and of creative solution to common problems, the more central text here is Marx's famous dictum that men, and today we would say and women, make their own history, but not in any way they please. The past weighs heavily and in the instances discussed here the power transnational capital and its state representatives weighs heavily, forming the ever-present constraint on what can be constructed. In Marxist terms both the drive to accumulate and the need to legitimate existing social relations and structures does produce an indeterminancy where struggle (and discussion) is possible and outcomes not determined a priori somehow given in structural determinism nor totally open to free agency.

Most theories of international organization have explained their creations in terms of transaction cost theories of one sort or another, how such costs can be overcome, and welfare improving decisions reached and enforced (Waltz, 1979; Keohane, 1984). Scholars give attention to how international organizations help decisionmakers, state leaders, and others, learn to learn (Haas and Haas, 1995). Social constructionists realize that interests are never totally given and are subject in any case to rethinking. Constructivism as an approach focuses on questions related to how international actors "construct" their interests rather than simply taking them as either given or deriving them in some mechanical sense from proffered payoff matrices. Such perspectives allow for intervention in such conversations, allow scope to idealism, and promise mutual benefits and shared increased trust. They return an importance to the role to agency and the material power of ideas when embraced by social actors of sufficient political force. While sharing "a commitment to promote human progress, defined in terms of the welfare, liberty, and security of individuals with special attention to the principles of justice" (Keohane, 1988: 380) said to be embraced by students of international relations, this discourse tends to give insufficient attention to divergence of material interest.

Constructivists talk of the developing of international norms, expectations of proper behavior, shared understandings, and intentions as social facts reflecting consensus on legitimate social purpose. They speak of persuasion occurring when actors' preferences change in response to communicative acts. Constructivists focus on communication and persuasion that change actors' preferences and challenge or create new collective meanings and norms which are shared collective expectations about proper behavior. Regime creation in this perspective translates shared ideas and expectations into normative structures. But why one set of knowledge claims prevails is more than a matter of the quality of rhetorical skills. Ideas resonate for reasons and norm entrepreneurs rely on more than a dexterous reading of the Zeitgeist (Payne, 2001).

In addressing realist pessimism with regard to the role of ideas and idealism, constructivists avoid what becomes the absent center of the discourse, the way power is exercised and consensus coerced. Constructivists are less attuned to why certain participants, certain interests find their claims validated by a general consensus while others appear to passively accept the desires of such "norm entrepreneurs" who almost always represent the interest of hegemonic participants. Constructivism explains the emergence and evolution of regimes and organizations in terms of functional institutional efficiency making it the latest version of liberal IR theory and draw the same sort of critique (Sterling-Folker, 2001). The structures within which conversations and negotiations take place matter. They shape international norms, define acceptable behavior, and cue expectations, shared understandings, and reflect consensus on purposes deemed socially legitimate. But they also reflect preexisting power relations. Whether stressing the desirability of Habermasian communicative rationality, the strategies of norm entrepreneurs, or redefining of issues into a moral frame by social movements, persuasion and framing of issues now absorbs a great deal of the attention of IR and IPE scholars (Finnemore and Sikkink, 1998).

I am paying such extended attention to methodology because my capital logic emphasis is at great variance to mainstream IPE. It is important to be clear on the priors we initially accept. There is a solidity to the institutions of an era that reflect the overarching logic of the social structure of accumulation of the conjuncture. There is weight on existing institutions which result from the pressure exerted by the logic of accumulation. As the economic base changes and the possibilities inherent in the new forces and relations of production become more pronounced we expect greater demand for institutional reform. It is from such a structural historical matrix that international finance and trade institutions will be discussed.

The rules of a particular historical conjuncture reflect the dynamics of accumulation characteristic of the epoch. This awareness of the structured constraints which come from the social relations of production and material interests is absent from much IPE theorizing and needs to be brought back in. Traditional liberalism at least since Adam Smith has seen the economic function of the state as providing and enforcing a legal and institutional frame within which exchange takes place based on market principles. But the laissez faire stance appropriate to the period of entrepreneurial capitalism, 1770–1875 following John Dunning's (1997a) periodization, was less appropriate during the stage of hierarchical capitalism (1875–1980) when oligopolistic concentration encouraged regulation and systemic welfare provision or to the present stage of development, of alliance or flexible capitalism, a conjuncture in which strategic growth is based on information and learning capacities which creates assets heavily embodied in human capital in an innovation-driven economic systems. In the contemporary era this change in the dominant growth paradigm privileges increasing returns to scale favoring companies which function globally and are able to lower unit cost as they increase the scope of their activities. Transnationals therefore favor greater openness and the institutional capacity to enforce such openness. Given economies of scale and scope a level playing field helps the already strong in the marketplace, promoting greater concentration and centralization, which in turn provides for still greater market power and political influence.

The French Regulation School and in the United States the social structure of accumulation perspective (Kotz, 1994) have theorized from the mainline economics side of political economy, the underpinnings of the relatively stable institutional framing which prevail through a historic stage of capitalist development. The Regulation School approach suggests examining contemporary tensions over trade, investment, and finance in the global economy from the perspective of the effectiveness and problems within current governance regimes. Unlike the liberal institutionalist school these critical theorists are less volunteeristic in their analysis, seeing the mode of regulation following from the interplay of the balance of contending forces and the nature of the accumulation process of each historical conjuncture. What the regulationists and students of comparative political economy have demonstrated in studies of different societies is that each has a set of norms and institutional practices which are the outcome of deeply embedded compromises, the result of past struggles. From a regulationist perspective there is always contestation over the shape of institutions and their resolution while not permanent can be stable over extended periods.

The institutional frame results from the way forces and social relations of and in production create institutional orderings in particular societies which because of their own unique histories internalize similar pressures in differentiated ways. For these reasons globalization is met with different responses and not a single reaction in distinct social formations. The desire of the United States to impose a neoliberal international governance regime through such agencies as the IMF and the WTO reflect a preference for conformity in line with transnational capital's preferred institutional frame. While constructivists tend to see a voluntary process of discussion, persuasion, and negotiation, the view taken here is that they miss the key factors which shape institutional realignment of economic regimes, most centrally the role of transnational corporations and international financiers in directing these changes and the mediating role of the hegemonic state which reflects their interest in alliance with other governments whose internationalized sectors are natural allies in many matters.

THE GRAMSCIAN OPTIC

Marx and Engels were among the earliest and keenest observers of the globalization trajectory of capitalist development. Later Marxists have built on their insights and method. In the present era the branch of Marxist theory which has made the most profound impact within IPE is based on the work of Antonio Gramsci. Gramscian and neo-Gramscian thinking privileges ideological struggle and has been used to forcefully question mainstream views of globalization. Gramscians argue that the strongest states promote international regimes which are structured to favor their interests but are legitimated by presumptions of wider consensus over goals and rules. It is the state which creates and maintains conditions under which markets and hierarchies function. The Gramscian focus on the problematic of social reproduction investigates how prevailing patterns of dominance and material capacities are embedded in institutions and regimes which mainstream IPE is more likely to see as preserving harmonious order and enhancing efficient allocation of economic and social resources.

Gramscian theory is an approach to politics which asks how the prevailing order developed and considers the power relations behind institutional forms and performance. It asks not only how existing institutions are changing under guiding pressure from hegemonic coalitions but also how they might be changed from below. It is this latter moment of contingent indeterminacy and so the possibilities of agent efficacy by counter hegemonic social forces which seems worth highlighting and counterposing to the problem-solving logic of existing norms and valuations embodied in the public administration bias liberal institutionalism inherits from classic nineteenth-century German and early twentieth-century American political science. Gramscians focus on the contestability of, and the contradictions in, the neoliberal discourse, seeking to transcend the reductionism and economism they see dominant in discussion of globalization. While neoliberal theorists stress the liberatory potential of the new globalism, Gramscians find "neoliberal market civilization" an oxymoron in that civilization implies an active process that fosters "a more humanized, literate, and civil way of life, involving social well-being on a broad and inclusive basis" (Gill, 1995: 422). Rather than focusing on the gains from cooperation, those influenced by a Gramscian outlook see contestation, struggle among competing hegemonic projects. The embedding of globalization as part of a broad process which restructures state and civil society, political economy, and culture, takes place on different levels. For Gramscians the ideological defense of the spatial mobility of capital, and the imposition of destabilizing flexibility are central.

This idea, that an old order can be swept aside when it is clear that it is unable to cope with deep structural problems, offers a useful framework. The pattern in which long prevailing regimes—personalistic dictatorships such as Marcos in the Philippines or Suharto in Indonesia, or institutionalized one-party dominance such as the Christian Democrats in Italy or the Institutional Party of the Revolution (the PRI) in Mexico rot, disintegrate, and are swept aside by the forces of capitalist modernization is surely a familiar one. In an era of globalization rent seeking, repressive and clientelist regimes which once provided security against communism and social revolution have served their purpose. Revolutions in communication and transportation reconfigure national economies, reorienting their dynamics to new forms of participation in a global system, have created a host of crises of authority for once-strong governance systems. In this context, the neo-Gramscian theoretical perspective has been mobilized to foreground the role of global civil society, of actors contesting the normative structures and enforcement mechanisms of existing and proposed international regimes. The claims of Gramscian that the conversations involved in such negotiations are themselves ideologically fraught. Subordinate participants may have internalized hegemonic values even as they negotiate from a position of structural weakness.

The political contribution of Gramscian intellectual work is to focus on the desirability in periods of radical structural dealignment and economic crisis, of rethinking givens and business-as-usual premises, to look at the new conjuncture and seek outcomes potentially possible in the circumstances which would resolve questions in unexpected but desirable ways. The Gramscian *modus operandi* is to pose and hopefully resolve questions raised by new circumstances in such a way as to create new terrain for thought experiments, popular consciousness, and action rather than succumbing to an inevitability of dominant ideological presuppositions. Gramscians hope that the masses may be drawn by their perspective to a radical restructuring based on such expanded horizons and new social understandings of system realism in which recurrent conflicts can be analyzed.

While the prospect of the formation of a counter-hegemonic bloc drives the work of many Gramscians, the approach is useful here because of its concern with how consensus is produced, how hegemonic blocs emerge and make use of state resources. The next chapter looks at concentric club formation through soft law and applies a mode of analysis driven from a Gramscian approach to a consideration of international financial institutions. Realists and liberal institutionalists see the real decisionmaking as effectively excluding such counter-hegemonic forces. The question of how a counter-hegemonic bloc can be successfully formed is not easily answered but these matters are secondary to the purposes here at hand: to examine the way coalitions among economic and political actors are formed and operate to shape global state economic governance institutions.Whether the promise of the social justice movement has been fatally compromised by the way Establishment forces have linked opposition to corporate globalization and solidarity with the oppressed and exploited as well as concern for the planet to being anti-American in a time of attack by terrorists remains to be seen. It is unlikely however that these critiques will seem less valid or that renewed mobilization will not occur. Whether such movements and critiques can effectively counter neoliberalism depends a great deal on the centripetal destruction and degradations corporate globalization unleashes and the response of GSEGIs to the critiques made of their policies in the face of perceptions of globalization's trajectory. The next chapter initiates investigation of the first of these questions.

CHAPTER FIVE

The Postwar Economic Order and Global State Economic Governance Institutions

" . . . the enhanced role of the international monetary system in the affairs of modern states constitutes a virtual revolution in world politics."
—*Robert Gilpin* (1987: 119)

"The 'free' market being constructed is negatively free for elite decision makers in TNCs. Their freedom is our constraint."
—*Bailey, Harte and Sugden* (1998: 297)

The dominance of traditional diplomacy in IR theory has meant the last half of the twentieth century is seen through the lens of the Cold War. This has tended to obscure the ways American capital through the agency of the U.S. executive branch pursued its interests in the global arena. We will offer an alternative perspective in Chapter 6 focusing on the emergence of global state economic governance institutions. Here they are discussed in terms of the concentric club formation and negotiation processes, which build consensus for soft law regulation. In this chapter the postwar economic order is revisited. Its transcendence is the focal point for interpreting globalization trends to be considered in subsequent chapters embedding current debates historically. Throughout we are aware of the Bush Doctrine's bold assertion of U.S. dominance in place of the multilateral era's key terms "leadership" and even "partnership." This new doctrine signaled to the world that the Bush administration has important givens of the postwar world. While it has been widely argued that the postwar era was shaped by the Cold War, examining events from today's perspective suggests that in world historical terms the end of the Cold War is an overrated event. More significant is the building of the postwar economic institutions and the multilateral management of an American-led liberal political and economic system. From such a perspective the Truman Doctrine ("the founding moment of the containment order") pronounced before Congress March 12, 1947 is of less historic salience than Truman's speech six days earlier at Baylor University in which he proposed a new economic order which turned its back on the tariff policy of Hawley and Smoot and the economic wars of the 1930s and replaced them with new rules of trade and investment in which "the interest of all will be considered and a fair and just solution will be found" (Ikenberry, 1996: 84). The world did not however simply chose the American way. U.S. policymakers and corporate capital used a complex strategy with many sticks and many carrots to successfully lead it in this direction. Indeed, the Cold War can be interpreted in terms of such a purposive design.

U.S. provision of this new regime over the opposition of nationalist governments was a self-interested strategy rather than the altruistic provision of public goods based on some abstract commitment to free trade and market openness. The American dominated postwar economic order succeeded in a double containment, that of the Soviet Union as George Kennan in his famous "Mr. X" telegram from Moscow to the State Department had proposed and in the strategy aimed at building a global economic order based on a coerced openness which allowed U.S.-based capital to expand globally. The ultimate containment was not in the defeat of "the Evil Empire" but of other forms of capitalist development which had through the postwar period and into the 1990s seemed contenders. These ranged from the national development models of Western European socialism, social democracy, and corporatism, import-substitution in Latin America, and the regimes of state-led development of Japan and Korea.

Interpretation of these postwar events has undergone substantial shifts as the National Keynesianism of the period waned and the world entered an era of neoliberalism in which Welfare State protections and presumptive entitlement of citizenship are on the defensive and an open world economy has forced a serious rethinking of, if not outright retreat from, the liberal-labor and Social Democratic consensus of the postwar years. It is useful to see these developments through the now less than fashionable lenses of class, nationalism, and competition among capitals. I suggest that the conflicts and crises evident in the international political economy are related to the way the Washington Consensus, the terminological short hand for the *modus operandi* of the global state economic governance institutions from the late 1970s, has impacted on economies around the world. Neoliberalism more broadly created and intensified problems and tensions in the core as well. The mainstream economic models on which GSEGI rules are premised have come in for increasing examination and the view here is that they deserve far more critical scrutiny. The acceptance of the neoliberal agenda reflects the ideological hegemony of powerful interests which have benefitted from the policies the GSEGIs have followed, and so demonstrating the Gramscian claim that the conversations involved in their negotiations are ideologically fraught. Along with an institutionalist (and inclusive of some aspects of a revisionist neo-institutional approach) two frames, that of the Regulationists and the Gramscians, will inform the discussion of international financial institutions in this chapter's discussion of concentric club formation through soft law. We will be specific in identifying the lobbying efforts and the close working relationship between the individuals and associations representing the most globalized sectors of capital and the policies of key public decisionmakers.

APPROACHING REGIMES

Because political science easily gravitates to the management frame of public administration it is an easy step for IR experts and now IPE theorists to seek the role of advising on the implementation of governance regimes. Multilateral regulation and regulatory policy are after all extensions in an age of globalization of longstanding concerns at the national level. Whether the particular problem at hand is a conflict over cross-border effluent discharge or charges of economic dumping, international fora are found desirable even when particular parties may be unhappy with particular outcomes. Stable and orderly dealings proceed best from joint acceptance of principles; beliefs with regard to facts; causation and norms—standards of behavior defined in terms of rights and obligations—and prescriptive specific rules. Regime theory's growing popularity, liberal institutionalism's promises of the payoff from their negotiation, and realist warnings that cooperation is unlikely to be reached by consensus but by exercise of power all take for granted the basic frame. In considering the norms and rules, decisionmaking procedures and implicit and explicit principles around which actors' expectations converge in a given area of international relations, the core governance requirement of the formation and functional evolution of regimes have become central to IPE thinking.

With the growth of economic interdependence and openness regimes more routinely involve formal multilateral governance. Legal standards, arbitration, modes of enforcement of rulings become more important, eroding sovereignty in the interest of establishing secure internationally recognized property rights for transnational investors and other transactors. Just as "the courts of the dusty feet," established by itinerant merchants as commercial capitalism grew within the womb of feudalism to challenge the lord's court system—with its tradition-bound understandings not designed for, nor flexible enough to adjudicate commercial disputes—over time displaced longstanding practices in the legal realm, so today the law adjusts to the growing scope of transnational business and finance. And again the private sector participants themselves rather than the constituted legal authorities are taking the lead in the reformulation.

For political scientists such developments require a shift in perspective which is similar, if less extreme, than that required of the feudal lords to the emergent mode of exchange of early mercantile capitalism. Capitalism in an era of renewed and intense globalization requires a rethinking of sovereignty. International regime analysis has primarily focused on the behavior of sovereign states and only secondarily, if at all, on private entities. IR experts dealing with treaties on substances which are believed to deplete the ozone layer, or the proper way to catch fish without endangering dolphin and great sea turtles, are engaged in multilateral regulation enforcement as much as UN peacekeepers are. The focus of International Relations theorists on the diplomacy of international law has ignored private international law; the very term is unfamiliar and uncertain. Enforcement of rules on private commercial actors by emergent state accords involves cooperation on the part of such economic participants in early stages of multilateral policy formation. They pressure states and have major, often determining, impact on the rules, enforcement procedures, and the effectiveness of regimes. Profit-oriented corporate actors are often the major non-state interlocutors in such regime formation and enforcement.

The staffs of extant international organizations also influence the trajectory of the process. Such bureaucracies have organizational stakes in outcomes. In the view taken here such a public choice framing is not wrong, and can be quite helpful in understanding the development of governance institutions. It is however only one level of explanation. A richer understanding of how global state economic governance institutions are evolving and the role they play in shaping, and the ways they are shaped by developments in the world system require a deeper grounding. In presenting and employing such an analysis we rely on regulation school theory and a Gramscian perspective, both of which have roots in critical realist thinking, and the Marxist tradition which remains useful in decoding the nature of capitalist development.

THE PRE-BRETTON WOODS ORTHODOXY

In the years following World War I, European politicians especially in Germany and France were obsessed with inflation, seeing runaway prices as symptomatic of deeper problems resulting from and enlarging social divisions and likely to erode the prewar consensus regarding the distribution of income and fiscal burdens. Bitter dispute raged over whether to restore the old or move to a new fiscal pattern. Incapable of finding agreement on a package of tax increases, public expenditure, and reductions capable of balancing their budgets, some governments resorted to the printing press. The self-interested actions of national governments and the tenacity of the false belief in the gold standard's automaticity led to failure to reach accord on the need for and the specifics of central bank cooperation.

In the interwar years the French saw the proposal to institutionalize the gold-exchange standard as a British plan aimed at solidifying London's position as the world financial center at the expense of Paris (Eichengreen, 1996). The French demanded reparations from Germany before paying war debts to the United States. As long as America extended loans to Germany, other Europeans could finance their current account deficits with the United States. When the Fed increased interest rates in 1928, the recycling process stopped; the highly indebted European economies tottered. Deflation, pressure to increase exports, competitive devaluations, and growing protectionism were the product of the resultant crisis, not its cause. That world trade contracted even more because of these policies made matters worse of course; but to say that the Smoot-Hawley Tariff caused the Depression is not accurate. Extremes of protectionism were the result of the collapse of economic stability. Nations feel forced into protectionism when their economies are not working and international pressures are extreme.

Consider the famous collapse of Credit Anstalt, Austria's largest deposit bank. Its liabilities when it failed in 1931 were larger than the Austrian government's budget. Its short-term indebtedness was enormous. It also held a controlling interest in Hungary's largest bank. Hungary and Germany both had reparations obligations and the crisis logically spread from Austria to neighboring Hungary and Germany. Protectionism only intensified the problem of not being able to export one's way out of domestic crisis. Coordinated reflation could have addressed the crisis, but the orthodox medicine then, as now, was austerity. The League of Nations programs for Hungary and Austria had been harsh in the early 1920s and were viewed as intrusions upon the sovereignty of these nations, which had emerged from the breakup of the Hapsburg Empire. Through such episodes U.S. policymakers worked closely with financiers to penetrate other national economies using credit extension as leverage over their policy space. This was similar to the way U.S. financiers operated in the early decades of the twentieth century, when private bankers, most prominently House of Morgan operatives, played key roles in stabilizing, for a price, not only the fiscal condition of other countries, but of the U.S. economy as well, as J. P. Morgan himself had done in the 1907 panic, doing good while earning a great profit.

At the end of World War II the inner circles of Wall Street liberal internationalist orthodoxy proposed to reform the old order by "shifting its locus from the pound to the dollar, ending discriminatory exchange rate and trade practices" although, as Ruggie (1998a: 259) writes, "Opposition to such economic liberalism was nearly universal outside the United States." The problem was mass unemployment which was widely thought to have been the product of laissez faire free trade economics. Jacob Viner wrote at the time, "There are so few free traders in the present-day world, no one pays any attention to their views and no person in authority anywhere advocates free trade." Governments needed to insulate economies to prevent what today might be called a race to the bottom as competitive devaluation and beggar thy neighbor policies led the world into a downward spiral. The fifth principle of the Atlantic Charter for this reason called for the fullest collaboration among nations "with the object of securing for all improved labor standards, economic advancement and social security." Freedom from want was uppermost in the minds of most everyone. Liberalism, or what today in the United States is called neoliberalism, would in the view of critics create conditions not unlike those which had produced the crises of the interwar years and the Great Depression. Hubert Henderson working at the British Treasury made the argument that captured the general fear: "To attempt this would be not to learn from experience but fly in its face. It would be to invite the same failure, and the same disillusionment; the same economic chaos and the same shock to social and political stability; the same discredit for the international idea" (Gardner, 1980: 30).

In the postwar years matters did not turn out this way. As Europe rebuilt, trade and financial liberalization were accompanied by rapid growth. Yet in the decades following, financial liberalization generated exactly the cycles of overexpansion, speculative excess, and financial crisis which Henderson and others had seen as the logical outcome of such policies. Freeing financial markets unleashed instabilities which proved costly. One of the important parallels between the two periods is the consistency of policy advice. While the IMF today is not calling for the restoration of the gold standard, it is asking for the functional equivalent in the enforced free movement of capital to discipline national governments and high interest rates to maintain exchange rates. In the contemporary period this imparts a deflationary bias for debtors just as the gold standard did in the earlier period. And as IMF decisionmaking today is dominated by Americans, it is interesting to note that the League of Nations' secretariat's Economic, Financial, and Transit Department's directors between 1922 and 1931 were all British nationals (as was the League's Secretary General) and that in the years leading up to the outbreak of World War II the League's Economic and Financial Organization whose spokesmen described the EFO as "technicians" involved in scientific problems was, like the IMF today, a profoundly political organization. Some of its key players indeed were significant in the establishment of the IMF (Pauly, 1994). The leadership came from, and the technical staff was trained in, the financially dominant economies in each period. Part of concentric club formation reflects the technical dominance as well as the economic and political power of the hegemon.

In the interwar years treasury officials and private and central bankers made every effort to reestablish the pre–World War I international financial order. This goal dominated once again as the recovery period following World War II passed. The Bretton Woods Regime, which looms so large in the post-World War II era, can be seen in such an extended perspective as a deviation in a longer pattern of the dominance of finance. The acceptance of the Bretton Woods interventionist approach was of limited duration. It reflected the serious social cost and the deep, but temporary, crisis of confidence of the financial establishment. Whether in fifty or a hundred years Keynes's approach will once again appear as an irreversible revolution, or as only a brief interval in a liberal or neoliberal order remains to be seen. It will depend on how financial markets perform and the effectiveness of political pressures for reregulation.

BRETTON WOODS

It has been widely noted that the British in the early postwar period were profoundly distrustful of unregulated market-based financial coordination. Keynes's original proposals had included plans to prevent "hot money" from destabilizing national economies. He preferred controls of short-term capital movements and managed fixed exchange rates. Fostering international trade, Keynes thought, required financial order, stable currency relations, and institutional support from an international bank to provide loans to countries suffering balance of payments problems. He saw a fixed exchange rate system as imparting security to the global financial order and suggested provisions penalizing surplus countries (and not simply deficit ones) in order to keep capital flows balanced, a proposal the United States, the world's dominant surplus nation, rejected out of hand. However despite the overwhelming power advantage of the Americans, British negotiators were able to win meaningful concessions so that as it came into being the Bretton Woods system struck something of a balance between a liberal world market and the domestic responsibilities of the state. The most conspicuous victory for Keynes's position favoring national autonomy was Article VI of the IMF agreement, which shielded countries from speculative capital flows. Restrictions on hot money flowing in and out allowed Western European countries in the early years of Bretton Woods successful pursuit of high growth and full employment policies. The controls it permitted on current international transactions remained in place in major Western European countries into the early 1990s.

At the Bretton Woods conference in 1944, at which the last stage of a process that was begun by U.S. and British treasury officials designing the rules for a postwar monetary and trade regime were ironed out, the initial draft plan established a condition for membership in the new institutional organization. It proposed that a government agree "Not to accept or permit deposits or investments from any member country except with the permission of the government of that country." This provision offered debtors protection and could have provided for substantial control over international capital flows. Early plans for the International Monetary Fund gave it the authority to block changes in exchange rates and even provided that "any monetary or general price measure or policy" of a member government could be reversed with the approval of four-fifths of the votes of the IMF. Such proposals and Keynes's writing on self-sufficiency and social engineering were in direct response to the prolonged inability of free markets to move countries out of the widespread suffering evident in Europe in the 1920s and which spread widely in the 1930s (Crotty, 1999).

Unlike the 1980s and 1990s, when much of the world once again experienced abnormally high levels of unemployment—but transnational capital and national elites generally did well—in the 1930s all were pretty much in the same boat. The crisis of confidence of elites, the bankruptcies, and mass unemployment affecting nearly everyone provided a generalized sense of shared crisis and a situation out of control. A falling tide was lowering all boats, to say nothing of profits and living standards. In the 1980s and 1990s while poverty grew, inequality increased, and working conditions deteriorated for many. Stock markets soared and wealth grew at the top. Stagnant or falling wages for the many produced a bipolar economic situation. The emphasis on demand stimulation, important in the Great Depression and enshrined in the postwar national Keynesian consensus, was rejected in the 1980s and 1990s as a result of a revision to understandings of the role of the state in policy circles which harkened back to the pre-Keynesian orthodoxy and had become the conventional wisdom as the new century began.

Keynes had called for a strong global central bank. But he did not want the reestablishment of the gold standard or any other regime which would limit the autonomy of member countries to follow their own monetary policy and to pursue domestic full employment. Keynes regarded the gold standard as a "barbaric relic." He wanted generous liquidity based on a new international currency to be known as the bancor. It would be used by nations' central banks to settle accounts among themselves just as a nation's own currency was used by banks domestically. The United States as the world's largest creditor nation had serious reservations. It wanted the dollar used as the global settlement currency. It was eager to prevent easy access of debtors to other sources of credit and wanted to abolish exchange controls which the British and other nations did not wish to give up. This American desire for free capital markets was the policy of the hegemonic foreign power. These same priorities were evident once again in the late 1990s when Japan, China, and other regional governments offered plans for an Asian monetary fund to provide liquidity to their neighbors. In chapter 11 the story of the U.S. veto of this proposal is told. The continuity of design and interest is notable.

When speaking of American policy, one must not assume that all the decisionmakers within the United States preferred the same solution. Domestic differences matter. In the American system as opposed to a parliamentary one, they impact on the manner in which the executive branch can negotiate international agreements. In the case of the IMF, many influentials in the Congress and the business community were opposed to any international agency which might restrict American freedom. (Fear of foreign competition as shall be discussed later doomed the proposed International Trade Organization.) The British had their divisions as well. Keynes had to contest with those wishing to maintain an overvalued currency at an outmoded gold value (and the tight monetary policy it required which had kept Britain in a state of depression through the second half of the 1920s). The cost, in higher unemployment and industrial stagnation, while it benefitted financiers, had important contagion effects. When Britain finally devalued in September 1931 it put pressure on other countries which stopped attempting to defend their own gold parities. Runs on banks, widespread protectionism, the collapse of trade and beggar-thy-neighbor policies followed as each nation tried to produce a positive outcome in its foreign accounts to the collective detriment. Given this experience the need for instrumentalities capable of providing controlled flexibility was uppermost in many minds as representatives gathered at Bretton Woods to establish a postwar financial regime.

The British initial preference for a combination of strong multilateral regulatory agencies and respect for the view that national sovereignty took precedence over international mobility of capital. The clearing union would have to have overdraft allowance so that deficit countries would be permitted credits to finance payments deficits. Payment deficits (and surpluses) would appear as debits (or credits) in the accounts of the clearing union providing substantial liquidity to the international financial system. The availability of generous credits would reduce the pressure on deficit countries to take swift and possibly extreme measures to adjust. Under the proposal considered (but not adapted) surplus nations would be required to pay interest above a certain level of surplus so that they would be under pressure to return to a balance of current accounts payments by increasing their imports. This would extend deficit countries the space to pursue their own domestic policies with regard to creation of employment.

The American insistence that surplus nations (of which the United States was presumed to be the most important into the foreseeable future) would not be penalized was to come back to haunt the United States in the years of diminished U.S. competitiveness and massive net debtor position—but this was long in the future as the postwar international financial order was being negotiated. American desire for a more open trading system, as against most of the rest of the world's preference for nationalist developmentalist regimes, led the United States to temporarily accept existing capital controls as the price of agreement on greater openness with regard to trade.

Given the debtor position of no longer so great Britain, Keynes proposed monetary reform which would have increased liquidity and allowed easier, indeed automatic, borrowing for debtors. He was also concerned to prevent capital flight. These preferences were behind the proposals to which we have alluded that the United States rejected. The U.S. did accept what Ruggie has called embedded liberalism, a form of multilateralism compatible with the requirements of domestic stability. Under such a regime governments so committed presumably "would seek to encourage an international division

of labor which, while multilateral in form and reflecting *some* notion of comparative advantage . . . also promised to minimize socially disruptive domestic adjustment costs as well as any national economic and political vulnerabilities." (Ruggie, 1998a: 265) This embedded liberalism was a far milder
guarantee than what Keynes had proposed. Its own internal contradiction
became clearer as what came to be termed globalization took its course.

If Keynes's principle, that surplus nations had as much responsibility to
bring their international payments back into equilibrium as debtor nations
had been accepted, substantial pain would have been avoided in the years
which followed. The actual regime adopted was quite different. The U.S.
government was unwilling to cede power to international agencies which
might challenge its interests and these more far-reaching measures were
not included. The postwar order was based on the dollar and not some
paper gold (such as Keynes's proposed bancor) and was securely under
American economic leadership and voting dominance at the institutional
level. The United States not only enjoyed the privilege of seigniorage,
(each little green piece of paper inexpensively printed commanded real
resources on a global basis), but because by the 1960s it issued more dollars than were demanded, yet was able to prevail upon other countries central banks to hold them, it also imparted an inflationary bias to the rest of
the world economy, putting countries at the mercy of destabilizing monetary flows they could not control.

Financial openness reduced the autonomy of Welfare States and that
was all to the good from the perspective of finance capital, which gained
from the lower taxes as well as from the freedom to pursue higher returns
on a global scale with decreased restrictions. Freer capital markets reduced
the efficacy of domestic fiscal and monetary policy and of the interventionist state more generally. This too was welcome from what is now called
a neoliberal position because it forced government policymakers to be
more responsive to market pressures. The continuity of U.S. strategy is
demonstrated in IMF conditionality developed in the late 1940s and early
1950s (and so of long standing) which even then led developing countries
to withdraw requests for assistance. For the Europeans too, in these years
their need for liquidity came at a price. The United States demanded
structural adjustment of a sort not unfamiliar to debtor nations today.

Acceptance of the IMF by the U.S. Congress was by no means a foregone conclusion. The League of Nations had failed to win approval and
isolation was rampant at the end of World War II. The *Wall Street Journal* and the *New York Times* editorially condemned government management of exchange rates. Influential leaders of the financial community

such as Winthrop Aldrich, the prestigious chairman of the Chase National Bank, condemned the plan. Treasury officials worked hard to convince American capitalists as well as others that the Fund was essential to domestic prosperity. The arguments for acceptance of the Bretton Woods international financial institutions were the promise of greater economic growth, outlets abroad for U.S. investments, markets for U.S. products, and gains in efficiency along traditional comparative advantage lines.

Domestic politics and economic imperative came together in the case of the International Bank for Reconstruction and Development (later called the World Bank) where the unpopularity of giving money to foreigners was overcome by the support of internationalist corporate interests and an appeal to aid the home country to ethnic communities. While retellings of these events often stress the disinterested good will of America, it is well to remember that in the late 1940s American power was used to build international economic arrangements consistent with the interests of American capitalism. The result was an open international market under American leadership rather than of a supranational authority. Instead of an intergovernmental union, the world got a financial system dominated by private banks. While the current focus on constructivist approaches to negotiating international regimes focuses on open-ended interactions and discourse practices, the dominance of the U.S. postwar project demonstrated a unity of purpose which is remarkable in its constancy.

The crisis of the postwar order came in the 1968–75 years when the balance shifted to a preponderance of global market integration and the subordination of domestic economies. To see this as a shift totally external to domestic politics obscures a set of events which were parallel in the sense that in all countries those sectors aligned with transnational capital grew stronger and nationalist coalitions and the political left were unable to develop an effective response. At the same time countries did not all act in identical fashion. Differences in historical political cultures and institutions made for divergent reactions even if it remained the case that these years were a turning point everywhere to some degree. It is useful to look more closely at how these changes occurred.

FROM MARSHALL PLAN TO EUROPEAN UNION

In the immediate postwar period the United States had favored a more open financial order but was constrained by the world situation, especially by European realities. To reverse the statist direction of European economic policies at the end of World War II required that the United States offer incentives to governments which were moving leftward. This aid most famously took the form of the Marshall Plan. Initially neither Congress nor the American people gave the money at all willingly. The invocation of the immediate threat from the Soviet Union, fear that communism would triumph in war-torn states, and even a major war scare were needed before the Truman Administration could pry the money from an isolationist Congress. The condition for aid was that they open their markets, which to some extent helped thwart European desire to give their own domestic firms priority. Yet the United States could not push too hard. Europeans were not all that eager for the American close embrace. Polls showed that a third to a half of the public in Britain, France, and Italy wished to remain neutral in the Cold War (Hitchcock, 2003).

The story of international economic regime formation rarely makes a place for the Marshall Plan. It should. Recovery aid for Europe is best seen as an important element in the shaping of this emergent postwar governance regime. As Under Secretary for Economic Affairs William L. Clayton bluntly put the matter at the time: "Let us admit right off that our objective has as its background the needs and interests of the people of the United States. We need markets—big markets—on which to buy and sell." (Kunz, 1997: 167) The public relations campaign as noted stressed the Soviet danger and while polls showed few people had even heard of the Marshall Plan (one in seven could articulate even its broadest goals), the media portrayed it favorably and various constituencies were shown the ways it favored their interests (for example isolationist Kansas warmed as farm organizations told their members about the expected boom in agricultural exports).

Economists focus on the International Bank for Reconstruction and Development and its role in funding European recovery. The Bank committed more loans to Europe than any other region in its early years, more than $750 million between 1947 and 1953. However the Marshall Plan supplied Europe with roughly 20 times as much. In addition, the Marshall Plan aid came with fewer strings or "conditionality" than either the Bank or the IMF imposed. Such politics of economic aid is of some importance. For example, the United States kept British reserves at between $600 million and $1 billion—large enough so it wouldn't resort to controls, small enough so that it would not be independent of United States influence in the postwar period (Wood, 1986: 33). Throughout the second half of the twentieth century the United States refined the art of making sure the loans were large enough to induce cooperative behavior, of timing pay-outs, and of knowing when to tighten or loosen conditionality in order to encourage structural reform that would be in the best interests of the lender's economic, political, and financial priorities. The GSEGIs through the last twenty-five or thirty years have been the vehicle to implement these policies acting as the intermediary which distances Washington somewhat from the fallout of more directly coercive behavior.

The Marshall Plan's major target may not have been only preventing the expansion of the Soviet system but also capitalism in the form of national regimes in Europe, which were leaning toward models based on national planning. The Marshall Plan was developed to stop this "creeping national capitalism" (as well as the spread of communism). Different interpretations of these events are prevalent of course. Anne Krueger suggests that "Never before in history had the victors provided so much aid to the vanquished and recognized their interest in rebuilding the war-torn economies of allies and enemies alike. And rarely had a major power voluntarily provided eco-nomic organization that limited its own scope for unilateral action in favor of a world system" (Krueger, 1993: 7). The United States may better be seen however as following the hegemonic path of the British who had also claimed that the expansion of its power was not simply in its own national interests but the universal interest, that its intentions, its advocacy of free trade, and its restructuring efforts promoted the general well-being. This imperialism of free trade was both a manifestation of its power and a tool to increase that power, and to do well while appearing to do good.

We may see such a capacity following Joseph Nye (1990) as "soft power," the ability to achieve desired outcomes in international affairs through attraction rather than coercion, convincing others to follow, to agree to norms and institutional forms which produce the behavior desired. It was not in fact an easy sell. In Europe capitalism had been discredited along with fascism and most Europeans saw the United States, which held half the gold and currency reserves of the world and ran vast payments sur-pluses as the problem, not Europe. The United States needed to provide credits if it was to sell its goods and in the context of socialist and commu-nist influence, if not outright political hegemony in much of Europe, the Marshall Plan too had to be sold. The U.S. State Department and its agents engaged in a major propaganda effort targeting labor and other European constituencies such as mothers and children in its "Operation Bambi." For example, films, forty of them, were made and shown in town cinemas and by mobile projection units in countryside villages.

Accompanying the impacts of financial liberalization (to an extent fostering them, to some degree responding defensively to globalization), was a trajectory of institution building focusing on interstate negotiation and, for Europe, the creation of a transnational regional community. The process of institutionalizing a European Community started with the Treaty of Paris (1951) which established the European Coal and Steel Community Treaty that pooled sovereignties in these industries. The result was a supranational "higher authority" of six states (Belgium, France, Germany, Italy, Luxembourg, and the Netherlands). In 1958 these countries signed the Treaty of Rome, setting out the principles of a common market. In 1987 they were joined by Britain, Denmark, Greece, Ireland, Portugal, and Spain in agreeing to The Single Europe Act. Then, in 1991, this larger group agreed to the Maastricht Treaty for monetary union as well as the launching of a common foreign and security policy (officially The Treaty on European Unity). Other agreements have followed strengthening rules, as well as extending membership and procedures for EU governance. The EU continues to add functions and members. The European Commission has become an active rule setter.

The EU puts pressures on member governments to liberalize their economies. For example, in 1997 the European Commission insisted that IRI (the Instituto per la Ricostruzione Industriale) which at its height ran 500 companies with half a million employees had to shut down because it violated EU rules against state aid to industry. Three years later the great and the good of Italian politics and finance met for one last time at IRI's fascist era headquarters on the Via Veneto for a final company general meeting. It was an end of an era event in much the same way as the death a few days earlier of Enrico Cussia the head of Mediobanca, a legendary figure who had dominated Italian finance. IRI and Mediobanca had protected and developed Italian industry and banking for decades. In other countries major mergers and takeovers, privatizations, and closings punctuated what was in historical terms a major transformation of statist-corporatist models under the pressure of globalization of production and investment. Even the euro, which was seen as Europe's effort to "bulk up" to better compete with the U.S. and Asia, acted as a Trojan horse for liberalization. Unable to devalue to stay competitive, governments could tell the voters "TINA," there is no alternative. To accommodate the single currency and the loss of economic policy autonomy which accompanied it, national governments adopted all sorts of reforms and austerity measures, changes which voters opposed. The euro acted as a lever to force painful adjustments on unwilling citizens.

Soft power is exercised in the context of legitimation mechanisms. As neo-Gramscians among others have made us aware, hegemony is best exercised not by the mailed fist but the velvet gloved open hand offering benefits in exchange for cooperation and/or acceptance of a larger regime structure. In the postwar social structure of accumulation a central element of the global order embedded liberalism, especially in the advanced countries of Europe and North America, offered an accommodation to worker-citizen material interests which quieted fear of the consequences of a more open globalism. Not a dissimilar accommodation was reached in those parts of the periphery, primarily in Latin America, which were becoming integrated into the international division of labor as more than producers of primary products. The rising manufacturing interests in the nations with larger populations to serve as a domestic market—Brazil, Mexico, and Argentina most prominently—embraced a form of selective inclusion, typically under populist political regimes. Wide sectors of the urban working class found their interests addressed by politicians, often charismatic leaders, supportive of a development path opposed by the traditional rulers, the landed elites. Needing the support of increasingly vocal middle strata and popular classes, especially in the large cities, modernizing elites cooperated in a form of peripheral Keynesianism in which social safety net provisions and better wages and working conditions were promised to gain the support of these groups and provided the material base for import substitution industrialization. This alliance for political economic development broke down for reasons not unlike those which led to the dismantling of National Keynesianism in the core countries—but that is to get ahead of the story.

Summarizing reflections on the creation of the postwar economic governance institutions Ethan Kapstein (1994: 93) writes that "postwar leaders resolved to build a global economy that would be far more institutionalized and constitutionalized than it was in the 19th century, and they would do so in the interests of political stability, economic growth and social justice—all inextricably linked in the minds of postwar leaders." The shift since the Bretton Woods order collapsed has been to adjusting national economies to the exigencies of globalization rather than protecting farmers and workers from destabilizing forces originating outside the national economy—states as transmission belts from the global into the national economic sphere, in Cox's metaphor (1993: 260). If National Keynesianism in its peripheral form of populism and its core versions protected the politically better organized sectors of the popular classes in an era of general economic growth, then in a period of slow overall progress and uneven development, in which Global Neoliberalism became the dominant strategic orientation, protection of national industries was reduced or eliminated, while foreign investment was favored with inducements, taxation on capital was reduced, tax systems became increasingly regressive, and state spending on Welfare State functions declined. In addition, harmonization of regulation was pursued, and ideological rationales stressing individual responsibility flowered.

THE END OF THE BRETTON WOODS SYSTEM

In 1951, as President of the Board of Trade, Harold Wilson allowed the reopening of the London Commodity markets to international trading. Labour Party leaders defended the use of sterling as an international currency which made the pound subject to destabilizing speculation and forced a stop-go policy of macro management which "had the worst possible influence on British industrial management, on industrial relations and trade union bargaining strategies and on the investment decisions of banks and other influential financial institutions" (Strange, 1986: 37–38). In the 1960s, the U.S. and British governments by allowing the growth of the London Eurocurrency market provided extraordinary profit-making opportunity but created instability, volatility of currencies, and hurt the productive sectors in both economies.

This money market, like all markets, did not exist in a political vacuum. For much of the postwar period the parties of the Left had been strong enough to prevent speculation in their country's currencies, but as the global reach of what were then called multinational corporations grew to dominate more and more markets, and the corporations' political influence increased (certainly by the second half of the 1960s), the politics of fixed exchange rates had changed. While the Bretton Woods rules explicitly treated all countries equally it was clear that the dollar was the key currency and the numeraire of the system. As long as the United States provided a stable currency expanding it in line with the liquidity needs of the international economy the system would work. Over the years there were suggestions, such as Triffin's Plan (proposed in the mid-1950s by Robert Triffin and clearly descended from Keynes's Bretton Woods proposals) for the creation of a supranational bank which would function as lender of last resort and issue its own international currency. Triffin saw that the dollar shortage must turn into a dollar glut and that some new accommodation was needed. U.S. policymakers however showed reluctance to give up control over the world's money. By the late 1960s, the postwar dollar shortage had as Triffin forecast given way to a dollar glut. Over the next decades the United States and the European powers temporized.

The major challenge came from the policies of the United States, which reflected not only the growing power of U.S.-based capital but also domestic political conflict. The Vietnam War was unpopular. The Johnson Administration chose not to raise taxes to pay for it nor to cut domestic programs. Instead it pursued a policy of increased government borrowing. This had inflationary impact. President Nixon, while elected in part because he claimed to have a secret plan to end the war (which in reality amounted to widening the war rather than ending it), added to military spending and so to inflationary pressures. These policies left the United States without enough gold to back the huge build-up of U.S. dollars in the hands of foreigners. In August 1971 Nixon announced the U.S. had unilaterally suspended the convertibility of the dollar into gold at the fixed exchange rate. Those foreign allies which had built up huge dollar holdings to support the United States, as well as private investors holding dollar denominated assets, took a beating as the value of the dollar fell. Nixon's reneging on the American promise to redeem each of the billions of dollars held abroad if presented for payment, abruptly ended the Bretton Woods system. As Ronald McKinnon (1993: 39) writes: "In 1970–71 facing the clamor for dollar devaluation and greater exchange flexibility, the schizophrenic American government would not disinflate the American economy in order to defend the most successful international monetary regime the world had ever seen."

The inflation and general financial disarray of the 1970s is usually attributed to OPEC, the Organization of Petroleum Exporting Countries. But the large rise in the price of oil can more reasonably be traced to the instability in international relations and the inflation pressures that emerged in the aftermath of the end of dollar convertibility, itself the result of the inability or unwillingness of the United States to properly control the creation of dollars and so international liquidity. Triffin's observations (1978–79: 270–71) on the period are particularly salient: "World import and export prices, measured in dollars, rose by less than one percent a year in the 1960s, but by more than six percent a year from 1970 through 1972, and by as much as 30 percent in the last 12 months *before* the explosion of oil prices in the fall of 1973. This was not unconnected, to say the least," he wrote, "with the enormous and mounting U.S. deficits abroad which flooded the world monetary system, doubling world reserves from the end of 1969 to the end of 1972 . . . , i.e., increasing them by as much in this short time span of three years as in all previous centuries in recorded history."

The struggle of the United States to increase its freedom of action in international monetary affairs destroyed the old Bretton Woods system.

"Step by step," writes Fred Block (1977: 75) summarizing these events, "the United States either broke the rules of the old order or forced other countries to break them." A very different view is held widely in this country which sees the United States as victim of a system in which it had paid for the common defense by providing a stable world environment, the most important international public good, which allowed other nations to gain trade shares by undervaluing their currencies. From this perspective, Nixon's action in devaluing the dollar was simply an expedient to get the rest of the world to pay its share of the costs the U.S. incurred for the general well being. To others the collapse of Bretton Woods was a matter of U.S. irresponsibly and to many betrayal.

At an international level the constitutional political order built around the Bretton Woods accords, which had seemed so central to the rapid postwar recovery and growth, gave way to increasingly ad hoc arrangements. The shift resulted from the inability of the United States to supply "the right amount" of liquidity to the international economy. When in 1971 President Nixon admitted the inevitable, that the US could no longer honor the commitment to redeem dollars for gold at the established fixed exchange rate, and unilaterally devalued the dollar shock waves spread through the world economy. After two years of turbulence and discussion it was agreed that the fixed exchange rate could not be reestablished and that currencies would be allowed to float. The floating exchange rate system, which came into being following the demise of the Bretton Woods system, provided a flexible monetary tool that enabled the United States to avoid the adjustments which would otherwise have been required of a debtor nation. In a system of fixed exchange rates and gold convertibility, the United States would, "like every Third World country today, [have] to pay for its indebtedness, with a relative loss of sovereignty and highly unpopular measures," Noelle Burgi and Philip Golub (2000: 3) explain. "The new system also allowed the US to maintain a high standard of living at home by dipping into the planet's savings. Thanks to its political power and to the dollar, which was the world's only reserve currency, the US was able to keep its monetary sovereignty intact. Its allies could not question American policy without destabilizing the institutional fabric and the Cold War security system from which they derived undoubted benefits." The U.S. deficit was funded for decades by Japan and Europe.

Economists generally welcomed the floating exchange rate regime on the grounds that it offered a market solution to what the "right" price of a currency was at any point in time. Supply and demand and not monetary authorities would set the value of currencies on a day to day, hour to hour and even minute to minute basis. This would end fears that there would be devaluations and reduce speculative pressures. It did not turn out that way. In 1971, before the system of stable exchange rates collapsed, more than 90 percent of foreign exchange transactions were related to trade or future real investment while less than 10 percent was speculative. A decade or two later the percentages were reversed as speculation became the tail that wagged the foreign exchange market. Instead of such speculation stabilizing markets as most economists had predicted markets became more volatile and macroeconomic instability worsened as a result of such short-term flows.

With more deregulation, increased liberalization of markets, and lower transaction costs speculation increased even more dramatically. Globalization of financial markets proceeded at such a pace that by 1993 the value of UK international securities transactions equaled more than a thousand percent of the country's gross domestic product. The creation of the eurodollar market fed the scale of such transactions which ironically had originated in actions taken by communist financiers in the former USSR at the time of the Cuban missile crisis when, fearing having their U.S. dollar accounts frozen, they shifted their reserves to London. President Kennedy's Secretary of the Treasury Robert Roosa's effort to address a deteriorating balance of payments situation through a capital control tax on foreign investment prompted the deepening of the eurodollar and eurobond markets. The unanticipated consequence of the Kennedy Administration's decision to institute this tax had the effect of encouraging such transactions to move to London.

Traders can move against currencies quickly if they fear inflation or even if they do not like the tenor of a government's proposed labor legislation and its possible impact on costs of production. Market players become "a new class of stateless legislators"—the bond market seemingly more powerful than elected governments or the most brutal of dictators. All states must compete for credit ratings in the same manner as private market participants do. At the beginning of the twentieth century the enforcement agency for international capital was the U.S. marines and American presidents were praised for carrying "big sticks." By the century's end the International Monetary Fund and other GSEGIs acted as collection agencies and the bond market imposed discipline through threat of turning down credit requests or the rollover of outstanding loans. As the amount of available footloose money grew, currency speculators were emboldened to place large bets against particular national currencies where they saw national governments in trouble or likely to be unable to sustain policies. Many free market economists greeted this growing power of capital markets as a useful corrective to "bad" governmental policies. Any state running outsized deficits or attempting to impose too high a tax rate on investors would be penalized by capital flight and high interest rates. The usual discussion of what governments needed to do to avoid problems with capital markets focused on the areas of tax policy, spending levels, the extent of government debt, and the rate of expected domestic inflation. But behind these macroeconomic concerns was the larger issue of what the relation between state regulation and the economy was to be. The U.S. led, deregulating its financial sector prompting others to follow. Market dominance and government subservience increased as did both bank profits and the fragility of the financial system.

In the weakened economic condition of Western Europe in the early postwar years, the extent of capital flight was greater then the volume of U.S. aid being sent to Europe. If the United States had instituted controls over "hot money" flows from Western Europe, presumably Marshall Plan aid could have been at a much lower level. However, as in the case of the Third World debt crisis in the 1980s and other episodes such as the conversion of the former Soviet Union to a crude form of capitalism in the 1990s, capital flight was in the service of transitional politics. The statist regimes were dismantled because of an insistence on the dominance of market forces enforced by foreign capital and the choices of the hegemon whose interests were served by these coerced conversions. The U.S. banks made a great deal of money in each of these episodes by administering capital flight for large fees. They naturally opposed capital controls, putting their interests above international monetary stability and their influence over governmental policy made this strategic choice seem inevitable.

Foreign exchange trading in the 1970s became a major source of bank profitability and an invitation to excessive risk taking that caused some spectacular bank failures. For example, 1974 saw the downfall of the German Herstadt Bank and the Franklin, the twentieth largest national bank in the United States at the time. In September of that year the Comptroller of the Currency issued a warning to banks to stop borrowing short and lending long. Franklin National had nearly 50 percent of its loans covered by short-term funds. It was foreign exchange speculation, with borrowed monies due on short notice, which had brought the bank down. Others were close to the line, as the Comptroller's office knew. The Fed, fearing a domino effect throughout the financial system, stepped in to help smooth the failure of Franklin National, since Manufacturers Hanover Trust, one of a handful of large money center banks, was one of its biggest creditors.

The bank failures in 1974 were brought on to a significant degree by petrodollar recycling. OPEC had built up huge reserves and "decided" to put the money into low-interest bearing accounts mostly in U.S. banks. "Decided" is in quotation marks to reflect doubt as to whether this was the investment of choice. It was widely understood at the time that National Security Adviser Henry Kissinger had made clear to OPEC governments that any effort to use their tens billions of dollars to buy control of American companies (then selling at a significant discount due to depressed market conditions, themselves in significant part a result of the oil price jump) would not be tolerated. The banks then found themselves sitting on huge amounts of short-term deposits. They lent as much as they could to Third World governments and used other monies to speculate on their own account in foreign exchange markets. Petrodollar recycling was considered a success at the time, and by many subsequently, despite the disastrous debt crisis this lending engendered. Johannes Witteveen, the IMF's managing director, argued in early 1974 for public recycling of petrodollars to ensure an equitable and prudent process. While Western European governments supported the idea, the United States did not. The story of the Third World debt crisis, which is widely attributed to the way petrodollar recycling loans were made by private, predominantly U.S. banks might have had a different outcome if recycling had been handled by public institutions.

Washington pressures and the ideological climate of the 1980s upset the existing bargain with the state. Banks demanded and got greater protection from insolvency, enhanced protection of their profitability, and less regulation. This combination reduced the room within policymakers could maneuver, and encouraged more risky activity, raising the likelihood of panics and bankruptcies and rendering government ever more subject to the sentiments of the market. On this reading, policy ineffectiveness has a political origin. Loss of control by governments was simply the other side of the coin of lack of control over the movement of funds internationally and the related shift to overwhelmingly large speculative financial flows. As financial market liberalization advanced and the National Keynesian model went into decline, finance capital took center stage. The BIS 1998 triennial survey of 43 foreign exchange markets showed in current dollar terms that the volume of foreign exchange trading in these markets grew by 26 percent between April 1995 and April 1998, following a 45 percent increase between 1992 and 1995. In 1998 foreign exchange trading was about 60 times as great as trade in goods and services.

The increased liquidity of world money markets in the context of an inability of particular nations to limit capital inflow and outflow became a major problem. It was to become the basis for crises in European countries in the subsequent decades and a major reason for efforts to develop a European currency. The free flow of speculative investment was also responsible for the Latin American debt crisis which began in 1982 in Mexico and the East Asian financial crisis which was first manifest in Thailand in 1997. The difficulties of capitalist Russia with its structurally corrupt banking system and Argentina's failure to honor its foreign debts while maintaining dollar for dollar backing for its currency are other instances and will be discussed in chapters 6 and 7. The final chapter will explore the extent to which weaknesses of U.S. capitalism represents a variant of these wider deficiencies in the world system's economic order so that a next stage International Political Economy will have to revisit many of the assumptions about the system's basic stability.

THE MARKET RESURGENT

The tendency for financial policies to become less restrictive cannot be explained by considerations of efficiency. As Yilmaz Akyuz (1995: 63) writes: "A more plausible reason is the cost of financial openness (loss of policy autonomy, increased financial instability, and so on) being collective are anonymous in their incidence, whereas the benefits accrue to particular economic agents (especially international financial and non-financial enterprises, and financial opening therefore do not meet significant resistance." The extent to which there had been political pressure to change from the early 1970s to the opening years of this century, it was predominantly in the direction of greater freedom for capital and less regulation. Despite what appeared not too many years into the new century as structural weaknesses in the way financial markets generate and evaluate information and the basis on which investments are made those calling for re-regulation on a world scale have not been able to convince policymakers that serious dangers lay ahead if some of the presumptions of the neoliberal order were not examined more closely and, where found to be increasing global financial and economic fragility, replaced.

Keynes had warned of the situation produced by the free mobility of finance capital in which any country that attempts to follow policies speculators do not like is coerced to change its announced plans to avoid capital flight (Keynes 1943). It was presumed in 1944 that national government should protect their citizens from destabilizing speculative short-term movements within the context of an international financial governance regime of fixed but adjustable exchange rates, of exchange controls, and with a low degree of movement of private capital. After the experience of the 1930s, it was assumed that no government would endanger its economic stability by allowing either its own citizens or those of other countries to send money abroad if this would destabilize their economy. The idea that one day soon a Eurocurrency market would be allowed, and that governments would tie their own hands, declare themselves powerless to control their own currencies, their banks' activities and those of investors, would have appeared an ominous prospect, but also an unlikely one. Today trillions of dollars move daily outside the superintendence of sovereign states. There is only the most limited international regulation, without reserve requirements on unregulated accounts or taxation of short-term speculative movements, and speculators are permitted to engage in just those activities Keynes condemned.

Reformers since Keynes, looking at the world financial system in which most capital movement is unrelated to trade and long-term investment (enough currency passes through foreign exchange markets each day to finance months of trade), understand that business decisions become dramatically distorted. Corporations can be better off placing bets on the direction and magnitude of currency movements than on production costs and marketing considerations since such fluctuations can easily wipe out foreign currency denominated earnings. The decision to invest in a plant in another country is based significantly on expectations concerning that nation's future exchange rate. A hint of serious currency uncertainty is enough to discourage investment and trigger capital flight. The mechanisms which might shelter investors, futures markets, and the use of derivatives add to the cost of doing business—sometimes significantly. They transfer risk, but cannot eliminate uncertainty. Systemic risk in fact grows with rising volatility. In the postwar years, as capital regained confidence, the financial sector grew in importance relative to directly productive activity and became interpenetrated with it to a substantial degree. Financial profits became more important. Specialized interests formed a strong support group for greater financial openness.

THE STATIST ECONOMIES ON THE DEFENSIVE

In Europe a strategy of protecting and subsidizing national champions had been adopted to varying extent. The possibility of building a relatively high growth economy on subsidizing research and development, protection, and promotion of "buy locally" had worked through the postwar period for a number of European states (and spectacularly for Japan). However, by the 1980s and 1990s transnational corporations had outgrown their national boundaries. A French, or Italian, or Swedish auto producer for example had to compete with U.S. and then Japanese companies which enjoyed economies of scale to their brands, sourced widely, and assembled cars outside their home territory taking advantage of production cost and location advantages. As the cost of innovation grew, and the speed at which new products were introduced increased, it became essential to amortize development expenses more quickly. Products had to come to market sooner and everywhere at the same time before competitors introduced similar or better ones. Such a new economics of production with its increasing returns to geographical scale encouraged a wave of mergers and acquisitions at first within countries and later across national borders.

Cross border strategic alliances among leading firms in consumer electronics and other areas involved quicker, pooled specific capabilities short of permanent consolidation. Closer working relations between major retailers and original equipment suppliers in a number of nations and complex commodity chains for bringing products to market based on design in one place and parts produced and assembled in a host of others introduced a new model of production which eclipsed the national champion strategy. Countries holding out through nationalist protection of their domestic producers saw their companies fall behind technologically. Nations which tried to develop their own computer industry behind protective walls, India and Brazil with large domestic markets for example, found that they were unable to keep up technologically to cutting edge developments on the world frontier and abandoned these efforts, inviting foreign firms back in after costly experimentation with local development strategies failed. The idea of delinking in the Third World was discredited by the success of countries such as Singapore, which grew dramatically by welcoming a dependence on transnational corporate investment. They became vital sites of export oriented industrialization.

Globalization enlarges the market reach of transnational corporations. It offers local elites the opportunity and exerts pressure for collaboration with internationalized fractions of capital. Strategic alliances provide access to cutting edge technologies and marketing advantages. Innovation in transportation and communication allow sourcing from lower cost producers. As national borders offer less protection and national markets become too small for TNCs, the pressure exerted by globalism prompts neoliberal policies. Constituencies with the least mobility or ability to adjust to the forces of globalization lose leverage in the political arena. The questions for national elites, and for citizens, is not whether to insert their national economies into the global matrix but how to do so, how much bargaining power they have, and whether they can pursue their own designs or must submit to the wishes of more powerful players. The decision to adapt export-led industrialization strategies did not always mean opening investment, money, and product markets to foreign ownership and control. The state-led East Asian regimes retained control over their banks and subsidized national ownership and productive capacities. The biggest dragon of them all, market-Leninist China, was able to attract foreign capital on its own terms and under tight political control. Its unwillingness to pursue credit convertibility meant that when its own banks developed serious problems China did not face a great threat. Capital flight was not legally possible under its controlled currency regime. India too retained controls and a nationalist orientation even as it slowly began to open its economy. These countries escaped financial crisis in the late 1990s as the world's currency markets especially in Asia went into turmoil.

Globalization pressures have increased the appeal of the neoliberal agenda in Europe and made it harder for advocates of the Delors project of a social democratic Europe embedded in a federal union. Maastricht convergence criteria, the stability pact, and later the widening of the EU membership have diminished the attainability of the Social Charter and other social democratic items once on the EU agenda. Nonetheless popular pressure and general public opinion remains concerned over the impacts of neoliberalism and class politics continues fluid. This means the use of soft power in pursuit of the corporate globalization project remains central. Bastiaan Van Apeldoorn (1998: 12) speaks of the "tendential 'disembedding' of the market from postwar social and political institutions." European integration increases bias in favor of deregulation by establishing, he says, "the primacy of negative integration," that is liberalizing the competitiveness process, repealing barriers to capital's penetration of markets, and limiting social protections and provisions for social goods.

Behind the EU is the ERT, the European Round Table of Industrialists founded in 1983 by seventeen of Western Europe's most prominent corporate leaders which has since expanded its membership to others of the most transnationalized European companies. This club too has played a major role in initiating the EU and guiding its development through lobbying efforts at the highest level guided by awareness of transnational class interests. The ERT must be seen as an important force giving direction to the program of European integration. "In fact, the ERT provides a unique private forum for the European bourgeoisie for the arbitration of different (fractional) ideological and strategic outlooks into an integrated program of class rule." (Van Apeldoorn, 1998: 26) The ERT has been the forum in which European industrialists in the early 1980s worked out a protective regionalism strategy for its national champions and also where, in the 1990s the Germans and British with more secure globalist interests, initiated discussion of opening Europe to outside competitors on a basis of equality with Europeans. The ERT was not only the force behind the creation of Europe's internal market but also the adoption of a single currency and pressures for reducing Welfare State spending. It argued for stepped up spending for the channel tunnel and the Trans-European Networks involving over seven thousand miles of new expressways, high speed train links, and airport expansions. Pehr Gyllenhammar, who chairs CGNU, the UK's largest insurance group, is a former executive chairman of Volvo and was involved in establishing the ERT. In 2001 he became the first chair of the European Round Table of Financial Services (ERTFS) which he founded along with the chairs and chief executives of eleven other major European financial institutions. In the concentric club pattern, others were invited to join up after its basic operation was established. The ERTFS joins the ERT as fora in which European capital strategizes as it jockeys with U.S. and Japanese interests in the new competitive environment in which globalization rules.

Within each of the major negotiating economies low profile meetings are held among key corporate players to develop agreement on strategy and detailed proposals their governments are then expected to adopt and push for in international fora. In England, for example, a group of captains of finance who call themselves the British Invisibles, more formally the Financial Services International London Group, participate in private meetings of the Liberalization of Trade in Services (LOTIS) committee with Britain's chief services negotiator, the Bank of England, and other important players such as the International Chairman of Goldman Sachs who as it turns out is a former Director General of the World Trade Organization. Documents obtained by BBC television's Night News program and CorpWatch and by Greg Palast in *The Observer* report on their meetings. Britain's chief negotiator for the General Agreement on Trade in Services (GATS) circulated EU proposals for industry regulation to LOTIS members for their comments. These are documents the British government refuses to share with NGO watchdog organizations. Indeed, one of these groups, the World Development Movement was told that these papers did not exist (Palast, 2001).

While media investigators have detailed such matters, confirming the suspicions of conspiracy theorists, such close working relations would seem natural to the workings of what after all is a capitalist political economy. A confidential document entitled "Domestic Regulation: Necessity and Transparency" advised the British Invisibles in defending themselves from public criticism and further scrutiny by stressing not "public interest" but that trade bodies adopt an "efficiency principle." This would have the advantage, the document said, of allowing presidents and prime ministers hostile to environmental protection regulations to eliminate them not through votes of a nation's congress or parliament but through an edict from the WTO which a nation would be powerless to reverse. "It may be politically more acceptable," the memo said, "to countries to accept international obligations which give primacy to economic efficiency" (Palast, 2001: 3).

Spokespersons for Britain's Department of Trade and Industry, a leader in the EC Working Group, responding to the public discovery of the documents, claimed that the GATS changes as proposed would still allow nations their "sovereign right to regulate services" to meet "national policy objectives." The national interest was being decided by the self-interested parties and excluded other constituencies and interest groups which might be thought to have some role in the development of a consensus on what "national policy objectives" would best be. One of the functions of the GSEGIs is to take pressure off governments to act more democratically.

Representatives of the largest and most transnational businesses serve in government, using public office to overcome resistance from the general public and other interest groups to the designs of deregulation and global economic integration. This does not mean they may not be public spirited and attempting to serve the general interest as they see it, but rather that their background, and sometimes more specifically the interests of the firms from which they have come, can guide their actions as policymakers. Typically such actors use their official positions to involve those sectors of the corporate world interested in a proposal to achieve such goals and to ensure that government policies meet the specific needs of transnational capital. Sir Leon Brittan, the EU Commissioner for Trade, explains speaking at a gathering of the Conference of British Industrialists, "We and the American government . . . asked businessmen from both sides of the Atlantic to get together and see if they could reach agreement on what needed to be done next. If they could, governments would be hard put to explain why it couldn't be done. The result was dramatic.

European and American business leaders united in demanding more and faster trade liberalisation. And that had an immediate impact." (Corporate Europe Observatory, 1999a: 4)

Since it was established in 1995 the Transatlantic Business Dialogue (TABD) has annually brought together more than a hundred key corporate CEOs, government cabinet members, ministers, as well as commissioners to agree on trade and investment policy. It has working groups and some forty specialized subgroups which make recommendations and track their implementation. When TABD's detailed proposals are forwarded to negotiators the expectation that they will be implemented is not likely to be disappointed. Indeed, it presents its demand to the EU-US Summit in the form of a scorecard setting priorities and deadlines for their implementation. The Corporate Europe Observatory (1999: 6) cites an internal EC working document for the Commission staff which reads in part "Follow-up to the TABD recommendations is a high priority task. Vice-president Sir Leon Brittan and Commissioner Dr. Bangemann have therefore decided to personally oversee the process and will be in direct regular contact with the TABD co-chairmen on this matter."

Paula Stern (1997: 37) a former government trade negotiator has made clear the *lex mercatoria* logic of the role played by the TABD,

> by giving industry not a voice, but the initiative in trade negotiations. . . . the TABD can realize the benefits of "subsidiarity," the decentralization of responsibility to those most effected by a given issue. . . . It is more efficient to give the responsibility of identifying barriers to trade and of supplying recommendations to eliminate them to those that are most intimately affected by—and therefore, more intimately knowledgeable of—such issues. And when CEOs— whose talents combine decisiveness and organizational skillfulness— sit down to work together, decisions get made decisively. Business knows best what is in its best interests . . .

In the core countries such procedures are disembedding economies from the postwar Welfare State and corporatist regulatory framework and reembedding them into a privatized corporate-government "partnership" in which the state is reduced to a transmission belt for the formulation of a modern "merchant's law." For Third World countries such a procedure amounts to being totally shut out from the private sector fora where the real decisions affecting their futures are made. The governmental forum which has become most central to implementing the neoliberal regime is the thirty-member "rich nations club," the OECD, the Organization of Economic Cooperation and Development (created in 1961). Its role in pushing liberalization on the less developed countries was, as shall be seen, an important one. The codes it has adopted, liberalizing capital movements and provision for national treatment, are binding on all members. Although there is no formal dispute settlement mechanism, the OECD is a clubhouse for the creation of global governance process. The OECD expanded its membership from the small core of rich European countries and the United States to its present size by including South Korea and Mexico as recognition of the growing importance of newly industrializing economies. It operates as an intermediary forum in which the more powerful nations agree on trade and finance issues and then take them to the larger governance institutions like the IMF and the WTO.

THE GSEGIS AND NATIONAL POLICY CHOICES

Ruggie's use of the term "embedded liberalism" in 1982 to describe the postwar international order captured the balance of forces which had temporarily stabilized the system, a balance the importance of which Karl Polanyi (1944) had previously called attention to, as would his fellow Hungarian George Soros (1998). Laissez faire economics in its uncompromising pure form is from such perspectives unsustainable and undesirable. The reason is it becomes more likely that without the support of an underlying moral economy (as Adam Smith had also explained), the public good is to be sacrificed to an unconstrained greed. Excesses can become system threatening and mobilize opposition. Without the moral sentiment enforcing collective respect for the non-market principles of mutual responsibilities, the market itself is perceived to be dysfunctional and actually becomes so. In the twentieth century the lesson that the lack of institutions of collective responsibility breed disaster had to be learned repeatedly (most recently as this is written in a capitalist Russia whose oligarchs seem determined to run the country to ruin for the benefit of a fabulously wealthy elite which has stolen and misused the collective patrimony). The forms of capitalism in peripheral formations with yawning gaps of income and wealth and the rise of a risk society in the once more securely social democracies produced potential for destabilizing political and religious movements and the more diffuse opposition of large populations without hope, for whom violence was a possible path.

The discipline of the risk society imposes costs on many who are the

incidental victims of failed choices made by elites. This is either a necessary cost or an unacceptable imposition depending on valuations which
are subjective and based on class position and ideological commitment.
For David Gill (1995: 413) the orthodox position favored by what he calls
the new constitutionalism is "the imposition of discipline on public institutions, partly to prevent national interference with the property rights
and entry and exit options of holders of mobile corporate capital with
regard to particular jurisdictions. These initiatives are also linked to efforts
to define appropriate policy, partly by strengthening the surveillance
mechanisms of international organizations and private agencies." This
would seem an accurate description. Balancing the meaning(s) of such a
new constitutionalism is as noted a subjective judgment. Betting on the
success of its project seems more problematic than the general uniformity
of optimistic views among mainstream thinkers and policymakers would
suggest. What is so remarkable about the discourse concerning its likely
trajectory is that value statements vary so substantially and that with few
exceptions the academic literature has for the most part excluded views
from the South and those neo-Gramscians and other critics for whom this
central question of whether capitalism can retain an adequate moral economy grounding for its expansion and indeed self-preservation remains
unresolved and very much on the agenda of the twenty-first century.

   In the last decades of the twentieth century the form globalization was
encouraged to take allowed capital to substantially escape social controls.
The presumed alliance among labor, capital, and the state which had been
the basis of National Keynesianism in the postwar era eroded. Social democrats, socialists, and communists who had neither foreseen nor responded at
all effectively to globalization saw their political influence dramatically
decline. Such a turn in public philosophy produced disarray in the left-of-
center camp, which had seen a slow but sure evolution and seemingly irreversible movement toward a more humanized capitalism through the postwar period and for some to socialism. The legacy of the Great Depression
had been faith in state planning in one form or another in most countries.
The idea was that the liberal democratic polity had freed itself both from the
heavy hand of hierarchical political control and the determining power of
capital—that the state had achieved a relative autonomy which allowed it to
pursue the general interest (however defined). Such expectations were the
basis of the postwar pluralist version of reformist state theory.

   Early in the postwar period and through the 1970s nationalist sentiment
was strong outside the core and there were efforts to achieve an international New Deal for the developing economies, to impose rules on foreign

investors, and to address the consequences of Western economic dominance. By the 1980s a counter-offensive led by the United States in pursuit of open markets and laissez faire gained momentum. In the context of financial liberalization severe problems arose for most developing economies. The pendulum swung from faith that government could provide stability and prosperity to the view that laissez faire was in fact the best policy after all. Because the U.S. economy prospered in the second half of the 1990s while others faltered, and so escaped most costs of this new policy orientation, American academics and policymakers celebrated its vigor and in the absence of an obvious challenger were confident that it was the only possible model for human development. The story can be told in brief.

In the second half of the twentieth century the non-Western countries attempted a variety of institutional responses to the formal and informal governance structures which they believed dominated and coerced their economic prospects. The nonaligned movement had its formal founding in Bandung, Indonesia in 1954, where the leading figures of the independence movements—Nehru, Sukarno, Nasser and others—mobilized a counter to the imperial powers, continued domination of what came to be known as the Third World. These efforts continued through the 1964 meeting of the G-77, where the African, Asian and Latin American states gathering in the first United Nations Conference on Trade and Development (UNCTAD). In 1974, with the proclamation of the Decade To Establish a New International Economic Order and for the Charter of Economic Rights and Duties of States, in which the rights were those of the states and the duties mandated for the transnational corporations, a high point of sorts was reached for the Third World states' efforts to impose regulations on transnational capital. There was overwhelming numerical support in the UN General Assembly. However the United States, Great Britain, West Germany, Denmark, Belgium, and Luxembourg voted no and shifted venues to the OECD, which responded to these demands with a 1976 Declaration on International Investment and Multinational Enterprises. The declaration included a voluntary set of guidelines in the context of a liberalization frame for the developing economies. The tide then turned decisively. In 1985 the World Bank, following the OECD's lead, sponsored the Convention that established the Multilateral Investment Guarantee Agency which promoted investor rights to transfer profit and capital out of the host countries. A majority for the proposal and the philosophy it embraced was made easier became the OECD countries had 60 percent or so of the votes at the Bank unlike in the United Nations General Assembly, where a one country one vote rule prevails.

Greater reliance on market forces and protection of investors coincided with the decline in government-sponsored aid and the greater importance of private capital markets in the less economically developed parts of the world. In the 1950s and 1960s most of the long-term financial flow to developing countries was foreign aid of one sort or another originating from Western government sources. By 1990, the year after the collapse of the Berlin Wall, private capital accounted for about 45 percent and by 1996 about 85 percent of the total. With the end of the Cold War the richer countries aside from the Nordic nations and one or two other honorable exceptions cut back on foreign aid. U.S. policymakers stressed "trade not aid" and suggested openness to foreign investment and trade liberalization would stimulate growth for the less developed economies. Even though many countries did liberalize, 95 percent of all private flows went to only 26 economies in 1996 while 140 nations shared among them only five percent of the total. Even those successful in attracting foreign capital routinely suffered destabilizing bouts of speculative inflows, bubbles, and painful sudden capital flight, events which shall be considered more fully in later chapters.

Here it may be noted that in the early 1970s when financial markets were highly regulated, there was no apparent link between balance of payments and banking crises. By the 1980s, following widespread liberalization of financial markets, banking and currency crises often accompanied each other. Indeed, banking crises predict currency crises. Most such financial difficulties in the 1980s and 1990s were associated with liberalization. Kaminsky and Rein report that the probability of a banking crisis beginning being conditional on financial liberalization having taken place is higher than the unconditional probability of a banking crisis. It appears they write that "the twin crises may have common origins in the deregulation of the financial system and the boom-bust cycles and asset bubbles that, all too often, accompany financial liberalization" (Kaminsky and Reinhart, 1999: 480). Such an analysis suggests that those GSEGI officials and academic experts who focus on the importance of market confidence for stability and for reimposing stability after crisis may be missing the basis of the problem which is in the liberalization process itself.

The collapse of a currency deepens a banking crisis. The vicious spirals of the 1980s and 1990s, most prominently in the Latin American and Asian crises but found in all parts of the world, resulted from the reinforcing impact of high interest rates perpetrated in order to defend exchange rates and the foreign exchange exposure of banks. Such policies were necessitated by financial market liberalization which seemed to make the crisis inevitable. The bunching of financial crises is widely attributed to contagion effects. When trouble develops in one emerging market investors flee those they see as similarly positioned (Calvo and Reinhart, 1996). There is also evidence that external factors, especially foreign interest rates (Frankel and Rose, 1996) and most especially interest rates in the U.S. matter a great deal (Calvo, Leiderman and Reinhart, 1993).

Since the 1994–95 Mexican crisis the IMF has played a new kind of role. It acted as an *ex ante* lender of last resort. The idea is to make a large amount of foreign exchange available so that market confidence in the troubled currency is quickly restored. Risk diminishes because the Fund (in that case with deep pocketed U.S. support) is ready to make good on Mexican obligations paying in dollars. With such a guarantee in place capital flight abated and money returned. Structural adjustment could take place in a calmer atmosphere. The amount of money required to guarantee risk taking increases as such guarantees are put in place, since investors go in deeper than they would otherwise.

In Mexico rapid trade liberalization accompanied by economic and financial deregulation and extensive privatization redistributed income dramatically. It intensified inequality and imparted an inflationary bias to the economy even as imports of luxury items soared. The foreign capital inflow to finance the deficit created a structural imbalance which could not be sustained leading to capital flight and crisis. Between 1995 and 1997 more than a third of all Mexican businesses declared bankruptcy, millions of people lost their jobs. The absence of unemployment benefits and falling real wages (they fell by 25 percent), brought the cumulative decline from 1982 to a loss of two-thirds of workers purchasing power. The government spent the equivalent of 12 percent of GDP to assist the collapsed banking sector, more than twice what it spent on education and social development combined in those years. (S. Helleiner, 1998: 9). For many Mexicans the actions of their government and the IMF serveds to bail out foreign investors and the local elite at the expense of the people while structurally transforming the economy in ways which would make it difficult if not impossible for some future government to undo the policies.

Since borrowers can have an interest in misleading lenders, the problem of asymmetric information (borrowers know more than lenders) can lead to adverse selection (lenders make bad decisions based on lack of information, extending credit where it will turn out they should have exercised restraint) greater disclosure allows markets to function more efficiently as allocators of loan capital. The IMF-WB financial economists believe that greater transparency of capital flows by providing decision-makers with better information will lead to earlier self-correction by markets themselves and make future GSEGI interventions either unnecessary, or more realistically, less necessary. Proposals to strengthen the IMF's intelligence gathering and data disseminating capacities are designed with such ends in mind. Many borrowers prefer to maintain privacy and so their room to maneuver, although some, especially in the better run economies, see advantages in fuller disclosure as a confidence building strategy.

Paralleling the emergence of the neoliberal regime were efforts by corporations and economies to "bulk up," to create larger units to more effectively compete in the globalized economy. Corporate mergers and the creation of regional trading areas both reflect such pressures. Transnational corporations and international financial institutions will be considered in future chapters. This chapter is brought to a conclusion with a consideration of how the strategy guiding regional integration changed in the second half of the twentieth century in response to the pressures brought to bear by corporate globalization.

REGIONAL INTEGRATION

The European Union is the most important instance of an emergent supra-regional governance structure. It allows a bulking up of formerly national firms of the continent to better compete with U.S. and Japanese transnationals. Where early discussion of a social charter to defend living standards led to worries in the United States that it might be facing a "fortress Europe," business interests have been able to dominate the policy debate. Over the years as it has developed out of less extensive integrative schemes Europe made a transition from a defensive alliance aimed at protecting the gains of social democratic corporatism to embrace an awareness that unless the continent's economy is capable of contesting markets globally it is unlikely to succeed in defending its home markets. The pressure to dismantle restrictions to free trade and investment was evident in the ways regional common market-like arrangements changed focus (as shall be discussed momentarily). Yet deregulation challenged nationalistic aspirations and imposed social costs creating pressure for protection of home markets and a desire for greater local state autonomy. Both of these conflicting pulls were, and continue to be, intense. The movement has been from nationalism in the 1950s and 1960s, a period of crisis of development strategy in the 1970s, the adaptation to neoliberalism in the 1980s and 1990s, and in the new century to backlash to globalization.

In the postwar years the nationalist economic policies followed by many less developed nations, faced with the power of the core economies and their own competitive disadvantage in dealing with transnational corporations, followed the infant industry strategy propounded by Alexander Hamilton and Frederich List. While early efforts at regional integration were based on these import substitution strategies, later on regional organizations tended to be more open, welcoming foreign investment from outside the area. They saw growth of trade coming from reducing barriers to trade. For example, the Andean Pact was created in 1969 as a protectionist-integrationist arrangement to foster import substitution strategies, and it was modified under the impact of globalization in the direction of a more open common market for its members Bolivia, Columbia, Ecuador, Venezuela, and Peru. Mercosur,—the common market among Argentina, Brazil, Paraguay, and Uruguay—began in 1991 with a customs union structure on a model of open regionalism. It is a free trade area with free circulation of goods and services and productive resources (with some exceptions). It is a customs union with a common external tariff on imports from other countries. Mercosur attempts to coordinate southern cone macroeconomic and sectoral policies. Brazil in the late 1990s and early 2000s tried to employ Mercosur as a counterfoil in FTAA negotiations. The organization was powerless in addressing Argentina's currency crisis and has not yet proven a strong coordinating vehicle for independent regional policy. It does allow private parties to initiate proceedings for perceived violation of Mercosur rules.

NAFTA was created to foster open regionalism with minimal interference with the external economic policies of its member countries. Given domestic opposition to even the appearance of compromise of sovereignty, NAFTA's dispute settlement mechanisms and panel decisions are not automatically binding. Yet because the system is one in which domestic legislation is interpreted by international panels bound by domestic law standards with no regular appeal system, some writers suggest that "NAFTA panels constitute a significant step toward supra nationalization of settlements of disputes related to international cooperation treaties, with concomitant creation of a favorable transnational environment for the elaboration of legal rules and principles with no state court participation or interference" (Naon, 1996: 656). From a very different perspective Raul Hinojosa-Oeda believes that the NAFTA and side agreements represent "a significant milestone in the emergence of new social actors into the traditionally closed arena of international economic policy-making long dominated by a limited set of state agencies and economic interests, with potentially important global implications" (Hinojosa-Ojeda, 1999: 2). The manner in which these multi-level games get played out will reflect the mobilizing capacities of interested parties—corporate, bureaucratic, and from sectors of civil society. For Naon and others the side agreement experience is a step toward supra-national decisionmaking. To Hinojosa-Ojeda it is a reflection of the growing power of Latino, labor, and environmental groups in forcing a more progressive international agenda over which their influence may be increasingly felt. Previous discussion in this chapter has indicated serious doubts as to this latter position.

The United States at the 1994 Miami Summit of the Americas proposed a free trade area from Alaska to Tierra del Fuego. The 34 governments agreed to a 2005 deadline for completing negotiations. Such an FTAA would basically expand NAFTA to almost the entire hemisphere. The Brazilians, who wish to first link Mercosur and the Andean Group into a South American free trade area have proposed a slower negotiating schedule. They hope to gain greater bargaining strength before they come up against the United States. The United States Congress delayed matters by not renewing President Clinton's fast track authorization to enter negotiations. The labor and environmental support group in the Congress felt that the Clinton Administration had hardly lived up to its verbal commitments to incorporate their concerns and was not about to give the president carte blanche in negotiations, feeling that they were burned badly in the case of NAFTA. The administration of George W. Bush offered even less in these regards but its targeted concessions to some protectionist interests won over a still tentative majority for reauthorizing fast track. The issues raised by politics of regionalization are essentially similar to those which characterize the broader globalization debates, as is the resistance to the FTAA. While as shall be discussed in the next chapter the hegemon has the greatest influence in structuring such agreements, the perception of a general failure of neoliberalism in Latin American led to the election of a number of left-center governments, including in Argentina, Brazil, and Venezuela—countries that cooperate in setting alternative priorities to those proffered by a U.S.-designed one-sided NAFTA.

CONCLUSION

Bretton Woods in a real sense lasted a dozen years or so. The thinking among many mainstream economists in the years since has been increasingly to question whether that system deserves much credit for postwar stability which seems in their view to have been a matter of readjustment growth in which the Marshall Plan, the European Payments Union, and other postwar accommodations played greater enabling roles. They conclude that "the lesson" of Bretton Woods (and the European Monetary System) is that pegged exchange rate systems do not work for long, no matter how well they are designed (Bordo, 1993). Those who share such a view think the case for a new Bretton Woods is dubious. The market is simply too powerful for governments to control. The rise of efficient market theories, a return to pre-Keynesian orthodoxy, encourages such views. Governments simply cannot control market forces, and in this view, it is not healthy for them to attempt to do so.

The contrasting perspective is that while the instrumentalities may be different than Bretton Woods, today government should control markets both for their own good (financial markets do not find equilibrium states but are subject to costly excesses due to ever present excitable animal spirits which produce waves of over optimism and over pessimism) and because unless there is social control of financial markets achieving the goals of higher living standards, a more acceptable distribution of income, and the funding of social priorities through the public sector will not be possible. The social costs of financial disruptions, taxpayer cost of bailing out banking sector excesses, and social inequalities are simply too high to accept. It is this second view that the architects of Bretton Woods took for granted. They sought to achieve a compromise: states had responsibility to safeguard domestic welfare, but were to do so within the rules that aimed at a harmonization of economic policies followed by other nations. As market forces gained momentum and the pressures of globalization asserted themselves governments acting alone became hard pressed not to surrender domestic goals to preserve international balance. For some governments, regional intergovernment trade and an investment customs union, common market, or some other arrangement, which initially were attempts to respond by building up a protected market among neighboring states, became with time instruments of integration into an open world economy. It would have required full scale political mobilization and international solidarity of a sophisticated sort to fight such pressures. The politicians of the era and the social movements which would resist such forces were not up to such a task. However at the ministerial gathering in Seattle in 1999 through the failure of subsequent WTO meetings and in the failure to gain acceptance of the U.S. vision of an FTAA in Miami in 2003, a far more contested terrain of what sort of globalization the world would prefer and accept was evident.

In the next chapter the way powerful private business interests interceded in the construction of alternative regimes to the Bretton Woods order is discussed in historical perspective. The question that arises as this project is pursued and carried on in subsequent chapters as well is the broader one of the continuing revising of state-market relations. The changes stressed are in the evolution of the global state economic governance institutions. It needs to be emphasized that these developments take place within the broad context of the evolving world capitalist system, a process of combined and uneven development, and of the political responses of influential private and public actors. When looking forward, an encounter with what a half century later had become a globally central market-Leninist China in the 21st century, a relative strengthening of not only a wider economic and political zone in East Asia, but also an increasingly important India nearby, as well as a more powerful European economic and political entity, the world would come to look quite different than the immediate post World War II configuration. While these challenges lay a half century in the future, what they suggest is that how the United States (and others) understand its role is historically contingent upon developments in the broader world system and in the jockeying of powerful political and economic actors. While not exactly analogous the soft power a country exercises by commanding the voluntary allegiance of others, the presumption of credibility that attaches to its policy initiatives and suggestions for presumably positive sum international accommodations, has a parallel in soft law proposals put forward by industry groups of rules and regulations to facilitate the smooth operations of key market players. The agreements reached by private associations in a particular business sector, banking or accounting for example, are typically ratified by intergovernmental conventions. Both soft power exercised by powerful states' leadership and soft law promulgated by peak business interests impact on formal rule making in GSEGIs as we shall see in the next chapter. Both refer to the ability to shape the framing of plausible options and the reaction and behavior of participants. The power relations and how potency is exercised in any regime are crucial aspects of consensus formation.

CHAPTER SIX

Clubs, Soft Law and International Financial Governance

"The financial community's view of the world predominates—even when there is little evidence in its support. Indeed, beliefs on key issues are held so strongly that theoretical and empirical support of the positions is viewed as hardly necessary."

—*Joseph E. Stiglitz* (2002: A19)

"Our global open society lacks the institutions and mechanisms necessary for its preservation, but there is no political will to bring them into existence. I blame the prevailing attitude, which holds that the unhampered pursuit of self-interest will bring an eventual international equilibrium. . . . As things stand, it does not take very much imagination to realize that the global open society that prevails at present is likely to prove a temporary phenomenon."

—*George Soros* (1998: 53–54)

The question of what sort of limits should be placed on the financial sector in an age of globalization is far from settled. It is an issue which attracts attention beyond the community of interest within the financial sector and regulator fraternity. Yet it has been slow to engage the wider polity, perhaps because the issues seem too complex and technical. Considering challenges to financial stability at the international level is difficult. The number of participants in the discussion of global finance has increased dramatically even as cross currents of competing interests and understandings make following the overlapping conversations more demanding. Short of a painful financial crisis with widespread costs it is difficult to see how such a serious consideration of systemic weaknesses would gain a hearing by policymakers. This chapter considers the international economic and financial regulatory regimes from the perspective of the evolution of soft law applicable to aspects of the international financial regulatory regime and the evolution of GSEGIs as producers of club goods. It explores the discourses of sovereignty and governance and then the concentric club formation and soft law concepts. The possibility that estimates of the private costs and benefits to the powerful participants in such negotiations are not coterminous with the social costs and benefits to the larger global community do not enter such a discussion.

To reiterate our positioning of these issues, IR theorists have long discussed the role of the United States as a hegemon in terms of the provision of desirable global public goods (like security guarantees) from which all may benefit and none need be excluded. In our view however, rather than seeing the hegemon as supplying public goods for the international community it is perhaps more useful, at least for the cases we discuss, to understand the hegemon as establishing a set of concentric clubs in stages with larger and larger memberships as they evolve outward from the hegemon itself, to the key participants, and to a broader followership which has little part in negotiating the rules but are the "price takers" of the world political market system. Sequencing to build coalitions follows a simple logic. It is of course easier to start with the party or parties most likely to agree to your proposal and postpone approaching parties less likely to agree, to start negotiations with those in a position to deny you your objective through noncooperation, and to ignore those without power.

That clubs are rarely initiated by the less powerful is a significant feature of regime formation. Influence in rule design for each club is proportional to power resources which can be brought to bear. In instance after instance the hegemon proposes rules and negotiates them with the secondary participants it needs to join if the club is to be successful. It establishes rules with these states, often the G-7 or the OECD, sometimes first with only one other government as is often the case in finance where London and New York reach agreement and then others are induced to sign on. We shall see this procedure at work later in this chapter when we discuss the BIS, the Bank for International Settlements, and its capital adequacy guidelines. While such a process of regime formation may have seemed controversial before the Bush II Administration's claim that unrivaled power confers its own legitimacy, in the days after the build-up to war with Iraq, when the U.S. signaled willingness to act alone if necessary and cajoled, threatened, and bribed others to fall in line, the world saw how a determined hegemon could set up regime change as an imperative and enforce its preferences on an unwilling world. The regime formation processes which shall be discussed in this chapter represented a gentler version of hegemonic initiative.

Conventionally the key difference between club goods and public goods is that while the latter are characterized by nonexcludability and nonrivalry (once established all can enjoy them whether they contribute to the cost of their provision or not and without diminishing the amount of the good available to others), non-club members can be excluded and gain only if they accept membership terms. Much of what passes for public goods is initially club goods. As a result the goods are compromised because the universal terms offered to all are designed by those who establish the club, typically favor them differentially, and offer them to non-club members on a take it or leave it basis. In the case of the presumed public goods which interest us here and which begin their life as club goods, non-club members "take it" because the option of refusing is too costly. The terms of what is provided, how, and under what conditionality, typically result in greater benefits to the original club members and lesser benefits (along with possibly greater costs) to those who join later. We can call such pseudo-public goods concentric club goods to distinguish them both from public goods and the ambiguous club good designation for such arrangements. Much of the global governance discussion which focuses on cooperation and the establishment of regimes can be retheorized as a process whereby the G-7 or perhaps the G-1 imposes preferences on the world community. In economic and financial matters the intermediating instrumentality is often a global state economic governance institution.

GOVERNANCE AND REGIMES

The concept of governance, as Wyn Grant (1997: 320) has said "has a kind of assuring vagueness." But as used in IPE its compass is clear enough. As defined by the Commission on Global Governance, "Governance is the sum of the many ways individuals and institutions, public and private, manage their common affairs. It is a continuing process through which conflicting or diverse interests may be accommodated and co-operative action be taken. It includes formal institutions and regimes empowered to enforce compliance, as well as informal arrangements that people and institutions with either have agreed to or perceive to be in their interests." In a world system lacking global government but fraught with trans-state issues in need of resolution accommodating the interests of state and nonstate actors requires some form of authority. We understand international governance in regime terms as the bundle of formal and informal rules, roles, and relationships which define and regulate international practices and so constrain state and nonstate actors. Much of the discussion of governance has taken place in the context of regime theory and study of formal international institutions which serve a range of functions from information collection and exchange to adaption and enforcement of codes of conduct. Providing such a regulatory framework and corresponding enforcement mechanisms are clubs which can be understood as providing public goods that reconfigure sovereignty. This last point becomes clearer as we look at particular GSEGIs.

An international regime, in Stephen Krasner's (1985: 4) influential formulation, is seen as "sets of implicit or explicit principles, norms, rules, and decision-making procedures around which actors' expectations converge in a given area of international relations." Principles are beliefs of fact, caution, and rectitude. Norms are standards of behavior defined in terms of rights and obligations. On the political science side of IPE the emphasis is on process, incentives for cooperation and punishment for defection, use of linkages, and so forth. "Rules are specific prescriptions or proscriptions for action" and decisionmaking procedures are the practices prevailing for making "and complementing collective choices." (Krasner, 1985: 4) Such a definition of an international regime is very much that of a political scientist. Political economists on the institutional economics side of IPE are more apt to talk about regimes of accumulation with their particular historical logics of economic development and modes of regulation—the norms, laws, but also habits and conventional understandings, which have a state embodiment and are part of the cultural-political assumptions of the era. To such economists political regimes are important because they define basic property rights. They establish acceptable patterns of behavior and coordinate decisionmaking.

International organizations act as the governance structures needed to "oversee" global regimes. Organizations need to overcome the transaction, implementation and enforcement, costs that create problems of coordination where collective action problems exist. Regime theorists have a shared belief that regimes do not generally enforce rules in a hierarchical sense, but by changing the pattern of transaction costs they provide information which participants use rationally and so they reduce uncertainty. The focus is on expectations. Regimes of economic governance differ in the way the market and corporate organizational are formed. Economists put this in terms of transaction costs: assembling information about the nature of problems, evaluating alternative responses, reaching agreement, and overseeing solutions (implementing and monitoring). Regimes offer a structure of leadership, recruitment, and governance for what is deemed legitimate and how control is exercised. Internationally regimes define and mediate international relationships among countries and with nonstate actors. In the market companies are protected, promoted, privileged, and proscribed by the state. The balance between cooperation and competition among firms is often conditioned by the extant regime.

Mainstream economics suggests that since competition is efficiency producing, monopoly is inefficient, regulatory diversity is good, and a global monopoly by a single regulatory regime imposed by international bureaucrats is bad. Let each state decide its own regulatory framework and allow corporations to vote with their feet. "Bad" regulation will drive out business. "Good" regulation will attract vibrant economic growth. Given competition, "bad" regulation will be driven out by "good" (market-friendly regulation). The effort by politicians and technocrats to impose their views of the best regulatory order for the global economy if successful is likely, in the view of economists wedded to this understanding of competition and efficiency, to produce a less than optimal pattern of resource allocation than would be the case in a world of regulatory diversity. The dominant view among political scientists, especially in the liberal institutionalist camp, is cool to this economistic approach. IR and IPE scholars typically seek ways to enhance coherence through the political process, of harmonizing regulatory regimes so that an institutional regime framework at the level of the global political system assures market participants cannot engage in regulatory arbitrage, seeking out the least regulated environment, which while perhaps to their own advantage leads to socially costly outcomes. If all are compelled to play by common rules competitive fairness and a level playing field can be created.

The political economy perspective stresses that markets need to be regulated in the public interest. Heterodox political economists focus on the instability unregulated markets produce through their normal workings which are part of capitalism's crisis tendencies. Where mainstream economists see the working of the law of one price allocating resources more efficiently in response to new technologies that change relative costs and reorganize production in space, mocking legislative attempts to restrict activities within national borders and imposing costs on governments which attempt to limit market freedom, many political economists view this unbundling of territoriality as leading to a rearticulation of international political space which must be addressed in political terms. Markets need supporting governance institutions. Otherwise participants have incentives, given asymmetrical information and moral hazard problems, to take advantage of those in weaker bargaining positions by abrogating contracts and understandings where they feel safe from effective retaliation. For this reason many participants are willing to accept a bad bargain but one assuring stability in the long run. The effort to build international regimes that can address collective action problems is the result. Some of these accords, often in response to technological developments, create new forms of interdependence. The need to establish standards among available possibilities appears benign promising positive sum gains. Such regimes are surely not new phenomena—think of the 1865 International Telegraph Union and the 1906 Radiotelegraph Union (Murphy, 1994).

While a global state is emerging from the accretion of international regimes, the form this process is taking is a selective one. In most instances it does not deal extensively (or at all) with a host of distributional issues which are integral to nation-state level governance. It is formulated through horizontal cross-border negotiations in which those charged with authority in particular areas and their domestic constituencies bypass domestic decisionmaking processes and create international fora for nego-tiation and international regime formation typically excluding antagonistic domestic interests. This is usually with the tacit approval and sometimes the active leadership of the executive branch of government sympathetic to the internationalized interests involved. The insider parties proceed in this way dealing with complex questions they want resolved and rules and enforce-ment procedures they wish harmonized. Those not directly involved (although they may be significantly effected) are excluded, producing in some instances a profoundly undemocratic process.

While regimes mediate and help define international relations they have a problematic relationship to law at the level of individual nation states. The process begins with private sector communities of interest which are for-mulators of *soft law*. These are agreements on practices which are not backed by formal enforcement power and do not originate through speci-fications in international treaties; rather, they are negotiated on a consen-sus basis and followed voluntarily because individuals, organizations, and states find it in their interest to do so. Hard law, by contrast, defines a signed treaty or agreement which is precisely worded and sets out exact enforceable obligations. With the demise of the Soviet Union and the emergence of a unipolar power structure the niceties of such a process were eroded, yet the basic principles of global management stay the same even as coercion has become more central to their formation and operation.

When Krasner (1985: 5) in his classic discussion wrote that regimes define basic property rights, establish acceptable patterns of behavior, and coordinate decisionmaking he, like most IR scholars, imagined that such issues would be resolved through diplomacy. In the relatively short time since then, the formalization of global state economic governance institutions has created dispute settlement frameworks which represent significant progress toward an international jurisprudence. It is remarkable how quickly this reframing took place. Krasner had suggested the key distinction was the one between authoritative and market allocation in which "Authoritative allocation involves either the direct allocation of resources by political authorities, or indirect allocation by limiting the property rights of nonstate actors, including private corporations. A market-oriented regime is one in which the allocation of resources is determined by the endowments and preferences of individual actors who have the right to alienate their property according to their estimations of their own best interests" (Krasner, 1985: 5). In the early to mid 1980s it was still possible to unproblematically presume the superordinate position of governments over nonstate actors, including TNCs, and the existence of two kinds of political economies, free market economies and command economies. Governments were authoritative, stable, unitary, and predictable. Market economies despite the work of Shonfield (1965) and others, were still seen as the homogeneous advanced economies of the democratic West and contrasted to the communist bloc East.

There was modest awareness that developmental states such as Japan and the East Asian NIEs were a different model. Krasner made no distinction between European corporatist models and the Anglo-American one, which was taken as generic. Since then mainstream IPE's most obvious need as a political science subdiscipline has been to enunciate more clearly how and why different national economies have adjusted as they have to globalization and how they might individually and collectively grapple with the dislocations and opportunities it produces. It has not yet responded with a theory of the state adequate to the task. The way forward has been to privilege governance over government as the central construct for the rule making-adjudication-enforcement core of a revised state theory.

Some analysts suggest that outcomes of enforced cooperation are for the best since globalization produces large positive sum gains, if only after a period of major transformation of existing relations involving significant redistribution of income, wealth, and power. It is suggested that in the interests of the common good democracy needs to be restrained to prevent the slowing of the process. The wealthy are unlikely to submit to a one nation one vote procedure for (re)distributing their resources and will be able to avoid efforts at regulation which if fruitful would, it is said, only result in slower growth. It is further argued that while losers know what is at stake for them because many others will eventually be made better off (a group which includes those who are forced into painful short-term adjustment), there need to be mechanisms to prevent self-perceived losers from effectively interfering and limiting the process. National governments need to be coerced as well because what they see as acting in their narrow short term self- interest reduces global welfare. As the World Bank (1997b: 81) has argued "The rules and norms embedded in the policy making process should be designed to curb the kind of uncoordinated political pressures that can lead to poor decision making and bad outcomes. If politicians or bureaucrats pursue only their own or their constituents' immediate interests as they are voiced, the result may be collectively undesirable, even destabilizing as there is no invisible hand in statecraft, automatically shaping individual initiatives toward a common good." In the age of U.S. hegemony the American insistence that it knows best structures and constrains the boundaries of such discussions.

What the Bank and others have been less willing to see is that during capitalism's cycles of creative destruction (which are at the same time processes of redistributional growth) identifiable communities and much of a generation may be written off. The losses of these people, workers and small businesses which go uncompensated, provide resources appropriated by new growth sectors often controlled by TNCs. Ignoring the redistributive issues involved, asserting that efficiency demands such sacrifice and that the losers who organize to protect themselves, their families, and their communities are standing in the way of progress, serves the winners in the restructuring process. It is true that compensating losers is costly, slows adjustment, and is inefficient in a market sense. However a democratic polity might choose to do so with serendipitous gains in long term system stability. It is to frustrate such "meddling" that GSEGIs intervene to prevent 'short run," "political" considerations from entering the calculus of policymakers. To say such regimes are efficiency enhancing is therefore not the whole story. In welfare terms the issue is whether maximizing at each local frontier produces the best global results. The highest peak may not be attained by each group of climbers continuing blindly up whatever local mountain they find themselves on but rather by looking at the broader terrain for the highest greatest peak, retreating from the short-term choice, and regrouping to challenge the highest mountain. It is in such a sense that maximizing local welfare in each domain spatially and temporally fails to maximize collective social welfare.

Growing global interdependence might be thought to require that national decisionmakers consider more inclusive sets of relevant populations; the impact on policies beyond national borders on people who will not vote in local elections or directly have inputs into national level policy debates will both be affected by and have an affect on outcomes. By including social as well as private costs and benefits, the policymakers redress the omission of considerations absent from market only allocations. An inclusive rather than a divisive pattern of growth can construct the kind of peace with justice that is in the interest of long-term sustainable stability and growth. The core issue for a normative political economy is how to balance market incentives and social justice, efficiency and equity. From a critical perspective it is to be expected that the excesses of ungoverned market forces and resultant social destructiveness and mounting instabilities engender movements demanding protection, and that the dictates of the world's only superpower may on occasion provide for outcomes which are not altogether in the general interest.

By the start of this century the negative moment of destruction of postwar social structure of accumulation's rules, norms, and expectations while perhaps not complete had proceeded to the point where efforts to establish new rules and regimes of an emergent regulatory frameworks for the global terrain were proceeding rapidly. Lawyers, technocrats, and regulators are taking leading roles in the formation of the GSEGIs while diplomats take a back seat in the process. Rules for globalist economic and financial institutions, enforcement mechanisms, and dispute settlement issues call for legalistic skills. The focus shifts in a subtle way from structure to process, and while matters of sovereignty are typically not directly addressed, the impact of the GSEGIs on sovereignty is evident nonetheless. In terms of international relations, economics ministers and central bankers found their power increasing at the expense of the traditionally powerful diplomatic side of the state.

Basic international law has asserted GSEGI immunity from national jurisdiction and so has undermined to an increasing extent the traditional international law understanding of the prerogatives of national sovereignty in ways that have increased the power of the market. It had long been accepted that no state can be sued in courts of other states for acts performed in their sovereign capacity. Immunity had also been accorded state agencies so that individuals acting as agents for their country could not be brought before courts in another state for acts undertaken as the representative of their government. In the 1990s in a number of arenas (for example NAFTA and the WTO) such immunity has been revoked by international treaty. In the economic realm a host of such international agreements on trade and investment suspend sovereignty of state regulations and regulators which are judged in conflict with market prerogatives. In the name of freeing markets a stronger global state infrastructure is being crafted. These processes are a global re-regulation at the transnational level rather than merely deregulation taking place at the level of the individual nation state. It is useful to consider the meaning of state sovereignty from such a perspective.

THE WESTPHALIAN ORDER AND THE REALITY OF SOVEREIGNTY

For political philosophy the centrality of the sovereign state is evident in its creation myths. Life primordial in one such myth is a Hobbesian war of all against all. The framers of the creationism myths may see "noble savages in the beginning" with a capacity for self-governance and collective action for mutual support in a Rousseau fashion, or the state arising out of the realization that by giving power to a sovereign who can enforce order in exchange for a (hopefully) reasonable amount of tribute, all would be better off. In the "good stories" people who live in the same area and are dependent on the same natural resources discover they have not only individual interests but also collective ones and see the need for laws regulating conflict over property and other rights and for enforcement mechanisms. They get together and form a government. In the "bad stories" or dictatorial versions, ruler(s) enforce their will, and institute dispute settlement procedures which conveniently allow them also to take action against those who contest their power. The point of both types of stories is in the end the same and the political institutions created not so different. They produce collectively binding decisions and implement them, settle disputes, and punish rule breakers by consent of the governed, whether voluntarily offered or coerced. (Rothstein, 1996).

The stylized International Relations sovereignty story has its very own creation myth that begins with the 1648 Peace of Westphalia, which ended the Thirty Years War, and is understood to have legitimated the interstate system and to have created the accepted norm that states act independently within their territorial borders and that other states do not interfere in their internal affairs. The Treaty of Westphalia marked the defeat of Hapsburg designs for a universal monarchy and proclaimed the right of the individual state—and so the continued division of Europe into sovereign states—by codifying the concept of national sovereignty in the principled acceptance of *rex imperator in regno suo* or the king is sovereign within his domain.

National sovereignty in an anarchic world has had a powerful hold on the thinking of international relations theorists. Such a framing is restrictive if not misleading in the era of corporate globalization in which transnational capital and international financial institutions shape and constrain the possibilities of nation states and global state economic governance institutions take on crucial elements of stateness. The strong globalization argument declares the Westphalian system at an end because interdependence has grown to the point where national level economic policies are significantly neutralized. Economic interdependence, global production, and cross border environmental spillovers, it is said, mandate a break or at least strong qualification of Westphalian thinking concerning the autonomy of the member states. And of course as strict notions of sovereignty and the norm of nonintervention erode, and as conditionality schemes multiply, it becomes easier to enforce norms against weaker states. The economic base to globalization, driven as it is by market forces and new types of scale and scope economies comes from internetted access to arm's length suppliers and customers as well as to relational contracting alliances. The corresponding governance discussion has been of the norms and standards appropriate in the new circumstances, and the policies and institutions conducive to a more open political economy.

Nor is the traditional framing accurate for the earlier period for which it was conceptually designed. For most of the world's people the Westphalian System never worked as advertised. In the colonial period military occupation of territory for the purpose of extracting resources made nonsense of any concept of sovereignty for subject people. In the Cold War years following formal independence of former colonies, the United States often favored control by local military rulers capable of governing and of creating stability, preventing communist inroads, and allowing American corporations to do business in relative security. In the present period countries are controlled to a greater extent than ever before by market forces and international financial institutions which provide the disciplinary pressure to keep states open to international capital so that in most cases dictators who demand payoffs become an unnecessary expense. Democratically elected governments can sensibly be expected to provide hospitable conditions for foreign investors so that just as the imperialistic gunboat diplomacy of a century ago was made partially obsolete by a neocolonialism which coopted and controlled local rulers, providing their armies with training and equipment to ensure stability, so in the post–Cold War years in the absence of the Soviet Union capital markets backed by international financial agencies have proven capable of trumping national sovereignty even if military interventions remain not infrequent.

The "Westphalian states" did not achieve monopoly on transborder violence until well into the nineteenth century in the countries of the North America–European core of the world system, many of which had only recently taken their modern form. Reflecting on early nationalism we are more aware that these Westphalian states were synthetic constructs based on imagined communities (Anderson, 1983), historical creations even in their fabled versions, of a time and place in world history which is passing with the growing control exercised by GSEGIs. It is clear that the tale that begins "once upon a time in olde Europe," and stresses the "Westphalian moment," spawned a scholarly tradition that was both Eurocentric and ahistorical (Ferguson and Mansbach, 1999: 90). Typical of the American hypocrisy of an era in which other imperial powers saw no reason for such high sounding rhetoric, after fighting a war "to make the world safe for democracy," Woodrow Wilson had had no interest in any extended application of sovereignty to the darker peoples at home or abroad. Colonialism continued. Imperial exactions were expected. The Treaty of Westphalia and international norms until the post–World War II era were not intended for the lesser peoples, the non-white, the non-Europeans. Even formal sovereignty for most peoples was. if it existed at all, a post-World War II phenomenon.

After the demise of Soviet communism, in the absence of the Cold War (and so the lack of competition for the hearts and minds of the peoples in the newly independent states), these nations have seen a loss of autonomy and bargaining power within the international system which to some extent they had briefly enjoyed. Sovereignty seems in eclipse not only due to the marines and gunboats (or rather special forces and smart bombs). In addition the idea that how nations reach decisions concerning internal matters is no one else's business comes to be questioned with the recognition of spillover effects and the harm done by their negative impacts to others (as in environmental pollution or financial contagion), from a growing consensus on minimal norms to which all states are expected to comply (for example in human rights), and the increased power of neoliberal ideology to legislate through GSEGIs.

Acceptance of Westphalian System thinking about sovereignty gives ground under globalization pressures—the growth of an internationalized infrastructure which stands over and above individual states, especially less powerful ones. Introducing the idea of the emergent global stateness of

GSEGIs suggests the limits of traditional understandings of the interstate system in which sovereign governments are not subject to external regulation except by their own consent, a consent which can be withdrawn as per the very meaning of sovereignty. Issues of sovereignty, its definition and force, are central to these discourses as they are to globalization debates which dispute the very viability of sovereignty in the contemporary world economy. Reexamination of sovereignty is the necessary preface to consideration of governance and is closely related to the discussion of the origins of globalization. As an emergent commercial capitalism brought principalities together into larger state sanctioned market areas, the older legalist definitions of sovereignty, as Robert Cox (1994: 52) has commented, "conjuring up visions of ultimate and fully autonomous power" are no longer meaningful.

The challenge the twenty-first century international political economy holds for IR theorists is that it presents increased evidence that the legacy of the Peace of Westphalia is not a suitable model for, or description of, the contemporary world system. The reason is that the Westphalian system has been interpreted to mean that there is no authority above the sovereign states and that the world-wide political system implies stable international laws and long periods during which a balance of power operates between rather than above states. The Westphalian presumptions of rules legitimating the absolute rights of governments over mutually exclusive territories has increasingly been undermined by the GSEGIs. Moreover states are accomplices of their loss of sovereignty as nationally constituted groups with specific aims and interests turn to supranational means to meet their objectives, influencing their own governments to accept GSEGI jurisdictional claims. Self-interested actors enhance their own power vis-à-vis other domestic participants by reaching out to international organizations, a phenomenon evident in the actions of large corporations in the 1950s pushing for European economic integration, in their pressure for the adoption of the single currency in the 1990s, and in other episodes of economic transformation.

New versions of identity politics emerge from globalization's fallout as sovereignty is reduced to affirmation of cultural identity even as governments have surrendered control over the domestic economy. The new nationalisms which arise from the disintegration of state formations is different than the created nationalisms of the period of the rise of the nation state. Earlier nationalisms were integrative and produced bonding which brought disparate cultures into a single national identity. The modernizing capitalist state formations which emerged had this function and derived power from such a constructed unity. On the other hand, older empires unable to make the transition to modern capitalist economies fell apart as many of the failed states in this era of globalization have done and are doing. It was out of the decay of the Ottoman Empire that Kamal Ataturk's Turkish nationalism emerges and the disintegration of the Austro-Hungarian Empire fed the nationalisms which created much of modern Europe. At present there are also failed states and empires (the USSR being the most notable example). If modern political philosophy has been a debate about who holds sovereignty, modern IPE is about the decline of absolute sovereignty and the recognition of the increasingly conditional nature of sovereignty for all, or almost all states. Under such conditions the assertion of the need for the United States as the dominant military and economic power to take on the role promoting stability, the rule of law, and the enforcement of open markets seemed a natural and inevitable conclusion. But such assertion of the responsibilities of primacy follow a longer trajectory over which market logic has led state logic.

SOFT LAW AND THE LEX MERCATORIA

The term law derives etymologically from "binding." "By it one is bound to a certain course of action," as Thomas Aquinas wrote. A law is a rule enacted or customary in a community and recognized as enjoining or prohibiting certain actions enforced by the imposition of penalties. International law refers to the body of rules and principles of action which are binding upon states in their relations with one another. Much of the basis for GSEGIs is not formally embodied in treaty law, although much of it is underpinned by such formal, if generally only broadly worded agreements. It is shaped through processes of negotiation by quasi-official groupings and set forth in consensus agreements which are then voluntarily followed not only by those formulating the procedures and policies but typically by a far broader group of actors as well. In the previous chapter this soft law process of norm setting was contrasted with hard international law, defined as a signed treaty or agreement which is a precisely worded setting out of exact obligations undertaken by signatories. While there are no explicit enforcement mechanisms in the case of soft law, failure to obey incurs disutility once standards are agreed upon. An individual state's national interest as well as those of nonstate actors such as banks and corporations generally dictate a clear preference for following the rules or at least appearing to do so. Consequences such as loss of investment or of foreign aid may be compelling arguments for compliance. Reputation costs translate into lost opportunities through informal shunning. Self-interest undergirds international regimes and soft law regulation. A country agreeing to a soft law regime relinquishes domestic authority over issues to which the regime applies. The quasi-legal character of soft law norms derives from both the international consent they command and the expectation that nations will be constrained by them.

The particular type of soft law we are concerned with here can be understood as a contemporary formulation of the *lex mercatoria*, the medieval and early modern merchant law, which provided for nonstate arbitration for transnational business disputes where private contract practices might differ by community of origin and a common standard was enforced by the cross border business community. Desire to preserve reputation impelled following *lex mercatoria* procedures and strongly encouraged willing consent with judgments thus derived. GSEGI soft law raises many of the same issues as the law merchant since they both reflect the power relations of the business world and may be at odds with broader community values and procedures. They represent a consensus based on private power legitimated by state acquiescence and support. In both instances state authority is not the initiating factor although wise rulers have long accepted that a good business climate is beneficial to the realm. The feudal lord of old did not have to be integrally involved, but only allow "the courts of the dusty feet," the merchants' own dispute settlement mechanism, to function. In the modern era the state actively legitimates the consensus of transnational capital in a more active fashion and, like the lords of old who were powerful enough to do so, restricts capital's prerogatives when they conflict with basic state needs.

The medieval *lex mercatoria* was not part of the fabric of community life. It operated outside the norms of the communal economy, immune from its laws. The broad authority of local political regime provided safe conduct in exchange for tribute in a context of considerable autonomy. The merchant courts were independent, their transactions privately arbitrated by their peers, who rendered judgment and administered punishment. They were not constrained by canonical prohibitions on interest charges or requirements of the just price. Summarizing the situation Cutler writes (1999: 69): "The authority structure with regard to production and exchange was thus dualistic: local transactions were heavily regulated by religious and a diversity of political authorities, while long-distance and overseas exchange was conducted privately by merchants, under their own system of law, procedure, and institutions." Of course in Italy and Holland merchant states emerged which actively offered institutional support for the merchant class. The emerging Westphalian order of sovereign states allowed such domestically dominant interests to influence external relationships and specify treaty obligations which formalized their guild practices. The preference for a laissez faire international legal environment and liberal institutionalist notions of shared public resources was not born with the end of the Cold War and the thrust of America's new world order neoliberal agenda.

With the growth of the centralized state, the law merchant and its courts were incorporated into domestic legal systems. The separation of the economic from the political allowed private law, contracts, torts and a body of private international trade law and commercial law to operate neutrally among participants. In a mercantilist age political authority negotiated international commerce as a way to strengthen the state's revenue position and capacity to wage war. In the era of globalization the law merchant is being reconfigured, reconstituted in a contemporary form as a handmaiden of transnational capital. Transnational law typically lags the growing complexity of commerce. The impulse behind the law merchant was the ignorance of existing state powers unable to understand or be concerned with the needs of the merchants who for rulers represented at best a source of revenue but also epitomized the threat of an unknown modernism, if that term can be used anachronistically in this context.

In the latter part of the nineteenth century the fledgling transnational industry was facilitated by the separation of public and private law as the courts grappled with the relationship between contract and sovereignty involving conflict between the laws of the home and foreign state. Increasingly international organizations promulgated substantive rules to govern private transactions. This process that began in the United States in the years after the American Civil War, with acceptance of the principle of comity, which courts had used to reconcile property rights in human beings between slave states and free, extended and applied to international disputes. After the Second World War international rules increasingly supplanted national rules and standards in a host of economic applications. "International law increasingly is about the respective roles of international organs and private persons, with nation-states serving more as agents of international bodies than as their principals." (Stephan, 1999: 1556–57) A universalist school has emerged in legal theory which sees private international commercial law as transforming the traditional choice of laws (among and between national legal systems) to a set of material rules that regulate transnational dealings and activities. The idea is that the economic interdependence of states has rendered the concept of territoriality obsolete. This seems too extreme. State interests remain. Competing national legal systems favor the firms of that nation in their dealings with other nonnational firms and so the issue of whose national laws are the basis of the presumed universal international law remains a politically contested issue.

Harold J. Berman and Felix J. Dasser (1990: 21) argue that "The law merchant has been for centuries and continues to be today an international body of law, founded on the shared legal understandings of an international community composed principally pf commercial, shipping, insurance, and banking enterprises of all countries" and that "These shared legal understandings are reflected in the contract practices of those enterprises, and they continually find their way into judicial and arbitral decisions and also into national and international legislation." The activities of elite business groups and associations and their success in guiding the mandate of national negotiators in international fora who have for the most part succeeded in adapting rules and regulations embodied in regimes run by GSEGIs which meet the preferred property right definitions and enforcement procedures of the most powerful and internationalized sectors of Western capital suggest that the process today of developing a new law merchant reflects important continuities with the *lex mercatoria*, practices going back to the time of the crusades.

State-dominated justice systems may ignore the importance of what is customary and use criteria in decisions other than those to which the contracting parties themselves subscribe. This leads merchants to set up their own adjudication mechanisms which allow for spontaneous creation of new rules appropriate to emergent situations. Thus *lex mercatoria* grows organically as international exchange brings in people of different cultures, including legal cultures and business relations. The merchant law was, and is, concerned with business transactions among private actors but as nation states developed, a public international law was required to deal with relations among states. It was, and remains, true that the voluntary character of merchant communities can make its law uncertain and when it clashes with state interest sometimes ineffective. The law merchant in the final analysis needs at a minimum state acquiescence and often its sovereignty attribute of coercion and enforcement. The interplay between the *lex mercatoria* and not only state power but also global state economic governance institutions suggests the importance of pre-public negotiation and private consensus formation as well as a continuing interpenetration of private, governmental, and intergovernmental consensus. The interpretive rules which industry conferences develop today are modern *lex mercatoria* documents reflecting industry consensus on definitions, standards, and rules. There is also the *lex mercatoria arbitralis*, which is devoted to application of the proper law and enforcement in international arbitration agreements (Smit, 1990).

The *lex mercatoria* provides the mechanism for not simply voluntary cooperation but also the imposition of extraterritoriality by stronger actors and the application of their national commercial law while it allows entry into domestic legal arrangements. In this way it "provides a normative framework generated by a transnational elite, a mercatocracy, that comprises corporate and governmental actors whose interests are associated more generally with the transnational expansion of capital." (Cutler, 1999: 67) Cutler's useful term "mercatocracy" may be read as denoting a transnational business class that includes private actors in the corporate and financial sector who, often through the office of governments, facilitate the creation and operation of international institutions committed to consolidating the power and advancing the interests of the global accumulation of capital. For all the attention academics in a self-flattering manner have given to epistemic communities of disinterested experts, it is the larger structure of mercatocratic framing of regime construction which needs greater stress than it has received.

THE CONTEMPORARY LEX MERCATORIA

It would appear that the medieval law merchant and its institutions, which operated outside of both the local political economy and the local state, disappeared with the emergence of modern capitalism. However, contemporary developments are both mirroring and structuring developments in global capitalism and freeing merchant laws and institutions from national controls. "The law merchant is being reconfigured and reconstituted as a 'handmaiden' of transnational capitalism. . . . It provides the norms that structure international commercial activities in a manner consistent with 'disciplinary neoliberalism' and a 'new constitutionalism,' which are expanding the market opportunities for corporate capital" (Cutler, 1999: 61).

In the era of globalization there has been a development of *lex mercatoria* as a third legal order to fill the gap between national (or municipal) law and international law. It has grown important for the same reason it developed in the middle ages. Business people, who need a way to settle disputes among themselves and enforce their understanding of property rights against other conceptions which are embedded in local norms, hesitate to rely on government, which may be ignorant of the criteria believed exclusively relevant and attempt to impose settlements on bases rejected by disputants. Thus industrial codes exist, privately negotiated for transportation, insurance, and other activities involving international trade and investment which regulate the terms of commercial access and competition. In recognition of the difficulties of adjudication by outsiders who lack a grasp of technical details or might want to introduce other concerns as governing permissible outcomes we have the *lex maritima* dealing with maritime matters, the *lex constructionis* for construction contracting.

Other instances of such informal law have, in the contemporary period, been followed by the agreement of professional organizations for e-banking and e-commerce in much the same manner as codes and conventions for practices in the tradition of agreed upon forms for bills of lading and counter party forms based on specialized knowledge and negotiation of standards. Courts and legislatures come in later and in effect interpret existing and emergent private standards rather than applying any outside body of legal theory. The law governing international commercial standards, private international trade law, adjudicates when there is uncertainty as to whose law governs. Today private international trade law as an autonomous body of merchant law is being applied in a host of areas by voluntary agreement. It is the first stage of the process of concentric club formation.

Standardization is driven by corporations working through such instrumentalities as the Global Business Dialogue on Electronic Commerce, which presented the G-7 with a framework for economic and social policy in the age of globalization that became the foundation for their technology initiatives. This sort of law merchant is today called "partnership" between government and industry but is in actuality corporate rule making. It has been described by *Business Week* (2001: 196) as a paradigm in which "businesses are free to develop standard practices on their own, and these become the generally accepted rules of the road. No committee meetings. No draft reports. No political dealmaking." Well, no and yes. Government experts may meet less often and do fewer draft reports, although even this is doubtful since the sheer volume of regulation involved has multiplied. The point is that the meetings are held by private sector trade associations and smaller meetings of representatives of dominant firms. They have their own deal making. And of course congresses and parliaments are not totally rubber stamps so that political deals still occur as part of the larger process despite *Business Week* hyperbole. Nevertheless, it is becoming increasingly common for Western firms to write protections into contracts with local firms around the world with which they do business. Such protective clauses state that the contracts are not enforceable by local law but through international arbitration. Businesses want predictability and confidence that the terms they expect are in fact respected and private law proves more effective in seeing that this is how matters play out. This is especially the case in the area of intellectual property.

The idea of intellectual property can be traced back to the middle ages, when guilds held a proprietary view of their knowledge and restricted its dissemination and the terms under which a guild's products could be sold by authorized producers. In its genesis, therefore, intellectual property was not a right but a contingent privilege awarded in respect of specific social benefits. Today's most lively battles among national standards involve the conflict between social benefit and the right to exclude. The economics is particularly murky. Whereas property was once expressly a physical thing which its owner had the right to use, intellectual property is not about holding but withholding. Since most intellectual property, once known, can be replicated at little or no cost, the idea behind it involves creating scarcity where none existed.

Theoretically knowledge can be used by others at zero marginal cost to those who first developed it. Free access would be the economically justified solution except for the incentive problem. If new intellectual property is to be developed there must be ample reward for doing so. What is ample or adequate, especially in cases such as life saving medicines needed by poor people unable to pay the prices set by pharmaceutical companies who prefer to use generics, for example? It is the construction of scarcity which defines modern property rights and their enforcement standards. Patents reward inventors and so encourage development of new and valuable innovations. However they restrict the dissemination in use as when James Watt created the steam engine, received a patent in 1769 for six years, later renewed by the British Parliament for twenty-five years, during which time he continued to refuse to license his invention, perhaps holding back the development of the metallurgy industry for over a generation (Renouard, 1987 as cited in Sell and May, 2001: 472). The imposed scarcity the patent allowed prevents the social benefit of swift deployment and highlights the tension involved in balancing intellectual property rights and the social good.

The U.S. preference for proprietary consortia is at the center of its approach to intellectual property rights. It is an approach rejected by most other countries who see it as a rent seeking tactic by U.S.-based transnationals. While it is the Anglo-American approach to treat standards as proprietary goods and services to be traded in the marketplace and as contestable rights, corporate strategies in coordinated market economies treat standards as "an infrastructure for deeper cooperation." As Tate (2001: 472) notes, standards are an increasingly crucial component of economic competition in many industries. Battle over the definition of property rights for a globalized economy involves conflicts between national systems. They also reflect a pendula movement as overregulation leads to deregulation, abuse of monopoly rights to intellectual property produces abuses that generate new regulation. Sell and May (2001: 487), after describing the reaction to the elevation of monopoly rights through patent privileges "to nearly absurd levels" at the start of the twenty-first century, recall: "As happened in the seventeenth century over-protection, or extreme monopolization of intellectual property prompted a reaction. Technologies which emerge taking advantage of the increased protection become exemplars critics can seize on to demand a new settlement. The technological enhancement of protection prompts a rethinking of the amount of benefit an 'owner' of knowledge should receive."

Whether there will be a similar pendula swing, a move to antitrust enforcement and judicial attack on scope and validity of patents remains to be seen. The free market ideology of the contemporary period ironically has proven to have provided impressive coverage for the monopolization of socially important ideas once understood as generally belonging within the public domain. The extreme bias in favor of exaggerated claims to property rights over diffusion and competition, protection and exclusion over open protocols may in fact be slowing economic growth since defensive patenting and technology consortia favor the giants over the possible emergence of competitors and the ability of users to modify and improve what become fixed protected essential technologies. The GSEGIs have been central in expanding and rigorously enforcing the intellectual property rights of transnational corporations while denying such protections to indigenous peoples and traditional users who find their ancestral knowledge enclosed by such foreign companies. The TRIPs agreement, which will be discussed in chapter 9, "is intellectual property protection at its most developed and most geographically extended" (Sell and May, 2001: 494). The appropriations involved in a range of contemporary business practices are substantial. Not surprisingly they follow and reinforce existing distributions of wealth and power while being presented as a leveling of the playing field and a guarantee of property rights for all so as to encourage more rapid economic development.

Industry groups such as the U.S. Coalition for Service Industries and the Pharmaceutical Research and Manufacturers of America have shaped WTO rules by first developing the templates and then participating on the Advisory Committee on Trade and Policy Negotiations, whose forty-five members are appointed by the President of the United States, and on its six policy advisory committees, where the details of the proposals put forward by U.S. negotiators are worked out. The General Agreement on Trade in Services which will be discussed in chapter 10 is the product of a long campaign by the Coalition of Service Industries. Started in 1982 under the leadership of Citicorp, American Express and other financial conglomerates, it was designed to expand overseas markets through their government's active involvement in changing the rules under which they would be able to function abroad. Over the opposition of most developing countries its negotiating position papers were the basis for the policies of a number of administrations and the proposals it drafted became the basis for the Uruguay Round's treatment of services and eventually for GATS. The Japanese and Europeans have similar arrangements. The meetings of such business advisers even when government representatives are present are closed to the public, other interest groups such as environmentalists and trade unions and proceedings are secret even from legislators. The processes through which the modern *lex mercatoria* is formulated would hardly be novel to medieval merchants even if the sheer scale would be incomprehensible to them. They would no doubt be surprising to most citizens today as well.

Private arbitration and GSEGI enforcement are complementary. The values of commerce are part of a transnational corporate culture which is enforced in the contemporary era through GSEGIs, which usually execute agreements established by industry associations. Their lawyers, technical advisers, and specialized-knowledge holding executives are the articulators, the organic intellectuals of the hegemonic ideology of the emergent transnational class, and act as a steering force for the private regulation of contracts involving trade, investment, and finance. The GSEGIs provide the framing of neoliberal ideas into enforceable rules. They are the public face of a stateness which allows transnational capital and international finance to establish precedents and then restructure laws within countries imposing their privately agreed preferences for transborder adjudication procedures. The political significance of GSEGIs is that they provide the bankers and transnational producers a way private power can be legitimated and preferred regimes made acceptable. The new law merchant wins formal approval through international organizations.

Consensus formation in such bodies is little more participatory than the original formulation process of the modern *lex mercatoria*. It is not surprising that Third World critics see Eurocentric norms and values created and perpetuated in such practices. They reject the conceptual premise of a *lex mercatoria* because their views were never part of its negotiation. The common principles said to make up the law merchant which is used to arbitrate disputes between their governments and foreign investors were largely developed at a point in time when trading relationship with non-European territories were undertaken mainly for the benefit of Europeans in the context of a colonial political relationships. Accordingly, as the African lawyer Sampson Semposa writes, the developing countries "consider it inequitable for arbitrators chosen or selected to preside over their disputes with multinational companies to elect lex mercatoria as providing the rules of application in the face of a case they believe clearly requires application of the laws of the African State. African lawyers and impartial analysts believe that it is a mistake for Western arbitration lawyers to see the development of arbitration only through the eyes of Western trading entities." (quoted in Maniruzzaman, 1999: 691).

With the post–World War II rise of the nonaligned movement that created space for nationalist development regimes corporations have found that agreements among themselves were no longer sufficient. Where once imperial state power called simply for the disciplining of independent governments of the periphery, gunboats are a crude vehicle in this age. The development of a web of global state economic governance institutions results from corporate interest in transnational enforcement mechanisms within a rule based frame backed by measured sanctions imposed by powerful home countries on recalcitrant "partners" in the global economy. Not only are the recognized arbitration fora and procedures the creation of Western commercial societies and serve their interests, but the new constitutionalism which incorporates such *lex mercatoria* presumptions, and the GSEGIs which enforce its rules are seen as agents of private power, of key Western players and their TNCs by the less economically developed countries. The contemporary mercatocracy includes a transnational cast but it is the influence of participants from the United States who have been crucial in generating the rules and procedures which have been central to the emergence of the new *lex mercatoria*. In banking and insurance, information technology, and transportation, a process of industry self-regulation has taken place which has then been validated by government officials (many on loan from these very industries).

Treaties, legislation, and court decisions have increased the autonomy of private transnational business dispute resolution mechanisms, which has had the impact of privatizing decisions in which the pubic regulation is absent, as is the public interest as a basis for decisions reached. National regulatory law can be avoided so long as private parties agree they mutually benefit from the inclusion of only private interest criteria. As private arbitration is used extensively social norms are changed though such a process. This of course has ever been the case in *lex mercatoria*. Where contemporary private law disputes involve substantial public policy interests, this may not be an acceptable decision making norm. Indeed, it may reflect another area of privatization of once public functions.

DEREGULATION AND COMMERCIAL LAW

The permissive climate of deregulation encourages the formation of the new law merchant in the era of globalization. In a capitalist economy we would expect the capacities to structure a workable international regime to be found in just such a mercatocracy, a mercatocracy which is the leading element in the historic bloc committed to neoliberalism. If regulations are to be constructed by those who are most expert, it is likely that these experts will have been trained in and pursue careers which lead to a particular outlook. If bankers are the ones who write banking law they will be aware of their own problems and how these might best be addressed. They will act to meet their own concept of security and stability and will have a natural desire to maximize profits. A broader view (one lacking, for example, the perspective of consumer advocates, who might well see the need for social control of finance) is typically absent. The mechanisms of negotiation obscure the essentially political nature of such a development. Elected officials are unlikely to have an independent outlook or the technical competence to mount an alternative. Given the hold campaign finance has on the electoral process, and the power of the media which is itself big business, it is unlikely that an alternative framing will surface except in time of crisis.

In terms of the *lex mercatoria*, proposals in the closing years of the twentieth century favored global institutionalization of arbitration outside the framework of existing national laws and self regulation by industrial groups developed as soft law through concentric club formation and later endorsed by international agreements. The advantage of such a procedure was most obviously to provide a vehicle to overcome inconsistency in legal background of common law and civil law, Islamic law, and other interpretations of custom and precedent backed by diverse history and usage. But beyond such concern was the private business firm's interest in escaping social regulation and tailoring dispute resolution to the interests of the fraternity. International commercial arbitration allows for the resolution of commercial disputes between private parties by providing a neutral and potentially faster way of resolving disputes and so appeals to investors who hesitate to trust foreign courts whose law is generally unfamiliar to them and which they believe may be biased and inefficient.

The growth of private law in the area of arbitration importantly shapes globalization. States benefit from the use of private arbitration because it reassures potential investors that through independent adjudication they will be treated fairly. Investment is thus encouraged. One of the key functions of the International Chamber of Commerce (created in 1923) is to provide such arbitration services to members (http: //www.iccwbo/org/court). Arbitration broadly construed is involved in a host of technical areas involving national organizations of the same profession linking internationally as transnational interdependence develops in their particular area of business. It should not be surprising that the most internationally active firms take the lead in suggesting that a "club" should be formed and proposing the rules for members. The further step which then occurs is that related fields need to work out mutual accommodations. This takes place through informal discussions in which information is exchanged and the possibility of shared norm development discussed. Formal structural links develop after such discussions establish the likely shape of formal ties and agreement on harmonizing rules and procedures.

International arbitration confronts national differences in law merchant conventions. Some procedures and processes are more evident in coordinated market economies such as Germany's where the legal system grants companies a collective law making capacity carried out within trade associations and other nonstate institutions. Disputes can be settled within such industry frameworks which adjudicate disagreements between members. The legal expertise resides with the trade associations and lawyers for companies participate in working groups within them to create new industrial frameworks as needed and set technical standards and rules. When matters do go to court, judges use the standard practices generated by industry frameworks which are designed to be transparent to third party observers. In labor law too unions and employers associations are recognized within law and encouraged to create private agreements which are then legitimized by the state (Casper, 2001). In an era of globalization GSEGIs such as the WTO in the area of trade related issues become the courts of last instance. They formalize such arbitration, taking it in house, and imposing powerful sanctions on those who flout its rules and rulings.

If one wishes to look at commercial disputes in game theoretic terms it can be said that cross border corporate arbitration involves a two level game. The outcome reached must be acceptable at both the level of the *lex mercatoria* and of international law. In the case of most industry arbitration this is an uncertain process subject to conflicting legal judgments. However in a number of areas, most prominently in accounting and financial services, the process has become formalized in ways which suggest regime formation. Arbitrators render judgments that reflect the expectations of the international business community in the sense that whatever the outcome its rationale is accepted and is understood as growing out of the norms, customs, and expectations of that business community. "The context," as Maniruzzaman (1999: 714) writes, "includes the business community interests, needs, and expectations. The purpose of an application of the *lex mercatoria* is to promote common values in the international business community, irrespective of national divergence on such matters. The arbitrator's intuition will lead him to the community expectation, which will dictate the best choice he can make out of diverse rules and principles." The arbitrators' role in the development of *lex mercatoria* would be discredited and might well come to an end if they allowed national origin or personal interest to overcome balanced, careful assessment of business community interest. The emergence of global state consensus on universalized rules for dispute settlement follows these long standing procedures just as arbitration of disputes has meant settlements superseding when necessary individual state norms and jurisdiction. This procedure comes to be monopolized increasingly by the GSEGIs in areas in which dependent states have been unable or unwilling to accept Western norms as their own. The mutually reinforcing rewards and punishments the interlocking functioning of GSEGIs imposes make resistance extremely costly for less powerful governments.

The establishment of global institutional control proceeds in such a fashion that the normalization of transnational intercourse seems natural, inevitable, and beneficial. However because at root the process is the self-organization of business communities in which cooperation while desirable occurs in a larger context of competition and the parallel political governance regime of the nation state, confidentiality remains an issue. The goal of *lex mercatoria*, the maximization of the well being of the merchant community, remains at the heart of the GSEGIs even as they are formalized and legitimated by interstate agreements, thus increasing the "constitutionalization" of these organizations and the extent to which they are active in resolving disputes and forcing their way into the domestic legal fabric. The extent to which their supremacy is recognized represents the degree of member states' acceptance of a relinquished sovereignty. Increasingly treaties have been negotiated which leave their interpretation to some form of adjudicative body (rather than to further clarification through emendation or the creation of new law legislatively). This can create problems of perceived illegitimacy. The willingness of WTO arbitration panels to make far-reaching, sweeping decisions which appear to many to go beyond their mandate and to violate aspects of international and domestic law has raised concerns about a democratic deficit that has resulted from such procedures. The growing power of GSEGIs over presumably sovereign countries can be seen as a powerful extension of supra-national authority.

Lex mercatoria is perhaps even more likely than law in other realms to be subordinated to economic and political power. It is easily interpreted as an effort to legitimate as "law" the economic interests of transnational corporations. It results from the changed incentive structures these economies face in an era of transnational dominance of the globalization process. Just as some governments have been willing to offer tax holidays and other material incentives to attract foreign investment so too states have been willing to surrender long-standing elements of sovereignty. For example, while much is being made of recent investment agreements (to be discussed in later chapters) which give private businesses the right to initiate legal challenges and demand redress against laws and rulings which are seen as violating investment and trade rights, this is only a recent manifestation of a surrendering of sovereignty.

Securing the rights of transnational capital typically prevails over the interests of weaker local businesses and developing countries. Because the countries of the core have dominated in North-South disputes with some regularity since the Age of Exploration, the law merchant has proven to service their interests even as it takes on a presumed universality. To many who see themselves as part of the Third World, the new legal doctrines are part of a long historical relationship which has included the forcible recognition of unequal treaties, the use of diplomatic protection of foreign nationals and to safeguard the "civilized" countries' privileges and the use of law to legitimate the subjugation and pillage of "uncivilized" peoples and their lands. For most of the history of capitalism the relation between conquered and colonizers has not admitted to any legal rights for the subjugated peoples. The "club" was a small and exclusive one even as it claimed universal application and validity. As Mohammed Bedjaoui, the Algerian judge on the International Court of Justice (quoted in Mickelson, 1998: 371–72) has written:

> To keep in line with the predatory economic order, this international law was thus obliged simultaneously to assume the guise of: a) an oligarchic law governing the relations between civilized states, members of an exclusive club; b) a plutocratic law allowing these states to exploit weaker peoples; c) a non-interventionist law (to the greatest possible extent), carefully drafted to allow a wide margin of laissez-faire and indulgence to the leading states in the club, while at the same time making it possible to reconcile the total freedom allowed to each of them. . . . This classic international law thus consisted of a set of rules with a geographic basis (it was a European law), a religious-ethical inspiration (it was a Christian law), an economic motivation (it was a mercantilist law) and political aims (it was an imperialist law).

With the end of colonialism and the emergence of the nonaligned movement after World War II, international law ceased in theory to be exclusively the law of white colonialists, although it remained, in the view of many, the law of the great powers. Many Third World (and other) legal scholars believe it continues to serve the purposes of political colonialization and economic domination even if the rhetoric has shifted, the claims to universalism offered a bit more subtle, and forms of coercion claim impartial authority and neutrality.

Powerful states have the major advantage in negotiations in being able to link any particular dispute or demand to other economic incentives (foreign aid, access to their markets, and so on). Weaker states may join multilateral organizations in preference to having to negotiate bilaterally against such a power discrepancy but find that the rules of the GSEGIs too are stacked against them. Protesting the rules has costs, considering the many unilateral opportunities the hegemonic power and the core economies can exert. Local elites may find cooperation rather than confrontation in their best interest. The stronger secondary economies of the core are in a better position and, in response to the unilateral extraterritorial application of U.S. laws, many—including Australia, Britain, Canada, France— have implemented blocking statutes and "claw back" laws, which allow their nationals to go to their own courts to recover damages awarded against them in U.S. courts under U.S. laws involving extraterritorial claims. To avoid the need for such high profile and politically charged conflicts, corporations have tried to expand the arena of the law merchant to avoid the outbreak of nationalist conflicts generating international tensions which soon become highly charged politically.

To the extent that arbitrators like GSEGIs are similarly seen as the instrumentality of Western corporations and global finance they are less effective. Therefore, great effort is exerted to develop a balanced and formally neutral jurisprudence and administrative-enforcement procedures. In the law this trend nevertheless clearly reverses long-standing practices. The "Calvo Clause," developed in the mid-1800s in response to European diplomatic maneuvering in Latin American countries, highlighted two basic principles of "national treatment" (which provides that foreign nationals will not be accorded greater privileges than citizens) and "no diplomatic intervention" (which provides that the claims of foreign nationals cannot be pursued through either military or diplomatic interventions but rather under the statutes and constitutions of the Latin American states). These clauses traditionally prevented a state from submitting to arbitration claims by foreign nationals (Dalrymple, 1996).

Governments continue to be recognized as having full sovereign immunity. As long ago as 1882 U.S. courts decided that the United States may only be sued by its own consent except where Congress has provided in legislative authority (United States v. Lee 106 U.S. 196). There is recognition, as stated in the Foreign Sovereign Immunities Act of 1976, that "subject to existing international agreements to which the United States is a party at the time of enactment of this Act a foreign state shall be immune from the jurisdiction of the courts of the United States . . . " The establishment of GSEGIs by treaty raise questions about such long-standing sovereignty privileges.

LAW AND ECONOMICS

Sovereignty claims of member states and the GSEGIs themselves have interestingly also been challenged by efforts of global civil society to force onto GSEGI agendas concerns such as labor rights and environmental issues. Indeed, it is not so much sovereignty claims which are being challenged. The accusation is that such sovereignty has a class nature, that the state has acted to defend corporate interests to the exclusion of other interests. The state's class bias in favor of capital is reflected in the uses to which sovereignty is and is not directed. Social justice and environmental activists maintain governments and corporate interests have tried to minimize concessions on such "noneconomic issues" as labor rights and environmental protection requiring intervention by democratic polities into what has been almost the exclusively business preserve of international agreements on economic and financial issues. Corporations and their government defenders have claimed that social regulation of such issues is either extraneous and/or harmful to the purpose of achieving more efficient resource allocation.

Their position in this regard is supported by legal theorists writing in the law and economics tradition. In this influential legal doctrinal school it is asserted that the market should be the test of good law. Law should achieve public goals at minimum cost. This approach was pioneered and codified by Richard Posner in his 1973 book *Economic Analysis of the Law*; it has come to be known simply as "Economics and the Law," as if it were the only approach to the application of something we call economics to the topic of the law. This economic analysis of the law (EAL) approach employs simple neoclassical economic propositions to explain the structure of legal doctrine and suggest ways it should be reformed to be more compatible with efficiency in economic resource allocation. There is almost no awareness among mainstream economists that there is any other useful approach to the law. The IPE literature has tended to ignore corporate and legal theory although a field bringing together international relations and international law has emerged (Slaughter, Tulumello and Wood, 1998). Legal discourse offers the same opportunity to reflect from outside the discipline on the broader contestation to impose meanings on the ipe and to theorize the role of rules and regimes as does a consideration of the differences between a mainstream economics and a mainline political economy. While relatively new to the academy its origins go back perhaps to 1604 when the merchants who formed the Dutch East India Company commissioned a legal brief from a young lawyer, Hugo Grotius. His book, *Mare liberum* published in 1609, arguing that the high seas were a shared resource, was perhaps the founding document in international law. The brief's open access thesis supported the Dutch merchants seeking entrée to East Asian ports, making *mare liberum* an example of claiming the general interest to support self-interested policies (Magoffin and Scott, 1916). Grotius made the familiar argument that the free will of states and not the commands of God (or His papal legate) should decide precedent by using what today would be called economic efficiency criteria and seeking what would come to be known as a Pareto optimal outcome. Unfortunately for the prospects of the *lex mercatoria* as a legal order outside of state control, various merchant interests prevailed on their states and the strength of their navy and armed might to enforce exclusive trading rights (or to try to break those asserted by other states).

John Selden's *Mare clausum* while less famous, and ill fitting the "free trade is best" story, explained how British merchants could rely on their sovereign's military superiority. The English trading companies needed no tutor to make a deal with Queen Elizabeth to share the gains from public regulation of exports and imports, which drove foreign merchants out of England. State capture, bribes, rent seeking are not new phenomena. This division, between those who sought state support to eliminate competition and those who welcomed competition in the belief that such a regime would allow them to prosper, remains central to interest group interpretation of IPE debates. New stream international lawyers concerned with who is, and who is not, included and marginalized by international law see international law as constituted by discursive practices of exclusion reflecting the interests and preoccupations of the powerful (Cass, 1996).

As we turn to GSEGIs which constrain and enable economic actors in particular ways, we will consider how they have been created, the power relations behind their development, standards for their legal judgments, and related economic and political questions. We will explore how the manner in which conflict of interest takes place is typically negotiated within a narrow circle of actors. The wider society's stake in such regimes is represented by industry practitioners and regulatory bodies whose leadership and technical staff is perforce drawn from the relevant industries. It is in a forum such as the Basle Committee that the regulators from the leading banking nations discuss what prudential supervision should mean and how conscientious enforcement of agreed upon standards can be insured. This is partly a narrow technical matter of adopting generally agreed upon procedures but it also requires an understanding of countries' particular practices and the tensions among them. Reaching agreement on a single set of rules is contentious because of such differences. Since countries' domestic regimes reflect the balance of political forces as well as the organization of economic sectors and legal framework regulation unique to that country, efforts to harmonize regulation raise anew issues of how best to address industry preferences in way which respects the larger societies' best interests.

SOME SECONDARY FINANCIAL GSEGIS

In the remainder of this chapter we examine the Bank for International Settlement (the BIS) and then some of the less well known Gsegis, the International Organization of Securities Commissioners, the International Accounting Standards Committee, the International Association of Insurance Supervisors, and the regime formations they organize. When we examine these particular economic and financial regimes we see the centrality of two developments which have already been stressed and which represent movements away from conventional IR state-centric theorizing. The first is the growing power of market actors, transnational corporations, international banks, and other globalizing financial institutions. The second is the increasing functional autonomy and growing power of the GSEGIs whose principals play the two level game as best they can to exclude parliamentary oversight and unwanted public pressures. Both developments reflect a restructuring of rules governing the international political economy.

Just as an alliance of merchants and kings against the territorial lords emerged in periods of nation state formation so today international state emergence is occurring in the form of global governance institutions fostered through an alliance of transnational capital and globally focused participation of core states. These governments authorize actors charged with international economic policy (which include securities commissions and insurance regulators as well as industry lobbying groups and elected officials whose constituencies and major contributors have particular interests) to pursue technical discussions concerning standards harmonization. The fora created overcome differences recognizing their interdependence and common interests. This leads to regime formation. We start with the example of the Basle Accords and the role of the BIS (the Bank for International Settlements), one of the lowest profile actors among the GSEGIs. The BIS was established to supervise reparations and war debt payments after World War I. It was (and remains) a forum for central bankers, not of elected leaders or other public officials. The United States in fact initially gave its seat to an association of private banks seeing debt relief as primarily a matter to which the private sector could negotiate.

THE BIS

In areas such as money laundering the procedure of banks is to know their customers and accept that correspondent banks have exercised due diligence, and made proper investigative inquiries for depositors so that such monies can be accepted without further scrutiny. Because money moves over such lightly regulated electronic networks in a system best described as bank clubs run on the honor system, transactions coming in from another club member, from a Nigerian bank say, or going out to Jamaican or Columbian banks, are simply accepted without scrutiny. Experience has shown this to be inadequate, witness such highly publicized cases as the Bank of New York's acceptance of $10 billion in deposits of alleged criminal origin transferred out of Russia in the late 1990s. The bank had made a significant profit from its cash processing operations and had little incentive to examine them closely until accusations were made by government investigators and publicized widely in the press.

While the U.S. Treasury Department's Office of Foreign Assets Control sends banks detailed lists of countries, companies, and individuals who aren't allowed to receive wired funds, fronts are used to avoid detection, although sophisticated filtering systems have been used by some banks who have made it a priority to detect suspicious transfers with good effect. However the majority of banks have declined to take more responsibility in such areas and the American Bankers Association has fiercely resisted tighter regulation (Silverman et al., 1999). As electronic funds transfer moves into cyberspace monies may not pass through what we recognize as banks at all. This will raise still greater problems for regulators. We are faced with the development of problematic private clubs whose activities embrace criminal or quasi-criminal elements and therefore with the need for next generation regulation of an equally sophisticated sort. For the most part the issues are political and not technical. In the wake of the September 11 attacks the United States was able to trace funds believed to belong to the bin Ladin terrorist network. If there was equal resolve to address money transfers linked to tax fraud and other illegal white collar crimes an international regime to regulate capital could be put in place.

The risk that depositors will lose their money to banks registered in other countries which are insufficiently supervised is a very real problem—witness the 1991 collapse of the Bank for International Commerce and Credit International (BCCI). Had it not been able to evade both home and host country regulators so effectively it would have been unable to engage in so many shady transactions over so long a period and the loss to depositors from its collapse might have been considerably less. The BCCI collapse and scandal which made it clear how determined perpetrators could evade regulators led to the 1992 "Report on Minimum Standards for the Supervision of International Banking Groups and Their Cross Border Establishment" by the Basle Committee established by the BIS. It must be said that such efforts tend to be crisis driven and *ex post*. They address problems which have surfaced in a costly way, usually involving political scandal and the uncovering of widespread corrupt practices. After the fact it takes less imagination to see how in the future similar problems could easily arise. BCCI had set up a holding company in Luxembourg and a second corporate entity in the Cayman Islands. It then did business all over the world (but little business in either place of incorporation both of which had minimal supervisory capacities and strict secrecy laws). It was hardly the only such case. The incentives for and processes allowing looting were well understood (Ackerlof and Romer, 1993). There has been less political discussion of the experience of Long Term Capital Management's failure and government actions taken in its wake although its experience raises equally important questions for financial regulation (deGoede, 2001). Because of interbank lending the failure of a poorly managed or rogue financial institution can have a domino cascading effect and drag down otherwise sound institutions with loan exposure. There is as well the global systemic risk, the possibility that a significant failure can engender the collapse of the entire financial system. It was the seriousness of such a prospect which led the New York Federal Reserve Bank to arrange a bailout for Long Term Capital Management, the privately held hedge fund which borrowed well over a $100 billion on less than $3 billion in assets at the time of its threatened collapse in 1998.

Because banking law differs from country to country and it matters considerably which jurisdiction's rules apply, it is necessary to adopt common standards sensitive to domestic particularities, but which are still capable of preventing financial institutions from shopping for jurisdictions with lower standards. Because of the volume of transactional activities and the complications that could arise from the threat posed if a financial institution, formally under the jurisdiction of a less powerful regulator, were to threaten spreading insolvencies on a scale home jurisdiction agencies did not have resources to adequately address, the demand developed for international coordination and procedures to prevent such exposure. The need for such cross-border regulation raises the issue of extraterritoriality. Officials need to apply regulations to transactions and to persons not located in their jurisdiction. While international agreements exist with regard to extraterritoriality in specific cases, these tend to lag contemporary concerns (for example those stemming from electronic data transmission and cross border derivatives trading).

The 1992 BIS Report on Minimal Standards affirmed the view that international banks and banking groups should be supervised by a home country authority and proposed that host country regulators provide information so that the home country has access to consolidated financial statements of the bank's global operations and that there be means to satisfy regulators as to the completeness and accuracy of these statements. It also specified that host country regulators be able to satisfy themselves as to the home country regulator's capacities to prevent banks under their jurisdiction from establishing instrumentalities that circumvent supervision. If they were not satisfied they could refuse the establishment permission to function in their territory.

The BIS is a good example of an institution which generates soft law. Failure of the Herstatt and Franklin National banks in 1974 further highlighted the need to monitor safety across national boundaries. It led to the establishment of the Committee on Banking Regulation and Supervisory Practices, better known as the Cooke Committee after its chair Peter Cooke of the Bank of England, or simply as the Basle Committee formed in the wake of these destabilizing bank failures. In 1974 representatives from eleven countries met under BIS auspices to create guidelines for banking supervision. The Basle Committee on Banking Supervision has no staff, facilities of its own, or bylaws. Its existence was proclaimed only through a press release from the central bank governors issued through the BIS. While not a secret society it does keep a low profile and is a consummate two level game player. Its membership is small and exclusive. The BIS initially suggested regulations in the domestic arena without formally soliciting comments including those from regulated constituencies (except to the extent that the central bankers themselves informally sound out people they wish to hear on a subject). National regulators in conforming to BIS proposals implement regulations they have had a hand in developing offstage, away from possible oversight at the national level. The Basle Committee on Banking Supervision developed these guidelines for cross-border banking supervision in an effort to create a level playing field so as to limit the attraction of regulatory arbitrage and to promote a greater degree of protection for all concerned from risk of bank failure in the international financial system. They also acted to stem the loss of business from their financial centers to less regulated competitors. Countries in the industrialized core quickly adopted these guidelines as hard law, as did many others wishing to do business on a nondiscriminatory basis with Basle Group member economies and the "internationally active" banks in major market centers they regulated. Once the Basle Committee negotiators reached agreement there was tremendous pressure on jurisdictions regardless of their economic or political systems to come into conformity if they were to have access on preferred terms to international financial network benefits.

For some time the Basle Committee maintained a low profile and operate in secrecy due to its informal existence and the discrete power of the central banker fraternity. Its founding agreement was not released to the public until more than five years after these central bankers approved it. Such an unpublicized existence allowed it to work as it chose without interference and by consensus with a rotating chair and a great deal of informality permitted by the close personal contact maintained among national regulators, which encourages a convergence of views (Zaring, 1998). The working of the Basle Committee on Banking Supervision is thus a model of soft law. The capital adequacy standards it agreed to were quickly adopted even though the committee itself has no legal standing. Its suggestions are not treaty agreements. It has no enforcement powers. Yet its views are universally accepted (except perhaps by a rogue state here and there). Most are anxious to join the club and the more countries adopt the standards the better off all are in enhanced financial security. The accord is another instance of a concentric club formation. In this case the Anglo-American preferences were accepted to the detriment of the French, German, and especially Japanese banks. The U.S. and UK concluded a stringent bilateral agreement and threatened to apply its terms to foreign banks operating in their markets. This pressure led the others at Basle to accept the U.S. definition of bank capital, the risk weighted framework, treatment of off-balance sheet items, and other provisions. The Basle accords, while they provided for standardization, did not so much offer simple joint gains as they represent an instance of redistributive cooperation, a case of an international institution that intentionally reduces the welfare of some participants compared to the status quo (Oatley and Nabors, 1998: 36). The Basle Accord is as well an example of a framework in which nation state level hard law was initiated by prior soft law agreement, in this case by central bankers not elected bodies (Lee, 1998).

The accords were not binding in a legal sense even on the signatory countries, but this soft law approach is in a sense more powerful. There is no external coercion, simply a shifting of actors' calculation of objective costs and benefits in their voluntary acceptance of the standards. Country regulators who do not hold their financial institutions to such generally recognized standards may find others judging their possible default risk on interbank obligations unfavorably, increasing the cost of raising capital on the international market. Banks not wanting the perception of higher risk adopt BIS standards so they will not have to pay higher loan premiums or be closed out of money markets. This does not mean its actions have been free from criticisms. For all its technical expertise its judgments have not necessarily produced successful guidelines. The standards adopted by the committee in 1988 proved unsatisfactory in the implicit weighting to assets which did not in fact reflect risk very well and gave incentive for misallocating loan capital. For example the original Basle Accord put a zero weight on credit risk for central bank debt of all OECD countries which in 1994 included Mexico. This was a dubious judgment as confirmed by the peso crisis which resulted in part because banks around the world could hold Mexican government debt securities without providing for any capital reserves for assets which in fact carried substantial credit risk. U.S. banks were particularly exposed and global contagion fallout and a multi-billion dollar rescue package soon followed.

As a result, and again under prodding by the United States the committee moved toward accepting a revised procedure favored by the American bankers but opposed by others. The procedure adopted allowed use of internal credit ratings already developed by major U.S. banks rather than some external control procedure. The Basle committee's chairman, William McDonnough, who was head of the New York Federal Reserve Bank, said the aim was "to bring about a situation in which banks themselves are basically responsible for what capital they have" (Graham, 1999: 1), a recipe which could be a disaster in many parts of the financial world, and perhaps even for the U.S. banks which demanded that their own internal methods be the governing ones, became the accepted procedure everywhere. Efforts by the BIS to revisit capital adequacy standard have been controversial among bankers leading to a delay in adopting new standards and an extended period for public comment to give industry participants more time to present their ideas and hash out their differences. There has been little input from outside of the financial service sector even though issues of public concern are involved. The technical nature of the questions obscures the larger questions of public policy, the cost to tax payers of bailouts and contagion and so on.

In spring 1999 a newly established financial stability forum met. It was chaired by Andrew Crockett, general manager of the BIS (like Mr. McDonnough a former chief executive of a large transnational bank based in the United States), and consisting of officials from central banks, finance ministries, and financial regulators from the leading industrial countries. In yet another instance of concentric club formation the forum was set up after a report to a Group of Seven finance ministers' meeting in February of that year by Hans Tietmeyer, then president of the German Bundesbank, the most powerful of the European central bankers. Reporting on the group's first meeting in Washington Mr. Crockett said: "There was some concern that reforms in financial systems are in some cases not proceeding sufficiently rapidly" (Fidler and Malkani, 1999: 5). The initiates of the BIS club were not going to leave things to the politicians who would not be capable of acting quickly enough and who might be inclined to overreact and overregulate. Because unregulated institutions such as hedge funds and inadequately regulated financial institutions of other types, especially those in emerging markets, presented danger to the health of core banking institutions and perhaps to world financial stability, they decided to establish three working committees. The first would examine the operation of the hedge funds and related institutions. A second working party would look at offshore financial centers. These were of concern because they were used for transactions which escaped financial supervisors. A third would study short-term capital flows and how recipient countries could make their financial systems more resilient in the face of their inherently destabilizing volatility.

It is to be expected that the working groups would come up with specific proposals which would address these problems in a manner consistent not only with concern for greater safety of the financial system but also with mechanisms that would not be harmful to the specific interests of the large financial institutions whose representatives were the core club members. Any proposals they agreed upon would then be adopted by relevant national regulators without oversight hearings or further study by legislators. The BIS as a global state governance institution would effectively make rules which sovereign states would simply accept. The BIS and the instrumentalities created in its penumbra (to be discussed in the next section) both reflect and drive such change. They represent instances of the expansion of *lex mercatoria* in the contemporary period and have changed the nature of international law dramatically. In the area of finance— national sovereignty, the very idea that each sovereign state makes its own law which is all powerful within its territories (while interstate differences are handled through diplomacy, including the threats and eventually the capacity to make war), has been replaced by an extension of commercial law to the global marketplace backgrounding traditional concepts of sovereignty and state-level decisionmaking. While such a development is basically an extension of domestic U.S. legal practice to a global setting it is at the same time a dramatic change in our legal culture. The law now loses its mooring in democratic accountability. As Paul Stephan (1999: 1555) writes, "We have not yet asked whether this new international law satisfies the expectations we normally have of the law, whether it serves our interests as an organized society or instead undermines our political and moral institutions."

SOME MINOR GSEGIS: THE IOSCO, THE IASC, AND THE IAIS

In 1993 the Basle Committee was instrumental in establishing the Tripartite Group, a coalition of international banking, insurance, and securities regulators to jointly examine the ways of improving regulation of financial conglomerates by creating a wider international financial sector regulatory framework. This development came out of a longer working relation among the groups husbanded by the BIS which had worked with the International Organization of Securities Commissioners (IOSCO), the International Accounting Standards Committee (IASC), and the International Association of Insurance Supervisors (IAIS).

These are relatively new organizations. They have small bureaucracies and budgets, relying on their members to enforce regulations the group issues and to monitor the compliance of other members. They too operate informally and secretly. They see their task as substituting for, by pre-empting, state action. Their goal is improving the cooperation and coordination among members in order to provide effective surveillance and mutual support, a goal which is described as promoting fair and competitive markets. It is understood that the United States and the European Union basically control these organizations, granting and protecting their autonomy and authority. Policies are worked out not by elected officials or diplomatic representatives but regulators who come from, and often return to, the private industries they regulate. Such individuals spend their working lives in a narrow culture and it would take a great effort to admit the concerns of those outside their frame of reference. Since their business is carried out for the most part in secret it is difficult for even students of these international financial regulatory organizations (IFROs) to have a precise idea of how they operate and what considerations are uppermost in the minds of participants. These organizations do not have representatives in the legislative bodies.

The participating regulators don't represent their countries in the usual diplomatic sense. They view themselves primarily as representatives of their agencies and industries rather than their national governments. Regulators from different countries who participate in IFROs form a community of interest. By coming together they are able to strengthen their bargaining positions within their own national governments where they are competitors with the other regulators and often at odds with legislators. At the same time since each wants standards adopted that are beneficial to home institutions, they are also rivals. The gentlemen's agreements they enter into are not treaties, not legally binding hard law. But they are authoritative. They are complied with even though they would seem to have at best a quasi-legal quality. "The unsatisfactory legal character of IFROs has disturbing implications beyond the intellectual incongruities of its treatment," Zaring writes (1998: 305). "As these organizations remain unrecognized by international law, they remain unregulated and unprotected by it as well. IFROs suggest a broader international context in which relevant international actors operate outside the formal categories of state action that traditional international law recognizes."

Nation level regulatory regimes can differ from each other substantially. On the continent of Europe and in Japan government agencies and businesses rather than the accounting profession play the dominant role. In France the National Accounting Code is published by the French National Accounting Council, a French government agency, and French statutory law provides a standard chart of accounts. In Germany accounting rules are largely set by statute as they are in Japan and administered by the Finance and Justice Ministries (C.T. Myers, 1999). In these countries banks not only lend based on long-term relations, but typically are significant stockholders in the firms to which they lend. State planners play a more active role in managing the economy. In the United States, the United Kingdom, and in other countries whose practices they have influenced the accounting profession directly has the preeminent role in setting standards. In large part this is because accounting in the latter group of countries is oriented to the needs of investors and creditors for more and better information. In the former it is the preferences of government which guide rules and business obtains most of their capital from banks rather than the securities market, These banks tend to have intimate knowledge and are often represented on management boards.

Since the end of the postwar period as globalization of investment has increased the investor community has become more aggressive, supported by Anglo-American diplomatic pressures, in the pursuit of greater transparency as opposed to the practices of closely held more secretive European and Japanese managers and their close knit controlling interests. In 1973 the professional accounting groups from ten countries including the United States, United Kingdom, Germany, Japan, and France formulated and published international accounting standards for the first time. Since then it has issued dozens more. These have been adopted by other countries and are in widespread use. The International Accounting Standards Committee, the IASC, is now sponsored by accounting organizations in more than 140 countries, although since it has a 16 member board (13 of whom are chosen by accountancy bodies) which is responsible for overseeing the development and approval of all accounting standards, the original members retain control. The three members from developing countries on the board are more observers than initiating participants. The process is dominated by the western countries, particularly Anglo-American countries followed closely by countries in the continental cluster. (C.T. Myers, 1999: 10) While outside comments are solicited, they come from a universe of commentators which for all intents and purposes is the same tight knit community of interest which comments on draft American standards. There is little input from public interest groups. In some countries, including the United States, the standards can then be adopted by the regulatory agency without further legislative action. With the international diffusion of stock ownership the American style accounting model appears more desirable to investors, to those firms wishing to list on U.S. exchanges, and to states desirous of attracting foreign capital.

Standards-setting and decisionmaking are hardly conflict free. While the general pattern is one of sequential club formation in which the most powerful set the agenda for others to join, confrontation among powerful state actors is common. Sometimes situations develop in which the United States stands against many of the other major powers, and sometimes against almost all of the other players. For example the International Accounting Standards Committee has tried to persuade U.S. securities regulators to compromise and not insist that all other nations accept its Generally Accepted Accounting Principles (GAAP). After four years of negotiations, prompted by transnationals' desire to have a single set of standards everywhere, in 1999 the United States rejected the IASC's standards proposal. U.S.-based firms objected to their having to meet the tougher American (GAAP) standards while foreign rivals did not. The differences are substantial. For example in fiscal 1993, before Daimler-Benz merged with Chrysler, the company reported a $346 million profit. Under U.S. accounting rules it would have reported a billion dollar loss.

Conflicts exist in a number of areas of proposed harmonization of standards-setting and governance structuring. In the United States the Financial Accounting Standards Board is a stand alone, independent body in which industry insiders are represented by their own experts who work out technical standards. In Europe, we have noted, accountancy is a politically regulated practice and the Europeans want a body with political legitimacy and accountability. The Americans respond that the European rules are weaker than their own and that the international accounting standard setting group they propose is not sufficiently independent of governments, too strongly influenced by European style corporate governance norms. While the U.S. GAAP standard is the most widely used in capital markets they are very much an American approach and disliked in most other parts of the world. Further as a PriceWaterhouseCoopers study comments "even US GAAP's most ardent admirers would readily admit that US GAAP is too complicated and, as a result, is fully understood by too few. . . . [Its] detailed rules beget imaginative interpretations, which in turn, beget more detailed rules." (Morris and Ward, 1999: 1 cited by C.T. Myers, 1999: 13) America's investor culture and litigious propensities are of course suited to such a standard. The U.S. government is working hard to impose its norms on the world, and this is seen as a tool for achieving greater competitive strength. (A 1997 Securities and Exchange Commission report to Congress for example is titled: "Report on Promoting the Global Pre-eminence of American Securities Markets.") After a series of scandals involving Enron, WorldCom, and a number of other high profile U.S.-based firms and their accountants, most prominently the now defunct Arthur Andersen, the comparative advantage of U.S. practices was radically reassessed. But examining such matters would take us too far afield, as would be consideration of major European accounting failures, such as Parmalat.

This chapter has explored the method through which new rules for the world system are generated. The distinction between soft law and hard law, to be discussed further below, and the specifics of formal regime construction add concreteness to the more general formulations of IPE theorists which have tended to acceptance of a liberal institutionalist frame of reference. The absent center of these discussions is the place and the nature of democracy in the new global governance structures. There is a tendency to assert the advantages of cooperation in overcoming collective action problems. Even as realists privilege the unequal power involved in such bargaining and see outcomes as related to the resources of participants they too tend to neglect the larger economic system in which power is exercised. The connection between the exercise of power and the construction of specific international regimes within the world system needs, it has been suggested, a less binary debate. A final point—while the United States's hegomonic power in the capitalist world system from the end of the Second World War made it the central power in shaping international economic and financial regimes there has been both cooperation and competition among leading governments and transnational corporations domiciled in different parts of the world. Europe has its own global corporation (e.g., Royal Dutch Shell, Unilever, Nestle). Also U.S. capital has a mixed bag of "global" corporations some of whom are protectionist (steel, agriculture, etc.), and even among these firms some are protectionist and some are not. Mini-mills produce steel at competitive world prices; older giants with aging plants may not. Small banks have different interests than money center banks, and so on. And as we have seen, companies in accounting, law, and many other fields are molded by national regulatory systems, which creates differences of interests in discussions of whose rules will be adopted in global regime formation. There are issues of international political economy on which the French government and Washington are in accord even if on others they are far apart. Such differences always complicate the story.

While the worries we have discussed in this chapter involve technical harmonization of financial and related regulatory regimes, issues of conflicting interest which may arise and the problems of rogue operations of various sorts, there is a question of the larger financial system and how it "normally" operates. There is divided opinion. Many economists hold to an efficient market theoretical approach which sees markets tending to equilibrium and understand government efforts at regulation to be interference with market processes best left alone. Others see financial markets as prone to destabilizing behavior which can and do produce great social dislocation and so call for regulation on a world scale. In chapter 8 we consider these different views of the global financial system. But first we examine the Bretton Woods institutions, which most powerfully structure how the global financial regime impacts poor and debtor countries.

CHAPTER SEVEN

The Bretton Woods Institutions In Operation

"Protecting global economic order can be a chaotic business. It certainly was for Hubert Neiss, a top official of the International Monetary Fund, when he was dispatched to South Korea last November to strike a deal aimed at restoring investor confidence in the battered Korean economy. . . . Ordered by his alarmed superiors to complete a massive rescue package. . . . Neiss went without sleep for three straight days and nights to negotiate a record $57 billion bailout. Such is the life these days for the international economy's shock troops " the 1,000 economists from six continents, boasting PhDs from prestigious universities, who from IMF headquarters in downtown Washington, D.C., exercise extraordinary influence over the affairs of countries thousands of miles away."

—*Paul Blustein* (1998: 15)

"Palpable everywhere to an American traveling in central Africa was the virtually interchangeable influence of the United States and the twin organizations charged to help: the International Monetary Fund (IMF) and the World Bank. The agenda of these agencies was explicit and ubiquitous. They were committed to a free market ideology, which they applied more or less inflexibly as the price of their assistance to these countries, and they managed to be remarkably insensitive to native reactions to their efforts. It was all packaged under the antiseptically neutral rubric of 'Structural Adjustment Loans.' Stated baldly, these agencies said to sub-Saharan Africa: 'Reduce the size of the public sector and we'll offer loans.'"

—*Philip A. Klein* (1998: 385)

As the GSEGIs become more powerful there is the attempt to apply the same rules everywhere. What results can be called a global regime or perhaps a set of interlocking and mutually supporting regimes which together represent a mode of global governance. Financial issues have come to command attention beyond technocratic specialist circles as awareness has grown that disputes concerning the structure and operation of these insti-

tutions set the terms of a global *macro*economic policy regime. Their policy advice increasingly constrains *micro*economic market regulation as well
to produce procedural rules that lay down broadly what is appropriate to
do in what circumstances. Such a regime of supranational governance has
growing aspects of stateness, as we have said. This chapter discusses the
role of the Bretton Woods institutions (BWIs) and how the global political economy is to be governed. The third key GSEGI, the World Trade
Organization, carries on the work of the General Agreement on Tariffs
and Trade (GATT) which for half a century was the substitute for a still
born International Trade Organization (agreed to by U.S. and other
negotiators of the 1948 Havana Charter, but rejected by our Congress as
too compromising of U.S. sovereignty). The WTO will be discussed separately in chapter 10.

Until the early 1970s the IMF managed the fixed exchange rate system
and since then has increasingly been the lender of last resort to debtor
nations, advice giver to transitional economies, and enforcer of "conditionality" to both. The World Bank played a key role in postwar recovery
of the economies of Western Europe (when it was known as the International Bank for Reconstruction and Development) as was discussed in
chapter 5. Since then it has been a principal actor in the formulation of
economic policy and in lending to developing and transitional economies.
In recent years it has worked closely with the IMF (although often with
different emphasis) to guide debtor nations.

These Bretton Woods institutions represent in some respects a competing structure to those of the United Nations. This separation results from
the split between democratic impulse in favor of one nation–one vote in the
General Assembly and the exercise of power by leading core states and
transnational capital in the GSEGIs. The idea of a parliament of nations
suggested in the wake of the decolonization movements after World War II
gave impetus to the creation of the UN but the voting strength of the less
developed nations meant that the United States and the major European
economies saw value in keeping issues of trade, finance, and investment
away from UN venues, relegating them to other fora where voting was
based on economic strength and not on the one nation–one vote principle
and was safe from the Soviet Union's veto in the Security Council. While
on the organizational chart the World Bank and the International Monetary Fund are officially specialized agencies of the United Nations, in fact
they operate autonomously, not subject to its control or discipline. The
point was made clear at a 1995 meeting of the UN Economic and Social
Council at which the World Bank president James Wolfensohn explained

the relationship as he saw it in the following terms: "The World Bank can't do it alone. We can work better together with U.N. agencies, on the ground." He said he was "happy to work with" the UN but said "I don't want or need guidance from you. I want to work with you but not be coordinated by you . . . I have a job to do and I don't want to carry out my business according to some resolution made by the U.N."

This relationship may be changing. In March 2002 at the UN's Monterrey Finance for Development gathering both the IMF and the Bank were participants. Cynics suggested that their involvement was an effort to "Blue Wash" their tarnished image. Some realists proposed a contrary idea: their involvement was to demonstrate that in the post–Cold War era, a period of weakness for what was once the nonaligned movement, they were in a position to bend the UN to their will. The two interpretations need not be in conflict. Kofi Annan's UN Corporate Charter. which gives the organization's seal of approval to companies agreeing to a list of nonenforceable good behavior promises, could be seen that the UN leadership was aware that it could lobby powerful interests, offering carrots, but could only respect the distribution of relative power resources in the contemporary world system. A more positive spin, offered by constructivists, was that the dialogue had broadened and there was prospect of a UN influenced post-Washington Consensus emerging.

THE WASHINGTON CONSENSUS

My own view is that the Corporate Charter favors both a secretary general who would like to be seen as doing something to increase corporate responsibility (and indeed would like to make progress in this area) and a primary public relations effort by the companies involved.

John Williamson describes the policy of the Washington Consensus (so-named because the headquarters of the IMF and the World Bank happen to be in Washington D.C. and not because it is located in the capital of the United States, which some interpret as designing and enforcing such a "consensus") as fiscal discipline, greater respect for property rights, a redirecting of public expenditures to reduce waste, lower tax rates, interest rate liberalization, a competitive exchange rate, privatization, deregulation, trade liberalization, and liberalization of inflows of foreign direct investment (Williamson, 1990). These policies, part of the normal conditionality and structural adjustment to which debtor nations had to comply if they were to receive favorable treatment of debt and receive new loans from the BWIs, had been widely criticized in the developing world as intensifying crises rather than addressing the underlying problems the countries faced. They were seen as policies designed in the interests of the rich countries and not the poor who were forced to adopt them.

This was not the view from Washington. John Williamson (1993: 1334) himself wrote that the precepts of the Washington Consensus was "The common core of wisdom embraced by all serious economists." He dismissed those who challenged the consensus as "cranks." "The proof," he wrote (1993: 1330), "may not be quite as conclusive as the proof that the Earth is not flat, but it is sufficiently well established as to give sensible people better things to do with their time than to challenge its veracity." Nonetheless many seemingly sensible and respectable people, including a number of prominent economists, did question the Washington Consensus and the impact its adoption had on the poorer debtor nations.

A globalization framework can explain the failure of the Washington Consensus by stressing the unacceptability of its central premise: that economic and social trends within a country were explainable in terms exclusively of the government's failure rather than power relations in the larger global political economy which constrained its options and having coerced its past choices was once again controlling its destiny. Not only was this "normative internationalism" (Gore, 2000: 791) a contestable ideological reading but also the evidence of the impact of adopting even the most extreme market fundamentalism with respect to deregulation, capital flows, privatization, and so forth, was disappointing to say the least. The iatronic medicine prescribed by the Washington Consensus redistributed property rights on a vast scale. The question of whose interest governance regimes and particular conditionalities impose needs close interrogation. A change in rights whether the freeing of short-term speculative capital movements or redefining intellectual property claims revalues assets and rebalances bargaining power and distributional outcomes in markets. To keep the debate solely on the level of increasing the efficiency of markets can obscure central motivations and impacts.

Williamson and others become upset by those who would "politicize" the Washington Consensus, which they continue to see as "a technocratic policy agenda" (Williamson, 2000: 255). But this view has lost a great deal of support. Increasingly the Washington Consensus is seen as an aggressive instance of rent seeking by the privileged of the world system. While nations are always aware of such power imbalance, the focus of liberal institutionalism generally, and especially regime-building epistemic community members devoted to their formation and greater effectiveness, is to stress that such emergent relationships can help promote smoother negotiation of potentially divisive exchanges. These organizations are needed, in this view, to overcome the transaction costs which arise whenever desirable outcomes encounter coordination problems. They are needed to overcome collective action problems which frustrate policymakers' good intentions.

Many political scientists, especially those who see themselves as advisers to government and international agencies, adopt what may be called "the plumber attitude" toward international regimes. They are guided by the central concern: what does it take to keep the regime operating efficiently, to process and to enforce its decisions? They see the task as keeping things moving through the pipes as put in place by the architects and operated by agency and member practices. They do not overly concern themselves with what flows, or causes the system to back up except as such inquiry is necessary to get things moving again. The validity of dissent, the conflictual aspects of regimes, tends to be ignored or minimized, seen as secondary to a positive sum game (the problem seen as getting to "yes"). Everyone presumably benefits from such regimes even if in any particular case they do so to different degrees. While they may in a given instance feel slighted, in the longer run, in which numerous rounds are played, all benefit from the fact that such a regime operates to resolve conflict.

THE SHIFT IN DEVELOPMENT STRATEGIES

In the postwar years development economists tended to look favorably on import substitution industrialization and infant industry arguments. Advocates of Third World autocentric development point out that state policy is diminished with greater openness and financial dependency allows, if not encourages, speculation in asset and currency markets, while amplifying swings, increasing risk, and leading to higher interest rates. They argue that an alternative, perhaps a refusal to refinance debt on the terms imposed by the GSEGIs and a nationalistic model of autonomous development, would be more successful. Then as now, criticisms of GSEGI structural adjustment programs were motivated by the assertion that other forms of globalism are possible which respect local concerns, share burdens more fairly between rich and poor, and are motivated by equity considerations in place of the punishing version of "efficiency" embraced by the GSEGIs.

By the late 1990s criticism from the free market Right as well as the social justice Left opposition to global state economic governance institutions increased dramatically. The issue became not only the success or failure of attempts to elicit compliance, but also the legitimacy of regime goals, and the judgments of those empowered to coerce enforcement of emergent regime rules. In a climate of the ideological resurgence of a laissez faire approach to markets liberal internationalists found themselves under attack from libertarian free market conservatives. Where regime theorists focus on compliance systems, questions were raised concerning the very strategy of the GSEGIs even whether they were doing more harm then good. The charge was that the international bureaucrats substitute their own judgments for the greater capacity of the invisible hand prompting greater conflagration rather than putting out fires. Their expertise is, in this view, no match for the efficiency properties of the market. This school of criticism declares that without the credit guarantees extended by these agencies, foolish lending would not have gotten so out of hand. If creditors had to pay for their own bad judgment they would have more incentive to take greater care. Market liberalization and less government social engineering would mean countries that wanted to borrow would have to meet the market test. They would choose to comply, to respect contracts, provide transparency, and pay their debts or be shut out of future funding.

The argument, however, that banks and governments in developing countries need better regulation of the sort presumed to prevail in core nations ignores the way the world's largest banks (as we will have further occasion to note) routinely break the law, aiding capital flight and intensifying the problems of these countries. In addition crises in such presumably well managed banking systems as those of Sweden and the UK suggest that even the best practices of existing benchmark regulatory systems can be inadequate. A closely related issue as it turns out is that the rich and powerful are not in favor of better disclosure, especially with regard to the anonymous transfer of funds internationally. This is no small matter. The scope of tax avoidance and the scale of money laundering not only deprive the public sector of badly needed resources but also impart a destabilizing dynamic with macroeconomic implications. Such difficulties with the existing operation of the global financial regime need to inform discussions of the current role of the Bretton Woods institutions, the World Bank, and the International Monetary Fund. Their role has evolved from that of traditional financial stabilizers to strong financial liberalizers. This role repositioning is crucial to our larger discussion.

Not only have there been lost decades for Latin America and Africa but even in East Asia—the only region where growth has been faster in the last two decades of the twentieth century (to 1997) compared to the 1960–1980 years—the central story turns out to be the quadrupling of GDP in China which has 83 percent of the population of East Asia and has come to dominate the growth statistics of the region; others were not doing so well. China retained state control and limited entry of foreign capital, refusing to liberalize its foreign exchange while maintaining capital controls. It enjoyed record growth following a variant of successful East Asian models, which likewise rejected Western demands. By contrast, Russia accepted the IMF insistence that the country maintain an overvalued fixed exchange rate, which required it to raise interest rates as high as 150 percent. This led to excessive foreign debt burdens, maintained a speculative bubble, and starved the anemic real economic of funds, producing a worse peacetime decline in GDP of any country in historical experience. The Russian Federation GDP in 1997 was only 60 percent of what it had been before its transition to capitalism began in 1989.

From the Left, critics of market liberalization see these agencies as robbing debtor nations of their sovereignty and forcing upon them policies they would wish to reject had they the power to do so. The demands by the BWIs that public expenditures be cut, state enterprises privatized, services contracted out instead of provided directly by the state and so on—the policies of the Washington Consensus—were seen as unjust and counterproductive from a growth with equity perspective. The policies were driven by the imperative that the debt must be paid. Others asked different questions: are these policies good or bad for nations wishing assistance? Will they help them develop economically? Were state actors shifting blame to the BWIs for structural adjustment changes they understood to be necessary? The procedure in addressing these debates will be to describe these BWIs, their history, how they have operated, and then to discuss proposals for their reform. An interpretative frame for this discussion will be offered in the next chapter where finance will be discussed within a Keynes-Minsky framework.

Financial liberalizers believe that free global capital markets are essential to promote efficiency and that financial crises are caused by poor national economic management and cronyism. They believe that macroeconomic blunders and structural flaws, which produce microeconomic inefficiencies often the result of "politics," need to be addressed by governments which would do well to submit to market discipline. Liberalization requires greater transparency in corporate governance, a rule of law which includes impartial bankruptcy laws, and uncompromised bank supervision. Financial stabilizers place emphasis on a different level of regulation able to respond to the inherent instability of global capital markets which are by their nature crisis prone (Armijo and Felix, 1999). They say that strict regulation not only of international creditors but also debtors is needed as well as control of short-term speculative capital movements, perhaps using Tobin tax-like mechanisms. Many financial stabilizers are deeply critical of the performance of the BWIs. The costs of the programs they have imposed have become increasingly evident. They note that there is no region in the world to which the BWIs can point and claim their policies have succeeded.

It does appear that the BWIs' allegiance to the neoliberal agenda and the policies it has imposed have not done well by their clients. These measures have however increased the control of the core Western economies over the rest of the world. The hegemonic Washington Consensus, while correlated with slower growth and perverse income redistributions, has pushed the corporate globalization agenda with great success. The debtor countries understand their problems in significant measure to be the product of external economic factors including deteriorating commodity prices and the feast-or-famine availability of foreign loan capital. When loans are abundant borrowers find it easy to raise money. When credit markets contract, difficulties emerge (as when in 1982 Mexico faced crisis following decisions in the United States to raise domestic interest rates). Such an interpretation suggests a misdiagnosis of the problem by the BWIs or their unwillingness to confront the need for the richer countries to accept a more equitable regulatory order. Without suggesting any conspiracy it should be clear that those who establish such organizations and continue to control their policies have perhaps not coincidently chosen strategies from which they benefit. To understand what has become the central controversy of economic policy debate of our time it is useful to discuss the history and operation of these institutions.

THE WORLD BANK

The International Bank for Reconstruction and Development which was established at Bretton Woods in 1944 has since been profoundly reoriented and reorganized. The World Bank Group as it is now called (because the WB is composed of a number of different lending facilities), has a staff of more than 7,000 (about three times larger than the IMF) 95 percent of it in Washington, although the Bank maintains some 40 offices around the world and efforts are being made to put more of them in the field. The World Bank Group is composed of five organizations although most of the lending is done by two, the International Bank for Reconstruction and Development (IBRD) and the International Development Association (IDA).

The Bank's loans are increasingly to support the private sector (a shift in emphasis since its original incorporation disbarred it from directly financing private enterprises). IBRD loans are at market interest rates for development programs, although in recent years they have been extensively for "programs to help governments change the way they manage their economies." The International Development Association was established in 1960 to make soft loans (below market interest, 0.75% after a ten year grace period repaid in 40 years is typical) to the world's poorest countries although it too is introducing private sector lending with the same dubious authority given its mandate. The International Finance Corporation, established in 1956, is legally and financially separate and while charged to act as a development institution has lent preferentially to large TNCs. Its five largest shareholders control 46 percent of the votes and the policy bias tends to reflect their interests fairly directly. The Multilateral Investment Guarantee Agency, founded in 1988, encourages private investment in poorer countries by guaranteeing them against noncommercial losses and advises governments on how to attract more private foreign investment. Its staff expertise is in a range of fields important for evaluating development projects such as sewage and water supply projects, rural health delivery and transportation. It hires agronomists, urban planners, statisticians, lawyers, as well as economists and loan officers. In form it is an investment bank, a financial intermediary which make funds raised through the issue of bonds (it has enjoyed a triple A rating because its 180 member nations guarantee repayment) available to help low income countries "realize their economic potential."

The Bank's history suggests that it was its dependence on bond markets for the financing of its operations which exerted the determining influence on its ideology. Lending had to be done in a way that would not jeopardize its access to private capital markets. The Bank borrows and relends. It is able to borrow at low cost because creditors consider it a low risk borrower. This view has been challenged. Indeed, it has been suggested that the World Bank has "the riskiest portfolio in the world" since the loan repayment is so often impossible, is technically accomplished only by new lending to pay off maturing debt, and new borrowing is often equally unpayable when it falls due leading to yet new loans. From such a critical perspective the Bank "is a financial house of cards" (Adams, 1997: 171).

World Bank members provide contributions on the basis of the size of their economies. It is virtually unaccountable to the majority of its members, the developing countries toward whom the Bank plays a commanding role. The WB is not merely a financial institution. It is a lawmaking institution dictating legal arrangements through its leverage over the lending process. It can rewrite fiscal policy, procurement and budgetary policies, civil service procedures, labor and health laws. Its non-financial requirements stem from its understanding of the development process and what is deemed necessary to avoid a recurrence of problems Bank officials have been sent to solve. The professional staff making the recommendations appears to many in the former colonized world reminiscent of the colonial civil service and advisers to local rulers sent from the "mother" country. And like the colonial administrators they never seem to go away except to be replaced by a fresh adviser team with the same outlook and powers over the local economy and society.

Every member of the World Bank has its representative on the Board of Governors but real decision making resides with the 24 member Executive Board where a smaller subset of major financial powers have disproportionate influence. The five largest shareholders sit on this board along with the 19 directors elected by members or blocs of countries which pool their votes. Amendments to the way the organization works requires an 85 percent vote that only the United States acting alone can veto change. The President of the World Bank has always been a U.S. citizen, nominated by the U.S. director. (The IMF's Managing Director is "by tradition" a European.) While economists stress the professionalism of the Bank in making loans on the basis of expert knowledge of the issues and careful project evaluation, in political circles there is agreement among most observers that "The United States has payed closer attention to the Bank than has any other major shareholder and has frequently flexed its muscle. As a result," Catherine Gwin (1997: 247) writes in a collection of essays sponsored by the Bank in celebration of its 50th anniversary, "even with its relative loss of power in the Bank, the United States still dominates largely by default." Neither Japan nor the western European nations have challenged U.S. leadership. There is agreement that the U.S. government officials have "privileged access" that as Gwin (1997: 248) writes, "differs substantially from that of every other member." The United States is the only member that carries out detailed reviews of every Bank loan proposal, the only one to maintain the constant contact at this level of monitoring of loans (often questioning their wisdom and killing loan proposals at an early stage of evaluation), and the country likely to present policy dicta when loans are voted on with the objective of influencing the broad scope and direction of future lending. Nonetheless the World Bank Group has been under pressure from the United States Congress to justify its existence. The Bank reported in response that between 1993 and 1995 it had channeled nearly five billion dollars to U.S. companies. It continues to adjust its future lending in this direction out of fear of possible funding cuts.

There has been a consistency of such intervention starting in the immediate postwar period when the United States State Department informed France that it would have to remove any communist representatives in the cabinet of the coalition government to get loans from the Bank. In 1947 when Poland applied for a loan the Bank team returned from a site visit and reported favorably, the US State Department made it clear that it would oppose even a small loan. Bank President John McCloy made it known that he thought Wall Street investors would not approve, and since the Bank depended on loans from Wall Street Poland was out of luck. Poland and Czechoslovakia denied loans withdrew from membership. In its 1948 Annual Report the Bank wrote that "existing political difficulties and uncertainties presented special problems."

Other examples can be cited through the history of the Bank. It said no for example to the Aswan Dam loan, after initial approval, when Egypt nationalized the Suez Canal. It denied loans to Chile after the Allende government nationalized copper (the aid was reinstated quickly after General Pinochet seized power in a US-backed coup in which Chile's democratically elected president and thousands of other Chileans were killed). The US opposed loans to Vietnam and manipulated lending in Central America during conflicts in that region. Independent researchers found the Bank had not evaluated the Somoza dictatorship in Nicaragua, a US ally with an even hand, nor Mobutu's Zaire or Marcos's Phillipines. Despite such a pattern, when Ronald Reagan was elected the 1980, the Republican platform urged a return to bilateralism as a tool of American foreign policy. A planning memo for the new administration announced the "organs of international aid and so-called Third World development . . . were infected with socialist error" (Gwin, 1997: 229). While critics on the Left argued that the Bank has served US policy makers well, right wing figures in this country continue to see it soft on socialist-style government programs. Many conservatives see its efforts at social engineering to be a failure and call for the curtailment of their "excessive" interventionism. There has clearly been and continues to be controversy within US policy making circles over the way for the Bank operates.

BANK STRATEGIC ORIENTATION

The first of the Articles of Agreement establishing the International Bank for Reconstruction and Development declared its purpose: "To assist in the reconstruction and development of territories of members . . . " and "To promote foreign investment . . . " And while the World Bank has shifted emphasis from European recovery to Third World development and its strategic emphasis has changed from funding infrastructure to promoting basic human needs, the promotion of foreign investment has always remained central to its mission, and the security of foreign lenders has always been paramount. The rationale has been that without the confidence of private capital markets, development will not simply be difficult; it will be impossible. As a result of such a mandate and philosophy, its loans have been widely criticized by grassroots organizations, NGOs, and institutionalist oriented development economists. During its first two decades two-thirds of the Bank's assistance went to fund electric power and transportation projects; now, while these categories of assistance are still important, it has broadened its loans to include locally initiated projects in response to critics' complaints and as it "has gained experience with and acquired new insights into the development process," as the bank's promotional materials say. Critics saw the earlier concentration on infrastructure projects as dictated by multinationals interested in extracting resources from these countries, such as ports, roads, bridges and other indirectly productive investments which would not have been profitable for the private sector to create.

Under Robert McNamara, its president from 1968–1981, the Bank's profile rose, its staff increased from 1,500 to 5,200, and the dollar quantity of its loans increased sixfold. McNamara's focus was the war on poverty. This meant funding priorities such as safe water and family planning. In place of exclusive focus on cities there was more attention to rural development. Instead of capital intensive giant projects it chooses labor intensive construction where practical. These reorientations to some extent changed the World Bank's image, which had been that of a stodgy lender for individual projects which were not part of any coherent overall strategy. Toward the end of the period of greatest nonaligned movement bargaining strength McNamara offered long-term non-project aid.

For most of the 1980s (the Reagan-Bush years) the Bank saw the state in the developing world as the problem and insisted upon 'structural adjustment": liberalizing financial markets, ending quotas, subsidies, minimum wage and other regulations, privatizing state enterprises, and in general reducing, forbidding where it could, state interference with market allocation. Very little in development loans went to health care, education, or other development purposes. The poorest countries, mainly in Africa, used IDA loans to pay back other debt. In the first half of the 1990s nearly two-thirds of the Bank's loans went in payments for earlier loans. These terribly poor countries spent a large part of their foreign exchange earnings paying interest on the interest on principal which they are unlikely to ever be able to repay. At the same time their indebtedness is the occasion for the GSEGIs to dictate economic policy, raising questions of the degree to which sovereignty has been respected.

There are issues concerning whether market oriented policies are always best. For example privatization undertaken in the hope of increasing efficiency in service delivery may result in simply transferring a monopoly provider, e.g., a phone company or an electrical utility, to unregulated private owners who exploit consumers. The terms under which public facilities are privatized may be overly generous and benefit politically well connected interests. Even where market provision might increase economic efficiency it may result in pricing many citizens out of needed services through high prices. Although privatization has been greeted as generally successful in increasing choices and "empowering" consumers by marketizing formerly publicly provided services, it has done so only for those able to pay the higher prices of the often monopolistic providers who use the price mechanism to ration poorer users away from choosing to be "empowered" by consuming services they cannot afford. Health care and other once public services are provided at "class appropriate" level in two or more tier segmented markets. The quality of services improves for those able to pay but the public has little control over service provision, and most people want more and get less than under "inefficient" public provision or they do without.

The budget cutting and anti-government rhetoric which accompanies such drives make it harder for the public sector to recruit talented civil servants, with long-term costs to the society. These are not easy issues since overstaffed public bureaucracies which result from political appointments and lax standards are widespread in many countries. Yet cutting waste is harder and cutting public services to those who badly need them is easier so that simply shrinking the size of the government is poor policy. In its 1996 Annual Report the Bank disclosed that from 1980 to 1993 social spending as a percentage of GDP declined in half the countries studied and per capita spending dropped in two-thirds of them. The Bank has continuously through its Structural Adjustment Loans, in its detailed legal reforms, organized fiscal institutions of debtor countries to direct more resources to debt repayment and sought to reduce the public sector through privatization and the scaling back of government programs. As a result the World Bank's funds were employed for debt rollovers conditional on structural adjustment policies to wring revenues for repayment from these economies. Health care and basic education were cut to meet debt repayment. Forcing such measures impacted the quality of life and access to opportunity. Public funding for social and environmental programs declined as a proportion of GDP in half the countries studied between 1980 and 1993 as a result of structural adjustment programs, according to a 1996 World Bank report.

After a decade of what looked like an attack on the state in the developing world, and the failure of most of its structural adjustment programs, the Bank, first in a 1989 report on Sub-Saharan Africa, argued that the problem was not with its advice when its programs had not worked as well as hoped; it was because the governments involved had not carried them out correctly. Over the next decade the problem came to be seen as governance. In the 1990s the Bank placed increased emphasis on state capacity or governance, defined by the Bank in a 1992 report as "the manner in which power is exercised in the management of a country's economic and social resources for development." In a 1994 report it argued "Africa needs not just less government but better government—government that concentrates its efforts less on direct intervention and more on enabling others to be productive." The report stressed that states needed to ensure a political order, rule of law, and administration to facilitate market efficiency. It was the overextended state, with its bloated bureaucracy and rent seeking or capricious policies, which needed to be tamed and redirected.

In the 1990s then (after the collapse of the Soviet Union made the admission possible), the Bank responded to critics by acknowledging that economics cannot be separated from politics in tacit admission that the dictators Western powers had encouraged as the best achievable governance structure in Third World countries (and who demonstrated anticommunist attitudes in repressing popular movements) were in fact anachronistic obstacles to economic development. With the Cold War over the cost of maintaining these repressive regimes, both monetarily and in terms of their inefficiencies and the damage such politics reflected, became much greater. These regimes are no longer necessary nor functional to foreign investors and core state foreign policy makers. These regimes were dispensable and the Bank, which had eschewed discussion of political factors, came to stress the importance of a rule of law, an unbiased political, administrative, and legal framework which would enforce contract obligations and not seek economic rents through extortion of market participants.

The Bank sees the best transitional strategy as building state competence. The global state economic governance institutions are now playing a central role in changing the rules of the game by giving moral and financial support to officials who strive to create a rule of law which will treat foreign investors fairly and not favor domestic economic interests. Yet to blame these countries "for creating their own problems" seemed a bit disingenuous if not outright hypocritical. The change should be seen not in terms of these institutions discovering the costs of political corruption. Rather the end of the Cold War allowed 'seeing" these regimes created, sponsored, and kept in power by the Western powers, for what they had long been. It is surely true that a number of poor countries need changes in governmental functioning along these modernizing lines, but such developments are inhibited by the difficulties of a transition to democratic governance given the basic economic relations of their societies, the vast chasm in income and wealth distributions, and the role of the military and repressive police apparatuses—all of which had been encouraged under the neocolonialism of the Cold War era.

The question in many countries where corruption is a major factor is: under what conditions does it become more profitable for local elites to set up a rule of law, a more honest legal system capable of decisions which will have the respect of participants, including foreign investors and local communities? If it remains more profitable to simply rip off international agencies and foreign investors and abuse state power to favor elite interests then meaningful development will be difficult, if not impossible to achieve. The issue is further complicated in that it is not always clear when development strategies are geared primarily to rent seeking and when they are part of a defendable state-led strategy favoring the national interest.

By the end of the 1990s there was widespread criticism of the World Bank and other IFI lenders for creating an indentured status for low income countries which enables their policy priorities to be manipulated and their resources claimed by perpetual debt repayment. Awareness of the costs of such policies led to a break in the late 1990s between the World Bank and the IMF. While the latter continued to maintain the "no pain, no gain" stance, Bank officials broke ranks, calling attention to the social costs of the policy strategy. Addressing the directors of the World Bank

Group, its president James D. Wolfensohn (1998: 2) spoke in the most immediate terms to the devastating human costs of the policy: "The mother in Mindanao, pulling her child out of school, haunted by fear that he will never return. The family in Korea, with a mid-size scrap metal business, made destitute through a lack of credit. The father in Jakarta, paying a money lender three times in interest what he can make that day, falling deeper and deeper into debt. Not knowing how he will ever work himself free. The child in Bangkok, now condemned to work the streets, a child no longer." In calling attention to such human suffering he urged the board and other policy makers to go beyond financial stabilization and address the need for long term equitable growth and the institutional and structural changes needed for sustained development. "We must," he said, "focus on social issues."

Wolfensohn's assertion that without greater equity and social justice there will be no political stability, and that without political stability no amount of money put together in financial packages can bring about financial stability, represented a challenge to the more economistic IMF thinking which presumed that by getting the financial fundamentals in order all other good things will follow. The response to such talk among bankers, other decisionmakers in the financial community, and the IMF has been "easy for him to say." The World Bank, after all, is supposed to worry about the poor. "We are concerned with the solvency of the financial system, without which all is lost." It has proven difficult for the two perspectives to interact constructively. Many World Bank staffers were also resentful of Wolfensohn's implicit criticism of the priorities and practices they had followed.

An in-house evaluation (Dollar and Svensson, 1998: 4) concludes that the Bank has disbursed large amounts of aid into "poor policy environments," to governments that took the money but did not follow the advice. Adding more conditions doesn't work. More resources do not increase the probability of reform. Even in the case of ongoing obvious failure where policy conditions are not met the Bank fully disburses monies. Indeed the good governance focus seems to have come out of an awareness of the failure of programs. For example, decades into his kleptocratic rule Mobutu Sese Seko was allocating himself a salary in Zaire which exceeded government spending on education, health, and human services combined. To change such priorities the Bank would have to support revolution in a post-Mobutu Zaire (as well as many other countries). Bank officials in charge fear that to report on the true state of things in a country reflects badly on them and so they tend not to report failure as frankly as they might. This is still the case a decade after the Wapenhans Report, a study by the most senior vice president of the Bank just as he was retiring, showing 30 percent of Bank projects failing in their fourth or fifth year of implementation. This major problem rate, Wapenhans suggested, may have underrepresented the actual level of failure (World Bank Portfolio Management Taskforce, 1992: 96). One evaluator notes that the Wapenhans Report's critique of the Bank reads like the usual evaluation of a case of bad governance applied to one of its client countries (Cahn, 1993).

Conditionality, Bank officials said, is meant not only to raise expected repayments to the GSEGIs but also to force the adoption of "good" policies to increase returns to private-sector banks who lend in tandem with it. The World Bank thereby generates an externality, which further promotes development by encouraging the inflow of private funds into its client states. Such enforcement David Vines (1998: 68) suggests means, "In due course the supply of funds to its borrowing clients will increase, both as development proceeds and as funds are attracted by the Bank's own actions. This, in turn, will mean the Bank's clients will be able to obtain funds from private markets. . . . These countries can, and should, *graduate* from borrowing from the Bank." However too few actually graduate, and as Vines appreciates "too many" of the Bank's projects and programs appear to fail or underperform. This leads Vines and others to suggest that actually the function of the WB should not be to lend money but to encourage trade liberalization. Since free markets allocate resources more efficiently than governments can, government and international institutions would do well to retreat from involvement. The proper function of aid then is to stress conditionality and coerce market friendly behavior. The aid is, or at least should be, the carrot for behavior modification. The Bank has seen its role in such terms. In the 1980s, when debt crises struck many poorer nations, the Bank shifted its assistance to structural adjustment lending for countries facing serious balance of payments problems. The restructuring demanded by the Bank was directed at producing the kind of economic reform thought likely to produce sustained economic growth and avoid such crises in the future. These policies demanded far-reaching structural changes which produced much social pain which the Bank then saw as short-run and unfortunately necessary.

The Bank as noted earlier has come to stress the importance of good governance which is seen as requiring transparency, the free flow of information, a commitment to fighting corruption, and a well-trained and properly remunerated civil service. Governments should secure property rights, enforce contracts and competition. The bank in the late 1990s following NGO criticisms stressed in its president's words (Wolfensohn, 1998: 7) "[O]ur framework would call for policies that foster inclusion, education for all, especially women and girls. Health care. Social protection for the unemployed, elderly, and people with disabilities. Early childhood development. Mother and child clinics that will teach health care and nurture. . . . [O]ur framework would set forth objectives to ensure environmental and human sustainability so essential to the long-term success of development and the future of our shared planet " Specifically, he mentioned water, energy, and food security. The goals seem unexceptionable. The problem has been, critics say, that the Bank's programs have not fostered these desirable goals and in fact have impeded their achievement. They have also failed in their efforts to reform client governments.

After years of advocating a reduction in the state sector there was recognition that it is not primarily the size of the state sector which is most important but the quality of the services it delivers, the cost effectiveness with which it does so, and the centrality of an effective public sector to the development process. Inadequate and deteriorating infrastructure, poorly funded education and health care are serious problems and that the Bank's structural adjustment programs (SAPs) have exacerbated such problems. SAPs demand interest rate liberalization and increases in government borrowing which, given scarce funds and imperfect competition in the oligopolistic banking sector, results in sharply higher interest rates. Higher interest rates, devaluation, government spending cuts, and trade liberalization produce a climate of instability and have devastating effect on investment. Geoffrey Schneider (1999: 327), writing of such programs in sub-Saharan Africa, notes that "High inflation is another product of SAPs. Moreover, the inflationary effects of currency devaluation are exacerbated by an increase in domestic money supply, which results from an inflow of international money in response to higher interest rates, and by shortages of goods from cutbacks in production. Budget deficits do not necessarily decline, even in the presence of deep cuts in spending on infrastructure and social services. Devaluation, coupled with higher interest rates can actually increase budget deficits."

The Bank favors inward foreign investment, letting markets "do it," and an outward-oriented development model of export-led growth. Where before the Bank was accused of favoring large infrastructure projects because they served transnational interests (as contractors and as users of the infrastructure to move natural resources out of these countries), today criticism is more likely to be of the Bank's echoing IMF austerity demands and punishing governments for being insufficiently market-oriented. The World Bank's "structural adjustment" programs work closely with the Fund's "conditionality" in stabilization packages to reorient the direction of Third World economies along lines responsive to globalization demands. Reflecting on conditionality, Jacques Polak noted that the old demarcation lines between "short term and macro for the Fund, long term and micro (or structural) for the Bank—have tended to fade." Both institutions are now in "the structural adjustment business" (Polak, 1997: 489). Both now give medium-term balance of payments credits to the same countries. Critics suggest that this is simply a new generation "hard cop-soft cop" routine in which the Bank "feels your pain" while the Fund forces your society through the wringer for the benefit of the transnational financial institutions.

The reduction of state subsidies, public ownership, and interventions in resource allocation more broadly are at the heart of the Bank's instructions. The typical structural adjustment program has included measures which are designed to maximize reliance upon market forces and minimize government interventions and expenditures. The prospect that such policies may prove politically difficult or even impossible for the affected governments has not been considered (at least officially) as relevant. A program's failure is attributed to lack of "political will." Where a move from dictatorship to elections has occurred these have not necessarily produced democratic governance in any meaningful sense but typically have been exercises in intra-elite maneuvering for power and credibility in a context of domestic class polarization and a hostile global economic climate. The charge of crony capitalism in its many Third World manifestations, not always off base, has widely substituted for attention to the larger global constraints which affect these economies, the extent to which they are the victims of forces beyond their control, and the need for global governance reforms to defend against unequal bargaining relations and destabilizing forces of markets.

In the poor countries which have experienced decades of secular decline in the prices received for the commodity exports which account for a major share of their foreign earnings, Bank programs have been almost universal failures. Washington Consensus policies have persisted into what can be considered the long run with dire impacts on the living standards of millions of people around the world who suffer from the slower growth that the wage austerity and cuts in government spending have produced. Such policies have generally not provided increases in the overall competitiveness of these economies although some sectors have responded within an overall pattern of uneven development. Observers who look more carefully do see a difference in emphasis with the Bank still lending with a growth focus and the Fund typically demanding a cold bath approach and quick adjustment. However there has been increasingly vocal criticism of the Bank and a blurring of public perception so that the close working relation between the Fund and the Bank has threatened to reduce them in the public mind to the two arms of a single policy agenda.

The World Bank, the IMF, the WTO, and other GSEGIs despite their different specific missions have in fact acted as part of a coherent program so that the Bank despite its mission emphasis on alleviating poverty has been criticized along with the other GSEGIs as working for the rich and powerful and hurting the poor. Structural adjustment and related liberalization programs, especially since the start of the debt crisis of the early 1980s, were central in producing a rise in inequality globally. As one leading global political economy text explains: "Because SALs [structural adjustment loans] are intended to improve LDCs' balance of payments by reducing spending for social services, lowering wages, emphasizing production for exports over local consumption, and ending subsidies for local industries, it is the poorer, more vulnerable individuals in LDCs who are often the most severely affected. Thus a large body of literature exists on the effects of IMF and World Bank SALs on poor women and children in LDCs" (Cohn, 2000: 191). The more central problems are in the model itself, which underlies the work of the various GSEGIs and the pressures of the countries and their corporate interests which control the direction of the GSEGIs. This is seen even more clearly in the case of the International Monetary Fund.

THE INTERNATIONAL MONETARY FUND

The IMF is organized like a credit union. Its 184 members pay in a quota subscription proportionate to their economic size and strength. The IMF has had no major default in its history (largely because it has simply rolled over unpaid debts and more recently called on its richer members to pay the obligations of the highly indebted poorest countries). It holds $40 billion in gold reserves. The adequacy of its resources is reviewed every five years automatically, more often as needed, but this does not mean its members eagerly respond. After Mexico in 1994–95, Russia, East Asia, and Brazil, the sheer magnitude of funding needed by the end of the twentieth century to assure markets had increased dramatically. With a growing list of troubled economies asking for loans or potentially calling on the Fund its resources seem inadequate. While the IMF needed a huge infusion to continue operating on the scale of its ambitions the House of Representatives resisted. It refused President Clinton's requests for such replenishment and so created a major crisis of credibility for the organization. The Fund responded, as shall be further discussed, with reforms calculated to please the legislative critics in Washington. As of this writing the administration of George W. Bush has shown no interest in increased funding to GSEGIs.

The Fund's traditional standby arrangements lasting a year to a year and a half are designed to help finance temporary or cyclical balance of payments deficits. They have proven inadequate because countries do not adjust so quickly. Their problems are more deeply rooted. They come from the structure of their economies and the mode of their insertion into the global economy. The Extended Fund Facility recognized and supports a longer time frame for adjustments. The Enhanced Structural Adjustment Facility finances long-term programs at concessional rates of interest for low income countries. With the push for capital market liberalization, and in recognition of what they consider short-term adjustment costs of neoliberalism, the IMF created the Supplemental Reserve Facility in December 1997 to, as First Deputy Managing Director Fisher put it, "assist emerging market economies facing crises of market confidence, while providing strong incentives for them to return to market financing as soon as possible." These loans are at higher interest than the Fund normally charges. Institutional assertiveness has played a motivating role in these changes. By the mid-1970s the original IMF clients, the advanced economies recovering from war damage and displacement, no longer needed its assistance. The Third World debtors did, and the IMF responded by assuming the role of lender of last resort not only for short run balance of payments but also for structural crises.

Fund officials frequently point out that U.S. taxpayers do not give money to the IMF to bail out anybody. The idea that IMF money is not taxpayers' money since it comes from each subscriber country's central bank would suggest that central banks are somehow private organizations, a view many central bankers admittedly seem to hold, except when they petition their government for an increase in funding for the IMF. Technically what happens is monetary exchanges take place in which the member country receives an international reserve asset comparable to a convertible foreign currency so that these transactions are monetary exchanges and not budgetary receipts or expenditures. The member receives a liquid interest-bearing claim. The IMF pays interest on the dollars so lent. When testifying before Congress in the fall of 1998 Robert Rubin, then President Clinton's Secretary of the Treasury, was careful to describe U.S. transfers to the IMF as "deposits." He asserted that over the previous fifty years our contribution to the IMF had not cost the taxpayer "one dime." It is the case that during most of the 1980s the United States was receiving over half a billion dollars a year in returns from the IMF as a result of debt crisis lending by the Fund, in the 1990s even more.

The idea that since the IMF has not yet defaulted to its own creditors its policies now and forever are somehow immune from the possibility of market discipline has in different ways, from a number of perspectives, been challenged. In its own inimitable style, the *Wall Street Journal* pointed out editorially in 1999, "At best this is arrogant and maybe kind of dumb. At worst it is a lie." The *Journal* may not really be worried on that score; rather it is the ability of the Fund to avoid market discipline which troubles libertarian zealots. The same ideological proclivity is also evident among Congressional free market radicals, particularly those Republican lawmakers who see the IMF as a statist spanner in the international capital markets. The IMF from their viewpoint props up crony capitalism and bails out bankers. They think it should be abolished. While the George W. Bush Administration hardly went to such extremes, it called for more pre-crisis precaution and fewer bailouts.

The term bailout is appropriate when the matter is examined from the perspective of how the borrowed funds are used to compensate private investors and banks who are creditors. The IMF in effect socializes debt, pays off investors, and places the burden on the citizens of the debtor country. Even those who have made loans to private borrowers find these debts assumed by governments at the insistence of the Fund. Locals who had not themselves borrowed or assumed the financial risk find losses shifted to them. The people funding the bailout are the citizens of the affected countries, especially those who lose public services like health and education, or their jobs through austerity measures. The people pay back the loans and make significant sacrifices over extended periods, typically outlasting the financial crisis by many years. The central assumption of IMF lending is that its goal is repayment of existing loans and the establishment of improved credibility for the country in question. This mission is reflected in the performance criteria for releasing successive amounts of financial assistance the IMF developed in the 1950s which use a simple model needing as inputs only two sets of statistical series which were generally available in all countries—banking data and trade data. It focused on domestic credit creation understood to be both the key variable government could control and crucial to correction of balance of payments problems. This simple model predicts income and changes in foreign reserves as weighted averages of the values of past and current changes in domestic credit and capital inflows. It is this model with the same four basic equations which is used to formulate the IMF conditionality which is to guide the client economy's policymakers (Polak, 1997).

Over time the IMF divided its credit creation into a private sector component (to be encouraged) and credit created by the government sector (usually to be discouraged) and detailed the advice it gave on specific types of taxes and the expenditures it endorsed. In the 1980s policy prescription focused around a set of structural adjustments, privatization, trade liberalization, ending price, and other controls including deregulating labor markets. But none of these as Jacques Polak, former director of the IMF's Research Department and founding father of the IMF model has noted "could conveniently be captures in econometric equations." The scientific precision the IMF claimed for its model's financial programming targets have been discarded. Its lack of success in incorporating new equations controlling for capital inflow and outflow has meant the IMF has had to forego the comforts of its old model and base its conditionality increasingly ad hoc instruments which seemed to it plausible. As a result advice given over time became less driven by formal models and more strongly influenced by the desire to reshape government's attitude toward its role in the development process. The first element in this policy is enforcement of outward orientation. The second is reliance on the market and the discouragement of any activist role for the state in economic development.

There is a judgment here on how to address a fundamental contradiction in the natural operation of financial markets. The free flow of foreign capital into economies which have raised their domestic interest rates as a matter of stabilization policy expands the money supply and imports inflation. Putting a ceiling on the domestic money supply to counter the inflation depresses the economy. The flexibility of international capital movements cannot tenably be treated as exogenous as the IMF model has done because in a floating exchange rate system they depend on the domestic interest rate and exchange rate expectations. Specifically, capital flight under the "freedoms" insisted upon by the IMF are common, sizable, and destabilizing. Polak and others from the IMF recognize this. He describes this problem as presenting "a major challenge" to the IMF model. Domestic interest rates do not even appear in the simple IMF model nor does the exchange rate, which effects inflationary expectations that can trigger sudden loss of confidence and capital flight. Governments can block the inflationary impact of an inflow of foreign money by letting their currencies appreciate to discourage further capital inflow but this also discourages exports (bad for financing external debt). For this reason countries often peg or fix their exchange rates through interventions as needed. This expedient has now failed in a number of high-profile instances, most dramatically Argentina in the winter of 2001–2002, leaving developing countries without a strategy in confronting the globalized financial regime's penchant for destabilizing local economies due to rapid and overwhelming capital movements. Critics suggest that the cost of IMF conditionalities to their citizens and polities vastly exceeds financial inflows from the bailouts to the countries.

A different sort of moral hazard is involved in their loans. Bureaucrats take actions but others pay for their mistakes while they go unsanctioned so that they have little incentive to change harmful policies which they are ideologically inclined to follow. Devesh Kapur (1998: 126) writes "The steady expansion of institutional objectives (and loan conditions) has occurred because borrowing countries bear a disproportionate share of the political, economic and financial risks of IMF programs. There is little downside of these programs for the Fund's major shareholders, its management, or staff." The IMF takes over the economic management of the country, dictating demands on such issues as labor law and the ability of foreign investors to acquire local businesses, and whether it bungles its mission or succeeds (however one measures performance), it risks little since it almost always gets its money back even if this comes at great cost to the citizens of the country. This amounts Kapur (1998: 126) writes, "to a situation of taxation without representation."

There is widespread appreciation that the IMF, the World Bank, and other international financial institutions (IFIs) have not simply been concerned with getting repaid. "One of their central missions has been the restructuring of the domestic institutions and policies of borrowing states. In some instances IFI officials have occupied positions within the bureaucracies of states that have signed agreements" Stephen Krasner (1999: 143) writes. He points out that 'some of the missions of IFIs are not so different from the bankers' committees that assumed control of state finances in the Balkans in the nineteenth century or the customs receivership established in Nicaragua." David Law (1995) suggests the strategic design and role of the GSEGIs is a new constitutionalism seeing the process as an attempt to treat the market as a constitutional order with its own rules and

institutions that operate to protect the market order from political interference. The presumption in such a frame is that the state does not wither
but exhibits strength in new tasks of disciplining domestic constituencies
to accept that market regulatory institutions are beyond the reach of transitory political majorities. Such a constitutionalism attempts to construct
an economic governance structure of natural economic law and not of
voters or their representatives. Such a new economic constitutionalism is
not a freeing of the market from state intervention so much as it is an insu-
lating of regulatory GSEGIs and their local correspondents from political
interference protecting the market as reconstructed under GSEGI guidance from domestic politics.

IMF POLICY LOGIC

Graham Bird has suggested that the conventional policy prescriptions
have misdiagnosed the problem. He writes, "A large amount of evidence
shows that BOP [balance of payments] difficulties in developing countries
are caused by external factors such as adverse movements in the terms of
trade or increases in world interest rates as well as by domestic economic
mismanagement (Bird, 1996: 491) He cites IMF evidence showing little
support for the idea that it is massive monetary growth that distinguishes
those developing countries that turn to it from those that do not and
notes the neostructuralist analysis that IMF conditionality is not only irrelevant to the real problem but has a negative effect via stagnationary consequences. His own review suggests that theory could "cut either way"
and empirical evidence is divided, showing weak positive and in other
cases weak negative relationships between borrowing from the Fund and
borrowing from private capital markets. He concludes that case study evidence likewise is broadly consistent with the conclusion that IMF lending
does not have a strong catalytic effect. This conclusion, that "IMF
involvement was neither a necessary nor a sufficient condition for attracting capital from other sources" suggests that the Fund's 'seal of approval'
does not seem to carry a very high market value (Bird, 1996: 489). This
does not mean that the IMF does not exert important influence over the
design of economic policies in debtor countries which turn to it for financial assistance.

In another review of studies concerning the IMF and the World Bank
Tony Killick concludes that the high conditionality adjustment programs

have only rather weak revealed ability to achieve their own objectives although they have had major impact in shaping the contemporary intellectual climate and practices of debtor governments (Killick, 1997). Stephen Helleiner (1998: 7) summarizing the consensus of a number of IMF SAPs offers a not dissimilar conclusion: "The studies paint a consistent picture of an institution bent on fully opening economies to foreign investors on advantageous terms at almost any cost—the destruction of domestic productivity capacity and local demand, growing poverty and inequality, the deterioration of education and health-care systems, and as has been seen most recently and dramatically in East Asia, a dangerously expanding vulnerability of those economies themselves to forces external to their governments."

The heterodox political economy position understands the IMF's role not in terms of "mistakes" made. It sees the IFIs as tools of transnational capital and the hegemon's foreign policy priorities. The IMF's agenda is to open Third World markets and to use foreign debt as leverage to force structural changes favorable to transnational capital or as political payoff. Its crisis is that debtors resist its demands and that the cost of pursuing its goals have grown. The difficulty in separating the attack on rent seeking from that on the development state is unimportant to most free market economists for whom both are distortions unacceptable in an efficient properly managed economy. For others who see the Fund's approach as a way of imposing a new colonialism, a neo-imperialism of free trade on less developed economies, and to nationalists of many stripes, the Fund's doctrine is an unwarranted intrusion on sovereignty.

The IMF takes financial crises as opportunity to demand all manner of structural changes. Their doing so is widely criticized. Wyplosz (1999: 173), for example comments, "One striking feature of the Asian crisis has been the official denial that the lessons from the Great Depression and subsequent financial crises applied (especially the crisis of October 1987, as well as the Scandinavian, UK and US banking crises of the 1980s and 1990s)." Those lessons are that crises quickly produced a credit crunch followed by a sharp contraction with rising unemployment, business failure, and lost incomes—not to mention political crises with profound longer-term implications. The question Wyplosz and other critics ask is: Why not instead of deflation add liquidity to the local market? Jeffrey Sachs (1998a: 16) writes, "a careful examination of the actual record shows that the IMF, loyal to financial orthodoxy and mindful of creditors to the neglect of debtor countries, often pours oil on the flames." Former World Bank Chief Economist Joseph Stiglitz agrees that the IMF mishandles economic crises and should not be allowed to force such conditionality on debtors. Of the IMF's strategy in the East Asian crisis he writes, "They invoked bad economic analysis. Anybody who has taken Economics 101 would have anticipated there was going to be a recession or a depression [in the countries hit by the crisis]. In that case, you need to expand government spending; the IMF called for fiscal contraction. It also backed raising interest rates to very high levels. They focused on inflation in the midst of depression" (*Business Week*, 2000: 48).

The IMF continues to pursue such policies even after they produced disasters and used the same approach again and again leading some observers to see it as a creditor cartel and not an institution primarily concerned with the needs of its clients, of the majority of its member states (Dieter, 2000: 2) The Fund's policies are generally understood not to have been in the best interests of the effected economies. Such critics, on the basis of its orientation and impact, understand the mission of the IMF as the pursuit of the interests of its major shareholders, above all those of what much of the world sees as United States imperialism. Weakening rather than strengthening the prospects of autonomous economic development is the guiding principle. The rationalizations, whether sincerely believed by staff economists or not, are secondary to the goal of opening these economies to foreign control and weakening the power of sovereign states to pursue state-led nationalistic models of growth. If sovereignty means the ability to pick between alternative courses of action, the goal of IMF policies was to reduce the sovereignty of East Asian states. In January 1998 after then Secretary of the Treasury Rubin returned from Seoul, Rudiger Dornbusch quipped on CNBC that the "positive side" of the financial crisis was that South Korea was "now owned and operated by our treasury" (Panitch, 2000: 5). In such a revisionist view of IMF orthodoxy, it is the U.S.-dominated Fund which is the ultimate in crony capitalism, directing its tens of millions of dollars to the foreign banks which had made the shaky and imprudent loans at the expense of the people of those countries.

There is a more overtly political dimension to IMF operation which undermines the Fund's credibility in the present period. This is the less discussed (at least by economists) pressure the United States imposes on the IMF in pursuit of foreign policy objectives. During the Cold War loans were refused to leftist governments which met the Fund's loan criteria (such as Nicaragua's under the Sandinistas) but extended to right wing regimes such as El Salvador's which did not. More recently, the IMF and WB have become part of America's anti-terrorist arsenal as in such instances as when Croatia was denied an IMF loan even though its economic policies were deemed sound because it had failed to turn over alleged war criminals. Such transparent political criteria are not our central concern here but are consistent with the way Fund policy favors its most powerful members.

THE IMF RESPONSE

Whether one stresses IMF maneuvers as management opportunism or as a response to political pressure, is in a sense a matter of secondary importance to the inevitable trajectory in the growth of GSEGI's ever more powerful transformational goals and capacities. As in the case of the conditionality imposed on Latin American and other debtors in the 1980s, its prominent role in directing the transformation of Russia to market capitalism, and efforts to impose the Washington Consensus on East Asian economies from the last years of the 1990s, the IMF had moved powerfully into what was an increasingly controversial role as director of world financial governance restructuring. In the mid-1990s ninety countries were accepting Fund programs and so the Fund's impact was substantial. The Washington Consensus reflects an approach which is interventionist in philosophy and detail. The new "governance" doctrine was expressed in the new set of IMF guidelines issued in August 1997; through them the Board directed the staff that "it is legitimate to seek information about the political situation in member countries as an essential element in judging the prospects for policy implementation" and that the Fund "has assisted its member countries in creating systems that limit the scope for *ad hoc* decision making, for rent seeking, for undesirable preferential treatment of individuals and organizations."

The Fund has run into two difficulties in convincing others of its priorities. The first is the domestic cost its programs impose—high unemployment and inflation of the price of necessities, along with decline in public goods and resentment when economic growth slows and resources are channeled from domestic needs to foreign creditors. There have been riots, rebellions, and the occasional coups displacing governments which cooperated with IMF programs. Resentment toward the IMF as debt policeman and enforcer for policies preferred by transnational capital made it appear in the role of extortionist in the eyes of many in the Third World. The bankers on the other hand, both in the public and private sectors, tended to see matters differently. The countries had borrowed the money, the debtors had consumed beyond their means; now they had to meet their obligations. In mediating between debtors and creditors the IMF saw its mission as expediting repayment on the view that reestablishing good credit ratings would bring renewed private sector lending and so was in the best interest of debtors. Further local banks had often "lacked a commercial orientation" in the minds of core financiers. They had made loans to insiders at concessional terms, and often these were not repaid. Crony capitalism was also linked to anti-foreign investment policies. Questionable loans to national enterprises gave an unfair advantage. Outside investors often faced hostility and were discouraged by development state policies. "Crony capitalism" and domestic subsidization were inexorably intertwined in the minds of this second set of critics.

The IMF may have entered a new phase, perhaps a third phase in its more than half century history. In the first, its creators saw it as overseeing a system of currency convertibility based on fixed exchange rates in which currencies were tied to a fixed value of gold (or to the U.S. dollar; since the dollar was then valued at $35 an ounce other currencies could be fixed in dollar equivalents). The Fund offered short-term loans to countries which temporarily ran balance of payment deficits which they could not meet out of their own reserves of gold or convertible foreign exchange. With the demise of the fixed exchange regime, the result of outsized U.S. balance of payments deficits, dollar liquidity forced increasing inflation on the world. With the unilateral decision by the Nixon Administration to resolve the weakness of the dollar by breaking the dollar-gold fixed exchange link, the world moved into a period of floating exchange rates which was officially accepted in 1973 after two years of temporizing.

After five more years of negotiation the IMF's second stage began in 1978 with an amendment to its constitution that broadened its functions and supervisory role. This second phase turn is a direct repudiation of the Fund's charter goals. The purpose of the IMF as described in Article I of the IMF Agreement is to promote international monetary cooperation by providing machinery for consultation and collaboration on international monetary problems, to promote exchange stability, maintain orderly exchange arrangements among members, and to shorten the duration and lessen the degree of disequilibrium in the international balance of payments of its members. The first Article of Agreement reflected a commitment to the promotion and maintenance of high levels of employment and real income, and the development of the productive resources of all members as primary objects of economic policy. The conditionality the

Fund was imposing by the 1980s seemed to go well beyond what was envisioned in its Articles of Agreement or in subsequent guidelines on conditionality. The former Director of the IMF's Exchange and Trade Relations Department, C. David Finch, has expressed the traditional understanding: the IMF "has not been established to give guidance on social and political priorities, nor has its voting system been designed to give it the moral authority to oversee priorities of a noneconomic nature. Its functions have to be kept narrowly technical if it is to be effective in the exercise of its role as a promoter of the adjustment process. For this purpose, the Fund has to accept that the authorities of a country are the sole judges of its social and political priorities." (James, 1998 citing Finch, 1983). This is no longer the case. The Fund now sees its job as forcing a restructuring of domestic economic policies in countries which go to it for loans. David Felix is not alone in arguing that its Washington Consensus policies violate the IMF charter "in spirit and substance." The IMF continued to make short-term financing for balance of payments purposes available but became more active in monitoring member economies' performance, particularly watching inflation and balance of payment pressures. The IMF stepped up its advisory role, conferring regularly with members, analyzing their situations usually once a year, and issuing a report which the country is free to make public should it wish to do so. Countries had to promise reforms which in the IMF view would return its balance of payments to health.

In what may be a third phase of the institution's evolution the Fund management in 1998 sought change in its constitution to require the freeing of capital accounts by members. This effectively would end the possible use of controls on inflow and outflow of capital which have been used as defensive measures by nations who find themselves in crisis situations. The proposed rule change can be seen as part of a broader effort which includes the proposed multilateral agreement on investment to guarantee the freedom of capital to move without restriction across borders on equal terms with domestic investment. This third phase turn also repudiates the Fund's Charter goals. The objective of the Bretton Woods Articles of Agreement was to establish a postwar economic order in which international trade and investment would be as stable as possible. Fixed but adjustable exchange rates would not be changed to gain competitive advantage and the primary goals, progressive taxation and other elements of welfare capitalism, were to set limits on international markets. In pursuance of such policies international capital flows were to be controlled. Article VI requires the IMF to deny emergency credits if used "to meet a large or sustained outflow of capital," authorizes members "to exercise such controls as are necessary to regulate international capital movements," and mandated the IMF to ask for such controls.

In 1996, the year before the East Asian financial crisis exploded, the Fund had proposed rewriting Article VI to reverse its policy thrust. The IMF wanted to mandate the unimpeded flow of capital internationally as part of its constitutional charter. In September of that year the Fund declared that "international capital markets appear to have become more resilient and are less likely to be a source of disturbances" (*IMF Survey*, 1996: 294). In May 1997 it announced plans to amend its Articles of Agreement "to make the promotion of capital account liberalization a specific purpose of the IMF and give it jurisdiction over capital movements" (*IMF Survey*, 1997: 131–32) Within months the devastating impact of the East Asian financial crisis was being felt and the IMF said no more about the proposal. Waldon Bello (1998) suggests the GSEGIs were not worried about the huge inflow of capital into East Asia because it was to the private sector and not a matter of government borrowing. But even though the crisis was of the private sector, the IMF imposed its traditional solution: to cut back government expenditures. Even though there was little inflation, it insisted on high interest rates, insuring profit to foreign investors. Other observers likewise point out that given the austerity measures the Fund imposed, long-run growth was stifled for the foreseeable future. In the absence of economic growth continued long-term investment was modest, confined to bargain hunters looking for assets which Fund policies had caused to be written down for quick sale.

Before the East Asian crisis, Haggard and Maxwell (1996: 35)were concerned with the puzzle of the rush to liberalize capital movements and open domestic financial systems. They noted well documented cases showing the "extremely high cost of premature and ill-conceived liberalization efforts." They had in mind the Southern Cone experiments in Argentina, Chile, and Uruguay, and of course Mexico. Later analysis showed a continuing pattern in East Asia and elsewhere (Kaminsky and Reinhard, 1999). The point is that financial integration holds governments hostage to capital markets and forces upon them greater fiscal austerity than they might otherwise choose is a common theme in this literature. The reasoning is clear enough. The government must maintain a cleavage between the domestic economy and the international economy with respect to financial flows because, as Robert Wade (1990: 367) explains, "Without controls of these flows, with firms free to borrow as they wish in international markets and with foreign banks free to make domestic loans according to their own criteria, the government's own control over the money supply and cost of capital to domestic borrowers is weakened, as its ability to guide sectoral allocation." Further explaining what was indeed to transpire within the decade in the East Asian region, Wade writes, "Uncontrolled outflows can leave the economy vulnerable to an investment collapse and make it difficult for government to arrange a sharing of the burden of adjustment to external shocks between the owners of capital and others; 'the others' are likely to be made to take the burden, with political unrest, repression, and interrupted growth as the likely result."

During the Asian crisis China and India, whose currencies were not freely convertible, had not experienced problems while contagion brought down other currencies in the region, some by as much as 80 percent of their pre-crisis value. While IMF officials claimed "there is as yet little convincing evidence bearing on the benefits or costs of open capital markets (Fisher, 1999: 95), over at the World Bank Joseph Stiglitz was convinced by cross-country econometric studies that examined the impact of capital market liberalization on the likelihood of recession and confirmed the generality of such an adverse impact. He noted "it is clear that not only is there no compelling empirical case *for* capital market liberalization, there is a compelling case *against* capital market liberalization, at least until countries have found ways of managing the adverse consequences" and rather than openness increasing stability and policy flexibility for countries Stiglitz concludes "openness may impose costly *constraints* on the ability of governments to pursue legitimate objectives." (Stiglitz, 2000: 1084). Keynes had made the similar point a half century earlier that international financial markets are inherently unstable and countries are better advised to protect themselves, retaining control over capital flows in and out of their economies. Keynes believed that a stable trade regime required capital controls. It can be argued that the postwar "Golden Age" of rapid growth and stability was owed in substantial part to near ubiquitous capital controls.

The issue which is central as we bring this discussion forward is evaluation of the process and impacts of the transformation of the IMF, which was to have been something of a world central bank charged with restoring currency stability, and the World Bank, which was to have been a development agency—both becoming governance vehicles with characteristics of sovereignty setting economic and political priorities for their vulnerable member governments who become to a significant extent vassal client states. It is the expansion of their remit to detailed conditionalities and coercive micro guidance which characterizes their evolution in global state economic governance institutions.

IMF RESCUES

There are a number of apparently competing and even contradictory truths about the IMF rescues. They do manipulate the governments involved, are often responsive to U.S. foreign policy concerns, generate moral hazard issues with their implicit promise of more bailouts next time, interfere with markets by refusing to allow bankruptcy to occur, and do its work of revaluation of debt, hurt the poor most, and subsidize financial institutions and speculation. Differences of opinion are more substantial when it comes to what is to be done. Some demand that the IMF be abolished, for doing more harm than good; others advocate giving it more money so it has resources sufficient to avoid future financial meltdowns. Currently the most popular solutions in Washington is to cut back on their remit so they deal only with illiquid and not insolvent debtors, lending at penalty rates without micro management, and offering grants but not loans to the poorest countries with no access to the private financial market. To move in this last direction would be to rely on market forces and curtail use of debt by the Fund as a means to pressure the economic policy makers in these economies.

As a result, there is a three-way policy debate among those who would reform the IMF, and by extension other GSEGIs. From the Left the trouble is the pain conditionality imposes on the poor of the less developed economies by capitalism in general and specifically by the collection agencies for lenders in collaboration with local elites. The goal should be more equitable economic relations within and between countries. From the free market political Right, a laissez faire stance sees interventions as inefficient and politically motivated by social engineering hubris. Without such interference borrowers and lenders would act more cautiously or be disciplined by market forces. This, not government intervention, would encourage economic growth. Third, the traditional liberal internationalist position sees the GSEGIs as stabilizing an unstable situation, promoting growth, and working through carrot and stick policies to improve regulatory structures and overcome market and government failures in these countries. This last position, and now being attacked from both Left and Right, has traditionally dominated.

The orthodoxy behind the current policies, that these countries face liquidity problems and short-term financing addresses their problems, does not fit well with the long-term nature of non-repayment of the loans and is increasingly and widely questioned. Further the amounts involved increase given the moral hazard implicit in guarantees under the current set up. When combined with the austerity imposed by conditionality, which does not bode well for a quick reverting to growth, creditors aware that official funds are limited and that confidence will not quickly return, those who can will take the monies and run. Speculators with short-term asset positions get out while those with the sort of long-term direct investment positions that potentially contribute to development suffer losses from the impact of devaluation and austerity. This payoff matrix is hardly desirable from a developmental perspective (Griffith-Jones, Cailloux and Pfaftenzeller, 1998).

Timing of IMF assistance is as harmful as its conditionality. Markets move fast and contagion can be nearly instantaneous. The time it takes to put an IMF program in place and the limited assistance parceled out in small doses does not prevent panic. Often it only finances the withdrawal of short-term speculative capital. At the other end, such loans do not seem to get repaid. Sixty-nine countries have borrowed from the IMF for a total of more than twenty years and twenty-four of them for more than thirty years. Seventy-three countries have borrowed from the IMF for more than 90 percent of the years they have been members of the IMF (Vasquez, 2000). This is not exactly the sort of emergency, short-term lending envisioned when the Fund was established. The IMF's micro management of debtor nations also came in for increased scrutiny. Conditionality agreements with some countries (Russia and Indonesia for example) contained more than 100 conditions specifying privatization, tax administration, bankruptcy codes, budgetary allocation for health and education and other detailed instructions. The Fund's expertise, presumed to be in the area of macro economics, did not extend to these fields. In forcing such extensive changes in a time of crisis the IMF put tremendous pressures on governments and their people going well beyond what many considered their legitimate mandate.

In 2000, without any consensus on a meaningful reform program, the IMF sent a few hundred million dollars to Ecuador leading Charles Calomiris (2000: 88) to ask: "Why in the world is the IMF sending money to Ecuador? Some observers claim the IMF aid to Ecuador is best understood as a means of sending political payola to the Ecuadoran government at a time when the United States wishes to ensure continuing use of its military bases there monitoring drug traffic." He goes on, "Will that sort of IMF policy be likely to produce the needed long-run reforms in fiscal and bank regulatory policy? Has the IMF not learned anything from the failure of its lending to Russia in 1997–98?"

Calomiris raises similar questions about the U.S. government telling Pakistan, or so it is said, that its access to IMF subsidized lending depended on its willingness to sign a nonproliferation treaty. The use of such a carrot as a tool of foreign policy relies on a want of clear rules, a lack of transparency in the full loan conditionalities involved in particular cases, and the tendency of GSEGIs to depart from economic criteria, lead him to suggest: "If Congress wishes to delegate power over a limited amount of resources to a multilateral 'political emergency fund' financed by the G7 counties, then let it do so openly, establish the appropriate governance and oversight to accompany that delegation of authority; and keep the management and funding of that entity separate from the other multilateral institutions" (Calomaris, 2000: 100).

Calomaris is not recommending such a step but suggests that political motivated loans and assistance should be separated from aid based on transparent economic criteria. Since those U.S. officials who have used the GSEGIs to pursue political aims which they cannot do as easily or at all through unilateral action find lack of transparency a virtue, working through the GSEGIs is hardly a failing. No superpower gives up leverage where it finds stealth helpful. To answer the question of whether the costs of such slush funding exceed the benefits the country derives from the way they are being used: it depends. It is not "the country" which decides. A reshuffling of GSEGI priorities consonant with America's wars on terrorism and need for a broad alliance required even more blatant payoffs after September 11.

The power of the IMF and other GSEGIs over the details of economic structural adjustment and its micro-management represented the opposite pole from proposals made during the 1960s and 1970s for a New International Economic Order (NIEO) which was put forward by the former colonized and newly independent nations. Those demands were in essence for meaningful, effective sovereignty and more participation in decision-making (especially in economic matters concerning the international trade and finance regimes). In those years the Group of 77 representing the Global South called for greater equality between more and less developed nations, the sovereign right to nationalize private property within their borders, and a code of conduct for multinational corporations (Blanco, 1999). But in the 1980s and 1990s Third World governments were not making such demands. Power had shifted so dramatically that their attention focused on attracting foreign investment rather than seeking international compacts to control it. Some of these demands were taken up once again in the civil society activism at the WTO Seattle ministerial meetings and other gatherings. The Fund could afford to write off the debt of the most highly indebted poorest countries which it is widely recognized can never pay their debt. The IMF and the other GSEGIs choose not to do so. Instead the G-7 countries promise to finance such debt forgiveness (in exchange for new conditionalities for the debtors). The promised bailout of the GSEGIs is thus presented as debt forgiveness. It is not the same as debt cancellation of the bad loans which are unpayable. As anger at the GSEGIs grew it might have been a good time to revisit John Maynard Keynes' predictions concerning the consequences of the British and French governments demanding unreasonable reparations from a prostrate Germany and of America's fitful ignorance in insisting on repayment of its allies wartime debts. The resulting imbalance of international finances produced economic and social instability and invited calamity. We return to the question of debt forgiveness and possible debt cancellation in chapter 11.

CONCLUSION

In this chapter it has been argued that since the end of the post–World War II era the World Bank and the International Monetary Fund have moved further from the financial regime that was the framework for the Bretton Woods system. This change of direction corresponds to the desires of the most transnationalized sectors of finance capital. This new agenda and the policies which have been carried out have been costly to the majority of the world's nations that fell under its tutelage. These costs have occurred not because GSEGIs have "made mistakes" so much as that their agenda has addressed the interests of the leading private financial institutions based in the core countries and have served to strengthen the hold of the core on the periphery. In the next chapter an alternative Keynes-Minsky approach is presented which seems to better explain the repeated financial crises the world has experienced as the neoliberal agenda of the Washington Consensus has been pursued. None of what has been said should suggest that the developing or economically underdeveloped poor countries of the world do not need help. The issue of course is what sort of international financial regime will better meet their interests as well as provide stability to the international economy.

CHAPTER EIGHT

Finance: Orthodox and Heterodox

"The ability to build models creates an illusion that there is a scientific basis to the calculation of risk. But the exactitude lies only in the calculation of the formulas. Models will invariably fail to predict the future when there are sudden shifts in the structure of the markets, such as we have seen in the past year."

—*Henry Kaufman* (1999: 10)

"In recent years, there's been a trend toward democracy and market economies. That has lessened the role of government, which is something business people tend to be in favor of. But the other side of the coin is that somebody has got to take government's place, and business seems to me to be the logical entity to do it."

—*David Rockefeller* (*Newsweek*, 1999 cited by Daly, 1999: 1)

Without a smooth functioning financial structure the economy will not be able to perform well. Banking is a unique sort of business. It needs effective prudential controls because unlike other enterprises banks can be insolvent but not illiquid. Most businesses run out of cash and the ability to borrow as their net asset position deteriorates with falling profitability. Banks can maintain the illusion of solvency even when there is little real chance that borrowers will repay loans (which can be maintained on the books at face value). Banks can disguise their situation and continue to attract funds by offering higher interest rates protected by deposit insurance supplied by government and for the large financial conglomerates by an implicit guarantee extended to those too big to fail. Once they are in trouble financial institutions become attracted to high-risk gambles in hope of recouping. If they do not succeed their eventual losses are made up by taxpayers. If they profit and survive the risk is rewarded. If they do not, the loss to management and owners is no greater. Indeed, something very much like this can go on at the level of a national economy in which companies, investment banks, corporate lawyers and accountants, government regulators, and investment analysts all have a vested interest in hyping stocks, while their optimism self-levitates economies into a euphoric prosperity, which can come crashing down as doubt eventually sets in as expectations are seen to be unrealistic.

The vulnerability of the financial system increased in the late twentieth century as corporate fund raising moved from reliance on bonds with 25–30 year maturities to shorter term borrowing, Interest rate and exchange rate volatility increased, and high real interest rates persisted. Economic actors tried to protect themselves in the new circumstance by using financial instruments which did not exist, or certainly were not widely used, even a decade or two earlier. There was for example a global explosion of derivative markets. Most of these were for cross-border transactions for interest rate and exchange rate contracts. Their notional valuation was mind boggling. Some high-profile disasters led to a growing awareness of the need for greater prudential controls. By the second half of the 1990s there was widespread awareness that, as the 1998 World Bank's annual report put it, "Liberalization in the financial sector is not the same as deregulation. The case for regulating banking is as compelling as ever."

This chapter focuses on aspects of the globalization of finance since the demise of Bretton Woods. It first describes something of the financial irregularities unleashed or intensified by deregulation and the policies of neoliberalism in the closing decades of the twentieth century. It then contrasts the mainstream finance theory of efficient markets and rational expectations models to a Keynes-Minsky approach. The latter suggests that financial markets are prone to crisis tendencies as a result not only of exogenous factors or government policy errors but also the endogenous workings of finance capitalism. Structural instability requires social regulation in the Keynes-Minsky paradigm. The contrast between this approach and the mainstream one is sharp. The conventional view celebrates growth and speed, as well as the diversity and sheer efficiency of modern money markets. The Keynes-Minsky one worries about their tendency to overshoot and produce financial crises. Those holding to the latter perspective are not happy that long-term ties between producers and financiers have been replaced by one-off transactions for short term gain and high-risk plunges in place of long-term relational lending. An appeal to the empirical evidence does not resolve the debate since the facts are not in dispute. Rather the interpretation of the severe crises of recent years is quite different from the two perspectives.

There are two aspects to the story. One is the question of whether the normal operations of financial markets stabilize economies. A second is the extent of corruption and criminality in the system. It is not easy in the real world to separate the two. There is individually corrupt behavior. There are widespread structural relations which allow, if not encourage, such dishonesty. There is a lack of effective regulation which from an institutional political economy perspective is part of the system. The GSEGIs have been culpable of creating a moral hazard problem of some severity. Their policies have encouraged financial crises by offering loans to debtor countries which protect creditors to some extent against loss. Their solutions have often made matters worse (a contention which was argued in the last chapter). There was also by 2002–2004 widespread evidence of crony capitalism in the most mature national capitalisms of the United States and in Europe as corrupt dealings were revealed to be widespread and unpoliced by markets or regulators until it was too late and firms were forced to declare bankruptcy even as stock analysts continued to sing their praises sometimes up to the day of their collapse—one thinks of Enron and WorldCom among other failed corporate giants (a topic to be covered in the final chapter).

FINANCIAL LIBERALIZATION AND THE EXCHANGE RATE REGIME

It is impressive how rapidly financial liberalization was adopted and globalized money and capital markets have expanded. In 1973 foreign exchange trading was between $10 and $20 billion a day. By the mid-1990s daily foreign exchange trading was $1.3 billion, an amount equal to the entire world's official foreign exchange reserves, including its gold, and was 70 times the value of world trade. The inability to reach agreement on a revised fixed exchange system led to the floating currency era which *de facto* developed as the U.S. on January 1, 1974 abolished all restrictions on international capital movements (following the lead of Germany, Switzerland, and Canada, which had done so in 1973). Great Britain followed in 1979, Japan a year after that, then France and Italy in 1990, followed by Spain and Portugal in 1992. These actions set the conditions for a dramatic expansion of global liquidity.

As discussed in chapter 5, floating exchange rates were supposed to stabilize foreign exchange markets and avoid sudden devaluations from unsustainable fixed rates. Instead of markets functioning to smooth supply and demand, adjusting to changed situations and perceptions of risk (in some gradual fashion so the system is always in equilibrium as free market fans claimed would happen) there was growing financial instability. It was certainly true that efforts to maintain overvalued currency levels provoked speculative attack. The speed and intensity of such capital flight significantly moderated during the years of Bretton Woods. With its demise the financial sector tail came to wag the real economy dog. When George Soros shorted the British pound in 1992 (making a billion dollars over the weekend) many thought globalization had entered a new stage.

Walter Wriston, one of the key players who actively reshaped his industry while CEO of Citibank in the 1970s and 1980s, pushed the envelope in self-deregulation. In defending himself from charges of irregular and perhaps illegal practices he claimed that "[T]he new international financial system was built not by politicians, economists, central bankers, or finance ministers, but by technology" (Wriston, 1992: 8). While he may be right that technology has permitted dramatic change, the form these developments took were matters of policy choice by the key players as even a cursory view of the activities of Citibank in these years reveals. Consider that after a three-year investigation the Securities and Exchange Commission concluded that between 1973 and 1980 Citibank had improperly shifted a minimum of $46 million in profits to branches in the Bahamas to avoid taxes. By tracing what the SEC staff said were bogus transactions involving artificially low and high exchange rates, money was shifted with the direction and approval of senior Citibank management. It is hard to give credence to Wriston's claim that "technology made me do it." Citibank had been charged with violating currency control and tax laws in Switzerland, France and West Germany as well, and has paid many millions in back taxes and penalties.

Privately the Comptroller of the Currency had expressed concern to the Citibank board over its accounting and other procedures and the safety and soundness of its foreign exchange practices. The bank was powerfully connected. Reagan appointees to the Securities and Exchange Commission overruled its staff and refused to bring civil action against the nation's (then) second largest bank. Later as Citigroup it was to be number one. It is not "technology" itself but the uses it is put to that is determinative. The relation between freedom of capital movement and illegal financial dealings is not at all easy to separate in practice. The profits from moving illegally gotten gains, funds seeking to disguise their origins in graft and corruption, and in tax avoidance are major revenue sources for banks. They are related to, but not the same as, the larger issue of sovereign debt.

Pressure on regulators in core countries to let bankers have their way is intense. Reagan Treasury officials did try to close down the Netherlands

Antilles as a tax haven. (According to the Commerce Department, a good chunk of the Eurobond investments, and many billions in other investments, were channeled through that island.) Regulators were forced to quickly back off under the threat that their action "could undermine the free functioning of the Eurobond markets and that investor confidence in American securities, including the Treasury's own issues to fund the bloated United States budget deficit "would be eroded" (Rosen, 1987). The Treasury Department's action had caught a number of U.S. companies Eurobond offerings (Nabisco, J.C. Penney and others). The banks denied tax avoidance had anything to do with their preference for booking loans and other transactions offshore. Rather the issue was said to be customer privacy. But there were also huge tax advantages for this "routine practice" which extend to many types of paper transactions. For example, when a French airline buys a jet or rather leases it from a Dutch subsidiary of Citibank and the lease is refinanced 30 percent by the U.S. taxpayer (through the Export-Import Bank) and 70 percent by Citibank New York through its Nassau branch, taxes are avoided.

"The basic principles of customer privacy" were and are routinely used to obscure the flow of drug monies and other illegal activities. There have been decades of such practices which were especially important during the 1980s debt crisis in Latin America when the banks profited both from lending to countries and for channeling capital flight out (much of this illegally), monies which in effect returned as new loans. Rich foreigners paid generous fees and accepted lower interest rates if they could evade national regulations and move their loot to the U.S. Such "private banking" was the single most profitable activity of Citibank and other money center banks in the 1980s. Despite the 1986 Money Laundering Control Act Citibank continued to be the leading private banker for dictators, their families and friends in smuggling money out of their own countries, including tens of millions by the drug connected brother of Mexico's former president. About the same time this "Salinas Case" surfaced, investigators discovered Citibank New York was transferring Juarez drug cartel monies to Uruguay and Argentina for Mexican drug lord Amado Carrillo Fuentes. Carlos Hank Gonzalez, a former chief executive of the federal district, was similarly accused of links to drug traffickers. He, too, was a good Citibank client. The Citibank moved $40 million for him and his family along with hundreds of millions for others connected with the drug business according to investigators (Jáquez, 2001: 40).

In another instance, Citbank moved $130 million through a series of transfers in eight countries, laundering bribe monies and other illegally gotten gains for Gabon's President Omar Bongo. In exchange the bank received millions in fees, according to a Senate staff research document (Dwyer, 1999: 142). Citibank officials expressed dismay that such things could be happening at their bank, as they had when the Philippines inquired about their moving funds looted by their ex-president Ferdinand Marcos a decade earlier. Their "shock" was reprised in February 2001 when they were caught up in the corruption investigation surrounding another of their newly rich customers, Joseph Estrada, a second ousted Philippine president. Such recidivism hardly raises an eyebrow in the polite community of politically appointed bank regulators whose ability to discipline banks is circumscribed by elected officials who are beneficiaries of contributions and sometimes "loans" from the financial service industry.

A report released by Britain's Financial Services Authority (the country's main industry regulator) that same year claimed that its banks had allowed the equivalent of over a billion dollars to pass through accounts linked to the family of General Sani Abacha, the former military ruler of Nigeria. About the same time $3 billion was allegedly moved for Slobodan Milosevic and his entourage through banks in Greece, Cyprus and Switzerland (*Economist*, 2001: 64). Much of this "don't ask—don't tell" money moves through smaller banks of questionable status in complicated patterns. Abuses possible under the deregulated financial system include such episodes as the Antigua-based European Bank founded by two Russians. This Internet bank provided numbered accounts operated by password rather than signature. It offered confidentiality and higher interest rates, at least until it collapsed in 1997, when its officials disappeared along with its deposits. More famous is the case of the Bank of Credit and Commerce International (BCCI) set up by a Pakistani businessman with backing from the Sheik of Abu Dhabi and the Bank of America. Registered in Luxembourg, headquartered in London, it operated around the world via a web of offshore accounts. Losses were concealed in a Cayman Island subsidiary—the Cayman Islands are, it may be noted in passing, the fifth largest financial center in the world after London, New York, Tokyo, and Hong Kong. This equal opportunity bank laundered money for drug syndicates and covered arms traders and CIA activities when its criminality could no longer be ignored. It was finally shut down in 1991 by British banking authorities.

The operation of offshore financial centers so crucial to the ability of such operations to flourish call for debate concerning the uses of sovereignty in an era of free market financial globalization when, as Kavaljit Singh (2000: 17) writes, "sovereignty becomes just another commodity to be bought and sold in the market." Not only is secrecy of those willing to pay protected in the name of sovereignty but citizenship is sold to criminals seeking to avoid prosecution by their home governments. Such havens could not function except as part of a larger global financial system with inadequate regulation of those with which the world's leading bankers do business (Enrico and Musalem, 1999). Abuses by Russian government officials for example are extensive and include the Russian Central Bank with its front companies based in the British Island of Jersey through which IMF loans have been rerouted out of the country as well as being transferred to assist political campaigns of candidates favored by the country's financial oligarchies. Russian criminal organizations send money to Israel via Antwerp, through Gibralter into Spain, London, and New York and on to the Caribbean.

More normal transactions involve tax avoidance by citizens and large corporations of core states. They include techniques of under and over invoicing shipments to minimize taxes paid on a global basis. Impacts on the fiscal viability of states is substantial. Craig Murphy (1994: 241) has suggested that "if today's system of free trade in currencies had existed 30 or 40 years ago, governments would never have been able to institute the wage, pension, and social service legislation needed to secure the original domestic compromises, let alone engage in the kind of Keynesian counter cyclical spending they also required."

The OECD reports that from 1985 to 1994 foreign direct investment from G7 countries to low tax jurisdictions increased by more than fivefold. Even as that organization condemned the distorting effects of harmful tax competition, its members have been unable to agree to do anything to stop or markedly reduce such flows whose purpose is simply tax avoidance (Benvenisti, 1999). The investment community prefers competition among jurisdictions and has been supported by some key policymakers including Paul O'Neill, when he was George W. Bush's Secretary of the Treasury. The ideology of deregulation serves the interests of the strongest banking center institutions in New York and London and it has been the U.S. and British governments which have initiated repeated rounds of deregulation, coming to recognize as legal the practices long followed illegally by their leading financial institutions.

Other governments have had to follow or to lose financial activity to these less regulated venues. When advocates of deregulation speak of the benefits of competition, each jurisdiction experiments and economic actors "vote" for the one which best meets consumer preferences. In doing so they misrepresent this process of competitive deregulation as if it could be seen as an exercise in consumer sovereignty instead of a sort of Gresham's Law in which social regulation is driven out by competition from jurisdictions which give away, or rather sell, additional benefits to tax evaders and other criminals. If one country ends tax withholding on securities held by nonresidents or allows unregistered bearer bonds which can be negotiated anonymously, then other jurisdictions must offer equal tax avoidance mechanisms or become less attractive to footloose capital. If governments accept transactions from nameplate off-shore banks they will soon allow tax-free "foreign" banking at home. If transnational banks compete in a slack global regulatory environment for the business of transnational borrowers, other taxpayers will have to make up for the tax avoidance or governments will have to reduce their commitments to spending programs.

That the Netherlands Antilles (home of George Soros's Quantum Fund among other such instrumentalities) is a major supplier of capital to the United States says much about what central bankers and politicians in America and in other economically powerful countries are willing to allow. There has in fact been a process of competitive deregulation in which acceptance of tax havens, and what William Greider has called "the politics of escape" by Great Britain and the United States, puts great pressure on the more regulated financial systems such as those of France, Germany, and Japan to accept similar relaxation of rules or face loss of capital to such less regulated environments. The (temporary) advantage gained from further liberalization drives the process, sometimes to irresponsible lengths. Greider has called finance capital "the Robespierre of the globalization revolution" because, he says, its principles are "transparent and pure." Global financiers he writes, "will turn on anyone, even their own home country's industry and government" (Greider, 1997: 25). That is the maximization of return without regard to political or social consequence and so it is the disinterested enforcer of market imperatives. Politicians and the press express shock whenever the excesses of financiers come home to roost, yet this is the way things continue to work even after measures taken to trace money flows as part of the U.S. war on terrorism showed the capacity of the system to track funds. Serious and perhaps effective reform may be possible as a collateral benefit to attempts to limit terrorist funding moving through the international banking system. But this need have no positive impact on the related problem of debt buildup by debtor nations, much of which is due to capital flight, not all of which by any means involves illegal transactions.

THE INCIDENCE OF FINANCIAL CRISES

The growth of sovereign borrowing in the context of liberalized foreign exchange markets has produced painful financial crises. A 1996 IMF study found that 133 of the Fund's 181 member countries had suffered at least one crisis or episode involving significant banking difficulties between 1980 and 1995 (Lindgren, Garcia, and Saal, 1996). The World Bank identifies more than 100 major episodes of bank insolvency in 90 developing countries and transitional economies (former communist regimes) from the late 1970s to 1994. These crises were found in advanced and underdeveloped economies, newly industrializing, and transitional economies. While in each case policy errors could be blamed, the pervasiveness of financial sector crises suggested problems broader and more systemic were at work. Because banks are typically the major provider of loan capital to business, hold individual savings, and provide the electronic infrastructure for the payments system of a society, these crises were destabilizing and quite costly. In some cases bank subsidiaries or close working partners among finance and insurance companies were the immediate sites of crisis which then spread. The fact that two-thirds of IMF members experienced banking problems between 1980 and 1996 can hardly be coincidence. The very deregulation the global state economic governance institutions forced on these countries produced crises which in turn allowed GSEGIs to demand more deregulation resulting in still greater foreign control.

In more than two-thirds of the countries for which data are available the direct loss sustained by these governments was more than 3 percent of Gross Domestic Product, about the increase in the average country's output in a good year. Argentina in the early 1980s lost the equivalent of more than half its GDP and Chile more than 40 percent (World Bank, 1997: 66). Competent deregulation it turns out is not easy to achieve. Given the size of such losses in presumably well run systems such as those of the United States (the S&L debacle) and the Scandinavian countries in the late 1980s and early 1990s, banking crises can carry enormous fiscal cost even in countries that are supposed to know better how to maintain robust systems of prudential regulation. It is not simply that supervision is administratively demanding or that at the start of a crisis the situation itself and what measures should be taken are not always clear, but that subjective factors, including ideological ones and the political connectedness of financial institutions, can weigh on the side of forbearance and can prove enormously costly. Recapitalizing banks puts enormous strain on national economies. The IMF estimates that from 1980 through the mid-1990s tax-payers paid over a quarter of a trillion dollars in resolving banking crises. More than a dozen countries expended the equivalent of more than their annual GDP (Caprio and Klingebiel, 1997; Caprio and Honohan, 1999). As a point of comparison the serious U.S. Savings and Loan crisis of the 1980s cost the equivalent of only 2 or 3 percent of U.S. GDP and between 1931 and 1933 the negative net worth of failed banks in the United States was roughly 4 percent of GDP. Of the nearly 100 crises with losses of this or higher magnitude that occurred over the last two decades of the twen-tieth century, twenty resulted in losses in excess of 10 percent of GDP. Ten produced losses of 20 percent of GDP.

What is remarkable is how similar banking sector problems are across domestic economy regimes. Whether we talk about China's banks non-performing loans to state enterprises or Russia's "oligarches" banks which attract funds on the Roach Motel principle (the money comes in but doesn't get out), whether we look at the overextension of bank loans to the *chaebol* in Korea, the Indonesian banks lending on the family and friends plan, or to the well connected Mexican plutocrats who bought nationalized Mexican banks and ran them into the ground so that they had to be renationalized at incredible cost to taxpayers, it is the political power of borrowers and the implicit state guarantees which are crucial. The dominance of finance is subsidized by taxpayers everywhere. It results from a contradiction which is, and has always been, at the heart of inef-fectively regulated banking and which seems to be the natural order of finance capital in our economic system.

The growth of sovereign borrowing amplifies the problem. When the share of government revenue that go to debt service becomes large, inter-est rates which must be paid go higher. Such carrying charges consume more government revenue, leaving less for necessary expenses and threat-ening a vicious cycle in which lenders flee, no longer willing to roll over debt even at very high interest rates. Liberalization leads to massive influx of foreign monies, overinvestment, asset bubbles, and panic. Sweeping cap-ital market liberalization has accelerated and amplified this pattern for a number of nations. Capital flees faster than it came in with dire conse-quences for the local economy. The resulting debt deflation typically initi-ates a situation of deep recession or depression for the economy. The aus-terity measures urged by, or forced by, the GSEGIs typically deepen such crises by removing purchasing power and bankrupting local businesses.

It is not simply that the Latin American debt crisis or the Asian finan-cial crisis, and whatever lending scheme related crises come next, "raise grave questions" regarding the sustainability of the individual pattern of overextension. They raise much larger questions about the system of finance as the global problem of the contemporary ipe. As has been noted, many bankers and financial economists present such developments in international money matters as (1) inevitable, (2) the result of technology, and (3) desirable on both efficiency and political grounds. Some views are one pole of the debate. An alternative position favored here is that finance as a social construction reflects interest group influence and class relations. It is the result of a political process and the regulatory context of financial intermediation. It can be, and in fact is, frequently redesigned. Consciously developed configurations are produced through the interaction of human agency in an evolving environment based only partially on a path dependent evolution. Contingency and agency intersect to produce outcomes which are hardly inevitable. Technology can become manifest in different forms and serve competing ends. There is never only one technologically determined outcome and so we are almost never dealing in maximizing behavior among known alternatives.

In terms of outcomes mainstream economics deterministic models do not predict well. Enough is unknown and unknowable in any situation that markets can quickly swing from optimism to pessimism as consensus shifts suddenly based on new information, rumor, or hunch which seizes upon the imagination of market participants. The power of speculators has increased with the demise of the National Keynesian social structure of accumulation and now is framed in much mainstream discourse in terms of a fetishization of markets. As Irwin Kellner, then chief economist at Chase Regional Bank, put it: "You could say it's really the bond markets that run the country, not the President and not Alan Greenspan." (Hershey, 1996: D1) And so perhaps it is, so long as the political authorities allow the bond market this power. While some countries just adjust to bond market preferences, others try to set independent national policies of different sorts using capital controls, taxation of short-term monetary flows, and pegging their exchange rates to gain greater credibility with market participants. None of these alternatives have proven sufficient in the face of destabilizing market pressures.

We have noted that the IMF takes the position that liberalization of capital flows is an essential element of an efficient international financial system. It has for a long time advocated removal of controls and other regulations on capital movements in violation of its official original mandate. Changing the mandate has come to appear the better part of discretion and it proposed to do so in an official statement in September 1997

(Interim Committee of the International Monetary Fund, 1997). It was an ill-timed suggestion coming as it did months before the outbreak of the East Asian financial crisis, which many observers blamed on capital flow liberalization. The Fund had two main arguments to support its position. The first was that the case for free capital mobility was identical with that for free trade. At the analytical level it simply required a relabeling of the axes. Second it was argued that capital account liberalization along with deregulation of domestic financial markets "is an inevitable step on the path to development" (Citrin and Fisher, 2000: 1134).

While Stanley Fisher, First Deputy Managing Director under Camdessus, acknowledged there are risks in capital account liberalization others suggested that in fact such risks exceeded benefits for the countries involved. Additionally, there appears to be no evidence that countries which liberalized capital accounts have performed better than those which haven't, nor that countries without capital controls grew faster, invested more, or experienced lower inflation (Rodrik, 1999c). Most of the more than $1.5 trillion in daily turnover of foreign exchange at the end of the 1990s was traded in forward transactions, the largest proportion of which was speculation on interest rate movements, changes in money supply, and balance of payments trends. Very little of this had to do with financing actual goods and services being exchanged across international borders. As we have noted forex transactions dwarf world production.

The distinction increasingly made is between the benefits of the inflow of direct foreign investment through which foreign investors build, purchase, and manage local plants, bringing with them technology, organizational skills, marketing access, and other efficiency enhancing assets, as well as foreign currency debt creating short-term capital flows. The latter is closely correlated with risk of crisis, because with the inflow of speculative capital comes a bidding up of assets and an overvaluing of the local currency that favors greater imports and is detrimental to the country's export position. It is speculative capital inflows that produce balance of payments crises without adding to the capacity of the economy to create more exportable goods and services and so to repay foreign debt. That short-term loans must be repaid whenever creditors refuse to roll it over makes countries which choose this route vulnerable to even slight and temporary problems which trigger concern on the part of foreign lenders.

The IMF does not stop borrowers from borrowing or lenders from lending even when it sees trouble developing. It has no legal authority to do so in any case. But it itself does continue to lend to countries until a situation is widely understood to be hopeless. It does not go public with early warnings of impending crisis for fear that it will be blamed for bringing on panic, capital flight, and default. It has no procedure for allowing countries to declare a standstill on debt service payments while they negotiate with creditors. It does not have procedures to compel private sector bondholders to become involved in restructuring debt (a process called "bailing in" the private sector in contrast to bailing them out by making GSEGI funds available to repay them). As things now stand, when a country defaults on debt and tries to come up with a workout plan with creditors it and the creditors willing to do a deal are held to ransom by so-called vulture funds which buy up distressed debt and force governments to pay the full face value with the threat of seizing assets if they don't.

So far the sort of Chapter 11 procedure through which U.S. firms obtain protection from creditors while a solution is worked out has been resisted by international financiers who have not been willing to give up the right to pursue foreign governments. They fear that allowing the IMF power to impose a standstill to prevent private foreign creditors from suing governments during debt negotiations would increase the bargaining power of debtors at the expense of creditors, making it too easy for them to declare moratoria on interest payments. This opposition by foreign financiers has prevented more orderly restructurings and, given GSEGI willingness to bail out debtors, worked to their advantage.

Rather than allowing markets, and speculators, to produce large current account deficits which can have deleterious effects, countries are better advised to discourage such destabilizing hot money flows and to build up foreign exchange reserves. China, with its nonconvertible currency and huge foreign reserve holdings, was most immune to the contagion effects of the Asian financial crisis. (This is not to say that the devaluations of regional currencies did not impact on its prospects but that the protection nonconvertibility provided and the reserve cushion the country enjoyed were major benefits.) It is not clear that such a strategy will always work under the actual conditions most economies face in a globalized economy. Still such examples as China, Taiwan and even Malaysia (which instituted capital controls after crisis broke) suggest that the successful path may not be through total openness as recommended by the Fund. The determination of what is credible is a product of how speculative markets work.

By creating barriers to the ease with which short-term capital movements can destabilize an economy the coherence of the local policy consensus can increase an economy's credibility. Countries such as Japan and Korea, as well as Italy and France used long-term capital controls with some form of coherent development strategy and one version or another of national planning to successfully develop their economies. As globalization advanced the United States used its muscle to force financial liberalization which in case after case has proven disastrous to economies even as it has benefitted financiers. This is not to say that much government intervention has not been inefficient, if not downright corrupt and distorting of markets in ways which have done harm to the countries involved. There is fairly widespread agreement that this has been the case. But there is agreement too that too little government supervision and regulation create serious problems. Given appropriate qualification it appears that executed properly capital controls enhance the bargaining power of countries to negotiate with their own private sector and with foreign capital. Contra the IMF position Kavaljit Singh (2000: 138) maintains that imposition of capital controls "should be viewed as the beginning of a process whereby a country asserts its own right and ability to shape economic policy so that the ill effects of globalization and structural adjustment policies could be reversed. If judiciously used, capital controls can also become a vehicle to enhance the bargaining power of its citizens and working classes."

Why then was financial liberalization pushed so hard by the GSEGIs? This question can be answered on two levels. The first asks who stood to benefit most from the liberalization version of the globalization of finance? The most obvious answer is the United States and the leading international financial institutions concentrated in New York and London and supported by the governments of the U.S. and the UK who have both motive and means, as the prime time detectives would say. The advantages for the U.S. and UK from financial liberalization are clear. In a world of globally mobile capital the demand of foreigners for U.S. dollars and U.S. government securities to hold as reserves to protect against sudden capital outflows increases. To the British "the City," London's financial district, is one of the few strong points of their economy. The U.S. large current account deficit since 1981 has been balanced by these large net capital imports. In contrast, Western Europe as a whole and Japan had trade and current account surpluses; but as Armijo and Felix (1999: 12) note, despite being a large net capital importer (unlike most advanced industrial countries but like most developed ones), the U.S. was also a large exporter of capital and a large net exporter of financial services. That is to say, the foreign profits of private U.S. financial institutions made a significant positive contribution to the overall current account balance.

There are those who argue that these costs were unavoidable and in a historical sense inevitable given the unsustainability of the older regulatory regime. Many of those who take this financial liberalization perspective, the financial liberalizers, see the free market leading to greater efficiency in capital allocation, greater competitiveness, and openness maximizing global economic growth and well being. A second school, the financial stabilizers (Armijo and Felix, 1999), who acknowledge self-seeking behavior and believe in an era of globalization call for more sophisticated and more substantial international regulation to supplement and eventually restructure national-level regimes.

This second school understands that markets by their very nature produce financial crises and so sees the need for stronger reregulation. In their view, financial deregulation has unleashed forces that are driving the current global economy in the reverse direction than had been predicted. Freedom for capital movements and the floating exchange regime has brought higher real interest rates, not lower ones. The higher interest rates have slowed investment and lowered global growth. The longer term horizons of productive investment and the shorter term horizons of finance lead to destabilizing capital movements. Given the increased mobility of capital countries have been forced to placate investors. Unfortunately, capital tends to come when it is unnecessary and leave when it is least convenient. It is not surprising then that national governments try to protect themselves from destabilizing effects of adverse short-term capital movements. Governments worry not only about bank failures, but also about sudden capital flight, which can represent a further occasion for loss of confidence. Given the incentive to increase risk, which bankers have in the brave new world of liberalized finance, effective reregulation seems both necessary and much harder to achieve.

In terms of ideology and economic theory, it can be suggested that the GSEGIs were responding to what they perceived as the shortcomings of statist and protectionist regimes and the fiscal laxity which they understood to characterize highly indebted countries, overextended governments which in their misguided efforts to control their economies had sought escape in inflationary policies. Such policy failings characterized Latin America in the 1970s and brought on, in the views of the GSEGI policymakers, the crisis of the 1980s. Much of Europe was judged guilty of similar policy errors. It was the need to restore sound macroeconomic management which GSEGIs saw guiding their strategic advice. But we may ask: Did all of these governments by some coincidence make the same mistake at roughly the same time? Was the problem their ignorance of sound policy? or political pressure on governments to pursue policies which would be damaging in the not very long term? or were changes in

the global political economy to blame—changes which forced governments into unsatisfactory policies at the national level because they were
unable to address them in a coordinated fashion? Such questions lead back
to the role of the United States and its suspicion of Japanese and European social democratic schemes for global financial regulation, and again,
to restate the obvious absent center of the whole affair, to U.S.-based
financial institutions and by extension the U.S. economy's interests as
understood by key policymakers who stood to gain from financial liberalization and coerced deregulation.

Macroeconomic policy in the 1980s and 1990s became, in the light of
the power of the bond market, a game of credibility played with symbolic
gestures. In the face of inflationary pressures the idea was to stand firm
through strong austerity measures directed at wages and government
social spending. Again there was nothing new in this. At least since Montesquieu political commentators have emphasized the role of "capital
strike," constraining policymakers in a capitalist economy. Whether this is
a good thing (makes governments act more responsibly) or a bad thing
(prevents governments from addressing pressing needs by placing a fairer
burden on capital), is a matter of political perspective. The IMF's solution
to the East Asian financial crisis was a capital strike in this sense, a delaying of lending in order to force structural changes in the relationship
between these economies and the interests of investors of the core. We can
interpret the Latin American debt crisis and the politics surrounding the
adoption of the euro and the Maestricht convergence criteria in similar
fashion. The economic fallout from the events of September 11 complicated issues of investor confidence still further.

By the end of the twentieth century, the burden of bailing out national
banking systems had grown to the point where local elites found it increasingly difficult to commandeer tax levied funding for this purpose or to
obtain foreign loans which did not come with demanding conditionalities,
including the sale of bankrupt assets to foreign investors. At the same
time, the United States directly and through GSEGIs demanded financial
liberalization and national treatment for foreign financial institutions. This
position is not without merit. In countries in which it is politically possible to appoint a truly independent, competent, and powerful conservator
to oversee troubled financial institutions, there would be less need for foreign takeovers. But to detail the requirements for such restructuring
under existing political conditions suggests its difficulty. Under such pressures many weakened debtor countries removed obstacles to foreign ownership in their formerly restricted domestic financial sector opening the

flood gates to acquisitions by transnational finance capital domiciled in the United States and other market centers.

It has been observed that monetary and fiscal discipline did not necessarily translate into counter-inflationary credibility in the foreign exchange markets. Nor does laxness in these areas invariably impose costs in terms of market credibility. It depended to a degree on who controlled the government and which sectors' policies are favored. Tax incentives for business might create fiscal deficits but not be penalized while spending for Welfare State functions may be. As Helen Thompson (1997: 106) observes, as far as foreign exchange markets were concerned, "it was one thing for the British Conservatives to expand demand, suck in imports and create an inflationary boom, it was quite another when French socialists had done the same thing."

Is freedom to set progressive domestic policy therefore precluded? Geoffrey Garrett (1998 and 2000) argues the broader empirical evidence suggests that capital market integration has been associated with increasing divergence in most facets of tax and spending policy and that much of the variation continues to be explained by traditional domestic policy variables such as the strength of organized labor. Governments with strong conservative parties and weak organized labor movements have reacted to financial openness with cutbacks. Strong left-labor regimes have done the opposite.

Economists have generally been skeptical about the possible use of capital controls as a way of husbanding foreign exchange to service debt and meet import bills. Yet opinion has shifted somewhat to acceptance of control over short-term speculative movement. There is wide agreement that if capital controls are to be effective and not counterproductively foster inefficiencies and corruption, they need to be rule-based and transparent within a system which is accountable in terms of effective enforcement. This is important because there are really two sides of the battle around capital controls. The first is to protect an economy from the harmful effects of unwarranted rumors, the impact of contagion from events elsewhere, and the overshooting to which markets are prone and that can produce substantial harm. Where capital controls are confined to limiting speculative short-term capital movements stabilization and long-term growth goals can be supported. But it is also the case that systems of controls and licensing have corrupted both market and polity becoming a source of bribes, rent seeking, and favoritism.

Chile, for all the free market liberalization enthusiasms of the early Pinochet years, learned the painful lesson that a poorly regulated banking sector allowed to speculate in real estate and extend huge credit to bank owners was a recipe for disaster. It was neoliberal excess that led Chile to go against the ideological grain of its governing coalition to embrace capital controls. The effectiveness of Chile's controls on inflow did extend the maturity of its foreign debt but also raised the cost of borrowing, especially for small and medium sized businesses (which, unlike the largest firms, could not evade the controls). In Chile's case controls on capital outflows did produce corruption and have been largely ineffectual. The controls did protect Chile by preventing excessive inflows and cushioning it from small shocks, but they could not effectively prevent contagion effects from large ones.

This is hardly an argument against capital controls. Sebastian Edwards (1999: 77), in reviewing the literature on the most important experiment to date, suggests that "All in all, then, the evidence suggests that the controls on inflows allowed Chile's Central Bank to undertake a more independent monetary policy." Nonetheless he also reads the evidence to the effect that controls on capital inflows are clearly insufficient to eliminate financial instability. Such conclusions suggest to some that it is the global financial governance regime which is in need of change.

In Chile as in other parts of the world prudential regulation of the financial system was weak for what can be seen as class structure reasons. The whole paradigm of supervised capital adequacy and bank regulation more broadly presumes state officials, bank shareholders, and other claimants to the assets of the bank monitor the bank's risk portfolio and that bankers are motivated by seeking profits from arm's length lending based on sound collateral and risk assessment. The problem is typically, however, that local banks are owned by businesses and well connected families which dominate the local economies. Loans are often made for reasons having to do with the interests of bank owners and managers. Capital controls are avoided through collusive activities based on such self-interests in much the same way that their loan portfolio is biased toward self dealing and sweetheart loans with little or no collateral, often for speculative purposes. Bank authorities may lack the independence to prevent or even moderate such practices. Foreign borrowing can be as bad when creditors either make no effort to determine the position of borrowers, or worse know full well to whom they are lending and the purposes for which they are borrowing, but believe that their loans are protected and find it difficult to turn down substantial potential income even when careful risk assessment suggests it would be wise to do so. The moral hazard of implicit GSEGI guarantees compounds irresponsible lending.

Such realities lend support to the need for strict generalized control over speculative capital flows.

It was for just such a reason that in his 1941 "Proposals for an International Currency Union" Keynes (1943: 52–53) offered the view that central control of capital movements, both inward and outward, should be a permanent feature of the postwar system: "There is no country that can, in future, safely allow the flight of funds for political reasons or to evade domestic taxation or in anticipation of the owner turning refugee. Equally, there is no country that can safely receive fugitive funds that cannot safely be used for fixed investment." Keynes thought it necessary to control capital flows to prevent destabilizing economies and to maintain control over domestic interest rates for policy purposes. The experiences since the end of Bretton Woods with its repeated financial crises have driven home Keynes's concerns. After speculative bubbles have crashed and hot capital ran for the exit policy makers have drawn the harmful conclusion that the logic of the situation dictates the need for an even greater loss of local control.

Given the need to write-down local bank portfolios, opening bidding for distressed assets to foreign buyers and allowing better capitalized foreign banks, national treatment may make economic sense. This, however, may bring foreign control of the economy, a fate many developing countries have long resisted. For grass-roots movements these nationalist appeals have worn thin, given the self-seeking of local elites. It is possible, and in many cases likely, that local economies given the character of their local rulers will be better off with a greater foreign presence in national markets. Transnationals bring not only capital, technology, and management abilities, but also access to foreign markets for local exports and a counterbalance to rent extractions by local elites. It may also be more difficult for foreign firms to get away with exploitative practices since they are more likely to elicit emotionally powerful resistance where local employers engaging in similar practices do not, or at least not to anywhere near the same extent. In the long run, however, loss of national control makes it far more difficult for governments that decide to follow independent economic policies. Matters as always can be more complicated, as the case of Argentina's default in early 2002 illustrates. The biggest losers (aside from the Argentine people) were the foreign owned banks, utility companies, and other investors who had poured $40 billion into buying assets put on sale by that country's privatization drive of previous years during which Argentina was the poster child for GSEGI privatization policies.

It is not clear that bankruptcy-driven restructurings (when crises are widespread) restore confidence in a country's financial system. Bankruptcies may produce a cumulative deflationary cycle. It is a judgment call in individual situations. Unfortunately there are few neutral decisionmakers. In most countries such steps are not easily taken because the government is so profoundly compromised by long-standing connections and accommodating dealings with financial elites. Often they are one and the same. Under such conditions financial liberalization leading to foreign takeovers of domestic banking is not necessarily the worst solution to financial crises. It does, however, bring with it loss of control of a crucial, perhaps the crucial, sector of the economy. On another level, surrender to foreign control was to comply with pressures on local economies everywhere exercised through bond markets and demands by foreign investors for greater control. These demands impact on all countries whether of the poorest Third World nations or the affluent core.

Crisis in emergent market economies is typically the joint product of local and foreign greed. This is no less true in East Asia as it is in Russia or Latin America. In Thailand, for example, a Bangkok International Banking Facility (BIBF) was created in early 1991 to promote offshore transactions, so-called "out-out lending," which allow banks to borrow overseas and lend overseas so long as there is no connection to domestic transactions. Such facilities and their exemption from domestic banking regulation has a long history which in most cases shows the difficulty of keeping such foreign transactions from permeating local financial markets. In the case of Thailand, by early 1997 nearly two-thirds of all BIBF assets were "out-in lending," offshore borrowing by domestic companies (mostly short-term) and for speculation in local real estate and equity markets. Such lending typically went unhedged (that is, borrowing was in foreign currency liabilities unprotected against the possible decline in the value of the domestic currency). When the bubble burst Westerners, led by the United States Treasury and the IMF, did not blame risky lending and unfettered capital flows which were accepted as normal market operations but rather corrupt locals, the Asian model of development, and more broadly "crony capitalism."

In Asia, a focus on 'what was wrong with them' was not accepted. Rather their system had produced decades of the most rapid growth the world had seen. Financial liberalization, forced on Thailand and its neighbors by Western financiers, and the panicked withdrawal of funds were blamed. It was widely noted that the United States had prevented an Asian monetary scheme proposed by the Japanese which would have extended liquidity to address capital flight by offering loan assistance without the counterproductive conditionality of the IMF and the United States Treasury which prompted deep recession. Asians were not alone in seeing the depth of the disaster as a result of the coerced policy of a punishing austerity.

American policymakers forced the Japanese and other supporters of the proposal to withdraw the idea of extending liquidity to debtors. The United States saw an Asian run and controlled funding organization as undermining the necessary discipline it sought to assert over the economies of the region. Asians interpreted this as continuation of long-standing imperialist policy. As a report of a special study group on East Asia and the international system by the Trilateral Commission (Morrison, 2001: 4) characterized the situation, "Although much modified over the decades, the historical roots of the present system lie in the same state system responsible for colonial conquests, unequal treaties, and other forms of humiliation that remain potent memories in East Asia."

At the same time, the Asian system was and remains one which favors local elites subsidized by the state—where politics plays a major role in the outcome of bank failures and restoration is often achieved at great cost to taxpayers for the benefit of well connected owners, managers, and even borrowers, whose debt obligation is scaled back. It can be argued that a better approach is the Western bankruptcy model, in which an outside conservator offers a more dispassionate assessment of whether a troubled financial institution can be restored to health, placed in receivership to be merged with a stronger institution, or closed. The local citizenry, if it were able to influence decisions, might logically favor such an approach. The conservator's goal is to protect depositors, selected creditors, and the general public. The shareholders and managers come last, the reverse of the situation typically found when insolvency threatens under existing management. Institutions on the verge of insolvency need to be put under close supervision to prevent managers from taking even greater risks hoping to recoup losses. If these gambles fail they are not worse off (but the taxpayer will be on the hook for considerably more). The conservator often fires existing managers, closes branches, sells assets, and changes bank lending and other policies. The immediate task is to put the bank back on its feet, to restore solvency allow the restructured bank staff to operate effectively, pursuing profit opportunities in a prudent fashion. Western advisers may have favored such a model not only out of abstract commitment to efficiency but also because they stood to gain if it is adopted. The distressed assets would be sold at bargain prices and locals would be in no position to outbid foreign investors.

Addressing a Fund seminar on central banking, Stanley Fisher (1997b: 22–23) noted: "In the past ten years, well over half of the IMF's membership has experienced significant banking problems in one form or another. These crises have affected every region of the globe, and countries at every level of economic development. . . . Banking sector crises have been associated with economic slowdowns, higher fiscal burdens, higher inflation, and exchange rate crises." But the problems, from a Fund perspective, are caused by incompetence and errors by the banks in question and national level regulators who allow them to take dangerous risks. Mostly there has been a lack of transparency which prevents markets from judging situations accurately. With increased openness, he thought, markets will perform well and such crises will be minimized. The Fund supports "increasing openness in the world economy, greater economic liberalization, and greater market responsiveness" (1997b: 31). Others believe it is just such policies which have produced the crises.

Whether the relatively better performance of the United States in the second half of the 1990s and the problems elsewhere can be blamed on or credited to differences in banking systems is an open question. In Europe trust relations built up over years and the close ties of relationship banking have been put under strong pressure by mergers and even hostile bank takeovers. The practive of cross shareholding among banks, insurance companies, and industrial companies (in a system which depends on the close working together of an elite of fairly like minded managers mostly educated at the same schools and sharing a common culture) is under fire in the same way that in Japan a similar system (though embedded in a different cultural matrix) has been criticized as economic performance deteriorated there. These systems have also been more stakeholder oriented than the Anglo-American one. Workers, suppliers, and others are accorded protections unknown in the Anglo-American system. These statist policy regimes now appear inadequate in the face of the forces of financial globalization.

THE LOGIC OF FINANCIAL LIBERALIZATION VERSUS THE KEYNES-MINSKY PERSPECTIVE

Support for financial liberalization comes from what is known as the Fundamental Theorem of Welfare Economics, which tells us that the competitive market produces Pareto optimal equilibria combined with the Efficient Market Hypothesis (that financial markets use information efficiently). Support at the level of pure theory is reassuring for real world practitioners to the extent to which they believe its presumptions of perfect competition, a static economy with no externalities, monetary neutrality and so forth. If real markets do not work this way there may be a case for government intervention. Some market distortions may be stability and efficiency enhancing. Efficient market theory hardly predicted the likelihood of the numerous crises which have followed from the lack of regulation in an era of globalization of finance. In the real world there are both market failures and government failures. One needs to interpret the record and evaluate the proposals. Where contracts are long-term ones, for example wage contracts, or consumers are accustomed to certain product prices, proportional change may not be easy to achieve. Most importantly, because debt contracts are written in nominal terms, financial assets and real assets do not stay in sync as prices change. A growing group of political economists, many basing their thinking on Keynes's views on speculation and financial market instability and on the work of Hyman Minsky, discount the policy relevance of a presumed long-term monetary neutrality. They see financial markets as prone to crises because in the relevant short-run monetary neutrality does not apply. Minsky and economists thinking along similar lines explain crisis tendencies not only as the result of exogenous forces or of government policy errors (as mainstream finance theory typically does), but as the endogenous workings of the institutional arrangements of contemporary finance capitalism as well.

Keynes's famous remarks that speculators "may do no harm as bubbles on a steady stream of enterprise" but that "the position is serious when enterprise becomes the bubble on a whirlpool of speculation," and that when "the capital development of a country becomes a by-product of the activities of a casino, the job is likely to be ill-done" (Keynes, 1936: 158–59) have come back to haunt us at depressingly short intervals. In Keynes's understanding speculation is integral to the financial system, which means that even in the absence of implied government guarantees investors are inordinately influenced by short-term trends and so become overly optimistic in the upturn and, when the rate of growth slows, mass psychology changes producing disquiet, then panic, followed by sustained pessimism which prolongs the recession-depression just as naive optimism lengthens booms. In the context of the historical experiences of the 1920s and 1930s there was widespread although hardly universal acceptance of Keynes's views on the need to control short-term capital flows. As Ragnar Nurkse (1945: 8) wrote at the time of the Bretton Woods conference "There is now almost general agreement that, in the future, capital movements of this type [short term ones] had better be prevented, or at least curbed, by some form of control." To economists for whom an ordered rational system moves from one stable equilibrium to another such Keynes-talk of animal spirits and irrationally exuberant waves of overoptimism and overpessimism are congenitally distasteful. It was the reality of the Great Depression that made such heretical ideas temporarily acceptable, and even then most establishment economists demurred.

Gerhard Haberler speaks for many economists when he opined that the Great Depression was "not a crisis of capitalism," as Keynesians, Marxists, and others maintain, "but was a crisis of largely anticapitalist government policy, the consequences of horrendous policy mistakes" (Haberler, 1987). Many of those who agree would concur as well with Hayek's judgment of Keynes that "though his ideas seemed to constitute a revolution to the generation which they captivated, they will probably appear as no more than a passing phase in the history of economic thought" (Hayek, 1959: 238). Indeed, it came to pass that what is known as the Keynesian Revolution was undermined by a long postwar expansion during which pre-Keynesian orthodoxy in many forms (monetarism, supply side economics, the rational expectations, real business cycles, the New Classical Economics and the rest) have overwhelmed Keynesians and New Keynesians, although a spirited combat continues. This is not a debate we can revisit here, although I have discussed it elsewhere (Tabb, 1999).

I shall, however, pursue one aspect of the complex paradigm clashes in economics here, however: to examine not Keynesianism, but the ideas of John Maynard Keynes on the monetary economy, ideas which have not found a home in the writings of mainstream Keynesians. This does not mean that were Keynes alive today he would hold the exact views he held in his lifetime. Much liquidity has gone through the circular flow since Keynes wrote on such matters. Were he alive today, having been socialized into the present moment, he would respond contextually, so that what he wrote in a very different conjuncture cannot be read unambiguously. As Roy Harrod once remarked, "It would be most inappropriate for me to stand up here and tell you what Keynes would have thought. Goodness knows he would have thought something much cleverer than I can think of." It is therefore problematic to apply Keynes's economics (or Adam Smith's or Karl Marx's) to a new historical context. If economists of the rank of Harrod are hesitant surely it behooves the rest of us to be careful in making inferences (Harrod, 1974: 8; for a similar response see Pasinetti, 1983: 205). Nonetheless some economists have built on Keynes's ideas in ways which seem useful in their application to the current period.

Mainstream economists, as has been noted, believe in monetary neutrality, the idea that in the long run a change in the money supply will be matched by an equal change in the price level, so that the real money supply will be unchanged while other economic variables such as the interest rate and most important asset valuations will be unchanged in real terms. Therefore, in effect, nothing has changed. Monetary neutrality presumes, erroneously I believe, in the policy relevance of a perfectly competitive economy in which there are no long-term contracts and no participant is able to take advantage of, or will be disproportionately victimized by, changes in the price level. The problem in the real world however is that as the rush to hard cash proceeds, interest rates (the cost of money) rise, making it more expensive to carry assets funded with debt promises. An increase in perceived risk leads to a desire for the assurance of reduced leverage, for greater liquidity, and holding assets in hard currency. Assets must be liquidated when carrying charges cannot be met. The market value of assets falls relative to liabilities. For Minsky the critical element in explaining why financial instability occurs is the development over historical time of liability structures that cannot be validated by market-determined cash flow or asset values. It is exactly this instability which is made worse by the standard IMF conditionality (as was argued more fully in the last chapter). By forcing countries to devalue, the debt of businesses and the public sector becomes more expensive to carry since so much of it is denominated in foreign currency. Asset values for local firms are reduced and the economy sinks into stagnation.

Crisis is initiated by the very processes of capital inflow conventional analysis celebrates. Foreign funds undergird an expansion which produces the inevitable excesses of speculation in the presence of financial fragility to trigger disruption by seemingly transitory events; when banking systems are not strong enough, they do not evaluate risk well and tend to over-lend. Systemic fragility is the term Minsky uses to describe this weakness when the normal functioning of the economy reflects a shaky financial structure (Minsky, 1977). For Minsky, as for Keynes and for Marx, whenever something approaching stability is achieved, destabilizing processes are set off. Business cycles are endogenous, part of the way a money economy works. "Each stage, whether it be boom, crisis, debt-deflation, stagnation, or expansion, is transitory" (Minsky, 1986: 61). From a Keynes-Minsky perspective institutions can never create more than a conditional stability, a temporary order. They eliminate uncertainties and so produce overconfidence that the stability will last, which results in greater risk taking—unless governments effectively intervene. Market sentiment can inspire too much confidence and this reduces the caution which is required to prevent overextension. Capitalism is congenitally prone to periodic crises and so its nature means, as James Crotty (1994: 136) writes, that "The uncertainty-reducing institutions make the pursuit of permanently effective state control of the capitalist economy through traditional macropolicy perpetually illusive." What makes an economy work is an acceptable level of risk and specifically of debt/asset ratios.

As Keynes knew the economy is "a system of borrowing and lending based on margins of safety." It is important to grasp the generality of this proposition. We borrow against the future when we take out a car loan or a mortgage. We could lose our jobs and become overextended. We might have to move to a new job and sell our house in a falling market. Companies borrow to expand output or to finance a merger in the expectation that such actions will increase future profit flow sufficiently to pay back debt and leave a surplus. Because economic growth is not steady some of these expectations at times will not be fulfilled. Disappointments will grow for many economic actors at the same time because of market psychology accentuating cycles. Economies can and do experience waves of expansive optimism, collapse, and recession pessimism. Globalization, the increased role of information technology, and so forth produce a substantial degree of uncertainty, increasing some expected returns and devaluing other assets. Some individuals and particular businesses and communities gain. Others lose in a process of redistributional growth. Everyone in the modern world lives in a risk society.

Changed valuations of assets can radically modify debt/asset ratios reducing once secured loans to unviable propositions. Loans which seemed conservative can become bad loans under such circumstances. Consider the differences between sensible hedge financing in which the cash flow of an operation is used to meet payments on the one hand and risky speculation which comes about when an investor borrows presuming that cash flow will be sufficient not to pay off debt but to continue to refinance it on the other. By gaining control over more assets with borrowed funds it is possible that if these assets go up in value speculation will be successful. If the assets go down in value or do not rise sufficiently to cover borrowing costs the speculator will have to sell at a loss, dumping assets. If many investors do so at the same time values fall dramatically. This makes the position of other more conservative asset owners tenuous and some of them may be required to sell as well. Those with deep pockets are able to take advantage of such a market to buy at low prices. Something like this happened in many parts of the world in the second half of the twentieth century as financial crises led to bankruptcy and often to foreign firms, especially American transnationals, entering to gain control at bargain prices.

There is a third type of finance which Minsky calls Ponzi-style financing. It requires new borrowing to pay the interest on old debt. It works only if you can keep borrowing. Since finance costs are greater than income from assets in Ponzi-style finance, debt increases over time. Why then would someone engage in Ponzi-style financing? The reason is that one can control more assets using other people's money. If the value of such assets rise sufficiently, Ponzi-financing can turn into hedge financing. If not, it may still be possible to milk the assets under temporary control. Or it may turn out that foolishness is rewarded with a government bailout or IMF loans. Repayment is more likely in hedge financing than in speculative financing and is most questionable in Ponzi-style financing. However often it is not easy to tell which type of financing a particular loan will turn out to be. A transaction can start out as one and end up as another. Hedge funding can change to Ponzi-style financing if the economy turns down unexpectedly. This can provoke a general panic situation or what is called in German *torschlusspanik*—"door-shut-panic," one of those special-purpose compound German nouns signifying people crowding in a panicked fashion to get through the door before it shuts.

Minsky does not use the German term, but this relation of leverage to confidence and then panic is central to a Minskian understanding of financial cycles. An increase in confidence typically increases debt outstanding. The increase in confidence lessens the demand to maintain holdings of assets in the form of hard cash and so liquidity declines. Risk takers, inspiring more confidence that their credibility warrants, go further out on a limb. Speculative use of funds increases, returns are not matched in duration with growing short-term debt maturities, and so a downturn leaves individual investors, businesses, banks, and the financial system overextended and illiquid. At the first sign of a stalled expansion everyone rushes to the door, attempting to sell assets before they lose value, to transform assets to hard cash (which at the bottom they can use to repurchase assets at distress prices). Of course when it is *torschlusspanik* time everyone can hardly fit through the door at the same instant. Many are ruined with consequences felt more broadly.

Such an understanding of financial panics is hardly new. As Karl Marx, one of the pioneers of endogenous monetary theory wrote in Volume III of *Capital*, "In a system of production, where the entire continuity of the reproductive process rests on credit, a crisis must obviously occur—a tremendous rush for means of payment—when credit suddenly ceases and only cash payments have validity" (Marx, 1894: 490). Instability has existed under a wide variety of institutions and banking governance regulations and for as long as we have had financial markets so that one should not be too optimistic that reform is an easy proposition. It would be well to bear these thoughts in mind when we look at the efforts of the IMF and other GSEGIs to deal with financial crises. Most centrally such a view leads to rejection of the rational expectations stress in contemporary finance theory. Instead it takes account of the herd-like behavior of investors and addresses the cost to society when bubbles burst—as they inevitably do.

If enough loans turn bad because overextension produces asset devaluation the solvency of a bank or a banking system comes into question. To increase liquidity bank officials may be tempted, perhaps believing they have no choice, to attract funds by offering depositors extremely high rates of return. This is what happened for example during the U.S. Savings and Loan crisis in the 1980s. To increase returns S&Ls bought funds at high cost and invested in risky projects to earn the high returns necessary to pay for them. Insolvent banks have nothing to lose in pursuing such strategies. Many banks in developing countries have gone down this road. Once liabilities exceed assets (because the banks have lent to borrowers incapable or unwilling to repay obligations) banks must either sell off assets which are now worth far less and so take serious losses in order to gain needed liquidity or they must borrow at extremely high interest rates since the bank itself is now a risky borrower. As public confidence dries up there are major withdrawals. Since bank assets are in long-term loans and liabilities in short-run deposits such disintermediation makes them still more desperate for liquidity. Bank secrecy and asymmetric information mean such problems can develop before regulators have sufficient warning.

Greater reliance on debt fuels asset inflation in property and stock markets. Higher interest rates are produced to slow asset inflation which produces sudden contractions as over-leveraged borrowers are forced to liquidate assets. Countries that suffer from inflation and possible capital flight and raise interest rates to ward off their problems in so doing reduce investment in the real economy. To please financial markets countries bring on domestic recession. The Charybdis of the discipline of rentier governance and the Syllia of speculative bubbles constrain economic policymakers everywhere. Matters grew worse with financial liberalization because the size of speculative flows has increased so dramatically. "It is the ability to generate losses at a previously inconceivable rate," as Alan

Greenspan has noted, that has people worried. "It is probably fair to say that the very efficiency of global financial markets, engendered by the rapid proliferation of financial products, also has the capacity of transmitting mistakes at a far faster pace throughout the financial system in ways that were unknown a generation ago, and not even remotely imagined in the 19th century" (Greenspan, 1998: 249).

Once financial crises develop they affect the asset values of "good" companies as well as "bad" ones. Countries which otherwise would have had no problems can experience turmoil by contagion—by the effects of spreading investor panic. Such developments are analogous to the bank runs which at ten or twenty year intervals before the establishment of the Federal Reserve System swept the U.S. financial sector, producing devastation for farmers and business people tied to the credit and depository functions of banking. While some contemporary new classical economists suggest letting markets allocate resources freely, the case for regulation remains overwhelming. The problem is who regulates and how. This brings us back to state theory. Financiers dominate the regulatory process. Not only does the theory of regulatory capture explain the basic situation, but as globalization deepens and the possibilities of cross-border contagion impose potentially severe costs on citizens everywhere, the question of global governance institutions, their transparency, and their democratic accountability come to the fore.

Third World debt from the 1980s Latin American crisis (starting in August 1982 with Mexico's threatened default) through the East Asian financial crisis (initiated with Thailand's problems in summer of 1997) resulted from hedge borrowing moving into Ponzi financing territory complicated by the moral hazard created by the likelihood of GSEGI bailout. The necessary information was available. It was misinterpreted. Further it was presumed that IMF and U.S. Treasury lending would rescue reckless behavior on the part of banks and market speculators. Ironically, as advice to "just let the market do it" was given to developing economies, closer to home the Federal Reserve took steps on behalf of powerful American financial institutions which were diametrically opposite to those the United States was urging on debtor countries. The bailout of Long Term Capital Management arranged by the New York Fed was particularly embarrassing, giving rise to charges of Western-style crony capitalism from Asians who saw ostensibly public-sector regulators helping their friends in the private sector. This single hedge fund's exposure, exceeding a trillion dollars, meant bailing it out was considered by U.S. regulatory authorities the better part of discretion. Its collapse posed a threat, they said, to the world economy. Much of the money came from supposedly well regulated banks which would be in serious trouble in the event of default on these unsecured loans. It turned out that the sort of financial meltdowns experienced in Latin America and Asia could happen here. As to crony capitalism, the role of a former vice chairman of the Federal Reserve System working for LTCM as the firm's interface with leading financial institutions was particularly glaring. The Fed's call in the fall of 1998 for a quick cut in short-term interest rates, following an emergency meeting of the Fed's Open Market Committee by conference call, was widely seen as motivated in no small part by a desire to assist LTCM and other funds to unwind their positions. The IMF did not give foreign debtors such an opportunity.

LACK OF REGULATION AND RISK

In the United States, the President's Working Group on Financial Markets, the regulatory committee which studies the Long Term Capital Management episode, pointed out the need for all participants in the financial system and not only the banks and the hedge funds to face constraints on the amount of leverage they can assume. The weaknesses found in LTCM were evident in other market participants. Other highly leveraged Wall Street securities companies and financial industry participants were also betting with borrowed money. The top five investment banks they found had ratios of borrowed money to capital of 27: 1 The investment banks further used affiliated companies to carry on many high-risk operations, such as derivative trading; these affiliates went unregulated. The United States has declined to regulate or to design an international regime to regulate such offshore investment funds. President Bush's first Secretary of the Treasury, Paul O'Neill, was particularly hostile to such efforts.

The theory suggesting that greater spatial mobility of capital under the neoliberal regime should lower cost of capital and harmonize interest rates has proven false. Futures markets, which are supposed to protect against such risks, are themselves dominated by a momentum trading which acts like loose cannon balls on the deck of a ship as they slide from side to side destabilizing the vessel. Speculators see the trend and go with it, accelerating movements which lead to an overshooting and reversal which then takes on undesirable momentum overshooting in the opposite direction.

Interest rate volatility increases. Average real interest rates have risen to compensate for the higher risk resulting from this increased volatility.

Derivative markets are expanding because such convergence has not taken place. Instead interest rate uncertainty has increased, in large measure due to the way the derivative markets diffuse problems and encourage contagion, making macroeconomic stability an increasingly elusive goal for policymakers at the national level who are unable to insulate their capital markets from disturbances originating elsewhere. The dramatic increase in global liquidity makes their job far harder and many policymakers have found themselves incapable of positively influencing the economic situation of their countries. The dramatic increase in the amount of capital drawn to pure financial speculation and the high interest rates necessary to attempt protection of national economies from currency destabilization has reduced the supply of capital and increased its cost for productive investments in the nonfinancial economy. Financial liberalization is generally growth-distorting because it promotes new opportunities for directly unproductive profit seeking. By misallocating resources toward speculative activities with destabilizing effects, financial liberalization produces "speculation-led development," which is characterized by "a preponderance of risky investment practices, shaky financial structures, and ultimately by lower rates of real-sector growth than would otherwise prevail" (Grabel, 2003: 112).

In the 1980s, the U.S. Securities and Exchange Commission attempted to institute a requirement that all foreign financial institutions waive client confidentiality in return for the right to operate in United States markets but dropped the proposal under opposition from Swiss and other European banks as well as the Reagan Administration's Treasury Department, which argued that such a requirement would "constrain the free flow of investment capital across national borders" even though the IRS worried about the tens of billions of dollars moved offshore by tax evaders and other criminals using foreign secrecy laws as a shield. There have been increasing worries about the systematic risk such unregulated finance can unleash; yet political weight continues to favor further liberalization. This is the perspective shared by President Reagan's successors from Bush through Bush with only marginal differences in emphasis in the Clinton years.

By now both the pattern of overextension and collapse and an unwillingness to rein in the financial system should be clear. This does not mean however that the social costs of financial crises are not substantial, the danger of costly disruption ever present, and the eventual need for reregulation and a shift in the global financial regime inevitable. The problem is accentuated in developing market economies by the difficulties GSEGIs have in balancing efforts to manage systemic risks against the desire to have market participants bear the cost of imprudent risk taking. Regulators not wanting to be accused of inhibiting efficiency-enhancing risk-taking accept lax enforcement, which encourages socially costly risk taking. The supervisory and regulatory frameworks have not kept up to the evolution of financial market technological advances and product innovations. Certainly regulators do not know as much as the financial institutions about what the latter's exposures really are at any point in time. They lack the tools to encourage and enforce prudent behavior. The analytical frameworks within which regulators work were designed for simpler times and traditional banking activities, not to monitor the risks associated with derivatives and other off-balance sheet financial products which are now major profit vehicles.

National regulators are particularly handicapped by the transition to a globalized financial market in which they lack a total picture of what "their" institutions are doing in foreign markets. The rise of financial conglomerates compounds the problems and widens jurisdictional gaps. Regulators are loathe to tighten the rules in any case for fear that these institutions will simply do their business from a more friendly location. International regulation is impeded by collective action difficulties and the benefits of noncooperation which flow to less regulated markets. The greater openness of the world financial system occurs in the context of asymmetric dependence with the smaller, poorer economies far more influenced by consequences of the policies of leading economies than the reverse. Thus greater openness increases risk disproportionately for the weaker economies who have fewer resources to deal with their consequences. These economies in addition typically have weaker management capacities and less developed financial markets. It is hardly a wonder that financial liberalization has so frequently been followed by financial crises.

Forcing countries to allow capital flight and then to borrow in foreign currencies to pay for it is not, or should not be, the only permissible policy. The pain inflicted on the citizens of Latin America by the debt crisis and its aftermath were in good part avoidable (Felix, 1994). And these costs were severe. The crisis was preceded by the liberalization of their financial systems and followed by greater demands for further liberalization which in their weakened conditions were deemed unavoidable. The debtor countries could have proposed a comprehensive asset registry scheme and demanded creditor cooperation on penalty of unilateral suspension of debt service until an agreement was reached. For countries such as Argentina, Mexico, and Venezuela, each of which had a stock of private foreign assets about equal to its foreign debt in the 1980s, it would have been possible to avoid the massive austerity and the burden of public subsidies to the banks (Felix and Coskey, 1990). In the two world wars Britain required nationals to register their foreign securities with the Treasury which could sell them or use them as collateral with owners compensated in domestic currency. After World War II there was reparation of clandestine European flight capital as part of the Marshall Plan which included a clause requiring any government receiving Marshall Plan aid to "locate and identify and put into proper use" the foreign assets of its citizens (E. Heilleiner, 1994: 17).

For all of Latin America, government guaranteed bank loans rose from 40 percent in 1982 to 85 percent in 1987 with *ex post* guarantees adding $144 billion or 25 percent of the 1982 public foreign debt of the region. Creditor governments, primarily the United States, had in effect forced an adverse tradeoff on debtors: rollover of debt in exchange for *ex post* guarantees on private loans when they turned bad. As Felix (1994: 180) wrote, "Forcing an *ex post* change of contract terms in order to shift part of the burden to the debtors was a power play that violated both capitalistic moralizing about the inviolability of contracts and social norms of fairness." Economic weakness was intensified by forced devaluations following capital flight. Foreign creditors were bailed out at the expense of the citizens whose governments had not initiated what was basically private sector borrowing. The austerity measures such accommodations required further impoverished the masses. A steep decline in living standards was intensified by the high interest rates, rapid inflation, and greater dependence on foreign investment. The need to maintain an overvalued exchange rate was occasioned by the demands of foreign investors who were ready to flee with their hot money at the sign of a weakening currency. The massive devaluation of the peso in 1995 resulted in the virtual collapse of the Mexican private banks which set the terms for their availability for the foreign control which resulted over the next half dozen years. Mexican industry was crippled by the dramatic increase in interest rates to levels as high as 80 percent occasioned by the devaluation. Private debts to foreign creditors was assumed by the government as it had been in the earlier crisis round. Given this sequence of events foreign ownership of Mexican banking became both attractive and, given the constraints forced by the IMF and their neoliberal agenda, inevitable.

Multinational banks that physically operate in more than one country such as Citibank (with offices in more than ninety countries) do more than aid capital flight and money transfers more generally. As they gain significant market shares by attracting wealthy clients interested in their international services, local banks lose their biggest depositors and are less able to finance loans to local smaller and medium size businesses. The local banks must depend on smaller accounts for more of their deposits and these are more costly to service. The foreign banks also cherry pick borrowers leaving local banks to lend to lower quality customers. It is both more costly to process many smaller loans and typically more risky as well. It is true that the foreign banks bring modern operating systems which can be imitated by local competitors, but such information systems are costly and having lost their previously secure business with large depositors and borrowers they can ill afford such technologies. As a result of such pressures their ability to lend to local business is diminished. Less well capitalized than the foreign banks they may seek high profit margins through speculative activities contributing to the crises so prevalent in such countries (Weller, 2000 and 2001).

The so-called East Asian model, which relied on high debt ratios to finance growth, worked so long as expansion continued. The economic miracle Korean *chaebol* for example followed a growth strategy and ignored profit. So long as they could finance their dramatically high debt levels they borrowed to expand further using new assets as collateral for borrowing to purchase more assets. Kim Woo Choong, founder of Daewoo, Korea's second largest business group before its bankruptcy leaving $50 billion in debt, had been able to hold the country hostage while he bought auto factories from Poland to India to Uzbekistan in an effort to become one of the world's largest car and truck makers, borrowing to build despite poor returns on investments (Clifford, 1999: 56). Korea had grown faster than any other economy in recorded history over a decade and more by following just such a leveraged growth strategy. Were they wrong to do so? The difficulty is that when conditions change companies and governments lack the flexibility or perhaps willingness to adjust. Such questions therefore need to be considered in terms of Keynes's "animal spirits" and the business cycle. The case of Daewoo may be extreme but the Korean conglomerates are not alone in playing such high-risk games with debt. It may be said that regulators should not allow such practices given their inherent dangers when growth inevitably slows. But to say this is likely is to hope against historical experience.

At a deeper level, interpretations not only of Mexico's crisis, the Latin American debt crisis more broadly, the Asian crisis, and similar episodes over the last two or three decades underestimate the extent to which the problem is over-lending by foreign creditors. The mainstream literature critiques local institutions rather than the lenders from the North. Local citizens are forced to pay and debtor government sovereignty further eroded. Nor is it a secret that the rescues have not succeeded on their own terms. As a *Business Week* (1998: 113) Special Report sums up the testimony of academic experts: "To date, the IMF-led rescue plans for these nations do not appear to have worked. Unemployment and interest rates have soared, the value of their currencies has plummeted, and prosperity has turned into dislocation and riots. The flow of private funds into these countries has screeched to a halt." Of course these economies were to eventually grow again as the worst of the financial sector problems were to some extent addressed, but often only after the IMF policies were eased and reversed either because countries refused to accommodate further to them and the Fund relented under pressure.

The problem has grown to the point where it affects more than just developing countries. The many sided difficulties for regulators and the increasing systemic risk to the entire global financial structure are significant (Schinasi, Drees, and Lee, 1999; International Monetary Fund, 1998; and International Monetary Fund, 1999). The GSEGI demand for greater transparency is as noted earlier difficult to achieve in situations in which ownership of a private bank is essentially a means to extend credit to a favored circle. Comprehensive and effective regulation before unleashing the magic of the marketplace would theoretically have saved hundreds of billions of dollars. But this would have required a very different world view on the part of the Fund's leadership. It would not have been easy or perhaps possible given political realities.

The issues involved can be understood in the framework of the Mundell-Fleming model which demonstrates that governments, their economic policymakers, central bankers, and treasury officials cannot simultaneously maintain monetary policy independence, a stable exchange rate, and unrestricted capital movements. Two of the three are possible; not all three simultaneously. Free capital flows and stable exchange rates can be achieved by allowing interest rates to move in line with external pressures. It is possible by controlling capital movements to have exchange rate stability and to control domestic interest rates, and of course if exchange rates are allowed to adjust to market forces, and capital mobile, then monetary autonomy is possible. The Mundell-Fleming model tells us that under conditions of capital mobility governments must chose between macroeconomic policy autonomy and exchange rate stability but cannot have both (Mundell, 1963). Economists speak in terms of the "macroeconomic policy trilemma": "a desire to have fixed exchange rates to avoid instability; a desire to have free capital mobility, to ensure efficient allocation and permit smoothing; and a desire to engage in activist monetary policy to address domestic goals. As in all trilemmas only two of the three goals are obtainable at the same time. Free capital mobility has been the preferred goal, at least the preferred goal of the large private international financial institutions who benefit from such a policy. They have been influential in convincing regulators and other policymakers. For weaker economies it is however questionable whether even two of these goals can be satisfactorily achieved by most countries. The model assumes more autonomy in a globalized world economy than most nations have as well as price flexibility and factor mobility that their economies do not possess (as the studies we have cited show).

Fiscal policy, taxation and government spending, is also captive to international monetary pressures because flexible exchange rates and capital flows can make such policies ineffective. An open economy subservient to market forces reduces state economic policy independence and forces decisionmakers to adjust rather than to lead. If activism is attempted without capital controls and in the absence of an international governance structure which sets the terms of such movements, market pressures are likely to be destabilizing and regressively redistributional. Of course this too is a matter of degree. Public pressure on governments can be important in avoiding total capitulation to rule by what Keynes called "a parliament of banks." A "new financial architecture" could institute a very different governance structure but is unlikely without a severe global crisis. It is useful to return to Keynes's characterization of our economy as "a system of borrowing and lending based on margins of safety" as a frame of reference within which to consider conventions of acceptable risk and debt-asset ratios. The safety of emerging liability structures is subject to much dispute, but what it highlights is that investment is a financial phenomenon. In sensible investment, hedge financing employs cash flow from operations to meet payment commitments in the future. Risky speculation comes about when an investor borrows presuming that cash flow will be sufficient not to pay off debt, but to continually refinance it. This allows greater leverage and return on investment until the pendulum swings.

THE NEED FOR REGULATION

The foreign reserves the smaller countries are required to keep so they may have a cushion and discourage speculation against their currency comes at a substantial price. They typically need to borrow from commercial sources at high interest rates and then use these borrowed funds to purchase low-yield U.S. Treasury securities. The difference between what they pay and what they earn on such idle reserves is money they could spend on development needs if a global financial regime were in place able to reduce the excessive currency fluctuations the world has experienced in the wake of the breakdown of Bretton Woods and an inability or unwillingness of the major countries to establish an alternative stable system. One possibility would be, even in the absence of some arrangement to maintain a currency band within which major currencies would be held, not insisting on financial liberalization and allowing countries to control capital inflow and outflow could lend the system some stability in the opinion of some experts. This is a highly contested area. The use of the dollar as the reserve currency means that the United States keeps only the equivalent of one percent of its GDP in the form of foreign reserves compared to 14 percent or so for Asian economies and 7 percent for African countries. Because of the clout of the United States the dollar remains the international currency instead of some non-national medium of exchange such as Keynes's bankor or the greater use of SDRs, the Special Drawing Rights, which act as paper gold issued by the IMF. The United States also benefits from the fact that almost two-thirds of its currency circulates outside of its own borders, representing in effect an interest-free loan to the United States. Depending on the interest rate used in calculations this gift to the United States mostly from the poor and less stable economies is about equal to the foreign aid they get from Americans. And again, depending on the interest rate used in the calculation by having to hold these large dollar reserves which could be used for development purposes, these poor countries' growth rates are cut annually by a half a percent to two percent, a serious cost.

Rather than insist that nations have no choice but to submit to market forces no matter the domestic costs, it is more reasonable to argue that just as national markets came to be regulated as the periodic failures of banking systems compelled social supervision, so too, with the overwhelming dominance of global markets, a new regulation regime is needed. Global markets need to come under rules which will limit their disruptive capacity. From a regulationist perspective the growing financial fragility caused by the lack of international agreements or supranational authority adequate to the task. We can suspect that just as at the national level bankers and other financial elements profiting from the deregulated climate and fearing government regulation resisted such a development as long as they could (and moved to control as much of the regulatory machinery once its adaption became inevitable), so too on a global canvas we can expect both resistance and efforts at regulatory capture.

Financial conglomerates are subject to different regulators in their home countries who need to talk more in order to gain a better overview of the consolidated activities of transnational financial entities. Such changes require international cooperation between national bank, securities, and insurance industry regulators across national borders since firms do business on a global scale in ways which simultaneously concern these regulators. There is a question, as we saw in the last chapter, concerning who shall regulate the regulators and more generally how their goals and policies are shaped.

Preventing capital flight is difficult because there are numerous countries which stand ready to accept hot money when the rich feel it is time to move liquid wealth to safety. These range from small island states to New York and London. For a country like Switzerland with few natural resources its secrecy laws and willingness to accommodate have made it the third or fourth largest financial center in the world. Banks are not the only major player in the intermediation process. The growing role being played by securities firms, insurance and pension funds, and other nonbank financial institutions and the growth of the financial conglomerates have changed both the industry and the task of regulation at the national and transnational levels. The business of making money is remaking the world in many ways. Financial liberalization impacts domestic politics. As Haggard and Maxfield (1996: 37) explain: "Increasing interdependence increases the weight of domestic actors with foreign ties, expands the array of interests likely to benefit from and demand greater openness of financial markets, and thus tilts the balance of political forces in a more internationalist direction. Interdependence also implies greater political voice for foreign investors in the domestic policy process."

Home country control, the idea that it is the responsibility of each state to define and regulate their own financial institutions, is still the norm. The principle remains that every international bank is still accountable to a single national regulator. But this is hardly adequate. Host governments have taken a more active interest in foreign banks which can create domestic problems. Moreover, given the mergers in the EU, what happens when one of the new euro-behemoths gets into trouble? The European Central Bank, unlike the national regulators, has no decisive legal mandate to act as a lender of last resort. There is also the problem, as John Plender has noted (1999: 17) that "some governments will be spurring their banks into geographic expansion, while encouraging further exposure to the dangerous macho game of global investment banking." Meanwhile, increased competition will lead to a profit crunch: "the inevitable consequence of market liberalisation. Systemic risk will increase accordingly." While international cooperation is based on home country control there are increasing numbers of agreements and a deepening of efforts to jointly supervise the financial marketplace. If major economy banks refused to do business with any country which did not adopt and enforce global standards on capital movements these countries and their financial institutions would be brought under substantial control. Such a procedure was envisioned by the architects at the Bretton Woods. For countries seeking to attract foreign capital, financial liberalization is an attractive policy. The temptation for political leaders to liberalize can be overwhelming since the immediate impact is typically the inflow of foreign capital in quantity and a short term boom which can go on for some time even if the usual consequence is for the expansion to come to a precipitous end in crisis and capital flight. A rushed financial liberalization without proper safeguards (and there are almost never such safeguards in place since if done properly they can discourage speculative hot money and reduce the quick fix desired by almost all participants) generally comes to grief. While some mainstream economists consider financial and trade liberalization through the same optic it is best to examine each in quite different theoretical and empirical perspective. Before turning to a consideration of trade and investment (the topics of the next chapter) it is useful to comment on the importance for investors of defensive actions when they hold considerable assets in a currency under threat. They are driven to protect the value of their investments and so perforce everyone holding assets in any currency is forced to become a speculator. Foreign Direct Investment is about expected future real exchange rates rather than nominal rates in any case and so the connection between macro economic performance and investor decisions forces governments in their own policy making to think globally and act locally. If governments or investors ignore warning signs they invite possible losses so that finally it is not speculators who are "bad" if they are prescient in seeing future trends, even if sometimes their fears drive such changes or lead to herd overreaction. All players in a financial system which allows the sharp, sudden and uncontrolled currency movements play in a profoundly risk prone system. If the societal harm done by such destabilizing currency movements and financial crises are judged to be intolerable, solutions need to be found at the level of systemic reform.

CHAPTER NINE

Transnational Corporations and Trade Theory

"A country's foreign trade is something more than a number of dealings between individuals at home and abroad, it is the outcome the relations in which the industries that belong to her, that are a part of her life, and embody much of her character, stand to the industries of other countries. . . . And, when a country is growing in strength, a disproportionately large share of it is likely to belong to her export industries, and therefore to increase her trade: industrial leadership is thus reflected in foreign trade."

—Alfred Marshall (1923: 4, 16)

"superficial or apologetic analysts, in order to minimize exploitative aspects of the international economy, have merely assumed that 'modern' economies are 'interdependent.' By stating this platitude, they often forget that the important question is what forms that 'interdependency' takes."

—Fernando Henrique Cardoso and Enzo Faletto (1979: xxi)

For some time now the death of the state has been announced. The nation state was just through as an economic unit (Kindleberger 1969: 207). It was clear that there might be a problem. Raymond Vernon wrote, "multinational enterprises are not easily subjected to national policy" (1970: 373) and as trade barriers became less effective in the face of technological developments it was the state which would be in trouble, for multinational corporations unleash changes which "raise issues of sovereignty that may, in the end, dwarf the multinational problem" (Vernon, 1970: 399–400). There was increasing realization that it was not simply the projection of state power by the United States in the context of the Cold War which was shaping IR and global institutions, but also privately owned U.S.-based corporations, which were investing abroad and thus challenging local sovereignty in the economic and financial realms. In the 1980s and 1990s focus shifted to the Japanese challenge, to industrial policy, state-led development, and national competitiveness. The specter of deindustrialization and runaway plants framed the issue for many observers, especially industrial workers and their unions. Technological change in manufacturing was allowing more output with fewer workers. The issue of saving jobs was soon joined by attention to the new realities of lower wage, non-union service employment, the growth of temporary and contingent work which generally lacked benefits and job security. The growth of the service sector was changing the source of job creation in the advanced economies. Neither state theory nor trade theory explains development well.

Because trade models require drastically simplified assumptions in order to achieve their sweeping generality, political economists are able, by questioning the empirical validity of particular assumptions, to show how in real-world cases the model ignores central aspects of what is going on. For example, the model assumes all producers have access to the same technology and have the same production function. Specialization and trade result from different factor endowment. But in the real world most trade is intraindustry trade. The growth of interaindustry trade confounds neoclassical international trade theory, which presumes specialization based on resource endowment and predicts market conforming behavior in which individual countries specialize in line with given factor endowments. The neoclassical theory of production predicts convergence to one best practice organization of production within countries. Firms face the same price structures and have access to the same technologies. Indeed, those who will not, or because of information asymmetries cannot, conform will be driven from the marketplace. However learning curves, proprietary knowledge, team competencies, first comer advantages, economies of scope, innovative capacities, and scale effects would seem to undermine the generality of the simple price theory story as a guide to the real world of contemporary capitalism. The quantity of factors of production cannot be seen as some given amount abstracted from the uses to which they can be put at any particular time. Relative factor endowment and comparative cost are hardly given but are in a state of constant change depending on entrepreneurial ability and changing technological possibilities.

TRADE THEORY

Mainstream scientists, at least through David Ricardo, have understood economic science to deal with the idealized world based on avowedly

unrealistic assumptions, which nonetheless are considered to have powerful predictive capacity. Ricardo insists on the primacy of questions of principle over contextual facts. Pure theory explains outcomes in a deterministic fashion from a set of parsimonious assumptions. Mainline economists
of the heterodox persuasion have been receptive to Ricardo's friend and
interlocutor Thomas Malthus's criticism that such logic comes at the
expense of concrete analysis and favor verisimilitude of analytic assumptions (Tabb, 1999: chapter 4). Just as Adam Smith had maintained that it
was excessive fondness of simplicity that had led Descartes astray, so
Malthus criticized Ricardo. Ricardo's response was that Malthus had "the
immediate and temporary effects of particular changes" in mind, while he
fixed his "whole attention on the permanent state of things which will
result" from those changes.

In the Ricardian tradition the basic Heckscher-Ohlin trade model
assumes identical production functions in the same industry in all countries. Economists have maintained this assumption is realistic enough to
drive a powerfully predictive model. In the model the outflow of funds
from capital abundant nations raises its return within that country and
lowers it in the receiving nation. Similarly the labor abundant country is
made better off through trade that specializes in products using more
labor while labor in the labor scarce nation loses as production shifts to
capital intensive products. The predictions of the model are therefore that
capitalists in the capital rich core will gain from globalization and low-
skilled and semi-skilled workers in the wealthy countries will lose out. *If*
labor in the advanced economies can move to capital intensive industries
they will be better off. It is the assumptions of international factor immobility internationally and costless movement of factors among industries
domestically which imparts the trade optimism bias to the model. Neither
is acceptable in the contemporary global economy. Perhaps they never
were. As Marcello de Cecco (1984: 6) writing about the lack of applicability of the model notes: "We must, in other words, exclude from the model
the prime movers of modern economic history: great inventions, the differences in levels of development that have permitted colonisation, the
huge migrations of Europeans to the new continents, the massive exports
of investment capital to the new countries."

The theory suggests that countries are all better off accepting free trade
unilaterally. It explains the need for reciprocal treaties by reference to the
power of special interests to override the general good, for even if one
country discriminates it should still be in the interest of other countries to
trade freely. Countries which subsidize their exports simply give foreign

buyers a greater bargain. It is an irrational act from the viewpoint of pure trade theory. It is explainable however in that those who benefit from the export bounty have real gains even if their fellow citizens whose taxation finances the subsidy are the losers. (Rowley and Tollison, 1988). A more realistic estimate of transition costs and an acceptance of international factor mobility makes outcomes more uncertain than the pure trade model's confident assertion suggests. Ricardo in arguing for his preferred economic policies made little discrimination between reality and theory. He abstracted most importantly from the possibility that labor and capital are internationally mobile and that technology is not, but rather is proprietary, giving TNCs advantages whether they export or locate production abroad.

Nonetheless, Ricardo's strategy has proven politically effective. It enables the claim of scientific analysis for views which are not in fact proven in the real-world instance but implied to be correct from the limited abstract model. Many contemporary economists use the same gambit and are in sympathy with Ricardo's claim that his laws and tendencies, as he wrote Malthus, "are as certain as the law of gravity." Ricardo assumed that the features of his idealized case were the main ones in the real world. He dealt in such idealized models and did not confront the validity of the implied realism while using the conclusions as a basis for policy advice. So far as the characteristics of the actual world are supposed to be those described by the model, any departures were seen as 'temporary and accidental.' Today, economists who write in favor of the undoubted benefits of free markets and deregulation adopt this strategy to equally favorable effect.

Ricardo's theory of international trade is still the basis of modern mainstream thinking. His abstraction technique considers international trade from the vantage point of two nations existing at first in isolation from each other. This is a methodological instance of a wider epistemology of attempting to understand the nature of economic actors by examining them as autonomous atomistic units, existing separately from each other, who then come together from their states of isolation to interact. Without any consideration of the nature of each country's actual relation to the rest of the world (are they a colonial power? a target of imperial ambition? a landlocked country at the mercy of those who control access to the sea?), or investigation of the domestic politics and social structure of the country (a democracy? a dictatorship in which a small elite manipulates matters for narrow ends?), such a model by assuming two equal participants exchanging freely to mutual advantage is able to make generalizations which misrepresent the situation of the actual historical experience of most exchange relations among territories over human history.

The archetypal trade theorist assumes a free trade norm and declares interference of tariffs, subsidies, or lack of national treatment as interferences. But the system to the extent "free" trade existed was created by powerful state actors forcing their will on others. Even in the classic Ricardian example coercion played its part. As Joan Robinson noted, the real impact on Portugal of free trade with England was that " . . . the imposition of free trade on Portugal killed off a promising textile industry and left her with a slow-growing export market for wine, while for England, exports of cotton cloth led to accumulation, mechanization and the whole spiraling growth of the industrial revolution" (Robinson, 1978: 103). As she explains, "Free trade for *others* is in the interests of the strongest competitor in world markets, and a sufficiently strong competitor has no need for protection at home. Free trade doctrine, in practice, is a more subtle form of Mercantilism." (Robinson, 1977: 1336) It is not just the strongest competitor nations which want an open trading system but also the transnational firms which believe they have secure advantage over less competitive national firms.

To presume factors of production, labor, and capital, as somehow homogeneous and differing on quantity but not qualitatively as in the pure theory is to stay in the realm of an abstracted blackboard economics. To presume that twenty-first century international trade should now be theorized as occurring between equal entities called nation states rather than preeminently within transnational corporations and their affiliates is another questionable choice. More and more trade involves vertical specialization, when a producer uses imported intermediate parts to produce goods which it may later export rather than horizontal specialization wherein countries trade goods made from start to finish in one country. Perhaps half of all US-Mexican trade is vertical trade (Hummels, Rapoport and Yi, 1998). Company advantages lie in a firm's specific competencies. This may be a matter of patented technique, brand name, distributional networks, and after sale service capacity. Business school theorists stress the core competency of organizations and the specific skills of their employees as an ensemble. Such an approach allows economists to theorize multinationals, multiplant economies, and the gains from trade in different fashion (Markusen, 1984). An evolving literature on strategic trade theory (Helpman and Krugman, 1985) demonstrates that under conditions of imperfect competition, technological externalities and increasing returns free trade is not necessarily the best policy (Tyson, 1992: 3).

Something of a civil conflict has been taking place among trade theorists concerning the sources of comparative advantage (Leamer, 1984). By "relaxing," or better, reversing the usual neoclassical trade assumptions—presuming oligopolistic competition not perfect competition, increasing returns rather than constant returns, factor mobility internationally rather than total immobility, that technological capacities differ rather than all market entrants and potential entrants have access to the same technologies at no cost to recipients—it is possible to gain purchase on real-world trade and policy options in the age of globalization (Krugman, 1993; Brander, 1993). Basic concepts such as capital abundance are being rethought in the light of the United States attracting huge amounts of capital, despite supposedly having a strong comparative advantage in possessing abundant capital. The very notion of capital itself has always been problematic. In a world with high R&D costs, substantial learning economies, supernormal profits can be routine for many transnationals acting as discriminating monopolists earning temporary economic rents which can be renewed through continuous innovation. Empirical evidence does not appear to be consistent with the use of identical techniques of production worldwide, or even within groups of relatively homogeneous countries such as the European Union. As a result recognition of the importance of intra-industry exchange and the study of country-specific technological developments becomes important for understanding international trade. As Helpman (1999: 136) writes, "In the new economy there is plenty of man made comparative advantage and product cycles." Examples abound from developmental states in East Asia to the Third Italy.

Consider the instance of the growth of software production in Bangalore, the Silicon Valley of India. It was Bangalore's location, away from India's borders, which led the new post-independence government to establish a national defense laboratory there. It attracted other private research facilities. From the concentration in electronics and aeronautics industries came the development of computers and information technology. The Indian educational system and English law and language are also factors. In the mid-1980s India eased regulations on ownership for export-oriented firms and offered investment incentives to attract foreign software firms, including government provided office space and infrastructure. India was one of the first developing countries which granted software copyright protection to encourage foreign investment and collaboration with local software firms. A review of the case of Bangalore and similar growth poles suggests that the distribution of jobs worldwide is hardly an outcome of some natural process or given factor endowment but the result of an institutional process involving historical, political, and cultural factors of which resource supply conventionally understood is only one component (Champlin and Olson, 1999).

In moving beyond Heckscher-Ohlin-Samuelson models in which mutually beneficial trade is driven by different factor endowment proportions to constructing models reflecting contemporary trade patterns economists are focusing on financial markets and trade driven by differences in "knowledge" between countries. Such models suggest North-North trade and financial markets, as opposed to North-South trade and product markets are important components of the explanation of accelerating technological change, intraindustry skill upgrading, and rising wage inequality in advanced and developing countries (Dinopoulos and Seegerstrom, 1999). Trade policies which promise liberalization and greater efficiency can and typically do promote inequality as well. It is said that public policy can address such social costs. But this rarely occurs. Redistributional measures are becoming not only less important within countries but are rare between them as well (the EU is a partial exception). Those who may lose out knowing this resist the liberalization efforts.

Mainstream trade theorists suggest an open trading system respecting equal rights of all participants is more globally efficient, produces increased output and welfare, and is an optimal arrangement. The new rules are thus best for everyone. Ronald Reagan's famous "magic of the marketplace" opening speech to the annual IMF-WB meeting in September 1981 in which the American president most forcefully responded to Third World demands for developmental assistance is one of the most powerful presentations of these ideas. The U.S. position enunciated by President Reagan and still at the core of the American negotiating stance, however, confused uniform and universal rules. The entire "level playing field" norm imposes "an equal treatment of unequals" principle of justice. From the perspective of the weak a general rule commanding such a level playing field is unjust. It is one thing to say that in order to prevent partiality rules have to be universal. But this does not mean they should be uniform. They should pay attention to the varying characteristics and circumstances of different countries. Rules, in this view, to be fair to all players need to differentiate rights and responsibilities according to circumstance. In this vein, the World Bank has pointed out the high cost of liberalization for developing countries with weak or nonexistent safety nets. As Joseph Stiglitz (1999: 4) argues "provisions that look fair on the surface may have very different and unequal consequences for the developed and less developed countries. Accordingly, the power imbalances at the bargaining table are exacerbated by the imbalance of consequences."

Moving workers from a low productivity sector to unemployment does not increase output. In the actual world of high unemployment and underemployment in developing countries the greater efficiency of core producers results in a loss of social welfare in the developing markets which liberalize too rapidly and are unable to make accommodations for displaced workers.

TRANSNATIONAL CORPORATIONS AND THE STATE

Susan Strange in a 1991 essay noted that the role of transnational corporations (TNCs) was still no more than an addendum, "a kind of appendage to the main body of the subject" in textbooks and courses in international relations. She thought this quite wrong. The larger problem in her view was that, in their concern with the relations between states, theorists unnecessarily and counterproductively did not pay sufficient attention to the exercise of market power in the international political economy. "Big business is a big actor; its role central, not peripheral" (Strange, 1991: 245). There was also a problem in the tools with which political scientists examined TNCs. Having no conceptual schema to talk about nonstate actors outside the formal political process, how could IR understand TNCs or the complex nature of the ipe? As I see it part of the problem is again in the intellectual division of labor. A holistic IPE needs to follow the logic of corporate evolution in the era of globalization and trace its political implications. Discussions of the growth of the transnational corporation and the theory of international trade stand in distant relation. The TNC is being theorized in terms of transaction cost analysis with almost no intersection with mainstream trade theory which has not (until very recently) had much room for the factors which have produced the TNCs—increasing returns, economies of scope, market power, and state policy. In the remainder of this chapter the evolution and significance of TNCs will be discussed. The next chapter deals with the manner in which an international trade regime developed from the end of World War II.

The multinationals which emerged at the end of the nineteenth century and beginning of the twentieth transformed not only international trade but also the relationship between private business enterprises and public institutions. They were based on technological changes in metallurgy, mechanical engineering, chemistry, and electrical generation. Most important were those which affected transportation and communication:

the railroad, steamship, cable, and telegraph which so profoundly revolutionized mass production as well as distribution in ways so far-reaching that the era has been called a second industrial revolution. The resultant reorganization of the corporation was momentous. Writing of that second industrial revolution Alfred Chandler noted that "Of paramount importance were the innovations in the compilation, collation, and communication of business and industrial information" (Chandler, 1986: 442). His emphasis offers important perspective on the claim of the unique organizing capacities of the Information Revolution and the Knowledge Economy a century later. It was of that period a hundred years ago that Chandler reminds us: "scale is only a technological characteristic. The economies of scale, measured by throughput, require organizational input. Such economies depend on knowledge, skills and teamwork on the human organization essential to exploit the potential of technological processes" (Chandler, 1986: 413). Mass production, standardization, an extensive division of labor under one roof, the many layered management pyramids, and sharp line between transactions in markets and within companies were all characteristic of the Fordist Model that defined industrialism and marked its departures from earlier craft production and family enterprise.

This is not to say that a newer New Economy had not put in an appearance by the end of the twentieth century. As late as 1973 almost two-thirds of large industrial corporations in the world were clustered in food, chemicals, oil, machinery, and primary metals. In the United States, which dominated the listing of the world's largest corporations in that year, the same corporations which had dominated throughout the twentieth century still topped the chart (Chandler, 1986: 411, Table 13.2). The organizational structure of early twentieth century was still evident into the 1970s when one in five American industrial workers was employed by a Fortune 500 company. By century's end the ratio had dropped to less than one in ten as transnationals shed direct employees and used the labor of subcontractors and strategic partners, existing as the core of a global network thanks to advances in communications, transportation, and managerial capacity to supervise flexibly at a distance. Companies like Nike and Mattel control their brand while their running shoes and toys are produced by subcontractors around the world. Simple integration in which companies contract out routine production to sites in low-cost Third World venues in a product cycle mode (Vernon, 1961) was giving way to complex integration in which firms located activities according to the logic of the world market and dispersed decision making as well. Whereas simple integration maintained a Fordist command and control logic complex integration's organization chart is flatter and networked.

A third scientific revolution has been claimed for the end of the twentieth and start of the twenty-first century in which the computer and information processing and telecommunication more generally have allowed innovations in finance, production, and distribution which impact across the global economy, shrinking distance and compressing time. Technology empowered new organizational forms and corporate entities have succeeded by taking better organization further than it had gone before. Benetton and Wal-Mart's close integration of point-of-sale computer scanning and factory restocking changed the face of retail. Small batch production and multi-product factories which can shift lines swiftly are part of the new customer driven best practice firm. FedEx created revolutionary overnight delivery and then self-monitoring of shipments by customers. Such innovations allow manufacturers and retailers to be more attuned to and respond more speedily to shifting consumer tastes. Inventory levels can be kept low.

Much is made of the scale economies of production which characterized industrialism and set Fordist organization apart from the earlier craft-based model. Now the economist's stylized story of production cost, the "U" shaped cost curve by which the growth process is constrained by diminishing returns, gives way to the prospect of increasing returns to winner take all successful initiators. Knowledge and organization economies of scope (not simply of scale) allow a process of endogenous growth. Additions to knowledge, organizational capacities, focusing on new uses of core competencies all allow firms to become more profitable using the same or fewer material resources. Knowledge based economies grow faster from such increases in productivity, limited to be sure by the social relations of the society's ability to make use of potential output. Innovations are cloned and spread through the global economy at low marginal cost since once ideas are available they are easily replicated. Because adjustment in real markets take time, and shocks occur so that the system is never in equilibrium, temporary rents from innovations can be a continuous source of profit and growth. Firms defend their intellectual property as proprietary knowledge (as shall be discussed in the next chapter). The United States, with so much at stake in this area, was tireless in involving the WTO centrally in this task. American trade negotiators have been sensitive to the demands of economic interests in those sectors in which the United States has particular competitive advantage, especially in industries where there are important learning curve economies. The U.S.

power to set the trade agenda has meant that its leading exporters and rapidly growing sectors with a interest in expanding trade opportunities take precedence over the concerns of developing nations at the WTO. The rush to set up new trade rules reinforce and expand this advantage and are designed to preclude catchup on terms which would be favorable to the less developed economies.

Early discussion of transnational corporations in the contemporary period typically misspecified the nature of their contribution to host country development. The initial framework was one in which multinational corporations brought capital to poor countries which had low savings rates. Yet it was not, as economic theory at the time suggested, that these economies primarily needed capital. The domestic saving rate was often not the issue. The problem was its productive use. It took theorists a while to get beyond the belief that foreign direct investment is important because it brings "capital" (in the sense of funding). Its contribution is now understood to be in the package of competition-enhancing resources including such managerial and technical inputs as product design, quality control, and marketing skills. The transnational corporation's advantage is in technical quality, brand name, and ability to mass market based on product differentiation. Bringing these capacities to the developing economies led not only to increased production there for local sales, but also to a new export strategy made possible and reinforced by falling transportation costs. By 1995 multinational sales outside the home country were growing 20 to 30 percent faster than exports. Worldwide foreign direct investment was increasing three times as fast as total investment.

The continued growth of transnational capital could seem inevitable, but not always at all to the good. On the positive side, foreign investment can bring new and desired products and be an important agent of the transfer of managerial and technological knowhow. On the negative side, such a development concentrates economic and so political power, while the oligopolistic control and growing intrusion of external economic regulation necessary to protect investor rights compromises what remains of national sovereignty and in general leads to policies favoring capital over labor. The impact of TNCs on local producers and net employment could be devastating, producing displacement which would not be tolerated if it were the result of government policy in any wealthy democracy. It could, as already noted, bring with it asset bubbles and inflation followed by capital flight and economic collapse.

Often a distinction is made: while uncontrolled short-term capital movements are harmful to smaller economies that are unable to protect the value of their currency and are destabilized by the overwhelming impacts of short-term capital inflows and outflows, long-term foreign direct investment and an outward oriented export strategy are of unambiguous benefit. In such a light the growth of exports of developing economies in the final decades of the twentieth century to the point where they accounted for almost a third of world merchandise trade, and that manufactures made up 70 percent of developing country exports (and in some product categories made up half or more of world exports), was a sure sign that many developing countries had succeeded in moving into technology intensive export manufacturing. However with the exception of a few East Asian economies developing-country exports are still concentrated on products derived from exploitation of natural resources and the use of unskilled labor with no movement toward higher value added production necessary to raise living standards and provide long-term development. The statistics available at the start of the twenty-first century show that assertions of considerable expansion of technology-intensive, high-value-added exports from developing countries are misleading. This is because these countries are often involved in the low-skilled assembly stages of the international division of labor organized by TNCs in which most of the value added accrues to the corporations in the advanced countries.

The neoliberal policy logic which focuses on increasing the share of exports to GDP has reoriented development away from production for the local market and has successfully presented the earlier focus on import substitution industrialization, as practiced successfully in the previous two decades and more in Latin America, as a total failure. This too is a misrepresentation of the causes of the Latin American debt crisis of the 1980s which was the result of faulty macroeconomic policies and not industrial strategy. As a strategy for industrialization, import substitution worked well in a broad range of countries which experienced unprecedented rates of economic growth during the postwar period until the mid-1970s (Rodrik, 1999b: table 4.2). Why did things go differently after 1973? The problem was not the "exhaustion" of the model but the two major oil shocks, the abandonment of the Bretton Woods system, the Volcker interest rate shock of the early 1980s, and other contingent factors and the response of countries to them, as Dani Rodrik points out. "The actual story is straightforward. The proximate reason for the economic collapse was the inability to adjust macroeconomic policies appropriately in the wake of these external shocks." He explains that macroeconomic maladjustment gave rise to a range of syndromes associated with macroeconomic instability from high or repressed inflation to external payments imbalances and debt crises. "The culprits were poor monetary and fiscal policies and inadequate adjustments in exchange-rate policy, sometimes aggravated by shortsighted policies of creditors and the Bretton Woods institutions. Trade and industrial policies had very little to do with bringing on the crisis" (Rodrik, 2000: 7).

If import substitution industrialization did not fail the willingness to read the evidence to claim that only manufacturing export orientation can bring growth is equally false. As UNCTAD (2001: v) reports: "while the share of developing countries in world manufacturing exports, including those of rapidly growing high-tech products, has been expanding rapidly, the income earned from such activities by these countries does not appear to share in this dynamism." Although developed countries now have a lower share in world manufacturing exports, they have actually increased their share of world manufacturing value added over this period (from 1980 to 2000) "Developing countries, by contrast, have achieved a steeply rising ratio of manufacturing value added to GDP, but without a significant upward trend in the ratio of manufacturing value added to GDP. Accordingly, the increase in the share of developing countries in world manufacturing exports has not been accompanied by concomitant increases in their share of world manufacturing value added, and in several countries the two ratios have tended to move in opposite directions." The UNCTAD report concludes few of the countries that pursued rapid liberalization of trade and investment and experienced a rapid growth in manufacturing exports achieved a significant increase in their share in world manufacturing income over the last decades of the twentieth century (UNCTAD, 2001: v). As UNCTAD's Richard Kozul-Wright said in presenting the report, "We have seen a decoupling of the trade engine from the growth engine in developing countries over the last two decades." Mr. Kozul-Wright said it was time for the international community to abandon its 20-year "fixation with liberalization." Yet in this view, by opening up their markets developing countries have witnessed an exit route from poverty, and will continue to do so (Stewart, 2002).

The mainstream economics story can be seen to have a certain bias in favor of interpretations which see free market solutions and liberalized trade and investment as inevitably the best policy. Under the slogan "trade not aid" per capita assistance to the developing world was cut by a third in the 1990s. Developing countries liberalized their economies only to be faced with protected or restricted markets in the richer countries which were especially resistant to accepting agricultural and textile imports, product areas in which developing countries had comparative advantage.

When those affected raise concerns about job loss they receive the reply that markets create jobs and resources released from the protected sectors can be redeployed productively elsewhere. But all too often, "the jobs do not appear quickly enough for those who have been displaced; and all to often, the displaced workers have no resources to buffer themselves, nor is there a public safety net to catch them as they fall. These are genuine concerns," Joseph Stiglitz (1998: 2–3) writes. He goes on to ask rhetorically "What are developing countries to make of the rhetoric in favor of rapid liberalization, when rich countries—countries with full employment and strong safety nets—argue that they need to impose restrictive measures to help those adversely affected by trade? Or when the rich countries play down the political pressures within developing countries—insisting that their polities "face up to the hard choices," "but at the same time excuse their own trade barriers and agricultural subsidies by citing 'political pressures'?"

The world-wide mergers and acquisition wave on a global scale as the twentieth century became the twenty-first suggested that growing market concentration is and may be to a greater extent in the future abused and require regulation in the interests of workers, consumers and the public interest more broadly. GSEGIs have hardly been in the forefront of considering the need for such regulation. In the immediate postwar years the Japanese and Western Europeans preferred cartel-like arrangements, as they had through the twentieth century and even earlier. The strategy continued in the postwar years in the form of support for national champions who were helped to "bulk up" by Western European states to better compete with U.S.-based TNCs. Similarly a particular competitiveness strategy of state-led growth through administrative guidance which was pioneered by Japan offered another alternative to accepting open markets and foreign (U.S.) domination. The postwar period, as we saw in chapter 5, was widely based on such economic nationalist premises. Globalization has made such strategies difficult to pursue. Cross-border mergers are undermining the possibility of nationalist development along such postwar lines and the thrust of international agreements on trade and investment has been almost uniformly to extend TNC freedom to operate with fewer impediments globally. It is the freedom of sovereign states to regulate economic activity which has been restricted.

Oligopolizing the global economy is a complicated process. It encompasses efforts by new producers to seize markets from more established but less nimble and higher cost rivals. Thus East Asia in terms of biotechnologies may surprise the more established firms, Scandinavia in terms of multimedia wireless, or specialty high end and higher margin multimedia chip production in Taiwan and Singapore, upset the existing dominant firms in the industry. The transition from the possibilities of nationalist economic development to the open market demanded by globalization is reflected in the way corporate reorganization and the international trade regime changed over the last half of the twentieth century. Just as at the beginning of that century the young automobile industry at the national level underwent shake out and mergers, so at the start of the twenty-first century we witness the mega mergers such as that of Chrysler and Daimler-Benz (which has also acquired an influential stake in Japan's Mitsubishi Motors and of Fiat, the major Italian auto producer). There is also the beginnings of the formation of a transnational capitalist class with the interpenetration of ownership, global stockholding, and international management teams running corporations. When Sweden's ASEA and Switzerland's Brown-Boveri merged to form ABB, its headquarters moved to the heart of Europe, Zurich, where the German, Swiss, and Swedish managers do business in English and the books are kept in dollars. At the same time ABB calls its international organization "multi-domestic," meaning they strive to be a local company everywhere in the world they operate. The company is not alone in striving for a global organization without national bias. Because of the dramatic shifts such developments can cause in employment patterns, government revenues, and social service obligations, what transnational capital does is of central political interest to governments.

John Dunning (1997b: 13) has remarked that a typical global firm "will own or control subsidiaries, and engage in value-added business alliances and networks in each continent and in every major country. It will source its inputs of manpower, capital, raw materials and intermediate products from wherever it is best to do so, and will sell its goods and services in each of the main markets of the world." In doing so the TNC diversifies risk. If business in one market is off it can rely on sales elsewhere. When it has a winner it can introduce a product globally more quickly to accrue economic rents before competitors can bring out similar ones. It enjoys economies of scale. It can absorb the costs of R&D, distributing them over a larger sales base. It can subcontract globally. One indication of the importance of such linkages is 2000 United Nations *World Investment Report* data showing 70 percent of all international royalty payments between parent firms and foreign affiliates.

TNC advantages include brand reputation. Interbrand, a division of a large U.S.-based advertising group, has established the brand value based on net present value of future profits separating this return from return to physical and intellectual assets (such as patents, skills, and distribution systems). It found the Coca-Cola brand to be worth $84 billion at the end of the twentieth century. Coke's brand represented 60 percent of the company's market value by this calculation "more than its offices, manufacturing plants and all other assets combined" (Tomkins, 1999: 12). The advantage of size in expanding market power of TNCs is increasing, leading to a new wave of mergers and acquisitions. By the end of the 1990s there were clear signs that waves of mergers were recasting the face of business not only in the United States (Wayne, 1998) but globally (Lewis, 1997). Editorials began to appear in the financial press warning of the dangers of global monopolization (*Business Week*, 1997).

A transnational corporation benefits from getting a broad customer base. TNCs market a new product to a great number of consumers at the same time in many different countries. Success can create network effects where because technology is cutting edge it comes into wide use. Because others choose the same telecommunications system, software, or recording format it becomes sensible for still others to do so in order to better interact. Companies benefit from the advantage of the choices the larger market makes within the framework of a proprietary system. Thus being first in supplying network products is an important source of increasing returns. Once IBM accepted Microsoft's DOS system it became the industry standard. The more computers which used it (as with Windows), the more attractive it became for software writers to work with and for other programs to accommodate to it. The famous example illustrating this power of networks is Sony's Beta format losing out to the technically less desirable VHS for video recording, because the later offered more choice of movies; and once this advantage was perceived it became a self-reinforcing cycle which drove Beta from the market. Once Ticketmaster reached a certain scale, consumers in the United States had to pay its high service charges since the company had exclusive contracts to distribute desirable hot tickets. The rock group Pearl Jam tried unsuccessfully to mount a national tour without Ticketmaster's services. It could not be done without substantial financial loss. Fans simply have to pay the service charge as determined by Ticketmaster. For a large media conglomerate like Time-Warner or Disney being the company which provides the film, the CD of the sound track, the book, and related merchandise (perhaps sold in an own-brand chain of stores) and which then spins off a TV series, video game, or amusement park ride offers synergies which translate into a fatter bottom line.

TNCs bring exposure to best practice productivity enhancing processes and it is this indirect effect of trade and foreign direct investment which is perhaps even more significant then the direct effect (Baily and Gersbach, 1995). Thus a welcoming attitude toward TNCs has spillover effects for local producers. TNCs provide employment. In a dynamic sense it can be more useful to attract foreign owned firms which will be globally competitive than to try and protect existing jobs with less efficient local producers. It is a better policy to upgrade the skills of the country's workers in order to attract and hold high-waged jobs than to subsidize locally owned corporations which may grow but by increasing jobs elsewhere (Reich, 1990).

Strategic alliances can be a related source of market power for TNCs. For example McDonald's, Coca Cola, and Disney, the world's top three brands, are linked by a web of exclusive business arrangements based on film product tie-ins. McDonald's had acted to form such arrangements after watching the success Burger King had linking itself to Disney's *Toy Story, Lion King, Aladdin, and Beauty and the Beast*. Starbucks, the biggest American coffee chain, has stores inside Barnes and Noble, the country's biggest book seller. Alliances were estimated in 1998 to account for 18 percent of the revenues of America's biggest corporations (*Economist*, 1998). Hotels form strategic global networks, as do airlines through network partners to service global fliers with a seamless reservation, purchase, and frequent flier system. In the early twenty-first century corporate power assumed a centrality as mergers and acquisitions produced global oligopolies. In oligopolistic industries companies find they have to become global themselves or be part of a global alliance to defend home markets.

By the early 1990s about a third of total world trade was intra-firm. By 1993 UNCTAD reported that sales by companies' foreign affiliates were $5.2 trillion compared to the total value of all exports of goods and non-factor services of only $4.8 trillion (United Nations Conference on Trade and Development, 1994). Further, since so much trade is contracted between suppliers and brand name sellers, the reorganization of trade by TNCs (not the sort of arm's length market exchange stressed by classic trade theory) dominated late twentieth-century capitalism. Much of the production of the newly industrializing economies involves long term relational contracting and manufacturing to specification, tightly monitored and representing a form of dominance not so different in impact from direct ownership (although with cost savings to the dominant partner who leaves the consequences of sudden market shifts and other uncertainties to the supplier). Indeed, the extent to which local owners keep costs down, a version of franchise production seems preferable as far as risk and production cost minimization strategies for the TNCs concerned. Where local presence has important advantages and proprietary knowledge is judged best protected, or where comparative advantage is not easily transferable, actual ownership is preferable. Shopping via the Internet and express delivery services redefine these relationships even more dramatically, making traditional trade theory less relevant.

In time for the new millennium plans were made in the waning months of the twentieth century by a consortium of financial products firms to produce the world's first index of multinational businesses on the basis that investors saw companies like BP-Amoco and Daimler-Chrysler as having more in common with fellow global companies than with most other UK or German stocks. The identification of 200 global companies which derived more than half their sales from overseas markets and noting that the performance of such companies often had little in common with that of national firms in the local economy suggested a need for a trading platform which would match the investment horizons of globally conscious investors (Martinson, 1999). A more prosaic indicator of the impact of globalization is found in the extent of grey market reselling in which say a German auto dealer buys his German cars not from the company but from other dealers, perhaps in Spain, Italy, or Denmark, at a lower price and resells them at home. In Denmark the very high luxury tax on cars has induced the manufacturer to offer them to dealers there for less to stay in the market. In Spain average income is lower putting downward pressure on imported car prices. The reseller takes advantage of the differentials. Such arbitrage creates pressures for closer adherence to the law of one price. The Internet speeds this process. And in Europe the adoption of a single currency in 2002 made it easier for consumers to comparison shop.

Such changes suggest three important questions: To what extent do such developments represent a historical shift from past spatial-economic relations? To what degree do they reduce the usefulness of extant bodies of theory? What form of regulation is called for in the new circumstance of globalized markets? Historical patterns are broken and reframed by globalization's reorganizations. Some story telling helps clarify the ways in which continuity exists along side change.

TRADE PATTERNS IN HISTORICAL CONTEXT

For an economic historian of the modern age the key date for the end of European ignorance and isolation is perhaps not 1492, when Columbus lands in America, but 1498 when Vasco da Gama arrives in Calcutta after the first direct voyage from Europe to Asia. His journey inaugurates the global economy in the modern sense when he finds a sophisticated culture and the spice trade is initiated. The Dutch East India Company (the VOC) formed in 1602 was by 1670 the richest corporation in the world, paying an annual dividend of 40 percent, employing 50,000, including 30,000 fighting men and 20,000 sailors aboard 200 ships. Many of these vessels were heavily armed, since their success was based on piracy and conquest as well as what economists call trade. Four centuries later, when Dutch activists engaged in symbolic protest against the WTO, they chose an ancient ship, a replica of the VOC's *Amsterdam,* anchored in the city's harbor, which had contributed substantially to the huge profits that financed the beautiful canal houses tourists to Amsterdam love so much.

The early history of Western trade was one of piracy and conquest. An island in the Caribbean was conquered, its people enslaved, their lands taken by one European power, only to be snatched away by yet another. The nineteenth-century conquest of India, as literary classics tell us, made the fortune of many an English gentleman. This history plays almost no role in the contemporary discussion of either trade theory (which takes comparative advantage as given) or globalization. It should. Conquest and war, not exchange freely entered, characterized early globalization, although even as colonialism and imperialism characterized the reshaping of the world system, economists presented international exchange in totally different terms. The history of trade is the history of intimidation, the exercise of state and private power by the strongest economic and military formations of the era. The classical view of trade does not describe the complexities of the emergence of the world economy which, as is simply a matter of record, is a story of conquest and colonialism, the opening of territories by military force that established the modern world system.

The value of territorial control and the worth of any particular asset found at a given location change over time. Scarcity does not adhere in some abstract and timeless fashion to resources. The value of assets can be undercut or enhanced by developments in the forces of production which can dramatically modify relative prices. Wealth can be created and protected by monopoly control. The riches which flowed to those Europeans who monopolized pepper, nutmeg, and mace arose because spices preserved and flavored decayed foods in an era before refrigeration. When the Dutch had traded away a certain island on the East Coast of America which they had purchased for $24 in trinkets for another small island in Asia with nutmeg trees they thought it a pretty good deal. Monopoly control was the key to maintaining price and guaranteeing profit from such valued goods, which is why East and West Indies and other such companies were formed by association of merchants to share risk and reduce competition.

Although Adam Smith and others argued that colonies were a burden for the many, a benefit for the select few, the colonial system was ended by the successful rebellions of the colonized and not any new found free trade sensibilities of colonial reformers (Schuyler, 1945). Frederick List's criticism of Smith and comparative advantage theory (with its assumptions of nations freely trading as equals) pointed to the reality of his time. There was one major manufacturing and trading empire, the United Kingdom, and weaker emerging economies which were not capable of successfully producing manufactures for the world markets. The British navy protected UK traders wherever they went and "opened" new markets. Adam Smith, from such a vantage point "is seen not so much as a founder of a value-free social science but as an apologist for British economic interests" (Winch, 1998: 302). Except for Great Britain, the first industrial economy, all other late developers (Germany, the United States, Japan, and others) and late-late industrializers (such as Korea, Taiwan, and Brazil) used protectionism as a development strategy. Yet discussions by economists would lead us to believe that free trade has slowly won out as the better policy alternative over the last two and a half centuries as the logic of the free trade position made converts on the merits of its intellectual persuasiveness.

While economists at least since David Hume have celebrated the virtues of free trade, protectionism based on some version of mercantilist philosophy has been typically the norm. The free trade era can be considered to have started only in 1860. Before that Britain had been uninterested in and unable to impose free trade on other nations. Others, who were fighting tooth and nail to catch up, were hardly going to adopt free trade simply because British political economists suggested that it was in everyone's best interests. Even with regard to the famous 1860 Cobden-Chevalier Commercial Treaty with France, taken as symbolizing the opening of the free trade era, it is important to understand that political rather than commercial or considerations of academic theorizing motivated Britain's shift in policy. Britain and France looked to the commercial agreement as a basis for improving relations, which in turn could prevent a European war over Italy. (Stein, 1990: 289) And while the complications of nineteenth-century European politics are not our concern, the point is that this treaty was really a bilateral mercantilist agreement. Even when in the late nineteenth century Britain created and maintained a free trade regime, it did not include most nations. By the late nineteenth century the general decline in growth generated new protectionist pressures throughout Europe.

The United States was in any case not part of this limited free trade club whose members continued to have tariffs which most raised between 1870 and the start of World War I (1913 is the dating agreed upon in even the most optimistic accounts as the close of the free trade era). That the United States as the rising hegemon after the Second World War favored free trade and used its power to impose it to the extent it could is true enough; but it has had to deal, as the British before it, with an unwilling world. And like the British, the Americans in the postwar period used commercial agreements for political ends in trade matters often favoring allies over more narrow, immediate economic interests—the goal as we saw in chapter 4 being to strengthen capitalism in Western Europe. Later, due to Cold War interests, there were important exceptions to general policy in South Korea and Taiwan. The United States also backed away from free trade when in the 1970s its economic hegemony came under challenge. It forced "voluntary" export restraint agreements on Japan and other competitors for a wide range of products in which it faced serious competition. Free traders from Ronald Reagan to George W. Bush have protected important domestic constituents from foreign competition while continuing to force open other markets where U.S. corporations had the advantage. The rhetorical commitment to free trade doctrine must be looked at in the light of actual negotiating interests and how those able to renege do so when influential domestic constituent interests are involved. Trade negotiation is inherently a hypocritical undertaking.

The specifics of a historical conjuncture are crucial. While colonial powers had been careful not to allow industrial development in their dependencies to compete with home production, by the end of the post World War II period there was a rethinking of the place of peripheral and semiperipheral economies by transnational capital. Rather than discouraging competition from such territories, core producers came to see them as potential low-cost manufacturing sites. For American managers sent abroad in the postwar years such a posting was considered a career threatening move in what was an insular corporate culture. A decade or two later it would be a possible stepping stone to the top spot of a globalized corporation. By the early 1990s world trade had tripled from its 1950 level as measured by the ratio of exports to GDP at constant prices (Maddison, 1995: 37–38). It was not unusual for large U.S. companies to derive half or more of their annual sales, profits, and royalties from returns on overseas investments.

Awareness of what came to be called globalization becomes evident from the 1960s and 1970s when the growing power of what were then called multinational corporations reached public awareness in Europe and the United States. The multinationals were virtually all American and were seen as a threat by the Europeans who felt "invaded." In 1956, 60 percent of U.S. manufacturing investment in Europe was in the UK; by the 1970s it was widespread all over Europe, including the peripheries of Spain and Ireland, and by the end of the century it had reached eastward to the once-"captive" states of the now vanished "Evil Empire." Similarly in the 1950s 90 percent of U.S. investment in Asia was in India, the Philippines and Indonesia; countries soon outpaced by newly industrializing economy exporters. By the late 1970s it was clear that overseas export platforms made sense. For example the 'threat" of Brazilian auto exports displacing U.S. exports was not a threat for the Ford Motor Company unless the cars exported are Volkswagens rather than Ford's. Producing exports in Brazil was as profitable for Ford, if not more so, as producing them in the United States (Evans, 1979: 320–21). In the mid-1980s Latin America was the most important site for US FDI, mostly for natural resources and manufacturing for the local market (autos, TVs, and other consumer products like tooth paste and breakfast cereal). The United States plays a central role as the world's largest provider and recipient of international investment.

By the end of the 1980s a major shift in strategy was evident. TNCs are very selective as to where they make major investments. They choose a mere twenty countries for more than 80 percent of foreign direct investment. Fifty countries receive one half of one percent of the total. Thus the winners in export-oriented development based on foreign investment were relatively few. Two-thirds of US FDI was in the gang of four East Asian economies (Taiwan, South Korea, Singapore, and Hong Kong), geared not to raw materials or the local markets, but export oriented manufacturing (first with white goods—dishwashers and refrigerators, latter consumer electronics). What mattered to foreign investors was a stable political climate, a good education system, disciplined, skilled, low-cost labor. Innovations in transportation and communication made sourcing production to such economies a cost effective proposition.

Elsewhere in Asia by the late 1990s despite the financial problems of the region its homegrown TNCs were pursuing expansion strategies, as in South Korea's Daewoo offering to pay more than a billion dollars for Poland's inefficient state-owned auto company (Chang, 1998: 108–9). Overall, by the end of the twentieth century, manufacturing made up more than 70 percent of the exports of developing countries (Hertel and Martin, 1999).and the proportion was expected to increase to close to eighty percent by 2005. Most of these exports were enmeshed in the commodity web production arrangements of transnational corporations (Gereffi, Korzeniewicz, and Korzeniewicz, 1994). For other sites of substantial investment local markets were important. By the end of the 1990s China was the destination of 30 percent of US FDI outside the core. In the post-Soviet years its particular brand of market-Leninism and the size of its internal market made it an attractive venue for transnationals. Increased trade hardly lifted all boats. Of the 160 countries for which we have comparable data, fifty had negative per capita growth in GDP from 1990 to 1998. The theory of international trade which continues to be taught to most undergraduate economics students does not do a very good job of explaining what is going on and why.

By the mid-1990s most U.S. foreign direct investment was not in the primary sector where it had once been concentrated, nor was it manufacturing. Rather it was in the service sector. The major growth was in finance, insurance, and business services. Within manufacturing FDI the major increases were in food, drink, and tobacco. And, despite the rapid rates of increase, in 1994 only a relatively modest share of US FDI was to East and Southeast Asia (14%) and investment patterns are complicated. A third of all direct investment was for merger and acquisition activity as global concentration and centralization proceeded at a rapid pace. FDI flowed among the advanced economies of the traditional core. Intra-Asian FDI is growing rapidly and overseas Chinese, Taiwanese, and Hong Kong investors dominate China's inward investment (along with a good deal of round trip funds from within China, laundered and reentering as "foreign investment"). The Mexican-U.S. maquiladoras are often owned by European and Asian producers and diverse ownership relations occur in the German-East European border area. Patterns of subcontracting have become complex. Nike buys running shoes from Korean plants operating in Indonesia and in the Singapore-Malaysia-Indonesia growth triangle from Johor to Bitan more complex patterns exist

If the stylized facts of the era of National Keynesianism were co-respective behavior by the three or four firms which dominated industries, globalization has increased cross border competition and intensified pressures for cost cutting. The entry of new producers in Asia and elsewhere dramatically added global manufacturing capacity. The combination of downward pressure on wages and excess supply has been reinforcing as companies desperately seek to cut costs in an intensely competitive environment. Awareness that many will not survive the global shake out has meant that companies continue to add capacity in a desperate effort to gain enough size to survive as a global competitor in a process James

Crotty (2000a: 362) calls "coerced investment." Those who are successful will be the few, the proud, the gigantic. The process of consolidation should leave a half dozen or so dominant players in the world in each major industry segment. The very few auto producers, airline alliances, and pharmaceutical companies will then have vastly more market power. We are likely to see on a global scale the sort of co-respective behavior which was prevalent nationally in the postwar era. Without some form of social control/global governance there is likely to be less sharing of benefits with the workers of the world who will continue to be played off against each other through multi sourcing by the TNCs.

Competition policy has taken an odd twist in the era of globalization. In its traditional practice it includes measures to prevent companies from abusing their dominant market position (restrictive business practices such as price fixing for example). The focus has however become one of preventing state subsidies to industry and questioning public provision of services which are seen as discriminating against foreigners wishing to enter a domestic market. The focus is on domestic competition regulations, specifically market access, and developing common rules which the transnationals find helpful. This element, preventing national companies from turning to their governments for help, has been highlighted while efforts to integrate multinational competitiveness rules addressed at transnational corporate behavior has been avoided. Cooperation among authorities addressing anti-competitive practices at the level of the global market have been slower to develop and insufficient attention has been paid to growing concentration on a global scale through mergers and alliances. The merger of America Online, the largest Internet service, and Time Warner the giant entertainment conglomerate, or the combination of Vivendi, the French media, communications and utility conglomerate and TV provider, Canal Plus, and Seagrams the Canadian film and music business, raise profound regulatory questions the answers to which will shape the twenty-first century economy in the same way that the Standard Oil and U.S. Steel (and government policy toward such behemoths) shaped industrial structure and the broader political economy a century earlier in America.

An important difference between the two turn of the century periods is of course that at the start of the twentieth century the mergers and growing concentration took place within national economies as smaller competitors came together to form nationally dominant oligopolies. At the start of the twenty-first century these mergers and acquisitions produce global giants while anti-trust regulation remains for the most part national. Competitiveness policy is being shaped by the WTO bias toward freeing up restrictions of companies wishing to penetrate new markets and to a great extent, although competitiveness officials at the EU have made some high profile interventions to prevent consolidations (led by American companies) which would have had a deleterious effect on competitors in Europe. The clash between the gains from trade perspective of the trade theorists which encourages such concentration on efficiency grounds and anti-trust concerns over the growth of market and political power are coming into sharper relief. This clash in perspectives (and objective interests) will intensify. How it is resolved will deeply influence the shaping of the twenty-first century international political economy.

One development has been of a growing literature questioning the presumed gains from trade. It may contribute to the wider nascent discussion of how ideology and material interest influence the direction research takes. At this stage the countervailing power opposing U.S. transnational capital is more effectively competing capitals based in other centers of the core rather than popular movements troubled by the exercise of monopolistic power by TNCs generally. However the dis-ease widely felt by many of the developing economies and elements of global civil society also contributes to the discussion in what we have called the verb-noun conversation: what rules there will be for globalization or will governments continue to step back and let globalization rule.

INCOME DISTRIBUTION AND INTERNATIONAL TRADE

It is surprising given all of this that when economists try to measure the gains from trade they turn out to be very small. "For example, no widely accepted model attributes to postwar liberalization more than a very tiny fraction of the increased prosperity of the advanced industrial countries. Yet economists do believe that expanding trade was very important to this progress" (Rodrik, 1997a: 15–16). As to the developing countries and the GSEGI push for trade liberalization as a tool for addressing debt problems, Hugh Streton (1999: 670) looking at the record writes: "Free trade has not recently rescued a deficit-trading country from unbalanced trade or accumulating debt. There is no reason why it should. Even if the theory of comparative advantage were valid, there is no reason to expect that all countries will develop such complimentary patterns of comparative advantage that unaided market forces will balance their trade. Trade and exchange are freer now than they have been for a century, and the main deficit traders of twenty years ago are deficit trading still, and deeper in debt than they were."

Trade with labor abundant countries is supposed to reduce wages for the less skilled workers in the richer, capital abundant countries. That is what the standard factor endowment model predicts—that is where the gains from trade come from—trade alters the relative scarcity and returns to factors. Economists have carried out empirical studies of trade's impact on labor in the advanced countries and while most everyone is convinced these have been large, most of their studies do not find much impact. Unions believe imports are badly hurting domestic labor—which is true; but it is not the whole story, since jobs are created in exports industries which are in high wage sectors, balancing such loses. It is the case that since workers being laid off in one area are typically not hired for these jobs there are many who suffer ill effects of globalization. It is also the case that on balance the presumably huge gains from trade do not show up in the numbers. What "everyone" believes are the obvious benefits from globalization are not established empirically. "Hence," Dani Rodrik (1997a: 12) writes, "saying that the impact of globalization on advanced-country labor markets is quantitatively rather small in the real world and is overshadowed by other phenomena (such as technological change) is no different from saying that the gains from trade have in practice been small." Paul Krugman (1995a: 33) puts the matter sharply "the widespread belief that moving to free trade and free markets will produce a dramatic acceleration in a developing country's growth represents a leap of faith, rather than a conclusion based on hard evidence." If Krugman is right and "the reductions in real income that can be attributed to tariffs and import quotas are not all that large" (Krugman, 1995a: 32), then the question logically arises why do the GSEGIs press so single mindedly for them, insisting upon such policies regardless of the short run costs for the economy in question?

Most economists are committed to the principle of comparative advantage and free trade and therefore, as Ray Marshall (1994: 68) has written, "often become almost hysterical in attacking those who believe in anything other than commercial rules for international transactions." One of the most prominent defenses of not interfering with "market" forces is the claim that technological change is responsible and that technology is adapted because it reduces costs and increases efficiency. Indeed the claim is widely made that the "problem," if it can be called a problem, is not trade but technology which has been biased toward the employment of more skilled workers. While this may hurt the unskilled, it is said, this bias represents progress and should not be discouraged. Reviewing the evidence, as opposed to the back of the envelop calculations, Dani Rodrik concludes that the case for skill-biased technology as the alternative to globalization in causing rising wage inequality "is far from overwhelming." Hence when economists say that the effect of trade is "small," they are certainly not saying it is small relative to some other cause that they have actually identified. Statements of the sort "trade has been of secondary importance compared with technical change" are therefore in his view inaccurate (Rodrik, 1997a: 16). Skilled labor in the United States is better compensated, because of increased trade in skill intensive exports and because it competes in a larger labor pool. Low skilled American workers competing to make low wage, low skill intensive products do poorly (following the factor endowment model's logic). There is little doubt that rising inequalities in the United States are related to skill premiums in just such a manner (Richardson, 1995; Freeman, 1996).

A conservative welfare function with regard to income distribution suggests that any absolute reduction in real income for any significant section of the community should be avoided, that income increase be given relatively lower weight, and decreased incomes high weight (Meade, 1955). Most people are risk adverse, which may be why even though elites back free trade arrangements most working Americans are shown repeatedly in polling data to oppose arrangements such as NAFTA. On welfare economics grounds the case can be made for temporary tariffs, which will prevent sudden changes in income, giving time for other more direct methods of compensation to be implemented. It offers protection but is not protectionist. Adjustment assistance allows structural change but also raises its cost and so slows such transformations. It is a preferable method than protection since "it protects or at least supplements real incomes without embalming or protecting patterns of production" (Corden: 1997: 77). In Europe the EU Social Fund has been established on this logic, and for this purpose, and regional policies are based on such a conservative welfare function.

American mainstream economists rarely call for actual compensation, as they see it as slowing adjustment. The politics of globalization reflect the sharp, dramatic changes which have been so pervasive as to weaken the position of unionized workers. Whole localized sectors have lost clout to the growing influence of transnationals' capital. The adjustment strategy is for the most part to allow those dislocated by such changes to bear the burden without compensation in order to retain incentives for greater flexibility in labor response. If social costs had to be internalized these destabilizing changes would be slowed. Thus the economic cost-benefit calculation employed is dependent on wider societal perceptions influenced by material interests more than welfare economics theory. Part of the confusion in policy debates is a failure to distinguish two different groups which oppose free trade. The first group consists of firms and workers who benefit from existing trade restrictions in the form of rents, receiving higher income than they "should," or would without the trade restrictions. The second is workers who do not receive rents but whose industry specific skills are not transferable to other jobs elsewhere, who bear high moving costs, protracted periods of unemployment, and who crowd unskilled sectors further depressing wages there. In this second category are millions of workers who are seldom compensated and many who are relatively poor. The knock on effects of such developments can lead to cumulative cycling downward in living conditions for millions more. There is a rationale for social protection in this second case.

Along such lines economists have developed models which predict a "race to the bottom." With a continuum of goods which require increasing ratios of skilled to non-skilled labor such models predict that capital movements from high wage to low wage economies increases the wages of skilled labor in both regions. If the low wage economies increasingly upgrade technologies, unskilled workers in both regions will be worse off unless the price of goods and services falls so much as a result that they are compensated for what otherwise would be falling real wages (Feenstra and Hanson, 1996). This analysis raises basic questions about the fairness and distributional consequences of free trade.

Such a model stresses cumulative causation and focuses attention on the dynamic distributional costs of free trade. It has two consequences of note. Those who are qualified get higher compensation as demand for their talents expands. Those who are not able to make the transition crowd into other low wage jobs where their entry pushes wages lower. Such gains and losses are spread over time. Some who are forced out of their jobs may be pushed into involuntary early retirement because they find employers will not hire them at their age even though if they had been able to remain at their old job they might have had substantially careers. Some suffer losses from lower waged work for the rest of their working lives. Others may lose short term but recover over a longer horizon. The losers are easier to identify than the winners because it will not be evident in the transition period who will come out where. Jobs are created not only in export sectors but also in secondary employment created by the expansion of these sectors. In general we can say that winners will be younger and better educated. Having skills in high demand in the new and expanding sectors is of course an advantage. Losers will be less educated and older. The macroeconomic situation and state of the labor market more broadly are also important.

Factor specific models show trade favors (and disfavors) particular activities. Business owners and individual workers have high sunk costs. Mobility is costly. Some factors may be easily and costlessly mobile, but others far less so. Industries in decline as a result of trade result in real losses for labor and capital in these sectors. These distributional aspects of trade are politically salient. In a similar manner a nation's mix of fiscal and monetary policies have distributional effects. For example, Jeffrey Frieden suggests that the peculiar pattern of U.S. economic policy during the Reagan years is comprehensible given that administration's principal base of support among defense contractors, real estate developers, and international investors who benefitted from increased spending on nontradables so that the mix of loose fiscal and tight monetary policy which hurt U.S. competitiveness was not a mistake (as most macro economists believe) but a reflection of the interests of the dominant political coalition (Frieden, 1991). The weakening of industrial unions, which have been core supporters of the Democratic Party, has had political impact on electoral outcomes. Similar political trends can be observed in most countries.

In earlier chapters we saw how in the post World War II years leading sectors of U.S. corporate capitalism became internationalist. Following recovery from the war, corporations in other countries followed, selling to and increasingly producing products in a variety of countries, entering into cross-national strategic alliances, joint ventures, as well as subcontracting and licencing agreements. The compromises of National Keynesian regimes of the post World War II period with their embedded liberalism offering Welfare State protections as *quid pro quo* for a gradual liberalization led over time to the disembedding of economic relations—to neoliberalism, deregulation and privatization—and to the illusion that all you need is a free market to bring growth and prosperity. A retelling of the events and thinking which went into this process stresses both international conflicts of interest, shifting class alliances, and the designs of policy elites and the corporate lobbyists and advisers who influenced their judgments.

The greater mobility of capital and the relative immobility of labor has another impact. It breaks down the national identity of capital even as it intensifies nationalism among those who are harmed by the varied impacts of globalization. The owners of French firms are increasingly foreign not only because of the increase in transnational corporate investment in the country but also because of the international diffusion of portfolio investment. At the start of the twenty-first century 40 percent of the Paris Bourse was held abroad with some of the best known "French" firms, TotalFina, Alcatel, and Aventis majority foreign owned. Vivendi a 140-year-old firm, a very French water and sewage company, became a global media group headquartered in New York City with most of its assets outside of France, although it over-reached and by 2003 was selling off its prime U.S. holdings. The assumptions of international trade models are less plausible in such a world.

IPE has not made all that much progress in bringing the transnational corporation in. Matters have not changed considerably since Susan Strange wrote how the role of transnational corporations is "no more than an addendum, a kind of appendage to the main body of the subject." That is why it seemed to her that so many writers and teachers in conventional international relations "are like the orthodox theologians in Galileo's time. . . . Flat Earthers who refuse utterly to recognize that the earth is round and resolves around the sun" (Strange, 1991: 245). It is not however so much the need to bring the transnational corporation "in," or the state, but to understand the interconnectedness of dominant institutions in an era of globalization. Governance in the contemporary ipe must be involved in complex regulatory issues and conflicts between nation states, which result from developments in the forces of production and clashes of interest among transnational corporations.

New technologies raise important technical questions for regulators. The best and the brightest now concern themselves with such questions as: is the electronic delivery of music a different market separate from CD and video sales? The answer to such a question influences what companies will be allowed to control what. They must give attention to the trans-mission capacity and phone networks that back up the Internet and the content of websites which offer music or movies on demand. Integration of seemingly separate markets can create monopoly power. Control over so-called "gatekeeper" functions can prevent rivals from entering a new field. There are important economic, political and social consequences from how private companies restructure our world and in this era of neoliberal deregulation there has not been adequate thought to the extent to which important, formerly public issues are now being decided by giant corporations. As Wyn Grant (1997: 319) suggests, "firms are not well placed to act as agents of international governance, particularly if the insertion of public policy objectives in the decision-making process is thought to be desirable. International firms create the need for improved international governance, but they do not and cannot provide it." Gov-ernments need to negotiate a regulatory regime to do so. The manner in which they have done so is the topic of the next chapter.

CHAPTER TEN

From the International Trade Organization to the World Trade Organization

"There was nothing natural about *laissez faire*; free markets could never have come into being merely by allowing things to take their course. Just as cotton manufacturers—the leading free trade industry—were created by the help of protective tariffs, export bounties, and indirect wage subsidies, *laissez faire* itself was enforced by the state."
—*Karl Polanyi* (1944: 139)

"The WTO is devoted largely to bargaining over market access. 'Free trade' is not the typical outcome of this process; nor is consumer welfare what negotiators prioritize. Instead, the negotiating agenda has been shaped in response to a tug-of-war between exporters and multinational corporations in the advanced industrial countries on one side, and import-competing interests (typically, but not solely, labour) on the other. The differential treatment of manufactures and agriculture, or of clothing and other goods within manufacturing, the anti-dumping regime, and the intellectual property rights (IPR) regime, for example, are all a result of this *political* process. There is little in the structure of the negotiations to ensure that their outcomes are consistent with development goals, let alone that they seek to further development."
—*Dani Rodrik* (2001: 7)

As the nature of its economic interactions with the rest of the world evolves, the United States has taken the initiative in bringing the international trade regime into conformity with what it understands from its vantage point as the needs of the time. This has required a shift in emphasis favoring a new set of rules covering an expanded agenda of within-border issues. In the 1970s and 1980s U.S. producers of standard manufacturing goods used orderly marketing agreements and voluntary export restraints to slow the market penetration of Asian producers. At the same time many

American-based companies increased their sourcing from the region. Those unwilling to restructure on a global basis lost out to those who did. To varying extent American corporations in these years hollowed out their manufacturing capacities, retaining product development and marketing at home but increasingly sourcing production abroad. By the end of the 1980s globalization had transformed the U.S. economy and undermined the regime of National Keynesianism. Protecting declining manufacturing jobs from foreign competition no longer commanded the powerful political consensus it once did. As its international financial and business services grew, American negotiators sought new rules to strengthen their ability to penetrate foreign markets in the areas of services and direct investment and put special emphasis on protecting intellectual property rights. American negotiators sought and obtained stronger enforcement mechanisms in the resolution of trade disputes. The Uruguay GATT Round, which established the World Trade Organization, embodied many of the demands of transnational capital, as we shall see in this chapter. The WTO and its international trade regime which is the focus here is but the most obvious, institutional advocate and agent of the neoliberal international order. Like other such fora which act under the strong influence of the most internationalized capitals of the core, the World Trade Organization spreads acceptance of open, competitive free market norms using coercive sanctions and ideological weapons of legitimation.

The position the U.S. or any other government takes in any particular historical conjuncture is the result of a political process in which domestic interests clash and the state adjudicates among them under constraints and given opportunities offered by the larger world system at each point in time. Even in the most partisan laissez faire economies the role of the state in fostering capital accumulation turns out to be substantial. In the United States federal and state subsidies underwrote economic development from the railroads and agricultural extension to the development of commercial aviation, the computer, and the Internet; but when other nations pursued similar policies this successful innovator, like other hegemons in previous eras, objected. No currently advanced economy followed the policies they today push on developing countries. The U.S. did not follow laissez faire when it came to measures to promote business opportunity and key sector development yet it condemned state-led strategies followed by Japan and others when they challenged U.S. dominance. The United States, having outgrown the use of tariffs and subsidies to protect and encourage domestic industry, left behind such immature protectionist attitudes (albeit somewhat selectively) but only after protectionism had allowed its industrialization to succeed so that they were no longer needed and so the country could embrace free trade (as late as 1913 the United States had an average tariff rate of 44 percent on manufactured goods).

There is controversy in practice however as internationally oriented firms clash with weaker, domestically oriented producers who demand continued protection. Typically the executive branch of government takes the broad internationalist perspective of the most powerful (and globally oriented) corporations and the legislative branch represents smaller businesses whose market is local or national and where representatives seek protection for their constituents from foreign competitors. The outcome is rhetorical embrace of free trade and in practice protectionism for politically favored industries. Where competition is fierce ideological nationalism follows. Similar patterns are evident from Japan to France whose external negotiations are restricted by the continued political infighting among powerful voting blocks, and often by free floating xenophobic fears.

The balance of influence between internationalist and nationalist forces changes over time as does that between the countries of the core and those of the peripheries. In 1948 the United States Congress rejected the proposal for an International Trade Organization which its own executive branch had been so instrumental in negotiating. The ITO would undermine U.S. sovereignty, critics declared. Third World countries had participated in negotiating the Havana Charter and gained some concessions there in the areas of development finance and commodity agreements. The preferential treatment they won was not however incorporated into the GATT so that after the U.S. Congress rejected the ITO, the less developed economies felt little incentive to join GATT, since it would have required abandoning nationalist development strategies and allowing liberalized market access to TNCs and other foreign investors. In the Dillon Round of GATT negotiations in 1960–61 only seven LDCs participated. In the 1960s and 1970s membership by the LDCs did increase although they continued to seek differentiated treatment both within GATT and other venues.

From the Havana meetings on as we have seen there were competing yet parallel developments in which the OECD in 1961 adopted a Code of Liberalization of Invisible Operations and another Code of Liberalization of Capital Movements while the United Nations General Assembly adopted Resolution 1803, which proclaimed the inherent sovereignty of peoples and nations to permanent sovereignty over their wealth, natural resources, and economic activities, while establishing the legitimacy of nationalization (with appropriate compensation). This conflict between the two approaches had been evident in the Havana treaty. Even though it was drafted primarily by the United States with the goal of liberalizing, as fully as possible, resistance from most other participants in the conference (for whom national controls were important as part of efforts to stabilize their economies and avoid U.S. domination) forced compromise.

In the last third of the nineteenth century Latin Americans elaborated the Calvo Doctrine, fathered by the Argentine diplomat Carlos Calvo, as the basis for modern international law doctrine. This doctrine asserted the economic independence of politically sovereign states in legal disputes involving foreign capital on their territory. It declares transnational activities in subject to local courts' jurisdiction in order to forestall foreign interventions. There was thus a tension from the start of postwar trade negotiations between investor goals of greater openness and nationalist objectives of social control in the form of market regulation. The principle of the equality of all nations was enshrined as the Calvo Doctrine. The claim it made was that the intervention of foreign states in deputes between foreign nationals and host states was a violation of the territorial jurisdiction of the host country. It was this principle that transnational capital and the U.S. state worked assiduously to overturn in the name of creating a level playing field for all economic actors. In this effort they had to move countries away from the Calvo Doctrine and efforts at collective action including the demand for a New International Economic order in which their development needs and autonomous development plans would have priority over the rights of foreign investors.

During the Cold War the United States to a considerable extent put politics first, allowing Europeans to pursue tripartite planning (a strategy of cooperation between corporations and governments with organized labor to lessen the appeal of communist unions and political parties of the class struggle left) and allowed such practices as state subsidies for national champions. The United States viewed Europe's move toward a regional economic bloc in the context of the communist threat. Such economic policies were part and parcel of a larger strategy in which the Central Intelligence Agency generously funding conservative political parties. Often, these parties, such as the Christian Democrats in Italy, had been discredited by their association with fascist regimes, and would likely have lost free elections to communist and socialist parties without such U.S. involvement. The Marshall Plan commanded the resources the United States was committed to spend to create a favorable postwar political economy. Such spending was seen as important to integrate a Germany allied to the West into Europe. Recipients were thus encouraged to adopt broad political preferences supported by the United States.

Similar considerations were at work in East Asia in the Cold War era. U.S. economic aid gave priority to "front line" economies, in particular South Korea and Taiwan (then competing with North Korea and communist China as to which system would be more successful). They were encouraged to industrialize; their manufactures were given preference in U.S. markets. In Latin America there was greater sympathy with commodity producers' desires to protect the prices they receive from destabilizing market forces when these countries were seen to have greater strategic value. For example, the Inter-American Coffee Agreement was negotiated as World War II loomed and the U.S. wanted "good neighbors" so that its flank would not be exposed when war broke out. Later, the excitement the Cuban Revolution created throughout Latin America and the example it seemed to set led President Kennedy to proclaim an Alliance for Progress that included policies for which the United States had shown little sympathy in the absence of a perceived communist threat in the Western hemisphere. Numerous other examples could be cited.

In 1964, during the Vietnam War and the broader Cold War struggles for the hearts and minds of Third World people, the United Nations Conference on Trade and Development was created and became a forum for the nonaligned movement's G-77 advocacy of a New International Economic Order. In 1971 the Generalized System of Preferences (GSP) was negotiated. The richer nations accepted a two-tiered global economic system with special exemptions for developing countries from expectations of reciprocity. In 1977 the United Nations Center on Transnational Corporations (UNCTC) began negotiations on a voluntary Draft Code of Conduct on Multinational Corporations. The code delineated rights and responsibilities within a framework promoting national economic development. The draft measure provided for respect for national sovereignty and observance of domestic laws, regulations, and administrative practices, adherence to national economic goals and development objectives and acknowledged that states had the right to nationalize or expropriate assets of TNCs (with appropriate compensation). It included specific environmental protection provisions and respect for sociocultural and human rights objectives. Negotiations dragged on until 1992, when the UNCTC abandoned its efforts as a result of unrelenting U.S. pressure and a changed global context. By the 1990s attracting foreign capital took precedence over its regulation.

The OECD does have a set of voluntary guidelines to ensure that multinational enterprises "operate in harmony with the policies of the countries in which they operate." Member countries are supposed to promote compliance with such policies by their multinational enterprises. But in practice the usefulness of these guidelines has been limited. As a Friends of the Earth statement suggests, "They are moderate, non-specific, voluntary, poorly-implemented and fail to call for public disclosure of information regarding TNC breaches of the Guidelines. In addition, they are in many cases not well-known and in all cases poorly regarded." (Friends of the Earth—England, Wales and Northern Ireland, 1998: 5) Also, the ILO's Tripartite Declaration of Principles Concerning Multinational Enterprises and Social Policy (adapted in 1977) contains general principles and specific provisions concerning industrial relations. It is not a particularly powerful document and is voluntary.

The waning of OPEC's power and the unwillingness of its members to use their leverage to help establish other commodity cartels by the early 1980s had, along with the economic slowdown in the global economy, led to a drop in commodity prices and a rise in protectionism in the advanced economies including an increase in non-tariff barriers and the imposition of "voluntary" export restraints on developing economies by the countries of the core. By the mid 1990s, with the Cold War a fading memory, the ratio of trade in goods to trade in services was 4: 1 with the later growing fast and exceeding $4 trillion. Because more than 80 percent of U.S. employment is in services, liberalization of trade in that sector was a priority for American negotiators, supported by a host of domestic industries from banking and insurance to fast food franchisers and telemarketers. In the context of the negotiating leverage of the peripheral economies having weakened dramatically the U.S. demands for deregulation of trade in services brought a striking redefinition of property rights, a matter discussed later in this chapter. We begin with a closer look at the dynamics involved in the abortive effort to form the International Trade Organization.

THE ITO

When Britain in 1945 negotiated a desperately needed $5 billion loan from the United States, the Americans insisted the UK commit itself on joint proposals for establishing the ITO, and when representatives of eighteen countries of the Prepatory Committee met in London in 1946 it was the U.S. Proposals for the Expansion of World Trade and Employment which was the working document. The countries chosen to participate in definitive negotiations for the reduction of tariffs and other barriers to trade followed the design of the American presentation in preparing a detailed Charter for an International Trade Organization. After small group meetings in London and Geneva to discuss a purely American draft a more general invitation to participate was sent out in accordance with the usual pattern here called concentric club formation. Fifty-six countries sent delegates to Havana and others were observers. By 1948 when these nations met in Havana to accept an International Trade Organization there had been six years of extensive negotiations to establish a global trade regime.

The ITO was in significant ways more ambitious than the WTO with respect to its rules concerning international investment, labor standards, and government commodity agreements. Its design provided countries with a framework for adjusting to competitive international pressures without having to sacrifice goals of equity and social justice. The decisionmaking process was one nation-one vote and not the system of heavily weighted voting adopted by the IMF and World Bank. This Charter was the most comprehensive international economic agreement the world had seen to that point. Its provisions detailed most of the problems of commercial relations. In nine chapters and 106 articles they covered exchange controls and quotas, internal taxation and regulation, state subsidies, and restrictive business practices. The conflicts with the American proposal came on the one side from the British and the French who wanted greater freedom to discriminate in trade in favor of their former colonies (although they had basically been beaten down by America in pre-conference negotiations among core members of the new club). On the other side were countries like India and Latin American states which favored quotas and other protection to foster industrialization. Indeed, the conference opened with "a chorus of denunciation in which representatives of thirty underdeveloped nations presented variations on a single theme: the Geneva draft was one-sided; it served the interests of the great industrial powers; it held out no hope for the development of the backward states" (Wilcox, 1949: 47). Provision for international commodity agreements (ICAs), which would have helped the vast majority of developing countries who were primary producers, came in for special criticism from free-market economists and U.S. government officials, including some who were instrumental in achieving domestic protection for American farmers through not totally dissimilar government price supports. The developing countries in Havana found the proposed commodity agreements totally inadequate. As Mark Zacher (1987: 295) has written, "The charter's chapter on ICAs largely reflected the preferences of the Western developed countries, since the latter possessed overwhelming power over the international economic system and since the developing countries only became involved in the final stages of the negotiations." Concentric club formation was evident here too.

The U.S. Congress rejected the ITO on sovereignty grounds, even though the commitments it required, as Wilcox (1949: 173) wrote at the time, "are commitments either to do things which the United States is already doing, or to refrain from doing things which the United States is not doing and does not desire or intend to do." Others would have had a good deal of adjusting to undertake, but not the United States. Indeed, the most common criticism of the period from the rest of the world was that the ITO was the mandate of Wall Street, a predatory ploy aimed at world domination. In retrospect many free-market economists and policymakers were glad the ITO was never ratified. The Charter envisioned an ITO which proclaimed the need for full employment, control of restrictive business practices, intergovernmental commodity agreements, and tariff reductions; but such measures raised the hackles of U.S. business groups, which believed the Charter jeopardized the free enterprise system. Such observers suggest that the failure to bring the ITO into existence may have been a "blessing in disguise," since it might have embraced a regulatory regime including intergovernmental commodity agreements and other "bureaucratic" stabilizing mechanisms. Nonetheless laissez faire oriented economists such as Anne Krueger (whom the Bush Administration chose to be chief economist at the IMF in 2001) viewed the concessions made in the ITO draft charter as "a schizophrenic document; half of it was designed to enable countries to adopt whatever trade policies they deemed necessary to assure domestic objectives" (Krueger, 1999: 105). For such economists the task is to overcome such schizophrenia by the enforced liberalization of economic relations.

The General Agreement on Tariffs and Trade was drawn up in 1947 to provide a procedure for continuing international negotiation until the Havana Charter was implemented. By default it became the ruling framework for world trade when the U.S. Congress refused to accept the ITO. The most important elements of the GATT were its Article I of the General Agreement's most-favored-nation (MFN) provision, which stipulated that every privilege that a GATT member gives to any one country with regard to trade must be extended immediately and unconditionally to all other GATT members. National Treatment (Article 3) required members to treat foreign products which are imported into that country at least as favorably as domestic products in terms of regulation and taxation and not to protect domestic products or impede the importing of goods. The ITO provisions on fair labor standards were not included in the GATT, nor was the binding treaty obligation for dispute settlement with its appeal procedure to the International Court of Justice, nor the codes regulating the restrictive practices of international businesses, nor the protection of host economies which limited investor prerogatives.

The GATT had twenty-three signatories when it came into effect in January 1948. It was seen as the place the United States and European powers negotiated the rules for world trade. Because of its exclusive membership (and the U.S. Congress's decision not to risk loss of sovereignty in a more comprehensive formal organization), GATT's organization was makeshift. Its formal powers were weak and ambiguously defined. GATT's role evolved through improvisations in a series of negotiation rounds. But the organization remained saddled with a voluntary core. The sovereignty of members and its failure to develop a conflict resolution and sanction structure which could resolve disputes made it ineffective in addressing serious trade conflicts, most especially between core states. The various rounds of trade negotiation which took place under GATT auspices did liberalize trade, but it took until 1961 before the trading system (as it affected the non-Communist world) was as open as it had been after 1904 for a brief pre-war period under the Public International Unions (Murphy, 1994: 198) or in 1924, at the beginning of the brief interwar era of good feeling.

NEGOTIATING TRADE

Modern regulation of trade dates from the late nineteenth century with the 1890 Treaty Concerning the Creation of an International Union for the Publication of Customs Tariffs. It was interrupted by the Great Depression and the dislocations of the two world wars and adjustment periods. In the long view such international regulations of trade have been becoming more formalized for some time. Individual bilateral agreements go back for the United States to the Treaty of Amity and Commerce with France in 1778 (negotiated by among others Benjamin Franklin). Such early bilateral treaties of Friendship, Commerce, and Navigation (FCN) focused on shipping and trading rights although they also protected property of nationals. They did not include explicit investment protection provisions until after World War II. FCNs were reincarnated in the postwar era as bilateral investment treaties (BITs) which the United States has with most countries ranging from Ethiopia to Estonia, Pakistan to Paraguay.

The main purpose of the bilateral investment guarantee agreements was to settle disputes between the investor and the host state through international arbitration (and not the legal system of the host country). In direct response to the United Nations General Assembly debate on nationalization rights and just compensation the United States launched an aggressive Bilateral Investment Treaty offensive in 1977 (although it was not the first to do so, France concluded its first BIT in 1972 and the UK in 1975 with former colonies). The U.S. soon concluded Bilateral Investment Treaties with scores of countries. These agreements encouraged trade partners to adopt market oriented domestic policies and support for the development of international law standards consistent with core country investment objectives through their precedent setting value. BITs imposed obligations on the host state for the protection of foreign investment but no corresponding responsibility on the foreign investor or the home country to regulate their companies operating abroad (for example requiring them to not violate basic labor rights). These have become more extensive in their protections of foreign investment and in providing for prompt, adequate, and effective compensation for expropriations. The United States also uses BITs to limit the ability of trading partners to impose restrictions on the conversion of currencies.

BITs have afforded the stronger trading partner significant leverage in negotiations. As a deputy U.S. Trade Representative has indicated "The BIT Program supports key U.S. government economic policy objectives of promoting U.S. exports and enhancing the international competitiveness of U.S. companies" (Lang, 1998: 458). U.S. bilateral trade agreements are the most comprehensive of any major industrialized nation. In addition to providing for national treatment and most favored nation rights to enter and establish an entity, the U.S. agreements typically ban a large number of specific performance requirements, regulation of transfers of profits and capital in a hard currency, expropriation provisions, and state-to-state and investor-to-state dispute settlement procedures. Often the United States achieves breakthroughs in property rights redefinition in bilateral negotiations in which its preponderant power allows it to basically write rules as it sees fit. The bilateral approach it should be noted is contrary to the multilateral principle of Bretton Woods and the GATT. BITs are primarily a vehicle to extend rules favored by the stronger party or as the matter can also be put, of favoring regulatory competition. In 2002 82 BITs were concluded by 76 countries bringing the total number of BITs to 2,181 (United Nations Conference on Trade and Development, 2003:21). After the breakdown of the Cancún WTO ministerial discussed in this chapter there was fear that this number instead of going down might rise with the difficulties of achieving multilateral agreements.

Unlike the top down club formation process which gets the key players on board first and then extends membership on a take-it-or-leave-it basis to weaker states, the unilateralist "momentum strategy" puts pressure on larger states that have significant disagreements with the United States, and also significant bargaining power, by establishing precedents where hegemonic leverage is greatest. Thus a deal with Chile pressures its neighbor Brazil (Chile and Brazil are already closely tied in terms of trade and associated through Mercosur, the regional trade pact). The Bush II U.S. Trade Representative (USTR) Robert Zoellick calls this negotiating strategy "competitive liberalization," the idea that a bilateral trade agreement with one country puts pressure on others. Critics point out that such competition favors those with "the largest market access to offer, the largest security blanket to share, the greatest capacity to threaten negative consequences from non-compliance or exclusion" (Woods, 2002: 7). Imbalance in negotiating power is felt in such bilateral contests even more than in regional or global negotiations. To be excluded from the U.S. market or from the favorable opinion of Washington policymakers can be a heavy burden. While BITs stressed economic cooperation, treaties signed during the 1990s and thereafter were about guaranteeing greatly extended rights and reducing costs and risks for foreign investors. The U.S.-Chile Free Trade Agreement and a similar treaty with Singapore negotiated in 2002–3 extended investor freedoms, restricted the right of the host government to impose capital controls in financial crises, and included the concept of regulatory expropriation giving private firms the right to sue for compensation should they believe the host government regulations, rules, or actions precluded potential profit-making opportunities (texts of agreements are available at http://www.ustr.gov).

There was an additional aspect to Bush II post-September 11 BITs. While Chile had been expected to be the first country to sign such an agreement with the United States (theirs was completed before the one with Singapore), Chile had refused to support the American call for war with Iraq in the UN Security Council. When President Bush announced that the signing from Camp Lejeune, North Carolina during the war he said there would be a White House ceremony in recognition of Singapore not only for its economic strength and global trading strategy but also for being "a strong partner in the war on terrorism and a member of the coalition on Iraq" (Becker, 2003b: C4). As the U.S. ambassador to Singapore said, it was the administration's policy after the war in Iraq, "to work with friends." The United States proceeded to negotiate additional BITs with a number of small and economically weak countries which could be expected to accept the terms dictated by American negotiators— Morocco, the five small Central American economies, and the five members of the Southern African Customs Union. Once these precedents were established the Administration moved to larger but also vulnerable countries such as the Philippines and Indonesia.

While trade economists criticize BITs as distorting trade flows they have the advantage for the stronger negotiator of bargaining leverage at a time the WTO Doha Round had bogged down. The bilateral pacts required little by way of U.S. concessions. Free trade advocates are highly critical of such practices. As a leader in *The Economist* (2002d: 14) notes "The befuddling complex series of overlapping deals, each with its own pattern of preferences, schedules and exclusions, undoubtedly adds to the political and technical difficulties of negotiating a multilateral WTO deal. It makes it that much less likely that governments will even try. And, in the meantime, global trade takes place on a playing-field as level as the Himalayas, with the added spur to trade and investment of not knowing what the contours will be from one month to the next."

Even after its WTO victory in achieving the TRIPs agreement (to be discussed later in this chapter), the United States used bilateral treaties to impose even stronger intellectual property rights protections than provided under TRIPs as a way of pushing an agenda it hoped it could then get accepted by other more powerful states once the precedent had been established. Paralleling these bilateral arrangements, GATT limited the use of tariffs, quotas, and regulations which discriminated against imports and subsidies that distort trade, although it left exceptions on national security grounds, health and morals, and allowed temporary restraints of various sorts which the United States would have liked to remove but, faced with strong opposition, could not. The direction of change was unmistakable however. The United States consciously pursued what was known as the bicycle theory of trade policy; as long as there was forward motion the process would survive (Jackson, 1997). By the 1990s the balance of forces had shifted and the new regulatory framework proposals, most dramatically for a Multilateral Agreement on Investment, aimed to free capital from social constraints and reverse the priorities of the GATT charter and the ITO agreement which had recognized the importance for individual states of being able to control their local economies against destabilizing external capital movements and recognized the role selective and temporary trade barriers could legitimately play in a national development strategy.

In the years immediately following decolonization amidst Cold War struggle to win the hearts and minds of the nonaligned nations there was a period of greater U.S. respect for the juridical independence and formal equality of sovereign Asian, African, Latin American, and other states which were trying to find their place on the world stage through state guided mechanisms to accelerate economic growth. The formation of the United Nations Conference on Trade and Development in 1963, and the coming together of the Group of 77 at the first UNCTAD session in 1964, created a unity of purpose and cohesion which challenged the former colonial powers. The Joint Declaration of the Seventy-Seven Developing Countries made at the conclusion of this conference spoke of the "injustice and neglect of centuries" which needed to be addressed. UNCTAD set about negotiating for preferential tariffs for their goods, setting targets for official development assistance and "fair" commodity prices. UNCTAD's first Secretary General, Raul Prebisch, an economist who had pioneered the analysis of the terms of trade between the industrialized nations and the primary producers (and found substantial secular deterioration), was influential in this debate. At the third UNCTAD session in 1972 Luis Echeverria, then Mexico's president, declared that economic cooperation should be removed from the field of "good faith" and moved to the legal sphere, although little progress was made in this regard.

Efforts by the developing countries to follow state-led development strategies, for example, were opposed by the United States which worked hard in the 1960s and mid 1970s to force liberalization on what was through these years an increasingly vocal and effective nonaligned movement. The United States in these years lost a number of important battles, and not only at the UN. Its efforts to gain adoption of OECD proposals such as its Draft Convention on Foreign Property failed at the multilateral level in the mid-1960s. When the United States lost votes in the General Assembly in the 1960s and early 1970s it withdrew financial resources from international agencies. In 1977 the U.S. temporarily withdrew from the ILO. It refused to participate in World Court cases or the Law of the Sea Convention. It increased efforts to strengthen GATT as its vehicle for making the changes it wanted.

The high points of the campaign by the Group of 77 are probably the Declaration and the Program of Action on the Establishment of a New International Economic Order in 1974 and the negotiations begun in 1977 in the UN for formulation of a Code of Conduct on Transnational Corporations which would set norms for TNC behavior and treatment of TNCs by host countries. The Declaration spoke of the need to "redress existing inequalities" and "eliminate the widening gap between the developed and developing countries." These were nonbinding but they exposed the chasm which existed between the liberalization agenda of the core powers led by the United States and the demands of the Third World governments. Negotiation on the Code was officially terminated in 1992, but the momentum was gone long before then as the gathering force of the TNCs in the international political economy had set in motion a very different dynamic. Instead of TNCs competing to penetrate Third World nationalist oriented economies, serious competition among these economies to attract foreign capital had become the central dynamic. The rich countries responded to Third World pressures by venue shifting, demanding bilateral investment treaties with developing countries which promote and protect foreign investment and finally for the creation of the WTO and its liberalizing regime. Developing countries seeking to attract foreign investment signed such agreements with the core economies. Discussion of policy regimes affecting trade and investment priorities was increasingly committed to an expanded set of global state economic governance institutions.

GATT AND LOWERING TRADE BARRIERS

The operation of the GATT system in its early days reflected its particular club character. Its rules were built upon diplomatic vagueness, indirection, and a lack of precision. By keeping procedures informal, members could work out accommodations without having to grant access to the newly emerging nations and others with less power and with different agendas for the global system. Such an arrangement allowed deals to be consummated away from the glare of public involvement and avoided likely rejection in some instances by domestic protectionist interests. In the light of what we have said about conflicts between nationalist and internationalist interests in concentric club formation it is less remarkable than generally thought that GATT had no enforcement mechanism, no codified rules or administrative structure. The move in the latter years of the GATT's existence to a more rule-based regime rather than a dispute settlement system centered on diplomacy in substantial measure is attributable to increasing pressure from domestic constituencies, especially in the United States, trying to influence outcomes.

A rule-based system made it easier for liberal trade policies to prevail. In a rule-based procedure it was more difficult to argue for special treatment. This change was not consummated only with the formation of the WTO replacing the "less effective" GATT enforcement procedures as some believe. After 1980, the GATT dispute settlement procedure transformed itself into an institution based primarily on the authority of legal obligations. Its transformation into a more juridical instrument was importantly the development of these legal powers. Their acceptance by governments laid the foundation for even stronger legal powers under the WTO (Hudec, 1999).

There was a great deal of continuity from 1948 when GATT achieved the first multilateral accord to lower trade barriers since the Napoleonic era (the Treaty of Utrecht of 1713) through the ten "rounds" of global negotiations under GATT, each involving more countries and more areas (later negotiations concerned intellectual property rights, for example). Under U.S. guidance a regime evolved in the sense of a coherent ordering of discussion and negotiation on trade matters. Through these negotiating rounds free trade was expanded and tariffs lowered to the point where they were mostly inconsequential by the end of the century (except agriculture and some labor intensive products in which less developed countries had comparative advantage and for which constituencies in core countries successfully demanded protection). While these negotiating rounds are typically described as multilateral in character, in point of fact they were largely bilateral between the United States and Europe, certainly from the initial Geneva Round in 1947 through the Dillon and Kennedy Rounds. Even the rounds since have been primarily bilateral affairs between the United States and the nations of the European Union in the club pattern of concentric global state economic institution building.

The GATT's core principle is the most favored nation provision. As noted MFN treatment requires each nation to treat the imports of every other signatory no less favorably than they treat imports from another GATT member country. Disputes were addressed through the consultation provision which requires parties to settle differences through consultation and negotiation although there was no collective enforcement. Nonetheless there is widespread agreement that "The GATT stands as one of the most successful international organizations ever created" (Garcia, 1999a: 433), although its supporters are well aware that the GATT's credibility was not very strong with environmentalists and labor advocates (a topic to which we will turn in the next chapter).

Most countries in Latin America did not join GATT until the 1980s because it required them to eliminated all policy intervention that discriminated between domestic and foreign producers—the very basis of their import substitution industrialization strategies. They were unwilling to give up domestic content rules and subsidies to national firms which were part an alternative development strategy (and to some extent a political one by which ruling political elites provided jobs, contracts, and subsidies). The denationalization of these economies took place under the hammer of the debt crisis which plagued the region in the 1980s which the United States and the GSEGIs worked to resolve within a framework requiring acceptance of liberalization by debtor economies. These events set the stage for the U.S. negotiating victories within the GATT as well as increasing pressures to join GATT and submit to its rules, thus bringing the world trading system to a new stage and completing a process begun in the aftermath of World War II.

The original ITO agreement was a compromise to the extent that it recognized the special situation of developing economies and the right of all countries to follow policies of their own choosing to promotion of growth and full employment. As the various GATT negotiating rounds proceeded a regime shift is evident as the principles, rules and norms for decisionmaking increasingly came to deny formerly recognized national sovereignty rights and to stress deregulation of markets. By the time the WTO was established at the conclusion of the Uruguay Round (1986-1994) the "trade and . . . " issues which had been part of the ITO mission were declared outside the WTO mandate. Its focus, at the insistence of the United States and transnational corporate interests, was liberalization of matters once considered the domestic province of sovereign nations, issues such as the use of local content requirements and export commitments, technological transfer, and control of remittances which governments negotiated with investors entering their economies.

The U.S. attack on "trade distorting practices" was resisted by developing countries. At the 1982 GATT meeting Brazil and India spearheaded such efforts, expressing fear that the developing nations would be forced to open key sectors such as banking, communications, and transportation to foreign companies as the price of access to the markets of the advanced economies. This was precisely the bargain and the threat the United States offered while resisting any regulation of foreign investor behavior. Given Third World resistance, the investment issue was not mentioned in the final declaration of the 1982 meeting, much to the disappointment of the American negotiators. Ambassador Brock warned the United States would "protect its interests" and if necessary pursue its "legitimate complaints perhaps in a more unilateral and confrontational manner than would have occurred, if the GATT ministerial had made more progress in this area" (Smythe, 1999).

The redoubled U.S. efforts at the new round of GATT negotiations in 1986 were the result of strenuous lobbying by U.S.-based TNCs, especially in the area of trade in services. By the end of the 1980s the trend toward liberalization had reversed the momentum toward control of transnationals, a less restrictive stance toward foreign investment and a *de facto* abandonment of the Calvo Doctrine. Companies such as Federal Express and Citibank formed a Coalition of Service Industries to push this agenda. Arthur Andersen & Co the giant accounting and (at the time) consulting firm with operations in more than fifty countries was a close adviser to the U.S. Trade Representative. The European Community, which expected potential gains from increased trade in services, joined the United States. Together they were able to link sanctions enabling retaliation against the exports from countries which did not comply with the new agreement on trade in services (GATS) which became part of the WTO rules.

The WTO has been open to members of "civil society" who it sees as having proper business with the organization. At each WTO ministerial meeting,—in Geneva, Singapore, and Seattle—the most influential non-government actors were the corporate lobbyist-advisers. At its Singapore Ministerial gathering two-thirds of the accredited civic organizations were business interests. As Jan Aart Scholte (2000a: 119) writes, "organised non-governmental forces have on balance actually *favoured* the neoliberal status quo, not opposed it." This should not be surprising. The U.S. Commerce Department's International Trade Administration identifies its primary aim to be "helping US business compete in the global marketplace" and formal consultative committees are a prominent feature of preparation for these international negotiations.

Grass roots oppositional organizations have had no direct entry to the WTO. One reason demonstrators fill the streets is that business associations and individual firms routinely are a major influence in global governance while trade unions and NGOs were kept out of the meetings. The President's Advisory Committee for Trade Policy and Negotiations is a who's who of U.S.-based transnational corporations. The United States Council on International Business with a membership of more than 300 business associations, law firms, and other interested corporate actors issues detailed recommendations to U.S. negotiators in preparation for WTO and other such conferences. International coordination of the business agenda is ironed out with government leaders at such gatherings as the annual World Economic Forum in Davos Switzerland (another target for demonstrators). In Europe, as discussed in chapter 4, there is the European Round Table of the leading European-based TNCs—Philips,

Nestle, Bayer, Unilever and others—who have similar highest level access to government ministers and their technical staffs. The Transatlantic Business Dialogue is the informal forum for Europeans and Americans to develop a joint US-EU trade policy. Like other peak organizations its members are CEOs of the largest transnationals.

Most international agreements are initiated by negotiators from the rich countries on behalf of their corporations seeking access to foreign markets. Liberalization of services as in the Basic Telecommunications Agreement opened world markets to a sector dominated by government-owned monopolies. The Financial Services Agreement opened new opportunities in developing countries to foreign banks, insurance companies, and stock brokers. The problem is that such deregulation and privatization has contributed to financial crises in countries lacking proper regulatory oversight capacities. These agreements have been pushed through prematurely at the insistence of industry lobbyists whose role has been central. Indeed, according to David Hartridge, former director of the WTO services division, "without the enormous pressure generated by the American financial services sector, particularly companies like American Express and Citicorp, there would have been no services agreement" (Ainger, 2002).

At WTO gatherings core government representatives continue the effort by meeting first as members of the QUAD, the United States, the European Union, Japan, and Canada, which gather separately to work out policy for the organization, after which, in typical concentric club form, they hold a green room meeting with perhaps twenty of the players deemed by the United States to count. Finally the other hundred plus member nations are brought together in the full ministerial meeting which ratifies the decisions which the vast majority of country representatives had no part in deciding. The QUAD meets separately several times a year between General Council meetings establishing the priorities for the organization and making agenda decisions.

The initiation on policy formulation for QUAD meetings in turn originates with the peak business associations in each political territory. In Japan, there is Keidandren, the Japanese Federation of Economic Organizations through its industry and sectoral committees chaired by the most important individual CEOs. The Committee on Trade and Investment is headed by the CEO of Mitsubishi Electric, for example. The European Round Table of Industrialists, the U.S. Business Roundtable, and the President's Advisory Committee of Trade Policy Negotiations, and in Canada the Business Council on National Issues (modeled on the U.S.

Business Round Table) are the key groups. Like Keidanren, each represents the largest corporations and has pubic policy committees chaired by powerful CEOs who have their own direct links to governments. These are not the only players. There are trade association lobbyists and the International Chamber of Commerce which deals continually with the WTO policymakers. If there is reason to fear a loss of sovereignty to such organizations it is first and foremost the loss of democratic control to the transnational corporate class and the virtual exclusion of all other citizens.

The Uruguay Round formally ended in Marrakesh, Morocco on April 15, 1994 with the ratification of a 26,000 page document, perhaps the longest agreement in the history of the world. During these talks representatives from TNCs chaired and staffed all of the fifteen advisory groups set up by the U.S. administration to develop U.S. negotiating positions. It should not be unexpected then that the GATT and the WTO favored transnational over national capital interests. This bias in favor of open trade is after all the foundation of the GATT-WTO system. But more narrow economic interests were at work in both establishment of rules and negotiating exceptions to them. Where important domestic constituencies would be harmed the United States frequently negotiated trade restrictions as in the Multifiber Arrangement on Textiles and Clothing in effect for two decades from 1974 to 1994 to protect core domestic producers against Third World imports. In the 1970s and 1980s the United States forced Japanese industries like auto and steel to "voluntarily" limit their exports to the United States. These VERs, or Voluntary Export Restraints, raised prices for U.S. consumers as all such protectionist measures do, and stimulated Japanese investment in U.S. production sites. The United States kept higher tariffs on manufactures from Third World countries, restricting their exports at a cost which exceeded the foreign aid the United States gave to these countries. The U.S. continues when it is in its interest to do so to insist on practices which depart from its professed belief in free trade as for example the steel cartel worked out by the Bush Administration in 2001 and the tariff protection afforded the industry by the Bush Administration a year later.

There may be equity reasons a society may favor protectionist measures. The effective costs imposed on fellow citizens from freer trade may be considered too high by voters who may be willing as consumers to pay higher prices for domestically produced products to avoid costs liberalization forces on their fellow citizens who are employed in affected sectors. Moreover the nations of the world may find their citizens prefer a negotiation of what has been called fair trade inclusive of various protective mechanisms to the harsher (if in economistic terms more efficient) market outcome. We shall return to this argument. However for the executive branch negotiators representing the interests of transnational capital such a framing has been consistently rejected.

The establishment of the WTO out of the GATT process reflects the success of venue shifting by the United States and other advanced economy negotiators away from the United Nations system. Social and cultural development, emergency food relief, and such could be handled by the UN. But the core economic and financial issues which affected the well being of the world are worked out in closely controlled fora. GATT generally took a realistic attitude toward the distribution of power in the international political economy. For example, agricultural protection which was to remain a contentious issue for the life of the GATT had its origin in the double standard the United States introduced at its inception. Quantitative restrictions were forbidden for industrial protection (under Article XI) but protection was permitted in agriculture at the demand of the U.S. Department of Agriculture to allow continuation of its price support program. The Executive Secretary of the GATT, Eric Wyndham White, explained that the relevant provision, Article XI, "had been largely tailor-made to U.S. requirements" (Dam, 1970: 260 as quoted in Tussie, 1991: 84) Characteristic of this separation is a revealing minor incident in 1995 when the UN asked the GATT to contribute to a UN consultation on the realization of social, economic and cultural rights including the problem of foreign debt and the realization of "the right to development." The Director-General of the GATT issued a statement in response that "GATT had no relevant information to offer in regard to the subject matter" (Bunn, 2000).

THE WTO

The Tokyo Round Declaration (1973) recognized "the importance of the application of differential measures in developing countries in ways which will provide special and more favorable treatment for them in areas of negotiation where feasible." This was in keeping with various sections of the GATT code which allowed countries to renegotiate tariffs in order to promote the establishment of certain industries and conceded the principle of nonreciprocity by developing countries in trade negotiations. The 1979 Framework Agreement (the Enabling Clause) provided for what became the General System of Preferences (GSP), an arrangement which allows preferential market access for developing country exports to core economies. The scope of GSP was reduced dramatically with the establishment of WTO rules that require new concessions by the less developed economies on pain of being excluded from core country markets. The WTO removes the "special and different status" of the developing countries which was guaranteed by GATT. The WTO rule based system in creating "a level playing field" favored the advanced economies and took away, or set the agenda for taking away, the little in compensating arrangements the developing countries had had. The richer countries on the other hand negotiated delays in liberalizing textiles, clothing, footwear, and agriculture which effected politically well connected producers and employment in their economies (Salazar-Xirinachs, 1999).

"[T]o many in the developing world, trade policy in the more advanced countries seems to be more a matter of self-interest than of general principle. When good economic analysis works in favor of self-interest, it is invoked; but when it does not, so much the worse for economic principles," as Joseph Stiglitz (1999b: 16) has written. "'Yes,' the advanced countries seem to be telling the economies in transition (and the emerging economies), 'produce what you can—but if you gain a competitive advantage over our firms, beware!' Too often there is a not-so-subtle subtext: 'Clearly, if there were a level playing field we could outperform you. Since you seem to be underselling us, it could only be because you are engaging in unfair trade practices!" It can be said that countries agreed to the terms of these new agreements voluntarily. Yet there was a substantial threat involved should they have refused to do so—loss of access to the U.S. market. It was not in the interests of any country not to cooperate in a particular instance even to protect an important local firm or industry because of the retaliation its action would incur since any single violation was an attack on the total framework. National interest of core countries led to important conflicts and unwillingness to negotiate certain areas (agriculture in some cases for example) or to demand exemptions and limits (as for textiles), but the pressure for continued liberalization by developing countries was maintained.

The leverage the rich countries have over the poorer ones comes largely from control over access to their own markets. Poorer countries accept unfavorable terms rather than a system without international rules under which local constituencies wielding political influence easily gain politicians' attention. Because of their position of needing the agreements the situation is structurally one of inequality. In addition the resources available to the overwhelmed negotiators from the smaller, poorer countries are limited. The USTR has a $30 million annual budget, more than all of the poorer country negotiators together. This structural imbalance of power is applauded in effect by academic writers in the law and economics tradition who see the existence of competition among jurisdictions as providing restraints on inefficient state regulation. A competitive market in negotiating reduces trade barriers, tariff protections, and the use of state-led development strategies which by definition are inefficient because they interfere with the market. Those from the critical legal studies tradition see unequal bargaining as not only inherently unfair, but also in their outcomes denying development priorities favored by the poorer countries and as overriding their social and economic concerns. For example tariffs are often a major source of government revenues for poor countries which unlike richer, more developed ones, cannot easily switch to other revenue sources. Further, without the ability of local states to regulate foreign capital, they lose the ability to control an important part of their own economies and of course they are unable to use the development strategies all of the currently developed economies used to overcome their earlier backwardness.

By the early twenty-first century the biases favoring the rich countries came to be more widely understood. The wealthy nations continued to argue that the developing countries need to follow the rules of free trade and end such trade distortions as seeking preferential access to Western markets or protecting home markets. The costs to the developing countries of the numerous derogations to the basic GATT principles imposed by the rich nations remained. The rich countries have achieved exceptions through various informal agreements, formal conventions, and bilateral agreements—all of which "violate the letter and spirit of the principles of non-discrimination, multilateralism and transparency that the entire GATT scheme advocates," as Ernesto Hizon (1999: 93–94) writes of the special treatment the richer economies had demanded and received. He thinks the GPS instituted for the benefit of developing countries was no match for the exceptions such as the special agreements in textiles (the Multi-Fiber Agreement), agriculture (variable levy in the then European Community), and manufactures (Voluntary Export Restraints in footwear, electronics, automobiles, steel, computer chips) "which were artfully targeted at commodities exported by developing countries, and later, manufactures produced by the NICs." These exclusions from the general framework pertained to specific sectors that would allow the poorer countries "a fighting chance in the world market."

The domination of transnational corporations is illustrated by UN Conference on Trade and Development figures which show more than two-thirds of world trade involves at least one multinational. Half of all world trade occurs within the same multinational (intra-firm exports) suggesting, as I have argued, the traditional international trade theoretical frame is inadequate. It needs to be replaced by an IPE understanding of the unequal exchange involved between core and periphery and an understanding of the way global corporations (re)organize production and distribution. For transnationals the WTO is crucial not only to their agenda of operating unhindered in all parts of the world, but also for the definition and then enforcement of intellectual property and market access in services. The WTO precludes competition from the newly industrializing economies along the lines previously employed by late developers. It assures their subordinate role in the value added production chain. The key vehicles are TRIM, TRIP, and GATS provisions of the WTO and their enforcement in a manner which has ignored interests other than those of transnational capital, which will be discussed in the next chapter. In a longer historical perspective the work of TRIPs and other WTO agreements are seen by critics as a continuation of a process began with colonization, the propagation of Western standards and the tightening of foreign control. TRIPs are designed to secure these standards in the face of the considerable diversity of social, cultural, and economic practices. It is important to see these recent developments in historical perspective. Over time the means to such goals have varied from extraterritorial laws to informal commercial empires, but it has long been the case that "property rules are important became they promote—or impede—the internationalization of capital" (Lipson, 1985: 33).

WTO rules permit the imposition of antidumping duties if foreign goods are sold in their markets below cost of production which causes or threatens material injury to domestic producers. A country may also impose countervailing duties against imports which benefit from trade distorting subsidies. The United States was the first to use countervailing duties and was initially responsible for initiating the majority of such retaliations. Smaller economies were cautious and not as likely to attempt such measures against the United States and other large economies. Their actions in any case would be less effective given the disparity in market size. By 2000, however, the larger developing countries had become more likely to use anti-dumping actions and were responsible for more than half of the new anti-dumping instances recorded by UNCTAD. The EU has also initiated important suits against the United States. Still, over the

1995–1999 period, two-thirds of the 1,229 cases recorded were directed against poorer countries (P. Williams, 2000). Such practices have not been easily adjudicated within the WTO framework.

THE DISPUTE MECHANISM

The major change between the GATT and WTO is with regard to issues of dispute settlement. The WTO Dispute Settlement Body (DSB) establishes strict timetables for a series of stages in a process which is binding and allows compensation or retaliation. Unlike under the GATT procedures, parties cannot block or ignore the process and are duty bound to adopt panel recommendations or submit to penalties. There is an appeal process to a permanent Appellate Body comprised of seven members of recognized authority with expertise in law and the subject matters covered in trade agreements. Under the GATT procedure unfavorable panel reports could be blocked by the losing party, which was likely to delay for prolonged periods, sometimes indefinitely, the implementation of panel reports. The United States was among the most flagrant in this practice. Under the WTO the Understanding on Rules and Procedures Governing the Settlement of Disputes (at Annex 2 of the WTO Agreement), matters are binding and disputes are adjudicated as follows: a dispute is initially heard by a three-member panel of experts and can be appealed to an Appellate Body appointed by the Dispute Settlement Body (the DSB is comprised of all parties contracting to the agreement). The Appellate Body is limited to issues of law and legal interpretation. It may not remand a case (send it back for further study) on any grounds. It can only uphold, modify, or reverse the decision. WTO members pledge themselves not to take unilateral action against what they perceive as unfair trade violations by other nations, but instead accept the multilateral dispute settlement system of the organization and abide by its rules and findings; this is a victory for the principle of multilateralism agreed to in 1948 in Havana. (For a useful summary of the procedure see International Contract Adviser, 1996.)

The dispute settlement procedure is a little more involved than this: it first seeks mutually acceptable solutions through bilateral consultation between the governments concerned. Should they fail, and if both parties agree, the case is brought before the WTO Director who in *ex officio* capacity offers good offices, conciliation, or mediation to settle the dispute. If such consultations fail to arrive at a solution within sixty days the complainant can ask the Dispute Settlement Body, convened by the WTO General Secretary, to establish a three-person panel to examine the case. The panel does so and makes a finding which is the basis for a DSB ruling. Panels are created from lists of qualified persons and if difficulties in agreeing on their makeup occur the Director General appoints the panelists. While there is an Appellate Body, the panel's decision is adopted automatically unless WTO members decide by consensus not to do so. A decision that finds a legal violation will recommend the defendant government bring its practices into conformity. If that is not done the plaintiff government may take countermeasures of equivalent value.

The GATT approach was a diplomatic one; the WTO Dispute Settlement Mechanism is a legal procedure. Decisions hinge on fact-finding in which parties naturally have conflicting interests in what information panels receive. The quality of legal representation is crucial since technicalities now count for more. The poorer countries, always at a disadvantage in negotiations because of power imbalance, have an additional handicap in participating in such legalistic adjudications since they typically lack highly qualified legal personnel and there is no public defender-like mechanism. The technical assistance the WTO itself provides is exceedingly modest. Dispute settlement has strict time limits to avoid protracted procedures— for instance the panel has nine months, or twelve if the panel report is appealed. Since the disputing parties often are unable to agree on the framing of issues and standards such terms are imposed unless the parties agree otherwise within twenty days from the establishment of the panel. Other strict rules keep the proceedings moving and the judgments and consequences clear. The contrast with the GATT, which lacked clear and timely procedures, contained no provision for the automatic establishment of a panel, and allowed the losing party to block adoption of reports is evident.

While much of the literature on the WTO focuses on the importance of dispute resolution issues, it is useful to begin with a clear understanding of the political economy of the organization, for its remit dramatically shifted the balance between the most advanced economies and the countries seeking to close the gap with them by moving up to produce more technologically advanced, higher value added products. The problem many see with the WTO procedure is the "overreaching" by WTO panels which as Presley (1998: 185) writes "have a natural predisposition to favor integrational concerns over domestic concerns, conceivably resulting in interference with properly domestic matters." To many critics panel interpretations do more than this. They ride roughshod over local preferences as well as environmental and human rights concerns. The panels make trade liberalization the be-all and end-all criteria for their decisions overriding the safeguards and exceptions to trade *über alles* which have been written into both WTO rules and the domestic laws of member countries. If their interpretation moves beyond or in contradiction to the expectations of member states at the time they signed the agreement then their interpretation can be seen as in effect legislative action. Public interest NGOs are dissatisfied with the dispute resolution procedure since they often have a stake in the outcome but are not allowed to present evidence and viewpoints which the governmental parties involved do not see as relevant. Consumer rights, environmental concerns, and labor questions are viewed by NGOs as integral to trade norms yet they are given short shrift (Van der Borght, 1999). Such complaints are the basis of the charge that a secretive group of unelected bureaucrats and technicians is imposing a trade regime on the world and that the WTO as it operates is an illegitimate abuse of power.

SOVEREIGNTY ISSUES

By the close of the twentieth century the developing countries represented nearly a third of the exports of all goods and nearly a quarter of all exports of services. As these countries gained a larger role in world trade, on the one hand they almost totally accepted that foreign investment was "a good thing," but on the other they demanded a greater voice in governance of the global trading system so that international rules would not discriminate against national strategies they found congenial to their development goals. While they wanted to attract foreign investment they were aware it could have both good and bad effects and wanted to maximize positive effects while minimizing negative aspects. They wished to retain the right to regulate entry and the terms and conditions under which foreign firms operated in their economies. They saw efforts by the United States and others to establish "a level playing field" as a move to reduce their ability to regulate TNCs and to build locally owned firms to better compete internationally.

Many of the Third World countries feared a return to a colonial situation where the imperial powers would control their productive resources and their local markets (Khor, 1996). They saw unseemly haste and strong-armed pressure in the tactics used by the United States and other core

state negotiators to force the acceptance of trade related investment measures, agreements on intellectual property, and trade in services which
appeared to be new weapons the core economies aimed at the prospect of
their economies. Indeed, looking at the cases initiated within the WTO
framework there is evidence according to critics that their goal was to
impose discipline on developing economies in areas in which they were
challenging the core producers. There has been concern at the increased
number of cases against developing countries with reference to their failure to meet new obligations contained in the Uruguay Round agreements. Whether these countries should have to play by the rules preferred
by the developed countries once they have come to understand them
more fully and object to their costs remains a matter of some dispute. U.S.
trade negotiators have been adamant that there is no going back. American negotiators insist that there will be no reopening of past negotiations
after agreement has been reached.

The trajectory of U.S. negotiating strategy through the history of the
GATT was to take the multilateral trading regime concerned with the
cross-border movement of goods increasingly into new areas of importance
to U.S. transnationals in successive rounds— in particular by expanding the
focus from a trade regime to an investment regime, and then expanding the
scope of investment to include equal treatment in local economies for
transnational firms. Indeed, there is wide recognition that "Because the
benefits which the WTO brings to the world economy come primarily via
the impact of the WTO on investment decisions, it is no exaggeration to
say that investment is at the heart of the WTO" (WTO Secretariat, 1996:
39). For U.S. negotiators the important issue was overcoming the resistance of sovereign nations to the investment regime, which would compromise the ability of governments to pursue nationalist economic policies that
favored home industry vis-à-vis the penetration of transnational capital. In
negotiating the WTO the United States had pushed for recognition of the
value of brands and intellectual property more broadly. The Uruguay
Round moved negotiations from the border of participant states, agreements geared to reducing barriers to trade transactions, to regulation of
economic activities within sovereign territory. By addressing intellectual
property and trade in services the GATT moved beyond cross-border trade
to intrusion on domestic sovereignty.

To many Americans the WTO represented not the increased sovereignty of transnational capital and importantly U.S.-based TNCs but a
loss of national sovereignty for the United States of America to foreign
interests. In the 1996 presidential campaign Patrick Buchanan got an

enthusiastic response when he denounced the WTO, saying that "face-less foreign judges" would nullify American laws. The Republican nom-inee Bob Dole declared he favored legislation that would let the United States pull out of the WTO if the trade court trampled on our sover-eignty. "Our laws should continue to be a matter for Americans, not international judges to determine," he declared. But of course no new legislation was required. The United States could withdraw from the WTO. If it wanted it could ignore its rulings, although this was not in its long-term interest, as expressed by the executive branch, which got so much more from a general adherence to the GATT-WTO system as a vehicle to gain acceptance of principles it saw as in its interests. The United States, as noted, has used the dispute settlement mechanism more then any other country.

Buchanan and other right wing populists were correct that GSEGIs deprive U.S. citizens of rights they had previously in theory enjoyed, and their government of sovereignty; but there is in such an analysis a failure to connect the dots properly. The vast conspiracy theories are typically vague on who or what is surrendering our well-being to foreign powers, although the thought is that "traitors" and "black helicopters" may be involved. It is more difficult to see as villains in the narrative either the transnational CEOs who believe they are doing right while doing good in their global state economic governance institution build-ing, or the government officials, typically involved in a revolving door relationship with these same TNCs. However if one objects to the sys-tem being created it would seem more fruitful to interrogate the motives and the hegemonic ideologies involved in its creation, perpetu-ation, and transfigurations.

The U.S. executive branch is a hard negotiator for these interests in many fora, often settling up special purpose negotiations in areas of con-cern to its leading corporations. For example, in announcing approval of an accord to open global telecommunications markets in early 1997 the then acting United States Trade Representative Charlene Barshefsky declared: "The United States has effectively exported American values of free competition, fair rules and effective enforcement." Other countries felt they had been coerced into accepting American policies which favored American companies. There was a good deal of muttering with some countries calling this economic imperialism. Barshefsky had used the pow-erful weapon of access to the United States, the home of half the world's telecommunication market to force concessions If Buchanan and others object to such supra-national obligations they should focus on their own Washington policymakers.

To other countries the source of diminished sovereignty is clear enough. Consider: it was the United States which undercut national autonomy when it pushed for dismantling within-border traditional prerogatives as it did for example when it attacked the Japanese *keiretsu* system as an unfair trade practice. (A *keiretsu* is an interconnected group of companies which have privileged relations with each other typically cemented through cross ownership.) Japanese suppliers and distributors often have such ties which, said the United States in its Structural Impediment Initiative negotiations in the 1980s, violated Japan's own anti-trust laws. Of course these laws were promulgated at the insistence of the SCAP economists when American forces occupied Japan at the end of the Second World War and have been mostly ignored since they are not the way Japan deals with such questions (Tabb, 1995). As the Japanese economy liberalized but also weakened in the 1990s and U.S. pressures continued, the Japanese were less willing to make concessions. Having been told that they needed to allow markets to function freely they were frustrated by U.S. insistence that they accede to numerical targets to improve U.S. export performance. Nonetheless in 1995 the Clinton Team, led by Mickey Kantor, the United States Trade Representative, demanded "a momentous shift" that would "break the back" of the collusive networks that kept Japan's market closed to American producers. The White House wanted an accord that would "remake the world's second-largest economy and strike fear into the heart of Asian countries tempted to imitate Japan's model" (Sanger, 1995: D5). In May 1995 the United States threatened a GATT suit on the issue in a case involving the domestic distribution system for film in Japan. In 1998, however, the American film maker Kodak, which had complained to the WTO that Fuji Film's distribution system was unfair, was told by a panel that the WTO had no jurisdiction over competitiveness laws. Such a ruling did not end the matter since in the U.S. legal system, unlike those of most other nations, it is perfectly acceptable to breach a contract so long as one is willing to pay damages. Therefore even if by prematurely sanctioning Japan we violated the WTO accord, from Kantor's perspective this was not a problem. The question is whether, after breaching the contract, and paying Japan's losses, the United States stood to gain more. Hardball was the name of America's game. The United States continued to push the agenda of future rounds in the WTO to make its views on competition policy part of the organization's expanding mandate.

TRIPS, TRIMS AND GATS

In the 1990s U.S. trade negotiators took a more ambitious approach than simply applying the bicycle principle. The ratchet principle would be a better term. Once barriers are removed they are not to be permitted to be restored. Nonconforming practices to the general principle of free trade are to be enumerated under the WTO by countries which practice them and those not so itemized are prohibited. Exceptions are understood to be temporary and conformity to the level-playing-field nondiscrimination principle achieved as soon as possible. This set of understandings had its own language—of 'standstill" and "rollback" whereby national treatment principles were to be reduced in coverage and then eliminated through successive rounds of WTO negotiations, which would continually reexamine nonconforming measures. This new trade order locked in liberalization and prohibitions and could not be rescinded (the "standstill" provisions). Specific exceptions would be periodically reexamined and liberalized (through "rollback" provisions) in successive rounds. These procedures, embodied in TRIM, TRIP and GATS agreements, rested to a significant extent on new definitions of legal property. Traditionally accounting theory has recognized the measurement of asset value in terms of historical acquisition cost. The new regime defines intellectual capital, the intangible value of which is not based on cost but expected discounted earnings. The new rules allow for the recapture of lost opportunities as a result of state actions in restraint of trade (as understood by panel interpretations of the investment rules of the new trading regime) following a theory assuming that all such intangible assets constitute legally protected property and that judges can determine their universally recognized attributes.

This represents a revolution in the understanding of what property is. It puts emerging economies and poorer countries generally at a tremendous disadvantage against the larger states and the TNCs they represent in disputes in the WTO procedures. There are complex matters on which these countries lack expertise and the resources to mount effective legal battle. More than this, the wider definition of property rights gives transnationals wishing to compete with national governments of other core countries in the provision of certain services the ability to challenge the government decision to provide the service. Barshefsky noted "health care service in many foreign countries have largely been the responsibility of the public sector . . . [making] it difficult for US private sector health care providers to market in foreign countries." Under the WTO a challenge to "restrictive" licensing of health care professionals and "excessive" privacy and confidentiality regulations can be mounted in order to obtain market access and national treatment allowing provisions of all health care services cross-border as well as allowing majority foreign ownership of health care facilities. Susan George (1999: 4), writing from France, comments on such developments that should the U.S. sustain its position at the WTO "we can kiss goodbye our public health-care system in Europe." To some extent developing countries have been granted exemptions to particular provisions but usually in the context that these are time limited and will be brought into conformity after a transitional period. What such exemptions are allowed to mean will be resolved only after contentious battle.

Article 11 of the Code recognizes that subsidies aimed at eliminating economic disadvantage in particular regions, which reduce unemployment and so on are allowed. The provisions' interpretation in any particular instance however is a result of intense negotiation and provides employment for many lawyers and other trade experts as well as grist for the mill of politicians. The Subsidy Agreement provisions are extensive. To decide when a subsidy is deemed to exist and when they are prohibited and actionable is rarely without controversy (Edwards, Jr. and Lester, 1997). The position of many developing economies that government intervention is an effective means of promoting domestic industry and increasing national income, as we saw in the last chapter, has gained support from the strategic trade theory literature, which questions neoclassical model assumptions that trade is driven solely by comparative advantage in given resource endowments in perfectly competitive markets. However in discussions of TRIMs the advanced economies have wanted to ban practices which interfere with free markets outright, considering them without exception as inherently trade distorting. The developing economies wish to argue on a case by case basis for the legitimacy and usefulness of specific practices in particular contexts and argue that harm to complainant countries must be proven and not assumed. Other areas of dispute center around those subsidies which countries claim are granted in pursuit of valid economic and social policy and those which defensibly can be understood as depriving other countries of legitimate trade opportunities.

Because the WTO incorporated the U.S. view of investment, intellectual property rights, and the legal order, transnational capital in markets everywhere has built on these and other agreements incorporated into the final GATT negotiating round to claim extensive privileges as against the preferred practice of developing countries. There was a lot at stake. In 1995 U.S. firms received more than half of all global receipts to royalty and licensing fees. As intellectual property became more important, American trade negotiators looked for ways to prevent what they saw as intellectual piracy. They wanted to act quickly and decisively and were willing to do so unilaterally if other nations would not agree on an international governance framework which the U.S. considered adequate. Up until 1994 the GATT regime had dealt solely with trade in goods. But with the growing importance of services, which also faced barriers in the international economy, and of the returns to intellectual property—which were being compromised through free rider use of proprietary software, videos and other product forms—the U.S. pushed hard for enforceable agreements. It achieved the General Agreement on Trade in Services (GATS), the Agreement on Trade-Related Aspects of Intellectual Property (TRIPs), and Trade Related Investment Measures (TRIMs) as part of the Uruguay Round. These agreements set standards and rules for the protection and exploitation of property rights which bind participating states to liberalization of trade in these areas and to the expansion of the international juridicalization process into new realms.

The Agreement on Trade Related Intellectual Property Rights was directly aimed at the long-standing pattern through which late industrializers borrowed ideas from the leaders. The United States, after all, industrialized to a great extent by using, but not paying for, British manufacturing innovations. The Japanese borrowed American technology, paying as little as they could get away with for product and process technologies. The Koreans, among others, reverse engineered U.S. and Japanese products and copied production techniques. What economists have interpreted as the process of technological diffusion has now been redefined by the U.S. trade lawyers as late industrializer piracy. TRIPs prevents the process of industrial imitation, or at least makes it more difficult. Koreans and others now complain bitterly about the high tech mafia which they see as extorting exorbitant royalty payments from them. The technically more advanced TNC is better able to control the extent to which new rivals can compete with them while squeezing their profit margins through such charges.

Part I of TRIPS lays out principles for the protection of intellectual property. These are conventions under which the nationals of parties to the agreement are guaranteed no less favorable terms by other countries than these nations extend to their own citizens with regard to the protection of intellectual property and a most-favored-nation clause. Under these provisions, advantages given to any one nation can be claimed by other signatory's nationals and must be extended immediately and unconditionally (even if the treatment is better than that which the country in question accords its own citizens).

Part II of TRIPS enumerates rights to be protected. These range to topographies of integrated circuits and details of the control of licensing practices. The extent of the privileges which are being claimed under TRIPS are extensive. They range from patenting of human genes to definition of software knowledge patents which would create monopoly rights to what others see as the common inheritance of humankind. Intellectual property rights agreements were signed before most people and governments understood their social and economic implications. Monopoly control by pharmaceutical companies and attempts to patent genetic materials and biogenetic resources of Third World countries are areas of particularly heated dispute.

It is of course the rich countries which have intellectual property to protect. Their legal systems and regulatory infrastructure can easily accommodate the enforcement of TRIPs. The poorer countries, who stand to gain little or nothing, face the costly process of building the enforcement infrastructure from scratch to protect transnationals' property which means higher prices for their citizens and punishment for the governments if they fail to meet their TRIP obligations. As Ernesto Hizon (1999: 143) writes: "it is the height of naivete to assume that the less developed WTO members, with hardly the technological capacity to innovate or even replicate inventions, and with a limited market, can benefit from increased protection." Indeed, he suggests, "imposing foreign legal standards on unwilling states in the name of harmonization would be a sophisticated form of neo-imperialism."

Under TRIPs Western "bioprospectors" search the world's plants, animals, and microorganisms looking for materials for new drugs, crops, and other now patentable "discoveries." Developing countries are the source of an estimated 90 percent of the world's biological resources from which most of the world's frequently prescribed drugs are derived, often based on long-standing local knowledge which is appropriated by Western pharmaceutical companies. Developing countries who go uncompensated call this biopiracy. For example, in 1995 two researchers at the University of Mississippi Medical Center were granted a U.S. patent to use turmeric to heal wounds. Very often printed documentation is simply not available to peoples with oral traditions or those whose common law property is being taken do not appeal in the court system. In the turmeric case to get the patent rescinded, an ancient Sanskrit text was eventually entered into evidence to prove that in India this was a long standing procedure. The United Nations Development Programme (1999: 70) notes: "Without the consent of local people, the knowledge has been used to develop highly profitable drugs. In any other situation this would be called industrial espionage—theft of both the genetic materials and the long-acquired knowledge of suing them to develop medicines." The report pointed out that a mere two percent royalty on medicinal plants would yield $5 billion for developing countries. This is a modest fee. The United States Park Service secured a ten percent royalty share from a bioprospector for Yellowstone Park (United Nations Development Programme, 1999: 71). Examples such as a case in northwestern Mexico, where an American company infuriated local farmers by obtaining a patent and exclusive right to market yellow enola beans in the United States (which the Mexicans had long grown) is typical of another pattern. Again the patent was given but not for a novel invention. The patent however deprived the Mexicans of the right to export their crop to el Norte. The use of patents by TNCs to obtain market power and exclude less powerful competitors is growing more common.

Conflict exists over a host of other issues related to the scope of property rights versus the common inheritance. In Rome in the summer of 2001 negotiations were held at the Commission for Genetic Resources for Food and Agriculture, part of the United Nations Food and Agricultural Organization. The meeting foundered on the division between the United States and the rest of the world. The United States, having succeeded in getting the WTO to accept TRIPs, was attempting to apply this intellectual property regime to public seedbanks, specifically those run by the Consultative Group on International Agricultural Research based in Rome, which, to share resources internationally, arranges informal seed exchanges on the principle of common heritage. Hundreds of thousands of seeds for cabbage and corn and all manner of other plants are lent at no charge to traditional plant breeders and biotech genetic engineers to develop new crop varieties. Most delegates favored funding the project with mandatory royalties into a central fund. The United States opposed such a plan saying it probably violated TRIPs. The U.S. view was rejected by the Europeans and the G-77 delegates who said the costly American alternative would allow only for participation by the largest companies and countries and would lead to a serious lessening of biodiversity (Mason, 2001: 5).

While much critical attention has focused on such aspects of TRIPs and their proper interpretation, there also has been concern that transnationals have lost many billions in pirated software, entertainment products, and other potential sales involving counterfeit logos and knockoffs of a host of products. Legitimate videodisc sales in China are almost nonexistent. That country is sophisticated at placing pirated versions on sale almost immediately after the product is released in the West. China produces close copies of Yamaha, Suzuki, and Honda motorcycles sold as

Yameha, Zuzaka and Honnea; they cost half as much as the genuine article. Sales are huge. In Indonesia Chinese-made motorcycles reached a
quarter of all sales in just two years after first being offered for sale in
1998. As commodity manufacturing moves to newly industrializing
economies, businesses in the core unable to compete in standardized
products understand that their future is tied to the knowledge economy
and a defining of property rights so that their ability to innovate and
package unique proprietary products is protected. The degree to which
they can claim exclusive right to techniques and designs will determine
the extent others can legally offer them competition through imitation.
Trademarks and brand names have become the most valuable asset many
companies have. Much is at stake in just where property rights lines are
allowed to be drawn.

The legal regime becomes crucial. The U.S. has been eager to extend
property rights and does so more liberally than any other country; some
would say it has done so promiscuously (*The Economist Technology Quarterly*, 2001). The U.S. patent Office has shown willingness to expand the
traditional understanding of what is patentable, leading to court cases
over the granting of such ownership claims. Critics cite the example of
the patent extended to Amazon for a one click ordering system, Price-
line's patent for reverse auctions on the web, and E-Data's patent on selling "material in a download fashion via the Internet." The ability to
patent such trivial innovations, if allowed, conveys exceedingly valuable
rights and can be powerfully anti-competitive in impact. Technical application of software development if patentable generates huge royalty
streams. The British Patent Office has strictly limited this type of software
patenting and maintains that business methods should remain
unpatentable. The U.S. continues to aggressively allow patents, including those on genes and living organisms (including humans) setting up
conflicts among national patent regimes. Other countries (and many
Americans) oppose such privatization of basic knowledge and common
inheritance resources.

TRIMS AND GATS

TRIMs require WTO members to provide national treatment to imported
products and disallow quantitative restrictions on import or export of
goods; thus they limit the use of tools countries have long employed to

address balance of payments deficits and to favor local producers as part of development strategies. Nations have for hundreds of years imposed tariffs and quotas to limit foreign competition with domestic production. They may see performance requirements for foreign companies as part of their domestic development strategy and offer preferential benefits to domestic firms or for particular investments. Countries may wish to limit the extent of foreign control of particular industries on national security, cultural, or anti-monopoly grounds. Host countries find their freedom in these areas increasingly constrained by the trade related agreements to which they have acquiesced. These become areas of dispute under the Agreement on Trade-Related Investment Measures provisions. TRIMs preclude many of the techniques of Latin American nationalist development models, the Asian development states and European corporatism. Rules that restrict transnational penetration or insist on local production of components which TNCs must source locally (so-called domestic content rules) and used with success by many developing countries to move up the ladder to more technologically sophisticated goods are, for example, illegal under TRIM rules.

TRIMs and TRIPs interact. Trade Related Investment Measures include subsidies to domestic producers, government sponsored cartels, and R&D grants for domestic producers, as well as joint ownership and profit remittance restrictions for foreign investors designed to favor domestic economic development. Trade Related Intellectual Property Agreements protect rights of patent holders, proprietary designs, genetic engineering, trademarks, and so on. The third pillar of the new expanded trade regime is the GATS, the General Agreement on Trade in Services, also part of the Uruguay Round negotiations. It marks the first time that services have been brought into the legal framework of a trade agreement by requiring nondiscriminatory treatment to suppliers of services from any one country to other WTO members.

As a concession to the many countries which objected, national treatment can be withheld for specified sectors. A country indicates which service sectors it wishes to accord national treatment and specifies the terms, limitations, and conditions of market access for these services. GATS can either be seen as representing only a modest improvement or as a major "foot in the door" for service exporters. Whichever interpretation one prefers, there is agreement that continuous pressure is now exerted to reduce discretion and bring services further into conformity with the liberal trading regime.

I know of no detailed research which systematically canvases developing country negotiators, but there is widespread belief that the United States exerted inordinate pressure to achieve the TRIP, TRIM, and GATS provisions in the Uruguay Round. From a Third World perspective, P. Saiwing Ho suggests the several rounds of multilateral trade negotiations can be viewed as a story of the changing, and decreasing, degrees of freedom and autonomy enjoyed by Southern countries in their pursuit of national development-related policies (Ho, 1998). Chakravarthi Raghavan has described the acronym in terms of the proposals of the industrial countries aiming at "tripping the Third World efforts at industrialisation and developing and preventing them from emerging as competitors" (Raghavan, 1990: 63). Whether such steps will "trim" the chances of development or speed them is of course a matter of some debate. It will surely change the pattern of their development trajectories.

Western economists tend to point to the benefits of foreign investment in transmitting best practice technologies to local economies and see autocentric development as an inferior strategy. Yet even if this position is accepted on economic grounds, issues of democratic procedure arise when the proposals are adopted only under the threat by the powerful against the relatively powerless negotiators. As Tony Clarke (1999: 1) writes, "From the outset, the WTO was crafted like no other international agency. The architects of the final agenda of the Uruguay Round wanted to put in place a political institution that would oversee the building of the new global economic order." And so it has. Politics, the exercise of power to determine who gets what in these negotiations, has been the dominant operating factor. The politics in turn reflects perception of economic interest and the power of transnational capital which derives from the structural relations of capitalism as our economic system and the instrumentalist activities of the agents of transnational capital and international finance as reflected in the background of key negotiators and the influence exerted by trade associations and groups like the Business Roundtable, the European Round Table, and the Transatlantic Business Dialogue (organizations discussed in chapter 4, which have been integral to the sculpting of TRIMs, TRIPs and GATS). The U.S. government's hardball negotiators may have pushed through these corporate globalization regulations using the hegemon's power resources to effectively cajole resistant Third World nations but in doing they were seen by much of the world for whom such language and analysis is not foreign or beyond the pale as agents of the leading fractions of the capitalist class as surely as the marines and the big stick foreign policy toward "banana republics" did a century earlier. Indeed, this sort of attitude toward U.S. imperial designs and military interventions continues to shape opinion in many parts of the world regarding contemporary U.S. peacekeeping interventions.

CANCÚN AND THE FUTURE OF THE WTO

At the September 2003 the World Trade Ministerial Meeting in Cancún, Mexico many of the tensions which had been simmering between the rich nations and the poor countries boiled over. These strains, which had been evident in Seattle and at the meeting which followed in Doha, Qatar in 2001, led to a breakdown and early end to the Cancún gathering. Two issues were central. The first was agriculture; the second the so-called Singapore issues. The rich countries had long enraged many of the poorer countries which are dependent on agriculture. The poorer nations accuse the rich nations of hypocrisy in demanding more and more concessions from them while refusing to have free trade in areas in which the poorer countries have a comparative advantage, let alone respecting the needs and priorities of the developing nations for special and differentiated treatment in areas of strategic interest to them.

Two-thirds of poor people in the world live in rural areas and most are farmers. The rich countries heavily subsidize production and export of basic foods such as rice, corn and wheat allowing the dumping of basic food commodities in developing country markets and pushing them to produce export crops. In the poorest region of the world, sub-Saharan Africa, wheat imports, for example, increased by more than a third between 1996 and 2000. This dumping led the French-speaking West African countries to invest heavily in cotton production at the urging of the World Bank. At the time of the Cancún meeting cotton was Chad's largest export; it represented 75 percent of Benin's export revenues, accounted for half of Mali's hard currency resources, and in Burkino Faso 60 percent of export revenues and more than a third of its GDP. Unfortunately cotton prices dropped by half between 1997 and 2002. Low cotton prices are largely attributable to the more than $3 billion the United States government provides to its 25,000 cotton producers (with an annual net worth of over $1 million each). These huge subsidies have allowed the United States to become the world's largest exporter of cotton despite the higher U.S. production costs. It has also contributed directly to the suffering of the 10 million cotton farmers in West Africa, many of whom live on a dollar a day or less.

The delegates from these countries asked that the United States stop these subsidies which were killing their people. Ibrahim Maloum, president of the African Cotton Association said "Africa does not ask for any special treatment; on the contrary, it asks that World Trade Organization rules be respected by all." Of course it is not only cotton producers in rich countries but almost all farmers who are given such subsidies which allow them to compete unfairly with the farmers in the poorest countries, who are often more efficient in a free market but who face high tariffs on their exports in the rich countries and do not benefit from export subsidies as the rich farmers do. But it was the case of West African cotton which mobilized what became known first as the G-19, then the G-20, G-21, G-22, G-23 as more developing countries joined Brazil, India, China and other large and more powerful developing countries who supported the Africans in demanding dramatic change in the agricultural regime. Zambian Trade Minister Dipak Patel said "We're working hard to find a convergence with G23. We're trying to make it G80." (Mathiason, 2003). This group demanded a timetable to end to such unfair agricultural subsidies. The rich countries refused to consider such a change, which they said was unrealistic in terms of their domestic politics.

The second issue which led to the breakdown of the talks was the refusal of the EU to back down on its insistence that the four Singapore issues (investment, competition rules, transparency in government procurement, and trade facilitation) be included in the negotiations. The developing countries have never wanted to even talk about them. At Cancún this refusal was reiterated strongly by more than seventy developing countries. Since explicit consensus is required to go forward, in theory even one country can keep an item from the agenda. That half the membership objected angered the rich countries who had insisted these items be negotiated. Robert Zoellick, the U.S. Trade Representative, in accusing unnamed governments of sabotaging the talks, said he had a long list of countries who wanted to negotiate with the United States and he would proceed with them while he wait for things to "calm down" at the World Trade Organization (Becker, 2003c).

Charles Grassley (R-Iowa) the chair of the U.S. Senate Finance Committee said he would judge countries seeking deals with the United States by their behavior at Cancún. The poor countries would be under tremendous pressure as one by one they would have to face the Americans behind closed doors. But at Cancún they had stood firm. Some commentators suggested that at Cancún the balance of trade power had shifted strongly away from rich countries, marking the most significant change at the

WTO in fifty years. Others said the organization now faced marginalization, an indefinite period in limbo as members turned away and toward
bilateral and regional negotiations. Both of these positions could well be
right. When powerful actors have been unable to get their way at global
state economic governance institutions they have withdrawn and shifted
venues.

POLITICS AND TRADE CONFLICT

Despite its having engineered the WTO the United States, in the eyes of
many others in the world, has in important cases shown an unwillingness
to play by its rules. The litigious logic and the "in your face" hubris of a
hegemonic power is manifest in use of the so-called "super 301" amendment to the 1974 Trade Act strengthened in the 1988 Omnibus Trade and
Competitiveness Act which authorize retaliation against what the United
States determines is "unfair" competition. Super 301 gives the United
States permission to unilaterally respond to trading partners seen as causing it injury. It works to the extent it does because the United States can
ignore the WTO rules it was so central in creating should it wish to, given
its unique position as the world's hegemonic power. When frustrated by
the inability to win through trade resolution structures the United States
has acted unilaterally. That the procedure is widely considered as outside
and antithetical to the GATT has not mattered greatly. The trade acts
included provisions that require the executive branch to investigate and
impose retaliatory measures where foreign governments are found to violate an international trade agreement with the United States. When such
a practice, even if it does not violate any international agreement, is seen
by the U.S. as "unreasonable or discriminatory and burdens and restricts
United States commerce" Section 301(b) provides for "discretionary"
action. Under the "super 301" mechanism the U.S. Trade Representative
identifies "priority foreign country practices, the elimination of which is
likely to have the most significant potential too increase United States
exports," publishes a list annually of trading partners engaging in unfair
practices, and allows for punitive action against them.

In the 1970s and 1980s the United States acted as a hegemonic power
which no longer was winning in global economic competition. Certain
sectors adversely effected by the pressure of foreign competition
demanded selective protectionism through sharp unilateral retaliation.

Most countries, among them Japan, would back down from any confrontation with the United States. South Korea similarly has taken extraordinary steps to bring its trade practices in line with U.S. demands to avoid receiving a "priority" status. The United States used protectionist measures which have hurt other countries (and also American consumers), especially in periods when it appeared to have lost competitive advantage in important domestic industries capable of pressuring the government for protection. Diana Tussie notes that while the United States was hardly the only country in these years to face intensifying competition, "it was the only one that could and did turn its own need for protection into a global regulatory framework to manage trade" (Tussie, 1993: 83). There were at least a hundred cases of U.S. threats of sanctions under Section 301 affecting foreign producers of everything (from semiconductors to oranges as well as toy retailers) in which the United States chose not recourse to the GATT but unilateral action.

While America continues to demand that others play by the rules, which mean "play by our rules," there always seems to be Congressional pressure for retaliations which do not meet the requirements of the multilateral trade regime. The threat of U.S. unilateral action under Super 301 was effective—even when it violated WTO rules. The Clinton Administration called its hardball trade politics "WTO-plus," suggesting it was consistent with multilateral trade agreements and specifically WTO rules. Others saw it as "vigilante justice" (Hudec, 1999) and resistance to accepting its use grew among American trading partners. The United States backed away from Super 301 unilateralism when challenged and has seemed to have come to an understanding with the Europeans who have threatened to demand a WTO ruling if the U.S. did not back off. The ambiguity will remain since it is not in any nation's interest to push for a definitive ruling which could lead the United States to withdraw from WTO jurisdiction. At the same time the overwhelming thrust of the WTO has been to act "as the muscular sheriff of the world trading system," a role which has overwhelmingly pleased U.S.-based transnational business interests.

The most severe disputes have involved the U.S. exercise of extraterritoriality in politically charged cases. The Cuban Liberty and Democratic Solidarity (Libertad) Act of 1996, popularly known as the Helms-Burton Act, among other things, authorized U.S. nationals who have had property confiscated by the Cuban government since 1959 to sue companies "trafficking" in expropriated properties and bars the issuance of visas to aliens and their families who traffic in such property. Helms-Burton resulted in vociferous protests from both the business communities and governments of Europe, Mexico, and Canada as infringing on international law. Countries have adopted blocking and clawback legislation (anything taken in American courts would be taken back in home legal proceedings) and to legal challenges initiated within NAFTA and the WTO. Specifically, in May, 1996 the European Union asked for the formation of a dispute settlement panel under WTO rules challenging the extraterritorial reach of Helms-Burton. The United States responded that the panel did not have jurisdiction because Helms-Burton was a matter of "national security." After months of negotiation, diplomatic efforts led to understandings that the United States would not attempt enforcement and others would suspend legal challenges. Various face saving understandings were reached such as a US-EU "Transatlantic Partnership on Political Cooperation and an Understanding on Conflicting Requirements" designed to stall the hardliners in Congress.

The politicization of trade takes place on a number of levels and is a many sided debate. It involves not only the clash between nationalist versus transnational interests but also efficiency market arguments versus social justice perspectives. From the latter perspective a statement from members of international civil society signed as of August 1999 by 798 organizations from more than 75 countries opposing a millennium round of trade negotiations offers charges against the WTO expressed in the following terms: "The Uruguay Round Agreements have functioned principally to prise open markets for the benefit of transnational corporations at the expense of national economies; workers, farmers and other people, and the environment. In addition the WTO system, rules and procedures are undemocratic, untransparent and not-accountable and have operated to marginalize the majority of the world's people." Such critics are angered at actions by "unaccountable bureaucrats." Yet the present institutional framing and its enforcement rules were created by the representatives of transnational capital acting through their state executives. There are numerous other indications that the WTO as it is currently structured dictates the scope and content of the international rules in ways which many find objectionable. In the next chapter the issues at stake and some of the most important clashes over protecting the rights of workers, addressing forced labor as well as such concerns as fishing practices which endanger sea turtles and dolphins and other ecological issues will be addressed from legal, economic, and political perspectives.

CHAPTER ELEVEN

Market Efficiency Versus Labor Rights and Environmental Protection

"Let us not stop at financial analysis. Let us not stop at financial architecture. Let us not stop at financial sector reform. Now is our chance to launch a global debate on the architecture—yes—but also on the foundations of development. Now is our chance to show that we can take a broader and more balanced view. Now is our chance to recognize that there is a silent crisis looming on the horizon. . . . A human crisis that will not be resolved unless we address the fundamental issues of the essential interdependence of the developed and the developing worlds. A human crisis that will not be met unless we begin to take a holistic approach both to development and to how we respond to crisis—looking at the financial, the social, the political, the institutional, the cultural, and the environmental aspects of society—together."

—*James Wolfensohn* (1998: 11)

"Loyalty, solidarity and social cohesion know no frontiers other than those erected by history."

—*Mohan Rao* (1999: 79)

The rules and decisions of courts and international administrative organizations such as the WTO, the ILO, and the OECD impact more widely as the interconnectedness of economies increase. Linkages have grown more complex. Where once the organizations dealt mainly with cross-border disputes, increasingly controversies involve conflicting domestic practices and how different nations' laws are to be harmonized in a world of presumably sovereign states. High on some lists of international economic law issues for cross-border harmonization are labor rights and environmental protection. In an increasingly interdependent world will such international standards be established and enforced? And if so, how?

Optimists suggest that with economic growth environmental protection, labor and other human rights will be widely and effectively demanded. Such quality of life items appear to be income elastic above a certain level of development. This would argue that as nations grow richer, and without government interference, labor rights and environmental protection (being superior goods with high income elasticities) will be more in demand. Globalization need not be a race to the bottom; in this argument it is a process which spreads higher regulatory standards. A related thesis is that more transparent regulations, subject to impartial arbitration and effective contract enforcement, attract investors while more corrupt, rent seeking jurisdictions inhibit investment.

Others argue that, on the contrary, countries must fear that more stringent regulation will drive business to less regulated venues. In this second view companies have never voluntarily accepted the social costs of their activities if they could put them onto the larger society, nor pay more than they needed to in order to attract labor unless there is strong societal pressure to do so, and that as long as the world provides a vast reservoir of unemployed and underemployed many will continue to be forced to work for substandard wages as a result of competitive pressures. Only the activity of working people themselves, and the legislation and international agreements it stimulates, can provide for a leveling up instead of a race to the bottom.

A related difference exists between those who stress that social regulation reflects public values we choose collectively and those who reduce society to an aggregation of self-interested individuals each striving for his or her own autonomous ends without collective consciousness or the need for discursive democratic practice. The first position understands a community as a network of relations in which individuals interact to create collective values and binding organization in a process which is not reducible to the rational choice, individual actor model of mainstream economics. It gives credence to social identities and understands the nature of democracy, the proper scope of the market, and all the other big questions as open to collective control. These matters—individuals in society, market control, and market freedom—are ones with which social philosophers have long grappled. In the context of globalization they take the form of "trade and . . . " discussions. They not only divide nations with different interests in particular outcomes but also expose deep ideological fissure between those who prefer less regulation and market-favored outcomes to prevail and those who wish to protect the rights of affected groups from market forces operating at the international level. This philosophical division has been evident in our discussions of the IMF and the WTO.

Economic analysis stresses the market's superior capacity to determine welfare, assuming no externalities or transaction costs. However social issues are essentially about externalities and transaction costs. Politics is the imperfect arena in which preferences are divulged and debated, in which individual and group needs and desires, their distributional consequences, and welfare significance are argued and policies decided. Politics sets the terms within which markets function. To call for a reduced role for politics and a greater role for freedom of choice based on the existing distribution of wealth and power is of course a political position. Where externalities are international in impact, diplomacy, the GSEGIs, and global civil society interact to set these constraints and enabling rules. This chapter discusses the clash of values and analyses involved in the politics and economics of the trade and the environment and trade and labor rights debates. The focus is on social and environmental policy and disputes over how such "trade and . . . " issues are to be theorized.

The chapter first considers one of the issues which drew tens of thousands of protestors to its 1999 Ministerial Meetings in Seattle, that of the unwillingness of the WTO to internalize environmental costs into trade decisions. Not long before these demonstrations corporate greed and for some the capitalist system itself were blamed for such disasters as the *Exxon Valdez* oil spill off Alaska and to Monsanto's Bhopal plant disaster in India killing and injuring thousands. Environmental activist attention shifted to a considerable extent from corporate targets to the WTO and other GSEGIs in the second half of the 1990s. At the dawn of the twenty-first century global issues such as the need to address greenhouse gasses through collective action have taken center stage. Frustrated environmentalists see the global state economic governance institutions as standing in the way of meaningful progress to protect the environment. It has proven easier to mobilize against these targets than to challenge national governments. As public consciousness has been raised on ecological issues many corporations have taken individual action to "green" their public image while the corporate sector has backed the use of market mechanisms as the preferred approach to whatever government regulation emerges out of these debates.

These debates take place on two levels. The first is whether it is reasonable to consider issues such as labor rights and environmental protection in the context of agreements on international trade. Popular movements say they must be integrated. Many corporate and government spokespersons say they should be handled in different fora and not allowed to interfere with trade concerns. The popular movements have public opinion on their side and the principalities and powers are divided between moving toward compromise and continuing to hold the line. Even if "trade and . . . " issues are allowed onto the WTO agenda the question is hardly settled since how such issues are to frame and qualify trade is far from clear. The fault line among academics is between mainstream economics and the approach of mainline political economy. Included in the latter camp are non-neoclassical environmentalists and heterodox institutionalists.

CLASH OF VALUES

As awareness of a single global village grows legal norms taken for granted in an era of international political economics seem arbitrary and in need of revision. Ugo Mattei (2003: 404) offers an example relevant to the discussion in this chapter. "A child that gets damaged by a toy within Europe can seek and find redress in the law. Thousands of children who, during the process of production of the very same toy, are poisoned and have their health ruined, can seek no redress. Arbitrarily, the moment in which a product is considered for the purpose of liability is the moment in which it is introduced in the Western market." Taking advantage of the weak and vulnerable appears unfair and so unacceptable in such a framing. International codes of conduct seem less utopian and become viable demands in the minds of a large segment of global civil society. The separation of the moments of production and consumption, which is taken for granted in the international division of labor, a territorial extension of commodity fetishism more generally, is made visible by labor rights activists.

Some economists argue that low wages and greater exploitation of labor are a legitimate source for comparative advantage. Child labor may be the best resource countries have to sell. If the alternative is starvation they have a legitimate right to exploit children. Others argue that while child labor reflects family poverty and the low wages of parents, removing children from the work force might raise adult wages through decreased labor market competition which removes incentive to put children in to the workforce. There is also a collective action problem. If all families could work together they might not select child labor even though as things stand it may be rational for each individually to do so. This is the rationale for the government to ban child labor. After many decades of such discussions the core countries established child labor laws. Globalization renews these debates in the context of a larger discussion of the best ways to bring about economic development in economically under-developed nations in the context of interdependent labor markets.

It is illegal for the owner of a U.S. factory to employ underaged, undocumented workers sixteen hours a day under sweatshop conditions. To open a sweatshop in a country which does not outlaw this practice is to engage in an acceptable business practice consistent with trade and comparative advantage. Abundant low-cost labor is available to investors. It is a resource for that country.

Neoclassical economists do not ask the sources of different national labor relations regimes. They take them as given; the preferences of par-ticular societies. Anne Krueger for example argues free trade based on comparative advantage "is independent of why there might be cost differ-ences" between nations (Krueger, 1990: 70). Similarly if environmental degradation is the basis for comparative advantage this is a matter of pref-erence as well and it would be wrong for others to impose their priorities. Because mainstream economists in their models of perfect competition assert that wages equal the marginal productivity of labor, it is theoreti-cally impossible for workers to be underpaid. To insist that workers must be paid more than they are worth is to invite job loss.

In addition the sovereignty issue intrudes when the argument is raised at the international level. What right do rich Westerners have to impose their preferences on other countries? The answer is that consumers have a right to boycott products made under conditions they find morally unac-ceptable and that workers in repressive undemocratic regimes are not freely accepting practices which their rulers impose such as the prohibition against forming unions or not being able to vote for social legislation. Nations do not "choose" social policies in any transparent or meaningful sense. Policy outcomes result from struggle among differently positioned social actors. They reflect the inequality of political capabilities embedded in economic and political structures, cultural norms, and understandings. Again the argument is that democratic polities may accept some market inefficiency in the pursuit of social justice.

THE ECONOMISTIC ARGUMENT AND MARKET IMPERFECTIONS

Mainstream economics takes competitive markets as the norm and so sees the introduction of labor standards as a distortion which will lead to misallocation and inefficiencies. Western theories of justice from a normative standpoint can be employed to defend economic liberalization on the argument that it produces welfare gains from the unfettered operation of comparative advantage, thus producing efficiency in production for participants and a higher standard of living through mutually beneficial voluntary exchange. The claim to particularistic human rights can be understood as a source of competitive disadvantage and reason to disavow such market interference.

The presumption that something closely approximating a free market would exist if it were not for social regulation is surely questionable. If labor markets are seriously distorted by unequal bargaining power, say the ability of transnationals and local governments to impose a labor regime which is structured to hold wages down and enforce longer hours and oppressive working conditions, then labor standards that act as a countervailing force may go some way to moving these markets back toward allocative efficiency. Wages are being held below their "proper" level, workers are being denied the value of their product, and capital is gaining unearned income. The difference in wages received by workers in advanced economies which are democracies and less developed economies which are repressive police states is in part a matter of differences in productivity and part due to the denial of labor rights. "If industrialization and democratization create conditions that promote unionism, national tripartism, and joint regulation, then" as Frenkel and Peetz (1998: 306) write, "globalization and attendant market liberalization have the reverse tendencies, heightening the employer imperative for flexibility and cost minimization and increasing employer and state resistance to unions and their involvement in regulation at the national and workplace levels." Those who think it is all or mostly productivity differences could (perhaps to pursue the intellectual issue) support labor standards to ensure free bargaining and open elections as a way of testing their view empirically. This need not involve acceptance of a class analysis of why repression exists.

In the real world the elasticity of demand for the products of low waged labor will admit to some price increase. Direct labor costs of these workers is a tiny percentage of the price consumers pay. They are unlikely to notice much difference, and in any case it is a difference they are inclined to pay so fellow workers in other countries can live a little better. A 1995 survey of the American public indicates 78 percent of those polled would avoid shopping in a store that sold garments made with sweatshop labor and would pay a dollar more on a $20 item for a guarantee that the product came from a labor-friendly supplier. Such surveys show public preferences and undercut the argument that higher wages would price them out of the market. If all workers are organized or international agreements are in place which set a floor under wages and working conditions workers will have jobs under proper macroeconomic policies. Moreover, some sources of comparative advantage—slave labor or forced labor of prisoners—are now considered illegitimate even if an "efficient" source of low-cost exports. Politically nations may agree to ban imports produced on such a basis. To deny that they have a right to do so, as many neoclassical trade theorists do, when the issue is wages and working conditions is a political judgment with which one can take issue. It is hardly a scientific statement of economic principle. The argument that it is wrong to interference with the "free" market and the working of comparative advantage, no matter what the basis of that advantage compromises, is the same one made against unions in the advanced countries a century ago.

POLITICAL ECONOMY AND NORMATIVE JUSTICE

The context of choice is crucial. The effort of many mainstream economists to reduce all choice to market choice reflects a value orientation others may not share. The substance of social choice requires an ability to transcend economic calculation in the interest of higher criteria defining the good society. The choice of market values over social values is inherent in narrow economistic reasoning. Efficiency is itself a value and can be rejected in the name of other ideals such as fairness. When acting in the role of a citizen one may make choices one might reject in the role as consumer. This is neither irrational nor inconsistent. For many, the right order for society is one that espouses an inclusiveness and a participatory egalitarianism which uncontrolled market economics undermines. The reality of substantial inequalities, which can be worsened by operation of the "free" market, can erode the rights of the weaker party. Moreover economistic analysis, by focusing on net benefits, ignores distributional issues such as how markets allocate the costs and benefits, concerns which are part of a political economy of fairness. Social regulation reflects public values chosen collectively and can be expected to clash with interests we hold in our economic man persona. We have a choice of rationalities. It is perfectly reasonable to choose non-market-oriented criteria which satisfy our beliefs and values. Economists tend to be skeptical of the importance of allegedly morally worthy preferences as compared to self-interest motivations and tend to ignore the empirical relevance of other regarding behavior and concerns in decisionmaking. In this instance the economists' cost-benefit analysis can be seen as a framework to keep a public communicative rationality (Habermas, 1981) out of the debate, to remove citizenship from problem solving through privileging a dollarized measure of what is most efficient.

Dani Rodrik suggests international economists in particular have been too Panglossian with regard to the consequences of globalization, too quick to paint those who have taken a more concerned stance as "ignorant of economics" or "closet protectionists" (Rodrik, 1997a: 72). Because workers in one place can more easily be substituted for workers in geographical locations in other political jurisdictions crossing traditionally separated national labor markets, the postwar social bargain is undermined along with the power of trade unions and self-interest is joined with fellow feelings. He writes, "The notion of fairness in trade is not as vacuous as many economists think. Consequently, nations have the right—and should be allowed—to restrict trade when it conflicts with *widely* held norms at home or undermine domestic social arrangements that enjoy *broad* support" (80). From such a perspective it can be argued that economists could play a more constructive role if they accepted the tension between social stability and globalization and devoted intellectual energies to assisting rather than taking issue with these objectives or denying that the problem exists. Looking at the statistical relationships between openness to trade, government consumption, and debt to export ratios as determinants of growth, Rodrik finds none to be statistically significant. His coefficient of conflict is significant, however; and he suggests that how tensions are managed plays a key role in transmitting effects of external shocks onto economic performance.

The issue here echoes one of the key themes of this book, that it is not whether one globalizes, but how. The world market is a source of disruption and upheaval (as well as opportunity for growth). Without effective domestic governance, judicial, civil and political rule of law, social insurance, and serious public education, countries do not adjust well. Weak domestic institutions stifle adjustment capacities and so growth. Nation level efforts at regulation and redistributional programs are now complicated, and compromised by the role of the GSEGIs which many insist upon and enforce particular patterns of adjustment which nations do not easily carry out. Since its creation in 1995, the World Trade Organization has been most controversial in this respect since it in effect piles on unfunded mandates.

THE WTO AND THE TRADE REGIME

There are those who maintain that the WTO does not in any way compromise sovereignty or undermine nation level laws. This view is defended most strongly by mainstream economists who have devoted careers to advocacy of free trade. Thus, for example, Douglas Irwin the author of an influential book of the history of free trade (Irwin, 1996), in an opinion piece in *The Wall Street Journal* (1999) writes of "the misinformation and sophistry spread by anti-WTO protestors." He asserts that the WTO cannot prescribe the policies of its member states. Irwin points out, rightly, that Article XX of the WTO agreement allows a general exemption for domestic measures to safeguard public health and safety. WTO rules simply require that such measures be imposed in a nondiscriminatory fashion (Irwin, 1999).

Unfortunately the reason protestors were upset (prompting Professor Irwin's condemnation of their know-nothingism), was that WTO panels had not been finding environmental or labor protection laws to be acceptable even when they widely appear to other observers to be nondiscriminatory and thus falling within the scope of Article XX exemptions. The idea that the WTO "cannot proscribe policies to member states" is hardly credible when one examines the decisions rendered by WTO dispute resolution panels which have eviscerated Article XX. Critics demand that WTO dispute resolution return to a consensus-based form of dispute resolution or admit to basic due process procedure (including accepting *amicus* briefs from NGOs and other interested parties which are now refused) since the current practice lacks legitimacy by in effect creating WTO law through its expert panel's decisions. For example, the WTO's basic presumption is that its rules fostering trade and investment liberalization take precedence over all other goals. Its Trade Policy Review Mechanism does not evaluate impacts on the environment, on workers, consumers, communities; and surely it does not consider sustainable development an operational concern. The trade panels lack capacity and interest in such matters which are no part of their mandate as they understand it. How the benefits of trade are distributed and any adjustment costs addressed are matters for individual states. Any concern with trade related issues by the WTO is seen as striking at the heart of the efficiency model of the trade regime it was established to impose.

The trade organization's Agreement on Sanitary and Phytosanitary Measures establishes a new standard for nondiscriminatory treatment which, in the interests of free trade, prevents governments from keeping a product out of its market as a public-health, safety, or environmental precaution. Governments must prove the product dangerous. This reverses the approach typically taken to protect public health. For example the U.S. Food and Drug Administration and other federal agencies require products to be proven safe before they are placed on the market. By shifting the burden of proof the WTO disallows the precautionary principle as a guide to public policy. Its Agreement on Technical Barriers to Trade in its rules on process and production methods further takes away a polity's right to consider under what conditions a product is made. Child labor, cruelty, environmental destruction and dangerous extractive processes cannot be grounds for denying a product access to a market.

TRADE AND ENVIRONMENT

The basis for social regulation is that markets do not properly price all the goods they produce. Most prominently pollution is created by industry as a byproduct of profit-making activity but the cost of this pollution is externalized onto others. A factory without proper devices to keep its pollution from escaping uses its neighbors lungs as filters, at some cost to the people living downwind who are not compensated for this unpriced transfer. A country without environmental regulation encourages its producers to in many cases share the waste they produce not just within their own borders but with the world. Environmentalists insist on a polluter pays principle to make those responsible pay to repair any damage done, compensating those injured (including damage to the planet and its ecosystem) or better, to prevent the harm in the first place.

Critics say that the impacts of policies environmentalists would impose to address these perceived problems have impacts which are uncertain, ineffective, and fail to meet cost-benefit criteria of efficiency. Certainly, studies of environmental cost are all over the place. Some use linear cost functions. Others use quadratic and cubic functions of changes and so produce far different impact estimates. There are disagreements on the proper discount rate to be used. Very different estimates of costs and benefits follow (Nordhaus, 1994; Cline, 1992). In the absence of definitive evidence many participants suggest it is wasteful to impose high economic cost to deal with poorly understood environmental questions and to solve problems which may not exist.

The traditional view among economists was set forth by Pigou in the early part of the twentieth century. It defined the optimal level of pollution consistent with maximum social welfare at the point where the marginal cost of abatement equals marginal benefit. Through taxation, regulation, and the assignment and enforcement of property rights these two magnitudes can be brought to equality internalizing the externalities created when pollution costs are shifted to others as non-priced effects of activities. Economists estimate optimal pollution charges using cost-benefit analysis, quantifying in dollar terms all elements, the value of habitats, species, water quality, and so on. All utilities and disutilities are given dollar valuations. The traditional approach, command and control regulation which sets maximum discharge levels or prohibitions of various sorts, is criticized by mainstream economists for misallocating resources. The cost of reaching these proscribed levels may be higher than the benefits they produce. Mandating the use of specified technologies for pollution control may lock polluters into approaches which over time are not the best or lowest cost alternatives.

Economists favor the trading of the right to pollute using permits which can be sold to the highest bidder. In such a manner higher value products can pay to buy the right to pollute from lower value added products on the basis that some polluters can reduce their emissions at lower cost. It should be these polluters who cut back most rather than demanding all be cut by the same amount. Some mainstream economists believe that once property rights are established, the market can deal with "commons" problems like pollution. If citizens have a right to a certain level of air or water quality firms can be charged a sufficiently high price to pollute (high enough to cover the cost of clean up) or lower pollution on their own to meet standards by trading "the right to pollute" so that the least cost efficient polluters are closed down (thus reaching environmental goals at lowest cost). Through such market mechanisms, economists claim, pollution can be reduced most effectively.

Mainline political economists and most environmentalists respond that such an economistic approach cannot work where the sources of pollution are diverse, and difficult to measure in terms of cause, and in the face of differential impacts of different sources which are not linear. The nature of externalities is that prices established are likely to be too low. Not all risks can be insured or properly priced. Indeed, pricing is difficult (winds shift, threshold levels are uncertain). Further, citizens do not necessarily accept the pecuniary valuations set by economists. Many reject the idea that social costs can be or should be reduced to dollar values or that trade related objectives should take precedence over other goals such as environmental and human rights concerns. There are information problems and verification issues. It is in the interests of buyers and sellers and of governments promoting economic development goals to exaggerate the levels of pollution which are being traded. Authorities typically do not or cannot verify the amount of pollution involved, especially in international transactions, because of such serious information problems.

WTO PANEL DECISIONS

There have been a number of cases in which, first under the GATT and then the WTO, dispute settlement resolution panels have come out against domestic environmental legislation by for example characterizing particular environmental laws as protectionist and in violation of the principles of the international trade regime. One of the most prominent of these cases concerns the Marine Mammal Protection Act (MMPA) of 1972 which was declared by GATT panels to be a legislative imposition of U.S. environmental policy on non-citizen tuna fishers who were required to use dolphin friendly technology or have their product barred from U.S. markets. The decision did not accept the imposition of such a trade embargo upon nonconforming countries even though motivated by an American desire not to be complicit in the unnecessary killing of large numbers of dolphins. Two GATT panel reports, in 1991 and 1994 (known as Tuna/Dolphin I and Tuna/Dolphin II) declared the law an unfair trade practice on the grounds that how a product is produced cannot be a condition determining market access but is an effort to regulate foreign producers and thus an unacceptable imposition of extraterritoriality.

The U.S. Congressional explicit mandate that the MMPA be administered for the benefit of the protection of the species rather than for the benefit of commercial exploitation was rejected by the panels because the GATT criterion is free trade and so efficient markets are, if not the sole policy criterion, the preponderant influence. As the Panel I report concluded, "to accept that one contracting party might impose trade restrictions to conserve resources of another contracting party would have the consequence of introducing the concept of extraterritoriality into the GATT, which would be extremely dangerous for all contracting parties." In a similar vein, the Tuna/Dolphin II Panel Report concluded that such an embargo could only accomplish "the protectionist objective" of forcing other countries to change their own domestic policies in accordance with the policies of the U.S." (Urgese, 1998: 478).

A similar WTO panel decision of May 1998 which declared U.S. attempts to protect endangered sea turtles to be a violation of world trade rules was met by furious reactions in this country not only from people who had been activists in the protecting of endangered species, but also from many others who thought whatever the specific issue, legitimate U.S. sovereignty had been compromised by a foreign body. This case revolved around a federal law which prohibited importation of shrimp from countries that allow trawling with nets which are not equipped with trap doors to let the turtles escape before they drown (the same law applies in a nondiscriminatory fashion to domestic shrimpers). The panel found against the U.S. Endangered Species Act which banned shrimp whether from the U.S. or imported shrimp caught without the devices to protect sea turtles from being slaughtered in shrimpers' nets. The WTO ruled it an illegal encroachment on the sovereignty of other governments for the United States to set rules for what could enter its domestic market. While the WTO's preamble was designed to allow members to take steps to protect the environment, and its Article XX has language declaring that "nothing in this Agreement shall be construed to prevent the adoption or enforcement by any contracting party of measures . . . necessary to protect human, animal, or plant life or health . . . relating to the conservation of exhaustible natural resources if such measures are made effective in conjunction with restrictions on domestic production and consumption," the Panel in its decision wrote: "While the WTO Preamble confirms that environmental considerations are important for the interpretation of the WTO Agreement, the central focus of that agreement remains the promotion of economic development through trade; and the provisions of GATT are essentially turned toward liberalization of access to markets on a nondiscriminatory basis."

As to the derogations permissible under Article XX, they were seen as applying only so long as they "do not undermine the WTO multilateral trading system." Such reasoning appeared to many lawyers as preposterous and clearly to violate the intent of Article XX. (Trachtman, 1999: 359) The U.S. argued that the panel's interpretation (that the measure to protect the turtles was a "threat to the multinational trading system") was erroneous and that it was a legal error to "jump from the observation that the GATT is a trade agreement to the conclusion that trade concerns must prevail over all other concerns in all situations arising under GATT rules." The WTO panel in its decision ignored international treaties protecting the endangered turtles. In doing so they threatened the credibility of the WTO's dispute resolution system and for some the WTO itself.

The U.S. lost again on appeal to the Appellate Body. The ruling there is importance because it rejected the logic and some of the conclusions of the panel. The Appellate decision was the first time the WTO suggested that an environmental measure could potentially be consistent with WTO rules (Sakmar, 1999). WTO spokespersons were quick to make clear there is no automatic inconsistency between national environmental measures and the rules of the international trading system. Observers saw the decision as a politically driven one, an attempt by the WTO to maintain its legitimacy in the face of widespread outrage (Simmons, 1999: 453). It was, the WTO seemed to be saying, possible to craft a law to protect the environment, but this one wasn't it. Environmentalists thanks to the Internet quickly became aware of what the panel had decided and its grounds for doing so. While some saw a willingness to compromise most environmentalists were outraged. "The WTO has proven to be profoundly anti-environmental both procedurally and substantively, handing down environmentally damaging decision whenever it has had the chance to do so," writes Ken Conca (2000: 484) summarizing its record. "Fear of a race to the dirty bottom are proving prescient, and optimism that trade rules can be greened from within has waned appreciably."

Vermont Congressman Bernie Sanders is not alone in asserting that "the people of this country have the right to maintain the level of environmental and food safety standards that they feel are appropriate, and these standards should not be subject to challenge through the WTO by other countries with weaker standards" (Urgese, 1998: 495). However under GSEGI rules, it is not clear at all that the American people have this right. What is at issue is clear enough. "The recognition, assertion, or rejection of particular trade linkages alters the way we negotiate and design trade rules, the role and nature of international economic law institutions' response to linkage issues, the extent to which the international trading system upholds or defeats basic democratic values and calls into question or affirms its own legitimacy," Garcia (1998: 203–4) writes, continuing "Moreover, since linkages bring most major areas of global social concern into the ambit of trade law and institutions, linkage issues, and through them, the international trading system, will have a far-reaching impact on the future of global social policy generally." This is understood by partisans on both sides of the issue who have marshaled a host of economic and scientific arguments.

Among proposals to address this situation it has been suggested that other institutions be empowered to provide substantive expertise to which dispute panels are bound. For example the World Health Organization rather than three trade lawyers meeting in secret should determine whether a country's pharmaceutical compulsory licensing or parallel importing system actually serves public health goals. There could be an appeal procedure in which WTO panels' judgments would be reviewed by other institutional tribunals with broader mandates (Wallach, 2000). The WTO's mere existence has had a chilling impact on global political imagination as Conca (2000: 488) argues. "It is difficult to envision the conclusion, in today's economic climate, of an agreement such as the 1973 Convention on International Trade in Endangered Species, which deliberately delegitimizes a lucrative form of international trade. The 1994 amendment to the Basel Convention, which essentially bans the north-south trade in hazardous wastes, probably constitutes the end of an era of targeting the trafficking of environmental hazards."

The other GSEGIs have also been criticized for their environmental priorities. Critics suggest that the World Bank has been a powerful force in genetic erosion for the last thirty years and more, and that its current initiatives in the area of Biodiversity conservation and management are little more than Band Aids (Rich, 1994). Environmentalists see the Bank focus on cash crops and the Green Revolution's use of fewer and better high yield seeds as promoting monoculture and the accompanying chemical packages as causing environmental damage. NGOs have organized to gain better access to GSEGI policymakers and to win the right to file *amicus curiae* briefs with the WTO (currently only governments have standing at the WTO). More recent panel rulings have acknowledged that the accepting of nonrequested information from nongovernmental sources is not incompatible with the WTO dispute resolution mechanism. The Bank, despite its green professions, provides loans for environmentally and socially harmful projects. Both it and the Fund still promote export-led growth designed to encourage natural resource exploitation which endangers local communities that depend on these resources for survival.

A Friends of the Earth report (Durbin and Welch, 2000: 2) suggests that the Bretton Woods organizations have gotten better at public relations without improving their practice. "The World Bank's structural adjustment loans do not even follow the institution's environmental policies. And staff at the institutions rarely question how the structural adjustment loans they design will effect either the environment or the poor. . . . For example, though the World Bank has established environmental policies, its own studies find that it routinely fails to enforce them." They find that in 1998 more than half of all lending by the Bank's private sector division was for environmentally harmful projects while resources devoted to environmentally beneficial projects amounted to 1.02 percent of the institution's lending.

The two U.S. government export credit/investment insurance agencies (ECAs), the Overseas Private Investment Corporation and the Export-Import Bank of the United States, turn out in the opinion of environmentalists to be "world class climate destabilizers" (Wysham, Sohn and Vallette, 1999). From 1992 to 1998 they underwrote tens of billions in financing for oil, gas, and coal projects around the world which over their lifetimes would release more carbon dioxide than all global emissions together in 1996. OPIC and the Ex-Im Bank support for fossil fuel projects is especially strong in China and India, which are singled out by U.S. politicians to explain why the United States should not sign the Kyoto Accord or take other actions to curb greenhouse gas emissions until these economies do. Yet these projects "would not occur without their support" (Wysham, Sohn and Vallette, 1999: 10). The Ex-Im Bank spends as much to finance fossil fuel power projects as the World Bank does and OPIC almost as much. The disproportionate share of investment in fossil fuels by these ECAs leads environmentalists to question why the State Department argues for greater participation by China and India under the Kyoto Accord as a requirement for U.S. participation while their government finances the greenhouse emissions projects in these very countries. Under U.S. law OPIC and Ex-Im are required to prepare and take fully into account an environmental impact statement for any project significantly affecting the global commons outside the jurisdiction of any nation. The ECAs insist their projects don't have significant impact on the global commons to warrant impact statements being made even though their effects are in fact great. The impact of their subsidies on global warming is substantial.

The impact on developing countries, who are asked to bear the burden of preserving the environment by not doing things now the way the currently more developed nations did when they were poor, is said to demonstrate a kind of moral insensitivity on the part of environmentalists. Indeed, such environmentalist concerns over the impact of development assistance has been seen as eco-imperialism by many in the developing world. "The poor are not asking for charity. When the rich chopped down their own forests, built their poison-belching factories and scoured the world for cheap resources, the poor said nothing. Indeed, they paid for the development of the rich," Malaysian Prime Minister Mahathir Mohamad told the Earth Summit in Rio in 1992. "Now the rich claim a right to regulate the development of the poor countries. And yet any suggestion that the rich compensate the poor adequately is regarded as outrageous. As colonies we were exploited. Now as independent nations we are being equally exploited." (Mickelson, 1998: 390–91) Rather than telling countries what they must do, such critics say, if we are to talk of preserving the common heritage of humankind we need to discuss equitable burden sharing of the cost. There will have to be some sort of collective purchase of resources to be preserved funded progressively which is to say primarily by the countries of the core. Environmental protection has faced rough going as countries agree in principle that the environment should be protected but favor doing so in a way which will not be costly to them. Thus even the better agreements offer inadequate commitments, escape clauses, and voluntary compliance which weakens their effectiveness.

Against all obstacles there has been movement toward the development of consensus on the importance of collective action to protect the planet. Through a series of reports and global conferences the United Nations has provided an alternation analysis to the GSEGIs with regard to the environment and its relationship to economic development. The first major global conference on the environment, the United Nations Conference on the Human Environment in Stockholm in 1972, served as a consciousness raising exercise for a wider public and spread a recognition that collective action needed to be taken. The Stockholm Declaration's twenty-six principles included a recognition that national sovereignty could not preclude responsibility to ensure that activities within their jurisdiction or control did not cause damage to the environment of other states or of areas beyond the limits of national jurisdiction. The Declaration joined environmental protection and the recognition of the interdependence of nations. It proclaimed the need for economic and social development to be part of environmental protection.

The environmentalists concern with the interconnectedness of things, and it has garnered substantial popular support, is reflected in their holistic approach, which can be contrasted to the mainstream economists' marginalism and comparative statics approach. The Brundtland Commission (the World Commission on Environment and Development) in a 1987 report, *Our Common Future*, found that the four basic components of development—peace and security, proper governance, social development, and economic development require environmental protection. The report described the interconnectedness of contestation over scarce resources and military conflict, the opportunity cost of money spent on armaments taking potential resources from meeting human need, including safe drinking water and basic sanitation, the connection between patterns of economic development and degradation and destruction of the environment.

The problem, as the Brundtland Report declared in its opening line, is that "The Earth is one but the world is not." The short-termism of private calculation lead to among other things unsustainable agricultural practices contributing to loss of soil fertility, groundwater pollution, and destruction of tropical forests along with the disappearance of animal and plant species which might otherwise have become sources of medicines and other goods. At the June 1992 United Nations Conference on Environment and Development (UNCED) held in Rio de Janeiro in response to the Brundtland Commission challenge, delegates agreed to an analysis of the relationship between the problems of the environment and poverty and to an unprecedented global plan of action. Its twenty-seven principles embraced sustainable development and stressed social equity as the conceptual framework for its Agenda 21. However this idealism confronted economic realities of the competitive global economy in which profits are made by ignoring such "external" concerns. Amidst tax cuts to attract investment and increased military spending Agenda 21's comprehensive plan of action (covering topics from management of sewage and solid wastes and combating deforestation) were not supported with government commitments and funding.

The principles agreed upon are important. They include the polluter pays principle, that actors who cause pollution are charged for the cost of undoing the harmful effects they have caused and so are induced not to cause the damage in the first place. By internalizing the cost of pollution prevention into the price of goods and services the Pigouvian principle of adjusting prices to reflect social costs achieves a more efficient allocation of resources. The precautionary principle according to the Rio declaration states that "Where there are threats of serous irreversible damage, lack of full scientific certainty shall not be used as a reason for postponing cost-effective measures to prevent environmental degradation."

The United States, as will be discussed further below, has stood sometimes virtually alone against all other nations (as in the case of the 2001 rejection of the Kyoto Accords, because accepting them as negotiated President Bush said would be harmful to the U.S. economy). This unilateralist impulse warred with the postwar bipartisan consensus, which saw the United States as "leader of the free world" while other nations were encouraged to join a rule of law which in theory would be applied to all nations equally and fairly. While it may be the case that "whether due to altruistic social evolution, or merely from utilitarian recognition of the need for world order to preserve a stable economic market, the international community increasingly favors a law-centered model of relations over a power-based, anarchic model" (Presley, 1998: 174), unilateral action by the world's one superpower remains a serious problem and interpretation of these agreed upon principles of international environmental law has been contentious. Along the same lines there has been resistance to the principle of differentiated responsibilities, which suggests that the developed countries which have caused 80 percent or so of the man-made pollution of the last two centuries should make the greatest contribution to addressing the global environmental problem.

Despite such recalcitrance, there has been wide acknowledgment that the global environment will not be able to provide a reasonable standard of living for most members of future generations without intervention and a change in growth strategy to sustainable development (which the Brundtland Commission defines as "development that meets the needs of the present without compromising the ability of future generations to meet their own needs"). Advocates suggest that "Sustainable development is a pragmatic, coherent and positive response to the deteriorating global conditions," that "It would make governments more economically efficient, more socially productive and more environmentally protective" and that "As a framework for governance sustainable development also provides a response to many current trends undermining the legitimacy and effectiveness of national governments in general, particularly globalization of the economy and the free market ideology."(Dernbach, 1998: 8).

While the global justice movement, the NGOs, and the UN conferences have made steady inroads to the point where those who would insist on a total separation between trade and the environment are on the defensive, there is still overwhelming disagreement over what the connections are in individual instances and what is to be done. There remain disputes about the science, which continues to be far from settled on a host of environmental questions, the degree of evidence, plausibility of environmental damages, and so proper policy response. When powerful interests with much at stake are involved these uncertainties are the battle ground for powerful clashes. Sustainable development does not seem an operationally easily applied category in the minds of most business people and regulators, even if there is agreement that the good of future generations should be counted and not only the consumption of the current generation. The tradeoff between present growth (which increases the possibilities of future generations) and saving environmental resources for future generations involves choices of valuation. Often those interests challenged by the environmental movement win significant victories, avoiding regulation, agreeing to general "apple pie" principles, and conceding a rhetorical acceptance of the activists demands and the need for further study. Some governments have been unwilling to even grant these tactical concessions.

In 1997 160 nations agreed to the first ever binding pact to limit emissions of carbon dioxide and other greenhouse gases. The Kyoto Protocol, while a landmark framing agreement, falls far short of what the vast majority of climatologists and other scientists in related fields suggest needs to be done. At The Hague Conference in late 2000 (the Sixth Conference of the Parties as it was called) to decide on the concrete steps to carry out the Kyoto convention goals, the United States argued that since its forests absorb 300 million tons of carbon dioxide a year this should be counted as a contribution toward meeting the treaty goals (it would contribute half of the lower levels the United States was expected to contribute, making it easier for it to meet its target without making the costlier reductions in emissions from its high pollution cars and smokestacks). Kert Davies, a representative of Greenpeace USA lobbying the talks, suggested that "This is a major free ride for the U.S., a get-out-of-jail-free card the likes of which has never been seen before." (Revkin, 2000: A6)

The United States lobbied hard for acceptance of carbon sinks which would cover up to half of its annual reduction obligation under the Kyoto treaty thanks to the country's extensive forests and farm land "sinks." Monsanto sees massive amounts of carbon being bottled up in the soil if farmers reduce or stop plowing and instead use its herbicide, Roundup, which goes with its Roundup Ready genetically modified seeds. Such drastic tillage practice changes combined with engineered trees genetically modified to grow faster and store more carbon is another company project. This is not the place to rehearse the growing literature on the science of such approaches but Malte Meinshausen of Oxford's Environmental Change Institute and Bill Hare, Climate Director of Greenpeace International, challenge the assumption that temporary carbon storage lowers temperature levels and damages "at each point in time" in the future, as industry analyses suggest, since it does not take account of the carbon life cycle (Meinshausen and Hare, 2001: 1). The technicalities involved here create a loophole as large as the "hot air" loophole surrounding Russian and Eastern Europe pollution "savings," which derive not from ecologically conscious activities but deindustrialization of the former evil empire.

The United States argued that cost-effective reduction of emissions is best achieved through the selling of rights to emit greenhouse gases, that those who can reduce emissions at lowest cost should do so and sell the savings to those who can only reduce emissions at higher cost. The Administration's negotiators also wanted a pollution rights trading regime so the United States could buy cheaper reductions from other pollution producers (such as the Russians, whose deindustrialization meant they had surplus pollution reductions they could not use and would be willing to sell). The Global Climate Coalition, a U.S.-industry funded group, estimated that this market mechanism could reduce emissions overall at lower cost than command and control regulations. Industrialized countries, rather than reducing their own emissions, could pay developing countries to cut back where reductions can be achieved at lower cost.

This Clean Development Mechanism allows industrialized countries to buy inexpensive reductions in pollution levels from developing countries by selling technologies to reduce pollution in the developing country; thereby they obtain the right to that amount of pollution which they could deploy at home where it would be more costly to reduce pollution. Coal burning utilities in the American Midwest could preserve a forest in Guatemala (which would absorb the equivalent amount of pollution as the utility releases at home). Monitoring such trades would be a nightmare and there is no enforcement mechanism. Richer countries could buy their way out of having to make any changes at home. Environmentalists warned of the lack of a workable accounting system, but to no avail. There are also scientific questions about the use of forests as pollution sinks. Critics point out that many of the proposed projects are dubious in terms of their environmental effectiveness if nuclear plants, large hydro-electric dams and other coal and oil projects qualify (Corporate Europe Observatory, 2001).

Such programs raise a number of important issues. Should they would be implemented on a global basis there are difficulties of verification given the huge number of enterprises and large number of jurisdictions involved. Such trading schemes will invite abuse since both sides of the transaction have an interest in inflating the amount of pollution which is being traded. It will be difficult to check the validity of what may be data of dubious quality originating in the national accounting of many countries. There are issues of the initial assignment of what are likely to be very valuable property rights in pollution. How are these allowances to be allocated? If based on current levels this gives the now more developed countries rights to pollute which exceed those of countries which have not yet achieved their living standards and would have a harder time doing so under such an allocation rationale. The use of a 1990 baseline gives vast credits to the former Soviet economies whose virtual industrial collapse generates huge right to pollute surpluses. Should the right to pollute be sold by governments or some international body? Such sales could raise vast sums that could be used for socially desirable purposes. As the cost of pollution is internalized, consumers would pay more for products. Would there be rebates to low-income consumers who otherwise might experience a substantial fall in real income?

In a follow-up meeting held in Bonn, Germany to set enforceable standards in 2001 167 countries (with only the U.S. dissenting) adopted standards that were so modest that if the loopholes allowed were taken full advantage of, CO_2 emissions would actually increase. The government negotiators accepted the idea advocated forcefully by the United States for a cap-and-trade system under which those who produce less pollution have their allowance (each country could choose levels from 1990 to 1995) could sell their excess right to pollute to others. For a fixed amount of money going to reduce pollution to acceptable levels output is maximized and the cost per unit of reduced pollution would be lower. The United States has used such a system since 1995 to reduce acid rain by controlling sulfur dioxide emissions, mostly from electrical generation plants and large industrial users.

Environmentalists point out that such emissions-trading schemes rest on the dangerously simplistic idea that emissions reductions anywhere are equal to reductions anywhere else. The location of emissions reductions, however, does have consequences. One often overlooked result is that allowing polluters to offset their pollution in remote places does nothing to redirect the trajectory of technological development. If the most advanced countries are forced to reduce production of pollution "in house," they will push the curve in innovative techniques and modify their consumption patterns, changes which will then be diffused to the rest of the world. "Without a fundamental redirection of the dominant technological and consuming template at the core, efforts to find savings on the periphery will be swamped by the diffusion of those unreformed practices" (Conca, 2000: 491).

Together the loopholes likely to be available to the United States should it in fact adapt the Kyoto Protocol with the provisions negotiated in subsequent meetings would have incentives sufficient to remove the need for any change in American production of greenhouse gases (Meinshausen and Hare, 2000: 10). More importantly the five percent Kyoto reduction target by 2008–12 relative to 1990 even if achieved would have only marginal effect on the build-up of greenhouse gases in the environment. As in all such regime construction a great deal of wiggle room was left so that parties that seemingly have committed themselves to noble goals could use escape clauses and exemptions to protect their interests, allowing the continuation of energy-intensive lifestyles and corporate profit strategies to remain unchallenged. In Denmark, one of the countries which is most serious about taking action to avoid global warming, the term *klimasvindel,* or climate fraud, is widely heard in discussions surrounding implementation of the Kyoto Protocol. Given that the potential loopholes in the agreement far exceed the reduction requirements of the Protocol this usage does not seem too harsh.

Over the many follow-up rounds to negotiate the details of the agreement and their enforcement the climate treaty became more and more of an economic treaty as countries sought specifics that aided their own comparative advantage, making it harder to evaluate arguments. For example, European opposition to carbon sinks is perhaps justified on the basis of science, but the European position may result more from the fact that the continent has fewer forests and agricultural areas than the United States. The devils are always in the details. By allowing parties to choose between 1990 and 1995 base levels for computing required reduction individual countries can increase their possible future emissions substantially. Some adjustments which seem reasonable (special circumstances always prevail) can have the effect of opening huge loopholes. Allowing uncontrolled use of "hot air" to be sold as emissions credits is one such instance. For example the Russian and Eastern European surpluses from industrial collapse noted earlier has meant that pollution levels there are down by 30 to 45 percent from 1990 levels. The amounts in question are not trivial. Such emissions trades would be worth tens of billions of dollars a year. Generous interpretation of the terms afforestation, reforestation, and deforestation, and failure to control international aviation and shipping fuels, are other quantitatively significant examples.

Behind government negotiating positions, and especially that of the United States, the influence of powerful corporate interests is evident. The positions of their lobbyists prefigure government stances. In the run up to the Kyoto meetings the American Petroleum Institute warned that 2.4 million jobs would be lost and an average income decrease of $2,700 would result per U.S. household if the United States adopted the Kyoto limits on greenhouse gas emissions. At the same time it lobbied developing country governments to reject binding reduction commitments. It then used their unwillingness to make such commitments as another reason to urge the United States to reject the Kyoto Protocol (Levy and Egan, 2000). The Business Roundtable issued warnings concerning loss of trade, and of the tens of billions of dollars of GDP to be lost if the Kyoto standards were accepted by the United States. Such threats and warnings had impact. In 1998 the US Senate passed the Byrd-Hagel Resolution by a vote of 95–0. It states that the United States should not be a signatory to any protocol that excludes the developing countries from legally binding commitments or that causes serious harm to the U.S. economy.

The strategies of corporate lobbyists have changed to some degree over time. In 1990 the Global Climate Coalition (GCC) was established. Its members came from coal, auto, oil, cement, steel, chemical, paper, electric utility, and aluminum—major users of energy. A number of similar European TNCs joined its efforts to coordinate lobbying to discredit the global warming thesis. At first the GCC challenged the science of climate change arguing consensus among scientists on the issue was lacking and so no measures should be taken given the uncertainty. As evidence became more undeniable it switched its emphasis to the "unreasonable" cost of measures to curb emissions and as noted the lack of developing country commitment. It attempted to undermine the credibility and legitimacy of the Inter-Governmental Panel on Climate Change, which expressed the consensus of experts that global warming was a severe problem that needed prompt action. When its market research suggested the public did not find industry a credible source and that challenging the scientific consensus was producing a backlash, its approach became less strident. The GCC was undermined by defections by British Petroleum in 1997 (BP accepted the precautionary principle as grounds for the need to take action on global warming). Other majors soon followed: Shell in 1998, Ford in 1999 among others. The coming to Washington of George W. Bush with a vice president and key administration appointees from the oil industry may not have changed public opinion but it did alter federal policy. Bush's rejection of Kyoto was couched in almost verbatim terms as the GCC warnings that unrealistic targets and timetables are not achievable without severely harming the U.S. economy and all American families.

The World Business Council for Sustainable Development along with the International Chamber of Commerce joined other corporate groups in advocating what is called the doctrine of corporate environmentalism, which portrays the energy industry as part of the solution and not the problem. What began as a campaign for the international regulation of corporations and binding agreement on greenhouse gas emissions, thanks in significant measure to their efforts, morphed into a reliance on voluntary agreements without enforcement and market-based solutions which are touted as minimizing the economic costs of reducing pollution levels by encouraging the swift introduction of energy efficiency prompted by the profit motive and emissions trading. The International Chamber of Commerce's Working Group on Climate Change fielded executives from dozens of corporations and coordinated business lobbying groups at UN gatherings, meeting with officials. Its delegations are the largest and most influential NGOs at such negotiations. The ICC has a long history of lobbying to weaken international environmental treaties from the Convention on Biodiversity through the Kyoto Protocol. While it has signed on to the UN's Global Compact principles it continues to obstruct the achievement of its announced goals. The Global Compact is a joint UN-corporate effort to promote principles such as greater environmental responsibility and to support the precautionary principle. It has been denounced as "greenwashing" of corporate behavior or rather "bluewashing" (given the UN's seal of approval).

While major polluters devoted resources to such public relations efforts they also had to face the long-term impact of growing environmental awareness and the actions of more farsighted competitors who were positioning themselves for what they understood as the inevitability of new regulations and to take advantage of the reputational gains and learning economies of acting early rather than late to meet such environmental friendly criteria. In the face of competitive challenges such as the commercial launch of gas-electric hybrid cars by Toyota and Honda, American companies began to fear that when inevitably emissions standards were mandated they would be behind. More firms, pushed by business strategy, changed their tune. In 1998 the Pew Center on Global Climate Change was formed as a vehicle to legitimate the new "responsible" position on the environment in preference to state regulation with such founding members as Toyota, BP, Enron, 3M, and American Electric Power. There is division on strategy not only in the corporate but the environmentalist camps. Among environmentalists the Pew Center, the World Wide Fund for Nature and the Environmental Defense Fund are among the groups which promote emissions trading as part of the solution, earning the ire of others who see their position as lending legitimacy to the corporate agenda. These other environmentalists have been impressed with the difficulties of applying market principles in the context of corporate dominance of the specific regime formation and enforcement. In 2000 the Environmental Defense Fund was central in creating The Partnership for Climate Action which TNCs joined to develop a global emissions trading scheme. The World

Bank also established a public-private partnership between some national governments and large corporations and proposed investing in renewable energy sources in developing countries, projects which would earn carbon credits for the investing private firms under the Kyoto Protocol.

More radical analysts associated with the anti-capitalist wing of the movement see corporate globalization as a set of processes that mask the fundamental logic of capitalism as a system of power which, because it favors an exponential growth model, is unsustainable. The problem is that the drive for accumulation supersedes other goals and is enforced by the system of power under capitalism which puts capitalist imperatives ahead of all else and whose growth has historically been the motor behind the uncontrolled increase in greenhouse gases (Patterson, 1999) Other activists agree that the focus must be on the reduction of the use of fossil fuels and are anti-corporate, seeing transnational capital, if not capitalism, as the enemy of the environment. The evolving positions taken by each of these constituencies will depend on the actions of the other players and their relative effectiveness.

ENVIRONMENTAL AND LABOR PROTECTION AND THE COURTS

Because of the difficulties of convincing elected officials to move beyond fairly empty rhetoric on environmental and labor protection, activists have turned to the courts seeking redress for the actions of transnational corporations in other parts of the world. Many of these countries are run by repressive dictatorships and in such places legal redress has not proven possible in local courts. U.S. courts have long dealt with commercial international law cases but have been hesitant to accept jurisdiction in cases alleging human rights and environmental crimes. When such claims have been brought, the companies have argued that they should be heard on their merits in the courts of the countries in which alleged misconduct occurred, even where these countries are recognized to lack an effective, independent judiciary. Lawyers bringing such cases face U.S. courts reluctant to cast judgment on the courts of countries on good terms with their own government. Those bringing the cases have been more successful when the demand for relief is based on events initiated in this country.

Among the factors that determine the reasonableness of a U.S. court's jurisdiction is comity (the understanding that courts should avoid conflict with the sovereignty of other states). However the courts have made it clear this cannot be the end of the story. If it was dispositive it would prevent any suits against foreigners in U.S. courts and the courts have accepted a number of such cases on various grounds. The common law doctrine of *forum non conveniens* allows judges who believe a case would be more appropriately or conveniently tried elsewhere to decline jurisdiction. Human rights and environmental lawyers have argued in a number of instances of the lack of an adequate alternative forum. They continue to work to expand such instances where seemingly logical foreign venues are found inadequate for the case to be fairly heard and, on the grounds that in a world in which markets are global and strong interdependencies exist, that the doctrine of *forum non conveniens* enables corporations to evade their responsibilities and any legal control by the very virtue of operating transnationally. On such grounds U.S. courts are finding that to prevent human rights and environmental violations abroad U.S.-based transnationals must be liable under U.S. tort law. There is also of course resistance to making the United States the courthouse for the world (Rosencranz and Campbell, 1999). Nonetheless the activities of NGOs, investigations, and exposures, and perhaps more importantly the increased willingness of the United States and other Western governments to intervene with force in the face of a perceived humanitarian need, has made matters easier for human rights lawyers to get cases heard and decided in U.S. courts. As Sohail Hashmi (1997: 3) writes: "The universalization of human rights standards and the growth of nongovernmental human-rights monitoring agencies have seriously undermined the old idea of essentially 'domestic' affairs of a state that are beyond the purview of the international community. There is today a growing consensus that claims of state sovereignty should not be an impediment to international intervention in the face of humanitarian crises."

Human rights and environmental lawyers have argued that under common law a duty of care arguably arises so that U.S.-based transnationals, which exercise significant control over operations abroad, must protect the international environment and safeguard the rights of their employees rather than using a double standard by engaging in actions they would not be allowed at home. In one case initiated against Unocal in California based on activities in Myanmar (Burma) the assertion was made that the company is liable for human rights abuses including forced labor and torture. The plaintiffs held Unocal responsible for acts of "forced relocation, forced labor, torture, violence against women, arbitrary arrest and detention, cruel, inhuman or degrading treatment, crimes against humanity, the

death of family members, battery, false imprisonment and assault"
allegedly committed by the Burmese government in furtherance of a
pipeline project (Baker, 2000: 88). The plantiffs argue that Unocal should
have known what was going on. They cite a 1992 report by consultants
who warned the company that the military "habitually uses forced labor
to construct roads" (Markels, 2003: Business Section, p. 11). Earth Rights
International, a human rights group co-founded by Ka Hsaw Wah, has
collected sworn depositions from villagers documenting how the military
enslaved locals after agreeing to build a pipeline (a $1.2 billion project) in
1990. Villagers were enslaved, beaten, and tortured on behalf of the
pipeline construction (Eviatar, 2003: 16).

In another case, Shell has been sued in U.S. District Court for the
Southern District of New York by Ken Saro-Wiwa's son and brother based
on claims for relief under customary international law, U.S. common law,
and the Racketeer Influenced and Corrupt Organizations Act (RICO) for
complicity in the torture and summary execution of the internationally
known writer and Ogoni activist. The plaintiffs alleged that his death was
the result of a strategy devised by top Shell executives and high ranking
military officers (Rosencranz and Campbell, 1999: 183) There have been a
number of cases in different parts of the world where international oil
companies have been charged with collusion with repressive local states to
engage in environmental destruction and human rights violations. In
these cases political and economic power have been concentrated and
local citizens effectively excluded from meaningful participation in the
political system. Local courts offer no redress, judicial appointments are
part of the patronage system, and the rule of law honored only in the
breech for those without political influence.

In many isolated areas indigenous peoples are having their lands expropriated or despoiled through the collusion of international oil companies
and their own governments. The courts of these countries are inadequate
for meaningful redress. In one such instance it is reported that "The
Ecuadorian government has not implemented measures to verify environmental claims made by the industry, and there is no independent monitoring, transparency or accountability. Decisions are made behind closed
doors without meaningful participation by affected residents, and critical
environmental information is withheld from both residents and the public as a matter of policy" (Kimerling, 1995: 326). Such conditions, plaintiffs'
lawyers claim, are grounds for the case to be tried in the United States
since it involves U.S. oil companies allegedly responsible for irreversible
damages to local habitats. Such cases combine human rights and in some

cases labor rights and protection of the environment and the local people who depend upon it. Coca Cola is one of the companies accused by labor rights groups of using paramilitaries in Columbia to kill union leaders. Such a charge and the publicity surrounding it is serious for a company like Coke. Its brand represents most of the company's market value—more than all its other physical and intangible assets such as patents, skills, and distribution system—so whether U.S. courts, eventually it will be the Supreme Court, decides on the applicability of the 1789 Alien Tort Claims Act on which such cases are based, can be used in this way will be of substantial importance.

The Bush Justice Department in 2003 submitted a strongly worded brief in favor of Unocal as it had earlier on behalf of ExxonMobil in a case involving dealings with the military in Indonesia saying proceeding could hurt the fight against terrorism. It opposed use of U.S. courts in such cases more generally.

TRADE AND LABOR RIGHTS

Discussions of trade and human rights, including labor rights, take place in ways which appear to auger a new internationalism and labor solidarity, but also are interpreted as involving paternalism and moral insensitivity on the part of Western groups motivated by protectionist or profit motives. A number of highly charged questions are involved: Are trade unionist demands for international labor standard enforcement inspired by fellow feelings with sisters and brothers or driven by the protectionist goal of reducing competition from such workers? Are corporations who promise to hire workers in poor countries, thus helping these nations develop imposing conditions which are morally unacceptable, or are investors offering development best suited to uplifting these underdeveloped economies? Are local governments who forbid unions, beat and jail militants, and do the bidding of TNCs promoting the long-term interest of these workers or are they the junior partners of twenty-first century imperialism? It is a matter of viewpoint. From a neoclassical economics perspective, unions and government regulation make labor markets less efficient and should be discouraged. Full employment and growth are created by flexible, competitive markets. Labor activists and NGOs such as Oxfam call the "flexible" labor policies (praised by the GSEGIs) a euphemism for the creation of jobs at sub-poverty levels wages. Appalling working conditions are found in the miracle economies as workers' rights are denied in the interests of "labor flexibility." NGOs report on forced overtime, corporal punishment, harassment, and jailings even as the World Bank and other GSEGIs praise weak labor laws as freeing labor markets from "distortions."

It is the case that many workers in less developed countries typically prefer to work for transnationals to their other possible options for earning a living. In terms of the economics of the firm, foreign or domestic, workers will be hired so long as the marginal product of their labor adds more to profitability than the value of the wages and other incidental labor costs paid. Workers will take the job so long as the compensation is better than the opportunity cost of not taking the job (accepting the next best alternative). In a less than perfect market, the sort we see in such countries among others, between these two measures of the value of the worker's time there can be a large gap. The firm could afford to pay more and still earn at least the normal rate of return. But it does not have to pay more because of the weak bargaining power of the worker.

If we believe a more equitable division of the worker's product is desirable then we need to look at how the worker's bargaining power could be strengthened. Companies may employ goon squads to intimidate and brutalize militant workers. In some places government repression is a major factor in holding down wages. Workers attempting to form unions are beaten. Organizers are jailed and killed. Where outright violence is tempered the legal environment can be such that workers have no rights a company is obliged to respect and organizers are fired and prevented from getting other jobs by being put on employers' watch lists. This is a matter of degree. Even in advanced economies union density differs as a result of labor law. Union density is far higher in Canada because of legal protections workers seeking to bargain collectively enjoy versus the manner in which protections once guaranteed in the United States have been eroded.

In general wages are higher in more developed countries. As economies modernize populations come to have greater human capital capacities and more technology can be employed per worker, raising productivity and compensation. It is often argued that poor countries cannot afford to pay higher wages. Only after there is economic development can wages realistically be expected to rise, it is argued. But as noted earlier this is not exactly accurate. The gap between the surplus created for the firm by their workers and labor's reservation wage (the opportunity cost of not working for the firm) can be substantial. This wedge is distributed based on relative bargaining power between capital and labor. There is room for wages to rise even in poor countries. Labor costs cannot rise too much or employers will choose to close down, but transnationals can typically afford to pay more.

Moreover the poor countries must attract foreign investment with more than rock bottom wages. They do better providing a healthy, skilled work force, supporting infrastructure, and a safe environment with a respect for the rule of law that inspires confidence that contracts will be honored. To offer low waged potentially super exploitable workers is a low road strategy If the lowest possible wage is their major allure they must be committed to maintaining such a status with repressive machinery. This allows rent extraction in the short run, a strategy which may enrich local elites and some investors in a static frame, but is not a strategy for economic development in the longer run. Thus respect for labor and democratic rights more generally is to choose to depart from past social structures of accumulation and adopt a new regime with broad implications for class relations and political governance.

The labor rights debate is in many ways parallel to the one over workers well-being which took place in the more economically developed countries over centuries. Now, the global integration of labor markets, the international division of labor, and the spreading understanding of the connectedness of human rights re-creates these arguments and demands for reform on a worldwide level. The global social justice movement supports the right of workers to unionize and bargain free of government repression. Responding to such criticisms, the World Bank has prepared a draft set of "principles of good practice social policy" incorporating conclusions of the World Summit for Social Development held in Copenhagen in 1995. The UK Chancellor Gordon Brown suggested that all such international codes of conduct be brought within the remit of the IMF's Article 4 consultations (discussed in chapter 9) which are held with member nations. NGOs and agencies such as the UNDP call for an opening up of the process of soft law formulation to incorporate priorities of equity, sustainability, and human development. The private law model relying on market criteria is too narrow from such a perspective. Frank Garcia reminds us, "Efficiency Model adherents fail to recognize that while efficiency and welfare are undeniably important values in trade, their pursuit is necessarily part of an overarching effort to establish a just global order, an order in which other values are also central, values which are implicated and quite properly considered in trade law decisions" (Garcia, 1999a: 66).

If there is no such thing as a pure trade issue, mainstream economists and trade negotiators need to make room for concerns which they have considered extraneous or as veiled protectionism. They must face that their doctrinaire and nonnegotiable position that only efficiency counts is judged reductionist from the perspective of broadly accepted social values by many, perhaps most, people. That said the problem remains, and it is a major one: efficiency models offer a precision of conceptualization and of measurement which can guide decisionmakers in a clear and seemingly precise manner. Other approaches appear ostensibly subjective, value dependent. They cannot be as tightly operationalized since their proponents are typically unable to go beyond idealist aspirations to offer guidance on how much efficiency should be sacrificed for what gain. When economists raise concerns over how to measure costs and benefits at the margin, environmentalists and human rights activists assert a language of absolutes and conversation stops. I do not say they are wrong to do so but the impasse does not allow for a constructive linking of issues in the language of mainstream economics or provide alternative ground for common discussion. The issue at dispute is not however finally that of measurement but of values.

Because advocates for labor rights and environmental protection wish to establish protections from market forces, while the GSEGI presumption is that liberalization fosters efficient markets and optimal outcomes, there is a sharp, deep, and perhaps irreconcilable gap between two very different understandings of "trade-relatedness." Advocates wish to limit market freedoms to accommodate other goals. The GSEGIs by and large favor greater liberalization, deregulation, and privatization to raise all boats. They think restricting free exchange is counterproductive in terms of the general welfare. This tension returns us to divisions discussed in chapters 3 and 4 between competing approaches to economics/political economy and between the law and economics and critical legal studies traditions. The latter two in these pairings rejects the universal commodification by the former in which the rights which have primacy are property rights and justice is reduced to utility maximization in a market setting (Radin, 1989; Baron and Dunoff, 1996). While it is widely acknowledged that market rationality fails to capture much of what people believe to be important, that approach is nonetheless the prevailing academic policy discourse. The question the social movements raise for analysts is how can the demand for social justice be operationalized to replace the exclusive efficiency centered approach to trade and investment?

THE PUBLIC DEBATE

There have been major campaigns by activist groups in which media have picked up the story. This has been the case in the targeting of Nike in Asia, where an Indonesian worker is not paid enough in a month to buy a pair of Nike running shoes, and where the company moves its plants from one low-wage country to an even lower waged one should wages threaten to rise. Nike does not own its plants and has not wanted to monitor its contractors on safety and working conditions until pressured by labor rights groups in the West who have contrasted the tens of millions of dollars Michael Jordan received to publicize the daily wage of two dollars and small change the Indonesian workers were paid in factories where Nike's chief executive told the press his subcontractors' workers can earn double the minimum wage. Critics point out that such governments set labor standards unreasonably low and a worker's health cannot be maintained living on the minimum wage. In subcontractor plants overtime is mandatory and workers regularly faint from overwork. The press has reported unionists stories of chronic harassment and government pressure on companies to fire unionists and ban contact with organizers and the press. The intrepid journalist who reported the particular story on which this account relies, *Business Week*'s Mark Clifford (1996: 46), was detained for some time by plain clothes police demanding to know what he was doing. Locals are not treated so well.

After years of grass roots education and public protests which had successfully effected public opinion in the richer countries the company had been hurt by falling stock prices and weak sales. It has, as Philip Knight, its CEO and the sixth richest man in America said, been "pummeled in the public relations arena" by human rights activists. "The Nike product," he said, "had become synonymous with slave wages, forced overtime and arbitrary abuses and American consumers did not want to buy products made under such conditions" (Cushman, 1998). The company promised in 1998 to end child labor at its subcontractors and apply U.S. rules abroad. Labor activists say there has been little meaningful improvement. The damage done by the spread of information about working conditions in subcontractor plants has, however, brought changes. Transnationals, which not long before said they had no control over policies and practices in the countries in which they sourced their products and that it would be wrong, even "imperialistic," to interfere with these sovereign countries and their independent producers, have under witheringly effective organization by labor rights groups and growing consumer awareness established business practices complete with monitoring, sometimes accepting independent monitors, of practices in their contractors' plants. Under public attack by the Coalition for Justice to Coffee Workers, Starbucks promised to monitor conditions on a Guatemalan coffee plantation which is a major supplier and where horrendous abuses have been reported. Reebok not only has pledged compliance with higher standards but also gives annual awards to human rights campaigners.

The intervention by activist groups in reshaping the behavior of transnational corporations has been significant. They have offered a powerful moral critique which is from outside, and in opposition to, the framework of mainstream economic analysis. By broadening the discussion they have reintroduced issues which were central to political economy back in the period when economics was emerging as a discourse from moral philosophy. It remains to be seen whether such popular movements will have staying power. It is possible they will develop in a programmatic direction to reconnect to other political economy traditions such as the one enshrined in the Universal Declaration of Human Rights, which would operationalize their moral concerns by offering an alternative set of rules for economic and financial relations.

TRADE AND WELFARE CONCERNS

The question of internationally agreed upon labor standards is not a new one. It was first raised at the Congress of Vienna in 1815. But binding, enforceable agreement has not been forthcoming. Positive rights were accepted in the Havana Charter, which was to have established the International Trade Organization. The agreement recognized that all countries have a common interest in the achievement and maintenance of fair labor standards and that unfair labor conditions, particularly in export sectors that create difficulties in international trade. The Charter declared that each member "shall take whatever action may be appropriate and feasible to eliminate such conditions from its territory." The principle is accepted even though the language of "appropriate and feasible" failed to offer clear guidance, and of course the entire Charter was rejected.

In December 1996 at the first Ministerial Conference of the then just established World Trade Organization the WTO decided not to go on record in favor of labor rights. It was argued that core labor standards are not shaped by policies but by market outcomes and only as countries reach a higher level of development (through open trade) will they themselves adopt labor legislation. This position put the WTO at odds with the ILO which a year earlier had said that globalization gives "governments an incentive to dilute, or fail to enact, measures intended to protect the welfare of workers, or to turn a blind eye to infringements of legislation with this in mind" (International Labor Organization, 1995: 72–73). Informalization, increased subcontracting, and pressure for greater flexibility has eroded working conditions in many countries, the ILO reported. The International Confederation of Free Trade Unions (the largest labor federation in the world) declared the WTO's credibility undermined due to "Mickey Mouse having more rights than the laborers who make toys." They said trademarks are protected but not working people. The WTO responded that its job is trade and that it is the task of the International Labor Organization to attend to such matters.

The ILO has ratified more than 170 conventions although not all of them were signed by all ILO members. Between the organization's founding in 1919 and 1988 the United States adopted only eight ILO agreements, all were maritime conventions. It wasn't until the 144th ILO convention that the United States finally adopted a non-maritime convention. However with the exception of the Abolition of Forced Labor Convention, the United States has not ratified any of the other ILO ten conventions which deal with basic human rights (related to freedom of association, forced labor, and equality of opportunity and treatment) leading other countries to question U.S. commitment to international labor rights. America's seeming willingness to unilaterally enforce penalties against countries it deems not meeting such standards are suspect since this country appears to want other nations to uphold standards in conventions the United States refuses to ratify. The U.S. response is that these treaties fall largely under the authority of U.S. state governments and so it is not proper for the central government to sign them. Critics suggest unwillingness to surrender sovereignty and the prospects of becoming subject to external judgment on domestic policy has figured in the U.S. Congress's unwillingness to ratify such treaties.

The International Labor Code the ILO has promulgated already would guarantee a host of important labor rights if it was followed. But unlike the WTO, which has strong enforcement powers the ILO, can only use whatever moral pressure it can bring to bear to encourage compliance. Ironically perhaps it is the United States which has taken steps to force labor standards in developing economies through both extraterritorial application of U.S. labor law as part of its trade policies, albeit in an inconsistent way and with limited results. Specifically, the U.S. experience under the Generalized System of Preferences (GSP) has been disappointing to proponents of labor protection. The GSP Program, part of the 1974 Trade Act, is a unilateral procedure for granting developing nations access to

U.S. domestic markets on a duty-free basis. In 1984, in response to the promptings of labor activists and U.S. trade unions concerning both the exploitation of workers abroad and the relocation of U.S. factories to such "labor friendly" environments, the GSP was amended and an internationally recognized workers rights provision added. The core list of labor standards includes freedom of association, freedom to bargain collectively, discrimination in employment (governments and employers should not treat workers differently on the basis of non-work related criteria), prohibition of forced labor and child labor (for details see Taylor, 1998: 658–59). The amendment declared that "The President shall not designate any country beneficiary developing status . . . if such country has not taken or is not taking steps to afford internationally-recognized worker rights." Because benefits under the act could continue if a country was "taking steps" to extend employment rights, there was leeway for U.S. Administrations to punish countries they did not like for reasons having nothing to do with their labor policies and ignore abuses of friendly governments. This law did not serve the function advocates had hoped it would (Baltazar, 1998: 710–12). As in the case of trade and environment issues discussed earlier, trade and labor rights challenges have found their way to the courts.

LEGAL REDRESS

As has been noted, IR scholars have not until recently paid much attention to developments in legal theory, preferring to focus on diplomacy and treaty making. Yet legal challenges have a practical significance and so are crucial to understanding how the meaning of sovereignty is changing in the era of globalization. This is not to say that political scientists must become legal experts any more than they must become economists. Rather some amount of cross disciplinary study can be rewarded with a more comprehensive understanding of phenomena which are part of one's core area of interest. In instances cited earlier such as the challenge to Unocal for its dealings with the State Law and Order Restoration Council (SLORC), the military rulers of Myanmar where the misdeeds of the military junta are well known, the questions are the responsibility of the company under U.S. law for acts it may have committed in Burma and the rights of foreigners suffering human rights abuse and environmental injury in their own country allegedly at the hands of a U.S. transnational operating in their country to sue for redress in U.S. courts. Dismissal as we have seen is always sought on the basis of *forum non conveniens* or the doctrine of comity and usually granted unless the claimants can demonstrate that there is a violation of some norm which violates the law of nations, a *jus cogens* norm—that there are certain universally accepted criteria which are generally applicable in all nations whether they have passed a law or not regarding a particular panoptic principle (for some of the case law see Rosencranz and Campbell, 1999: 147–48).

There are very few *jus cogens* norms—torture, murder, slavery, genocide. Because a universal norm requires universal consensus, activists seek to establish rights through international conventions, which can then make violations actionable. Transnational public law litigation, even when it is not successful in supplying remedy, has powerful public relations impacts and can prompt publicity-shy corporations to change their ways and others to work to avoid similar compromising situations, possible exposure, and legal involvements. Labor rights activists have sought remedy in the courts where they have challenged a host of TNC labor practices. This tactic has not met with a great deal of success yet, although this may be changing. Under the Foreign Sovereign Immunities Act (FSIA) a foreign government enjoys general immunity from civil action for damages unless they occur in the United States or the matter falls within one of the enumerated exceptions. The definition of sovereignty thus is reworked in the context of legal challenges under the FSIA.

Some legal scholars studying the refusal of trade organizations to discuss enforcement of labor rights have suggested that the advocacy groups consider posing the issue not as one of human rights but as property rights, the property rights of workers in their labor. If workers are treated like property by capital this should entitle labor to at least the same protection as other forms of property are accorded. This would not demean labor. Labor is already demeaned by the practices of employers and governments which do not respect labor rights now. This formulation would be a parallel construction to the right of property as protected for capitalists under these agreements. It will be harder to refuse the protection of labor rights if they are conceptualized as property rights, it is argued. Viewing labor rights as akin to investment rights, intellectual property rights, and so forth would allow the adoption of core labor rights as just one more property right (Taylor, 1998: 650). Such a tactic suggests that defining labor rights as property rights would potentially better working conditions and enhance human dignity of workers. It could even mean that such rights come before property rights as defined by the WTO and other GSEGIs. If social rights were given the legal and practical status of property rights—and assuming that they would be made inviolable and granted as the basis of citizenship rather than performance—then this would entail a decommodification of the status of the individual vis-à-vis the market. Or so advocates of this approach suggest. This seems unlikely however. The right to one's labor is not the same as the ability to sell one's labor on terms one would like. The right to own one's labor means little without ownership of capital, or dramatically greater bargaining power in contract negotiation and enforcement vis-à-vis those who do own capital.

Not only are workers in many countries denied the right to free speech and to organize in independent labor organizations but also there are parts of the world where slavery is still very much an issue. In 1999 the ILO annual conference passed a resolution denying Burma (Myanmar) any technical aid except help in eliminating forced labor. The International Confederation of Free Trade Unions estimates that 800,000 people are subject to forced labor in Burma and describes the practice as "a crime against humanity." While Burma signed the ILO's forced labor convention in 1955 the ILO points to that country's "flagrant and consistent failure to comply." Thousands of villagers are conscripted to work, by its military rulers, on roads or as porters, or on farms and railroads. Burma is hardly alone (Williams, 1999a: 8). The case law which is being developed around a challenge to its egregious practices are likely to be precedent setting. Here too questions of self-interest have been raised. It is pointed out that the West had little interest in labor rights in the periphery until these countries became competitive in products which compete with core production. Human rights concerns and sanctions are seen as cynical protectionist mechanisms. And again the rejoinder is that resistance to labor rights is not an assertion of national sovereignty but of the interests of the elites of these countries wishing to continue to profit from the exploitation of "their" workers and that pressure needs to be put on repressive governments to respect labor rights, prevent forced labor and child labor, and meet minimal wage and working conditions. The use of trade sanctions to achieve these ends has been problematic in many cases however.

The United States has imposed unilateral economic sanctions on at least seventy-four countries at a cost of tens of billions of dollars to U.S. business and consumer interests and to lost jobs and sales for the countries involved. This has led to the charge that human rights and the economic sanctions Washington seems so willing to impose are "the new imperialism" (Wall, 1998) and has opened this country to the charge of having a double standard and of hypocrisy not only for its unilateralism, ignoring the jurisdiction of the relevant international organizations, but also because the United States has entered extensive reservations to such treaties which do exist in the human rights field and "refusing to itself be bound by many provisions within them" (as the 1997 Amnesty International Report points out). Other critics suggest that the only human rights that the United States has consistently fought for has been the freedom from socialism and the freedom to make a profit. An extensive literature exists in the law journals detailing the positions on such linkages and rule making (Taylor, 1998; Cappuyns, 1998). Third World workers organizations further call attention to the double standard in which capital is encouraged to be internationally mobile and impediments to its freedom discouraged while workers cannot move internationally in search of better opportunities. If the movement of one factor of production increases global well being, why not movement of the other?

It is no longer possible for diplomats or technocrats to negotiate such issues outside the glare of public attention. They do so pressed on one side by their corporations and on the other by grass roots movements and NGOs representing human rights, environmental, and labor advocacy groups as they make choices concerning the financial, trade and investment regimes of the global political economy. Meetings of the WTO or the IMF-WB have been the occasion for massive street demonstrations, intense lobbying, and alternative meetings. The GSEGIs are no longer able to insulate themselves. They have however tried to keep concerns which they consider not germane to their tasks out of their operational mandates and left in the rhetorical realm of "goals." The most prominent examples of sequestering have involved concerns for labor rights and environmental protection which have been kept to side agreements separate from the operational rules of trade and investment treaties, as in the case of NAFTA.

NAFTA SIDE AGREEMENTS

The discussion of whether labor rights and environmental regulation are 'side issues" or perhaps even counterproductive interference when it comes to trade and investment matters is derivative of the broader bifurcation between those who privilege efficiency versus equity considerations in constituting political economy. The "side issue" formulation represents something of a compromise which gives market forces priority but says social costs should not be ignored, even if they are secondary to the efficiency enhancing mechanism of free market allocation.

For those who consider quality of life issues primary and would define profitability in a larger context of social costs and benefits this is not a satisfactory outcome, especially as experience with this side agreement practice has been to give short shrift to their concerns. The NAFTA side agreements can be seen not as a way of addressing the concerns of environmentalists and labor activists so much as a move aimed at taking the steam out of organizing efforts and to promote an easier acceptance of the agreement itself. The NAFTA model of cross-border monitoring and enforcement did little to contribute to the goal of establishing uniform standards or a floor of labor rights. "The NAFTA Labor Side Agreement's cross-border enforcement model does not raise or equalize labor standards. To the contrary," Katherine Stone (1995: 1023) writes, "it provides disincentives for member states to legislate labor protections because each state can be sanctioned for not enforcing its own labor regulations." Furthermore, because NAFTA removes trade barriers without providing uniformity in labor regulation, each country stands to lose business if it imposes a higher level of regulation than do other countries. "Therefore," she believes, "cross-border monitoring encourages race-to-the-bottom and regulatory competition, resulting in the lowering of labor standards."

If the goal of a trade regime is to increase trade and eliminate labor conventions which act as a barrier to trade then the best model is the one that minimizes regulation, lowers labor standards, and discourages regulatory uniformity, which critics argue is what NAFTA does. Any effort to enforce NAFTA labor side agreement provisions would be a long, drawn out, and cumbersome undertaking since the qualifiers and exceptions are many and the degree of evidence for assertion of violations is substantial. A "persistent pattern of failure" "to effectively enforce" a nation's laws is a hard standard. "There is almost no instance, at least under U.S. labor law, in which government failure to enforce a labor law cannot be characterized so as to fall within one of these exceptions." After reviewing the provisions Stone (1995: 1011) concludes "The exceptions found in Article 49 provide a legal excuse for almost all nonenforcement. In light of these broad exceptions, it is difficult to imagine any situation in which the agreement's procedures for obtaining labor law enforcement would apply."

If the agreement is looked at from the point of view of investors the evaluation is somewhat different. Stephen Canner, Vice President for Investment Policy and Financial Services at the United States Council for International Business (1998: 659) explains, "From the perspective of an international investor, NAFTA rules on investment were a quantum leap forward. The rules not only established a floor under a number of measures Mexicans were liberalizing on their own account, but also provided for new liberalizations and an investor-to-state dispute settlement mechanism through binding arbitration." This right to private action was a major breakthrough. NAFTA gives those corporations which perceive themselves as hurt by public policies the right to sue for damages. This can make it costly for state and local governments and discourages legislation in areas which may prove sensitive. For example public provision of auto insurance at the provincial level in Canada was challenged by large North American insurance companies as "unfair." As privatization and contracting out become increasingly prevalent one can contemplate more suits of this nature. The Methanex Corporation of Vancouver, British Columbia famously sued for damages because California banned imports of a gasoline additive they sold which had been leaking into the West Coast water supply. In another case Canada paid $13 million to settle a claim by the U.S.-based Ethyl Corporation over its allegedly dangerous gasoline additive.

All manner of claims are being arbitrated including those involving movement of hazardous waste. Tobacco firms from the United States contemplate suing the Canadian government, which requires health warnings on cigarette packages to be bigger than the brand name. They claim that this amounts to appropriation of intangible assets. The United States, given its litigious culture, has long used legalistic approaches to settling trade disputes and increasingly it is such a model which is being generalized under American pressure. Such suits may become a familiar presence in the deregulated global economy under the emergent international trade regime. To many non-U.S. critics, like the Canadian political scientist David Law (1995: 415) there appear to be no transnational citizenship rights "other than those accorded to capital, and these are defined to favour US-registered companies." NAFTA from his perspective can be seen as an exercise in which the United States government is using access to its vast market as "a lever of power, linked to a reshaping of the international business climate, by subjecting other nations to the disciplines of the new constitutionalism" (Law, 1995: 415). But of course the Canadian government signed up for NAFTA. It did so because the alternative was less appealing to Canadian (and Mexican) decisionmakers. It was better to have a set of rules theoretically binding on all members than to face a situation in which a neighboring 800 pound gorilla could be expected to pursue its own interest in less predictable ways.

Fast track authorization was first adopted in 1974. It allows a president to negotiate trade agreements, including free trade agreements such as NAFTA, following objectives agreed to by the Congress which must be notified in advance of any signing of an agreement. The idea is that Congress votes the treaty up or down but cannot modify it. Without fast track other countries, where typically the executive speaks for a legislative majority, are hesitant to enter into negotiations with the U.S. executive branch since the president's team cannot make commitments for the government. Plans for a Free Trade Area of the Americas which would expand NAFTA to almost the entire hemisphere were back burnered as a result until George W. Bush revived this effort initiated during his father's presidency. In the wake of Mr. Bush's ninety percent approval rating following September 11, and thanks to some generous payoffs to members previously opposed to fast track, Mr. Bush obtained passage of the enabling legislation by one vote in the House of Representatives in late 2001. The White House did not do so well in its negotiations with the Latin Americans (especially the key player Brazil), in gaining acceptance of its views on trade and investment which were designed to open the markets of its neighbors to the South while protecting key domestic constituencies. This selective openness sat uneasily with professions of free trade. At the same time the U.S. negotiators hammered away at social provisioning.

The thrust of the new international trade regime is to prevent the provision of goods and services on a non-market basis either directly by public providers who do not meet commercial criteria or in ways which restrict the freedom of capital. The claim is that any social protections or priorities which do not meet market criteria are prima facie "inefficiencies" and so not to be permitted. From the point of the government negotiators and their corporate advisers, however (at least according to their critics), any government policies which restrict business should be outlawed and this is, or should be, unacceptable (Ranney, 1993). Thus regional integration rather than competing with, and standing in the way of, a free and open global economy is proving an intermediate step consistent with corporate globalization. The significance of any tensions between the separate rules of such agreements and the universalizing designs of GSEGIs are secondary to this larger social reality. The international system envisioned at Bretton Woods continues to be eroded.

CHAPTER TWELVE

Redecorating and New Architecture

"If people like me can crash a currency system, there is something wrong with the system"

—*George Soros*

"If talk about reforming the international financial architecture were equivalent to action, the last few years would have seen a spectacular transformation in the way the world works."

—*Alan Beattie* (2001: 11)

The capacity of those exercising power to frame the agenda in the areas which have been a key topic this study is illustrated by the extent to which official concern has focused on the need to develop new financial architecture, a discourse initiated by the countries of the core fearing a financial global meltdown. Of course other countries would suffer from such a calamity but it is not their interests which guide this discussion, nor are issues of development, poverty eradication, social justice, workers' rights, or the environment arguably central concerns of elite decisionmakers beyond a certain rhetoric of good intentions. Instead discussion of financial architecture took center stage when the questions of how the present pattern of globalization needs to be modified were discussed in the 1990s in those influential circles where real differences are produced.

There was a change in focus in the post September 11 world view as enunciated by the Bush Administration and its unilateralist approach to an array of international concerns and at the same time a demoting of discussion of alternatives to the export oriented development model dependent on inflow of foreign investment and loan capital denominated in hard currencies, above all dollar denominated debt. The excess capacity visible on a global scale, downward pressure on prices, the threat of deflation, and the impact of desperate countries seeking to compete by ignoring labor rights and environmental concerns produce a shallow and uneven development. Income inequalities within countries and between countries and the crisis-prone architecture of financial and trade regimes have not gotten the attention they merit given Washington's focus on a perpetual war on the evil ones.

Among disputes which took central attention among the leading economies were questions of the Bush Administration's endorsement of huge agricultural subsidies and protection of the domestic steel industry widely understood to violate professions of commitment to free trade in the service of electoral ambitions. The United States by underwriting its corporate farmers to the extent that they are able to flood global markets with inexpensive corn, soybeans, wheat, and rice—some of which are sold at half their cost of production—has disastrous ramifications for farmers in poor countries who are unable to compete with subsidized U.S. exports. The largest agribusiness firms received the largest share of the subsidies.

The European Union is an even worse offender. For all products agricultural subsidies in the United States equaled 21 percent of farm income in 2001. For the OECD countries as a whole agricultural subsidies exceeded $300 billion and in the EU 35 percent of total farm income came from government subsidies. Nonetheless the 2002 Bush approval of an 80 percent increase in farm subsidies has made a discussion of reducing their trade barriers far more difficult. Such trade disputes are common and persistent irritants. They relate to larger problems of profit realization linked not simply to overcapacity but to the increased importance of financialization. While trade disputes have potential to be destabilizing it is debt which has become central to the global system at a level never before approached. And while the Bush Administration's war on terrorism was a dramatic change of subject for the world, these previously central questions of trade, investment development, and especially the centrality of debt, have not gone away. Nor could they be ignored for long.

Excessive borrowing by companies, households, or governments has been at the root of almost every economic crisis of the last decades of the twentieth century, from Mexico to Japan, to Russia (similar overextension is a problem in the United States as well). Financial crises as we have discussed were occurring with regularity and their costs were high, in the area of 15 percent of GDP for countries ranging from Benin, Hungary, Mauritania, Mexico, Spain to Venezuela (Wyplosz, 1999: 154 Table 1). Analysis of more than 300 economic crises in more than eighty countries from 1973 to the late 1990s showed that while output growth recovered to pre-crisis levels in a year or so on average—as did macroeconomic balance generally, exchange rate, balance of payments, and so on—real wage growth takes on average four years to recover and unemployment growth five years (United Nations Development Programme, 1999: 40). There are worries that the inability to expand debt from its already high base constrains future growth. As a reaction to these widespread failures there were increasingly vocal criticisms of the IMF for mishandling the emerging market crises and its failure of vision.

As the cost to the low-income countries of the new international trade, finance, and investment regimes becomes more evident the countries of the core proclaim the need for the next round of global negotiations to be "a development round." But as Peter Sutherland (2001: 15), former director of the WTO, notes the richer countries "have responded so woefully to the issues that developing countries want addressed right now" and so why should the less developed nations accept a new round with "the inevitable new commitments which will ensue?" He thought soothing words about a new development round "have no credibility if the promoters cannot demonstrate good faith up-front." Because they have not done so, governments in poor countries "can recognize empty political spin." The rich countries continue to protect their vulnerable industries while demanding that the poor countries accept elaborate and costly protection of the TNCs intellectual property and unfettered market access. The Bush Administration's hardball unilateralism put serious constraints on the prospects of the Doha Round and on the future of the WTO. Failure to make concessions on agricultural subsidies was a key contributing factor.

As globalization deepened the specifics of a proposed neoliberal global economic and financial governance regime have emerged more clearly. These efforts have centered on the International Monetary Fund's assumption of new functions and efforts under the auspices of the Organization for Economic Cooperation and Development to produce a Multilateral Agreement on Investment, "a new constitution for the global economy," as Michel Camdessus termed it. They have come in for extensive criticism from voices ranging from academic and political establishment figures to well-organized grassroots and NGO protestors. The proposed new constitutionalism met with counter formulations including debt cancellation/forgiveness campaigns and the models of human development given widespread exposure in the work of the United Nations Development Program. Such alternative approaches contest a perceived and narrow economism of the market efficiency model of globalization.

This chapter discusses reform efforts and alternatives. It highlights as well three important areas of international negotiation. The first is the effort by transnational capital to legislate a Multilateral Agreement on Investment bypassing nation state level legislative debate in secret negotiations designed to impose a more constricting and irreversible version of market-driven globalism. The second is the intense negotiations over the handling of the debt crisis afflicting the most heavily indebted poor countries. The third is the attempts by East Asian governments to come together, mobilize regional resources, and support alternatives to control by the GSEGIs. Each of these negotiations, like the continued sometimes heated negotiations between the United States and the European Union and its member countries, in their own way illustrates the complexity of the politics of economic policymaking in the era of globalization.

FORMULATING THE QUESTIONS

In terms of a new financial architecture, what would a more equitable agenda look like? The objectives commonly shared by developing countries can be easily listed: more balanced and "symmetrical" treatment of creditors and debtors, more stable exchange rates among the key currencies, IMF surveillance of the policies of the rich countries with regard to trade and especially capital flows, less intrusive conditionalities, and of course more democratic and participatory multilateral institutions and processes (United Nations Development Programme, 2001: 76). They have yet to have much success in achieving these goals. Developed countries account for 17 percent of voting strength in the United National General Assembly but over 61 percent in the Bretton Woods institutions. The G-7, where the governing consensus on important issues is often reached, gets no systematic input from the developing world. The G-20, a creation of the G-7 which, while expanded to include some of the larger economies of the developing world, adheres to an agenda submitted by the G-7. Given power asymmetries it is hardly surprising that the demands for transparency are addressed to the debtor countries, who are expected to bear the adjustment costs of market failures while the GSEGIs and Western states and financial institutions are not forced to live up to similar standards. What could compel them to do so? Asymmetric impacts suggest core-periphery tensions over regime design do not get resolved in favor of the latter.

The problems disorderly exchange rates pose are not so damaging to the United States (or to Euroland and Japan). Large economies less dependent on international trade in relation to GDP can lend, borrow, invest, and accept investment in their national currency and so do not have the same experience as small, more trade dependent countries for whom fluctuating exchange rates are far more destabilizing and for whom efforts to peg currencies can lead to disaster. The most influential negotiators establishing the rules of the international financial regime have a different cost-benefit calculation than the weaker economies.

A crisis-prone system increases the need for the latter to hold more international financial reserves in key currencies (primarily in dollars) to the advantage of those who provide such currency. Individual small economies cannot avoid the impact of erratic currency fluctuation and volatile capital markets. To place the blame on their poor supervision of domestic banking is to mistake the central nature of the problem. The presumption is that the less developed economies must change their internal behavior despite the evidence of financial crisis so widespread that we can conclude it is systemic problems related to the excessive volatility of unregulated capital flows that need to be addressed. The continued direction of demands being made by the GSEGIs for greater capital account convertibility, deregulation of foreign investment, and liberalization of financial services fly in the face of the past impacts of such polices which typically have been regressive in their incidence. Financial liberalization has been an important source of wealth creation and distribution in the countries of the core where higher real interest rates and uncontrollable capital movements have been responsible for the increased share of total income going to rentiers (rentier income is entrepreneurial income of the financial sector and interest receivable) which increased between the 1960s and 1970s to the 1980s and 1990s by a hundred percent and more in the United States and the UK (Epstein and Power, 2002).

More attention has been paid to the issue of capital flight and to cases such as that of the late Ferdinand Marcos of the Philippines, some of whose billions in Swiss banks was recovered by the government of his country after a twelve year effort. In 1998 Switzerland finally enacted legislation to address accusations that its banks were turning a blind eye to wealth inflows stripped from poor countries. A year later the Nigerian government was taking them to court to retrieve a billion or so dollars stashed in their banks by Sani Abacha the former dictator of that country. Switzerland has been the location of preference for Slobodan Milosevic of Yugoslavia, Jean-Claude Duvalier of Haiti, Benazir Bhutto of Pakistan, and Mobutu Sese Seko of Zaire (Olson, 2002: 5). The International Monetary Fund showed little interest in such instances even though it is often its loans which were being "recyled" in this manner to the detriment of the poor of the world whom the loans were allegedly to help. It was only after September II that the United States government demanded a detailed tracking of criminal funds (but only those related to possible terrorist activities, not the vast sums associated with corrupt practices of the governing classes and criminal elites often favored by American policymakers). Nor has regulation of illegal capital flows or movements to hide legitimately acquired funds from tax authorities been central to the reform agenda. The call for new financial architecture is confined for the most part to reforms to protect the banks.

There are two very different emphases in discussion of the need for greater transparency in financial markets. First, there is the conflict between those who suggest uncoerced financial markets are rational and work efficiently to allocate resources in optimal fashion or that they would do so given adequate disclosure. The competing view asserts that financial markets are by their nature prone to speculative instability, waves of overoptimism, panic, and pessimism due to those famous animal spirits and crowd psychology a la Keynes-Minsky and that it is the job of government to take seriously their responsibility to regulate financial markets. In this second perspective it is not information *per se* which is understood to be the problem but rather the swings in subjective interpretation of information. The sudden reversal in market psychological mood is the trigger. The costs of repeated crises produced a general consensus that some sort of international judicial process needs to be established to allow bankrupt governments to restructure debt without being sued by private creditors, some sort of "sovereign chapter eleven," (after similar rules in the U.S. domestic bankruptcy law). The creation of a single international judicial entity to arbitrate disputes and bind all creditors to a single settlement avoids individual creditors shopping for jurisdictions most likely to favor their interests, a common practice of bottom feeding hedge funds which buy debt at deep discount and then extort payment at the expense of other more cooperative creditors.

There nonetheless remains division on the issue of who should be regulated. Most attention is focused on the debtor nations and efforts to strengthen creditor protections. However a greater offense in dollar terms, and more severe in a larger social sense, is the impact of tax avoidance by the rich and powerful, individuals and corporations, and the resultant erosion of the public sector's possibilities. The problem of financial irresponsibility and widespread dishonesty by the rich and powerful suggests a need to regulate the Andorras, Liechtensteins and Panamas, the "don't ask because we won't tell" havens which shelter vast sums from the tax collectors and which disappear the ill gotten gains of corrupt officials and elites. In addition, many legitimate U.S. companies reduce the taxes they pay to the American government on profits earned in the United States by transferring them to, for example, a paper company in Barbados where they become expenses that can be deducted on U.S. tax returns. Major corporations encouraged by their lawyers and accountants participate in such activities. The deductible expenses can be declared royalties for the use of the company's logo or fees for management advice. In Bermuda, where there is no income tax, income earned becomes tax free dollars which can be used anywhere in the world.

THE LIMITED CALLS FOR REFORM

In the closing decades of the twentieth century many condemned American use of the IMF as part of its own effort to stage manage the evolution of global capitalism. There were critiques of the Fund's "mission creep," its expanding role in the global economy, and of the self-interest some saw behind its policy approach—high interest rates to defend currencies to the advantage of creditors and elites wishing to move monies into other currencies. The use of tax payer monies and the focus on retaining the "confidence" of markets whatever the cost to ordinary people and local businesses, the prolongation of the burdens of unpayable debt, the punishing public sector austerity its "consensus" demanded, and resultant recessionary impacts were widely criticized as the wrong medicine. The generalized failure of the GSEGIs signaled to many that a new financial architecture was needed. The difficulty was a fundamental division over what changes were appropriate. A state-centered regime such as Bretton Woods with fixed rules seemed restrictive to many advocates of greater market freedom. Others feared the emergence of a powerful international state under U.S. dominance could overwhelm sovereignty by forcing market conforming limits to economic independence.

President Clinton speaking at a Monica-moment before the Council on Foreign Relations in the October 1998 said that "This is the biggest financial challenge facing the world in half a century." It was time to "adapt the international financial architecture to the twenty-first century." Tony Blair, ever quick to second a U.S. initiative, expressed the thought that perhaps a new Bretton Woods "for the next millennium" was needed. But few specifics of a new global governance regime in these waning years of the second millennium were proposed and the need for action soon passed as the world's financial system seemed to become somewhat more stable. The mood changed in the years immediately following, when the financial situation seemed to recover. Now, suggestions were more along the lines of plumbing improvements or perhaps interior redecorating rather than new architecture. It is possible that serious crisis in the core economies especially if they were to affect the United States in some dramatic fashion will focus reform efforts in a way which has not been in evidence since Bretton Woods. Serious problems elsewhere have not had this effect. When George W. Bush took office, the global financial system was no longer showing obvious crisis signs, even though the growth of the U.S. and global economies had slowed. There was little sign of contagion from events in Argentina and Turkey in significant part because investors had been cautious about jumping back into the so-called emerging markets.

The Bush Administration criticized its predecessors in the Clinton Treasury for having micro-managed the IMF and having focused too much on bailouts to troubled debtors. Treasury Secretary Paul O'Neill said the Bush approach would be to prevent crises rather than to spend taxpayer monies on bailouts. Mr. Bush, committed to a more free market approach and unilateralist foreign policy than his predecessor, backed away from international treaty agreements ranging from missile testing and deployment to the Kyoto Accord on the reduction of greenhouse gas emission. He and his Secretary of the Treasury distanced the United States from the GSEGIs rather than closely managing of these institutions as their immediate predecessors had done. Nevertheless, when confronted with a possible Turkish default on international obligations, they supported an IMF loan rather than accepting the consequences of default for an important NATO ally and key player in a region of strategic interest to the U.S.

When the administration supported an August 2001 loan package to Argentina, the action was widely seen as throwing good money after bad—the new loan did not change matters and Argentina soon had to go off its currency-board-fixed link to the dollar and devalue anyway. When after this initial commitment the United States abandoned Argentina, a country which had aligned itself more closely with the U.S. in its economic programs and foreign policy than any other country in the region (it had enthusiastically liberalized and privatized), this seemed to confirm to many that the United States was a fickle and undependable ally. Argentina's default triggered economic depression in that nation without parallel since the Great Depression; its economy was sinking at a double digit annual rate causing widespread suffering and the destruction of most of its middle class. The cases of Argentina and Turkey were not different in kind from the impact in other countries submitting to neoliberalism. Deep financial integration with low export capacity meant downturns in foreign exchange earnings triggering debt crises and currency crashes. The Washington Consensus brought stagnation and in some places chaos.

The Bush economic team seemed unsure of what to do. Its instincts were to wash their hands of the problem but the costs of doing so were simply too high. In the next test, Brazil, while eventually approving (in August 2002) the largest IMF bailout package ever, it heavy handedly prefaced aid with a very different message which adversely impacted markets making solution to the crisis more difficult. Secretary O'Neill only two months before the decision to aid Brazil had insisted that "Throwing the US taxpayer's money at a political uncertainty in Brazil does not seem brilliant." (It was the frankness of such off the cuff comments which greased his subsequent exit from government service.) A month before the record bailout he was insisting he would not approve of loans which would likely end up in Swiss banks. Only after markets panicked from such a response did he agree to the loan. It was to be extended in segments with most not being released until after the upcoming presidential election to be sure that the leftist Workers Party candidate, ahead in the polls, would be tied to continued toeing of the Washington Consensus policy line which the voters of Brazil and many other observers concluded was an ineffective, painful, and counterproductive policy design.

Although Bush's Treasury Department was less involved in the day-to-day operations of the Fund than its predecessors were, the administration did not want to give up the option of using the fund for strategic ends. Talk of a new financial architecture continued camouflaging what was in fact the continuing effort by the United States executive branch, its allies in other governments, and leading internationalist elements of the corporate sector to liberalize the world economy and to further free trade and capital movements from national regulations. "Even more telling, the Bush Treasury is not keen to make structural reforms for the Fund which would limit future bailouts. Many European governments favour explicit limits laying out, in advance, how much a country can borrow. The main opponent of such a change is the United States," as the *Economist* (2002: 71) reported.

At the same time these debates were taking place the United States itself was continuing to go deeper in debt to the rest of the world as its current account deficit soared. In an intricate flow of funds the U.S. sucked capital in from the rest of the world (including flight capital from many debtor nations) to finance consumption as well as relending to other parts of the world producing unsustainable debt levels among not only Third World borrowers but also the United States itself, creating potential systemic dangers which went uncommented upon in the discussion of how to reform the global financial governance regime.

THE MISSION OF THE GSEGIS

As was discussed in earlier chapters, the IMF was seen to have outlived its function when, after President Nixon ended the system of fixed exchange rates in 1973. Countries then left currencies to float so that minute by minute the price of their money could be set by supply and demand conditions on foreign exchange markets. This development seemed to obviate the central function of the IMF which was to help countries whose currencies had become misaligned. A freely floating currency would eliminate, or so economists generally thought, persistent balance of payments troubles without outside support (as was discussed in chapter 6). By definition countries which allowed their currency to float would always be in equilibrium. A shortage or surplus would trigger price movements and automatically the price mechanism would restore proper valuation. In the early 1980s, when many countries were hit by massive capital flight, orthodoxy saw these developments as the result of faulty government policies. Governments had overvalued their currencies, intervened in markets creating costly rigidities, hidden unpleasant information, and as a consequence suffered because when adjustment came it was sharp and deep. The IMF created a new mission for the organization by helping them adjust. The Fund it was pointed out did not have a mandate to re-create itself in this way. Such a role of "lender of last resort" increased moral hazard, the chance that greater risks would be taken because of the implicit safety net offered. Its strategic demands for quick financial liberalization produced greater problems for reasons discussed in chapters 6 and 7.

As evidence of the failures of IMF policies mounted some formidable figures, William Simon and George Schultz, former secretaries of the Treasury, and the Republican majority leaders of the Senate and the House, Trent Lott and Dick Armey, were strongly opposed to an IMF with a mission of imposing its vision of global governance, reinventing itself further with more Washington Consensus regulations, detailed conditionality, and disciplinary enforcement procedures. What they saw was bureaucratic empire building and social planning usurping the market. Critics from the Left stressed the challenge to sovereignty and the riding roughshod over the ability of democratic polities to pursue their chosen economic and political priorities. While critiques differed there was a significant overlap between Right and Left views of the IMF's self-declared new mission.

Supporting the growing GSEGI role was the internationalist fraction in American politics, especially transnational corporations and finance capital with the firm support of the executive branch of the government and those members of Congress favoring the continuation of the American state's historic mission of overseeing the opening of the international economy to U.S. investors. To liberal institutionalists the gains from such openness are obvious and it is therefore beneficial, indeed necessary, for international organizations to act to overcome collective action problems to the smooth functioning of global markets by creating proper rules and enforcing them. In this view the IMF was acting to facilitate more efficient allocation of resources and so increasing overall prosperity. It should be supported by policymakers, voters, and taxpayers. As a major player in the world economy it was in the interests of the United States and its financial institutions that the IMF be strengthened and capable of exercising greater leverage on recalcitrant governments.

In addition to broad philosophical issues concerning how the world economy would best function, technically difficult matters also needed to be addressed. Among the most important of these was whether floating or quasi fixed exchange rates were better. This question had been debated intensely from the early 1970s when the Bretton Woods system ended. As has been noted, economists had thought floating rates would equate supply and demand in constant small steps as needed so that large and sudden changes, as when fixed exchange rate regimes devalued, could be avoided. On the other hand, because expectations concerning a country's economic fortunes can change suddenly and dramatically when investors in a herd mentality decide to flee a country, floating rates encourage extreme volatility. Inflows of "hot" monies looking for short-term speculative gain by gambling on the immediate future of asset prices are very different from long-term investment which can bring technological know how, management skills, and access to foreign markets.

When amounts involved in short-term capital flows are great few countries have enough foreign reserves to protect their stability through foreign exchange interventions. Those who do hold huge resources, typically in the form of U.S. Treasury bonds earning low interest rates compared to the much higher interest paid for the short-term borrowing these reserves back. The demand that these countries hold greater foreign reserves to defend against the destabilizing prospect of possible capital flight is therefore a request that they devote still more of their scarce resources to further subsidize the United States Treasury Department and ease the burden of the national debt to U.S. taxpayers. Experience quickly showed that floating rates tended to overshoot and produced unexpected instability and continuous turbulence. But holding large reserves was also costly.

By pegging their exchange rates (interfering in markets to maintain the value of their currencies by buying and selling foreign reserves) countries could impart the expectation of stable rates which dampened speculation and increased investor confidence. By keeping one's currency in line with major trading partners a country avoids loss of competitiveness. The advantages of economic integration are strengthened it was claimed through the adoption of currency boards, currency unions, or the outright use of a stronger currency in place of one's own (as in "dollarization"). The advantage is a dependable currency the value of which is guaranteed by a core economy central bank. The price is a loss of autonomy and inability in recession to use monetary policy to stimulate the domestic economy when unemployment and bankruptcies threaten. Policymakers can do little to intervene if they surrender currency independence.

There can be costs to the loss of the possibility of active monetary policy as Argentina so painfully came to know in the winter of 2001–2002. A creditable pegged exchange rate policy, or any policy that does not allow markets to fully set the value of a country's currency requires such reserves to allow intervention to influence the currency's value in foreign exchange markets or capital controls of some sort to limit its convertibility. At one extreme is a strategy of controls on capital flows, especially short-term speculative movements such as Chile's 30 percent tax on incoming portfolio investments, refundable after a year, which is often given as the sort of measure that discourages destabilizing flows.

However matters are not so simple. Chile's innovative tax was repealed due not only to the prevalence of smuggling, bribery, and false invoicing to conceal capital flows, but also in order to better attract capital to Chile's financial markets. Effective capital controls involve substantial interference with markets, which is not appreciated by investors and so not undertaken lightly by any single country acting alone. In normal times capital controls appear too costly and in time of crisis too late. But in a deep crisis which augers to get worse they may be the lesser of evils. When Malaysia adopted them in the wake of the East Asian financial crisis there were dire warnings on the one hand and great interest on the other. The country discontinued trading in its national currency, the ringgit. Outside Malaysia it became worthless after thirty days. Foreign investors in the country were forced to remain for one year and nonresidents could not cross the border with more than a thousand ringgit (then $263) at the government fixed exchange rate.

While most economists frowned on such interventions some, including Paul Krugman, favored capital controls for East Asian economies. He observed "We're seeing a general loss of patience with trying to satisfy the international marketplace. International investors demand a lot," he said, "and it's starting to look like these countries can't do it while rebuilding their economies" (interviewed in Landler, 1998: B2). As matters worked out the Asian financial situation improved, lessening the incentive for neighbors to follow Malaysia's example. Part of the turn around can be credited to the IMF's reversal of policy, its easing pressure for deflation and allowing growth in the region (to some extent out of fear of more Malaysia-like rebellion in the region). A year later, when Malaysia removed its controls, capital able to pull out did not do so. The experience can be viewed as a successful strategy measure although other policies of the Mahathir regime cloud the issue.

The basic problem for countries is that free access to foreign finance, especially short-term finance, is incompatible with financial stability. The three main goals nations have with regard to their financial regime have been called the impossible trinity. Governments want to maintain their sovereignty. They want the benefits of global capital markets and they want to regulate and supervise their financial markets to avoid corruption and for safety purposes. But too much regulation and attention to sovereignty discourages foreign investment. Free flowing investment means regulation only by market forces and a loss of sovereignty as we have noted.

PROMOTING STABILITY

In the wake of the East Asian financial crisis and the subsequent trend toward recovery there were various post mortems and proposals for new strategies. In the United States President Clinton suggested the IMF act earlier, making funds available before disasters strike through a contingent credit line (CCL). His Secretary of the Treasury explained that if investors knew a country has adequate resources to fall back on, they would not pull out in a panicked reaction fearing default by the country on its obligations. Such a line of credit might help a nation whose economy was basically sound avoid the impact of contagion when others got in trouble. Of course deciding who would qualify would be a tricky matter. It will not be clear when the fundamentals are in fact sound. In almost all crisis there are claims that there is really no serious problem. Indeed, the prospect of such a guarantee increases moral hazard since politicians and bankers in emerging and other markets will be tempted into undertakings knowing that the IMF will come in with liquidity should they run the boat aground. Critics suggest that these funds will be absorbed by elites, foreign banks, and others to finance their exit from the troubled economy. Providing the wherewithall for speculators to profit no matter their mistakes is hardly consistent with market principles. Such doubts increase the pressure for greater oversight and regulatory enforcement powers for the IMF and other GSEGIs.

The carrot of such an offer might be used to encourage governments to conform to structural changes favored by the Fund. But what if a country was declared to be qualified and then conditions changed and it was dropped? Could the IMF do this without panicking investors and precipitating the contagion the CCL was designed to avoid? Further, loans need to be repaid and this typically is done through austerity measures. Such measures frequently bring on political crisis. Investors fearing chaos or even just political uncertainty are unlikely to be convinced by a cash cushion even if they think the economy might be sound in some hypothetical long run. Thus the availability of such loans could be inadequate inducement for investors. States might hesitate to draw on such lines of credit if they are not actually facing imminent danger for fear of triggering panic and capital flight. No country applied for a CCL.

If the development banks are to become lenders of last resort should they not also be empowered to shut down local financial institutions and manage central banks which act irresponsibly? The administration of George W. Bush inclined not to grant loans to debtors unable to meet obligations, favored measures to ensure problems would not develop in the first place. Their emphasis was on meeting the test of the market rather than bailouts when market failure occurred. This however is easier said than done. While the Bush team preferred leaving investment decisions to the market, they too became drawn into regulatory questions. How much should national sovereignty be compromised as the price for lender of last resort protection once the IMF goes down this road? Should the Fund certify that restructuring is needed and supervise the equivalent of a Chapter II (of the U.S. bankruptcy code) type system globally? What procedures should be negotiated for debt rescheduling and what is the proper forum for such a discussion? Should the market price risk and taxpayer insurance be withdrawn? Others asked: Shouldn't the Fund become more of a rating agency and less of a fire fighter and the debt police? Should countries facing capital flight be encouraged to impose controls as the better alternative to punishingly high interest rates and economic repression which the IMF demands as part of its current conditionality? How can governments prevent putting the interests of speculators before jobs for their citizens and safety net programs when crisis strikes? Investors look for decisiveness and institutional structures which inhibit policy reversals. Should elections be eliminated? Democracies are messy. What price should countries pay for market credibility? Should the monopoly the IMF has achieved as the agency dealing with financial crises be ended and competition allowed so that other (non-IMF strategies) be allowed? Competition would permit us to see if other approaches helped countries in trouble more that the Washington "Consensus," which after all is a consensus only within a limited circle. The scope of the questions conveys the breadth of viewpoints reform proposals elicit.

Behind these questions still others lurk: Was the growth of speculation the demise of the Bretton Woods unleashed creating a financially driven economy? Were bubbles becoming a more potent force destabilizing the world economy as a whole? Was the deflationary bias GSEGIs policies imposed on the world producing slower growth and dangerous deflationary tendencies in the world system? When so many countries continually face the same set of recurring problems are there systemic issues which need to be faced?

This latter set of questions would be considered seriously only in a period of severe systemic strain. In the absence of such deeply threatening occurrences reform would tend to be modest and within the context of an acceptance of market deregulation and financial decontrol. For example, in the second half of the 1990s the IMF instituted some minor reforms. It introduced (in 1996) the Special Data Dissemination Standard (SDDS), a code for collection and disclosing of information to international investors concerning the state of key financial magnitudes by national governments. Most "emerging" and "transitional" economies did not participate in the SDDS or at least do not fully comply. The debate continues over how complete a picture can be ensured for such key variables as usable central bank reserves, including forward liabilities (one of the most frequent methods used to obscure the real reserve position of a central bank). Issues of size, composition, and maturities of foreign currency liabilities of not only governments and banks but also other major players get complicated as private debts are hidden, but in the event of problems they can quickly become public obligations. How far should the Fund go in reversing the extent of such financial engineering?

Article IV provides for consultations and analysis of the current economic situation and IMF Board recommendations for economic policy reforms. Approximately once a year its staff prepares an Article IV report for each country. It is an in-depth analysis of its policies and performance. These have been secret because markets tend to "overreact" when the IMF expresses concern. If they were made public the Fund fears it would come to be denied access to potentially damaging information. And if countries had to disclose details of their Letters of Intent and Policy Framework Papers prepared in order to obtain IMF loans, the effect might be for countries not to negotiate with the Fund until matters became far worse. This would raise the cost of bailouts and make eventual adjustment more painful.

Responding to critics Stanley Fisher, then the Fund's chief economist (later he would join Citibank where he would deal with many of these same "emerging market" countries) asked rhetorically: "should the IMF have gone public with its fears of impending crisis? While we knew that Thailand was extremely vulnerable, we could not predict with certainty whether, or when, crisis would actually strike. For the IMF to arrive on the scene like the fire brigade with lights flashing and sirens wailing before a crisis occurs, would risk provoking a crisis that might never have occurred" (Fisher, 1998: 9). The IMF argues that capital account liberalization will make international financial markets more efficient. It grants that liberalization will increase the magnitude of capital movements and concludes that it is likely that there will be fewer, but more serious, crises. It therefore needs greater financial resources, the Fund says, to insure that it can adequately help economies if problems arise. Its ability to gain cooperation from the countries in question and their willingness to conform to its policy advice depend on its ability to provide such financial assistance in time of crisis.

But if bailouts are expected moral hazard grows. The practices of lenders will remain more reckless than if they had to bear the full cost of their actions. To encourage more responsible lending the suggestion has been made that creditors should shoulder a greater share of the cost when debtors were unable to repay and nations should be discouraged from so much reliance on short-term capital. Such shifts may be a step in the right direction but the devil still resides in the details. Major differences exist in how for example bankers are to be "bailed in," i.e., take on part of the burden when debts cannot be repaid. American policy makers favor a voluntary, *ad hoc* approach. The Europeans think a voluntary approach will end up being unfair and relies too much on American arm twisting. They want something more formal. Michel Camdessus, when head of the IMF, proposed that the Fund's articles of agreement be changed to give it the right to declare a temporary debt moratorium. Bankers strenuously object to this proposal and prefer the American voluntary approach. What is at issue are the very different economic philosophies which ensure this debate will not easily be resolved.

While the United States continues to insist that countries should be dealt with on a case-by-case basis, America's critics remain unconvinced. "I would not accept that *ad hoc* solutions have been acceptable or successful in any way," says Richard Portes of the London Business School to the *Financial Times*, "They play Pakistan one way, Ecuador another and Romania a third, depending on what US policy priorities are" (Crooks and Beattie, 2000: 14). In the wake of September 11 the U.S. coalition building required completely dropping the pretense that GSEGIs made decisions only or even primarily based on objective economic criteria as America's new allies in the war against terrorism were able to demand and were granted huge concessions by the GSEGIs proportional to their perceived contribution to the US anti-terrorism campaign. Well before September 11, the Europeans complained that the top ten borrowers from the Fund were dominated by those of strategic interest to the United States. The Americans think Europe over represented on the IMF's executive board and among the officials who run the IMF, including the managing director who, as we have noted, is by convention a European. The United States went so far in the wake of the emerging market crisis of the late 1990s to convene (without any source of formal legitimacy) a Group of 22 "systematically significant nations" omitting the smaller European states and including more emerging market nations of importance to the Americans.

By the negotiations held early in the twenty-first century a group of twenty became favored. It too was an example of concentric club formation in that it was the Group of Seven at its September 1999 Washington, D.C. meeting which announced the creation of the Group of Twenty as an international forum of finance ministers and central bank governors representing nineteen countries, the EU and the BWIs. The creation of the G-20 fulfilled the G-7's commitment made at a previous meeting "to

establish an informal mechanism for dialogue among systematically important countries within the framework of the Bretton Woods institutional system." The G-20 was established to address "the lack of emerging market
representation in the G-7 [which] limits its ability to deal with some issues
related to developments in the international economy and financial system" (G-7,n.d.: 2). It had no representative of the poorest nations and their
priorities nor did it address the imbalance between creditor and debtors in
decision making on global financial policies suggesting to some inadequacies of the G-20 format since its creators were not interested in an expansion of the agenda to the concerns of the majority of less developed
economies or in improving representativeness of this key forum.[*]

Any new Bretton Woods would need address both a North-South division between creditors and debtors and more generally the gap between
those who had benefitted from corporate globalization and those who had
not. The contemporary imbalance at the heart of why the IMF and other
GSEGIs behave as they do would have to be addressed. The emphasis in
new financial architecture discussions was however quite different and as a
result George Melloan writing in early 1999 in the *Wall Street Journal*
notes, the "new architecture" amounts to "trying to save the old architecture." While academics debate what the best sort of architecture would be
(for the most part using liberal institutionalist presumptions concerning
the common good goals), one should also look at the contradictions at the
core of global governance regimes. Miles Kahler (1999: 4) is not alone in
noticing that the burden of adjustment falls as it usually has "largely on
national governments in the developing countries." Most of the elements
of the new architecture commit countries to adoption of market-oriented
economic policies and Anglo-American regulatory standards. It is these
governments which are called on to provide greater transparency and not
private actors or the GSEGIs. There was no regulation of hedge funds and
market makers despite the experience of Long Term Capital Management

---

[*]The "G-ization" of global governance is creating some overlaps and confusion. There
is also a G-24, the Intergovernmental Group of Twenty-Four on International Monetary Affairs established decades earlier (in 1971). Its main objective is to concertize
the positions of developing countries on monetary and development finance issues.
At the Cancún WTO Ministerial in 2003 what was momentarily called a G-23 emerged
led by Brazil, India, South Africa and supported by China which opposed the G-7
agenda. U.S. pressure caused some members to quickly leave this group although an
oppositional nucleus remained. The Brazil-led group consolidated as an interlocutor
in trade talks as "G20" on the grounds that it was formed August 20, just before the
Cancún talks.

and Enron. The only agreement is that markets need to receive better information (on the presumption that they are always the most efficient allocators) and should not be interfered with by state agency.

Discussion of new financial architecture takes place within a relatively small policymaking circle and there has been an unwillingness to consider a stable system of exchange rates or coherence in macroeconomic policy by the major industrial countries which would provide the necessary stability the smaller countries so desperately need. The most powerful economies, and above all the United States, refuse to surrender or seriously compromise sovereignty over their own monetary flexibility such coordination would require. Nor are private financial institutions of the core willing to consider any involuntary mechanisms compelling standstill or rollover of debt (Goldstein, 2000). The assumptions and policy measures of the new financial architecture being discussed looked very much like a reinvention of the Washington Consensus (Soederberg, 2001).

To achieve regulation would have required major changes in the way financial markets were allowed to work, and this governments were not powerful enough or independent enough to achieve. The problem was clear. Without a credible "first tranche" of private loss, moral hazard would continue to plague any attempt by governments or GSEGIs to provide liquidity. As Charles Calomiris (1998: 8) writes, what is needed is "a set of transparent credible rules that impose a margin of private loss on bank claimants, which limits the exposure of taxpayers to bailout costs *ex post*, and in so doing, limits banks' willingness to undertake risks *ex ante*. Putting those safeguards into place should be a requirement of membership in the IMF." Such a proposal would, if adopted, ensure that the IMF would return to its original mission which is to provide liquidity to illiquid banking systems and not bailouts to insolvent ones. It is a seemingly sensible and necessary proposal but unlikely to be easily achieved. Since the private lenders have not been willing to compromise their freedom of action and the IMF has stood ready to make up losses, other proposals focus on preventing the shifting of unpayable debt to the IMF (which then has simply rolled it over in an effort to obscure its essentially unpayable nature).

There is no country in the world, not least the United States, in which the financial system does not have the power to coerce bailouts from the state. In most countries the distance between the personnel of government leadership and bank ownership is a short one. This is why in so many developing country crises bailouts have had priority over national interest more broadly conceived. In the advanced countries such personal linkages are not absent but such protection seems more a structural characteristic of the system's organization than an instrumentalist personal intervention, although numerous cases of revolving door personnel in public service are in obvious evidence. This does not mean that there was not awareness that what is needed are mechanisms to force private banks and investors to take responsibility for the costs they now shift to the public. The problem was political. The banks and other international financial institutions were able to resist any efforts to impose meaningful controls.

By the start of the twenty-first century the amounts involved in bailouts were becoming simply too great and taxpayer resistance too substantial to keep funding the GSEGIs at higher and higher levels. This led to two kinds of proposals. The first was the establishment of collective action clauses of the sort which exist under English law which force individual creditors to restructure based on majority vote of creditors rather than the American rule requiring unanimous consent of all creditors, a process which allows any bondholder to sue the issuer, which makes the crisis worse. This approach was endorsed by Anne Krueger, the number two at the International Monetary Fund. It would allow a country temporary legal protection when it suspends payment of debts in return for a promise to negotiate in good faith with creditors and pursue sound economic policies as approved by an impartial adjudicator who would act as the international equivalent of a bankruptcy judge. The country would get working capital which would be senior to previously contracted debt for a workout. Creditors and debtors would each have to make concessions.

Of course agreeing on such an arbitrator and allowing the power usually welded in such a bankruptcy proceeding would be complicated. The "CEO" of the misperforming economy could hardly be removed and an alternative national leadership team imposed. National governments, including the U.S. Congress would have to approve such a change and working out details to which all parties could agree would not be easy. Without statutory protection of debtors, negotiations with creditors for restructuring loans could not be expected to result in equitable burden sharing. Indeed, as the *World Development Report* (UNDP, 2001: 69) pointed out, in recent examples of negotiated settlements the creditors have not borne the consequences of the risk they have taken; rather, they have forced the developing country governments to assume responsibility for the private debt and accept a simple maturity extension at penalty rates.

In the fall of 2002, following a meeting among G7 officials, bankers, and several large emerging market governments including Mexico, Korea, and Brazil, the G7 officials announced broad agreement to change sovereign bonds by adding collective action clauses to make debt restructuring easier by allowing a majority of creditors to impose a deal. Agreement on details of a juridical procedure to arbitrate between creditors in case of default would not come as easily. The Wall Street bankers and brokerage houses had opposed the move, warning that investors would move their money out of developing countries rather than having their funds impounded in any international bankruptcy proceeding, and some developing economy governments expressed fear that they might be forced into bankruptcy (they preferred new loans from the GSEGIs, even on harsh terms). The IMF plan, which was modeled on British bankruptcy laws, allowed the right of a country to declare bankruptcy and negotiate with lendors, a majority of whom could decide the terms binding on all other creditors; that would prevent bottom fishing operators from buying up debt at a discount and forcing countries to pay them ahead of others on threat of creating a collapse before other creditors could negotiate any adjustment. Under the new arrangement while a deal was worked out the IMF could allow the country to impose temporary foreign exchange controls to prevent capital flight. The banks, having lost on the principle of the arrangement, would fight over the arbitration process.

The second orientation was proposed by the Meltzer Commission (International Financial Institutions Advisory Commission, 2000). It suggested maturities on IMF loans be cut back to a maximum of 120 days with only one allowable rollover. Its rationale is that the IMF should lend in cases of illiquidity, which is characteristically a short-run problem as a way to buy time for restructuring of debt but not in insolvency crises, and that it do so at penalty rates of interest. In making the proposal the commission noted that 24 of the Fund's debtors had been in arrears for thirty or more of the previous fifty years and 46 more countries in debt for at least twenty of those years. There has been much talk of Bagehot's classic council (1873) that official lender of last resort credit should be available only at penalty rates of interest so as to discourage all but essential borrowing and to act as a disincentive to careless lending. The problem with this advice is that borrowers, while nominally representatives of the people of the debtor nation, have often proven to be personally corrupt officials who care little for the long-term consequences to others of their self-serving actions.

Money borrowed finds its way into crony projects and Swiss banks. That the nation will eventually pay at high penalty rates is not a major concern to such people. As importantly if the illiquidity and not insolvency criteria is enforced few debtors among the less developed economies which have suffered such crises would qualify for IMF support. Because the Meltzer approach would exclude the vast majority of current recipients of IMF funds social chaos would follow financial meltdowns with dire consequences not limited to these particular economies. The Meltzer Commission's response is that these countries need grants not loans. They are unable to pay loans so why disguise the nature of the subsidies?

The Bush Administration supported such a shift from loans to grants but not a sufficient increase in U.S. aid, which was as a percentage of GDP the lowest of any of the advanced economies. The Europeans opposed a change from loans to grants as likely to seriously diminish the financial support available to less developed countries. The post-September 11 White House made foreign aid loan guarantees subject to the imperatives of the anti-terrorism campaign favoring nations whose support was needed over those in need who were otherwise better qualified and deserving. Aid withdrawal became a tool to ensure cooperation, agreement to base troops in a country, or a vote in the Security Council. None of this was new but the undisguised vulgarity of the White House, or so it was seen by much of the world, increased fear and resentment. It did not make friends for the United States despite a promise to raise overall aid.

The problem of politicization of the loan process, the pressure on the IMF by its most powerful members (above all of course the United States itself) to bail out countries where their interests were substantially involved and then the inability of the policies imposed to actually create conditions which allowed the loans to be repaid and the IMF involvement to end was of course not a new one. It is related to the second issue: duration over which client states stay dependent on Fund and Bank loans which are never repaid, only rolled over. This puts them in somewhat the same position as miners dependent on the company store or sharecroppers perpetually in debt to the landowners. The dependency is criticized from both the political left and right. Such enduring debt keeps the countries under the control of foreign overlords whose grip on their budget is a life and death matter and so the country effectively loses its sovereignty. This is imperialism, debt as a tool of control by the rich creditors says the Left. This is social engineering run to its usual excess, says the Right. Such a pattern promotes dependency instead of encouraging countries' leaders to take responsibility for their nation's future. Reflecting the concern of the latter perspective the first report of the IMF's independent evaluation office (created to investigate these basic problems) concluded in September of 2002, that the Fund lent too much and for too long. The watchdog group noted that the institution of such policies contrary to the stated mission of short-term stabilization was partly a reflection of pressure from shareholder governments. The policies, they said, often failed in their desired objectives and put the institution's credibility at risk (Independent Evaluation Office of the IMF, 2002).

The inadequacy of much-heralded debt relief undertaken at the initiative of the G-7 and prompted by movements of global civil society was affirmed by a second study released at about the same time by the staff of the joint ministerial steering committee linking the IMF and the World Bank. It reported that half the countries going through the well publicized debt relief program were likely to exceed their sustainable debt targets. The report made clear that "Earlier projections often contained overly optimistic macroeconomic assumptions, reflecting . . . inadequate analysis of the likely sources of growth and the expected impact of planned policies," something NGOs had predicted as shall be discussed later in this chapter. (See Staff of the IMF and World Bank Heavily Indebted Poor Countries [HIPC] Initiative: Status of Implementation, 2002). The report considered various proposals from NGOs to address the problem but concluded they would be too expensive and noted that there was no general sentiment in the Bank's board to modify the heavily indebted poor country initiative.

From the perspective of both types of critique the reforms have been limited and for the most part ineffective. At the same time, such governance reforms have displaced earlier emphasis on "special and different treatment" with a commitment to bring developing countries under conventional financial market rules. The presumption has been that somehow sustainable economic growth will follow as a result of renewed private capital flows. Because this has rarely occurred, however, it is suggested that the governments themselves have been responsible for faulty implementation and that if they followed advice to liberalize more completely they would see capital inflows. The G-7 has called for greater transparency in developing markets in the belief that better information will allow investors to avoid the sort of problems the financial system experienced on such a broad scale. The Report of the G-7 Financial Ministers at the Cologne summit (1999: 11) made the case that "An efficient social system, by equipping people for change, builds trust and encourages people to take the risks which are a necessary part of the competitive modern market. This in turn helps to mitigate the risks and spreads the benefits of globalisation."

Critics suggest that the risk to society is a great deal easier for the affluent to accept than those living on the margins of survival without safety nets. IMF policy documents discuss social needs relatively briefly and in general terms. References to safety nets have figured prominently in the Fund's pronouncements at least since the early 1990s but practical measures to combat poverty have not advanced to the heart of IMF-supported programs. Good governance, which plays an increasingly central role in GSEGI strategy, likewise refers to protection of property rights and becomes the responsibility of debtor governments, not the international community. A more progressive global financial architecture would stress full employment in a return to the original purposes of the Bretton Woods agreement. It would reverse the trends toward high real interest rates, widespread unemployment, slow or declining economic growth, high poverty levels, and stagnant incomes that prevail in most of the world's economies at this writing. The literature on new financial architecture is driven as we have seen by very different concerns, those of the international financial lenders of the cost of potential default to their stockholders.

If there were muscle behind it, a proposal which would have a positive impact would be the expanded use of special drawing rights (SDRs) as a way to increase global liquidity, reduce dependence on the dollar, and perhaps meet progressive social goals. The SDR is a basket currency based on the movement of the dollar, yen, euro, and sterling and can be freely created by the IMF and used in transactions between governments. In 1997 the IMF board proposed a $27 billion allocation of SDRs but it has not received the 85 percent majority needed to go into effect. Were the United States to put its 17.2 percent voting weight behind the proposal it would be ratified. However since the last SDR allocation in 1981 the United States has resisted further expansion of the use of SDRs. George Soros (2002) suggested that President Bush announce at the United Nations 2002 gathering in Monterrey, Mexico to discuss Financing for Development that he would ask Congress to approve the 1997 special issue on the condition that the rich countries agree to donate their SDRs to a trust fund that would be used for the provision of public goods on a global scale. Monies would be spent on public health (especially fighting infectious diseases like AIDS), education, and strengthening the legal systems. The president was not receptive although at the Monterrey meeting he did announce he was committing an additional $5 billion to foreign aid, a welcome change since the United States gave a mere one tenth of one percent of its GDP for this purpose, far less than the Japanese and rich European countries.

Although the Europeans promised to increase their aid by far more, and from a higher base, Mr. Bush's announcement made the headlines.

He promised to increase aid by this amount in 2006 (after his current term in office was over). While he might be reelected and some of the increase could come before then, the perception of change exceeded the tenuous reality of the proposal. As to SDRs, it seems unlikely that the United States would allow increased reliance on a source of liquidity which would come at the expense of the dollar as the international unit of account and store of value. Since most of the U.S. money supply, approaching two-thirds of the total, is outside the country and U.S. external debt was close to half a trillion dollars, the interest payments saved by gaining access to foreign currencies by printing green pieces of paper (seigniorage) was substantial. It has been suggested that all of this represents "foreign aid" to the United States from the rest of the world.

As matters transpired the United States came to be widely viewed as having offered little. In September 2002 Secretary of State Powell was jeered, heckled, and abused as he attempted to defend his country's foreign aid policy at the World Summit on Sustainable Development in Johannesburg. He was booed again when he insisted that the United States was committed to solving global warming. It was the culmination of a series of increasingly vocal and bitter incidents in which the United States had become increasingly isolated from world opinion on a host of multilateral issues. In one telling instance the Bush Administration was denounced at the gathering as part of "an axis of oil" (Dao, 2002: 9). Its own problems had begun to emerge in a more unpleasant light as well, a matter to which we return in the next and final chapter.

What about reform of the global trade regime? We have seen that the WTO acts to enforce the demands of transnational corporations, frequently over the objections of less developed countries. Its adjudication system favors the powerful and the mere threat of anti-dumping action by the United States or the EU discourages small developing countries. When large countries ride roughshod over the weak the latter do not have the resources to mount successful legal contests through the WTO procedure and typically find no value in the proposed remedy should they win (the right to retaliate they are granted usually is an ineffective deterrent against a far larger economy). The issues the WTO focuses on, its procedures and priorities, are not those of the poor countries. As Gerald Helleiner (2001: 16) asks in his Prebisch Lecture:

What sort of World Trade Organization is it, after all, that doesn't seriously concern itself with trends and fluctuations in its members' terms of trade, particularly those of its weakest and most vulnerable members? Or with the "burdensome surpluses" (as the ITO Charter called them) in primary commodity markets? Or with restrictive business practices and abuse of dominant power in international goods and services deeply into such *domestic* policy issues as intellectual property regimes, domestic investment and subsidy policies and some would even push it into labour standards and environmental practices, all of which may or may not, be "trade-related"?

It is the costs to the northern-based transnational corporations that dominate trade discussions and guide the proposals offered by their governments. In a like manner banks and financial stability of core economies dominate the new financial architecture discussion. Despite their numbers the poor and their allies in the core countries have not been able to effectively challenge the club structures set up by the former colonial and imperial powers. Both the trade and finance regimes show no sign of fundamental progressive change despite the discussions of reform. Indeed there is evidence that transnational capital is working to lock-in neoliberal constraints in powerful ways. Maneuvering to buy friends and reward supporters of U.S. preemptive war policies further complicated matters undermining the sense that all were to be treated equally based on economic conditions and needs.

PROPOSALS FOR A MULTILATERAL AGREEMENT ON INVESTMENT

While discussion of new financial architecture faded with the immediacy of a possible global economic meltdown, advocates of corporate globalization advanced an agenda for radical restructuring. At the heart of their design was a dramatic rebalancing of the rights and responsibilities of governments and investors. Corporate globalization's device is a legal framework in which capital's rights are defined as having priority over the state's ability to regulate. In the late 1990s discussion of broad proposals for a legally binding new regime on foreign investment reached an advanced stage. Advocates stressed the benefits of a rule of law enforced at a supranational level which would protect investors, and treat all comers equally by ending (or substantially reducing) discrimination against non-nationals by governments. Clear definition of property rights and speedy, effective dispute settlement procedures would, it was said encourage greater investment, job creation, consumer choice and lower prices by undercutting monopolies in protected local markets. This would end inefficient subsidies which amount to rent seeking by self-serving officials who sell benefits while imposing dead weight losses on the economy. On both equity and efficiency grounds the advocates of a multilateral agreement on investment (MAI) urge its adoption and painted opponents as selfish while they claimed to represent the broad public's welfare. The U.S. Council for International Business, a peak organization of key corporations, was central to the formation of MAI proposals which the United States tried to push through and failed, but the other three Quad members have reintroduced into the WTO Doha Round discussions.

Critics, while not disputing the importance of the benefits that can come from foreign investment, questioned what kind of rules would be best for their citizens and businesses and what pattern of economic development they would prefer. The near-total right to unlimited entry for short-term foreign capital seemed to them dangerously excessive. Control of local economies by foreign capital can, and repeatedly has, worsened balance of payments instability. It can produce what is seen as a recolonizing of a country's economy, bringing it under foreign control and reducing the role its own government can play in influence over the nation's future. While its advocates understand the MAI as aiming to create a fair, transparent, and predictable investment regime, opponents see it as a power grab by the transnational corporations of the world's dominant economies. It is worth examining the philosophy and provisions of this proposal because while the MAI was withdrawn from consideration in 1998, its approach is central to subsequent liberalization schemes, for example the Free Trade Agreement for the Americas.

Advocates of an MAI argued that attempts at auto-centric development have failed. Developing countries which try to go it alone are doomed to failure, slow growth, and poverty. Development requires up to date production skills and exposure to best practice technologies which come from the countries of the core. Foreign investment is the best way to get access to such benefits. While opponents to MAI-type regulation agree that trade and investment can be advantageous for all parties, they point out that benefits are typically shared very unequally. They argue against complete removal of barriers, favoring instead selective adaptation of foreign processes and products through licensing and, as technical competence builds through reverse engineering and emulation, protecting local industries so that they will not be overwhelmed by foreign companies. Protecting the local market has been the time honored way by which all late developers have succeeded. The United States, Germany, and Japan used this technique as did the late, late industrializers such as South Korea and Taiwan, which borrowed technology from the industrial leaders. Local industries do not have to reinvent cutting edge techniques; they need merely adopt and modify them. What is important is maintaining control over national economic choices. MAI was seen as intended to remove the capacity of development states to engineer their own growth strategies. These countries did not wish to permanently close themselves off from the rest of the world but to protect their own development trajectory so that they could become more open on terms which favored continued advancement. Examining the provisions of the MAI proposal illustrates the extent to which it favors a development model dependent on transnational corporations and other foreign investors.

One hint that benefits under the agreement would not be equitably shared was that there was little or no public debate, or even announcement that negotiation of the MAI was taking place until a Canadian NGO obtained a copy of the draft agreement in 1997 and posted it on the Web. The treaty negotiations had been a secret matter. It was understood that such governance regulation along corporate globalization lines is not popular. Indeed, as a result of activist efforts to raise awareness, in November of 1997 twenty-five members of the House of Representatives sent a letter to the President of the United States saying it had come to their attention that a multilateral agreement on investment was being planned. They pointed out that while the Administration claimed that it needed fast track authorization from Congress to negotiate such agreements here was one nearly completed and much more complicated than NAFTA or GATT, which had been going on without Congress even knowing about it. Negotiation had been happening for years without any Congressional consultation and oversight. How could that be? It is Congress' exclusive constitutional authority to regulate international commerce? Their statement asked "Why would the U.S. be willing to cede sovereign immunity and expose itself to liability for damages under vague language" included in the proposal—language that seemed to give TNCs broad powers to sue countries for a host of damages, a power never before given them?

If American legislators were concerned, when those in countries that had not been invited to participate in negotiations found out what was being considered many of them were far more upset. Any small company which has ever found itself in an American court facing the array of legal talents at the disposal of a Fortune 500 company might sympathize with foreign firms and governments which fear having to submit to arbitration procedures premised on the legal framework of the strongest economies, most centrally the United States, whose case law and precedents shape the new investment regime.

Between 1991 and 1995 approximately 70 preparatory studies were made for the OECD Committee on International Investment and Multilateral Enterprise (CIIME) and its Committee on Capital Movements and Invisible Transactions (CMIT). When it came time for negotiations these were held in secret—outside of the formal OECD committee structure, in a high-level Negotiating Group. The group was chaired by three individuals: an American, a European, and a Japanese national. Some outreach occurred with key decisionmakers around the world and a small number of nations were granted observer status. The focus of these discussions was the optimal extent of liberalization and what, if any, exemptions would be allowed. Issues that others (not privy to these negotiations) might consider central to any new regime—labor rights, the environment, taxation issues, and anti-trust protections were not even secondary considerations; judging by the draft proposal which emerged, they were never discussed at all. The U.S. Council for International Business, the main corporate lobbying group behind MAI, NAFTA, and other extensions of global state economic institutionalization of freedom for transnationals, made clear, as its President wrote in a letter March 21, 1997 to senior U.S. officials: "We will oppose any and all measures to create or even imply binding obligations for governments or business related to environment or labor."

The MAI was not a new departure. Its general principles are the same as the GATT and its successor the WTO. The focus of nondiscrimination is, however, different in an agreement on investment than it would be in a trade regime. National Treatment and Most Favored Nation provisions are addressed to equal standing for trading nations. The nondiscriminatory provision in the MAI draft went further. It was written not to ensure equal treatment but only treatment no worse than that accorded national firms, leaving open incentives to attract foreign investment which would favor them over local firms. Such formulations are troubling in the light of state incentives to attract investment from other states within the United States that provide huge subsidies. They prompt increased competitive concessions by governments eager for foreign investment. More importantly, the rights of corporations as investors are codified in the MAI in a manner that gives them equal standing with other "contracting parties"—that is, to sovereign states. This equal legal status allows them to sue governments who interfere with their profit-making freedoms.

The advocates of such an agreement seek to outlaw such formerly accepted practices and policy options by awarding "national treatment" to all foreign investors. Laws inhibiting their ability to make a profit as has been noted would be interpreted as a "regulatory taking." The line between what is considered proper government exercise of regulatory power and such regulatory taking would be moved substantially by adoption of MAI criteria. The MAI constrains governments but frees capital. By establishing a general right of establishment the MAI creates a general "open door" principle which once required gunboats. The proposed MAI's national treatment clause brings into question the validity or application of a range of regulatory measures maintained by all states to some degree (Picciotto, 1998: 752). Such affected laws include everything from taxation and intellectual property to competitiveness policies and industry-specific regulation of telecommunications or banking. The tribunal established to resolve disputes would base its decision not on national law of the country in question but on the rules of the investment treaty. It would be foolish to think the formal withdrawal of the proposal in 1998 ended the matter. These goals remain on the corporate agenda.

As in the case of NAFTA state enterprises are required to act "solely in accordance with commercial considerations." Any discounts the state water or electric authority gives which do not meet these criteria can be seen as unfair to private competitors and the occasion for suits to recover damages. Awards can be prospective. State enterprises or government regulations which compromise future potential profit opportunities are interpreted as expropriating property rights. In the past it was recognized that companies must receive permission to operate from the governments of jurisdictions in which they wished to do business. The MAI represented a major shift in property rights and how they would be defined. Corporations are no longer creatures of the state but their equals within a regime which grants them privileges which governments cannot abrogate. The binding dispute mechanism compromises sovereignty in a dramatic fashion. This provision is included as well in the proposed FTAA agreement and is implied in the U.S. interpretation of the WTO's GATS agreement.

The rollback clauses of the MAI require national laws which are not in conformity with its principles (reservations which would have to be described in "the most precise terms possible") to be reduced and eventually limited (the rollback provision of the law). Any exceptions must be specified and no new nonconforming ones can be added (under so-called standstill rules contracting governments agree not to introduce any new nonconforming policies, regulations, or laws). The sunset provisions would over time reduce and eliminate any nonconforming national regulation (the so-called ratchet effect). Change could only be in the direction of liberalization. Future governments could not therefore reverse the agreement by choosing nonconforming alternative regulations. Nor is there any mention of the right of states to take legal action under the agreement on behalf of citizens. Individuals, community groups, or NGOs: none would have legal standing under the agreement.

The draft MAI provision prohibiting governments from expropriating foreign investment "directly or indirectly" or "take any measure having equivalent effect" would allow companies to sue to recover damages if state policies affected their future profits from a planned investment. The long accepted norm that states were always free to keep out foreigners would be repealed. International law under the MAI regime would compromise these essential aspects of sovereignty. Contracting parties under the draft agreement would not be able to withdraw from the MAI until five years after it had come into force and MAI rules would continue to apply to existing investments for another fifteen years. This twenty-year lock would be supplemented by a requirement that any change in the agreement would have to be ratified by all parties. Thus the later one signed on, the less influence a country would have on club rules. Early members, those who set up the club, propose a set of principles and operating procedures. Those invited to join face accepting these rules or not being admitted to the club in a situation where the costs of exclusion are substantial. Many representatives from governments of less developed economies reject the MAI approach and its assumptions., While they fear the consequence of free remittances of profits and capital without reference to the ability to make payments and the external account viability of host countries, they doubt they can do much to stop the core countries from imposing such regulation (Rasiah, 1997).

The premises of the proposed MAI regime were the opposite of the attempts in previous decades to draft a UN Code of Conduct for Transnational Corporations. The latter would have restricted the behavior of foreign companies in the perceived interests of host countries. Rules concerning profit repatriation, labor conditions, technology transfers, environmental protection, taxation, and such matters would have protected host governments and their citizens, conditioning the terms under which foreign investment was welcomed and allowed. The UN Code of Conduct for TNCs was consistent with the accepted principle that sovereign nations decided the conditions under which foreigners did business in and with their country, whether foreigners could own TV stations, banks, or energy reserves for example. Rules could limit foreign owners to minority control of companies or require them to hire a certain percentage of management from among nationals. It was accepted that voters could decide to limit or to prohibit imports from countries whose policies they found repugnant (apartheid in South Africa was the occasion for boycotts of that country's products, for example).

In contrast, under the proposed MAI investors would be guaranteed the free and immediate right to transfer currencies related to an investment. This would make capital controls illegal and make it more difficult for countries to address balance of payments problems. In terms of our earlier discussion of the desirability for governments to limit short-term capital inflow as a way of protecting against sudden capital flight should international conditions change, the MAI would forbid such measures. State-led development strategies which fine tune liberalization and regulation to ensure the best mix of foreign investments would, as noted, be illegal discrimination under MAI. The ability to import products from countries which violate human rights would no longer be a strategy social activists could use. Efforts to reserve some segment of local markets to locally owned small businesses, or minority owned firms, would be illegal. State provision of low-cost health care would be unfair competition with private health providers.

The MAI was negotiated to provide a predictable rule of law for TNCs, a *lex mercatoria* for the twenty-first century, to protect their rights and establish a dispute resolution regime which met their self-perceived needs. Corporate spokespersons complain that TNCs cannot invest freely where access is constrained, protection inadequate, or treatment discriminatory. They argue for MAI-like rules so that investment decisions can be based upon "the laws of economics, not the laws of politics; upon economic rationalism; not economic nationalism" and speak out against "arbitrary exercise of unfettered bureaucratic discretion" and "inadequate enforcement of private and public obligation" (Messing, 1997: 124). As the UNDP (1999: 35) suggests "no consideration went to their responsibilities to people—their responsibilities to limit their behavior, to bind their obligation to respect human rights and to promote the development interests of the communities they touch." Acceptance of the MAI would abrogate commitments made under the International Labor Organization and at the Rio Earth Summit as well as more broadly the 1974 Charter of Economic Rights and Duties of States adopted by the United Nations (which provide that every state has the inalienable right to regulate foreign investment within its national borders).

Similar debates over what should be considered proprietary knowledge and patentable resources often divide developed and developing societies. Less economically developed countries find their gene pool, seeds, and traditional medicines claimed as property of TNCs, as was noted in chapter 9. Environmentalists and social justice activists urged that these treaties have equal standing and be respected by the investment and trade regimes being negotiated. It was suggested that a rights-enhanced MAI should affirm a broad set of labor rights and labor standards such as those approved by the International Labor Organization and allow unions, NGOs, and governments to file complaints for alleged violation of those labor rights norms (such as the right to freely form trade unions). This could be done by strengthening the already existing OECD Guidelines for Multinational Enterprises and making them binding (Compa, 1998: 711-12).

Feeling the pressure of grass roots criticism and the spreading bad press it engendered, a formal consultation with NGOs was organized in October 1997. The meeting was attended by representatives of more than thirty groups from all regions of the world. In response to their critiques preambular language was included directed at a number of objections raised. The MAI was to be implemented "in a manner consistent with sustained development as reflected in the Rio Declaration . . . and Agenda 21." There was to be "observance of internationally recognized labor standards," a proviso securing consideration of living and nonliving exhaustible natural resources, and annexing of the OECD Guidelines on Multinational Enterprises to the text of the MAI (without changing its nonbinding nature). Such rhetorical concessions were hardly enough. The opposition of domestic constituencies and by some governments (the opposition of the French and the Canadians on cultural matters was particularly important) led to a suspension of the negotiations. The internationally coordinated campaign against the MAI was a landmark in the growing power of NGOs and nationalist sentiment to effect global governance and challenge the new constitutionalism.

The self-imposed April 27, 1998 deadline passed without agreement to adopt the MAI, suggesting it was dead. This seems far from the case for two reasons. First many of its provisions are already adopted as part of other international agreements currently in effect. That the MAI was called "NAFTA on steroids" suggests that the basic ideas had been accepted in other agreements even if the extremes of the MAI have not. Second, having failed in this effort, the forces which are pushing the new constitutionalism have pursued other gambits. Some of these may lead to the further successful *de facto* acceptance of MAI basic principles. Many of its strongest advocates ended up preferring no agreement to a watered down one which would have formalized compromise. They continue to work expanding corporate property rights under TRIPs, TRIMs, and GATS. While U.S. negotiators met resistance in global fora, they pushed forward in the Western Hemisphere where their leverage was greatest, demanding their version of property rights be accepted in exchange for access to the huge U.S. market.

DEBT RELIEF

Debt and defaults are nothing new. There have been episodic recurrences in the 1930s, the 1880s, 1840s, and on back to the South Sea Bubble. In each case there is always the question of how far creditors can push debtors for repayment. As Joseph Hanlon (2000: 889–90) writes,

> Since the late 19th century, it has been recognized that human rights take precedence over debts, however those debts were acquired. Most countries now have bankruptcy laws. If a company goes bankrupt, no one expects the children of the owners or employees of that company to drop out of school to work to pay the company's debts. Similarly, if a man runs up huge debts through drinking or gambling, no one any longer expects his children to leave school to work to pay the debts.

Yet these principles, he notes, are not applied at the level of nations within the global economy. Under disciplinary neoliberalism children are forced to drop out of school because the money which would have gone for their education is taken to pay debt the children were in no way responsible for incurring. Health clinics are closed, hunger spreads, and creditors are paid. To say that a nation borrowed too much, spent irresponsibly, and now must meet its obligations is to assume a unitary state actor, a responsible agent of its own fate. The nature of most debtor economies is quite different. The great majority are undemocratic, presided over by a small elite and often led by military strongmen with Swiss bank accounts. Lending to such governments is safe to the extent the governments of the core and the GSEGIs enforce debt collection on them or their successors.

To recapitulate our earlier argument, what is different about the contemporary period is that the GSEGIs are able to coerce repayment where in the past default would have removed the burden or U.S. Marines were set up at the customs house to garner repayment. This happens to a lesser extent thanks to the effectiveness of GSEGIs as collection agencies. Behind them are the United States and the other nations where the major international banks and most other lenders are domiciled. The debate over debt relief raises some of the same issues discussed in the context of the MAI, and some broader ones. Debt can be understood as a coercive instrument which has resulted in major income transfers from the poor to the rich so that there is an intensification of environmental degradation and labor exploitation. By putting debt repayment before all other goals a set of priorities is enforced consistent with a particular model of economic development. Elites profited from existing relations and were in no hurry to change them in any real way while the people who had not been extended credit, who would be laughed out of a bank or rudely escorted to the door if they had even dared apply for loans, suddenly became liable for the debt of privileged elements in their country owed to foreign creditors that the IMF insisted be rolled into the obligations of the nation.

The issues of what those who control certain undemocratic states have as their priorities is not irrelevant to the discussion. Performance criteria are unlikely to be effective in kleptocracies where local elites hold their own people in contempt and live in luxury while the vast majority of the citizens suffer from intense deprivation. The broader issue of the responsibility of outside states is complicated by the colonial past and the dependencies perpetuated under post-independence regimes and continued intervention in the internal affairs which did not end with the Cold War. While the focus here is on the consequences of what turn out in retrospect to be socially and financially costly market decisions to lend, or to insist on preferential access to markets for the less powerful governments of the world, trade and investment policies are hardly separate from those issues usually considered to be matters of national security. The coddling of governments with vile human rights records—for example, repressive Middle Eastern states created by the oil companies in the middle years of the twentieth century create anger and resentment.

The blinkered insistence on protecting preferential access to oil has unleashed hatred of the United States and created fertile ground for terrorists. The commonalities involved, and of course the very important distinctions to be made in each individual case, suggest that economics and politics are closely intertwined here too. Consideration of particular tinderbox locations involves a much larger complex of issues than can be dealt with here, yet the absent center of all such discussions is not all that different than that of many corrupt debtor nations: issues of class oppression, lack of participatory democracy, and the inability of ordinary citizens to have an impact on, let alone take active control over, governance of their societies. This failure has its roots not only or primarily in the faulty ethics of locals but also in the structural role these economies play in the world system. It has been more convenient to pay local strongmen who exercise military sway over a population than to address the economic inequities without outside help in the early stages of democratization or, equally important, to respect the autonomy of the many democratic states of the Third World.

The issue is further complicated by overriding dominance of market criteria and so the fear that forgiveness will set precedents which end up making it more difficult for poor countries to borrow in the future. Further the most indebted are to a considerable extent the most badly managed governments. It is not clear that debt forgiveness will lead to needed reforms. In most developing countries the legacy of colonialism and the Cold War has been to leave in place undemocratic regimes, often dominated by military officers trained by the West or politicians put in place by the CIA or other covert agencies of Western governments. When a democratic opposition comes to power, cancellation of the odious debt is called for since the people of these nations are not to blame. It was exactly on this basis that the United States following the Spanish-American War declared Cuba's debt (Cuba having become a dependency as a result of U.S. victory over Spain) to be "odious debt" not needing to be repaid to Spain setting forth a position accepted in international law. When U.S. banks are owed the money the very notion of odious debt has been forgotten. Some say the forgiveness is unfair to relatively less indebted governments who have worked hard to pay down debts and have a greater percentage of their populations living in poverty (such as India). Others suggest that since most of this debt comes from heavy borrowing in the 1970s undertaken when interest rates were low and commodity prices higher, and mushroomed with higher world interest rates and dramatic declines in commodity prices (both beyond the control of these nations' governments), debt relief is not unreasonable.

Third World debt rose from $100 billion to $600 billion over the ten years between 1970 and 1980. Initially most of this money was owed to private creditors. The amount had grown considerably under the inexorable logic of compound interest but the ownership of the debt changed hands. By 1997 four-fifths of the enlarged debt was owed to GSEGIs. While studies showed that the debt was essentially unpayable (interest on interest on interest was rising well beyond the capacities of these stagnant economies to cope), the GSEGIs did not want to consider forgiveness of debt because of the precedent it could set and possible impact on their own credit rating and so borrowing costs. They have favored new loans when old ones could not be paid. As a result of what *Financial Times* columnist Martin Wolf (1999b: 14) calls "the world's most effective single issue initiative," political leaders have been forced to address the demands of activists. These groups made the case not only on grounds of ethical considerations but also by showing in concrete studies the effect of adjustment programs—programs which have created more debt even as they have deepened misery by cutting social spending while they have foreclosed the prospects of longer term development by starving health and education programs. In 1998, Tanzania for example was spending a third of its budget on debt payments (four times the amount it spends on education in a country half of whose population is illiterate). Such a burden was widely understood to have created a dead-end situation. Continued debt payment sentenced the country to perpetual underdevelopment yet the amounts owed were modest from the point of view of creditors.

Jubilee 2000, the church-related advocacy group, argued that the world's poorest countries have the right to set aside a percentage of their income to spend what is needed to meet internationally agreed upon targets for poverty reduction. Such efforts had remarkable grass roots support. In June 1999 rock star Bono went online to talk about debt relief with 36,000 other people in a chat room. The Microsoft Network reported that by the end of the day two million people had downloaded the transcript of the session. The Internet was an important source of information for many in the huge crowd attending a June 13, 1999 rally in Trafalgar Square and the 50,000 who formed a human chain on the banks of the Thames which followed. Giant demonstrations accompany meetings of the Group of Seven Finance Ministers and the IMF-WB and WTO annual meetings. What was remarkable about these manifestations of popular democratic expression was the degree to which mainstream political science continued to see them as marginal to "real" politics, defined only as what the powerful do and what takes place in elections. The size and enthusiastic activism of the global justice movement for the most part is not driven by programs proposing national solutions. While seeing the GSEGIs as the immediate target perhaps a majority of participants do not look to strengthen national sovereignty given existing social and class relations. Their demand is a more utopian call ("be realistic, ask the impossible," as their forerunners from 1968 would have said) for international solidarity and participatory democratic globalization which is for many of them anti-capitalist in a moral sense. How far this tendency develops will depend on how reform (and reformist) efforts are perceived.

The financial bankruptcy of the poorest countries had been evident for a decade or two and the rich, in delaying solutions to the problem, had perpetuated suffering. It was in part the pride of the IMF and the World Bank that their loans never go bad which prevented an earlier resolution. Instead they insisted on new loans so that old loans appeared repaid. Taking all the HIPCs together their nominal debt to the United States was by 1998 about $6 billion but was actually "worth" perhaps $600 million, the amount experts thought could realistically be recovered. Economic ministers from poor nations spend all of their time negotiating to stay a step ahead of default, without the time or financial stability to address long-term problems. The only winners, critics said, are the staffs of the IMF and World Bank which have invented a perpetual motion machine for endless missions to these hapless countries. Under widespread pressure for relief for the HIPCs from organizations such as Jubilee 2000 the GSEGIs offered an initiative which would have reduced debt after a period of six years of "good behavior." The thinking was that these countries needed deep structural reforms and until then lower debt burdens would be wasted.

In the summer of 1999 the G-7 agreed to implement a swifter debt relief which would lower the target ratio of debt service to export earnings and fiscal revenues in the Cologne debt initiative. The public relations quality of this announcement was not matched by concrete details of how the promise was to be paid for and how it would be implemented. The UNDP (1999: 107) suggested lowering the debt sustainability ratio considered manageable from 200-250 percent of a country's annual exports to 100 percent or less and debt repayment deemed bearable from 20–25 percent to 10 percent or less so that there are resources to reestablish growth. *Business Week* (1998c) wrote at a nadir of global pessimism concerning the international financial regime that given the situation not simply in Africa, but also in Russia, Asia, and parts of Latin America where "*de facto* default may be the best choice among evils" it was time to consider a global write-down. "It is time for a clean financial slate. New lending and new easing are needed to get everyone back in the growth game."

When relief finally started to come for these countries it made a significant difference for the small number of HIPCs which actually benefitted from forgiveness programs. Uganda, the first to receive some relief from a World Bank and IMF program used money saved to eliminate fees the country had charged for primary school attendance. In two years the percentage of children attending school jumped from 54 percent to 90 percent. In neighboring Zambia, which spends five times more each year on debt than on education, school fees had to be raised and enrollment declined. For other countries this system of forgiving debt for money spent on social programs cannot work because the country has no money either for debt repayment or social purposes. It is not that such countries have the money and can choose how to use it. They are bankrupt; creditors have already squeezed to the breaking point. If the richer countries want to help they need to accept debt cancellation and come up with new real resources for the needed programs. Even then where local governments are in the hands of unscrupulous officials they must closely monitor spending and insist that local efforts however inadequate be maintained when additional funds for worthy purposes are made available.

This dimension of new financial architecture has been forcefully raised and will not easily be shunted aside even in the post September 11 world. To an important degree the terms of the discussion have shifted. This is demonstrated by the struggle over the pricing of AIDS medicines in disease-ravaged low-income countries, especially in sub-Saharan Africa. The focus of this controversy in the late 1990s was between the South African government and the United States over AIDS drugs. Even without a MAI the United States asserted that the South African government did not have the right to parallel import (buying drugs from companies in countries which are not signatories to the international copyright agreement) at far lower cost and to require multinationals to license local producers of AIDS drugs. In 1999, as this dispute erupted, 16 percent of South Africa's adults were HIV-positive and experts did not expect the epidemic to peak for at least another five years. Few victims could afford the prices the Western drug companies were charging. The South African health ministry claimed that the basic life preserving needs of these people came before the profits of transnational pharmaceutical companies. Vice President Al Gore, who chaired the bilateral commission on U.S.-South African relations, quickly became a target for AIDS activists in the United States. The moral and political debates around the issue were hurting his presidential campaign prospects and the Clinton Administration looked for a way out.

More such conflicts seem inevitable as the United States pushes for greater property rights protections for its TNCs. It took until 2001 for the pharmas, the large transnational pharmaceutical companies to withdraw their suit against the South African government and to offer reduced prices in an effort to head off generic production and parallel importing—as well as to limit what was shaping up as a public relations disaster. The Canadian and U.S. threats to break Bayer's Cipro patent protections in the face of a handful of anthrax related deaths further weakened this negotiating stance and the need to secure the moral high ground in holding together its anti-terrorist alliance led the Bush Administration to make concessions on the issue at the 2001 WTO meeting in Doha, Qatar although these appear to have been withdrawn in subsequent negotiations.

The launch of the Fourth Ministerial Conference of the WTO in November 2001 was celebrated as the "Doha Development Agenda," and calculated to trade concessions from the rich countries of importance to the less developed economies in exchange for an expansion of the areas over which the WTO would substitute treaty obligations desired by the rich countries in areas formerly acknowledged to be under national sover-eignty. Once again critics charged that "the Doha Promise" had been sac-rificed to powerful protectionist interests in the rich countries as deadlines passed without producing agreement on such central issues as the reduc-tion of trade barriers by the North to exports of agricultural and labor intensive manufacturing from the South, especially textiles. The Bush Administration's farm bill of May 2002, which raised subsidies received by U.S. farmers by 80 percent and new tariffs on imported steel, did not help. European concessions which changed the form in which they extended agricultural subsidies brooded as a major concession did not open EU markets to the farmers of the South as their negotiators had demanded. The disagreements persisted through the Cancún, Mexico, WTO Minis-terial in 2003, leading to the early end of that meeting as Third World resistance to further concessions hardened. In Miami a few months later FTAA talks went nowhere because of similar basic conflicts.

AN ASIAN ECONOMIC ZONE

An interesting aspect of the discussion which receives little comment when financial architecture is discussed are the efforts by East Asian govern-ments to escape what they understand as the clutches of the Western run GSEGI structures, especially the IMF. While China and Japan are com-petitors in the region and the smaller countries that are economically pow-erful (Singapore and Taiwan) lack corresponding clout in policymaking circles, these countries came together on the need for new financial archi-tecture following the East Asian crisis. They were initially unsuccessful in achieving the sort of regional autonomy they saw as in their collective interest. The episode illustrates the difficulty of challenging a regime created and maintained by the global hegemon. In September 1997 given the spreading and deepening East Asian financial crisis, Japan proposed the establishment of an Asian Monetary Fund which was to raise $100 billion (half from Japan, the rest from China, Hong Kong, Singapore, and Taiwan) to provide liquidity against speculative attacks on regional currencies. Pointedly, the loans were to be made without the sort of conditionality the IMF typically requires. The U.S. demanded, and got, the withdrawal of the proposal which was seen as undermining IMF authority and detrimental to U.S. interests in the region. A substitute proposal backed by the United States, the Framework to Promote Financial Stability, was accepted by regional governments at a November 1997 meeting. This Manila Framework was confined to monitoring and surveillance. The Japanese were allowed a $30 billion package to help the region. The plan was made consistent with the Washington Consensus and accepted by the United States.

Since 1997 the governments of the region have continued discussing regional cooperation and have slowly marshaled their resolve to set up a competing regional club. At the November 1999 ASEAN, the Association of South East Asian Nations summit (the six original members of that organization Singapore, Indonesia, Malaysia, Thailand, the Philippines, and Brunei expanded to ten by the admission of former enemies—Vietnam, Laos, Cambodia, and most controversially Burma or Myanmar—and including at the meeting the participation of Japan, China, and South Korea) there was discussion of a public regional liquidity fund. The ASEAN ten plus three (where the United States is not represented even though the organization was founded in 1967 at its instigation) has emerged as an important potential pole in the restructuring debate. Its continued discussions of a regional initiative were phrased in deference to opposition from outside the region not to be an East Asian Monetary Fund but a regional liquidity aid system. In a crisis the participant countries' central banks would have speedy access to the currency reserves of participating states. Not wanting confrontation with the United States it was stated clearly that the aim of the proposed cooperation was not to bypass the IMF. Yet it was hard to avoid the conclusion that the plan is aimed at exactly that, challenging the IMF's monopoly on crisis management. Adoption of the plan could substantially undercut the Washington Consensus and the power of the IMF. An alternative safety system whose policies contrast with those the IMF has insisted upon would provide an alternative blueprint for developing countries and diminish the capacities of disciplinary neoliberalism.

Efforts to establish a Pacific Economic Cooperation Conference and other Asians-only fora had not succeeded until ASEAN, a Cold War legacy instrument, expanded its mandate and associated membership. Now the ASEAN plus three grouping has taken shape reflecting an awareness, concern, and indeed dissatisfaction throughout the region that the global finance and trade regimes administered by the GSEGIs are a continuation of the Western system which has long kept them in a subservient position. "Although much modified over the decades, the historical roots of the present system responsible for colonial conquests, unequal treaties, and other forms of humiliation that remain potent memories in much of East Asia," Charles Morrison observes. As a result these regimes are not endowed with the legitimacy and moral authority attributed to them by the "international community," a term that to many in East Asia appears to refer mainly to dominant Western public and political opinion. The Asians of course benefit to some extent from participation in the GSEGI regimes but as in all such concentric club structured regimes, suspect the system operates to the relative advantage of its creators and constrains the ability of the latecomers like themselves to assume equal status. Thus as Morrison and others suggest a lasting effect of the Asian financial crisis and "the Western triumphalism associated with it" was to help the East Asian countries to come closer together (Morrison, 2000: 18). Not only in the area of currency support but also in trade these countries are learning to work together.

A multi-currency placement mechanism reflecting this diversification objective does appear to be developing. The eventual proper monitoring of capital flows and an effective regional surveillance process are hardly assured, or even clear in their possible design, but a common currency area is a viable and realistic option over the not too long term. In May 2000 the finance ministers of the ASEAN plus three countries met in Chiang Mai, Thailand and agreed to an initiative to deal with destructive currency fluctuations and international capital movements. The signatories to the Chiang Mai Initiative agreed to contribute $40 million each to a common swap fund to protect threatened currencies of the group. The interdependence of the region in terms of trade, investment, and financial flows is substantial and the capital flight following the 1997 crisis was devastating. At the time of the crisis, in July 1997, China and Hong Kong each had provided a billion dollars with the understanding that the IMF would contain the crisis within Thailand. But as Henry C.K. Liu, an astute observer of the Asian financial scene noted (in a restricted-circulation list-serv post), "Instead, the IMF exploited the crisis to promote dollar based global market fundamentalism. The East Asian region therefore must accept the fact that it has to rely on itself more than on outside help alone." The ability of Hong Kong with its huge dollar reserves to withstand speculative attacks was widely appreciated. The view that Asian countries suffering from financial illiquidity should not be allowed to plunge into crisis if they can collectively prevent it is now widespread in the region. Liu suggests a Regional Financial Arrangement to complement the existing international facilities be recognized and within such a framework emphasis be placed on regional currencies (and not the dollar).

In the 2000 meeting the leaders of ASEAN plus three commissioned a one-year feasibility study based on a proposal made by China to link the ASEAN economies to those of China, Japan, and South Korea. It was quickly stated that the proposed free trade area was not intended to discriminate against the United States. ("This is not, I repeat, not an attempt to shut out Washington from east Asia," Goh Chok Tong, Singapore's prime minister and chair of the meeting stressed.) In late 2001 China announced it had agreed to negotiations to form a trading bloc with ten Southeast Asian countries encouraging Japan to seek new bilateral agreements. Japan, the third largest trading nation after Germany and the United States, felt itself under increasing pressure from China. Of the world's thirty largest economies Japan, China, Korea, and Taiwan were the only ones without such free trade agreements but as the twenty-first century began they too sought to negotiate bilateral trade agreements. The negiotations were led by Japan, whose economy faltered through the 1990s and into the 2000s. As it came to feel more isolated and under increased competitive pressure, the Japanese government moved away from reliance on GSEGI framing of trade and toward promoting bilateral agreements. These East Asian regional developments bear watching. They have potential to challenge a U.S.-dominated system. China's growth to a world superpower is about to change a great deal.

In 2002 China and ASEAN agreed to eliminate tariff and non-tariff barriers on goods and services by 2010 and so to create the world's largest free trade area with more than 1.7 billion people. The move was prompted both by the fear of China's neighbors that they were being bypassed as China grew at ASEAN's expense and also by China's efforts to woo Southeast Asia as allies in global diplomacy as the United States sees China to some degree as its next enemy in geopolitical terms. The overvaluation of China's currency and huge trade surplus with the United States were major issues of contention. In total Asian foreign exchange reserves had more than tripled between 1993 and 2002, reaching $180 billion, despite the region's financial crisis of 1997–98. The sterilizing of these capital inflows kept Asian goods artificially cheap and distorted local economies, keeping domestic consumption below what it would otherwise have been and preventing a more balanced relationship between production and consumption in the region. On the other hand these huge surpluses Asia kept in dollars helped fund the increased U.S. military expenditures and tax cuts of the period and the American half trillion dollar current account deficit.

Efforts to reform global regimes will continue to be contested. Whether the Asians (or the Europeans) are able to create an economic and political counterweight to the power of the United States remains to be seen. Whether meaningful debt cancellation comes to pass and whether it can be linked to domestic reforms so that new obligations will be taken on after due consideration and with greater democratic accountability and participation remain to be seen These are matters of degree rather than all or nothing matters. The negotiations will continue even in a global environment in which American power at least in the military area is unrivaled, but runs into trouble on the ground when the job turns to nation rebuilding. If regime change and finding terrorists set the global agenda than many of these concerns will recede in importance or at least lose out in competition for public and policymaker attention. We cannot know the future, but as indicated briefly in the first chapter, the presumed strength of the United States does not quite so confidently extend from the military realm to the economic. In the latter there are challengers or at least potential challengers and countries who cannot be easily dismissed but whose wishes must be taken into account in serious negotiations. There is another issue as well. The stability of the global system depends very heavily on the United States and there are imbalances both within the U.S. economy and between the U.S. and the rest of the world which need to be examined more closely. In the next and concluding chapter some of these questions are examined in what is of necessity a somewhat more speculative manner.

CHAPTER THIRTEEN

The Evolving Political Economy

"Even the US cannot achieve global prosperity on its own. Nor can it expect others to obey rules that it refuses to follow itself. Here, then, it is bound to the idea of international law. Yet how long will a country used to being unquestioned judge and jury in its own cause accept the judgments of others in its economic life?"

—*Martin Wolf* (2003: 13)

"Chief executives are beginning to worry that globalization may not be compatible with a foreign policy of unilateral preemption. Can capital, trade, and labor flow smoothly when the world's only superpower maintains such a confusing and threatening stance?" "U.S. corporations may soon find it more difficult to function in a multilateral economic arena when their overseas business partners and governments perceive America to be acting outside the bounds of international laws and institutions."

—*Bruce Nussbaum* (2003: 34)

Globalization has many faces. This book has examined its features in the hope of broadening the perspective with which we examine the interrelated phenomena associated with the emergence of global state economic governance institutions and the regimes of which they are a part. My central argument has been that the interests of transnational corporations and international financiers prompted the creation of a new law merchant in cooperation with government policymakers in the most powerful states. Above others the United States, through a process of soft law agreements and concentric club formation, has produced rules and regulations for global finance, trade, and investment regimes through the instrumentality of global state economic governance institutions. Popular participation has been for the most part lacking, which has produced complaints of a "democratic deficit." Nor, as was discussed in the last chapter, has meaningful reform of these regimes been possible despite their well recognized failures.

One less tangible development in the opening years of the new millennium was a tendency not only for the claims of the GSEGIs to technical efficiency to be challenged as instead often being of a political nature (Porter, 2003) but their moral authority has come to be questioned (Best, 2003). In the context of disclosure of pervasive corporate dishonesty efforts to explain corporate corruption by political economists now flirt with systemic questions (Demski, 2003) and awareness of state capture at the hands of foreign corporate interests became a crucial issue under investigation (Kaufman, 2003).

There has been a powerful ideological component to regime failure resulting from a too single minded application of idealist neoclassical models of perfect competition that assume full employment and social efficiency are assured by private maximization of individual agents without sufficient consideration to justice issues as seen by many ordinary citizens. This bias is challenged in the mainline tradition of political economy, which suggests orthodoxy does not describe or explain the real world accurately. Critique of mainstream models is supported by empirical data on the distributional consequences and instabilities produced by the operation of the Washington Consensus. Instead of greater growth and stability the decades during which globalization on neoliberal terms has been dominant have brought the world disappointing economic results and for many countries retrogression and crisis, as this book has argued.

Mainstream theorists have been wrong about the likely effects of neoliberal policies. The promises were that freeing capital markets would move monies from the rich countries where is was abundant to the poor countries where it was scarce. Instead savings move from what are called developing countries (although many, perhaps most, cannot really be described as developing in any realistic sense of the term), to the rich countries. The result has been, not floating exchange rates that stabilize international finance, but wide swings and destabilizing movements. Free capital movements were supposed to have lowered the cost of borrowing. Instead real interest rates have gone up as a result of the uncertainty the new dispensation has brought as chapters 6 and 7 have explained.

Finally the world was promised more rapid economic growth. Instead growth rates declined even as instability increased. A deflationary tendency threatens the world as all countries compete to attract capital by reducing government spending and lowering labor costs. The informal sector of economies which should be shrinking as the modern sector absorbs labor are instead growing. Income inequalities have increased and a lack of attention to social need, most vividly to the AIDS pandemic, threaten the future of entire nations. The objective failures of the Washington Consensus in all of these areas requires a continued interrogation of how the interests of the world's most powerful governments, economic actors such as transnational corporations and international financial interests, and the global state economic governance institutions frame policy.

Earlier chapters have detailed the manner in which the period from the late twentieth to the early twenty-first century has been an era not only of globalization but also of expansion of international institutions with strong aspects of stateness. These GSEGIs provide a governance structure in which most nations are limited by legalistic agreement and supranational organization rules. It has been suggested that in the process of international regime formation, at least in the economic and financial areas which have been considered, soft law is the crucial vehicle in a process of concentric club formation in which the most powerful forces in the global political economy seek rules and enforcement procedures that best meet their goals. This process has not been an uncontested one. Not only have states once on the periphery of the world system been active in contesting self-serving club rules but also non-state actors including grass roots activists and NGOs have played important roles in expanding the context of decisionmaking. The presumption that the economic components of the Washington Consensus and the neoliberal approach more generally are anchored in universally accepted "good economics" has been widely discredited and so its technocratic implementation is essentially a nonpolitical undertaking. These policies are intrinsically political. The fact that policymakers impose obligations, often very painful obligations, on others who have little or no say over them and that the GSEGIs are themselves far from transparent or taking responsibility for the consequences of their own actions has been widely noted.

There has been unrelenting pressure from the richer, more powerful countries to expand global governance regulation into highly contentious areas before these governments show willingness to make concessions on long standing grievances in the areas of textiles and agricultural protectionism which hurts the poorest economies. In addition the IMF's ever more intrusive conditionalities in place of a global development agenda and a regime which would control destabilizing currency movements and capital flows to produce more balanced trade and growth has been widely criticized. Global governance has been shown to be a systematically biased procedure. This is seen attempts to further constitutionalize global governance through not only concentric club mechanisms, but also secret negotiations (as in the case of the Multilateral Agreement on Investment discussed in the last chapter), in the informal and closed discussions by key players before and during WTO ministerials, and in enforcing acquiescence to a consensus imposed by powerful members of the world community in the interests of preserving collegiality.

U.S. military capacity and its ability to organize the capitalist world in terms of alliances to contain the Soviet Union in the postwar period also in effect contained America's competitors in Western Europe and Japan. The end of the cold war offered an opportunity for Europe to develop its own currency, the euro (and to make the suggestion that the Organization of Oil Exporting Countries denominate oil sales in euros rather than dollars), and a common market which has the potential to challenge U.S. hegemony. There is also opportunity for Japan, Korea, China and the ASEAN countries to do the same in the East (where the Chinese have floated the idea of the yuan becoming the regional currency). The United States, by focusing on NATO enlargement to the East and its ability to veto the emergence of an East Asian economic financial bloc, has limited these possible initiatives but its insistent unilateralism in response to September 11 encourages formation of independent counter alliances to resist its domination. In discussion of how economics and politics have co-determined the shaping of the postwar regimes and GSEGIs since World War II short shrift has been given to military power which underlay the ability of the United States to shape the rules of the world system; but this has not been an unimportant factor. Application of the Bush Doctrine raised the question of whether democracy can be practiced at the global level or whether the world system, which has been characterized as a realm of anarchy in IR literature, now needs reconceptualization in terms of a quest for American Empire as a possible project.

The predilection of the administration of George W. Bush to make unilateral decisions, to "de-join" agreements other presidents (including his father) had signed on to, and to show disregard for world opinion has hardened opposition to U.S. hegemonism. Existing regimes negotiated by elites and enforced by GSEGIs have been rejected by the increasingly vocal, organized, and growing constituency of advocacy groups and popular movements. The further question arises as to what extent Mr. Bush's unilateralism has transformed the international political economy and requires reconsideration of the presumptions of contemporary international political economy. This book concludes with a consideration of these issues, which must of necessity be handled speculatively. They are signaled by the two passages by *Financial Times* columnist Martin Wolf and by *Business Week*'s editorial page editor Bruce Nussbaum that introduced this chapter and that convey a new and disturbing note into the IPE discourse which come in response to the U.S. invasion of Iraq in 2003. A further element of worry is added by the weakness of the world economic order and especially the imbalance between the United States and its trade partners on current account. The degree to which the Bush II Administration represents a long-term shift cannot be known; surely there are substantial issues which George W. Bush's successors may be forced to rethink. This final chapter looks at the ways in which the U.S. economy at the time of writing seems to have characteristics familiar from earlier discussion of financial and economic problems elsewhere.

NEGOTIATING GLOBALISM

The process of globalization is a dual one of market penetration and state practices. As firms from one location seek out markets, production venues, and other opportunities in territories their own government does not control they encounter resistance from those whose economic well being is threatened by their incoming presence. If the affected economic actors are politically powerful, local governments can be expected to place, or attempt to place, controls on such foreign penetration. What is required from the perspective of foreign capital is the reorientation of the local state to facilitate accumulation on terms favorable to their interests. Thus the penetration of capital presupposes the penetration of the state. In an earlier era this was arranged through direct conquest and colonization. Over the centuries, as independence movements have succeeded, indirect control through carrot and stick has been no less impressive as a mode of pressuring governments. In the contemporary conjuncture the GSEGIs play a central mediating role, although bilateral negotiations are hardly unimportant, especially those involving the hegemonic American state. Negotiations among core economies set the terms for regimes later opened to weaker players who sign on. Bilateral negotiations set precedents which are embraced in these wider agreements.

The importance of initiation and negotiation among peak business organizations and the concentric club formation model call attention to the density of business sector networks in the powerful states. The penetration of neoliberal ideas and norms into local states is the subsequent step in the process of globalization. The innovation of a G-20 announces the emergence onto the world stage of players once peripheral but now consulted. Bringing these key developing countries on board and accustoming their political leaders to the internal procedures of club membership is to at the same time transform these states. South-South networks are thinner in part because the GSEGIs are organized for North-South transmission of rules and procedures central to conditioning the possibilities of the developing economies of the periphery. The formation of policy remains for the most part the prerogative of the center. So too the dominant interpretation of these negotiations is the one offered by the major actors representing the core.

Following the Doha Round meetings of the WTO, which were unsatisfactory to many in the Third World, the organization's then Director General, Michael Moore, announced, "By any standard, the 4th Ministerial Conference of the WTO was an extraordinarily successful meeting. We tend to talk rather glibly about the historic importance of such events, but this time, for once, the claim is not exaggerated, the meeting at Doha will be remembered as a turning point in the history of the WTO and the trading system and in relations between developed and developing countries within that system." The U.S. Trade Representative put the matter more directly: "We have removed the stain of Seattle." But of course they had not. The Pakistani WTO Ambassador spoke for many when he said: "We didn't like it but it's a question of whether we will have to swallow it" (Haque, 2002: 1098). As discussed in chapter 10 at the Cancún WTO meeting the countries of the global South decided that they didn't have to do so. The question of what pressures are to be placed on the developing nations to adjust to Washington's desires is one that takes on new significance given the Bush's unilateralism in foreign policy. The collapse of the 2003 Cancún meeting only heightened the tension.

At the World Bank's annual meeting in fall 2003 (following on the heels of the breakdown of the Cancún WTO talks) there were attempts to put serious institutional reform on the agenda, but little progress was made, in significant measure because the United States took the lead in blocking proposals that would reduce its formal voting weight. Trevor Manuel, chairman of the Bank's development committee and South Africa's Finance Minister said of the debate, "There will be deep disagreements" but that such a move had "such profound logic that it's actually embarrassing to try to argue against it. But power is a strange thing," he observed, "It is not something easily given up." Mr. Wolfensohn, speaking after meetings which made little progress on increasing developing countries' say came close to openly siding with the developing countries, noting that after Cancún it had become clear that "This is a world out of balance" (Beattie, 2003:4).

Five important phenomena were discussed in the last chapter which shed light on Washington's dominance. The discussion of the possible emergence of an economic zone in East Asia is perhaps the most important instance of a challenge in the long run although the refusal of "Old Europe" to rubber stamp the Bush Doctrine may engender new energies for an EU project of an alternative and independent pole in the global political economy which, given Europe's strengths, could prove crucial to globalization's future. Second, the efforts to solidify a coherent single regime that will embrace the various elements of the global economy, of finance, investment, and trade in the MAI approach, have widespread support among transnational corporate and financial interests., However, those efforts continue to be widely resisted by popular forces and some governments who despite often intense pressures find ways to pursue national interests. The continued support for broader discussion of "trade and . . . " issues may also further an alternative globalization. Third, it is clear that there are large parts of the world where countries are falling further behind and are not developing despite their government's enthusiastic following of Washington Consensus policies. Most of Sub-Saharan Africa fits this category. Democracy, while it may be necessary for basic change in direction to occur in many poor countries, is hardly all that is needed. On debt, the HIPC initiative was an inadequate beginning and efforts to encourage good governance from outside had only limited impact. Fourth, there is resistance to the current pattern of globalization even in relatively well off countries where unequally shared benefits and fear of a future out of control and without security feed discontent. Finally, the movements of civil society propose a discourse of social justice to protest the GSEGIs from a space outside traditional party politics.

An internal criticism leveled at the Augmented Washington Consensus from within the economics profession and policymaking community suggests it is "an impossibly broad, undifferentiated agenda of institutional reform. It is far too insensitive to local context and needs. It does not correspond to the empirical reality of how development really takes place" (Rodrik, 2002: 1). The problem from this perspective is that the global state economic governance institutions are still trying to straightjacket all countries into a one size fits all development model. This is inappropriate because there have been many routes to success, most quite unexpected and combining unpredictable elements of sectoral specialization and governmental support arrangements (Haussman and Rodrik, 2002). The neoclassical model presumes universally available knowledge, capacities to apply existing technologies, and transparent access to all market information. It is surely unrealistic. For most participants in low-income countries adoption and adaptation are problematic undertakings. Uncertainty is pervasive, access to resource markets limited and often on unattractive terms. Success depends on contingent factors about which it is not easy to generalize beyond saying that a proper balance between state functioning and the role of the market is key (Amsden, 1989; Wade, 1990; Evans, 1995).

Some critics of the approach taken by neoclassical economist policy-makers would reform international regimes to make them fairer to the less developed countries and their people by protecting local producers and the autonomy of local control to the greatest extent possible so that international exchange is truly based on mutual consent and is shared fairly. The issue is how is this to be done? Is reform of existing structures and institutions possible? Is more fundamental transformation based on different class relations essential? These questions bring us to criticism coming from NGOs and civil society groups which offer a more basic critique of corporate globalization and capitalism. To the social justice movements class power and the imperialism are the core problematic. The domination by market criteria over social need and the power of transnational capital and the most powerful governments of the world (above all by the United States) who establish rules for their own benefit come at the expense of the weaker parties, the subordinate nations and classes within state formations of the contemporary world system.

The question of what the rich owe the poor takes many forms. On an explicitly normative level, to mainline political economists freedom of choice does not exhaust the ideal of freedom nor should freedom of choice based on the existing distribution of income, wealth, and power come before all other freedoms. As a matter of charity in the original biblical sense of that word the poor are deserving of compassion and this is not an option for a person whose religion calls on them to share with their less fortunate sisters and brothers and the stranger in their midst. Such sharing is needed by both the giver and the recipient. Economic justice can be understood to require addressing the structural barriers to equal participation, especially to the degree that they have been created by colonialism, imperialism, and their legacies which include the establishment and perpetuation of local elites which serve foreign interests (as well as their own more narrowly selfish ones).

Whether the outcome of next-stage neoliberalism would be poverty reduction or increased accountability of the local state to its own citizens is debatable. The political strategy has shifted from the cold-war era scheme of privileging rent seeking local elites once necessary to defeat revolutionaries to a new emphasis on diminishing the share going to these rent seeking, now less necessary, or even costly local liabilities. That these elites oppress their people is now admitted, and condemned by Western leaders who find denunciation of human rights abuse to be a useful charge with which to flog such regimes. The free market answer is one which positions foreign capital to take over the dominant role in these economies. Next stage neoliberalism stresses transparency, the rule of law, and a level playing field in the marketplace, not in the society as a whole. Unequal access to government would continue for the vast majority of citizens. The distribution would be from incumbent elites to foreign capital whose bargaining power would be improved substantially by the strict enforcement of the good governance rules. From this more radical perspective it is argued that reforms being suggested are system reinforcing and that it is class rule and imperial domination which must be replaced. The growing strength of what is called the anti-globalization movement or the alternative globalization movement is testament to this critique. There was also a progression from a weak public presence in the form of global civil society to stronger public forms a globalizing democracy without a state and a global constitutionalism from below.

THE CONSEQUENCES OF THE BUSH II APPROACH ON THE POLITICAL ECONOMY

The administration of George W. Bush in opposition both to the liberal institutionalists of the Clinton White House and the conservative realists who dominated his father's policymaking staff, embraced a neoconservative assertiveness breathtaking in its ambition to remake the world under U.S. unilateral control. For the liberal institutionalists who labored mightily to construct an interdependent set of international regimes which, though dominated by the United States served, in their view, broader purposes, this sort of naked unilateralism seemed ill advised. Realists who do not flinch from military resolutions when deemed necessary were vocal about the risks inherent in the new doctrine of preemptive wars. To both of these traditions the idea of perpetual war on evil was alarming. To many traditional conservatives and others in the corporate world it was seen as bad for business to invite such potential instability. As political economy issues were re-securitized in the Bush II Administration, foreign policy imperatives guided bilateral dealings with America's friends as well as perceived foes. By using free trade deals in the war against terrorism the Bush Administration angered many of the Republican Party's business allies who complained that "such grand diplomacy makes for poor trade policy" (Magnusson, 2003: 29).

As discussed in chapter 4 IPE as a subdiscipline in political science emerged from IR in the last decades of the twentieth century with the demise of the Soviet Union, in recognition that the "high politics" of diplomacy and war was being displaced by the "low politics" of trade, investment and finance. The Bush Administration's response to September 11 brought a reassertion of the uncontested centrality of the military and displaced neoliberalism and globalization or rather each was reframed in the light of the assertiveness of the Bush Doctrine. Much depends on the pertinacity of U.S. unilateralism. As Chris Patten, the European Union's foreign affairs commissioner said at the time with regard to Iraq (and in doing so raising larger concerns), "It will be that much more difficult for the European Union to cooperate fully and on a large scale—also in the long-term reconstruction process—if events unfold without proper UN cover." He pointed to the solicitation of Iraq reconstruction contract bids exclusively from American companies as "exceptionally maladroit" (Cowell, 2003: W7).

If war and terrorism are to frame the world's prospects a number of costly consequences follow for important sectors such as the travel industry, airlines and hotels, and more widely in such aspects as the cost of insurance coverage for buildings, ships, and factories for which premiums jumped in a number of locations in the wake of military activity in the Persian Gulf. Security concerns add to the cost of transporting goods and can have an impact on industries whose products are considered strategic. William Archey, president of the American Electronics Association, fearing more restrictions on sales, spoke for the thousands of companies he represented of the impact of export controls. Two years after the high tech bubble had peaked, the sector had lost over half a million jobs, and fear of a security state augured to make matters worse. Archey's members, he said, "are worried that politicians will take a short sighted approach to national security that will not make us more secure but will harm our economy" (Foremski, 2003: 1). U.S.-based producers were losing out to overseas competitors who were profiting from those restrictions. The group was also alarmed at massive cutbacks to education from squeezed state budgets. "We need well-educated people; it is what feeds the high tech sector," he said adding that loss of a skilled workforce would push firms to go abroad. His was not the only industry which expressed such concerns.

THE AMERICAN ECONOMY— THROUGH A GLASS DARKLY

At the end of 2001 foreign investors owned $9.2 trillion worth of U.S. assets including bonds, stock, and other ownership claims. U.S. holders of foreign assets held only $6.9 trillion worth of foreign assets (Tille, 2003: 1). The $2.3 trillion difference was a measure of American net debt position, an obligation which had doubled over only the two previous years, so that by the start of 2004 the U.S. current account deficit was running at 4 to 5 percent of GDP (enough to destabilize any other country's currency), and was impacting the value of the dollar as foreign investment into the U.S. slowed. In the eight years, 1995–2003 about 60 percent of the cumulative growth rate in world output came from the United States, almost twice America's share of world GDP, reflecting its growth in domestic demand at twice the rate as the rest of the richer group of countries. But much of this spending was with money borrowed from foreigners. The United States, the world's largest debtor by far; it was borrowing to fund asset values and an unsustainable level of consumption, piling up debt at a rate which could not be sustained for long, and which promised problems ahead. For the United States to come back into a trade balance with the rest of the world would threaten global slowdown if America was no longer to be the insatiable consumer of last resort.

Years after the telecom bust the market was still receiving jaw dropping news in large doses as the extent of the misallocation of resources in the bubble years became more evident. In 2003 WorldCom said it was writing down its assets by $80 billion, a remarkable sum. While a little over half of this was in what it had overpaid to acquire other companies, the value of its property, plant, and equipment had also been inflated by tens of billions of dollars—its presumably "hard assets" were worth 75 percent less than what they had cost. The market asked "Who's next?" "How bad will this continue to be?" "How much can we trust the next wave of optimism?"

In 2003 the Securities and Exchange Commission found the annual reports of 350 of the 500 biggest companies in the U.S. seriously compromised. These companies did not say how they did the math as to what they counted as revenues, or how they treated brands, good will, and other aspects of their accounting policies and interpretations of the rules as to what they reported as profit. Decisions on when to keep debt off the books (as Enron famously did) and how they recognized revenues from long-term contracts were among the factors used to dress up poor performance and mislead investors. One of the important vehicles was accounting for acquisitions and mergers, which allows for flexible treatment of costs and returns so that stock values could climb rapidly, funding further rounds of expansion using the overestimation of value to buy still other companies with more inflated stocks. Through these and other methods profits of nonfinancial corporations were able to rise far faster than their historical trajectory totally out of relation to growth in GDP. Over the dozen years to 2003 the actual earnings of the Standard and Poor's 500 companies according to Generally Accepted Accounting Principles (GAAP) was 17 percent less than the numbers given to Wall Street analysts and to investors, the SEC said. In 2001 and 2002 this divergence widened to 40 percent (Henry, 2003: 72).Of course the GAAP figures are themselves suspect. The Financial Accounting Standards Board (FASB), which sets the rules for the bookkeepers, was raising uncomfortable suggestions on how companies might better disclose their pension assumptions and how they accounted for stock options among other practices (Hill, 2003: 30) To add to these concerns the huge U.S. deficit—the result of a massive, irresponsible ten year tax cut and inordinate military spending in the Bush II years—threatened larger problems. Forecasts remained widely distributed on the optimism-pessimism scale and of course the economic situation elsewhere looked worse.

The question of what version of national capitalism and what set of international financial and trade regimes made sense both remained open. It is of course the level of strain in the world economy which prompts discussion of such matters. Without serious crisis there is unlikely to be serious consideration of dramatic reforms. In the presence of serious breakdowns a window is forced open in which radical ideas are taken seriously and only then are dramatic alternatives on the agenda. Hence the problem for those who see troubles developing. For them to be taken seriously by those who would be discomforted by change things must get worse before they gain a serious hearing. If the crisis passes, or it is hoped that by doing nothing it may resolve itself, or does not seem imminent politicians and others will ignore dangers. Far reaching changes in regulation and structure are always difficult.

CONCLUSION

The cold war, with its focus on military confrontation, led to the separation of an IR which focused on security studies and IPE. This, as Buzan and Wæver (1998: 15) argue, would have seemed bizarre at any other time during the previous two centuries but during those years seemed normal. We need to ask, as the war on terrorism replaces the cold war and security issues crowd out other concerns which had taken central stage during the post Cold War-pre-September 11 period in which IPE flourished, whether liberal institutionalists will seem as naive as they did in the wake of the failure of the Wilsonian project close to a century ago.

Will the victory of the neoconservatives' regime changing enterprise have lasting power and marginalize the multilateralist IPE project focused on strengthening the GSEGIs? Buzan and Wæver (1998: 8) argue, the liberal demand has been to create greater openness in economics and politics so that states and other social actors "agree to narrow the range of things that they treat as security issues." This liberal ideal to increase trade and intercourse so much that war becomes unthinkable among interdependent nation states would, its advocates have long argued, de-escalated securitization (meaning a focus on preparation for war) and so the legitimacy of the use of force would decline. The neoliberals put markets first, making these larger assumptions about the trajectory of the world system that would result. In doing so they set in motion economic and societal insecurities which contributed to large-scale, rapid labor market displacement and social breakdown and were criticized by social justice advocates for unleashing such risk society norms.

The debate between these two groupings has been decentered as the war on terrorism has reversed this neoliberal trajectory. The neoconservatives make security concerns the overwhelming priority and are seemingly insensitive to the economic costs of doing so. Where liberals would use human rights as the lead issue to demand changes in the behavior of repressive regimes by using economic sticks and carrots, neoconservatives advocate regime change by force where necessary. They are willing to change the long standing rules of the Westphalian order openly and self-consciously rather than as the neoliberals would through a gradual extension of the governance powers of global state institutions. In doing so they offer a challenge not only to other nations who have different approaches to the sort of world order worthy of construction but to the study of IPE as well.

If we are unhappy with any of the seeming givens of contemporary global realities there needs to be space for vision and consideration of meaningfully alternative arrangements which can make a difference. This would seem an idealist hope except that at each historical juncture there have been in fact theorists whose prefigurative perspectives have illuminated the new era to come. There is no reason to believe this will not continue to be the case. I have suggested that IPE as well as PE more generally needs to be historical, comparative, and institutional in their emphases and less centered on Anglo-American hegemonic presumptions in its theorizing. But they need to be something else as well, suggesting to some the demand for greater pragmatism in what had become an altogether too open ended theorizing of international relations (Haas and Haas, 2002). Part of its mission is to be prefigurative. After examining contemporary realities and how they have emerged out of the relations of the past, having considered problematic aspects of the political economy of the present conjuncture, along with examining alternative theorizations and the programmatic suggestions of varied perspectives, it is possible that room can also be made for an approach to the social world informed by moral philosophy concerns and a return to the framing of economics and politics characteristic of the classical social theory of the eighteenth- and nineteenth-century pioneers of political economy. A return to this traditional approach might well be taken through a very American Deweyan pragmatism of method, which makes possible maintenance of objectivity in inquiry while exercising ethical judgment. However a revitalized mainline political economy returned to the center of social science and public intellectual discourse would be welcome and would have positive implications for the understanding of, and contributing to social justice in, the broader international polical economy.

REFERENCES

Abbott, Kenneth W. 1996. "The Decline of the Nation State and Its Effects on Constitutional International Economic Law: 'Economic' Issues and Political Participation; The Evolving Boundaries of International Federalism." *Cardozo Law Review*, December.

Abu-Lougod, Janet. 1989. *Before European Hegemony: The World System A.D. 1250–1350*. Oxford: Oxford University Press.

Ackerlof, George A. and Paul M. Romer. 1993. "Looting: The Economic Underworld of Bankruptcy for Profit." *Brookings Papers on Economic Activity*, 2.

Adams, Patricia. 1997. "The World Bank's Finances: an International Debt Crisis." In Caroline Thomas and Peter Wilkin eds., *Globalization and the South*. London: Macmillan.

Aglietta, Michael. 1987. *A Theory of Capitalist Regulation: The US Experience*. London: Verso.

Agins, Teri. 2000. "To Track Fickle Fashion, Apparel Industry Goes Online." *Wall Street Journal*, May 11.

Ainger, Katherine. 2002. "European Commission Demands to Deregulate Services Spell Disaster for the Developing World." *Guardian*, April 18.

Akyuz, Yilmaz. 1995. "Taming International Finance." In Jonathan Michie and John Grieve Smith eds., *Managing the Global Economy*. Oxford: Oxford University Press.

Akyuz, Yilmaz. 2000. "The Debate on the International Financial Architecture: Reforming the Reformers." Discussion Paper No, 148 United Nations Conference on Trade and Development.

Alesina, Albert and Alan Drazen. 1991. "Why Are Stabilizations Delayed." *American Economic Review*, December.

Allen, Chris. 1998. "The Machinery of External Control." *Review of African Political Economy*, March.

Author's Note: All the works cited here appeared as references in the final version of this book or in earlier drafts. In the case of the latter they have been left, since their influence remains and the citations may be useful to readers.

Almond, Gabriel A. 1991. "Rational Choice Theory and the Social Sciences" In Kristen R. Monroe ed., *The Economic Approach to Politics*. New York: Harper-Collins.

Almond, Gabriel A. 1996. "Political Science: The History of the Discipline." In Robert E. Goodwin and Hans-Dieter Klingemann eds., *Handbook of Political Science*.

Amam, Alfred C., Jr. 1998. "The Global State: A Future-Oriented Perspective on the Public/Private Distinction, Federalism, and Democracy." *Vanderbilt Journal of Transnational Law*, October

Amsden, Alice H. 1989. *Asia's Next Giant: South Korea and Late Industrialization*. New York: Oxford University Press.

Amsden, Alice H. 1992. "Otiose Economics." *Social Research*, Winter.

Anand, Sudhir and Amartya Sen. 2000. "Human Development and Economic Sustainability." *World Development*, December.

Anderson, Benedict. 1983. *Imagined Communities: Reflections on the Origins and Spread of Nationalism*. London: Verso.

Anderson, Sarah and John Cavanagh. 1997. "In Focus: World Trade Organization." *Foreign Policy In Focus; Internet Gateway to Foreign Policy*, January. http://www. foreignpolicy-infocus.org

Andrews, David M. 1994. "Capital Mobility and State Autonomy: Toward a Structural Theory of International Monetary Relations." *International Studies Quarterly*, June.

Andrews, David M. and Thomas D. Willett. 1997. "Financial Interdependence and the State: International Monetary Relations at Century's End." *International Organization*, Summer.

Anghie, Antony. 1999. "Finding the Peripheries: Sovereignty and Colonialism in Nineteenth-Century International Law." *Harvard International Law Journal*, Winter.

Armijo, Leslie Elliott and David Felix. 1999. "Reform of the Global Financial Architecture: Who Wants What and Why?" Paper presented to the annual meetings of the American Political Science Association, Atlanta, September 2–5.

Arestis, Philip and Murray Glickman. 2002. "Financial Crisis in Southeast Asia: Dispelling Illusions the Minskyan Way." *Cambridge Journal of Economics*, March.

Asher, Mukul G. and Ramkishen S. Rajan. 2001. "Globalization and Tax Systems: Implications for Developing Countries with Particular Reference to Southeast Asia." *ASEAN Economic Bulletin*, April.

Atkinson, Glen. 1999. "Developing Global Institutions: Lessons to Be Learned from Regional Integration Experiences." *Journal of Economic Issues*, June.

Augelli, Enrico and Craig N. Murphy. 1997. "Consciousness, Myth and Collective Action: Gramsci, Sorel and the Ethical State." In Stephen Gill and James H. Mittelman eds., *Innovation and Transformation in International Studies*. Cambridge: Cambridge University Press.

Avramovich, Michael P. 1998. "The Protection of International Investment at the Start of the Twenty-First Century: Will Anachronistic Notions of Business Render Irrelevant the OECD's Multilateral Agreement of Investment?" *John Marshall Law Review*, Summer.

Axelrod, Robert and Robert O. Keohane. 1986. "Achieving Cooperation Under Anarchy: Strategies and Institutions." In Kenneth A. Oye ed., *Cooperation Under Anarchy*. Princeton: Princeton University Press.

Axworthy, Lyoyd. 1997. "Canada and Human Security: The Need for Leadership." *International Journal*, Spring.

Ayoub, Lena. 1999. "Nike Just Does It—and Why the United States Shouldn't: The United States' International Obligation to Hold MNCs Accountable for Their Labor Rights Violations Abroad." *DePaul Business Law Journal*, Spring/Summer.

Bailey, David, George Harte, and Roger Sugden. 1998. The Case for Monitoring Policy Across Europe." *New Political Economy*, July.

Baily, Martin Neil and Hans Gersbach. 1995. "Efficiency in Manufacturing and the Need for Global Competition." *Brookings Papers on Economic Activity*, Microeconomics.

Bairoch, Paul. 1996. "Globalization Myths and Realities: One Century of External Trade and Foreign Investment." In Robert Boyer and Daniel Drache eds., *States Against Markets: The Limits of Globalization*. London: Routledge.

Baker, Dean. 2002. "Dangerous Minds? The Track Record of Economic and Financial Analysts." Center for Economic and Policy Research." December. http://www..cepr.net.

Baker, Lauren. 1999. "A Different Tomato: Creating Vernacular Foodscapes." Deborah Barndt ed., *Women Working the NAFTA Food Chain; Women, Food, and Globalization*. Toronto: Second Story Press.

Baker, Mark B. 2000. "Flying Over the Judicial Hump: A Human Rights Drama Featuring Burma, the Commonwealth of Massachusetts, the WTO, and the Federal Courts." *Law and Policy in International Business*, 32.

Baker, Stephen, Marsha Johnson, and William Erikson. 1998. "Europe's Privacy Cops." *Business Week*, November 2.

Baltazar, Lisa G. 19998. "Government Sanctions and Private Initiatives: Striking a New Balance for U.S. Enforcement of Internationally-Recognized Workers' Rights." *Columbia Human Rights Law Journal*, Summer.

Bardhan, Pranab. 1997. "Corruption and Development." *Journal of Economic Literature*, September.

Barlow, Maud. 2001. "The Free Trade Area of the Americas and the Threat to Social Programs, Environmental Sustainability and Social Justice in Canada and the Americas." Council of Canadians, http://www.canadians.org/campaigns/campaigns-tradepub-ftaa2.html.

Barnett, Michael N. 1997. "Bringing in the New World Order: Liberalism, Legitimacy, and the United Nations." *World Politics*, July.

Barnett, Michael N. and Martha Finnemore. 1999. "The Politics, Power, and Pathologies of International Organization." *International Organization*, Autumn.

Baron, Jane B. and Jeffrey L. Dunoff. 1996. "Against Market Rationality: Moral Critiques of Economic Analysis in Legal Theory." *Cardhouse Law Review*, January.

Barry-Jones, R. D. 1995. "International Interdependence and Globalisation: Economic Liberalism, Marxist, economic realist and structuralism approaches." *Globalisation and Interdependence in the International Political Economy*. London: Pinter.

Basu, Susan and Alan M. Taylor. 1999. "Business Cycles in International Historical Perspective." *Journal of Economic Perspectives*, Spring.

Bean, Charles R. 1992. "Economic and Monetary Union in Europe." *Journal of Economic Perspectives*, Fall.

Beattie, Alan. 2001. "An Architecture That May Be Put to the Test." *Financial Times*, November 30.

Beattie, Alan. 2003. "Give the Poor World a Bigger Voice, Bank Chief Urges." *Financial Times*, September 24.

Becker, Elizabeth. 2003a. "U.S. Unilateralism Worries Trade Officials." *New York Times*, March 17.

Becker, Elizabeth. 2003b. "Bush Signs Trade Pact With Singapore, a Wartime Ally." *New York Times*, May 7.

Becker, Elizabeth. 2003c. "Poorer Countries Pull Out of Talks Over World Trade." *New York Times*, September 15.

Becker, Elizabeth and Edmund L. Andrews. 2003. "Performing a Free Trade Juggling Act, Offstage." *New York Times*, February 8.

Becker, Gary S. 1976. *The Economic Approach to Human Behaviour*. Chicago: University of Chicago Press.

Bell, Janet and others. 1999. "Patenting Piracy and Perverted Promises. Barcelona, Spain: Genetic Resources Action International. Available at http://www.grain.org.

Bello, Walden. 1997. "Fast-track Capitalism, Geoeconomic Competition and Sustainable Development Challenge in East Asia." In Caroline Thomas and Peter Wilkin eds., *Globalization and the South*. Houndsmills, England: Macmillan.

Bello, Walden. 1998. "Testimony of Walden Bello before Banking Oversight Subcommittee, Banking and Financial Services Committee." April 21. http://www.igc/dgap/walden.html.

Benvenisti, Eyal. 1999. "Exit and Voice in the Age of Globalization." *Michigan Law Review*, October.

Bergsten, C. Fred. 1992. "Commentary." In Federal Reserve Bank of Kansas City, Long-Run Economic Growth: A Symposium Sponsored by the Federal Reserve Bank, August 27–29, 1992.

Berman, Harold J. and Felix J. Dasser. 1990 "The 'New' Law Merchant and the 'Old': Sources, Content, and Legitimacy." In Thomas E. Carbonneau, ed. *Lex Mercatoria and Arbitration* 22. Transnational Juris Publications.

Bernard, Mitchell. 1997. "Globalisation, the State and Financial Reform in the East Asian NICs: The Case of Korea and Taiwan." In Geoffrey R. D. Underhill ed., *The New World Order in International Finance.* New York: St. Martin's Press.

Bernard, Mitchell B. and John Ravenhill. 1995. "Beyond Product Cycles and Flying Geese: Regionalization, Hierarchy, and the Industrialization of East Asia." *World Politics* 47, no. 2.

Best, Jacqueline. 2003. "Moralizing Finance: the New Financial Architecture as Ethical Discourse." *Review of International Political Economy* (August).

Best, Michael. 1990. *The New Competition: Institutions of Industrial Restructuring.* Cambridge: Polity Press.

Bhagwati, Jagdish. 1998. "The Capital Myth: The Difference Between Trade in Widgets and Trade in Dollars." *Foreign Affairs,* May–June.

Bhagwati, Jagdish and Daniel Tarullo. 2003. "A Ban on Capital Controls is a Bad Trade-Off." *Financial Times,* March 17.

Bienefeld, Manfred. "Is a Strong National Economy a Utopian Goal at the End of the Twentieth Century?" In Robert Boyer and Daniel Drache eds., *States Against Markets: The Limits of Globalization.* London: Routledge.

Bierstecker, Thomas. 1995. "The 'Triumph' of Liberal Economic Ideas in the Developing World." In Barbara Stallings ed., *Global Change, Regional Response: The New International Context of Development.* Cambridge: Cambridge University Press.

Birchfield, Vicki. 1999. "Contesting the Hegemony of Market Ideology: Gramsci's 'Good Sense' and Polanyi's 'Double Movement'." *Review of International Political Economy,* Spring.

Bird, Graham. 1996. "The International Monetary Fund and Developing Countries: A Review of the Evidence and Policy Options." *International Organization,* Summer.

Bird, Graham. 1998a. "Exchange Rate Policy in Developing Countries: What Is Left of the Nominal Anchor Approach?" *Third World Quarterly,* June.

Bird, Graham. 1998b. "The Political Economy of the SDR: The Rise and Fall of an International Reserve Asset." *Global Governance,* July/September.

Bird, Graham and Dane Rowlands. 2000. "The Catalyzing Role of Policy-Based Lending by the IMF and the World Bank: Fact or Fiction? *Journal of International Development,* October.

Birdsall, Nancy and Augusto de la Torre. 2001. *Washington Contentious: Economic Policies for Social Equity in Latin America.* Carnegie Endowment for International Peace and Inter-American Dialogue.

Blackhurst, Richard. 1981. "The Twilight of Domestic Policy." *The World Economy* 4, no. 4.

Blackhurst, Richard. 1998. "The Capacity of the WTO to Fulfill Its Mandate." In Anne O. Krueger ed., With the assistance of Chonira Aturapane. *The WTO as an International Organization.* Chicago: University of Chicago Press.

Blanco, Sandra. 1999. Pursuing the Good Life: The Meaning of Development as

It Relates to the World Bank and the IMF." *Transnational Law & Contemporary Problems*, Spring.

Bleakley, Fred R. 1995. "Developing World Gets More Investment." *Wall Street Journal*, December 15.

Blecker, Robert A. 1996. "NAFTA, the Peso Crisis, and the Contradictions of the Mexican Economic Growth Strategy." Working Paper Number 3, Globalization, Labor Markets and Social Policy, Center for Economic Policy Analysis, New School for Social Research.

Block, Fred L. 1977. *The Origins of International Economic Disorder: A Study of United States International Monetary Policy from World War II to the Present.* Berkeley: University of California Press.

Blustein, Paul. 1998. "The IMF's Faceless Commandos." *Washington Post National Weekly Edition*, April 6.

Bohman, James. 1996. *Public Deliberation: Pluralism, Complexity, and Democracy.* Cambridge: MIT Press.

Booker, Salih and William Minter. 2001. "Global Apartheid." *The Nation*, July 9.

Boland, Vincent. 1999. "Dow Jones Launches Index of 'Titans'." *Financial Times*, July 15.

Boltho, Andrea. 1996. "Has France Converged on Germany? Politics and Institutions Since 1958." In Suzanne Berger and Ronald Dore eds., *National Diversity and Global Capitalism*. Ithaca: Cornell University Press.

Bonturi, Marcos and Kiichiro Fukasaku. 1993. "Globalization and Intra-Firm Trade: An Empirical Note." *OECD Economic Studies*, Spring.

Bordo, Michael D. 1993. "The Bretton Woods International Monetary System: A Historical Overview." In Michael D. Bordo and Barry Eichengreen eds., *A Retrospective on the Bretton Woods System: Lessons for International Monetary Reform*. Chicago: University of Chicago Press.

Borosage Robert L. 1997. "Fast Track to Nowhere." *The Nation*, September 29.

Bourdieu, Pierre. 1999. *Acts of Resistance: Against the Tyranny of the Market.* Richard Nice, trans. New York: New Press.

Bowles Samuel and Herbert Gintis. 1996. "Efficient Redistribution: New Rules for Markets, States, and Communities." *Politics and Society*, December.

Bowles, Samuel and Herbert Gintis. 1993. "The Revenge of Homo Economicus: Contested Exchange and the Revival of Political Economy." *Journal of Economic Perspectives*, Winter.

Boyer Robert. 1996. "State and Market: A New Engagement for the Twenty-first Century?" In Robert Boyer and Daniel Drache eds., *States Against Markets: The Limits of Globalization*. London: Routledge.

Boyer, Robert. 1997. "The Variety and Unequal Performances of Really Existing Markets: Farewell to Doctor Pangloss?" In J. Rogers Hollingsworth and Robert Boyer eds., *Contemporary Capitalism: The Embeddedness of Institutions*. Cambridge: Cambridge University Press.

Brander, James A. 1993. "Rationales for Strategic Trade and Industrial Policy." In

Paul R. Krugman ed., *Strategic Trade Policy and the New International Economics*. Cambridge.: MIT Press.

Braudel, Fernand. 1981. *The Structure of Everyday Life*. New York: Harper and Row.

Brecher, Michael. 1999. "International Studies in the Twentieth Century and Beyond: Flawed Dichotomies, Synthesis and Cumulation." *International Studies Quarterly* June.

Brierly, J. L. 1963. *The Law of Nations: An Introduction to the International Law of Peace* 6th edition. Humphrey Waldock trans. Oxford: Clarendon Press.

Broadway, Robin W. and Anwar Shaw. 1995. "Perspectives on the Role of Investment Incentives in Developing Countries." In Anwar Shah ed., *Fiscal Incentives for Investment and Innovation*. Oxford: Oxford University Press.

Bronfenbrenner, Kate. 1997a. *The Effects of Plant Closings or the Threat of Plant Closings on the Rights of Workers to Organize*. Ithaca: School of Industrial and Labor Relations.

Bronfenbrenner, Kate. 1997b. "We'll Close! Plant Closings, Plant-Closing Threats, Union Organizing and NAFTA." *Multinational Monitor*, March.

Buchanan, James M. 1984. "Politics Without Romance: A Sketch of Positive Public Choice Theory and Its Normative Implications." James M. Buchanan and Robert Tollison eds., *The Theory of Public Choice II*. Ann Arbor: University of Michigan Press.

Bunn, Isabella D. 2000. "The Right to Development: Implications for International Law." *American University International Law Review*, 15.

Bunting, Gerald A. 1996. "GATT and the Evolution of the Global Trading System: A Historical Perspective." *St. John's Journal of Legal Commentary*, Spring.

Burchell, Scott. 1996. "Liberal Internationalism." In Scott Burchell and Andrew Linklater with Richard Devetak, Matthew Paterson, and Jacqui True eds., *Theories of International Relations*. New York: St. Martin's Press.

Burgi, Noelle and Philip S. Golub. 2000. "Has Globalization Really Made Nations Redundant? The State We Are Still In." *Le Monde Diplomatique*, April.

Business Week. 1997. "Monopolies: Time to Debunk the Myths." Editorial, June 16.

Business Week. 1998a. "How to Reshape the World Financial System." Special Report, October 12.

Business Week. 1998b. "Needed a New Financial Architecture." Editorial, October 12.

Business Week. 1998c. "Needed: A New Deal on Global Debt." September 7.

Business Week. 1999. "Deutsche Bank's Chinese Puzzle." April 15.

Business Week. 2000. "Acid Words for the IMF." April 24.

Bustany Christine and Daphne Wysham. 2000. "Chevron's Alleged Human Rights Abuses in the Niger Delta and Involvement in Chad-Cameroon Pipeline Consortium Highlights Need for World Bank Human Rights Investment Screen." Institute for Policy Studies, Washington, D.C., April 28.

Buzan, Barry. 1994. "The Interdependence of Security and Economic Issues in the 'New World Order'." In Richard Stubbs and Geoffrey R. D. Underhill eds., *Political Economy and the Changing Global Order*. Toronto: McClelland and Stewart.

Buzan, Barry and Ole Waever. 1998. "The Contradictions of the Liberal Leviathan." Copenhagen Peace Research Institute Working Paper 23.

Bybee, Roger. 1996. "Sweatshops Are the Workers' Friend." *Extra!*, November/December.

Cahn, Jonathan. 1993. "Challenging the New Imperial Authority: The World Bank and the Democratization of Development." *Harvard Human Rights Journal*, 6.

Calder, Kent E. 1993. *Strategic Capitalism: Public Purpose and Private Enterprise in Japanese Industrial Finance*. Princeton: Princeton University Press.

Callaghy, Thomas R. 1993. "Visions and Politics in the Transformation of the Global Political Economy: Lessons from the Second and Third Worlds." In Robert O. Slater, Barry M. Schutz and Steven R. Dorr eds., *Global Transformation and the Third World*. Boulder: Lynne Rienner.

Calomiris, Charles W. 1998. "Blueprint for a New Financial Architecture." Hoover Institute, October 7. http://www.imfsite.org/reform/calomiris.html.

Calomiris, Charles W. 2000. "When Will Economics Guide IMF and World Bank Reform?" *Cato Journal*, Spring/Summer.

Calvert, Randall L. 1995. "The Rational Choice Theory of Social Institutions: Cooperation, Coordination, Communication." In J. S. Banks and E. A. Hanushek, eds., *Modern Political Economy: Old Topics, New Directions*. Cambridge: Cambridge University Press.

Calvo, Guillermo A, Leonardo Leiderman, and Carmen M. Reinhart. 1993. "Capital Inflows and Real Exchange Rate Appreciation: The Role of External Factors." *International Monetary Fund Staff Papers*, March.

Calvo, Sara and Carman M. Reinhart. 1996. "Capital Flows to Latin America: Is There Evidence of Contagion Effects?" In Guillermo A. Calvo, Morris Goldstein, and Eduard Hochreiter eds., *Private Capital Flows to Emerging Markets*. Washington, D.C. Institute for International Economics.

Camdessus, Michel. 1997. "Address to the United Nations Economic and Social Council." July 2. http://www. imf.org/external/pubs/exrp/govern/ govindex.htm.

Cameron, Maxwell A. and Brian Tomlin. 2000. *The Making of NAFTA: How the Deal Was Done*. Ithaca, New York: Cornell University Press.

Campbell, John L. and Leon N. Lindberg. 1991. "The evolution of governance regimes." In John L. Campbell, J. Rogers Hollingsworth and Leon N. Lindberg eds., *Governance of the American Economy*. Cambridge: Cambridge University Press.

Canner, Stephen J. 1998. "The Multilateral Agreement on Investment." *Cornell International Law Journal*, 31: 657.

Canova, Timothy A. 1999. Banking and Financial Reform at the Crossroads of the Neoliberal Contagion." *American University Law Review*, 14: 1571.

Caporaso James A. and David P. Levine. 1992. *Theories of Political Economy*. New York: Cambridge University Press.

Cappuyns, Elizabeth. 1998. "Linking Labor Standards and Trade Sanctions: An Analysis of Their Current Relationship." *Columbia Journal of Transnational Law*.

Caprio, Gerhard and Patrick Honohan. 1999. "Restoring Banking Stability: Beyond Supervised Capital Requirements." *Journal of Economic Perspectives*, Fall.

Caprio, Gerhard and Daniela Klingebiel. 1997. "Bank Insolvency: Bad Luck, Bad Policy or Bad Banking?" In Michael Bruno and Boris Pleskovic eds., *World Bank Annual Conference on Development Economics*. Washington: World Bank.

Cardoso, Fernando Henrique. 1973. "Associated-dependent Development: Theoretical and Practical Implications." In A Stephan ed., *Authoritarian Brazil*. New Haven: Yale University Press.

Cardoso, Fernando Henrique and Enzo Faletto. 1979. *Dependency and Development in Latin America*. Berkeley: University of California Press.

Carmody, Pàdraig. 1998. "Constructing Alternative Structural Adjustment in Africa." *Review of African Political Economy*, March. Casper, Steven. 2001. "The Legal Framework for Corporate Governance: The Influence of Contract Law on Company Strategies in Germany and the United States." In Peter A. Hall and David Soskice eds., *Varieties of Capitalism: The Institutional Foundations of Comparative Advantage*. Oxford: Oxford University Press.

Cass, Deborah Z. 1996. "Navigating the Newstream: Recent Critical Scholarship in International Law." *Nordic Journal of International Law*, 96.

Cassese, Antonio. 1986. *International Law in a Divided World*. Oxford: Clarendon Press.

Castañeda, Jorge G. 1993. *Utopia Unarmed: The Latin American Left After the Cold War*. New York: Alfred A. Knopf.

Cerny, Philip G. 1994. "The Infrastructure of the Infrastructure? Towards 'Embedded Financial Orthodoxy' in the International Political Economy." In Ronan P. Palan and Barry Gills, eds., *Transcending the State-Global Divide: A Neostructural Agenda in International Relations*. Boulder: Lynne Rienner.

Cerny, Philip G. 1996. "Globalization and Other Stories: The Search for a New Paradigm for International Relations." *International Journal*, Autumn.

Cerny, Philip G. 1997a. "Paradoxes of the Competition State: The Dynamics of Political Globalization." *Government and Opposition*, Spring.

Cerny, Philip. 1997b. "The Search for a Paperless World: Technology, Financial Globalisation and Policy Response." In Michael Talalay, Chris Farrands and Roger Tooze eds., *Technology, Culture and Competitiveness: Change and the World Political Economy*. London: Routledge.

Champlin, Dell and Paulette Olson. 1999. "The Impact of Globalization on U.S. Labor Markets: Redefining the Debate." *Journal of Economic Issues*, June.

Chandler, Alfred D., Jr. 1986. "The Evolution of Modern Global Competition." In Michael E. Porter ed., *Competition in Global Industries*. Boston: Harvard Business School Press.

Chang, Ha-Joon. 1994. *The Political Economy of Industrial Policy*. New York: St. Martin's Press.

Chang, Ha-Joon. 1995. "Explaining 'Flexible Rigidities' in East Asia." In Tony Killick ed., *The Flexible Economy: Causes and Consequences of the Adaptability of National Economies*. London: Routledge.

Chang, Ha-Joon. 1998. "Globalization, Transnational Corporations, and Economic Development: Can the Developing Countries Pursue Strategic Industrial Policy in s Globalizing World Economy?" In Dean Baker, Gerald Epstein, and Robert Pollin eds., *Globalization and Progressive Economic Policy*. New York: Cambridge University Press.

Charnovitz, Steve. 1998. "The Moral Exception in Trade Policy." *Virginia Journal of International Law*, Summer.

Charnovitz, Steve. 2000. "World Trade and the Environment: A Review of the New WTO Report." *Georgetown International Environmental Law Review*, no. 12.

Chase-Dunn, Christopher. 1981. "Interstate System and Capitalist World-Economy: One Logic or Two? *International Studies Quarterly*, March; reprinted in George T. Crane and Abla Amawi eds., *The Theoretical Evolution of International Political Economy: A Reader*. 2nd ed., New York: Oxford University Press.

Chayes, Abram and Antonia Handler Chayes. 1995. *The New Sovereignty: Compliance with International Regulatory Agreements*.

Cheng, Tun-jen. 1990. "Political Regimes and Development Strategies: South Korea and Taiwan." In Gary Gereffi and Donald L. Wyman eds., *Manufacturing Miracles: Paths of Industrialization in Latin America and East Asia*. Princeton: Princeton University Press.

Choate, Robert. 1999. "Lobbying Hard for a Place at the Table." *Financial Times*, May 28.

Chossudovsky, Michael. 1997. *The Globalisation of Poverty: Impacts of IMF and World Bank Reforms*. London: Zed.,

Chinkin, C. M. 1989. "The Challenge of Soft Law: Development and Change in International Law." *International and Comparative Law Quarterly*, October.

Council on Foreign Relations. 1999. *Safeguarding Prosperity in a Global Financial System: The Future of International Financial Architecture,*. New York: Council on Foreign Relations.

Cowell, Alan. 2003. "British Ask What a War Would Mean for Business." *New York Times*, March 18.

Chu, Yun-han. 1995. "The East Asian NICs: a state-led path to the developing world." In Barbara Stallings ed., *Global Change, Regional Response: The New International Context of Development*. Cambridge: Cambridge University Press.

Chu, Yun-han, Fu Hu and Chung-in Moon. 1997. "South Korea and Taiwan: The International Context, in Larry Diamond, Marc F. Plattner, Yun-han Chu, and Hung-mao Tien eds., *Consolidating the Third Wave Democracies: Regional Challenges*. Baltimore: Johns Hopkins University Press.

Citrin, Daniel and Stanley Fisher. 2000. "Strengthening the International Financial System: Key Issues." *World Development*, 28:6.

Clarke, Tony. n. d. "Mai-Day! The Corporate Rule Treaty." http://www.aidc.org. za/archives/mai_corporate_treaty.html.

Clarke, Tony. 1999. "Who Owns the WTO?". Washington, D.C.: Corporate Watch., http://www.corpwatch.org/trac/feature/wto/2-clarke.html.

Clarke, Tony and Maude Barlow. 1997. *MAI: The Multilateral Agreement on Investment and the Threat to Canadian Sovereignty*. New York: Apex Press.

Clifford, Mark L. 1999. "Daewoo's Boss Is Playing a Dangerous Game." *Business Week*, August 16.

Cline, William R. 1992. *The Economics of Global Warming*. Washington, D.C.: Institute for International Economics.

Coase Ronald. 1937. "The Nature of the Firm." *Economica* 4, reprinted in Oliver Williamson and Sidney G. Winter eds., *The Nature of the Firm: Origins, Evolution, and Development*. New York: Oxford University Press, 1991.

Coase, Ronald H. 1960. "The Problem of Social Cost." *Journal of Law and Economics*, October.

Coase, Ronald. 1991. "Nobel Lecture: The Institutional Structure of Production." In Oliver E. Williamson and Sidney G. Winter eds., *The Nature of the Firm: Origins, Evolution, and Development*. New York: Oxford University Press, 1993.

Cobb, Clifford, Ted Halstead, and Jonathan Rowe. 1995. "If GNP is up Why is America Down?" *Atlantic Monthly*, October.

Cobb, Clifford W. n.d. "The Roads Aren't Free: Estimating the Full Social Cost of Driving and the Effects of Accurate Pricing." Working Paper Series on Environmental Tax Shifting No. 3, Redefining Progress, San Francisco.

Coffee, John C., Jr. 1999. "The Future as History: The Prospects for Global Convergence in Corporate Governance and Its Implications." *Northwestern Law Review*, Spring.

Cohen, Benjamin J. 1999. "Capital Controls: Why Do Governments Hesitate?" paper presented to the annual meetings of the American Political Science Association, Atlanta September 2–5.

Cohn, Theodore H. 2000. *Global Political Economy: Theory and Practice*. New York: Addison Wesley Longman.

Collier, Peter. 1997. "The Failure of Conditionality." In C. Gwin and Joan Nelson eds., *Perspectives on Aid and Development*. Washington, D.C.: Overseas Development Council.

Compa, Lance. 1998. "The Multilateral Agreement on Investment and International Labor Rights: A Failed Connection." *Cornell International Law Journal*, 31: 683.

Conca, Ken. 2000. "The WTO and the Undermining of Global Environmental Governance." *Review of International Political Economy*, Autumn.

Cooper, James M. 1999. "Spirits in the Material World: A Post-Modern Approach to United States Trade Policy." *American University International Law Review*, 14:957.

Cooper Richard. 1968. *The Economics of Interdependence: Economic Policy in the Atlantic Community.* New York: McGraw-Hill.

Cooper Richard N. 1972. "Economic Interdependence and Foreign Policy in the Seventies." *World Politics*, January.

Corbridge, Stuart. 1993. "Discipline and Punishment: The New Right and the Policing of the International Debt Crisis." In Stephen P. Riley ed., *The Politics of Global Debt.* Houndsmith, England: Macmillan.

Corden, W. Max. 1997. *Trade Policy and Economic Welfare* 2nd ed., Oxford: Clarendon Press.

Corporate Europe Observer. n. d. "'Better Regulation': For Whom? EC Prepares to Dismantle Business Regulation and Expand Corporate Control." Issue 9.

Corporate Europe Observer. n. d. "Post-Seattle Retaliation: US Business Rallies to Keep Neoliberal Globalisation on Track. " Issue 9.

Corporate Europe Observatory. 1999. "Transatlantic Business Dialogue: Putting the Business Hourse Before the Government Cart." Briefing Paper, October 25.

Cox, Robert W. 1992a. "Global Perestroka." In Ralph Miliband and Leo Panitch eds., *The New World Order? Socialist Registrar 1992.* New York: Monthly Review Press.

Cox, Robert W. 1992b. "Towards a Post-Hegemonic Conceptualization of World Order: Reflections on the Relevancy of Ibn Khaldun. In James N. Rosenau and Ernst-Otto Czempiel eds., *Governance Without Government: Order and Change in World Politics.* Cambridge: Cambridge University Press.

Cox, Robert W. 1993. "Structural Issues of Global Governance: Implications for Europe." In Stephen Gill ed., *Gramsci, Historical Materialism and International Relations.* Cambridge: Cambridge University Press.

Cox, Robert C. 1994. "Global Restructuring: Making Sense of the Changing Political Economy." In Richard Stubbs and Geoffrey R. D. Underhill eds., *Political Economy and the Changing Global Order.* Toronto: McClelland and Stewart.

Cox, Robert W. 1995. "Critical Political Economy." In Bjorn Hettne ed., *International Political Economy: Understanding Global Disorder.* London: Zed.,

Cox, Robert W. 1999. "Civil Society at the Turn of the Millennium: Prospects for an Alternative World Order, " *Review of International Studies*, January.

Crooks, Ed and Alan Beattie. 2000. "Global Warning." *Financial Times*, May 17.

Crotty, James. 1994. "Are Keynesian Uncertainty and Macrotheory Compatible? Conventional Decision Making, Institutional Structures, and Conditional Stability in Keynesian Macromodels." In Gary Dymski and Robert Pollin eds.,

New Perspectives in Monetary Macroeconomics. Ann Arbor: University of Michigan Press.

Crotty, James. 1999. "Was Keynes a Corporatist? Keynes's Radical Views on Industrial Policy and Macro Policy in the 1920s." *Journal of Economic Literature*, September.

Crotty, James. 2000a. "Slow Growth, Destructive Competition, and Low Road Relations: A Keynes-Marx-Schumpeter Analysis of Neoliberal Globalization." Joint Conference on the Future of the Korean Economy in the Context of Globalization at Suanbo, Korea, June 22.

Crotty, James. 2000b. "Structural Contradictions of the Global Neoliberal Regime." *Review of Radical Political Economics*, September.

Crotty, James and Gerald Epstein. 1999. "A Defense of Capital Controls in Light of the Asian Financial Crisis." *Journal of Economic Issues*, June.

Crotty, James Gerald Epstein, and Patricia Kelly. 1997. "Multinational Corporations and Technical Change: Global Stagnation, Inequality and Unemployment." to appear in Economic Policy Institute's volume *Globalization and Progressive Economic Policy; What are the Real Constraints? What are the Real Options?*

Cumings, Bruce. 1984. "The Origins and Development of the Northeast Asian Political Economy: Industrial Sectors, Product Cycles, and Political Consequences. In Frederic C. Deyo ed., *The Political Economy of the New Asian Industrialism*. Ithaca: Cornell University Press.

Cumings, Bruce. 1991. "Trilateralism and the New World Order." *World Policy Journal*, Spring.

Curtin, Philip. 1984. *Cross-Cultural Trade in World History*. Cambridge: Cambridge University Press.

Cushman, J. H., Jr. 1998. "Nike Pledges to End Child Labor and Apply U.S. Rules Abroad." *New York Times*, May 13.

Cutler, A. Claire. 1995. "Global Capitalism and Liberal Myths: Dispute Settlement in Private International Trade Relations." *Millennium: Journal of International Studies*, Winter.

Cutler, A. Claire. 1999. "Locating 'Authority' in the Global Political Economy." *International Studies Quarterly*, March.

Dahl, Gordon B. and Michael R. Ransom. 1999. "Does Where You Stand Depend on Where You Sit?" *American Economic Review*, September.

Dalrymple, Christopher K. 1996. "Politics and Foreign Direct Investment: The Multilateral Investment Guarantee Agency and the Calvo Clause." *Cornell International Law Journal*

Daly, Herman. 1999. "Feasta Lecture" to the International Society for Ecological Economics. http://www.feasta.org/article_daly.htm accessed September 24, 2001.

Dao, James. 2002. "Protestors Interrupt Powell Speech as U. N. Talks End." *New York Times*, September 5.

D'Arista, Jane. 2000. "Reforming International Financial Architecture." *Challenge*, May–June.

De Angelis, Massimo. 2000. "Globalization, New Internationalism and the Zapatistas." *Capital and Class*, No. 70.

de Goede, Marieke. 2001. "Discourses of Scientific Finance and the Failure of Long Term Capital Management." *New Political Economy*, July.

Dell, Sidney. 1981. *On Being Grandmotherly: The Evolution of IMF Conditionality*. Princeton: International Financial Section, Department of Economics, Princeton University. Essays in International Finance Number 144.

de Cecco, Marcello. 1979. "Origins of the Postwar Payments System." *Cambridge Journal of Economics*, March.

de Cecco, Marcello. 1984. *The International Gold Standard: Money and Empire*. London: Frances Pinter. second edition.

de Larosière, Jacques. 1996. *Financing Development in a World of Financial Flows: The Challenge for Multilateral Development Banks in Working with the Private Sector*. Washington, D.C.: Per Jacobson Foundation.

DeMartino, George. 1999. "Global Neoliberalism, Policy Autonomy, and International Competitive Dynamics." *Journal of Economic Issues*, June.

Demski, Joel S. 2003. "Corporate Conflicts of Interest." *Journal of Economic Perspectives* (Spring).

Denemark, Robert A. and Robert O'Brien. 1997. "Contesting the Canon: International Political Economy at UK and US Universities." *Review of International Political Economy*, Spring.

Dernbach, John C. 1998. "Sustainable Development as a Framework for National Governance." *Case Western Reserve Law Review*, Fall.

Destler, I. M. 1995. *America's Trade Politics* Third Edition. Washington, D.C. Institute for International Economics and New York: The Twentieth Century Fund.

Devetak, Richard and Richard Higgott. 1999. "Justice Unbound? Globalization, States and the Transformation of the Social Bond." *International Affairs*, July.

Dewey, John. 1984. "The Public and Its Problems." In Jo Ann Boydston ed., *John Dewey, The Later Works, 1925-1953*. Volume 2: 1925–1927. Carbondale: Southern Illinois Press.

Deyo, Frederic C. 1987. "Coalitions, Institutions, and Linkage Sequencing— Toward a Strategic Capacity Model of East Asian Development." In Frederic C. Deyo ed., *The Political Economy of the New Asian Industrialism*. Ithaca: Cornell University Press.

Deyo, Frederic C. 1995. "Capital. Labor and the State in Thai Industrial Restructuring: The Impact of Global Transformations." In David A. Smith and Jozsef Borocz eds., *A New Global Order? Global Transformation in the Late Twentieth Century*. Westport, CT: Greenwood Press.

Diamand, Robert W. and Mohammed H. I. Dore. 2000. "Keynes's Casino Capitalism, Bagehot's International Currency, and the Tobin Tax: Historical Notes on Preventing Currency Fires." *Journal of Post Keynesian Economics*, Summer.

Dicken, Peter. 1998. *Global Shift: Transforming the World Economy* 3rd ed., New York: Guilford Press.

Dieter, Herbert. 2000. "Monetary Regionalism: Regional Integration Without Financial Crises." Institute for Development and Peace, Duisburg University, Germany.

Dinopoulos, Elias and Paul Seegerstrom. 1999. "A Schumpeterian Model of Protection and Relative Wages." *American Economic Review*, June.

Dixon, Anne M. n.d. "From Harvard to Paris to Washington: Making Marshall's Plan A Reality." *The European Recovery Program*, Marshall Foundation. http://www. marshfnd.com

Dogan, Mattei. 1996. "Political Science and the Other Social Sciences." In Robert E. Goodin and Hans-Dieter Klingmann eds., *A New Handbook of Political Science*. Oxford: Oxford University Press.

Dollar, David and Jocob Svensson. 1998. "What Explains the Success or Failure of Structural Adjustment Programs?" Macroeconomics and Growth Group, World Bank.

Drozdiak, William. 1999. "The Moment of Truth." *Washington Post National Weekly Edition*, March 29.

Drysek, John. 1996. "Foundations for Environmental Political Economy: The Search for *Homo Ecologicus.*" *New Political Economy*, 1, no. 1

Dunning John H. 1991. "Enterprises: From Confrontation to Co-operation?." *Millennium: Journal of International Studies*, Summer.

Dunning John H. 1993. *Multinational Enterprises and the Global Economy*. New York: Addison-Wesley.

Dunning John H. 1997a. "Governments and the Macro-Organization of Economic Activity: An Historical and Spatial Perspective." *Review of International Political Economy*, Spring.

Dunning John H. 1997b. "The Advent of Alliance Capitalism." In John H. Dunning and Khalil A. Hamdani eds., *The New Globalism and Developing Countries*. Tokyo: United Nations University Press.

Dunning, John H. 1998. "An Overview of Relations with National Governments." *New Political Economy*, July.

Dunning, John H. and Khalil A. Hamdani eds., 1997. *The New Globalism and Developing Countries*. Tokyo: United Nations University Press.

Dunoff, Jeffrey L. 1999. "Does Globalization Advance Human Rights?" *Brooklyn Journal of International Law*, 25: 125.

Durbin Andrea, John Cavanagh, and Martin Khor. 1999. "A Call to Action: A Citizen's Agenda for Reform of the Global Economic System. http://www.twn.org.sg/ifgcall-cn.htm.

Durbin, Andrea and Carol Welch. 2000. "In Focus: Greening the Bretton Woods Institutions." *Foreign Policy In Focus*, September. http://www. foreignpolicy-infocus.org/briefs/vol5/v5n33bretton.html.

Dwyer, Paula. 1999. "How to Wring Out Money Launderers." *Business Week*, November 22.

Eatwell, John. 1995. "Disguised Unemployment: The G7 Experience." Trinity College, Cambridge, August.

Eatwell, John. 1996. "International Capital Liberalization: The Record." New York: New School for Social Research., August, a Report to the UNDP. SSA no. 96–049.

Eatwell, John and Lance Taylor. 2000. *Global Finance at Risk: The Case for International Regulation.* New York: New Press.

Eatwell, John and Lance Taylor. 1998. "The Performance of Liberalized Capital Markets." Center for Economic Policy Analysis, New School for Social Research, Working Paper No. 8.

Economist. 1998. "The Science of Alliance." April 4.

Economist. 2001. "Through the Wringer." April 14.

Economist. 2002a. "America and the IMF/World Bank: What Leadership?" April 20, 2002.

Economist. 2002b. "Special Report World Economy." January 26.

Economist. 2002c. "The Unlikeliest Scourge." July 13–19.

Economist. 2002d. "World Trade Coming Unstuck." November 2.

Economist Technology Quarterly. 2001. "Patently Absurd?" June 23.

Eden, Lorraine. 1991. "Bringing the Firm Back In: Multinational Corporations in International Political Economy." *Millennium: Journal of International Studies*, Summer.

Eden, Lorraine and Fen Osler Hampson. 1997. "Clubs Are Trump: The Formation of International Regimes in the Absence of a Hegemon." In J. Rogers Hollingsworth and Robert Boyer, eds., *Contemporary Capitalism: The Embeddedness of Institutions.* New York: Cambridge University Press.

Edwards, Robert H., Jr. and Simon H. Lester. 1997. "Towards a More Comprehensive World Trade Organization Agreement on Trade Related Investment Measures." *Stanford Journal of International Law*, Summer.

Edwards, Sebastian. 1993. "Openness, Trade Liberalization, and Growth in Developing Countries." *Journal of Economic Literature*, September.

Edwards, Sebastian. 1999. "How Effective are Capital Controls?" *Journal of Economic Perspectives*, Fall.

Ehrlich, Marc S. 1997–8. "Towards a New Dialogue Between International Relations Theory and International Trade Theory." *UCLA Journal of International Law & Foreign Affairs*, Fall/Winter.

Eichengreen, Barry. 1996. *Globalizing Capital: A History of the International Monetary System.* Princeton: Princeton University Press.

Eichengreen, Barry. 1999. "Building on Consensus." *Financial Times*, February 2.

Eichengreen, Barry. 2000. "Taming Capital Flows." *World Development*, 28:6.

Eichengreen, Barry and Jeffrey Frieden eds., 1994. *The Political Economy of European Monetary Unification.* Boulder: Westview Press.

Eichengreen, Barry and Peter B. Kenen. 1994. "Managing the World System under the Bretton Woods System: An Overview." In Peter B. Kenen ed., *Man-

aging the World Economy: Fifty Years After Bretton Woods. Washington, D.C.: Institute for International Economics.

Elson, Diane. 1991. "Male Bias in Macrco-Economics: The Case of Structural Adjustment." In Diane Elson ed., *Bias in the Development Process.* Manchester: Manchester University Press.

Enrico, Luca and Albert Musalem. 1999. "Offshore Banking: An Analysis of Micro- and Macrco-Prudential Issues." *IMF Working Paper*, Number 99/5.

Epstein, Gerald. 1996. International Capital Mobility and the Scope for National Economic Management." In Robert Boyer and Daniel Drache eds., *States Against Markets: The limits of Globalization.* London: Routledge.

Epstein, Gerald A. amd Dorothy Power. 2002. "The Return of Finance and Finance's Return: Recent Trends in Rentier Incomes in OECD Countries, 1960–2000." Political Economy Research Institute, November.

Epstein, Gerald A. and Juliet B. Schor. 1991. "Macropolicy in the Rise and Fall of the Golden Age." In Stephen A. Marglin and Juliet B. Schor eds., 1991. *The Golden Age of Capitalism: Reinterpreting the Postwar Experience.* Oxford: Oxford University Press.

Erickson, Christopher L. and Daniel J. B. Mitchell. 1999. "The American Experience with Labor Standards and Trade Agreements." *Journal of Small and Emerging Business Law*, Summer.

Esty, Daniel C. 1994. *Greening the GATT: Trade, Environment and the Future.* Washington, D.C.: Institute for International Economics.

Esty, Daniel C. 1998. "Linkages and Governance: NGOs at the World Trade Organization." *University of Pennsylvania Journal of International Economic Law.* Fall.

Evans, Peter. 1979. *Dependent Development: The Alliance of Multinational, State, and Local Capital in Brazil.* Princeton: Princeton University Press.

Evans, Peter. 1992. "The State as Problem and Solution: Predation, Embedded Autonomy, and Structural Change." In Stephan Haggard and Robert R. Kaufman eds., *The Politics of Economic Adjustment.* Princeton: Princeton University Press.

Evans, Peter. 1995. *Embedded Autonomy: States & Industrial Transformation.* Princeton: Princeton University Press.

Evans, Peter. 1997. "The Eclipse of the State? Reflections on Stateness in an Era of Globalization." *World Politics*, October.

Eviatar, Daphne. 2003. "Profits at Gunpoint." *The Nation*, June 30.

Falk, Richard. 1997. "Resisting 'Globalisation-from-above' through 'Globalisation-from-below'." *New Political Economy*, 2, no. 1.

Federal Reserve Bank of New York, Research and Market Analysis Group. 1998. *Research Update*, July.

Feenstra, Robert C. and Gordon H. Hanson. 1996. "Globalization, Outsourcing, and Wage Inequality." *American Economics Review*, May.

Feldstein, Martin. 1998. "Refocusing the IMF." *Foreign Affairs* March/April.

Felix, David. 1994. "Debt Crisis Adjustment in Latin America: Have the Hardships Been Necessary?" In Gary Dymski and Robert Pollin eds., *New Perspectives in Monetary Macroeconomics.* Ann Arbor: University of Michigan Press.

Felix, David. 1998. "In Focus: IMF Bailouts and Global Financial Flows." In Martha Honey and Tom Barry eds., *U.S. Foreign Policy In Focus* 3, no. 5 April. A project of the Institute for Policy Studies and the Interhemispheric Resource Center.

Felix, David and John P. Coskey. 1990. "The Road to Default: An Assessment of Debt Crisis Management in Latin America." In David Felix ed., *Debt and Transfiguration? Prospects for Latin America's Economic Revival.* Armonk, NY: M. E. Sharpe.

Ferguson, Yale H. and Richard W. Mansbach. 1999. "Global Politics at the Turn of the Millennium: Changing Bases of 'Us' and 'Them'." *International Studies Review,* Summer.

Fidler, Stephen and Gautam Malkani. 1999. "Fear on Pace of Financial Systems Reform." *Financial Times,* April 15.

Finance Ministers of G7. 1999. "Strengthening the International Financial Architecture—Report of the G7 Finance Ministers to the Köln Economic Summit, Cologne, June 18–20. http://www.g8cologne. de/06/00122/ index.html.

Findlay, M. C. and E. E. Williams. 2000–2001. "A Fresh Look at the Efficient Market Hypothesis: How the Intellectual History of Finance Encouraged a Real 'Fraud-on-the-Market'." *Journal of Post Keynesian Economics,* Winter.

Finlayson, Jock A. and Mark W. Zacker. 1983. "The GATT and the Regulation of Trade Barriers: Regime Dynamics and Functions." In Stephen D. Krasner ed., *International Regimes.* Ithaca: Cornell University Press.

Finnemore, Martha and Kathryn Sikkink. 1998. "International Norm Dynamics and Political Change." *International Organization*

Fioretos, Orfeo. 2001. "The Domestic Sources of Multilateral Preferences: Varitieties of Capitalism in the European Community." In Peter A. Hall and David Soskice eds., *Varieties of Capitalism: The Institutional Foundations of Comparative Advantage.* Oxford: Oxford University Press.

Fisher, Stanley. 1997a. "Capital Account Liberalization and the Role of the IMF." International Monetary Fund., September 19. From IMF web page. http://www.imf.org/

Fisher, Stanley. 1997b. "Banking Soundness and the Role of the Fund." Charles Enoch and John H. Green eds., *Banking Soundness and Monetary Policy: Issues and Experience in the Global Economy.* Washington, D.C.: IMF Institute and Monetary Exchange Affairs Department.

Fisher, Stanley. 1998. Statement in Los Angeles in response to criticism by Martin Feldstein, March 20. IMF web page. http://www.imf.org/

Fisher Stanley. 1999. "On the Need for a Lender of Last Resort." *Journal of Economic Perspectives.* Fall.

Fishlow Albert and Catherine Gwin. 1994. "Overview: Lessons from the East

Asian Experience." In Albert Fishlow, Catherine Gwin, Stephan Haggard, Dani Rodrik, and Robert Wade *Miracle or Design? Lessons from the East Asian Experience*, Policy Essay Number 11. Washington, D.C.: Overseas Development Council.

Finch, C. David. 1983., "Adjustment Policies and Conditionality." In IMF Conditionality, ed., by John Williamson. Washington: Institute for International Economics.

Foremski, Tom. 2003. "High-tech Sector No Longer US's Biggest Employer, *Financial Times*, March 19,.

Foreman-Peck, James. 1995. *A History of the World Economy: International Economic Relations Since 1850*. 2nd ed., New York: Simon and Schuster., Second Edition.

Foss, Pal. 1995. "Introduction: On the Economics of Institutions and Organizations." In Pal Foss ed., *Economic Approaches to Organizations and Institutions: An Introduction*. Aldershot: Dartmouth.

Fderguson, Yale H. and Richard W. Mansbach. 1999. "Global Politics at the Turn of the Millennium: Changing Bases of 'Us' and 'Them.' *International Studies Review*, Summer.

Frankel, Jeffrey and Andrew K. Rose. 1996. "Exchange Rate Crisis in Emerging Markets." *Journal of International Economics*, November.

Freeman, Richard. 1996. "Will Globalization Dominate U.S. Labor Market Outcomes?" Susan Collins ed., *Imports, Exports, and the American Worker*. Washington: Brookings Institution.

Frenkel, Stephen J. and David Peetz. 1998. "Globalization and Industrial Relations in East Asia: A Three Country Comparison." *Industrial Relations: A Journal of Economy & Society*, July.

Frey, Bruno S. 1984. "The Public Choice View of International Political Economy." *International Organization* 38:

Frieden, Jeffry A. 1981. "Third World Indebted Industrialization: International Finance and State Capitalism in Mexico, Brazil, Algeria, and South Korea." *International Organization* 35, no. 1; reprinted in Jeffry A. Frieden and David A. Lake eds., *International Political Economy: Perspectives on Global Power and Wealth*. New York: St. Martin's.

Frieden, Jeffry A. 1991. "Invested Interests: The Politics of National Economic Policies in a World of Global Finance." *International Organization*, Autumn.

Frieden, Jeffry A. 1996. "Economic Integration and the Politics of Monetary Politics in the United States." In Robert O. Keohane and Helen V. Milner eds., *Internationalization and Domestic Politics*. New York: Cambridge University Press.

Friedman, Jeffrey ed., 1996. *The Rational Choice Controversy: Economic Models of Politics Reconsidered.*, New Haven: Yale University Press.

Friends of the Earth—England, Wales, and Northern Ireland. 1998. "A History of Attempts to Control the Activities of Transnational Corporations: What

Lessons Can Be Learned?" Washington: International Forum on Globalization.

Fukuyama, Francis. 1995. "Recent Books on International Relations." Reviewing Jean-Marie Guéhenno's *The End of the Nation-State*, *Foreign Affairs* November/December.

Galbraith, John Kenneth. 1980. "The No-WIN Society." *New York Review of Books*, June 12.

Galeano, Eduardo. 2003. "Our World is a Great Paradox That Turns Around in the Universe." http://www.portoalegre2003.org

Gallagher, John and Ronald Robinson. 1953. "The Imperialism of Free Trade." *Economic History Review* Second Series, 6, no. 1; reprinted in Jeffry A. Frieden and David A. Lake eds., *International Political Economy: Perspectives on Global Power and Wealth*. New York: St. Martin's.

Gamble, Andrew. 1995. "The New Political Economy." *Political Studies*, September.

Gamson, William. 1993. *Talking Politics*. Cambridge: Cambridge University Press.

Garbade, Kenneth D. and William L. Silber. 1978. "Technology, Communication, and the Performance of Financial Markets, 1840–1975." *Journal of Finance*, June.

Garcia, Frank J. 1998. "The Trade Linkage Phenomenon: Pointing the Way to the Trade Law and Global Social Policy of the 21st Century." *University of Pennsylvania Journal of International Economic Law*, Summer.

Garcia, Frank J. 1999a. "Trade and Justice: Linking the Trade Linkage Debate." *Journal of International Law*, Summer.

Garcia, Frank J. 1999b. "Trading Away the Human Rights Principle." *Brooklyn Journal of International Law*, 25: 51.

Gardner, Richard. 1980. *Sterling-Dollar Diplomacy in Current Perspective: The Origins and Prospects of Our International Order*. Berkeley: University of California Press.

Garrett, Geoffrey. 1996. "Capital Mobility, Trade, and Domestic Politics of Economic Policy." In Robert O. Keohane and Helen V. Milner eds., *Internationalization and Domestic Politics*. New York: Cambridge University Press.

Garrett, Geoffrey. 1998. *Partisan Politics in the Global Economy*. New York: Cambridge University Press.

Garrett, Geoffrey. 2000. "Shrinking States? Globalization and National Autonomy." In Ngaire Woods ed., *The Political Economy of Globalization*. Houndsmills, UK: Macmillan.

George, Susan. 1999. "Globalising Designs of the WTO." *Le Monde Diplomatique*, July.

Gereffi, Gary. 1990. "Big Business and the State." In Gary Gereffi and Donald L. Wyman eds., *Manufacturing Miracles: Paths of Industrialization in Latin America and East Asia*. Princeton: Princeton University Press.

Gereffi, Gary, Miguel Korzeniewicz, and Roberto P. Korzeniewicz. 1994. "Introduction: Global Commodity Chains." In Gary Gereffi and Miguel Korzeniewicz eds., *Commodity Chains and Global Capitalism.* Westport, CT: Praeger.

Germain, Randall D. 1997. *The International Organization of Credit: States and Global Finance in the World-Economy.* Cambridge: Cambridge University Press.

Gibbs, David N. 2001. "Washington's New Interventionism: U.S. Hegemony and Inter-Imperialist Rivalries, *Monthly Review*, September.

Gilbert, Christopher L., Gregor Irwin and David Vines. 2001. "Capital Account Convertibility, Poor Developing Countries, and International Financial Architecture." *Development Policy Review*, March.

Gill, Stephen. 1995. "Globalisation, Market Civilization and Disciplinary Neoliberalism." *Millennium: Journal of International Studies.* Winter.

Gill, Stephen. 1997. "Transformation and Innovation in the Study of World Order." In Stephen Gill and James H. Mittelman eds., *Innovation and Transformation in International Studies.* Cambridge: Cambridge University Press.

Gill, Stephen. 1998. "European Governance and New Constitutionalism: Economic and Monetary Union and Alternatives to Disciplinary Neoliberalism." *New Political Economy*, March.

Gills, Barry and Ronan Palan eds., 1994. *Transcending the State-Global Divide: A Neo-structuralist Agenda in International Relations.* Boulder: Rienner.

Gilpin Robert with the assistance of Jean M. Gilpin. 1987. *The Political Economy of International Relations.* Princeton: Princeton University Press.

Gilpin, Andrew,. 1998. "Internal and External Constraints on Egalitarian Policies." In Dean Baker, Gerald Epstein and Robert Pollin eds., *Globalization and Progressive Economic Policy.* New York: Cambridge University Press.

Glyn, Andrew, Alan Hughes, Alain Lipietz and Ajit Singh. 1991. "The Rise and Fall of the Golden Age." In Stephen A. Marglin and Juliet B. Schor eds., 1991. *The Golden Age of Capitalism: Reinterpreting the Postwar Experience.* Oxford: Oxford University Press.

Goldstein, Morris. 2000. "Strengthening the International Financial Architecture: Where do we Stand?" Working Paper 00–8. Washington: Institute for International Economics., October.

Goodin, Robert E. and Hans-Dieter Klingemann eds., 1996. *A New Handbook of Political Science.* New York: Oxford University Press.

Goodman, John B. and Louis W. Pauly. 1993. "The Obsolescence of Capital Controls? Economic Management in an Age of Global Markets." *World Politics* October.

Goodstein, Eban. 1998. "Malthus Redux? Globalization and the Environment." In Dean Baker, Gerald Epstein and Robert Pollin eds., *Globalization and Progressive Economic Policy.* Cambridge: Cambridge University Press.

Gore, Charles. 2000. "The Rise and Fall of the Washington Consensus as a Paradigm for Developing Countries." *World Development*, Fall

Gourevitch, Peter. 1978. "The Second Image Reversed: The International Sources of Domestic Politics." *International Organization*, Autumn.

Grabel, Ilene. 2000. "The Political Economy of 'Policy Credibility': The New-Classical Macroeconomics and the Remaking of Emerging Economies." *Cambridge Journal of Political Economy*, January.

Grabel, Ilene. 2003. "Averting Crisis? Assessing Measures to Manage Financial Integration in Emerging Economies." *Cambridge Journal of Economics*, May.

Graham, Edward M. 1996. *Global Corporations and National Governments*. Washington, D.C.: Institute for International Economics.

Graham George. 1999. "Radical Banking Reforms Announced.," *Financial Times*, June 4.

GRAIN. 1998. "Biopiracy, TRIPs and Patenting of Asia's Rice Bowl. http://grain.org/publications/reports/rice.htm.

Gramsci, Antonio. 1971. *Selections from the Prison Notebooks of Antonio Gramsci*. Eds., Q. Hoare and G. Nowell Smith. New York: International Publishers.

Grant, Wyn. 1997. "Perspectives on Globalization and Economic Coordination." In J. Rogers Hollingsworth and Robert Boyer eds., *Contemporary Capitalism: The Embeddedness of Institutions*. New York: Cambridge University Press.

Grassman, Sven and Erik Lundberg eds., 1981. *The World Economic Order: Past and Prospects*. Basingstoke, UK: Macmillan.

Gray, H. Peter and Jean M. Gray. 1994. "Minskian Fragility in the International Financial System." Gary Dymski and Robert Pollin eds., *New Perspectives in Monetary Macroeconomics*. Ann Arbor: University of Michigan Press.

Green, Philip. 1985. *Retrieving Democracy: In Search of Covil Equality*. Totowa, New Jersey: Roman and Allenheld.

Greenspan, Alan. 1998. "The Globalization of Finance." *Cato Journal*, Winter.

Greider, William. 1997. *One World, Ready or Not: The Manic Logic of Global Capitalism*. New York: Touchstone.

Greider, William. 1998. "Breakdown of Free-Market Orthodoxy." *Washington Post National Weekly Edition*, October 12.

Griffith-Jones, Stephany. 1991. "International Financial Markets: A Case of Market Failure." In Christopher Colclough and James Manor eds., *States or Markets? Neo-liberalism and the Industrial Policy Debate*. Oxford: Clarendon Press.

Griffith-Jones, Stephany with Jacques Cailloux and Stephan Pfaffenzeller. 1998. "The East Asian Financial Crisis: A Reflection on Its Causes, Consequences, and Policy Implications." Institute of Development Studies, Sussex University, IDS Discussion Paper 367.

Grindle, Merilee S. 1994. "Sustainable Economic Recovery in Latin America: State Capacity, Markets, and Politics." In Graham Bird and Ann Helwege eds., *Latin America's Economic Future*. San Diego: Academic Press.

Grossman, Gene M. and Ephanan Helpman. 1999. "Competing for Endorsements." *American Economic Review*, June.

Gwartney, James, Randall Holcombe, and Robert Lawson. 1998. "The Scope of Government and the Wealth of Nations." *Cato Journal*, Fall.

Gwin, Catherine. 1997. "U.S. Relations with the World Bank, 1945–1992." In Devesh Kapur, John P. Lewis, and Richard Webb. 1997. *The World Bank: Its First Half Century*. Washington, D.C. Brookings Institution. Volume I History.

Haas, Ernest B. 1980. "Why Collaborate? Issue-Linkage and International Regimes." *World Politics*, April.

Haas, Ernest B. 1992. "Introduction: Epistemic Communities and International Policy Coordination." *International Organization*, Winter.

Haas, Ernest and Peter Haas. 1995. "Learning to Learn: Improving International Governance." *Global Governance*, September–December.

Haas, Peter M. and Ernest Haas. 2002. "Pragmatic Constructionism and the Study of International Institutions." *Millennium: Journal of International Relations* 31, no. 3.

Haberler, Gottfried., 1987. "Liberal and Illiberal Development Policy." In Gerald Meier ed., *Pioneers in Development*. Oxford: Oxford University Press.

Habermas, Jurgen. 1981. *The Theory of Communicative Action*. Boston: Beacon Press.

Hagapian, Frances. 1993. "After Regime Change: Authoritarian Legacies, Political Representation, and the Democratic Future of South America." *World Politics*, April.

Haggard, Stephen and Sylvia Maxfield, "The Political Economy of Financial Internationalization in the Developing World." *International Organization*, Winter 1996.

Haggard Stephen and Steven B. Webb. 1993. "What Do We Know About the Political Economy of Reform?" *World Bank Research Observer*

Hall, Rodney. 1999. *National Collective Identity: Social Constructs and International Systems*. New York: Columbia University Press.

Hall, Stuart. 1988. *The Hard Road to Renewal*. London: Verso.

Hallett, Graham. 1990. "West Germany." In Andrew Graham with Anthony Seldon eds., *Government and Economies in the Postwar World: Economic Policies and Comparative Performance, 1945–85*. London: Routledge.

Hamilton, Nora. 1982. *The Limits of State Autonomy: Post-Revolutionary Mexico*. Princeton: Princeton University Press.

Hamilton-Hart, Natasha. 1999. "The World Financial Order in Asia." Paper to the American Political Science Association, September 2–5.

Hancher, Leigh and Michael Moran. 1989. "Organizing Regulatory Space." In Leigh Hancher and Michael Moran eds., *Capitalism, Culture and Economic Regulation*. Oxford: Clarendon Press.

Hanlon, Joseph. 2000. "How Much Debt Must Be Canceled?" *Journal of International Development*, August.

Haque, Inaamul. 2002. "Reflections on the WTO Doha Ministerial: Doha Development Agenda: Recapturing the Momentum of Multilateralism and Developing Countries." *American University International Law Review*, 17.

Harmes, Adam. 1998. "Institutional Investors and the Reproduction of Neoliberalism." *Review of International Political Economy*, Spring.

Harmon, Mark D. 1997. *The British Labour Government and the 1976 IMF Crisis.* Houndsmills, UK: Macmillan.

Harrison, Bennett. 1994. *Lean and Mean: The Changing Landscape of Corporate Power in the Age of Flexibility.* New York: Basic Books.

Harrod, Roy F. 1974. "Keynes' Theory and Its Applications." In D. E. Moggridge ed., *Keynes: Aspects of the Man and His Work.* London: Macmillan.

Hart, Jeffrey A. 1992. *Rival Capitalists: International Competitiveness in the United States, Japan, and Western Europe.* Ithaca: Cornell University Press.

Hart-Landsberg, Martin. 1993. *The Rush to Development: Economic Change and Political Struggle in South Korea.* New York: Monthly Review.

Harvey, David. 2001. "Cosmopolitanism and the Banality of Geographical Evils" In Jean Commaroff and John L. Commaroff eds., *Millennial Capitalism and the Culture of Neoliberalism.* Durham: Duke University Press.

Hasenclever, Andreas, Peter Mayer, and Volker Rittberger. 1997. *Theories of International Regimes.* Cambridge: Cambridge University Press.

Hashmi, Sohail H. 1997. "Introduction." In Sohail H. Hashmi ed., *State Sovereignty: Change and Persistence in International Relations.* University Park: Pennsylvania State University Press.

Hausmann, Ricardo and Dani Rodrik. 2002. "Economic Development as Self-Discovery." Kennedy School of Government, Harvard University.

Hawes, Gary and Hong Liu. 1993. "Explaining the Dynamics of the East Asian Political Economy: State, Society, and the Search for Economic Growth." *World Politics*, July.

Hawley Jim. 1979. "The Internationalization of Capital: Banks, Eurocurrency and the Instability of the World Monetary System." *Review of Radical Political Economics*, Winter; reprinted in Jeffry A. Frieden and David A. Lake eds., *International Political Economy: Perspectives on Global Power and Wealth.* New York: St. Martin's.

Hay, Colin. 1997. "Divided by a Common Language: Political Theory and the Concept of Power." *Politics*, February.

Hay, Colin and David Marsh. 1999. "Introduction: Towards a New. International. Political Economy?" *New Political Economy*, March.

Haydn, Björen. 1995. "Introduction: The International Political Economy of Transformation." In Haydn ed., *International Political Economy: Understanding Global Disorder.* London: Zed.

Hayek, F. A. 1959. "Symposium on Keynes: Why?" Bruce Caldwell ed., *Contra Keynes and Cambridge: Essays, Correspondence.* The Collected Works of F. A. Hayek. Volume 9. Chicago: University of Chicago Press, 1995.

Held, David, Andrew McGrew, David Goldblatt and Jonathan Perraton. 1999.

Global Transformations: Politics, Economics and Culture. Stanford: Stanford University Press.

Heilbroner, Robert. 1996. "Reflections on a Sad State of Affairs." In John Eatwell ed., *Global Unemployment: Job Loss in the '90s*. Armonk, NY: M. E. Sharpe.

Helleiner, Eric. 1993. "When Finance Was the Servant: International Capital Movements in the Bretton Woods Order." In Philip G. Cerny ed., *Finance and World Politics: Markets, Regimes and States in the Post-hegemonic Era*. Aldershot, UK: Edward Elgar.

Helleiner, Eric. 1994. *States and the Reemergence of Global Finance: From Bretton Woods to the 1990s*. Ithaca: Cornell University Press.

Helleiner, Eric. 1996. "Post-Globalization: Is the Financial Liberalization Trend Likely to Be Reversed?" In Robert Boyer and Daniel Drache eds., *States Against Markets: The limits of Globalization*. London: Routledge.

Helleiner, Gerald. n.d. "Globalization, Liberalisation and Markets." *Third World Network*. http://www.twnside.org.sg/title/gerry.htm. Accessed August 2001.

Helleiner, Gerald K. 2001. "Markets, Politics, and Globalization: Can the Global Economy be Civilized?" *Global Governance*, July/September.

Helleiner, Stephen. 1998. "Testimony Regarding Congressional Funding of the International Monetary Fund." Subcommittee on General Oversight and Investigations, Committee on Banking and Financial Services." U.S. House of Representatives, April 21. http://www.igc.dgap/imfsteve.html.

Hellman, Joel S., Geraint Jones and Daniel Kaufmann. 2000. "Seize the State, Seize the Day: State Capture, Corruption and Influence in Transition." World Bank Policy Research Working Paper No. 2444, September.

Helm, Dieter. 2000. "The Assessment: Environmental Policy—Objectives, Instruments, and Institutions." *Oxford Review of Economic Policy*,14, no. 4.

Helpman, Elhanan. 1982. "Increasing Returns, Imperfect Markets, and Trade Theory." Ronald W. Jones and Peter B. Kenen eds., *Handbook of International Economics*. Amsterdam: North-Holland.

Helpman Elhanan. 1999. "The Structure of Foreign Trade." *Journal of Economic Perspectives*, Spring.

Helpman Elhanan and Paul R. Krugman. 1985. *Market Structure and Foreign Trade: Increasing Returns, Imperfect Competition, and the International Economy*. Cambridge: MIT Press.

Henderson, David. 1993. "International Economic Cooperation Revisited.," *Government and Opposition*, Winter.

Henry, David. 2003. "Ouch! Real Numbers." *Business Week*, March 24.

Heredia. Zubeta, Carlos. 2000. "The Mexican Economy: Six Years into NAFTA." Talk delivered to forum sponsored by the Development Gap and the Economic Policy Institute, Washington, January 21.

Hershey, Robert D., Jr. 1996. Nintendo Capitalism: Zapping the Markets." *New York Times*, May 28.

Hertel, T. W. and W. Martin. 1999. "Would Developing Countries Gain from

Inclusion of Manufacturing in the WTO Negotiations? Paper presented to the Conference on the WTO 2000 Negotiations, Geneva, September 20–21.

Highet, Keith. 1989. "The Internationalization of Law and Legal Practice: The Enigma of the *Lex Mercatoria.*" *Tulane Law Review*, February.

Higgott, Richard. 1999a. "Economics, Politics and International Political Economy: The Need for a Balanced Diet in an Era of Globalization." *New Political Economy*, March.

Higgott, Richard. 1999b. "Justice and the World Economy." Proceedings of Centre for the Study of Globalization & Regionalization 75th Anniversary of *International Affairs.*

Hill, Andrew. 2003. "Regulators Close the GAAP on Earnings Differentials." *Financial Times*, March 18.

Hinojosa-Ojeda, Raul. 1999. "Institution Building with the NAFTA Context: An Evaluation of Policy Initiatives from the Transnational Grassroots." BRIE Working Paper. http://www. brie.berkeley.edu/~briewww/pubs/wp/wp95.html.

Hirshman, Albert O. 1992. "The Concept of Interest: From Euphemism to Tautology." *Rival Views of Market Society and Other Recent Essays.* Cambridge: Harvard University Press.

Hirst Paul and Grahame Thompson. 1996. *Globalization in Question.* Cambridge, Mass.: Blackwell.

Hitchcock, William I. *Struggle for Europe: The Turbulent History of a Divided Continent, 1945–2002.* New York: Doubleday.

Hizon, Ernesto M. 1999. "Virtual Reality and Reality: The East Asian NICs and the Global Trading System." *Annual Survey of International & Comparative Law*, Spring.

Ho, P. Sai-wing. 1998. "Multilateral Trade Negotiations and the Changing Prospects for Third World Development: Assessing From a Southern Perspective." *Journal of Economic Issues*, June.

Hobsbawm, Eric. 1996. *The Age of Extremes: A History of the World 1914–1991.* New York: Random House.

Hodgson, Geoffrey M. 1988. *Economics and Institutions: A Manifesto for a Modern Institutional Economics.* Cambridge: Polity Press.

Hoekman, Bernard M. and Michael M. Kostecki. 1995. *The Political Economy of the World Trading System: From GATT to WTO.* Oxford: Oxford University Press.

Hoffman, John. 1997. "Can We Define Sovereignty?" *Politics*, February.

Hoffman, Philip and Kathryn Norberg eds., 1994. *Fiscal Crises, Liberty and Representative Government, 1450–1789.* Stanford: Stanford University Press.

Hollingsworth, J. Rogers. 1998. "New Perspectives on the Spatial Dimensions of Economic Coordination and Social Systems of Production." *Review of International Political Economy*, Autumn.

Holloway, Steven. 2000. "U.S. Unilateralism at the UN: Why Great Powers Do Not Make Great Multilateralists." *Global Governance*, July/August.

Holman, Michael. 1999. "Nigeria Told to Accept IMF Monitors." *Financial Times*, May 4.

Holsti, K. J. 1991. *Peace and War: Armed Conflict and International Order 1648–1989*. Cambridge: Cambridge University Press.

Hooke, A. W. 1983. *The International Monetary Fund: Its Evolution, Organization, and Activities*. Washington, D.C. International Monetary Fund.

Hopkins, Terence K. and Immanuel Wallerstein. 1996. "The World-System: Is There a Crisis?" In Terence K. Hopkins and Immanuel Wallerstein eds., *The Age of Transition: Trajectory of the World-System, 1945–2025*. London: Zed Books.

Horsefield, J. Keith. 1969. *The International Monetary Fund 1945–1965*, Volume III. Washington, D.C.: International Monetary Fund.

Hossein-Zadeh, Esmail. 1997. "NAFTA and Sovereignty." *Science and Society*, Summer.

Haussman, Ricardo and Dani Rodrik, "Economic Development as Self-Discovery." National Bureau of Economic Research Working Paper 89523, May, 2002.

Howes, Candace and Ann R. Markusen. 1993. "Trade, Industry, and Economic Development." In Helzi Noponen, Julie Graham, and Ann R. Markusen eds., 1993. *Trading Industries, Trading Regions: International Trade, American Industry, and Regional Economic Development*. New York: Guilford Press.

Hudec, Robert E. 1999. "The New WTO Dispute Procedure: An Overview of the First Three Years." *Minnesota Journal of Global Trade*, Winter.

Hummels, David, Dana Rapaport, and Kei-Mu Yi. 1998. "Vertical Specialization and the Changing Nature of World Trade." *Economic Policy Review* of New York Federal Reserve Board, 4, no. 2.

Humphries, Jane. 1998. "Towards a Family-friendly Economics." *New Political Economy* 3, no. 2 July 223–240.

Huntington, Samuel. 1999. "The Lonely Superpower." *Foreign Affairs*, March/April.

Hurrell, Andrew and Ngaire Woods. 1995. "Globalization and Inequality, *Millennium: Journal of International Studies*, Winter.

Hutton, Will. 1996. "Relaunching Western Economies: The Case for Regulated Financial Markets." *Foreign Affairs*, November/December.

Hymer, Stephen H. 1970. "The Efficiency. Contradictions. of Multinational Corporations." *American Economics Association, Papers and Proceedings*, May.

Ikenberry, G. John. 1992. "A world Economy Restored: Expert Consensus and the Anglo-American Postwar Settlement." *International Organization*, Winter.

Ikenberry, G. John. 1993. "The Political Origins of Bretton Woods." In Michael D. Bordo and Barry Eichengreen eds., *A Retrospective on the Bretton Woods System: Lessons for International Monetary Reform*. Chicago: University of Chicago Press.

Ikenberry, G. John. 1996. "The Myth of Post-Cold War Chaos." *Foreign Affairs* May/June.

Interim Committee of the International Monetary Fund. 1997. *Statement on Liberalization of Capital Movements*. Washington, D.C., April.

Independent Evaluation Office of the IMF. 2002. *Evaluation of the Prolonged Use of Fund Resources*, September 25. http://www.IMF.org/ieo

International Contract Adviser. 1996. "GATT and the Resolution of International Trade Disputes." *Law Journal Extra!* http://www.jextra.com/practice/internat/GATTdisp.html.

International Financial Institutions Advisory Commission. 2000. *Report*. Washington, D.C.: Congress of the United States.

International Labor Organization. 1995. *World Employment Report*. Geneva: ILO.

International Monetary Fund. 1998. *World Economic Outlook and International Capital Markets: Interim Assessment*. Washington: International Monetary Fund.

International Monetary Fund. 1999. *International Capital Markets: Developments, Prospects, and Key Policy Issues*. Washington: International Monetary Fund.

Irwin, Douglas A. 1995. "The GATT in Historical Perspective." *American Economic Review*, May.

Irwin, Douglas A. 1999. "How Clinton Botched the Seattle Summit." December 6.

Islam, Iyanatul and Anis Chowdhury. 1997. *Asia-Pacific Economies: A Survey*. London: Routledge.

Israel, Jonathan. 1995. *The Dutch Republic: Its Rise, Greatness and Fall, 1477–1806*. Oxford: Oxford University Press.

Iversen, Torben. 1998. "The Choices for Scandinavian Social Democracy in Comparative Perspective." *Oxford Review of Economic Policy*, Spring.

Jackson John H. 1997. *The World Trading System: Law and Policy of International Economic Relations*. Cambridge, Mass.: MIT Press. Second Edition.

Jackson, John H. 1998a. "Designing and Implementing Effective Dispute Settlement Procedures: WTO Dispute Settlement, Appraisal and Prospects." In Anne O. Krueger ed., With the assistance of Chonira Aturapane. *The WTO as an International Organization*. Chicago: University of Chicago Press.

Jackson, John H. 1998b. *The World Trade Organization: Constitution and Jurisprudence*. London: Pinter for Royal Institute of International Affairs.

James, Harold. 1998. "From Grandmotherliness to Governance: The Evolution of IMF Conditionality." *Finance & Development*, December.

Jáquez, Antonio. 2001. "Following the Money Trail—to Citibank." *Process*, March 25. In translation *World Press Review*, June.

Jayasuriya, Kanishka. 1998. "Globalization, Authoritarian Liberalism and the Development State." Paper presented International Workshop on Globalization and Social Welfare in East Asia, Research Center on Development and International Relations, Aalborg Denmark, March 12–13.

Jha, Raghbendra and Mridul K. Saggar. 2000. "Toward a More Rational IMF Quota Structure: Suggestions for the Creation of a New Financial Architecture." *The World Economy*, June.

Johnson, Chalmers. 1984. "Political Institutions and Economic Performance: The Government-Business Relationship in Japan, South Korea, and Taiwan." In Frederic C. Deyo ed., *The Political Economy of the New Asian Industrialism.* Ithaca: Cornell University Press., pp. 136–64.

Johnson, Chalmers. 1998a. Cold War Economics Melts Asia; Events Reinforced the Need for an Asia Model, Not Repudiated It." *The Nation*, February 23.

Johnson, Chalmers. 1998b. "Economic Crisis in East Asia: The Clash of Capitalisms." *Cambridge Journal of Economics*, November.

Jones, C . 1987. *International Business in the Nineteenth Century: The Rise and Fall of a Cosmopolitan Bourgeoisie.* New York: New York University Press.

Kaiser, David. 1990. *Politics and War, European Conflict From Philip II to Hitler.* Cambridge: Harvard University Press.

Kahler, Miles. 1992. "External Influence, Conditionality, and the Politics of Adjustment." In Stephan Haggard and Robert R. Kaufman eds., *The Politics of Economic Adjustment.* Princeton: Princeton University Press.

Kahler, Miles. 1999. "The New Financial Architecture and Its Limits." In G. Noble and John Ravenhill eds., *The Asian Financial Crisis and the Architecture of Global Finance.* New York: Cambridge University Press.

Kaldor, Nicholas. 1934. "The Equilibrium of the Firm." *Economic Journal*, 44.

Kambhu, John, Frank Keane, and Catherine Benadon. 1996. "Price Risk Intermediation in the Over-the-Counter Derivatives Markets: Interpretation of a Global Survey." *Federal Reserve Bank of New York Economic Policy Review*, April.

Kaminsky, Graciela L. and Carmen M. Reinhard. 1998. "Financial Crises in Asia and Latin America: Then and Now." *American Economic Review*, May.

Kaminsky, Graciela L. and Carmen M. Reinhard. 1999. "The Twin Crises: The Causes of Banking and Balance-of-Payments Problems." *American Economic Review*, June.

Kantor, Rosabeth Moss. 1995. *World Class: Thriving Locally in the Global Economy.* New York: Simon and Schuster.

Kapstein, Ethan B. 1994. *Governing the Global Economy: International Finance and the State.* Cambridge: Harvard University Press.

Kapur, Devesh. 1998. "The IMF: A Cure or a Curse" *Foreign Policy*, Summer.

Kapur, Devesh, John P. Lewis and Richard Webb. 1997. *The World Bank: Its First Half Century.* Washington, D.C. Brookings Institution. Volume I History.

Kardam, Nuket. 1993. "Development Approaches and the Role of Policy Advocacy: The Case of the World Bank." *World Development*,

Katzenstein, Peter J. 1978. "Introduction: Domestic and International Forces and Strategies of Foreign Economic Policy." In Peter J. Katzenstein ed., *Between Power and Plenty: Foreign Economic Policies of Advanced Industrial States.* Madison: University of Wisconsin Press.

Katzenstein, Peter J., Robert O. Keohane, and Stephen D. Krasner. 1998. "Preface: *International Organization* at Its Golden Anniversary." *International Organization*, Autumn.

Kaufman, Henry. 1985. "Reshaping the Financial System." *New York Times*, July 14.

Kaufman, Henry. 1999. "Too Much on Their Plate." *Financial Times*, February 4.

Kaufman, Robert. 1990. "How Societies Change Development Models or Keep Them: Reflections on the Latin American Experience in the 1930s and the Postwar World." In Gary Gereffi and Donald L. Wyman eds., *Manufacturing Miracles: Paths of Industrialization in Latin America and East Asia*. Princeton: Princeton University Press.

Kaufmann, Daniel. 2003. "Rethinking Governance: Empirical Lessons Challenge Orthodoxy. Washington: World Bank, discussion draft March 11.

Kaul, Inge, Isabelle Grunberg, and Marc A. Stern. 1999. "Defining Public Goods." In Inge Kaul, Isabelle Grunberg, and Marc A. Stern eds., *Global Public Goods: International Cooperation in the 21st Century*. New York: Oxford University Press.

Kearney, A. T. 2001. "Globalization Index." *Foreign Policy*, January/February.

Kelman, Mark. 1987. *A Guide to Critical Legal Studies*. Cambridge: Harvard University Press.

Kenny, Sara York and Robert K. Larson. 1995. "The Development of International Accounting Standards: An Analysis of Constituent Participation in Standard Setting." *Journal of International Accounting*.

Keohane, Robert. 1984. *After Hegemony: Cooperation and Discord in the World Political Economy*. Princeton: Princeton University Press.

Keohane, Robert O. 1989. "International Institutions: Two Approaches." In Robert O. Keohane ed., *International Institutions and State Power: Essays in International Relations Theory* . Boulder: Westview.

Keohane, Robert O. 1997a. "International Relations and International Law: Two Optics." *Harvard International Law Journal*, Spring.

Keohane Robert O. 1998b. "Problematic Lucidity: Stephen Krasner's 'State Power and the Structure of International Trade'. " *World Politics*, October.

Keohane, Robert O. 1998a. "International Institutions: Can Interdependence Work?" *Foreign Policy*, Spring.

Keohane, Robert O. 2000. "Governance in a Partially Globalized World." Address to the American Political Science Association Convention, Washington, D.C., August.

Keohane, Robert O. and Joseph S. Nye. 1977. *Power and Interdependence: World Politics in Transition*. Boston: Little, Brown.

Keynes, John Maynard. 1920. *The Economic Consequences of the Peace. The Collected Writings of John Maynard Keynes*, Volume 2. London: Macmillan.

Keynes, John Maynard. 1931. "Consequences to the Banks of the Collapse of Monetary Values." *The Collected Writings of John Maynard Keynes*, Volume 21. London: Macmillan.

Keynes, John Maynard. 1936. *The General Theory of Employment, Interest, and Money*. New York: Harcourt, Brace. Reprinted in *The Collected Writings of John Maynard Keynes*, Volume 7. London: Macmillan.

Keynes, John Maynard. 1943. "Proposal for the International Clearing Union." In *The International Monetary Fund, 1945–68*, Volume III, Documents. Washington, D.C. International Monetary Fund, 1969.

Keynes, John Maynard. 1963. *Essays in Persuasion*. New York: W. W. Norton. Reprinted in *The Collected Writings of John Maynard Keynes*, Volume 9. London: Macmillan.

Khor, Martin. 1996. *The WTO and the Proposed Multilateral Investment Agreement: Implications for the Developing Countries and Proposed Positions*. Penang, Malaysia: Third World Network.

Killick, Tony. 1997. "Principals, Agents, and the Failings of Conditionality." *Journal of International Development*, 9, no. 4.

Kim, Eun Mee. 1997. *Big Business, Strong State: Collusion and Conflict in South Korean Development, 1960–1990*. Albany: State University of New York Press.

Kimerling, Judith. 1995. "Rights, Responsibilities, and Realities: Environmental Protection Law in Ecuador's Amazon Oil Field." *Southwestern Journal of Law and Trade in the Americas*, Fall.

Kindleberger, Charles. 1969. *American Business Abroad: Six Lectures on Direct Investment*. New Haven: Yale University Press.

Kindleberger, Charles P. 1989. *Manias, Panics, and Crashes: A History of Financial Crises*. New York: Basic Books.

Kindleberger, Charles P. 1993. *A Financial History of Western Europe*. New York: Oxford University Press.

Kinnear, Douglas. 1999. "The 'Compulsive Shift' to Institutional Concerns in Recent Labor Economics." *Journal of Economic Issues*, March.

Kiriyama, Nobuo. 1998. "Institutional Evolution in Economic Integration: A Contribution to Comparative Institutional Analysis for International Economic Organization." *University of Pennsylvania Journal of International Economic Law*, Spring.

Kirshner, Jonathan. 1995. *Currency and Coercion: The Political Economy of International Monetary Power*. Princeton: Princeton University Press.

Kirshner, Orin ed., 1996. *The Bretton Woods-GATT System: Retrospect and Prospect After Fifty Years*. Armonk, NY: M. E. Sharpe.

Klein, Philip A. 1998. "Rethinking American Participation in Economic Development: An Institutionalist Assessment." *Journal of Economic Issues*, June.

Koekman, Bernard M. and Petros C. Mavroidis. 2000. "WTO Dispute Settlement, Transparency and Surveillance, *The World Economy*, April.

Kotz, David M. 1994. "The Regulatory Theory of the Social Structure of Accumulation Approach." In David M. Kotz, Terrence McDonough and Michael Reich eds., *Social Structures of Accumulation*. New York: Cambridge University Press.

Kowalewski, David. 1989. "Asian State Repression and Strikes Against Transnationals." In George A. Lopez and Michael Stohl eds *Dependence, Development and State Repression* Contributions in Political Science No. 209. New York: Greenwood Press.

Kozyrev, Andrei. 1995. "Address." *Copenhagen 1995 The Annual Meeting of the Trilateral Commission*. New York: Trilateral Commission.

Krasner, Stephen D. 1976. "State Power and the structure of International Trade." *World Politics* 28, no. 3

Krasner, Stephen D. 1985. *Structural Conflict: The Third World Against Global Liberalism*. Berkeley: University of California Press.

Krasner, Stephen D. 1988. "Sovereignty: An Institutional Perspective." *Comparative Political Studies*, April.

Krasner, Stephen D. 1993. "Westphalia and All That." In Judith Goldstein and Robert Keohane eds., *Ideas and Foreign Policy: Beliefs, Institutions, and Political Change*. Ithaca: Cornell University Press.

Krasner, Stephen D. 1994. "International Political Economy: Abiding Discord." *Review of International Political Economy*, Summer

Krasner, Stephen D. 1999. *Sovereignty: Organized Hypocrisy*. Princeton: Princeton University Press.

Kratochwil, Fredrich. 2000. "Constructing a New Orthodoxy? Wendt's 'Social Theory of International Politics' and the Constructivist Challenge." *Millennium: Journal of International Studies*, 29, no. 1.

Krishnan, Raghu. 1996. "December 1995: 'The First Revolt Against Globalization'." *Monthly Review*, May.

Kristof, Nicholas D. 1998. "Experts Question Pouring Flow of Global Capital, *New York Times*, September 20.

Krueger Anne O. 1990. "Free Trade is the Best Policy." In Robert Z. Lawrence and Charles L. Schultze eds., *An American Trade Strategy: Options for the 1990s*. Washington, D.C.: Brookings Institution.

Krueger Anne O. 1993. *Economic Policy at Cross-Purposes: The United States and the Developing Countries*. Washington, D.C. Brookings Institution.

Krueger Anne O. 1998. "Whither the World Bank and the IMF? *Journal of Economic Literature*, December.

Krueger Anne O. 1999. "Are Preferential Trading Arrangements Trade-Liberalizing or Protectionist?" *Journal of Economic Perspectives*, Fall.

Krugman, Paul R. 1993. "New Thinking About Trade Policy." Paul R. Krugman ed., *Strategic Trade Policy and the New International Economics*. Cambridge: MIT Press.

Krugman, Paul R. 1995a. "Dutch Tulips and Emerging Markets." *Foreign Affairs*, July/August.

Krugman, Paul. 1995b. "Growing World Trade: Causes and Consequences." *Brookings Papers on Economic Activity*, 1.

Kunz, Diane B. 1997. "The Marshall Plan Reconsidered.," *Foreign Affairs*, May/June.

Kydd, Jonathan, Janet Haddock, John Mansfield, Charles Ainsworth, and Allan Buckwell. 2000. "Genetically Modified Organisms: Major Issues and Policy Responses for Developing Countries." *Journal of International Development*, November.

Lambert, Rob and Donella Caspersz. 1995. "International Labour Standards: Challenging Global Ideology?" *Pacific Review* 8, no. 4

Landler, Mark. 1998. "Goodbye World!" *New York Times*, September 11.

Lang, Jeffrey. 1998. "The International Regulation of Foreign Direct Investment: Obstacles and Evolution." *Cornell International Law Journal*, 31:455.

Lash, William H., III. 1996. "The Decline of the Nation State in International Trade and Investment." *Cardozo Law Review*, December.

Lawson, Tony. 1995. "A Realist Perspective on Contemporary 'Economic Theory'. " *Journal of Economic Issues*, March.

Lazonick, William and Mary O'Sullivan. 2000. "Maximizing Shareholder Value: A New Ideology for Corporate Governance." *Economy and Society*, February.

Leamer, Edward E. 1984. *Sources of International Comparative Advantage*. Cambridge: MIT Press.

Lebowitz, Michael. 1988. "Trade and Class: Labour Strategies in a World of Strong Capital." *Studies in Political Economy* 27.

Lee, Lawrence C. 1998. "The Basle Accords as Soft Law: Strengthening Banking Supervision." *Virginia Journal of International Law*, Fall.

Levinson, Jerome I. 1999. "The International Financial System: A Flawed Architecture." *Fletcher Forum of World Affairs Journal*, Winter/Spring.

Levy, David L and Daniel Egan. 1998. "Capital Contests: National and Transnational Channels of Corporate Influence on the Climate Change Negotiations." *Politics and Society*, September.

Levy, David L. and Daniel Egan. 2000. "Corporate Political Action in the Global Polity: National and Transnational Strategies in the Climate Change Negotiations." In Richard Higgott, Geoffrey Underhill, and Andreas Beiler eds., *Globalisation and Non-state Actors*. London: Routledge.

Lewis, Paul. 1997. "Euro to Igniter Boom, Analysts Say." *New York Times*, December 27.

Lewis, Paul. 1998. "World Bank Worried by Pressure for Quick-Fix Fiscal Action." *New York Times*, October 5.

Lim, Linda Y. C. 1998. "Whose 'Model' Failed? Implications of the Asian Economic Crisis." *Washington Quarterly* 21, no 3 (Summer): 25–36.

Lindgren, Carl-Johan, Gillian Garcia, and Mathew I. Saal. 1996. *Bank Soundness and Macroeconomic Policy*. Washington, D.C. International Monetary Fund.

Lipietz, Alain. 1987. "Question of Method." *Mirages and Miracles: The Crisis of Global Fordism*. London: Verso.

Lipson, Charles. 1985. *Standing Guard: Protecting Foreign Capital in the Nineteenth and Twentieth Centuries*. Berkeley: University of California Press.

Little, Adrian. 2000. "Environmental and Eco-social Rationality: Challenges for Political Economy in Late Modernity." *New Political Economy*, 5, no. 1.

Loasby, Brian. 1976. *Choice, Complexity and Ignorance: An Enquiry into Economic Theory and Practice of Decision Making*. Cambridge: Cambridge University Press.

Loriaux, Michael. 1992. *France After Hegemony: International Change and Financial Reform*. Ithaca: Cornell University Press.

Loriaux, Michael. 1997. "The End of Credit Activism in Interventionist States." In Michael Loriaux, Meredith Woo-Cummings, Kent E. Calder, Sylvia Maxfield, and Sofia A. Perez *Capital Ungoverned: Liberalizing Finance in Interventionist States*. Ithaca: Cornell University Press.

Loriaux, Michael. 1997. "Capital, the State and Uneven Growth in the International Political Economy." In Michael Loriaux, Meredith Woo-Cummings, Kent E. Calder, Sylvia Maxfield and Sofia A. Perez *Capital Ungoverned: Liberalizing Finance in Interventionist States*. Ithaca: Cornell University Press.

Love, James Packard. 1997. "A Consumer Perspective On Proposals As They Relate To Rules Regarding Intellectual Property." Comments for the Working Group on Intellectual Property Rights, Third Ministerial and American Business Forum, Belo Horizonte, Brazil, May 13–16. http://www.cptech.org.

Lowi, Theodore J. 2001. "Our Millennium: Political Science Confronts the Global Corporate Economy." *International Political Science Review*, April.

Lukausakas, Arvid. 1999. "Managing Mobile Capital: Recent Scholarship on the Political Economy of International Finance." *Review of International Political Economy*, Summer.

Machlup, Fritz. 1967. "Theories of the Firm: Marginalist, Behavioral, Managerial." *American Economic Review*, March.

MacIntyre, Andrew. 1998. "The Political Economy of the Asian Economic Crisis." *Review of International Political Economy*, Autumn.

McKinnon, Ronald. 1993. "International Money in Historical Perspective." *Journal of Economic Literature*, March.

McMichael, Philip "The New Colonialism: Global Regulation and Restructuring of the Interstate System." In David A Smith and Jozsef Borocz eds., *A New Global Order? Global Transformations in the Late Twentieth Century*. Westport, Ct.: Greenwood Press.

McNulty, Paul J. 1984. "On the Nature and Theory of Economic Organization: The Role of the Firm Reconsidered.," *History of Political Economy*, Summer.

Magoffin, Ralph van Deman translator and James Brown Scott editor. 1916. *Hugo Grotius, The Freedom of the Seas*. Oxford: Oxford University Press.

Magnusson, Paul. 2003. "Bush's Free-Trade Diplomacy Has Corporate America Steaming." *Business Week*, July 7.

Magnusson, Paul with Stephen Baker. 1998. "The Explosive Trade Deal You've Never Heard Of." *Business Week*, February 9.

Manchester Philip. 1999. "An essential ingredient of success." *Financial Times*, April 28.

Mander, Jerry. 1996. "The Dark Side of Globalization; What the Media Are Missing." *The Nation*, July 15-22.

Maniruzzaman, Abul F. M. 1999. "The Lex Mercatoria and International Contracts: A Challenge for International Commercial Arbitration?" *American University International Law Review*, 14: 657.

Mankiw N. Gregory. 1992. "Commentary." In Federal Reserve Bank of Kansas

City, Long-Run Economic Growth: A Symposium Sponsored by the Federal Reserve Bank, August 27–29, 1992.

Mankiw N. Gregory. 1995. "The Growth of Nations." *Brookings Papers on Economic Activity*, 1.

Mann, Charles C. 1998. "Who Will Own Your Next Good Idea?" *The Atlantic*, September.

Mann, Michael. 1997. "Has Globalization Ended the Rise and Rise of the Nation-State?" *Review of International Political Economy*, Autumn.

March, James G. and Johan P. Olsen. 1984. "The New Institutionalism: Organizational Factors in Political Life." *American Political Science Review*, September.

March James G. and Johan P. Olsen. 1998. "The Institutional Dynamics of International Political Orders." *International Organization*, Autumn.

Marden, Emily. 1999. "The Neem Tree Patent: International Conflict Over the Commodification of Life." *Boston College Environmental Affairs Law Review*, Spring.

Marichal, Carlos. 1989. *A Century of Debt Crises in Latin America: From Independence to the Great Depression, 1820-1930*. Princeton: Princeton University Press.

Markels, Alex. 2003. "Showdown for a Tool In Rights Lawsuits." *New York Times*, June 15.

Markusen, James R. 1984. "Multinationals, Multiplant Economies, and the Gains From Trade." *Journal of International Economics*, .

Marshall, Alfred., 1923. *Industry and Trade: A Study of Industrial Technique and Business Organization; and of Their Influences on the Conditions of Various Classes and Nations*, 4th Edition. New York: Augustus M. Kelley, 1970.

Marshall, Ray. 1994. "Internationalization: Implications for Workers." *Journal of International Affairs*, Summer.

Marshall, T. H. 1950. *Citizenship and Social Class*. Cambridge: Cambridge University Press.

Martin, Lisa L. 1992. "Interests, Power, and Multilateralism." *International Organization*, Autumn.

Martin, Lisa L. 1999. "An Institutionalist View: International Institutions and State Strategies." In T. V. Paul and John A . Hall eds., *International Order and the Future of World Politics*. Cambridge: Cambridge University Press.

Martin, Lisa L. and Beth A. Simmons. 1998. "Theories and Empirical Studies of International Institutions." *International Organization*, Autumn.

Martinson, Jane. 1999. "Index of Multinationals May Be Launched This Year." *Financial Times*, February.

Marx, Karl. 1894. *Capital: A Critique of Political Economy*, Volume 3 edited by F. Engels. Moscow: Progress Publishers, 1971.

Mason, John. 2001. "Future of World's Seedbank in Doubt." *Financial Times*, June 22.

Mathiason, Nick. 2003. "Poor Rattle Doors of WTO Club." *The Observer*, September 14. Internet edition.

Mattei, Ugo. 2003. ""A Theory of Imperial Law: A Study of U.S. Hegemony and the Latin Resistence, *Indiana Journal of Global Legal Studies*, Volume 10.

Matthews, Jessica T. 1997. "Power Shift." *Foreign Affairs*, January/February.

Maxfield, Sylvia. 1990. *Governing Capital: International Finance and Mexican Politics* . Ithaca: Cornell University Press.

Meade, James. 1955. *Trade and Welfare*. London: Oxford University Press.

Meinshausen, Malte and Bill Hare. 2000. "Temporary Sinks Do Not Cause Permanent Climate Benefits." September. Available at http://www.carbon-sinks.de.

Meinshausen, Malte and Bill Hare. 2001. *Cheating the Kyoto Protocol: Loopholes Undermine Environmental Effectiveness*, Greenpeace International, July.

Meltzer, Allan H. 1998. "Asian Problems and the IMF." *Cato Journal*, Winter.

Mercuro, Nicholas and Steven G. Medema. 1997. *Economics and the Law: From Posner to Postmodernism*. Princeton: Princeton University Press.

Messing, Joel W. 1997. "Toward a Multilateral Agreement on Investment." *Transnational Corporations*, April.

Meyerson, Roger B. 1999. "Nash Equilibrium and the History of Economic Theory." *Jounral of Economic Literature*, September.

Mickelson, Karin. 1998. "Rhetoric and Rage: Third World Voices in International Legal Discourse." *Wisconsin International Law Journal*, Summer.

Miller, James N. 2000. "Origins of the GATT—British Resistance to American Multilateralism." Jerome Levy Economics Institute at Bard College, Working Paper No. 318.

Miller, Marcus and Lei Zhang. 1999. "Creditor Panic, Asset Bubbles and Sharks: Three Views of the Asian Crisis." University of Warwick, March.

Miller, Victoria. 1998. "The Double Drain with a Cross-Border Twist: More on the Relationship Between Banking and Currency Crises." *American Economics Review*, May.

Milner, Helen V. 1998. "Rationalizing Politics: The Emerging Synthesis of International, American, and Comparative Politics." *International Organization*, Autumn.

Milner, Helen V. and David B. Yoffie. 1989. "Between Free Trade and Protectionism: Strategic Trade Policy and a Theory of Corporate Trade Demands." *International Organization*, Spring.

Milward, Alan. 1984. *The Reconstruction of Western Europe 1945-1951*. London: Methuen.

Milward, Alan. 1992. *The European Rescue of the Nation State*. London: Routledge.

Minford, Patrick. 1995. "The Lessons of European Monetary and Exchange Rate Experience." In Sebastian Edwards ed., *Capital Controls, Exchange Rates, and Monetary Policy in the World Economy*. Cambridge: Cambridge University Press.

Minsky, Hyman. 1977. "A Theory of Systematic Fragility." Edward I. Altman and

Arnold W. Sametz eds., *Financial Crises: Institutions and Markets in a Fragile Environment*. New York: John Wiley.

Minsky, Hyman P. 1986. "The Emergence of Financial Instability in the Postwar Era." *Stabilizing an Unstable Economy*. New Haven: Yale University Press.

Minsky, Hyman P. 1996. "Uncertainty and the Institutional Structure of Capitalist Economies." *Journal of Economic Issues*, June.

Minton-Beddoes, Zanny. 1995. "Why the IMF Needs Reform." *Foreign Affairs*, May–June.

Minton-Beddoes, Zanny. 1999. "Global Finance." Survey *The Economist* January 30.

Mishkin, Frederic S. 1997. "Understanding Financial Crises: A Developing Country Perspective." Michael Bruno and Boris Pleskovic eds., *Annual World Bank Conference on Development and Economics, 1996*. Washington, D.C.: International Bank for Reconstruction and Development.

Mishkin, Frederic S. 1999. "Global Financial Instability: Framework, Events, Issues." *Journal of Economic Perspectives*, Fall.

Mitchell, Ronald B. 1994. "Regime Design Matters: International Oil Pollution and Treaty Compliance." *International Organization*, Summer.

Mitchell, Ronald B. 1998. "Sources of Transparency: Information Systems in International Regimes." *International Studies Quarterly*, March.

Modigliani, Franco and Merton H. Miller. 1958. "The Cost of Capital, Corporate Finance and the Theory of Investment." *American Economic Review*, June.

Montiel, Peter J. and Carmen M. Reinhart. 1998. "The Dynamics of Capital Movements to Emerging Economies During the 1990s." In S. Griffith-Jones and M. Montes eds., *Short-term Capital Movements and Balance of Payments Crises*. New York: Oxford University Press.

Moravcsik, Andrew. 19997. "Taking Preferences Seriously: A Liberal Theory of International Politics" *International Organization*, Autumn.

Morris, David and Gerald Ward. 1999. *One Global Corporate Reporting Standard: Nightmare? Dream? Or Reality?*. New York: PriceWaterhouseCoopers., May.

Morrison, Charles E. 2000. "East Asia and the International System." *Trilateral Commission 2000 Meetings*.

Morrison Charles E., coordinator. 2001. *Report of a Special Study Group, East Asia and the International System*. New York: The Trilateral Commission. Triangle Paper 55, April.

Mundell, Robert A. 1963. "Capital Mobility and Stabilization Policy Under Fixed and Flexible Exchange Rates." *Canadian Journal of Economics and Political Science*, November.

Murphy, Craig N. 1994. *International Organization and Industrial Change: Global Governance since 1850*. New York: Oxford University Press.

Murphy, Craig N. and Roger Tooze. 1991. "Getting Beyond the 'Common Sense' of the International Political Economy Orthodoxy." In Craig N. Murphy and Roger Tooze eds., *The New International Political Economy*. Boulder: Lynne Rienner.

Murphy, James Bernard. 1996. "Rational Choice Theory as Social Physics." In Jeffrey Friedman, ed., *The Rational Choice Controversy*. New Haven: Yale University Press.

Myers, Charles T. 1999. "The Development of International Accounting Standards: The Public/Private Nexus." Paper presented at the American Political Science Meetings September 2.

Myers, Steven Lee. 1999. "South Africa And U.S. End Dispute Over Drugs." *New York Times*, September 18.

Myerson, Roger B. 1999. "Nash Equilibrium and the History of Economic Theory." *Journal of Economic Literature*, September.

Nakamae, Naoko. 1999. "CS 'Offered Tokyo Sowa Scheme To Hide Bad Debt'." *Financial Times*, June 12-13.

Naon, Horacio A. Grigera. 1996. "Sovereignty and Regionalism." *Law and Policy in International Business*, Summer.

Neuber, Alexander. 1995. "Adapting the Economies of Eastern Europe." In Tony Killick ed., *The Flexible Economy: Causes and Consequences of the Adaptability of National Economies*. London: Routledge.

Nicolaides, Phedon. 1994. "The Changing GATT System and the Uruguay Round Negotiations." In Richard Stubbs and Geoffrey R. D. Underhill eds., *Political Economy and the Changing Global Order*. Toronto: McClelland and Stewart.

Nordhaus, William D. 1994. *Managing the Global Commons*. Cambridge: MIT Press.

North, Douglass C. 1990. *Institutions, Institutional Change and Economic Performance*. New York: Cambridge University Press.

North, Douglass C. and Barry R. Weingast. 1989. "The Evolution of Institutions Governing Public Choice in 17th Century England." *Journal of Economic History*, November.

Notermans, Tom. 1993. "The Abdication from National Policy Autonomy: Why the Macroeconomic Policy Regime Has Been So Unfavorable to Labor." *Politics and Society*, June.

Notermans, Tom. 1997. "Social Democracy and External Constraints." In Kevin R. Cox ed., *Spaces of Globalization: Reasserting the Power of the Local*. New York: Guilford.

Nurkse, Ragnar. 1945. "Conditions of International Monetary Equilibrium." *Essays in International Finance*. Princeton: International Finance Section. reprinted in American Economics Association, *Readings in the Theory of International Trade*. Philadelphia: Blakeston Company, 1949, Volume 4.

Nussbaum, Bruce. 2003. "The High Price of Bad Diplomacy." *Business Week*, March 24.

Nye, Joseph P. 1990. "Soft Power." *Foreign Policy*, Fall.

Oatley, Thomas and Robert Nabors. 1998. "Redistributive Cooperation: Market Failure, Wealth Transfers, and the Basle Accords." *International Organization*, Winter.

Obstfeld, Maurice. 1995. "International Currency Experience: New Lessons and Lesson Relearned.," *Brookings Papers on Economic Activity*, 1.

Odell, John S. 1999. "The Negotiating Process and International Economic Organizations." Paper presented at the American Political Science Association September 2–5.

Odell, John and Barry Eichengreen. 1998. "The United States, the ITO, and the WTO: Exit Options, Agent Slack, and Presidential Leadership." In Anne O. Krueger ed., With the assistance of Chonira Aturapane. *The WTO as an International Organization*. Chicago: University of Chicago Press.

Ohmae, Kenichi. 1993. "The Rise of the Regional State." *Foreign Affairs*, Spring.

Olson, Elizabeth. 2002. "Nigeria to Recover $1 Billion From the Family of a Late Dictator." *New York Times*, April 18.

Orlando, Brett. 1998. "The Kyoto Protocol: A Framework for the Future." *SAIS Review*, Summer/Fall.

Overseas Development Council. 2000. *The Future Role of the IMF in Development: An ODC Task Force Report*, April.

Palast, Greg. 2001. "Inside Corporate America." *The Observer*. http://www.gregpalast.com accessed January 3, 2001.

Palley, Thomas I. 1999. "The Case for Labor Standards: Theory and Evidence." AFL-CIO Public Policy Department Economic Policy Paper EO36.

Palley, Thomas I. 2000. "Labor Standards and Governance as Public Institutional Capital: Cross- Country Evidence from the 1980s and 1990s." AFL-CIO Public Policy Department Technical Working Paper T030.

Panitch, Leo. 2000. "The New Imperial State." *New Left Review*, March/April.

Parkinson, Fred., 1977. *The Philosophy of International Relations: A Study in the History of Thought*. Beverly Hills: Sage.

Pasinetti, Luigi L. 1983. Comment on Axel Leijonhufvud, "What Would Keynes Have Thought of Rational Expectations?" In David Worswick and James Trevithick eds., *Keynes and the Modern World*. Cambridge: Cambridge University Press.

Patterson, Matthew. 1999. "Globalization, Ecology and Resistance." *New Political Economy*, 4, no. 1.

Paul, Joel R. 1995. "Interdisciplinary Approaches to International Economic Law: The New Movements in International Economic Law." *American University Journal of International Law and Policy*, Winter.

Pauly, Louis. 1994. "Promoting a Global Economy: The Normative Role of the International Monetary Fund." In Richard Stubbs and Geoffrey R. D. Underhill eds., *Political Economy and the Changing Global Order*. Toronto: McClelland and Stewart.

Pauly, Louis. 1995. "Capital Mobility, State Autonomy and Political Legitimacy." *Journal of International Affairs*, Winter.

Pauly Louis W. and Simon Reich. 1997. "National Structures and Multinational Corporate Behaviour: Enduring Differences in the Age of Globalization." *International Organization*, Winter.

Payne, Rodger A. 2001. "Persuasion, Frames and Norm Construction." *European Journal of International Relations*, March.

Peck, Joe and Eric S. Rosengren. 19997. "The International Transmission of Financial Shocks: The Case of Japan." *American Economic Review*, September.

Picciotto, Sol. 1996–7. "Restructuring Global Governance." *Journal of International Law and Business*, Winter/Spring.

Picciotto, Sol. 1998. "Linkages in International Investment Regulation: The Antinomies of the Draft Multilateral Agreement on Investment." *Journal of International Economic Law*, Fall.

Pieper, Ute and Lance Taylor. 1997. "The Revival of the Liberal Creed: The IMF, the World Bank, and Inequality in a Globalized Economy." *Working Paper Series: Globalization, Labor Markets, and Social Policy*, Center for Economic Policy Analysis, New School for Social Research, June.

Piore, Michael J. and Charles F. Sabel. 1984. *The Second Industrial Divide: Possibilities and Prosperity.* New York: Basic Books.

Plender, John. 1999. "Crisis in the Making." *Financial Times*, April 12.

Polak, Jacques J. 1997. "The IMF Model: A Hardy Perennial." *Finance and Development*, December.

Polanyi, Karl. 1944. *The Great Transformation: The Political and Economic Origins of Our Time.* Boston: Beacon Press, 1957.

Pollin, Robert. 1998. "Can Domestic Expansionary Policy Succeed in a Globally Integrated Environment? An Examination of Alternatives." In Dean Baker, Gerald Epstein and Robert Pollin eds., *Globalization and Progressive Economic Policy.* New York: Cambridge University Press.

Porter, Michael E. and Claas van der Linde. 1995. "Toward a New Conception of the Environment-Competitiveness Relationship." *Journal of Economic Perspectives*, Fall.

Porter, Tony. 1999. "Representation, Legitimacy and the Changing Regime for World Financial Regulation." Paper to American Political Science Association, September 2–5.

Porter, Tony. 2003. "Technical Collaboration and Political Conflict in the Emerging Regime for International Financial Regulation." *Review of International Political Economy* (August).

Portes, Richard. 2003. "Resolution of Sovereign Debt Crises: The New Old Framework." London Business School, EHESS and CEPR, May.

Posner, Richard A. 1998. "Creating a Legal Framework for Economic Development." *World Bank Research Observer*, February.

Prasad, Eswar, Kenneth Rogoff, Shang-Jiin Wei and M. Ayhan Kose. 2003. "Effects of Financial Globalization on Developing Countries: Some Empirical Evidence." International Monetary Fund, March 17.

Presley, Mari. 1998. "Sovereignty and Delegation Issues Regarding U.S. Commitment to the World Trade Organization's Dispute Settlement Process." *Journal of Transnational Law & Policy*, Fall.

Pressman, Steven and Gale Summerfield. 2000. "The Economic Contribution of Amartya Sen." *Review of Political Economy*, 12, no. 1.

Pryor, Frederic L. 2000. "The Millennium Survey: How Economists View the U.S. Economy in the 21st Century." *American Journal of Economics and Sociology*, January.

Putnam, Robert. 1988. "Diplomacy and Domestic Politics: The Logic of Two Level Games." *International Organization*, Summer.

Putterman, Louis. 1986. "The Economic Nature of the Firm: Overview" Louis Putterman ed., *The Economic Nature of the Firm: A Reader*. New York: Cambridge University Press.

Radelet, Stephen and Jeffrey D. Sachs. 1998. "The East Asian Financial Crisis: Diagnosis, Remedies, Prospects." *Brookings Papers on Economic Activity*, 1.

Radin, Margaret J. 1989. "Justice and the Market Domain." John W. Chapman and J. Roland Pennock eds., *Markets and Justice, Nomos 31*

Rasiah, Rajah. 1997. "Toward a Multilateral Framework on Investment." *Transnational Corporations*, April.

Ranney, David C. 1993. "NAFTA and the New Transnational Corporate Agenda." *Review of Radical Political Economics*, Winter.

Rao, J. Mohan. 1999. "Equity in a Global Public Goods Framework." In Inge Kaul, Isabelle Grunberg, and Marc A. Stern eds., *Global Public Goods: International Cooperation in the 21st Century*. New York: Oxford University Press.

Rasiah, Rajah. 1998. "Busting the Bubble: Causes of the Southeast Asian Financial Crisis." Paper presented at the conference "Implications of the East and Southeast Asian Financial Crisis for the World Economy." Brussels: European Institute of Asian Studies and Friedrich-Ebert Stiftung, January 20.

Raghavan, Chakravarthi. 1990. *Recolonization: GATT and the Uruguay Round and the Third World*. Panang, Malaysia: Third World Network.

Reich, Arie. 1997. "From Diplomacy to Law: The Jurisdicization of International Trade Relations." *Journal of International Law & Business*, Spring.

Reich, Robert B. 1990. "Who is Us?" *Harvard Business Review*, January/February.

Revkin, Andrew C. 2000. "U.S. Moves Improves Chance For Global Warming Treaty." *New York Times*, November 20.

Reynolds, Alan. 1998. "The IMF's Destructive Recipe: Rising Tax Rates and Falling Currencies." In Kevin Dowd and Richard Timberlake, Jr. eds., *Money and the National State: The Financial Revolution, Government and the World Monetary System*. New Brunswick, N. J.: Transaction Publishers.

Rich, Bruce. 1994. *Mortgaging the Earth: The World Bank, Environmental Impoverishment and the Crisis of Development*. Boston: Beacon Press.

Richardson, J. David. 1995. "Income Inequality and Trade: How to Think and What to Conclude." *Journal of Economic Perspectives*, Summer.

Rittberger, Volker ed., 1993. *Regime Theory in International Relations*. Oxford: Clarendon Press.

Roach, Stephen. 1997. "Angst in the Global Village." *Challenge*, September–October.

Robinson, Joan. 1977. "What Are the Questions?" *Journal of Economic Literature*, December.

Robinson, Joan. 1978. *Aspects of Development and Underdevelopment*. Cambridge: Cambridge University Press.

Robinson, William I. 1996. *Promoting Polyarchy: Globalization, US Intervention, and Hegemony*. New York: Cambridge University Press.

Rodgers, Gerry ed., 1994. *Workers, Institutions and Economic Growth in Asia*. Geneva: International Labor Organization.

Rodriquez, Francisco. 2000. "Inequality, Economic Growth and Economic Performance." A Background Note for the World Development Report 2000, Department of Economics, University of Maryland, College Park.

Rodrik, Dani. 1994. "King Kong Meets Godzilla: The World Bank and the East Asian Miracle." In Albert Fishlow, Catherine Gwin, Stephan Haggard, Dani Rodrik, and Robert Wade eds., *Miracle or Design? Lessons from the East Asian Experience*, Policy Essay Number 11. Washington, D.C.: Overseas Development Council., pp. 13-54.

Rodrik, Dani. 1997a. *Has Globalization Gone Too Far?* Washington, D.C.: Institute for International Economics.

Rodrik, Dani. 1997b. "The 'Paradoxes' of the Successful State." *European Economic Review*, April.

Rodrik, Dani. 1998a. "Globalisation, Social Conflict and Economic Growth."

Rodrik, Dani. 1998b. "Understanding Economic Policy Reform." *Journal of Economic Literature*, March.

Rodrik, Dani. 1998c. "Who Needs Capital Account Convertibility?" *Should the IMF Pursue Capital- Account Convertibility?* Essays in International Finance, Number 207, International Finance Section, Department of Economics, Princeton University, May.

Rodrik, Dani. 1999a. "Democracies Pay Higher Wages." *Quarterly Journal of Economics*, August.

Rodrik, Dani. 1999b. "Governing the Global Economy: Does One Architectural Style Fit All?" Paper prepared for the Brookings Institution Trade Policy Forum conference, April 15-16.

Rodrik, Dani. 1999c. "Whose Trade?" *The Nation*, December 6.

Rodrik, Dani. 2000. "Developing Strategies for the Next Century." Paper presented to conference, Institute for Developing Economies, Chiba, Japan, February.

Rodrik, Dani. 2001. "Trading in Illusions." *Foreign Policy*, March–April.

Rodrik, Dani. 2002. "After Neoliberalism, What?" Paper presented to the Alternatives to Neoliberalism Conference sponsored by the New Rules for Global Finance Coalition, May 23–34.

Rogoff, Kenneth. 1999. "International Institutions for Reducing Global Financial Instability." *Journal of Economic Perspectives*, Fall.

Rosen, R. Eliot. 1987. "Treasury Blunders in Paradise." *New York Times*, October 4.

Rosenau, James N. 1992. "Citizenship in a Changing Global Order." In James N.

Rosenau and Ernst-Otto Czempiel eds., *Governance Without Government: Order and Change in World Politics*. Cambridge: Cambridge University Press.

Rosenau, James N. 1997. *Along the Domestic-Foreign Frontier: Exploring Governance in a Turbulent World*. Cambridge: Cambridge University Press.

Rosenberg, Emily S. 2000. *Financial Missionaries to the World: The Politics and Culture of Dollar Diplomacy 1900–1930*. Cambridge: Harvard University Press.

Rosenberg, Nathan. 1994. *Exploring the Black Box: Technology, Economics, and History*. Cambridge: Cambridge University Press.

Rosencranz, Armin and Richard Campbell. 1999. "Foreign Environmental and Human Rights Suits Against U.S. Corporations in U.S. Courts." *Stanford Environmental Law Journal*, June.

Rosow, Stephen J. 1997. "Echoes of Commercial Society: Liberal Political Theory in Mainstream IPE." Kurt Burch and Robert A. Denemark eds., *Constituting International Political Economy*. Boulder: Lynne Rienner.

Rothstein, Bo. 1996. "Political Institutions: An Overview." Robert E. Goodin and Hans-Dieter Klingmann eds., *A New Handbook of Political Science*. Oxford: Oxford University Press.

Rowley, Charles K. and Robert D. Tollison. 1988. "Rent Seeking and Trade Protection." In Charles K. Rowley, Robert D. Tollison and Gordon Tullock eds., *The Political Economy of Rent Seeking*. Boston: Martinus Nijhoff.

Rowthorn, Robert and Ramana Ramaswamy. 1997. "Deindustrialization—Its Causes and Implications." International Monetary Fund, Economic Issues No. 10.

Ruggie, John G. 1982. "International Regimes, Transactions and Change: Embedded Liberalism in the Postwar Economic Order." *International Organization*, Spring; also in Stephen D. Krasner ed., *International Regimes*. Ithaca: Cornell University Press,1983.

Ruggie, John G. 1993. "Territoriality and Beyond: Problematizing Modernity in International Relations." *International Organization* 47

Ruggie, John G. 1995. "At Home Abroad, Abroad at Home: International Liberalisation and Domestic Stability in the New World Economy." *Millennium: Journal of International Studies*, Winter.

Ruggie, John G. 1998a. "Introduction: What Makes the World Hang Together? Neo- utilitarianism and the Social Constructivist Challenge." In *Constructing the World Polity: Essays on International Institutions*. London: Routledge.

Ruggie, John G. 1998b. "What Makes the World Hang Together? Neo-utilitarianism and the Social Constructivist Challenge." *International Organization*, Autumn.

Rupert, Mark. 1995. *Producing Hegemony: The Politics of Mass Production and American Global Power*. New York: Cambridge University Press.

Rupert, Mark. 1997. "Contesting Hegemony: Americanism and Far-Right Ideologies of Globalization." In Kurt Burch and Robert A. Denemark eds., *Constituting International Political Economy*. Boulder: Lynne Rienner.

Ryan, Colleen. 1998. *Austrian Financial Review* of October 17, 1997; as reprinted in *World Press Review*, January.

Sachs, Jeffrey D. 1989. *Developing Country Debt and the World Economy: Structural Adjustment Policies in Highly Indebted Countries*. Chicago: University of Chicago Press.

Sachs, Jeffrey. 1998a. "The IMF and the Asian Flu." *The American Prospect* March/April No. 37.

Sachs, Jeffrey. 1998b. "Global Capitalism; Making It Work." *The Economist*, September 12.

Sachs, Jeffrey D. 1999. "A Millennial Gift to Developing Countries." *New York Times*, June 11.

Sachs, Jeffrey D. and Andrew Warner. 1995. "Economic Reform and the Process of Global Integration." *Brookings Papers on Economic Activity*, 1.

Safire, William. 1999. "On Language." *New York Times Magazine*, March 7.

Sagoff, Mark. 1994. "Should Preferences Count?" *Land Economics*, May.

Sakmar, Susan L. 1999. "Free Trade and Sea Turtles: The International and Domestic Implications of the Shrimp-Turtles Case." *Colorado Journal of International Law and Policy*, Summer.

Salazar-Xirinachs, Jose M. 1999. "The Trade-Labor Nexus: Developing Countries' Perspectives." Overseas Development Council/Friederich Ebert Stiftung Conference on Trade, Labor Standards and the WTO, Washington, D.C., November 15.

Samuels, Warren J. 1981. "Maximization of Wealth as Justice: An Essay on Posnerian Law and Economics as Policy Analysis." *Texas Law Review*, December.

Sanger, David E. 1995. "Cars, Trade Sanctions and a Legacy of Frustration." *New York Times* May 8.

Sanger, David E. 1998a. "As Economies Fail, the I. M. F. Is Rife With Recriminations." *New York Times*, October 2.

Sanger, David E. 1998b. "Dissension Erupts at Talks on World Financial Crisis." *New York Times*, October 7.

Sanger, David E. 1999a. "America Finds It Lonely at the Top." *New York Times*, July 18, Section 4, p. 4

Sanger, David E. 1999b. "Rubin Proposes Modest Limits on Lending Risk." *New York Times*, April 22.

SAPRIN. 1998. "Global Civil Society Endeavor to Assess the Impact and Shape of the Future of Economic-Reform Programs." March.

Sayer, Andrew. 2000. "Moral Economy and Political Economy." *Studies in Political Economy*, Spring.

Schachar, Ron and Barry Nalebuff. 1999. "Follow the Leader: Theory and Evidence on Political Participation." *American Economic Review* June.

Schadler, Susan. 1996. "How Successful Are IMF-Supported Adjustment Programs?" *Finance and Development*, June.

Scharping, Rudolph. 1994. "Rule-Based Competition." *Foreign Affairs*, July/August.

Scherrer, Christoph. 1998. "Protecting Labor in the Global Economy: A Social Clause in Trade Agreements." *New Political Science*, March.

Schinasi, Garry J., Burkhard Drees, and William Lee. 1999. "Managing Global Finance and Risk." *Finance and Development*, December.

Schmidt, V. 1995. "The New World Order, Incorporated: The Rise of Business and the Decline of the Nation-State." *Daedalus*, Spring.

Schneider, Andrea Kupfer. 1999. Getting Along: The Evolution of Dispute Resolution Regimes in International Trade Organizations." *Michigan Journal of International Law*, Summer.

Schneider, Geoffrey E. 1999. "An Institutionalist Assessment of Structural Adjustment Programs in Africa." *Journal of Economic Issues*, June.

Scholte, Jan Aart. 2000a. "Cautionary Reflections on Seattle." *Millennium*

Scholte, Jan Aart. 2000b. "Global Civil Society." In Ngaire Woods ed., *The Political Economy of Globalization*. Houndsmills, UK: Macmillan.

Scholte, Jan Aart with Robert O'Brien and Marc Williams. 1998. "The WTO and Civil Society." Centre for the Study of Globalization and Regionalisation, University of Warwick, CSRG Working Paper No. 14/98.

Scholtz, Wesley. 1998. "International Regulation of Foreign Direct Investment." *Cornell International Law Journal*, 31: 485.

Schotter, Andrew. 1981. *The Economic Theory of Social Institutions*. Cambridge: Cambridge University Press.

Schoultz, Lars. 1982. "Politics, Economics, and U.S. Participation in Multilateral Development Banks." *International Organization*, Summer.

Schuyler, R. L. 1945. *The Fall of the Old Colonial System; A Study in British Free Trade, 1770–1870*. New York: Oxford University Press.

Schumpeter, Joseph. 1919. *Imperialism and Social Classes*. New York: Meridian Books, 1996.

Schumpeter, Joseph. 1947. *Capitalism, Socialism, and Democracy*. New York: Harper and Row.

Schwartz, Anna. 1998. "Time to Terminate the ESF and the IMF." *Foreign Policy Briefing*, Number 48, Cato Institute, August 26.

Schwartz, Herman. 1992. "Hegemony, International Debt, and International Economic Instability." In Chronis Polychroniou ed., *Perspectives and Issues in International Political Economy*. Westport, CT: Greenwood.

Sebanius, James K. 1996. "Sequencing to Build Coalitions: With Whom Should I Talk First?" In Richard J. Zeckhauser ed., *Wise Choices: Decisions, Games, and Negotiations*. Boston: Harvard Business School Press.

Sell, Susan and Christopher May. 2001. "Moments in Law: Contestation and Settlement in the History of Intellectual Property." *Review of International Political Economy*, Autumn.

Sen, Amartya. 1999. *Development as Freedom*. New York: Knopf.

Sen, Amartya. 2002. "How to Judge Globalism." *The American Prospect*, Special Issue, Winter.

Sengenberger, Werner and Frank Wilkenson. 1995. "Globalization and Labor

Standards." In Jonathan Michie and John Grieve Smith eds., *Managing the Global Economy*. Oxford: Oxford University Press.

Shachar, Ron and Barry Nalebuff. 1999. "Follow the Leader: Theory and Evidence of Political Participation." *American Economic Review*, June.

Shambaugh, George E. 1999. "Globalization, Sovereignty and Sovereign Control Over Economic Activity." Paper presented at the American Political Science Association, September 2–5.

Shapiro, Helen and Lance Taylor. 1990. "The State and Industrial Strategy." *World Development* 18:6.

Shaw, Martin. 1996. *The Global Revolution in the Social Sciences: The Globalization of State Power as a Defining Issue*. Falmer: Sussex University Press.

Shaw, Martin. 1997. "The State Of Globalization: Towards a Theory of State Transformation." *Review of International Political Economy*, Autumn.

Sheehan, Jim. 1998. "The Case Against Kyoto." *SAIS Review* 18, no. 2.

Shemrod, Joel. 1995. "Tax Policy Toward Foreign Direct Investment in Developing Countries in Light of Recent International Tax Changes." In Anwar Shah ed., *Fiscal Incentives for Investment and Innovation*. Oxford: Oxford University Press.

Shonfield, Andrew. 1965. *Modern Capitalism*. New York: Oxford University Press.

Sica, Vincent. 2000. "Cleaning the Laundry: States and Monitoring of the Financial System." *Millennium*, 29, no. 1.

Silverman, Gary with Margaret Coker, Joseph Weber, Laura Cohn and Carol Matlack. 1999. "Dirty Money Goes Digital." *Business Week*, September 20.

Simmons, Benjamin. 1999. "In Search of Balance: An Analysis of the WTO Shrimp/Turtle Appellate Body Report." *Columbia Journal of Environmental Law*, 24.

Singh, Ajit. 1994. "Openness and the Market-friendly Approach to Development: Learning the Right Lessons from Development Experience." *World Development*, 22:16,

Singh, Kavaljit. 2000. *Taming Global Financial Flows*. London: Zed.,

Slaughter, Anne-Marie, Andrew S. Tulumello, and Stepan Wood. 1998. "International Law and International Relations Theory: A New Generation of Interdisciplinary Scholarship." *American Journal of International Law*, July.

Smis, Stefaan and Kim Van der Borght. 1999. "The EU-U.S. Compromise on the Helms-Burton and D'Amato Acts." *American Journal of International Law*, January.

Smit, Hans. 1990. "Proper Choice of Law and the *Lex Mercatoria Arbitralis*." In Thomas E. Carbonneau ed., *Lex Mercatoria and Arbitration: a Discussion of the New Law Merchant*. Dobbs Ferry, N. Y.: Transnational Juris Publications.

Smith, Craig S. 1995. "Unofficially, Lending in China is Growing." *Wall Street Journal*, December 21.

Smith, Geri Smith. 1999. "Mexico: Could This Scandal Sink the PRI?" *Business Week*, August 2.

Smith, John Grieve. 1999. "A New Bretton Woods: Reforming the Global Financial System." In Jonathan Michie and John Grieve Smith eds., *Global Instability: The Political Economy of World Economic Governance*. London: Routledge.

Smith, John Grieve. 2002. "Exchange Rate Management." Paper presented to the Alternatives to Neoliberalism Conference sponsored by the New Rules for Global Finance Coalition." May 23–24.

Smythe, Elizabeth. 1999. "Agenda Formation and the Negotiation of Investment Rules at the WTO: The History of a Campaign." Paper presented at the International Studies Association, February 16–20.

So, Alvin Y. and Stephen W. K. Chiu. 1995. *East Asia and the World Economy*. Thousand Oaks, California: Sage.

Soederberg, Susanne. 2001. "The Emperor's New Suit: The New International Financial Architecture as a Reinvention of the Washington Consensus." *Global Governance*, October–December.

Solomon, M. Scott and Mark Rupert. 1999. "Eight Theses in Search of a Nail: Historical Materialism, Ideology, and the Politics of Globalization." Paper presented to the International Studies Association, February 16-20.

Soros George. 1998. "Towards a Global Open Society." *Atlantic Monthly*, January.

Soros, George. 2002. "Address to Panel." New Proposals on Financing for Development Conference, Center for Global Development, Washington, D.C., February 19–20.

Spegele, Roger D. "Is Robust Globalism a Mistake?" *Review of International Studies*, April 1997.

Spiro, Joan E. 1996. "U.S. Foreign Policy and International Financial Institutions." U.S. Department of State Dispatch v. 7, April 29.

Sprance, William R. 1998. "The World Trade Organization and United States Sovereignty: The Political and Procedural Realities of the System." *American University International Law Review*, 13: 1125.

Staff of the IMF and World Bank "Heavily Indebted Poor Countries. HIPC. Initiative: Status of Implementation." http://www.imf.org, September 23.

Stegmann, Klaus. 1989. "Policy Rivalry Among Industrial States: What Can We Learn From Models of Strategic Trade Policy?" *International Organization*, Winter.

Stein, Arthur A. 1994. "The Hegemon's Dilemma: Great Britain, The United States, and the International Economic Order." *International Organization*, Spring.

Stein, Arthur A. 1990. *Why Nations Cooperate: Circumstance and Choice in International Relations*. Ithaca: Cornell University Press.

Stein, Howard. 1995. *Asian Industrialization and Africa*. New York: St. Martin's Press.

Stephan Paul B. 1999. "The New International Law—Legitimacy, Accountability, Authority, and Freedom in the New Global Order." *Colorado Law Review*, Fall.

Sterling-Floker, Jennifer. 2001. "Competing Paradigms or Birds of a Feather? Constructionist and Neoliberal Institutionalism Compared." *International Studies Quarterly*, March.

Stern, Paula. 1997. "New Paradigm for Trade Expansion and Regulatory Harmonization: The Transatlantic Business Dialogue." *European Business Journal*, 9, no. 3.

Stephens, Philip. 2003. "Present at the Destruction of the World's Partnership." *Financial Times*, March 7.

Stewart, Frances and Albert Berry. 1999. "Globalization, Liberalization, and Inequality: Real Causes," in Andrew Hurrell and Ngaire Woods eds., *Inequality, Globalization, and World Politics*. Oxford: Oxford University Press.

Stewart, Heather. 2002. "Poor Miss Out as Rich Nations Cream Off Their Trade." *The Guardian*, April 30.

Stigler, George J. 1965. "The Economist and the State." *American Economic Review*, March.

Stiglitz, Joseph E. 1996. "Some Lessons from the East Asian Miracle." *The World Bank Research Observer*, August.

Stiglitz, Joseph E. 1999a. "Two Principles for the Next Round; Or, How to Bring Development in from the Cold." Geneva, September 21.

Stiglitz, Joseph E. 1999b. "What Have We Learned from the Recent Crises: Implications For Banking Regulation." Remarks at the Conference "Global Financial Crises: Implications for Banking and Regulation." Federal Reserve Bank of Chicago, May 6.

Stiglitz, Joseph E. 2000a. "Capital Market Liberalization, Economic Growth, and Instability." *World Development*, June.

Stiglitz, Joseph. 2000b. "Democratic Development as the Fruits of Labor." Keynote Address, Industrial Relations Research Association, Boston, January.

Stiglitz, Joseph E. 2001. "Failure of the Fund: Rethinking the IMF Response." *Harvard International Review*, Summer.

Stiglitz, Joseph E. 2002. "Globalism's Discontents." Special Supplement *The American Prospect*, Winter.

Stiglitz, Joseph E. and Marilou Uy. 1996. "Financial Markets, Public Policy, and the East Asian Miracle." *The World Bank Research Observer*, August.

Stone, Katherine Van Wezel. 1995. "Labor and the Global Economy: Four Approaches to Transnational Labor Regulation." *Michigan Journal of International Law*, Summer.

Storper, Michael. 1997. *The Regional World: Territorial Development in a Global Economy*. New York: Guilford Press.

Steiner, Daniel. 1997. "The International Convergence of Competition Laws." *Manitoba Law Journal*, 24: 577.

Stewart, Frances and Albert Berry. 1999. "Globalization, Liberalization, and Inequality: Real Causes." In Andrew Hurrell and Ngaire Woods eds., *Inequality, Globalization, and World Politics*. Oxford: Oxford University Press.

Strand, Jonathan R. 1999. "Regional Voting Blocs in the International Monetary Fund." Paper presented to American Political Science Association, September 2–5.

Strange, Susan. 1983. *"Cave! Hic Dragones.* A Critique of Regime Analysis." In Stephen D. Krasner ed., *International Regimes.* Ithaca: Cornell University Press.

Strange, Susan. 1986. *Casino Capitalism.* Oxford: Blackwell.

Strange, Susan. 1991. "Big Business and the State." *Millennium: Journal of International Studies,* Winter.

Strange, Susan. 1994a. "Rethinking Structural Change in the International Political Economy: States, Firms, and Diplomacy." In Richard Stubbs and Geoffrey R. D. Underhill. New York: St. Martin's Press.

Strange, Susan. 1994b. "Wake Up Krasner! The World *Has* Changed." *Review of International Political Economy,* Summer

Strange, Susan. 1995a. "The Defective State." *Daedalus,* Spring.

Strange, Susan. 1995b. "The Limits of Politics." *Government and Opposition* 30, no. 3 Summer.

Strauss George, ed., 1998. "Comparative International Industrial Relations." Special Issue *Industrial Relations,* July.

Stretton, Hugh. 1999. *Economics: A New Introduction.* London: Pluto Press.

Stumberg Robert. 1998. "Direct Investment: Sovereignty by Subtraction; The Multilateral Agreement on Investment." *Cornell International Law Journal,* 31.

Summers, Lawrence H. 1999. "Distinguished Lecture in Economics and Government: Reflections on Managing Global Integration." *Journal of Economic Perspectives,* Spring.

Summers, Lawrence H. 2000. "The troubling aspects of IMF reform." *Financial Times,* March 23.

Sutcliffe, Bob. 1998. "Freedom to Move in the Age of Globalization." In Dean Baker, Gerald Epstein and Robert Pollin eds., *Globalization and Progressive Economic Policy.* New York: Cambridge University Press.

Sutherland Peter. 2001. "Doha and the Crisis in Global Trade." *Financial Times,* September 4.

Swenson, Peter. 1991. "Bringing Capital Back In: Employer Power, Cross-Class Alliances, and Centralization of Industrial Relations in Denmark and Sweden." *World Politics,* July.

Syrquin, Moshe. 1995. "Flexibility and Long-Term Economic Development." In Tony Killick ed., *The Flexible Economy: Causes and Consequences of the Adaptability of National Economies.* London: Routledge.

Tabb, William K. 1995. *The Postwar Japanese System: Cultural Economy and Economic Transformation.* New York: Oxford University Press.

Tabb, William K. 1999. *Reconstructing Political Economy: The Great Divide in Economic Thought.* London: Routledge.

Tabb, William K. 2001. *The Amoral Elephant: Globalization and the Struggle for Social Justice.* New York: Monthly Review.

Tabb, William K. 2002. *Unequal Partners: A Primer on Globalization.* New York: The New Press.

Tate, Jay. 2001. "National Varieties of Standardization, in Peter A. Hall and David

Soskice eds., *Varieties of Capitalism: The Institutional Foundations of Comparative Advantage*. Oxford: Oxford University Press.

Taylor, C. O'Neal. 1998. "Observations on Trade and Investment and Trade and Labor." *Journal of International Economic Law*, Summer.

Taylor, Lance, ed., 2000. *External Liberalization, Economic Performance and Social Policy*. New York: Oxford University Press.

Taylor, Lance. 2001. "Capital Market Crises." In Jim Stanford, Lance Tayor, and Ellen Houston eds., *Power, Employment, and Accumulation: Social Structures in Economic Theory and Practice*. Armonk, NY: M. E. Sharpe.

Taylor, Peter J., ed., *1995. Political Geography of the Twentieth Century: A Global Analysis*. London: Belhaven.

Taylor, Robert. 1999. "ILO Seeks Ban on Worst Child Labour Abuse." *Financial Times*, June 6. *World Development*, 28:6.

Tett, Gillian. 1999. "Bank Staff Obstructed Inspectors, CS Admits." *Financial Times*, May 22.

Thelen, Kathleen. 1994. "Beyond Corporatism: Toward a New Framework for the Study of Labor in Advanced Capitalism." *Comparative Politics*, October.

Thelen, Kathleen and Ikuo Kume. 1999. "The Effects of Globalization on Labor Revisited: Lessons from Germany and Japan." *Politics and Society*, December.

Thomas, Caroline. 2001. "Global Governance, Development, and Human Security." *Third World Quarterly*, April.

Thomas, Chantal. 1999a. "Causes of Inequality in the International Economic Order: Critical Race Theory and Postcolonial Development." *Transnational Law and Contemporary Problems*, Spring.

Thomas, Chantal. 1999b. "Does the 'Good Governance Policy' of the International Financial Institutions Privilege Markets at the Expense of Democracy?" *Connecticut Journal of International Law*, Fall.

Thomas, Chantal. 2000. "Balance-of-Payments Crises in the Developing World: Balancing Trade, Finance and Development in the New Economic Order." *American University International Law Journal*, 15.

Tomkins, Richard . 1999. "Assessing a Name's Worth." *Financial Times*, June 22.

Thompson, Helen. 1997. "The Nation-State and International Capital Flows in Historical Perspective." *Governance and Opposition*, Winter.

Tille, Cedric. 2003. "The Impact of Exchange Rate Movements on U.S. Foreign Debt." *Current Issues in Economics and Finance*. Publication of the New York Federal Reserve Bank., January.

Tilly, Charles. 1990. *Coercion, Capital, and European States AD 990–1992*. Oxford: Basil Blackwell.

Tollison, Robert D. "Public Choice, 1972–82." In James M. Buchanan and Robert D. Tollison eds., *The Theory of Public Choice II*. Ann Arbor: University of Michigan Press.

Tollison, Robert E. and Thomas D. Willett. 1979. "An Economic Theory of Mutually Advantageous Issue Linkage in International Negotiations." *International Organization*, Fall.

Trachtman,, Joel P. 1999. "The Domain of WTO Dispute Resolution." *Harvard International Law Journal*, Spring.

Trachtman, Joel P. 1994. "Reflections on the Nature of the State: Sovereignty, Power and Responsibility." *Canada-United States Law Journal*, 20: 399

Transition Newsletter. 1999. "A New World Bank–NGO Initiative: Joint Review of Structural Adjustment." The World Bank's "Newsletter About Reforming Economies." July/August.

Triffin, Robert. 1978–79. "The International Role and Fate of the Dollar." *Foreign Affairs*, Winter.

Turner, Adair. 2003. "What's Wrong With Europe's Economy?" Queen's Lecture, Centre for Economic Performance, London School of Economics, February 5. http://cep.lse.ac.uk.queens.

Tussie, Diana. 1993. "The Uruguay Round and the Trading System in the Balance: Dilemmas for Developing Countries." In Manuel R. Agosin and Diana Tussie eds., *Trade and Growth: New Dilemmas in Trade Policy*. New York: St. Martin's Press.

Tyson, Laura D'Andrea. 1992. *Who's Bashing Whom?*. Washington, D.C.: Institute for International Economics.

Uchitelle, Louis. 1997. "A Bad Side of Bailouts: Some Go Unpenalized.," *New York Times*, December 4.

United Nations Conference on Trade and Development. 1994. *World Investment Report, 1995*. New York: United Nations Commission on Trade and Development.

United Nations Conference on Trade and Development. 2001. *World Investment Report, 2001*. New York: United Nations Commission on Trade and Development.

United Nations Conference on Trade and Development. 2003. *World Investment Report 2003*; FDI Policies for Development: National and International Perspectives. New York and Geneva: United Nations.

United Nations Development Programme. 1999. *Human Development Report 1999*. New York: Oxford University Press.

United Nations Development Programme. 1999 and 2000. *Human Development Report*. New York: United Nations.

United States Department of Labor. 1994. *By the Sweat and Toil of Children: The Use of Child Labor in American Imports*. Washington, D.C.: Department of Labor.

Underhill, Geoffrey R. D. 1991. Markets Beyond Politics? The State and the Internationalisation of Financial Markets." *European Journal of Political Research*, 19.

Underhill, Geoffrey R. D. 1994. "Introduction: Conceptualizing the Changing Global Order." In Richard Stubbs and Geoffrey R. D. Underhill eds., *Political Economy and the Changing Global Order*. Toronto: McClelland and Stewart.

Urgese, Joseph J. 1998. "Dolphin Protection and the Mammal Protection Act Have Met Their Match: The General Agreement on Tariffs and Trade." *Akron Law Review*, 31.

Utting, Peter. 2000. "Business Responsibility for Sustainable Development." United Nations Research Institute for Social Development, June.

Van Apeldoorn, Bastiaan. 1998. "Transnationalization and the Restructuring of Europe's Socioeconomic Order." *International Journal of Political Economy*, Spring.

Van der Borght, Kim. 1999. "The Review of the WTO Understanding on Dispute Settlement: Some Reflections on the Current Debate." *American University International Law Review*, 14.

van der Pijl, Kees. 1984. *The Making of an Atlantic Ruling Class*. London: Verso.

van der Pijl, Kees. 1997. "Transnational Class Formation and State Formation." In Stephen Gill and David Mittelman eds., *Innovation and Transformation in International Studies*. Cambridge: Cambridge University Press.

Van der Wee, Herman. 1987. *Prosperity and Upheaval: the World Economy 1945–1980*. Berkeley: University of California Press.

Vander Stichele, Myriam. 1997. *Globalization, Marginalization and the WTO*. Amsterdam: Transnational Institute, September. WTO Booklet Series, Volume 2.

Vander Stichele, Myriam. 1998. *Towards a World Transnationals' Organization?* Amsterdam: Transnational Institute., April. http://www.tni/wto/booklets/wto3.htm.

Vandevelde, Kenneth J. 1998. "The Political Economy of a Bilateral Investment Treaty." *American Journal of International Law*: 92.

Vasquez, I. 2000. "The International Monetary Fund: Challenges and Contradictions." In International Financial Institution Advisory Commission, *Expert Papers*, March. http://phantom-x.gsia.cmu.edu/IFIAC.

Vernon Raymond. 1966. "International Investment and International Trade in the Product Cycle." *Quarterly Journal of Economics*, May.

Vernon, Raymond. 1970. "Future of Multinational Enterprise." In Charles P. Kindleberger ed., *The International Corporation*. Cambridge: MIT Press.

Vines, David. 1998. "The WTO in Relation to the Fund and the Bank: Competencies, Agendas, and Linkages." In Anne O. Krueger ed., with the assistance of Chonira Aturapane. *The WTO as an International Organization*. Chicago: University of Chicago Press.

Vogel, David. 2000. "The Environment and International Trade." *Journal of Policy History*, 12, no. 1.

Wachtel, Howard. 1998. "Labor's Stake in the WTO." *The American Prospect*, March/April.

Wade, Robert and Frank Veneroso. 1998. "The Asian Crisis: The High Debt Model Versus the Wall Street-Treasury-IMF Complex." *New Left Review*, March/April.

Wade, Robert. 1990. *Governing the Market: Economic Theory and the Role of Government in East Asian Industrialization*. Princeton: Princeton University Press.

Wade, Robert. 1994. "Selective Industrial Policy in East Asia: Is *The East Asian Miracle* Right?" In Albert Fishlow, Catherine Gwin, Stephan Haggard, Dani Rodrik, and Robert Wade *Miracle or Design? Lessons from the East Asian Experience*, Policy Essay Number 11. Washington, D.C.: Overseas Development Council.

Wade, Robert. 1996. "Globalization and Its Limits: Reports of the Death of the National Economy Are Greatly Exaggerated.," In Suzanne Berger and Ronald Dore eds., *National Diversity and Global Capitalism*. Ithaca: Cornell University Press.

Wade, Robert. 1998a. "The Asian Debt-and-Development Crisis of 1997–9?: Causes and Consequences." *World Development*, August.

Wade, Robert. 1998b. "From Miracle to Meltdown: Vulnerabilities, Moral Hazard, Panic and Debt Deflation in the Asian Crisis." draft, June 1.

Wæver, Ole. 1998. "The Sociology of a Not So International Discipline: American and European Developments in International Relations." *International Organization*, Autumn.

Wall, Christopher. 1998. "Human Rights and Economic Sanctions: The New Imperialism." *Fordham International Law Journal*, December.

Wallace, Don and David B. Bailey. 1998. "The Inevitability of National Treatment of Foreign Direct Investment with Increasingly Few and National Exceptions." *Cornell International Law Journal*, 31: 615.

Wallach, Lori. 2000. "Unmasking the WTO: Access to the System: Transparency in WTO Dispute Resolution." *Law and Policy in International Business*, 31: 773.

Wallerstein, Immanuel. 1998. "The Rise and Future Demise of World-Systems Analysis." *Review* 21, no. 1.

Walter, Andrew. 1991. "The Global Financial Revolution: Causes and Consequences." *World Power and World Money: The Role of Hegemony and International Monetary Order*. Hemel Hempstead, England: Harvester Wheatsheaf.

Walter, Andrew. 1998. "Do They Really Rule the World?" *New Political Economy*, July.

Waltz, Kenneth. 1979. *Theory of World Politics*. Reading, MA: Addison-Wesley.

Waltz, Kenneth. 1999. "Globalization and Governance." *PS: Political Science and Politics*, December.

Warren, Bill. 1973. "Imperialism and Capitalist Industrialization." *New Left Review*, September/October.

Waters, Richard. 1999. "US Regulators Stand In The Way Of Global Rules." *Financial Times*, March 25.

Watson, Matthew. 1999. "Rethinking Capital Mobility, Re-regulating Financial Markets." *New Political Economy*, 4, no. 1.

Wayne, Leslie. 1998. "Wave of Mergers Is Recasting Face of Business in U.S." *New York Times*, January 19.

Webb, Michael C. 1991. "International Economic Structures, Government Interests, and International Coordination Of Macroeconomic Adjustment Policies." *International Organization*, Summer.

Weingast, Barry. 1997. "The Political Foundations of Democracy and the Rule of Law." *American Political Science Review*, June.

Weisbrot, Mark, Dean Baker, Egor Kraev, and Judy Chen. 2001. "The Scorecard on Globalization 1980–2000: Twenty Years of Diminished Progress." Center for Economic Policy Research, July 11.

Weiss, Friedl. 2000. "From World Trade Law to World Competition Law." *Fordham International Law Journal*, 23.

Weiss, Linda. 1998. *The Myth of the Powerless State.* Ithaca: Cornell University Press.

Weiss, Linda. 1999. "State Power and the Asian Crisis." *New Political Economy*, November.

Weiss, Linda. 2000. "Developmental States in Transition: Adapting, Dismantling, Innovating, Not 'Normalizing'." *The Pacific Review*, 13, no. 1.

Weller, Christian. 2000. "Financial Liberalization, Multinational Banks and Credit Supply." *International Review of Applied Economics,*

Weller, Christian. 2001. "Financial Crises After Financial Liberalization: Exceptional Circumstances or Structural Weakness." *Journal of Development Studies,*

Wendt, Alexander. 1992. "Anarchy Is What States Make of It: The Social Construction of Power Politics." *International Organization*, Spring.

Wendt, Alexander. 1999. "A Comment on Held's Cosmopolitanism." In Ian Shapiro and Casiano Hacker-Cordon eds., *Democracy's Edges.* Cambridge: Cambridge University Press.

Whitley, Richard. 1998. "Internationalization and Varieties of Capitalism: The Limited Effects of Cross-National Coordination Of Economic Activities on the Nature of Business Systems." *Review of International Political Economy*, Autumn.

Wilcox, Clair. 1949. *A Charter for World Trade.* New York: Macmillan.

Wilkin, Peter. 1996. "New Myths for the South: Globalization and the Conflict Between Private Power and Freedom." *Third World Quarterly* 17, no. 2.

Wilkins, Mira. 1970. *The Emergence of Multinational Enterprise: American Business Abroad from the Colonial Era to 1914.* Cambridge: Harvard University Press.

Williams, David and Tony Young. 1994. "Governance, the World Bank and Liberal Theory." *Political Studies*, March.

Williams, Frances. 1999a. "ILO Boycott Urged Over Burma 'Slavery'." *Financial Times*, June 16.

Williams, Frances. 1999b. ILO's child Labour Treaty Set for Adoption." *Financial Times*, June 15.

Williams, Frances. 2000. "Report Reveals Change in WTO Actions." *Financial Times*, December 7.

Williams, Karle. 2000. "From Shareholder Value to Present-Day Capitalism." *Economy and Society*, February.

Williamson, John. 1990. "What Washington Means by Policy Reform." In John Williamson ed., *Latin American Adjustment: How Much Has Happened?.* Washington, D. C, Institute for International Economics.

Williamson, John. 2000. "What Should the World Bank Think About the Washington Consensus?" *The World Bank Research Observer*, August.

Williamson, Oliver E. 1979. "Transaction-Cost Economics: The Governance of Contractual Relations,: *Journal of Law and Economics* 22, no. 2.

Williamson, Oliver E. 1985. *The Economic Institutions of Capitalism: Firms, Markets, and Relational Contracting*. New York: Free Press.

Williamson, Oliver E. 1996. "Efficiency, Power, Authority and Economic Organization." In John Groenewegen ed., *Transaction Cost Economics and Beyond*. Boston: Kluwer.

Williamson, Oliver E. 1998. "The Institutions of Governance." *American Economics Review*, May.

Winch, Christopher. 1998. "Listian Political Economy: Social Capitalism Conceptualized?" *New Political Economy*, July.

Winzer, Jane. 1999. "Cross National Demands for International Labor Standards." paper prepared for American Political Science Association, Atlanta, September 2–5.

Wolf, Martin. 1999a. "Blair's Model." *Financial Times*, April 5.

Wolf, Martin. 1999b. "The Debt Myths." *Financial Times*, June 23.

Wolfensohn, James D. 1997. "The Challenge of Inclusion." Address to the Board of Governors, Hong Kong, China. Washington: World Bank Group., September 23.

Wolfensohn, James D. 1998. "The Other Crisis." Washington: World Bank Group, October 6.

Wolfensohn, James D. 2003. "A Better World Is Possible." Washington: World Bank Group, January 24.

Woo-Cumings, Meredith. 1991. *Race to the Swift: State and Finance in Korean Industrialization* . Ithaca: Cornell University Press.

Woo-Cumings, Meredith. 1997. "Slouching Toward the Market: The Politics of Financial Liberalization in South Korea." In Michael Loriaux, Meredith Woo-Cumings, Kent E. Calder, Sylvia Maxfield and Sofia A. Perez *Capital Ungoverned: Liberalizing Finance in Interventionist States*. Ithaca: Cornell University Press.

Woo-Cumings, Meredith. 1998. *The Development State in Historical Perspective*. Ithaca: Cornell University Press.

Wood, Robert E. 1986. *From Marshall Plan to Debt Crisis: Foreign Aid and Development Choices in the World Economy*. Berkeley: University of California Press.

Woods Ngairi. 2000. "The Challenge of Good Governance for the IMF and the World Bank Themselves." *World Development*, May.

Woods, Ngaire. 2002. "Accountability in Global Governance." Human Development Report 2002 Background Paper, United Nations Development Program.

Woolcock, Michael. 1998. "Social Capital and Economic Development: Toward a Theoretical Synthesis and Policy Framework." *Theory and Society*, April.

World Bank Portfolio Management Taskforce. 1992. *Effective Implementation: Key to Development Impact*. Washington: World Bank. Known as the Wapenhans Report.

World Bank. 1995. *World Bank Development Report: Workers in an Integrated World*. New York: Oxford University Press.

World Bank. 1997a. *Global Economic Prospects and Developing Countries*. Washington, D.C.: World Bank.

World Bank. 1997b. *World Development Report: Fostering Markets: Liberalization, Regulation, and Industrial Policy*. New York: Oxford University Press.

World Trade Organization Secretariat. 1996. "Trade and Direct Foreign Investment." October 9. http://www.wto.archives/chpiv.html.

Wriston, Walter. 1988. "Technology and Sovereignty." *Foreign Affairs*, Winter.

Wriston, Walter. 1992. *The Twilight of Sovereignty: How the Information Revolution is Transforming Our World*. New York: Charles Scribner's Sons.

Wyplosz, Charles. 1999. "International Financial Stability." In Inge Kaul, Isabelle Grunberg and Marc A. Stern eds., *Global Public Goods: International Cooperation in the 21st Century*. New York: Oxford University Press.

Wysham, Daphne, Jon Sohn and Jim Vallette. 1999. "OPIC, Ex-Im and Climate Change: Business as Usual. An Analysis of U.S. Government Support for Fossil Fueled Development Abroad, 1992–1998". Washington": D.C.: Institute for Policy Studies, Friends of the Earth and the International Trade Information Service.

Yaghmaian, Behzad. 1998. "Globalization and the State." *Science and Society*, Summer.

Yarbrough, Beth V. and Robert M. Yarbrough. 1987. "Cooperation in the Liberalization of International Trade: After Hegemony, What? *International Organization*, Winter.

Yergin, Daniel and Joseph Stanislaw. 1998. *The Commanding Heights: The Battle Between Government and the Marketplace that is Remaking the Modern World*. New York: Simon and Schuster.

Yergin, Daniel. 1999. "Uncertainty—the One Sure Thing." *Financial Times*, March 8.

You, Jong-Il and Ju-Ho Lee. 1999. "Economic and Social Consequences of Globalization: The Case of South Korea." School of Public Policy and Global Management, Korea Development Institute.

Young, Oran R. 1989. "The Politics of International Regime Formation: Managing Natural Resources and the Environment." *International Organization*, Summer.

Zacher, Mark W. 1987. "Trade gaps, Analytical Gaps: Regime Analysis And International Commodity Trade Regulation." *International Organization*, Spring.

Zaring, David. 1998. "International Law by Other Means: The Twilight Existence of International Financial Regulatory Organizations." *Texas International Law Journal*, Spring.

Zevin, Robert. 1992. "Are World Financial Markets More Open? If So, Why And With What Effect?" In Tariq Banuri and Juliet B. Schor eds., *Financial Openness and National Autonomy*. Oxford: Oxford University Press.

Zupnick, Elliot. 1999. *Visions and Revisions: The United States in the Global Economy*. Boulder: Westview Press.

Zysman, John. 1983. *Governments, Markets and Growth: Financial Systems and the Politics of Industrial Change*. Ithaca: Cornell University Press.

Zysman, John. 1996. "The Myth of a 'Global' Economy: Enduring National Foundations and Emerging Regional Realities." *New Political Economy*, Summer.

INDEX

Abacha, Sani, 225, 377
ABB company, 273
Abolition of Forced Labor Convention, 365
Abu-Lougod, Janet, 46
accounting standards, 179, 180–182, 428
accounting theory, on asset value, 318
acid rain, 352
acquisitions. *See* mergers and acquisitions
actors. *See* global state economic governance institutions; individuals; transnational corporations
Afghanistan, 53
African Cotton Association, 327
agency, structure vs., 84
Agenda 21 (environmental action plan), 348
agents of globalization, 41–42
Agreement on Sanitary and Phytosanitary Measures, 339–340
Agreement on Technical Barriers to Trade (WTO), 339–340
Agreement on Trade Related Aspects of Intellectual Property Rights (TRIPs), 161, 300, 311, 320–323, 324
agricultural protectionism, 308, 326–327, 374
AIDS, 44–45, 411
airline companies, 275
Akyuz, Yilmaz, 124
Alcatel company, 288
Aldrich, Winthrop, 113
Alien Tort Claims Act, 359
Alliance for Progress, 293
America. *See* Argentina; Brazil; Canada; Central America; Chile; Ecuador; Latin America; Mexico; United States
America Online, 282
American Bankers Association, 173

American Business Abroad (Kindleberger), 73
American Electronics Association, 426–427
American Petroleum Institute, 353–354
American social scientists, subjectivity, 89
Amity and Commerce with France, Treaty of, 297
Amsden, Alice H., 75
Amsterdam (Dutch East Indies Company ship), 277
Andean Pact, 137
Anghie, Antony, 52
Anglo-American economic model, 62–65, 75–76, 79, 241
Annan, Kofi, 186
antidumping duties, 311
antitrust authority, global, 67, 282
antitrust laws, 317
Appellate Body (of WTO, for trade disputes), 312, 313, 344
Aquinas, Thomas, 154
arbitration, 162, 164–165, 166, 371
arbitrators, constraints on, 166
Archey, William, 426–427
Argentina, 207, 228, 238, 380–381, 384
Armey, Dick, 382
Armijo, Leslie Elliott, 233
Arthur Andersen & Co., 305
Articles of Agreement (Bretton Woods), 213
ASEA company (Sweden), 273
ASEAN (Association of South East Asian Nations), 413–415
Asia
    Chiang Mai Initiative, 414
    economic zone, 412–416, 420
    financial system, 240
    free trade area, proposal for, 415

Index compiled by Fred Leise

Asia (*continued*)
  United States, views on, 240
  U.S. manufacturing investments in, 280
  See also East Asia
Asian Monetary Fund, 110, 413
assets, 20, 277–278, 318, 427
Association of South East Asian Nations
  (ASEAN), 413–415
Aswan Dam, 194
Ataturk, Kamal, 154
Atlantic Charter, 107
Augmented Washington Consensus, 3–4, 9,
  423
Austro-Hungarian Empire, 154
authoritative allocation of resources, 147
automotive industry, 273, 276, 355
Aventis company, 288

Bagehot, Walter, 393
bailouts, 205, 388
  See also debt
bancor (Keynes's proposed international
  currency), 110
Bangalore, 264–265
Bangkok International Banking Facility
  (BIBF), 239
Bank for International Commerce and
  Credit International (BCCI), 173–174
Bank for International Settlements (BIS),
  173–179
  Basle Committee on Banking Supervi-
    sion, 174, 175–176
  financial stability forum, 177–178
  origins, 172
  Report on Minimal Standards, 175
Bank of Credit and Commerce International (BCCI) d.p., 225
Bank of New York, 173
bank regulators, 225
bank runs, 248
bankers, views on IMF, 211–212
banking crises, 134–135, 189, 228–229, 229,
  235
  See also financial crises
bankruptcy, 232, 238–239, 240
  See also debt
banks
  failures, foreign exchange trading and,
    122–123
  financial crises' effects on, 228
  global central, 110
  illegal activities, 189, 223, 224–225
  insolvency vs. illiquidity, 220
  insolvent, treatment of, 240

lendees, relationships with, 180
local banks, 252–253
multinational, 252–253
private banking, 224
regulation of, 123–124, 173–179
risk-taking, 220
U.S., opposition to capital controls, 122
  See also Bank for International Settle-
    ments; International Monetary Fund;
    World Bank; World Bank Group
Bardi (Italian family), 47
Barnes and Noble, 275
Barshefsky, Charlene, 316, 318
Basel Convention, 1994 amendment to, 345
Basic Telecommunications Agreement, 306
Basle Accord, 176, 177
Basle Committee on Banking Supervision
  (Committee on Banking Regulation
  and Supervisory Practices, Cooke Com-
  mittee, BIS), 174, 175–176
Battle of the Methods *(Methodenstreit)*, 77
Bayer company, 412
Baylor University, 103
Bedjaoui, Mohammed, 168
Bello, Waldon, 214
Benetton, 268
benign hegemon, United States as, 18–21
Benin, 326
Bergsten, C. Fred, 62
Berman, Harold J., 157
Beta video format, 274
Bhagwati, Jagdish, 7
Bhutto, Benazir, 377
BIBF (Bangkok International Banking
  Facility), 239
bicycle theory of trade policy, 300
bilateral investment treaties (BITs),
  297–298, 299–300
bilateral trade agreements, 297, 298–300,
  415
biopiracy, 321–322
bioprospectors, 321–322
Bird, Graham, 208
BIS. *See* Bank for International Settlements
Bismarck, Prince Otto, 52
BITs (bilateral investment treaties),
  297–298, 299–300
Blackhurst, Richard, 70
Blair, Tony, 379
Block, Fred, 120
Bloomberg company, 23
bond market, 121–122, 230
Bongo, Omar, 225
Bono (rock star), 409

Bordieu, Pierre, 26
borrowing. *See* debt; leverage
bourgeoisie, emergence of, 47
brands, values of, 273–274
Brazil, 138, 299, 304, 381
Brenner, Robert, 64
Bretton Woods conference, 109, 213
Bretton Woods institutions (BWIs)
  arguments for acceptance of, 113
  criticisms of, 190–191
  developed countries' voting strength in, 376
  neoliberalism, problems with, 191
  operation of, 184–219
  UN, as competition to, 185–186
  See also International Monetary Fund; World Bank; World Bank Group
Bretton Woods system, 108–113, 118–124, 139–140
Britain
  Department of Trade and Industry, 129
  deregulation, preference for, 226
  Keynesian capital controls, preference for, 108–109
  League of Nations, influence on, 108
  merchants, reliance on military superiority, 171
  Patent Office, 323
  protectionism, 278
  U.S., postwar dependence on, 115
  See also United Kingdom
British Invisibles (Financial Services International London Group), 129
British Petroleum, 354
Brittan, Leon, 130
Brock (U.S. Ambassador), 304
Brown, Gordon, 361
Brown-Boveri company (Switzerland), 273
Brundtland Commission (World Commission on Environment and Development), 347–348, 349
bubbles, speculative, 25, 135, 246–247
Buchanan, James, 83
Buchanan, Patrick, 315–316
Burger King, 275
Burgi, Noelle, 120
Burkino Faso, 326
Burma (Myanmar), 357–358, 366, 368
Bush, George W.
  crusade, call for, 53
  foreign aid announcement, 396–397
  Free Trade Area of the Americas, support for, 372
  Kyoto Accord rejection, 354

political economy, approach to, 425–427
  protectionism, 279
  unilateralism, 380
Bush Administration
  AIDS drugs, actions on, 412
  as axis of oil, 397
  Clinton IMF actions, criticism of, 380
  farm bill, 412
  fast track authorization, 138–139
  financial crises, response to, 381, 386–387
  GSEGIs, funding for, 204
  IMF and, 205, 381
  loan restructuring, policy on, 393
  on power, legitimacy of, 142
  preemptive war doctrine, 10
  protectionism, 307, 374
  single-mindedness, 44
  unilateralism, 10, 373, 375, 420
  Unocal, support for, 359
  war on terrorism, influence of, 7
Bush Doctrine, 8, 102, 420, 426
Business Council on National Issues (Canada), 306
business cycles, 244
business methods, patenting of, 323
business-to-business communication, 48–49
business-to-business relationships, 70
Business Week
  on corporate rule making, 159–160
  on debt relief, 410
  Special Report, on financial rescue plans, 254
Buzan, Barry, 429
BWIs. *See* Bretton Woods institutions
Byrd-Hagel Resolution, 354

Calomiris, Charles, 217, 218, 391
Calvert, Randall, 83–84
Calvo Clause, 169, 305
Calvo Clause (Calvo Doctrine), 292
Camdessus, Michel, 375, 389
Canada, 63, 306, 360, 371
Canal Plus, 282
Cancún, Mexico, World Trade Ministerial Meeting in, 326–328, 422
Canner, Stephen, 370
capital
  Greider on, 227
  mobility, vs. labor mobility, 287–288
  power of, 29, 30
  rights of, states' rights vs., 398
  speculative, effects of, 231
  states, influence on, 31

capital (*continued*)
  transnational capital, 29, 56, 325
  See also capital controls; capital movements
capital account liberalization, 231, 388
  See also capital movements
capital adequacy standards, 176, 177
capital control tax, 121
capital controls
  British preference on, 108–109
  British preferences, 111
  in Chile, 236–237
  economists' views on, 236
  effective, 384
  effects of, 233, 236
  global settlement currency, 110
  growth rates, relation to, 231
  Keynes on, 238
  under multilateral agreement on investment, 404
  Mundell-Fleming model on, 254–255
  U.S. banks' opposition to, 122
  See also Bretton Woods system; capital movements; currency markets; financial liberalization; International Monetary Fund

capital flight
  debt buildup, cause of, 227
  dictators', 377–378
  effects of, 234
  exchange rate as trigger, 206–207
  Keynes on, 125
  in Latin American debt crisis, 252
  prevention of, 257
  Western Europe, postwar years, 122
  See also capital movements
capital flow. *See* capital movements
capital market liberalization. *See* financial liberalization
capital markets
  expansion, 222
  free, U.S. desire for, 110
  integration, dispute over time of, 48
  liquidity, effects of, 124
  power of, 122
  resurgence of, 124–126
  technology and, 22
  U.S. leadership of, 113
capital movements
  controls on, 237, 242–243
  effects of, 7, 418
  IMF position on, 230–231
  Mundell-Fleming model on, 254–255

restrictions on, abolishment of, 222
  short-term capital flows, 178, 383–384
  social control of, 117, 132–133, 213–214, 227
  See also capital controls; capital flight
capital strikes, 235
capitalism
  moral economy grounding, 132
  nature of, 36–37
  postwar European view of, 115
  as redistributive growth, 49–50
  social democracy, conflict with, 93
  transnational, *lex mercatoria* and, 158
  transnational corporations' domination of, 275
  versions of, deregulation and, 20
Capitalism, Socialism and Democracy (Schumpeter), 89
capitalist class, 31
carbon sinks (for greenhouse gases), 350, 352
Carr, E. E., 77
cars. *See* automotive industry
Cayman Islands, 225
Central America, 194, 300
central banks, 4, 106, 204, 257
  See also European Central Bank; Federal Reserve Bank; World Bank
Central Intelligence Agency (U.S.), 292
Chad, 326
chaebol (Korean business groups), 253
Chandler, Alfred, 267
change, effects of, 89
charity, 424
Charter for an International Trade Organization, 295
Charter of Economic Rights and Duties of States, 133–134, 404
Chartist movement, 92
Chiang Mai Initiative, 414
child labor, 334–335
Chile
  Brazil, relationship with, 299
  capital controls, 7, 236–237, 384
  GDP loss during financial crisis, 228
  U.S.-Chile Free Trade Agreement, 299
  World Bank loans to, U.S. influence on, 194
China
  Asian economic zone, efforts on, 412–413, 415
  capital controls, 127, 190
  contagion effects, immunity to, 232
  during East Asian financial crisis, 215

East Asian financial crisis and, 232, 414
fossil fuel projects, 346
GDP, growth in, 190
globalization and, 19
intellectual piracy, 322–323
regime clubs, preparation for joining, 68
U.S., relationship with, 281, 415–416
WTO, entry to, 52
choice, context of, 337
Christian Democrats, 79, 292
CIA (Central Intelligence Agency, U.S.),
    292
Cipro (drug), 412
Cisco Systems, 22–23
Citibank, 224–225, 305
citizenship, corporate vs. individual, 43
the City (London financial district), 233
civil society oppositional politics, 36, 218
Clarke, Tony, 325
class interest, 88, 237
classical liberalism, 79–81
clawback legislation, 330
Clayton, William, 114
Clean Development Mechanism, 351
client confidentiality, 224, 250
Clifford, Mark, 363
climate, destabilization of, 346
    See also greenhouse gas emissions
climate fraud (klimasvindel), 352
Clinton, Bill, 138, 204, 379, 385–386
Clinton Administration, 138, 317, 329
club goods, 142–143
Coalition for Justice to Coffee Workers,
    363–364
Coalition of Service Industries (CSI), 11,
    162, 305
Coase, Ronald, 74
Cobden-Chevalier Commercial Treaty, 278
Coca Cola company, 274, 275, 358
Code of Conduct for Transnational Corpo-
    rations, 301–302, 403–404
Code of Liberalization of Capital Move-
    ments (OECD), 291
Code of Liberalization of Invisible Opera-
    tions (OECD), 291
coercion
    benefits, 147–148
    coerced globalization, 17
    coerced investment, 282
    debt as, 407
    in market access, 309
    in restructuring, 93
    soft law approach instead of, 176–177
    in trade history, 277

trade theory's lack of attention to, 263
World Bank on, 148
Cold War, 102, 114, 151, 198
collective action, 88, 332, 334
collective action clauses, 392, 393
collective social welfare, 148
colonialism
    developing countries' fear of return to,
        314–315
    end of, 278
    new, IMF policy as, 209
    sovereignty and, 51–52, 151
    subjugated peoples, legal rights of, 168
Columbia, 359
Columbia University, 77
comity, principle of, 156, 356–357
commercial law. See lex mercatoria
Commission for Genetic Resources for
    Food and Agriculture, 322
Commission on Global Governance, 143
Committee on Banking Regulation and
    Supervisory Practices (Basle Committee
    on Banking Supervision, Cooke Com-
    mittee, BIS), 174, 175–176
Committee on Capital Movements and
    Invisible Transactions (CMIT, of
    OECD), 401
Committee on International Investment
    and Multilateral Enterprise (CIIME, of
    OECD), 401
Committee on Trade and Investment
    (Japan), 306
commodity chains, 126
common good. See social considerations
common heritage, 322
Communism, spread of, 115
communities, individuals vs., 332
community of interests. See concentric club
    formation
companies. See corporations
comparative advantage, 334, 335, 337
comparative advantage theory, 263–264,
    278, 283, 284
comparative political economy, 77, 98
competition, 161, 171, 282–283
competitive deregulation, 226–227
competitive liberalization, 299
competitive markets, 81, 335–336
competitiveness laws, 317
computer industries, 126–127
Conca, Ken, 344, 345
concentric club formation
    conflicts in, 181–182
    by corporate leaders, 128–129

description of, 35
examples of, 177–178, 389–390, 403
hegemons and, 108, 142
in ITO negotiations, 295, 296
opposition to, 419
private international trade law and, 159
process of, 142, 421
professional organizations' role in, 165
rule making, control of, 35
unilateralist momentum strategy vs., 299
See also Basle Committee on Banking
    Supervision
concentric club goods, 143
conditionality (of IMF loans)
    criticism of, 217, 419
    as expansion of IMF purpose, 212–213
    formulation of, 206
    instability, effects on, 244
    Polak on, 202
    problems of, 207, 210, 216
confidentiality, 224, 250
conflicts, 338
consensus formation, in GSEGIs, 163
conservatives, 189, 194
constitutionalism, of GSEGIs, 207–208
constructivism, 74, 95–96, 97, 99
Consultative Group on International Agri-
    cultural Research, 322
consumer debt, 64
contagion (financial)
    in capital markets, 250
    derivative markets' effects on, 250
    description of, 248
    in financial crises, 177, 215, 232, 237
    of fixed exchange rates, 111
    instantaneous nature, 217
    sovereignty and, 152
containment, 103
contingent credit lines (CCLs), 385–386
contract law, 46, 67, 317
    See also lex mercatoria
contract manufacturing, 22–23
controls. See capital controls
Convention on International Trade in
    Endangered Species, 345
Cooke, Peter, 175
Cooke Committee (Basle Committee on
    Banking Supervision, Committee on
    Banking Regulation and Supervisory
    Practices, BIS), 174, 175–176
Cooper, Richard, 73
cooperation, 95, 147–148
    See also coercion
coordinated market systems, 67

See also Germano-Japanese economic
    model
copyright, on software, 264
core countries
    Basle Committee recommendations,
        adoption of, 176
    business sector networks, density of, 421
    concerns of, 373
    developing countries, relationship with,
        309–310
    intellectual property, protection of, 321
    international institutions and, 35
    international state, role in emergence of,
        172
    power, 168–169
    protectionism, 326–327, 375
    special treatment of, 310
    wealth creation in, 377
    See also Japan; United Kingdom; United
        States
corporate environmentalism, doctrine of,
    354–355
Corporate Europe Observatory, 130
corporations
    corporate globalization, 31–32, 35,
        398–406
    global horizons, 50
    government, partnerships with, 130–131
    international citizenship, vs. individual
        national citizenship, 43
    multi-domestic, 273
    multilateral agreement on investment,
        status under, 401, 402
    rule making, 159–160
    strategic alliances, 126
    in U.S., 379, 427–428, 428
    See also multinational corporations;
        transnational corporations
corruption
    capital flight resulting from, 377–378
    corporate, explanations of, 418
    in debtor states, 408
    in developing countries, 4
    in financial markets, 222
    rule of law, change to, 198
    technology as excuse for, 223
cotton production, 326–327
Council on International Business, 305,
    399, 401
counter-hegemonic forces, 101
countervailing duties, 311
countries. See states
courts (legal), 26, 105, 155, 356–358, 356–359
    See also law

courts of last instance, 166
courts of the dusty feet, 105, 155
Cox, Robert, 6, 55–56, 57, 153
creation myths, 80, 150–151
creative destruction, 89, 148
Credit Anstalt (Austrian deposit bank),
    106–107
creeping national capitalism, 115
crime. *See* corruption
criminal funds, tracking of, 378
crises. *See* banking crises; financial crises
Croatia, 211
Crockett, Andrew, 177–178
crony capitalism, 202, 212, 222, 248, 249
Crotty, James, 245, 281–282
crusade, as term, 53
CSI (Coalition of Service Industries), 11,
    162, 305
Cuba, 408
Cuban Liberty and Democratic Solidarity
    (Libertad) Act (Helms-Burton Act),
    329–330
Cuban Revolution, 293
currencies, 110, 119, 256
    See also bancor; dollar; eurodollar;
    exchange rates; gold standard; special
    drawing rights
currency crises, 134–135
currency independence, 384
currency markets, 118
Cussia, Enrico, 116
customer privacy, 224, 250
Cutler, A. Claire, 155–156, 158
Czechoslovakia, 194

da Gama, Vasco, 276–277
Daewoo, 253, 280
Daimler-Benz, 182
Dasser, Felix J., 157
Davies, Kert, 350
de Cecco, Marcello, 261
debt
    consumer debt, 64
    costs, 229
    debt relief, 395–396, 406–412
    foreign currency debt, 231
    global issue of, 374–375
    grants, change to, 393
    moratoria, 389
    odious, 408
    recycling of, 393, 410
    repayment of, World Bank's requirement
        for, 197
    restructuring, 232, 392–393

sovereign chapter eleven, 378
    of U.S., 427
    See also financial crises
Decade To Establish a New International
    Economic Order, 133
Declaration on International Investment
    and Multinational Enterprises, 134
defense spending, U.S., 2
democracy, 35–36, 37
democratic deficit, 417
Democratic Party, 287
Denmark, 276, 352
Department of Trade and Industry
    (Britain), 129
dependency, 57
dependent territories, 51
deregulation
    competitive, 226–227
    European integration and, 128
    ideology of, beneficiaries of, 226
    lex mercatoria and, 164–165
    liberalization, difference from, 221
    reasons for, 20
    See also financial liberalization; regulation
derivative markets, 221, 250
destructive creation, 89, 148
developing countries
    EXTERNAL RELATIONS
    colonialism, fear of return to, 314–315
    IMF, views of, 211
    influence, lack of, 131, 218
    legal expertise, lack of, 313, 318
    WTO's lack of focus on, 397–398
    FINANCIAL AFFAIRS
    balance of payments difficulties, 208
    capital controls, 133–134
    debt, level of, 408
    financial bankruptcy, 410
    financial crises, 123, 239
    financial liberalization, desire for review
        of, 25–26
    foreign capital, competition for, 302
    foreign reserves, costs of, 255–256
    IDA loans, use of, 196
    liberalization, effects of, 7, 24
    new financial architecture, objectives
        for, 376
    reserves, 377
    INFLUENCES ON
    colonialism, legacy of, 408
    environmental protections required of,
        346–347
    global constraints on, 202
    global integration, 23

developing countries (*continued*)
  norm enforcement against, 151
  rich countries' leverage over, 309–310
  INTERNAL AFFAIRS
  biological resources, 321–322
  globalization, responses to, 36
  growth strategies, control of, 399–400
  improvements, effects of failure at, 8–9
  labor rights, 359–362
  TRADE
  agricultural protectionism against,
    326–327
  antidumping practices against, 311–312
  contract manufacturing, 22–23
  international commodity agreements,
    views on, 295–296
  lex mercatoria, views on, 163, 167–169
  manufacturing exports, 270, 271,
    280–281
  market restrictions, 271–272
  trade negotiations, nonreciprocity in,
    308
  TRIMs, effects of, 324
  TRIPs, enforcement of, 321
  world trade, proportion of, 314
  See also economic development; struc-
    tural adjustment programs
development strategies, 188–191, 206, 404
developmental state model, 68
dictators, 197–198, 224–225
differentiated responsibilities, on environmental problems, 349
Dillon Round of GATT negotiations, 291
diplomacy, 34–35, 70–71, 149
direct foreign investment, 231
disclosure, 189
Disney company, 275
Dispute Settlement Body (DSB), 312, 313
dispute settlement mechanisms, 138, 147,
  312–314, 342–356
  See also arbitration
divine rights doctrine, 80
Dogan, Mattei, 73
Doha Development Agenda, 412
Dole, Robert, 316
dollar (U.S.), 118–119, 120, 212, 256
dollarization, 384
domestic content rules, 324
domestic credit creation, 206
domestic money supply, 206
domestic politics, 70
"Domestic Regulation: Necessity and
  Transparency" (confidential document),
  129

Dornbusch, Rudiger, 210
DOS operating system, 274
double movement theory, 91–92
Draft Code of Conduct on Multinational
  Corporations, 293
Draft Convention on Foreign Property,
  301
drugs, low-cost, 411–412
Dunning, John, 98, 273
Dutch East India Company (VOC), 47,
  170, 277
Duvalier, Jean-Claude, 377

e-banking, 159
e-commerce, 159
Earth Rights International, 358
East Asia
  capital controls, 385
  economic models, 253
  economic zone, 412–416, 420, 423
  economies of, 19, 127
  FINANCIAL CRISIS
  causes of, 124, 231
  contagion effects, 215, 232
  IMF response to, 210, 214–215, 235
  reasons for, 239–240
  results of, 209
  U.S. aid to, 293
  See also Asia
East Asians, society, understanding of, 79
East India Company (Dutch), 47, 170, 277
Eastern Europe, 353
ECAs (export credit/investment insurance
  agencies), 346
Echeverria, Luis, 301
eco-imperialism, 346–347
economic adjustments, 33
  See also structural adjustment programs
economic aid. *See* foreign aid
Economic Analysis of the Law (Posner), 170
economic analysis of the law (EAL)
  approach, 170–172
Economic and Financial Organization
  (League of Nations), 108
economic crises. *See* banking crises; financial crises
economic development, 188–191
economic efficiency, 36–37, 85, 124, 170–172
  See also markets, efficiency of
economic growth, 418
economic imperialism, 316
economic law. *See under* law
economic liberalism, 116–117
  See also neoliberalism

economic models, 62–65, 71–72, 75–76, 79, 241
economic nationalism, 272
economic restructuring, 43–46
economic theory. *See* finance theory; trade theory
economics
    as field of study, 73–74
    moral philosophy framing of, 430
    political economy, presumption of abandonment of, 73–74
    politics, relationship to, 156, 407
    rational choice models, 81
    as social science, 79–82
    usefulness, lack of, 74
economics and the law, 170–172
economies of scope, 268
The Economist, 300, 381
economistic analysis, 337
economists
    on environmental costs, 340–341
    mainstream, on Augmented Washington Consensus, 9
    neoclassical, views on politics, 75
    politics, views on, 18
    social issues, removal from efficiency considerations, 338
    uncertainty, views on, 18
economy
    global, oligopolization of, 272–273
    Keynes's explanation of, 245–246
    politics' place in, 70
    See also international political economy; world economy
Ecuador, 217, 358
education cutbacks, 426–427
Edwards, Sebastian, 237
efficiency. *See* economic efficiency; markets, efficiency of
Efficient Market Hypothesis, 25, 241
electronic funds transfer, 173
electronic-manufacturing service providers, 22–23
electronics industry, 426–427
elites, 3, 15–16, 425
Elizabeth, Queen, 171
embedded liberalism, 112, 131
emergent market economies. *See* developing countries
emissions. *See* greenhouse gas emissions
employment, 49–50
    See also unemployment; workers
"The End of Laissez-Faire" (Keynes), 33
Endangered Species Act, 343

Endangered Species Act (U.S.), 343
enforced cooperation. *See* coercion
Engels, Friedrich, 99
Enhanced Structural Adjustment Facility (IMF), 204
entrepreneurial diplomacy, 34–35
environment, 340–357
    collective action, recognition of importance of, 347
    corporate lobbyists on, strategies of, 354
    differentiated responsibilities for, 349
    disregard of, in multilateral agreement on investment, 401
    environmental costs, determination of, 340
    environmental disasters, 333
    holistic approach to, 347–348
    protection of, conditions supporting growth of, 332
    as side issue, 369–370
    spending on, 197
    trade and, 340–342, 349–350
    WTO panel decisions on, 342–356
    WTO's disregard for, 339
environmental activists, 356
Environmental Defense Fund, 355
equal treatment, 292, 401
Ericsson company, 61
ERT (European Round Table of Industrialists), 128, 305–306, 325
ERTFS (European Round Table of Financial Services), 128
Estrada, Joseph, 225
Ethyl Corporation, 371
EU. *See* European Union
eurodollar (euro), 116–117
eurodollar market, 121
Europe
    accounting, political regulation of, 180–181, 182
    banking practices, 241
    crony capitalism, 222
    information technology industry, 61
    isolation, end of, 276–277
    national regimes, Marshall Plan and, 115
    neoliberalism, appeal of, 127
    policy failings, 234
    trade models, 33–34
    U.S. influence on IMF, response to, 389
    U.S. manufacturing investments in, 280
    U.S. policy stance toward, during Cold War, 292
    Western, U.S. constraint on, 420
    World Bank, role in postwar recovery of, 185
    See also European Union; *specific countries*

European Bank (Internet bank), 225
European Central Bank, 257
European Coal and Steel Community Treaty, 116
European Commission, 116
European Round Table of Financial Services (ERTFS), 128
European Round Table of Industrialists (ERT), 128, 305–306, 325
European Union (EU)
  agricultural subsidies, 374
  antidumping actions, use of, 311
  benefits from, 136–137
  competition policy, 34, 283
  eurodollar, 116–117
  European Round Table of Industrialists and, 128
  Helms-Burton Act, challenge to, 330
  policy debate, corporate domination of, 137
  social agenda, decreased attention to, 127
  Social Fund, 285
European Unity, The Treaty on, 116
exchange rate regime, 222–227
exchange rates, 207, 254–255, 377, 384
  See also fixed exchange rate system; floating exchange rate system
exclusion, in international law, 171
executive branches, internationalist perspective, 291
export credit/investment insurance agencies (ECAs), 346
Export-Import Bank of the United States, 346
exports, 39, 261–262
Extended Fund Facility (IMF), 204
extraterritoriality, 174–175, 329–330, 342
ExxonMobil, 359

factor endowment model, 284, 285
fair trade, 32
FASB (Financial Accounting Standards Board), 182, 428
fashion, 23
fast track authorization, 371–372
FCN (Friendship, Commerce, and Navigation) treaties, 297, 298
FDI. See foreign direct investment
Federal Express company (FedEx), 268, 305
Federal Reserve Bank (the Fed), 123, 248–249
Federal Reserve Board of Kansas City, 62
Felix, David, 213, 233, 252
finance

free markets in, effects of structures of, 19
  as social construction, 230
  See also capital; financial system
finance theory, 221, 241
Financial Accounting Standards Board (FASB), 182, 428
financial architecture, new. See new financial architecture
financial controls. See capital controls
financial crises, 228–241
  capital market liquidity and, 124
  causes, 228, 248, 253–254, 374–375
  contagion effects, 135
  costs of, avoidance of, 252
  currency crises, 134–135
  effects, 248, 375
  GSEGIs' encouragement of, 222
  Keynes-Minsky view of causes of, 244–245
  lessons learned from, denial of, 209
  liberalization's effects on, 134–135
  mainstream economists' views on, 12–13
  models for, 33
  rescue plans, 254
  responses to, 238
  ubiquity, 240–241
  U.S. economy and, 19
  See also banking crises; East Asia, financial crisis; Latin America, debt crisis; Mexico; World Bank
financial cycles, 246
financial instability, 223, 244, 247
  See also financial stability
financial institutions, 46, 207, 209
  See also banks; Bretton Woods system; International Monetary Fund; World Bank
financial integration, 214–215
financial liberalization
  banking and currency crises, linking of, 134–135
  beneficiaries of, 233
  competitive liberalization, 299
  critics of, on GSEGIs, 190
  demands for, 235
  deregulation, difference from, 221
  developing countries' views of, 272
  differing approaches to, 190–191
  EFFECTS OF
    banks, foreign control of, 239
    on domestic politics, 257
  exchange rate regime and, 222–227
  growth-distorting nature, 250
  IMF's views on effects of, 214–215

increased crisis risk, 7
instabilities from, 107–108, 229
Keynes-Minsky perspective vs., 241–249
laissez-faire view of, 133
requests for reviews of, 25–26
reregulation, as evidence for, 234
on speculative bubbles, 247–248
wealth creation, as source of, in core
    countries, 377
See also capital controls
financial liberalizers, 190, 234
financial panics, 246–248
financial sector, 38, 141
See also banks
Financial Services Authority (Britain), 225
Financial Services International London
    Group (British Invisibles), 129
financial stability, 199
See also financial instability
financial stability forum (BIS), 177–178
financial stabilizers, 190–191, 234
financial system
    controls, costs of lack of, 250
    exchange rate regime, liberalization and,
        222–227
    financial crises, incidence of, 228–241
    government supervision of, need for, 233
    ineffective regulation of, 229
    Keynes-Minsky perspective, 242–249
    need for, 220
    new financial architecture, 373–416
    post–Bretton Woods, 220–258
    regulation, need for, 255–258
    regulation, risk and, 249–255
    social construction of, 230
    speculation's role in, 242
    state bailouts of, 391–392
    states, constraints on, 60, 151
    systemic risks, 254
    vulnerability, late twentieth century, 221
    See also Bretton Woods system; capital
        markets; fixed exchange rate system;
        markets
financialization of global economy, 24–25
financiers, 227, 232
Finch, C. David, 213
FISA (Foreign Sovereign Immunities Act),
    169, 367
Fisher, Stanley, 204, 231, 240, 388
fixed exchange rate system, 109, 111, 118,
    120, 185
Flextronics International, 22
floating exchange rate system, 120–121, 212
    financial instability, 223

purpose, 222
self-equilibrium of, 382
volatility, 383, 384
force, 27–28
forced labor, 368
Ford Motor Company, 280, 354
Fordist Model of industrialism, 267
foreign aid
    cutbacks in, during 1990s, 134
    politics of, 114–115
    purpose, 200
    reduction in (1990s), 271
    from U.S., 393, 396–397
foreign capital, local economies' control by,
    399
foreign currency debt, 231
foreign direct investment (FDI)
    flows of, 281
    growth of, 39, 269
    impact, 23, 269
    in service sector, 281
    short-term vs. long-term, 269–270
    theoretical analysis of, 269
    by TNCs, 280
    by U.S., 280, 281
    See also capital movements
foreign exchange trading, 121, 122–123, 124,
    222, 231
foreign investment, 195, 231, 314, 325,
    398–399
    See also foreign direct investment (FDI)
foreign reserves, 232, 255–256, 383–384, 416
Foreign Sovereign Immunities Act (FSIA),
    169, 367
foreigners, suits against, 357
forex transactions. *See* foreign exchange
    trading
forum non conveniens (common law doc-
    trine), 357, 367
Foss, Pal, 82
fossil fuel projects, 346
Framework Agreement, 308–309
Framework to Promote Financial Stability
    (Manila Framework), 413
France
    accounting standards, setting of, 180
    capital controls, 232–233
    corporate ownership in, 287–288
    gold-exchange standard, views on, 106
    standards, method for setting of, 66
    World Bank loans, requirements for,
        194
franchise production, 275
Franklin National Bank, 123, 175

free trade
  coercive nature, 263
  costs of, 307
  effects of, 283–284, 286, 287, 425
  era of, 278, 279
  fair trade vs., 32
  as GATT criterion, 342
  groups opposing, 286
  myth of, 278
Free Trade Area of the Americas, 372
free trade classical liberals, 93
freedom from want, 107
French National Accounting Council, 180
Frenkel, Stephen J., 336
Frieden, Jeffrey, 287
Friends of the Earth, 294, 345
Friendship, Commerce, and Navigation
  (FCN) treaties, 297, 298
Fuentes, Amado Carrillo, 224
Fuji Film company, 317
Fundamental Theorem of Welfare Eco-
  nomics, 241
futures markets, 249
  exchange rate regime and, 222–227
  growth-distorting nature, 250
  IMF's views on effects of, 214–215
  Keynes-Minsky perspective vs., 241–249

G-7 (Group of Seven)
  debt relief, actions on, 219, 393, 410
  developing countries, input from, 376
  on developing markets, transparency of,
    395
  Financial Ministers' report, 395
  foreign direct investment to low tax juris-
    dictions, 226
G-20 (Group of Twenty), 376, 389–390,
  421–422
G-22 (Group of Twenty-Two), 389
G-24 (Intergovernmental Group of
  Twenty-Four on International Mone-
  tary Affairs), 390n
G-77 (Group of Seventy-Seven), 133, 218,
  293, 301–302
GAAP (Generally Accepted Accounting
  Principles), 181, 182
game theory, 53–54, 56–57, 74, 166
gang of four East Asian economies, 280
Garcia, Frank, 361
Garrett, Geoffrey, 236
gas-electric hybrid cars, 355
gatekeeper functions, 288
GATS. See General Agreement on Trade in
  Services

GATT. See General Agreement on Tariffs
  and Trade
GCC (Global Climate Coalition), 351, 354
GDP. See gross domestic product
General Agreement on Tariffs and Trade
  (GATT)
  concentric club characteristics, 302
  core nations' preference for, 58
  core principal, 303
  developing countries' attitude toward,
    291
  dispute settlement mechanisms, 312, 313
  dispute settlement panels, environmental
    decisions, 342–343
  elements of, 296
  intellectual property, extension to, 320
  Latin American members, 303–304
  negotiating rounds, bilateral nature of,
    303
  problems with, 297
  rule-based regime, move to, 302–303
  sovereignty rights, reduction of, 304
  U.S. influence on, 303, 304–305
  See also World Trade Organization
General Agreement on Trade in Services
  (GATS)
  CSI's influence on, 11
  EU proposals, sharing of, with corporate
    leaders, 129
  importance, 324
  national treatment under, 324
  origins, 162
  sanctions under, 305
  U.S. desire for, 320
General System of Preferences (GSP), 309
general welfare. See social considerations
Generalized System of Preferences (GSP),
  293, 365–366
Generally Accepted Accounting Principles
  (GAAP), 181, 182
genetic erosion, 345
genetic material, patenting of, 321
George, Susan, 319
Germano-Japanese economic model,
  62–63, 64–65
Germany, 62, 66–67, 165–166, 180
Gershenkron, Alexander, 75
Gill, David, 132
Gilpin, Robert, 75
Global Business Dialogue on Electronic
  Commerce, 159
global civil society, 16, 100, 170
Global Climate Coalition (GCC), 351, 354
Global Compact (UN), 355

global financial governance restructuring,
211
global settlement currency, 110
global society, 41
global state, 146
global state economic governance institutions (GSEGIs)
ACTIONS
agreement enforcement, 162
debt repayment, enforcement of,
406–407
financial crises, encouragement of, 222,
229
financial liberalization, push for, 233,
234
intellectual property rights, role in
enforcing, 161
international state, role in emergence
of, 172
regime formation, intermediators in,
143
rent-seeking behavior, 86
sovereignty, granting of, 52
standard-setting, role in, 68
EXTERNAL VIEWS OF
American right-wing populists on, 316
environmentalists', 333
financial, secondary, 172
global social justice movement's, 28
moral authority, questioning of, 418
opposition to, 188–189
INFLUENCE
growth of, 29, 211
on national policy choices, 131–136
political significance, 162–163
on postwar economic order, 102–140
on regulations, 4
states, relationship to, 156
OPERATIONS
bases for, 154
central contradiction of, 26–27
as collection agencies, 122
as concentric club formation, 35
control of discussions of, 58
as courts of last instance, 166
democracy in, 182–183
extra-legal nature of, 26
formation of, participants in, 149
governments, reasons for membership
in, 58
as lenders, 408–409
missions of, 382–385
models of, 25–26
objectivity, end of pretense of, 389

purposes, 5, 129, 167
role of, as new constitutionalism,
207–208
stateness and, 5
U.S. policy, implementors of, 115
U.S. role in, 55
POLICIES
debt reduction plans, 410
development model, problems with,
423–424
disregard of past impact of, 377
on free trade, 284
liberal market economy bias, 65
on liberalization, 362
policy coordination among, 203
policy debate over, 216
political agendas of, 59
public choice theory, application of, 86
rule of law, support for, 198
strategy, critique of, 37
under rational choice theory, 84–85
See also Bank for International Settlements; International Monetary Fund;
World Bank; World Trade Organization
global system for mobiles (GSM), 61
global trade regime, 314–317, 397–398
global warming, 346, 354
See also greenhouse gas emissions
globalization, 15–38
agents of creation of, 41–42
characteristics, 41, 91
civil society approach to, 35
corporate, problems of, 356
debate on, 39–68
differing responses to, 99
fault line of, 43
governance frameworks for, 49
government's role in, 17
in history, 46–50
impact, 17–18, 44, 276
IPE as core issue of, 18
method of, 338
models of, 58
political nature of, need for recognition
of, 57
politics, role of, 15
process of, 421–425
responses to, 36–38, 423
rules of (See rules)
societal forces and, 91–94
technology and, 22
as term, defining of, 40–42
theorists on, separation among, 11
in world system terms, 47–48

globalization (*continued*)
　See also global state economic governance
　　institutions; *lex mercatoria;* sovereignty
globalization rules (verb) perspective, 16–17
Goh Chok Tong, 415
gold reserves, 203
gold standard, 106
　See also fixed exchange rate system; float-
　　ing exchange rate system
Golden Age of real output, 50
Golub, Philip, 120
Gonzalez, Carlos Hank, 224
Gore, Al, 411
Gourevitch, Peter, 70
governance
　central contradiction of, 26–27
　Cox on, 6
　definition of, 143–144
　global, 184, 248, 390
　global, biased nature of, 419
　good, 200–201, 396
　government vs., 147–148
　OECD's role in creation of, 131
　organizations providing, 289–330
　regimes and, 143–150
　role of, 288
　society and, 49
　universal mechanisms for, limitations of,
　　58–59
　See also European Union; global state
　　economic governance institutions;
　　International Trade Organization; sov-
　　ereignty; World Trade Organization
governance regimes, 13, 58–59, 104–105
　See also regime theory
governments
　autonomy, 43, 148 (See also sovereignty)
　under classical liberalism, 79–80
　corporations, partnerships with, 130–131
　effects of financial integration on, 214–215
　financial pictures of, 387–388
　globalization, role in, 17
　GSEGIs, outsourcing of functions to, 29
　legal immunity, 169
　under public choice theory, 83
　transnational capital, accommodation of
　　desires of, 29
　See also states
Gramsci, Antonio, 99
Gramscian theory, 99–101
Grant, Wyn, 143, 288
grants, debt restructuring as, 393
Grassley, Charles, 327
Great Depression, 110, 133, 243

greenhouse gas emissions, 346, 350–352, 352,
　355
Greenspan, Alan, 247–248
Greider, William, 227
grey market, 276
gross domestic product (GDP), 39, 63, 190,
　228–229
Grotius, Hugo, 170–171
Group of Seven. See G-7
Group of 20. See G-20
Group of 22. See G-22
Group of 77. See G-77
groups, under rational choice theory, 84
growth, economic, 418
GSEGIs. See global state economic gover-
　nance institutions
GSM (global system for mobiles), 61
GSP (General System of Preferences),
　309
Guidelines for Multinational Enterprises
　(OECD), 405
guilds, medieval, 160
Gwin, Catherine, 193
Gyllenhammar, Pehr, 128

Haberler, Gerhard, 243
Haggard, Stephen, 214
Hague Conference (Sixth Conference of
　the Parties), 350
Hamilton, Alexander, 137
Hanlon, Joseph, 406
Hapsburgs, 150–151
hard law, 68, 146, 154
　See also soft law
Hare, Bill, 350
harmonization, 60–62, 65–68, 94–95
Harrod, Roy, 243
Hartridge, David, 306
Hashmi, Sohail, 357
Havana Charter (of ITO), 291, 292, 364
Hayek, F. A., 243
hazardous wastes, trade in, 345
　See also pollution
health services, 318–319
Heavily Indebted Poor Country (HIPC)
　Initiative, 390n, 395, 423
Heckscher-Ohlin trade model, 261–262
hedge financing, 245, 246
hedge funds, 178, 378
hegemonic power, 32, 101, 117, 328, 420
hegemons, 2, 5, 18–21, 142
　See also neoliberalism (Washington Con-
　　sensus)
Helleiner, Gerald, 397–398

Helleiner, Stephen, 209
Helms-Burton Act (Cuban Liberty and Democratic Solidarity (Libertad) Act), 329–330
Helpman, Ethanan, 264
Henderson, Hubert, 107
Herstadt Bank, 123
Herstatt National Bank, 175
hierarchical capitalism, era of, 98
Higgott, Richard, 43
high politics, 6
high technology, 61
Hinojosa-Oeda, Raul, 138
HIPC (Heavily Indebted Poor Country) Initiative, 390n, 395, 423
historical contexts, economic theory and, 243
Hizon, Ernesto, 310, 321
Ho, P. Saiwing, 325
Hobbes, Thomas, 80
Hobsbawm, Eric, 48
Holland, 156
    See also Dutch East India Company
home country control, 257, 258
Honda company, 355
Hong Kong, 280, 414
horizontal trade, 263
hotel companies, 275
House of Morgan, 107
human rights, 36–37, 357–359, 406
    See also labor rights
Huntington, Samuel, 20
Hurrell, Andrew, 35

IAIS (International Association of Insurance Supervisors), 179
IASC (International Accounting Standards Committee), 179, 181
IBM, 274
IBRD (International Bank for Reconstruction and Development), 192, 195
ICAs (international commodity agreements), 295–296
IDA (International Development Association), 192
ideas, socially important, 161
identity politics, 56, 153
IFIs (international financial institutions), 207, 209
IFROs (international financial regulatory organizations), 179–180
illegal activities. See corruption
IMF. See International Monetary Fund
immunity (legal), 149–150, 169

imperialism, 56, 316
    See also colonialism
import substitution strategies, 137, 270–271
imposed regimes, 58
income distribution
    1930s vs. 1980s and 1990s, 110
    adjustment strategy on, 285–286
    during business cycles, 245
    inequalities in, 418
    international trade and, 283–288
    in Mexico, in 1990s, 135–136
    social protection and, 286
    See also wealth
India
    Bangalore, software production in, 264–265
    conquest of, 277
    during East Asian financial crisis, 215
    fossil fuel projects, 346
    at GATT meeting (1982), 304
    nationalist orientation, 127
    regime clubs, preparation for joining, 68
individuals, 37, 43, 79–80, 90, 332
Indonesia, 300, 359, 363
industrial codes, 159
industrial revolutions, 47, 267
industrial workers, 267
industrialists, European, 128
industry self-regulation, 163–164
    See also lex mercatoria
inequality, 50, 51, 56, 58, 203, 209
infant industry strategy, 137
inflation, 106, 119, 201
information technology, 22, 61, 65–66
innovation, 20
instability, 223, 244, 247
institutionalists, in IR and IPE, 75
institutions
    forces acting on, 89
    international, 34, 35, 301
    left and right hand institutions, 27
    political economy, importance to, 90–91
    under rational choice theory, 84
    social structure context for, 97–98
    socially efficient, 88–89
    See also financial institutions; global state economic governance institutions; International Monetary Fund; left hand institutions; liberal institutions; non-state institutions; United Nations; World Bank; World Trade Organization
Instituto per la Ricostruzione Industriale (IRI), 116
integration, global, 22–23
intellectual capital, 318–319

intellectual property rights (IPR), 160–162
    agreements on, 320
    defense of, 268
    disputes over, 322
    human rights vs., 36–37
    importance, 323
    international state enforcement system
        and, 29
    nature of, 59
    under neoliberalism, 187
    new definitions of, 318–319
    rules on, 16–17
    sovereignty vs., 105
    under TRIPs, 320–322
    U.S., importance to, 315
    U.S. protection of, 160–161, 290, 300,
        320, 323
    See also lex mercatoria
Inter-American Coffee Agreement, 293
Inter-Governmental Panel on Climate
    Change, 354
Interbrand company, 273–274
interconnectedness, 39
interest rate uncertainty, 250
Intergovernmental Group of Twenty-Four
    on International Monetary Affairs (G-
    24), 390n
Internal Revenue Service (U.S.), 250
International Accounting Standards Com-
    mittee (IASC), 179, 181
international arbitration, 158, 165–166
International Association of Insurance
    Supervisors (IAIS), 179
International Bank for Reconstruction and
    Development (IBRD), 192, 195
    See also World Bank
International Chamber of Commerce, 165,
    307, 354, 355
international commodity agreements
    (ICAs), 295–296
International Confederation of Free Trade
    Unions, 365, 368
International Development Association
    (IDA), 192
International Finance Corporation, 192
international financial institutions (IFIs),
    207, 209
    See also International Monetary Fund;
    World Bank
International Financial Institutions Advi-
    sory Commission (Meltzer Commis-
    sion), 393–394
international financial regulatory organiza-
    tions (IFROs), 179–180

international financial system. See financial
    system
International Labor Code, 365
International Labor Organization (ILO),
    294, 301, 364–365
international law
    on arbitration, 158
    biases in, 168
    changes in nature of, 51
    description of, 154
    founding document of, 170
    on GSEGIs, 149
    under multilateral agreement on invest-
        ment, 403
    national law, supplantation of, 156
    public, 157
    See also lex mercatoria
International Monetary Fund (IMF),
    203–219
    ACTIVITIES
    debt recycling, 410
    debt writeoffs, lack of, 219
    Ecuador, loans to, 217
    goal of, 205–206
    Independent Evaluation Office, 393–394
    influence of, 208
    information gathering capacities, 136
    loans, 215, 217
    loans from, 393
    reforms, institution of, 387
    rescues by, 216–219
    stability, promotion of, 385–396
    See also conditionality; World Bank
    characterizations of, 122, 185, 204, 210
    EXTERNAL RELATIONS
    Asian economic zone as challenge to,
        413–414
    GSEGIs and, 382–385
    Russia, effects of demands on, 190
    United Nations, competition with,
        185–186
    U.S. Congress's acceptance of, 113
    U.S. influence on, 210–211, 379, 389
    World Bank, relationship to, 198–199,
        202, 203
    FINANCIAL CRISES
    announcements of, 388
    banking crises, costs of, 229
    early warnings of, 232
    East Asian, 235, 385
    rescue plans for, 254
    role in, 135, 209–210
    study of, 228
    views on reasons for, 241

ORGANIZATIONAL ISSUES
creation of, context for, 87
evolution, stages in, 212–214
funding of, 204–205
influences of and on, 4
membership rules, proposed, 109
mission of, 212–213, 382–383, 391
operations, method of, 205
organization of, 203–204
resources supporting, 203–204
strategic orientation, 199
subsidiary organizations, 204
POLICIES, 108
bias of, 379
on capital flows, 230–231
on credit creation, 206
on criminal funds, 377–378
debate on, 216
logic of, 208–212
problems of, 209–210
results of, 24
PROBLEMS WITH
bureaucrats' accountability, lack of, 207
criticisms of, 375
lending model, 206–207
market discipline, need for, 205
opposition to, 110, 111, 211–212
programs, domestic costs of, 211
International Monetary Fund (IMF)
Agreement, 109, 113, 212, 213–214, 388
International Organization of Securities
Commissioners (IOSCO), 179
international political economy (ipe)
crises in, source of, 103
future of, 417–428
influences on, 30–31, 59
power, distribution of, GATT on, 308
rules governing, restructuring of, 172
violence capacities, 16
See also mainline political economy; mainstream political economy
international political economy, academic
study of (IPE)
academics' role, own view of, 30
as American social science, 71
core issues, 17–18, 60, 154, 362
democratization of, 35
differing approaches to, 79
economics, as social science, 79–82
emergence of, 72–77, 79, 426
Gilpin on, 75–76
goal of, 94
Gramscian theory, 99–101
GSEGIs, model of, 25

idealism vs. realism in, 30
international politics and economic issues,
framing of, 6
international relations' role in, 77–79
mainline political economy and, 83–88
nature and scope of, 69–101
origins, 31, 77–78
overview, 30–33
PROBLEMS WITH
corporate and legal theory, lack of
attention to, 170
narrowness, 31
theorizing, issues absent from, 98
transnational corporations, lack of
attention to, 266, 288
U.S.-centrism of, 75
world trade, lack of understanding of,
311
rediscovery of, 78
social choices, treatment of, 88–91
state-centric focus, 30–31
international regimes, 55, 105, 144, 188
international relations (IR)
as American social science, 71
bifurcation of, 36
domestic politics, relationship with, 70
as field, emergence of, 77–79
law-centrism, 349
most important issue in, 43–44
political economy, isolation from, 78
sovereignty story, creation myth of, 150–151
international state, emergence of, 172
international systems, 29, 70
international trade, efficiency assumption.
See efficient market hypothesis
International Trade Administration (U.S.),
305
International Trade Organization (ITO),
185, 291, 294–297, 304
internationalists, attacks on, 189
internationalization, 46
See also globalization
Internet, 409
interoperability, 274
investment, 255, 398–406
See also foreign direct investment (FDI);
foreign investment; multilateral agreement on investment; speculation
investment agreements, 167
investment banks, 249
investment regime, 315
investment vehicles, 276
investors, 181, 370–371
ipe. See international political economy

IPE. *See* international political economy,
    academic study of (IPE)
IR. *See* international relations
Iraq, 53, 299–300, 426
Irwin, Douglas, 339
Italy, 46, 116, 156, 232–233, 292
ITO (International Trade Organization),
    185, 291, 294–297, 304
    1930s vs. 1980s and 1990s, 110
    1930s vs. 1980s and 1990s, 110

Jackson Hole Wyoming Symposium (Fed-
    eral Reserve Board of Kansas City), 62
Japan
    accounting standards, setting of, 180
    Asian economic zone, efforts on, 412–413
    banking practices, 241
    bilateral trade agreements, 415
    capital controls, 232–233
    Committee on Trade and Investment,
        306
    keiretsu system, 317
    market policy, postwar years, 272
    per capita income growth, 62
    standard coordination in, 65–66
    U.S. constraint on, 420
Japanese Federation of Economic Organi-
    zations (Keidandren), 306
Jerusalem, 53
The Johns Hopkins University, 77
Johnson Administration, 119
Joint Declaration of the Seventy-Seven
    Developing Countries, 301–302
Jordan, Michael, 363
Juarez drug cartel, 224
Jubilee 2000, 409
jus cogens norm, 367
justice, 85, 336, 362, 424
justice movements, 16, 409
    See also social justice movements
justice systems, 157

Ka Hsaw Wah, 358
Kahler, Miles, 390
Kaminsky, Graciela L., 135
Kantor, Mickey, 317
Kapstein, Ethan, 117
Kapur, Devesh, 207
Keidandren (Japanese Federation of Eco-
    nomic Organizations), 306
keiretsu system, 317
Kellner, Irwin, 230
Ken Saro-Wiwa, 358
Kennan, George, 103

Kennedy, John F., 293
Kennedy Administration, 121
Keohane, Robert O.
    on global debate, participants in, 49
    on institutions and regimes, 90
    neoliberal institutionalism, 74
    on realism, 94
    *Transnational Relations and World Poli-
        tics,* 73
    utility maximization, criticism of, 85
Keynes, John Maynard
    on capital mobility, 125
    on economic policy making, 33
    on the economy, 245
    financial controls, preferences in, 109, 110
    on financial openness, 48
    on gold standard, 110
    Hayek on, 243
    on IMF, 215
    monetary reform proposals, 111–112
    policies, opposition to, 111
    on Ponzi-style financing, 246
    "Proposals for an International Currency
        Union," 238
    on speculation, 242
Keynes-Minsky finance theory, 221, 241–249
Keynesian Revolution, 243
Keynesianism, National, 33, 118, 132–133,
    287, 290
Keynesianism, peripheral, 117
Killick, Tony, 208–209
Kim Woo Choong, 253
Kindleberger, Charles, 73
kings, sovereignty of, 151
Kissinger, Henry, 123
kleptocracies, 407
klimasvindel (climate fraud), 352
Knight, Philip, 363
knowledge-based economies, 268
knowledge differences, 265
Kodak company, 317
Korea, 232–233, 253
Kozul-Wright, Richard, 271
Kozyrev, Andrei, 44
Krasner, Stephen, 144, 146, 147, 207
Krueger, Anne, 115, 296, 335, 392
Krugman, Paul, 284, 385
Kyoto Accord (Kyoto Protocol), 346, 348,
    350, 352–354

labor
    costs of, consumer elasticity on, 336–337
    disregard of, in multilateral agreement on
        investment, 401

mobility of, vs. capital mobility, 287–288
See also workers
labor law, 166
labor markets, 24, 336, 359–360
labor rights
  in developing countries, 359–362
  growth, conditions supporting, 332
  market efficiency vs., 359–372
  in NAFTA, 370
  at Nike plants, 363
  as property rights, 367–368
  public activism on, 362–364
  as side issues, 369–370
labor standards, 335–337, 364–366, 370
laissez faire, 91, 98, 290
late industrializers, 320, 399–400
Latin America
  Calvo Doctrine, preference for, 292
  debt crisis (1982), 124, 224, 251–252,
    270–271, 304
  European encroachments, response to, 169
  as GATT members, 303–304
  neoliberalism, perception of failure of, 139
  policy failings, 234
  social accommodation, 117
  U.S. foreign direct investment in, 280
law
  definition of, 154
  democratic accountability, loss of, 179
  economic analysis of, 170–172
  etymology of term, 154
  forum non conveniens (common law doc-
    trine), 357, 367
  jus cogens norm, 367
  literature on, 32
  rule of, 8, 348–349
  theory on, 156–157
  TYPES OF
    competitiveness laws, 317
    contract law, 46, 67, 317
    economic law, 331–332
    labor law, 166
    local law, 160
    merchants' (*See lex mercatoria*)
    private law, 105, 156, 159, 164–165
    public law, 156, 157
    transnational, 156, 366–369
  WTO's creation of, 339
  See also hard law; international law; pri-
    vate law; soft law
Law, David, 207, 371
law and economics tradition, 170–172
law merchant. *See lex mercatoria* (merchants' law)

law of one price, 276
Law of the Sea Convention, 301
leadership, U.S. exercise of, 13–14
  See also hegemonic power
League of Nations, 106–107, 108
Lee, United States v., 169
left hand institutions, 27
left hand of the state, 26
legislative branches, protectionist perspective, 291
lender of last resort, 185, 204, 382, 386–387,
  393
level playing field theory, 265, 309, 318
leverage, 249
lex constructionis (construction contracting
  law), 159
lex maritima (maritime law), 159
lex mercatoria (merchants' law)
  contemporary, 34–35, 158–164
  deregulation and, 164–169
  developing countries' view of, 163,
    167–169
  extra-communal status, 155
  game theoretical view of, 166
  goals, 167
  growth, method of, 157
  GSEGIs as extension of, 167
  history of, 155–158
  importance, reasons for, 159
  as international law, 157
  Maniruzzaman on, 166
  multilateral agreement on investment as,
    404
  private international trade law, 159
  public good in, lack of, 164
  purpose, 166
  secret formulation of, 162
  soft law, comparison with, 155
  state power and, 157
  See also arbitration; intellectual property
    rights
lex mercatoria arbitralis (international arbitration law), 158
liberal ideal, 429
liberal institutionalism, 93–94, 94–99, 100
liberal institutions, 42
liberal market economies, 64, 65
  See also Anglo-American economic
    model
liberalism, 79–81, 98
liberalization, 221, 299, 318, 401
  See also capital account liberalization;
    deregulation; financial liberalization;
    trade, liberalization of

Liberalization of Trade in Services
     (LOTIS) committee, 129
libertarian free market conservatives, 189
licensing payments, 319–320
List, Frederich, 137, 278
Liu, C.K., 414–415
living standards, 252
loan capital, 136
lobbyists, 354
the local, 41, 45
local banks, 252–253
local law, 160
localisms, 45
Locke, John, 80
London Eurocurrency market, 118–119
Long Term Capital Management, 174,
     248–249, 249
losers, compensation of, 148
LOTIS (Liberalization of Trade in Ser-
     vices) committee, 129
Lott, Trent, 382
low politics, 6
low wage economies, 286
     See also developing countries

Maastricht Treaty (1991), 116
macroeconomic policy regime, 185, 235
macroeconomic policy trilemma, 254–255
Mahathir Mohamad, 346–347
MAI. See multilateral agreement on invest-
     ment
mainline political economy
  choice, context of, 82
  description of, 32–33, 71
  mainstream political economy, critique of,
     418
  pollution, approach to, 341–342
  public choice theory and, 83–88
  on social analysis power, 93
  social economy, relationship to, 89–90
  supporters of, 334
mainstream economists, 337, 339, 361–362,
     418
mainstream finance theory, 221, 265,
     271–272
mainstream political economy, 71–72, 81, 82,
     93, 145
Malaysia, 232, 384–385
Mali, 326
Maloum, Ibrahim, 327
Malthus, Thomas, 261
Manhattan, Dutch sale of, 277
Manila Framework (Framework to Pro-
     mote Financial Stability), 413

Maniruzzaman, Abul F. M., 166
Mankiw, N. Gregory, 62
Manuel, Trevor, 422
Manufacturers Hanover Trust, 123
manufacturing, 271, 281
     See also production
March, James, 34, 83, 84
Marcos, Ferdinand, 377
Mare clausum (Selden), 171
Mare liberum (Grotius), 170–171
Marine Mammal Protection Act (MMPA),
     342
market forces, 68, 151
market society, 92
markets
  under classical liberalism, 80
  concentration in, 272
  currency markets, 118
  deregulation of, 20
  EFFICIENCY OF
  deregulation and, 20
  environmental protection vs., 340–357
  and GSEGIs, 189
  issues affecting, 334–335
  labor rights vs., 357–372
  negotiation imbalances and, 310
  problems of, 248
  as a value, 337
  fetishization of, 230
  fundamental contradiction in, 206
  global, 48, 256–257
  good law, as test of, 170
  governance institutions, need for, 145–146
  imperfections of, 335–337
  increasing power of, 149
  labor markets, 24, 336, 359–360
  liberalization of, U.S. approach to, 318
  liberalized capital, impact of, 24
  power and, 58–60
  rationality, social justice vs., 43–44, 80
  regulatory framing of, 3
  resource allocation, 147
  self-expansion, 91–92
  social regulation of, 59–60, 92, 145, 340
  transparency, approaches to, 378
     See also bond market; capital markets;
        derivative markets; futures markets
Marshall, Ray, 284
Marshall Plan, 114–116, 252, 292
Marx, Karl, 99, 246–247
materialism, 97–98
Mattei, Ugo, 334
Mattel, 267
Maxwell, Sylvia, 214

May, Christopher, 161
McCloy, John, 194
McDonald's company, 275
McDonnough, William, 177
McKinnon, Ronald, 119
McNamara, Robert, 195
Medema, Steven G., 86
Medici bank, 46–47
medicines, low-cost, 411–412
Mediobanca, 116
Meinhausen, Malte, 350
Melloan, George, 390
Meltzer Commission (International Finan-
   cial Institutions Advisory Commission),
   393–394
mercatocracy, 158, 163, 164
merchant courts, 155
merchants' law. *See lex mercatoria*
Mercosur, 137, 299
Mercuro, Nicholas, 86
mergers and acquisitions, 272, 273, 274, 275,
   282, 428
   See also antitrust authority
Methanex Corporation, 371
Methodenstreit (Battle of the Methods), 77
Mexico
   financial crisis (1982), 191
   OECD, membership in, 131
   peso crisis (1994–95), 135–136, 177, 252
   yellow enola beans, U.S. patenting of, 322
MFN (most-favored-nation) provision (of
   GATT), 296, 303
Miami Summit of the Americas (1994), 138
microeconomic market regulation, 185
Middle East, 53, 407
military power, 420, 426
military rulers, 151
Milosevic, Slobodan, 225, 377
Minsky, Hyman, 242, 244, 246
mobile telephone standards, 61
models
   developmental state model, 68
   economic models, 62–65, 71–72, 75–76, 79,
   241
   factor endowment model, 284, 285
   of globalization, 58
   Mundell-Fleming economic model,
   254–255
   neoclassical growth model, 75–76, 424
   rational actor model, 88–89, 332
   trade model, 261–262
   trade models, 33–34, 260
momentum trading, 249
monetarism, as necessary evil, 34

monetary policy, 236, 242, 244
   See also capital controls
money laundering, 173, 189, 224–225
monoculture (agricultural), promotion of,
   345
monopolies, 145, 196, 277–278
Monsanto company, 350
Monterrey Finance for Development gath-
   ering, 186
Montesquieu, Charles de Secondat, Baron
   De la Brède et de, 47
Moore, Michael, 422
moral economy, 132
moral society, 87
Morgan, J. P., 107
Morocco, 300
Morrison, Charles, 414
most-favored-nation (MFN) provision (of
   GATT), 296, 303
motorcycles, 322–323
multi-domestic corporations, 273
Multifiber Arrangement on Textiles and
   Clothing, 307, 310
multilateral agreement on investment
   (MAI), 399–406
   Camdessus on, 375
   concentric club characteristics, 403
   individuals, status under, 403
   NGOs, status under, 403
   opposition to, 405, 423
   purpose, 300
   secrecy of negotiations for, 376, 400–401
   social rights enhancements for, 405
   TNCs, favoring of, 400
Multilateral Investment Guarantee Agency,
   134, 192
multilateralism, 14, 299–300, 312
   See also unilateralism
multinational banks, 252–253
multinational corporations
   awareness of, 280
   Draft Code of Conduct on Multinational
   Corporations, 293
   fixed exchange rates, influence of, 118
   growth, 33
   index of, 276
   influence, 266–267
   OECD guidelines on, 293–294
   output, size of, 24
   See also transnational corporations
Mundell-Fleming economic model, 254–
   255
Murphy, Craig N., 75, 226
Muscovy Company, 47

Muslims, 53
Myanmar (Burma), 357–358, 366, 368

NAFTA (North American Free Trade
    Agreement), 137, 138–139, 285, 369–372
Naon, Horacio A. Grigera, 138
Nash equilibrium noncooperative games,
    74
National Accounting Code (France), 180
National Keynesianism, 33, 118, 132–133, 287,
    290
National Treatment (in GATT), 296
nationalisms, 153–154, 272
nations. See states
negotiations, orderly, 104
neo-Gramscians, 56, 75
neo-institutionalism (new institutionalism),
    83–84
neoclassical economics, 81–82
neoclassical economists, 75, 335
neoclassical growth model, 75–76, 424
neocolonialism, 151
neoconservatives, 429
neoliberal institutionalism, 74
neoliberal market civilization, 100
neoliberal order, 64
neoliberalism (Washington Consensus)
    assessments under, nature of, 25
    on capital costs, 249
    criticism of, 186–187
    effects of, 103, 381, 429
    failures of, 3, 139, 187, 202–203, 418–419
    global, 33
    globalization and, 17
    Gramscians on, 100
    of IMF, problems with, 213
    implementation of, political nature of,
        419
    interventionist nature, 211
    neorealism, convergence with, 74
    new financial architecture as, 391
    Polanyi on, 91
    policy elements, 186–187
    post–World War II views of, 107
    pressure for, 127
    property rights under, 93
    as rent seeking, 187
    social systems and, 103
    success, 191
    tenets of, 3
    See also neoliberalism
neorealism, 74
Netherlands Antilles, 223–224, 227
network effects, 274

new constitutionalism, 132, 375
New Deal perspective on international
    order, 33
new economy, 22, 63–64
new financial architecture, 373–416
    Asian economic zone, 412–416
    contradictions of, 390–391
    debt relief, 406–412
    discussions on, limitations of, 391
    formation of, 376–379
    limited content of discussions of, 398
    multilateral agreement on investment,
        300, 375, 376, 398–406
    nature of, questions concerning, 386–387
    problems facing, 390
    progressive, characteristics of, 396
    reforms, 379–382, 424, 425
    stability, IMF and promotion of, 385–396
new institutionalism (neo-institutionalism),
    83–84
New International Economic Order
    (NIEO), 218, 293
new political economy, 82
New World Order, 55
New York Federal Reserve Bank, 174
The New York Times, on exchange rate
    management, 113
NGOs (nongovernmental organizations),
    16, 314, 403
NIEO (New International Economic
    Order), 218, 293
Nigeria, 377
Nike company, 267, 281, 362–363
Nixon, Richard, 119, 120, 382
Nixon Administration, 212
Nokia company, 23, 61
non-European world, 51–52
    See also Asia; developing countries; East
        Asia; Japan; Latin America
non-U.S. capitalist developments, 103
nonaligned movement, 133
    See also developing countries
noneconomic issues, corporate minimiza-
    tion of, 170
nongovernmental organizations (NGOs),
    16, 314, 403
    See also global state economic governance
        institutions
nonreciprocity, 308
nonstate actors, 30
    See also global state economic governance
        institutions
nonstate institutions, 55–56
normative internationalism, 187

norms, 144, 154
North, Douglass, 74
North American Free Trade Agreement
    (NAFTA), 137, 138–139, 285, 369–372
Nurske, Ragnar, 242–243
Nussbaum, Bruce, 420
Nye, Joseph S., 49, 73, 115

odious debt, 408
OECD countries, 374
Office of Foreign Assets Control (U.S.),
    173
offshore activities, 178, 223–224, 225–226,
    239, 249
oil companies, 357–359
old-economy industries, 22
oligarches banks, 229
Olsen, Johan, 34, 83, 84
Omnibus Trade and Competitiveness Act,
    328
O'Neill, Paul, 226, 249, 380, 381
OPEC (Organization of Oil Exporting
    Countries), 119, 123, 294
openness, 48, 124, 215, 241, 251
    See also transparency
Operation Bambi, 116
Operation Infinite Justice, 53
OPIC (Overseas Private Investment Cor-
    poration), 346
oppositional politics, 36
Organization for Economic Cooperation
    and Development (OECD)
    Declaration on International Investment
        and Multinational Enterprises, 134
    Guidelines for Multinational Enterprises,
        405
    importance, 131
    liberalization codes, 291
    member countries' growth rates, 62
    multilateral agreement on investment,
        preparation for, 401
    multinational corporations, guidelines on,
        293–294
Organization of Oil Exporting Countries
    (OPEC), 119, 123, 294
organizations. See corporations; global state
    economic governance institutions; insti-
    tutions
Ottoman Empire, 154
Our Common Future (Brundtland Com-
    mission), 347–348
out-in lending, 239
out-out lending, 239
outflows. See capital flight

outsourcing, international, 23–24
over-lending, 253–254
overinvestment, 50
overseas investments, of U.S. companies,
    279
overseas postings, 279
Overseas Private Investment Corporation
    (OPIC), 346

Pacific Economic Cooperation Conference,
    414
Pakistan, 218
Panitchpakdi, Supachai, 7
Paris, Treaty of (1951), 116
parliament of banks, 255
Partnership for Climate Action, 355
Patel, Dipak, 327
patents, 160, 161, 322, 323
Patten, Chris, 426
Patterson, Matthew, 41
Peace of Westphalia, 150
Pearl Jam (rock group), 274
Peetz, David, 336
pegged exchange rate policy, 384
per capita income, 62, 64
peripheral economies, 279
    See also developing countries
peripheral Keynesianism, in Latin America,
    117
Peruzzi (Italian family), 47
peso crisis (Mexico, 1994–95), 135–136, 177,
    252
petrodollar recycling, 123
Pew Center on Global Climate change, 355
Pew Global Attitude surveys, 9
pharmaceutical companies, 411–412
Pharmaceutical Research and Manufactur-
    ers of America, 162
pharmaceuticals, trade determinations on,
    345
Philippines, 300
Pigou, Arthur C., 341
Pinochet, General, 194
piracy, intellectual, 322–323
Plender, John, 257–258
Polak, Jacques, 202, 206
Poland, 194, 280
Polanyi, Karl, 91–92, 131
policy analysis, 76
policy coordination, 20–21
policy making, 33
political economy
    core issue of, 149
    influences on evolution of, 47

political economy (*continued*)
  nature of, 90
  See also mainline political economy; main-
    stream political economy
political issues, in 1970s, 69–70
political parties, 79, 205, 287
political process (political discourse), 51, 86
political science, 89, 409
political scientists, 16, 75, 145, 188
political stability, 199
political voices, 42–43
politicians, 31, 82
politics
  civil society oppositional, 36
  economics, relationship to, 156, 407
  economy, place in, 70
  of escape, 227
  global, U.S. domination of, 10
  globalization, role in, 15
  individual preferences and, 37
  international, realists' view of, 78
  as market interference, 18–19
  social considerations and, 333
  trade conflict and, 328–330
  in WTO negotiations, 325
"Politics without Romance" (Buchanan), 83
pollution, 340–341, 345, 348, 351–352
  See also environment
Ponzi-style financing, 246
poor, 36–37
poor countries. *See* developing countries
Portes, Richard, 389
Posner, Richard, 170
postwar economic order
  Bretton Woods system, 108–113
  Bretton Woods system, end of, 118–124
  crisis in (1968–1975), 113
  description of, 12
  European Union, 116–117
  financial markets, resurgence of, 124–126
  governance regimes, 104–105
  GSEGIs and, 102–140
  Marshall Plan, 114–116
  pre-Bretton Woods orthodoxy, 106–108
  regional integration, 136–139
  statist economies, defensive posture,
    126–131
  Truman's economic proposal and, 103
  U.S.-centric nature, 103, 112
postwar international order, 33
poverty reduction, 195, 409
Powell, Colin, 397
power (authority)
  asymmetries of, 57, 97, 376
  concentration of, 39
  in decisionmaking processes, 58
  economic, inequality of, 59
  economists' views of, 72
  hegemonic, challenges to, 16
  private, *lex mercatoria* and, 155
  soft power, 115, 117, 128
  structural imbalance of, 310
Pratt, Edmund, 11
pre-Bretton Woods orthodoxy, 106–108
Prebisch, Raul, 301
Precautionary principle, WTO disregard of,
    339–340
preemptive war doctrine, 10, 425
President's Advisory Committee for Trade
    Policy Negotiations, 305, 306
President's Working Group on Financial
    Markets, 249
Presley, Mari, 313
price theory, 81
PriceWaterhouseCoopers, 182
principles, definition of, 144
private arbitration. *See* arbitration
private banking, 224
private law, 105, 156, 159, 164–165
  See also arbitration
private sector, World Bank loans to, 192
privatization, 196, 238
product liability, 334
product placement, 18
product safety, 339–340
production
  astatist nature, 46
  complex integration of, 267–268
  conditions of, market access and, 342
  economics of, 126
  neoclassical theory f, 260
  outsourcing of, 290
  spaces of, 22–24
  U.S. proportion of, 2
profit inflation, 63–64
Program of Action on the Establishment of
    a New International Economic Order
    (G-77), 301
property rights, 351–352, 362, 367–368, 402,
    411
  See also intellectual property rights (IPR)
"Proposals for an International Currency
    Union" (Keynes), 238
Proposals for the Expansion of World
    Trade and Employment, 294
protectionism, 106, 278, 285, 290–291, 374
  See also tariffs
public choice theory, 83

public goods, 25–26, 83, 142–143
public interest, 164
Public International Unions, 297
public law, 156, 157
public policy issues, 288
public services, 196
pure market society, 93

QUAD (United States, European Union, Japan, and Canada), 306
quality, workforce's effects on, 66–67

Raghavan, Chakravarthi, 325
railroads, 89
ratchet principle, 318, 403
rational actor model, 88–89, 332
rational choice theory, 74–75, 81, 82, 94
rational institutionalists, 54
rationalists, 75
rationalities, choice of, 337
R&D, U.S. proportion of, 2
Reagan, Ronald, 194, 250, 265, 279, 287
real output, slowing of growth of, 50
realism, 77, 78
Reebok, 364
regime theory, 54–58
    actors in, 55, 56
    GSEGIs, literature on public good of, 25–26
    neo-Gramscian, 56
    premises of, 74
regimes
    challenges to, 16
    change, 142, 429
    exchange rate regime, 222–227
    failures of, reasons for, 418
    formation of, 87, 172
    global, 184, 416
    global trade regime, 314–317, 397–398
    governance and, 143–150
    governance regimes, 13, 58–59, 104–105
    imposed, 58
    international, 55, 105, 144, 188
    investment regime, 315
    Krasner's description of, 146–147
    long prevailing, disintegration of, 100
    macroeconomic policy regime, 185, 235
    nature of, 144–145
    negotiations, unequal outcomes of, 29
    regulatory, 180
    repressive, 197–198, 224–225
    rule enforcement by, 144
    states as enforcers of, 21
    trade regime, 339–340

See also concentric club formation; global state economic governance institutions
regional integration, 136–139, 372
regulation
    of accounting, 180–182
    of banking, 173–179
    of IFROs, 180
    international, richer nation's views of, 34
    international market success and, 23
    labor markets, effects on, 359
    lack of, risk and, 249–255
    need for, 183, 255–258
    of offshore investment funds, 249
    of pollution, 340–341
    transnational corporations' influence on, 34–35
    See also capital controls; deregulation; harmonization
Regulation School, 98
regulators
    constraints on, 225
    in IFROs, 179–180
    knowledge, lack of, 251
    national, 251
    new technologies' effects on, 288
    private industry, relationship with, 179
regulatory regimes, 180
regulatory taking (expropriation), 299, 402
Reinhart, Carmen M., 135
rent seeking
    coercion of state policies as, 15
    by GSEGIs, 86
    locus of, 24
    neoliberalism as, 187
    theories of, under New Political Economy model, 82
rentier income, 377
Report on Minimal Standards (BIS), 175
"Report on Minimum Standards for the Supervision of International Banking Groups and Their Cross Border Establishment" (Basle Committee), 174
repressive regimes, 197–198, 224–225
Republicans (U.S.), 205
research, influences on, 283
research and development, U.S. proportion of, 2
resolution 1803 (UN General Assembly), 291
resource allocation, 147
return, maximization of, 227
reverse engineering, 320
Ricardo, David, 79, 260, 261, 262
rich countries. See core countries

right hand institutions, 27
right hand of the state, 26
rights, 4, 16, 85, 86–87
  See also human rights; intellectual property rights; labor rights
ringgit (Malaysian currency), 385
risk
  Basle Accord assessment of, 177
  of capital movements, 231
  diversification of, by TNCs, 273
  of IMF programs, 207
  and regulation, lack of, 249–255
  responses to, 244
  uncertainty, relationship to, 18
  of World Bank portfolio, 192
Robinson, Joan, 71, 263
Rodrik, Dani, 270–271, 284, 285, 338
Rogoff, Kenneth, 6
rollback provisions, 318, 402
Rome, Treaty of (1958), 116
Roosa, Robert, 121
royalty payments, 273, 319–320, 322
Rubin, Robert, 205
Ruggie, John G., 70, 107, 112
rule making, 159, 162
rule of law, 8, 198
rules
  definition of, 144
  fairness, 265–266
  from industry conferences, 158
  institutional, 90
  nature of, 16–17
  on property rights, 16–17
  under rational choice theory, 84
  social embeddedness, 3, 49
  See also globalization rules; law; *lex mercatoria;* norms; standards
rural development, 195
Russia
  financial abuses, 226
  IMF, acceptance of demands of, 190
  oligarches banks, 229
  oligarchs, actions of, 132
  pollution surpluses, 351, 352, 353
  regime clubs, preparation for joining, 68
Russian Central Bank, 226

Sachs, Jeffrey, 209
safety nets (financial), 396
Salinas Case, 224–225
Samuels, Warren, 86
Samuelson, Paul, 81
Sanders, Bernie, 344
SAPs. *See* structural adjustment programs

scarcity, construction of, 160
Schneider, Geoffrey, 201
Scholte, Jan Aart, 305
Schultz, George, 382
Schumpeter, Joseph, 75, 89
scientific revolution, third, 268
SDRs (Special Drawing Rights), 256, 396, 397
sea turtles, protection of, 343–344
Seagrams, 282
second industrial revolution, 267
secrecy, 176, 179–180, 400–401, 419–420
Securities and Exchange Commission, 223, 250, 427–428
securitization, 429
security concerns, 429
seedbanks, 322
seigniorage, 397
Seko, Mobutu Sese, 199, 377
Selden, John, 171
self-deregulation, 223
self-interest, 33, 155, 170–171, 309
self-regulating market, 92
Sell, Susan, 161
Semposa, Sampson, 163
September 11 terrorist attacks, 9
  See also war on terrorism
service sector, 281, 294, 305, 306, 318
  See also Coalition of Service Industries; General Agreement on Trade in Services
Seventy-Seven Developing Countries. *See* G-77
Shell company, 354, 358
shipping, speed of, 23
Shonfield, Andrew, 77, 147
short-term capital flows, 178, 383–384
shrimp, U.S. policies on, 343
Silicon Valley of India (Bangalore), 264–265
Simon, William, 382
Singapore, 7, 127, 280, 299–300, 412–413
Singapore issues (at Cancún WTO negotiations), 222
Singh, Kavaljit, 225–226
The Single Europe Act, 116
Sixth Conference of the Parties (Hague Conference), 350
skilled labor, 285
slavery, 368
small countries. *See* developing countries
Smith, Adam, 80, 87, 261, 278
Smoot-Hawley Tariff, 106
Social Charter (EU), 127
social considerations

in decisionmaking process, need for
    inclusion of, 149
economists' disregard for, 338
in globalization, 91–94
importance of, Wolfensohn on, 199, 201
market efficiency vs., 331–372
social choices, 88–91
social good, 36–37, 131–132, 160
social justice, 32, 43–44
social policy, 236, 335
social regulation, 165, 170, 337, 340
social spending, 196, 197
social welfare, collective, maximization of,
    148
WTO's disregard for, 339
See also social justice movements
social democracy, 93
Social Democrats, 79
social economy, 89–90
social justice movements
    global, 28, 423
    globalization problems, identification of,
        424
    nature of, 35
    objectives, 409–410
    on Uruguay Round Agreements, 330
    workers rights, support for, 361
social world, artificial vs. natural in, 93
societies
    basic principles in, 91–92
    differing norms of, 98–99
    global, 41
    global civil society, 16, 100, 170
    societal decisionmaking, importance of,
        90
soft law, 154–158
    Basle Committee as model for, 176
    description of, 68, 146
    enforcement mechanisms, 154–155
    importance, 419
    institutions creating, 175
    lex mercatoria, comparison with, 155
    priorities of, 361
    self-interest and, 155
    See also lex mercatoria
soft loans, 192
soft power, 115, 117, 128
software patenting, 323
Soros, George, 131, 223, 396
South Africa, 411
South Korea, 131, 210, 280, 293, 329
Southern African Customs Union, 300
Southern Cone, 214
sovereign borrowing, 229

sovereign chapter eleven, 378
sovereignty
    capital penetration of, 125, 421
    as commodity, 225–226
    of developing countries, 196
    devolution of, 45–46
    financial limits to, 47
    hypocrisy in, 51–52
    imperial past, 50–54
    INFLUENCING FACTORS
        finance sector, 178–179
        financial contagion, 152
        Foreign Sovereign Immunities Act,
            367
        global trading system, 314–317
        GSEGIs, 149
        humanitarian crises, 357
        IMF intrusions, 209, 210
        perpetual debt and, 393
        regime clubs, 68
        restrictions on, 152, 167, 272, 304,
            402–403
        U.S., 317
    IPE, as core issue of, 18
    labor issues and, 335
    legal redress and, 366
    Montesquieu on, 47
    nature of, 50–51, 60, 153–154
    property rights vs., 105
    states' surrender of, 167
    Treaty of Westphalia as codification of,
        150–151
    UN resolution on, 291
    U.S. respect for, during Cold War, 301
    of U.S., on environmental issues, 344
    See also concentric club formation; gover-
        nance; states
Sovereignty at Bay (Vernon), 73
Soviet Union, 103, 121
Special Data Dissemination Standard
    (SDDS), 387–388
Special Drawing Rights (SDRs), 256, 396,
    397
speculation
    financial liberalization's effects on, 250
    in foreign exchange transactions, 121–122,
        231
    in futures markets, 249–250
    hedge financing vs., 245
    Keynes on, 242
    need for control of, 19
    power of, growth in, 230
    problems of, 125
spices, monopolies of, 277

Standard and Poor's 500 companies, 428
Standard Oil, 282
standards
  in banking law, 174–177
  capital adequacy standards, 176, 177
  corporate role in, 159
  French method for setting, 66
  in Germany, 66–67
  harmonization of, 60–62, 65–68
  market approach to, 65, 66
  need for, 146
  treatment of, 161
  See also labor standards; rules
standstill provisions, 318, 402
Starbucks, 275, 363–364
stateness, 5, 34, 152–153, 162, 185
states
  ACTIVITIES
    actions of, under NAFTA, 402
    economic function, 98
    economies of, 220–221, 229, 255
    financial regimes, goals of, 385
    functions, new, 50–51
    global economy, role in, 6
    globalization, advocacy of, 51
    in globalization, transformation to, 59
  CHARACTERISTICS
    capital bias, 170, 290
    complex nature, 60
    differences among, rules and, 171
    inequality in, 51
    interconnectedness, as globalization, 41
    nature of, 5
    power, differentials in, 30–31
    sovereignty, loss of, 125, 153, 167
    stability, AIDS and, 45
    as unitary actors, 31
  Cox on changing role of, 57
  creation myths of, 150–151
  failed, 154
  financial system, bailouts of, 391–392
  governments, size vs. quality of, 201
  influences on, 31, 156, 266–275
  international, emergence of, 172
  left hand of the, 26
  origin myth, 80
  policies, 131–136, 323–324
  political economy and, 3
  private arbitration, benefit from, 165
  right hand of the, 26
  security, 44
  TREATMENT OF
    under multilateral agreement on invest-
      ment, 402

  under New Political Economy model, 82
  under public choice theory, 83
  undemocratic, 407–408
  See also sovereignty
statist development, theorists of, 57
status quo bias, 34
steel industry cartel, 307
Stephan, Paul, 179
Stephens, Philip, 8
sterling (currency), 118
Stern, Paula, 34–35, 130
Stiglitz, Joseph
  on capital market liberalization, 24, 25, 215
  on displaced workers, 272
  on IMF failures, 209–210
  on rules, fairness of, 265–266
  on trade policy, self-interest in, 309
Stockholm Declaration, 347
Stone, Katherine, 370
Strange, Susan, 57, 69, 70, 266, 288
strategic alliances, 126, 127, 275
strategic trade theory, 263, 319
Streton, Hugh, 283
strong states, influence, 5
Structural Adjustment Loans, 197
structural adjustment programs (SAPs)
  criticisms of, 188–189
  effects, 203, 209, 409
  failures, reasons for, 202
  objectives, ability to achieve, 208–209
  problems with, 197, 201
  World Bank's insistence on, 195–197, 200
structural adjustments, nature of, 186–187
structure
  agency vs., under public choice theory, 84
  constructionism on, 95–96
structured constraints, 98
sub-Saharan Africa, 326, 423
subsidies, 319
  See also rent seeking
Subsidy Agreement, 319
Summers, Lawrence H., 15, 18
Summit of the Americas, Miami (1994),
  138
super 301 amendment (1974 Trade Act),
  328, 329
Supplemental Reserve Facility (IMF), 204
surplus nations, 111
sustainable development, 349–350
Sutherland, Peter, 375
sweatshops, 335, 336
Switzerland, 257, 377
systemic fragility, 244
systems, international, 29, 70

TABD (Transatlantic Business Dialogue),
130–131, 306, 325
Taiwan, 280, 293, 412–413
Tanzania, 409
tariffs
ASEAN agreement on ending, 415
developing countries, importance to,
310
domestic production, as protection tools
for, 324
reduction of, 303
temporary, 285
in U.S., 307
See also protectionism
Tarullo, Daniel, 7
Tate, Jay, 161
tax avoidance, 189, 226, 227, 378–379
taxes, capital control tax, 121
taxpayers, 229
Taylor, Lance, 15, 19, 25
technology
computer industries, 126–127
cost reductions of, 22
diffusion vs. piracy of, 320
effects, 13, 284–285
globalization and, 22–23
illegal actions, influence on, 223
information technology, 22, 61, 65–66
network effects, 274
politics' effect on, 17
technology bubble, 63–64
telecommunications markets, 316–317
territorial boundaries, 43–44
territories, dependent, 51
terrorism. See September 11 terrorist
attacks; war on terrorism
textbooks, 266
Thailand, 124, 239
Thatcher-Reagan policy revolution, 33
theory
game theory, 53–54, 56–57, 74, 166
Gramscian theory, 99–101
price theory, 81
public choice theory, 83
rational choice theory, 74–75, 81, 82, 94
regime theory, 25–26, 54–58, 74
See also trade theory
Theory of International Politics (Waltz),
73–74
third industrial revolution, 47
Third Italy, 45
third scientific revolution, 268
Third World countries. See developing
countries

Thompson, Helen, 236
Ticketmaster, 274
Tietmeyer, Hans, 178
time-space compression, 48
Time Warner, 282
TNCs. See transnational corporations
Tokyo Round Declaration, 308
Tooze, Roger, 75
torschlusspanik (door-shut-panic), 246
TotalFina company, 288
Toyota company, 355
trade
authority structures for, 155–156
barriers to, 305–308 (See also tariffs)
benefits from, 283–284
civilizing nature of, 52
conflicts on, politics and, 328–330
dispute settlement, 312–314
early Western, history of, 277
environmental considerations and,
340–342, 349–350
fairness in, 338
goods vs. services, 294
growth, relationship to, 271
income distribution and, 283–288
international , during mercantilist age, 156
intra-firm, size of, 275
liberalization of, 130, 200
meaning of, 7
models of, 33–34, 260, 287
modern regulation of, 297–302
negotiations for, 279, 297–302
patterns of, historical context, 276–283
politicization of, 330
of pollution rights, 341
theories of (See trade theory)
vertical vs. horizontal specialization, 263
Zoellick on, 7
See also free trade; General Agreement on
Tariffs and Trade; intellectual property
rights; International Trade Organization; markets; World Trade Organization
Trade Act of 1974, 328, 329, 365–366
trade agreements
Agreement on Sanitary and Phytosanitary
Measures, 339–340
Agreement on Technical Barriers to
Trade (WTO), 339–340
bilateral investment treaties, 297–298
effects of, 26
fast track authorization, 371–372
social issues, consideration of, 333–334
TRIMs, 319, 320, 323–326

trade agreements (*continued*)
TRIPs, 161, 300, 311, 320–323, 324
Understanding on Rules and Procedures
Governing the Settlement of Disputes,
312
U.S. bilateral approach to, 298
See also General Agreement on Tariffs and
Trade; International Trade Organization; World Trade Organization
trade associations, 165
Trade Policy Review Mechanism (WTO),
339
trade regime, 339–340
Trade Related Investment Measures
(TRIMs), 319, 320, 323–326
trade theory
approaches to, 260–266
on comparative advantage, 263–264
early, on transnational corporations, 269
economists, influence on, 72
Heckscher-Ohlin trade model, 261–262
manufacturing export orientation, 271
presumptions of, 262
trade history, lack of attention to, 277
transnational corporations, lack of attention to, 266
transaction cost theories, 87, 96
Transatlantic Business Dialogue (TABD),
130–131, 306, 325
Transatlantic Partnership on Political
Cooperation and an Understanding
on Conflicting Requirements,
330
transnational capital, 29, 56, 325
transnational capitalist class, 273
transnational corporations (TNCs)
ACTIVITIES
environmental lobbying, 353–354
operating methods, 273
overinvestment by, 50
patents, use of, 322
advantages, 269, 273–274
freedom, 272
INFLUENCE
effects of, 274–275
growing dominance, 39–40
on income distribution, 283–288
national corporations, competition
with, 126
on regulations, 34–35
of representatives of, 130–131
on WTO, 306–307
influences on, 127, 362–364
investments, selectivity of, 280

multilateral agreement on investment
and, 399, 400
multinational corporations, comparison
with, 66
openness, favoring of, 98
piracy, losses from, 322–323
public policy issues, decisions on, 288
regulatory understanding of, 257
standards, need for, 61–62
the state and, 266–276
strategic alliances, 275
U.S.-based, duty of care, 357
world trade, domination of, 311
transnational law, 156
Transnational Relations and World Politics
(Keohane and Nye), 73
transparency, 19, 332, 378
See also openness
travel industry, 426
treaties, 167, 297, 298
Treaty Concerning the Creation of an
International Union for the Publication
of Customs Tariffs, 297
Treaty of Amity and Commerce with
France, 297
Treaty of Paris (1951), 116
Treaty of Rome (1958), 116
Treaty of Westphalia, 150–151, 152
The Treaty on European Unity, 116
trees, 350
Triffin, Robert, 119–120
Trilateral Commission, 240
TRIMs (Trade Related Investment Mea-
sures), 319, 320, 323–326
Tripartite Declaration of Principles Con-
cerning Multinational Enterprises and
Social Policy, 294
Tripartite Group, 179
tripartite planning, 292
TRIPs (Agreement on Trade Related
Aspects of Intellectual Property Rights),
161, 300, 311, 320–323, 324
Truman, Harry S., 103
Truman Administration, 114
Tuna/Dolphin I and II reports, 342
Turkey, 380
turmeric, 321
turtles, endangered, 343–344
Tussie, Diana, 329

Uganda, 410–411
UK. *See* United Kingdom
uncertainty, 18
See also risk

UNCTAD. *See* United Nations, Conference on Trade and Development
UNCTC (United Nations Center on Transnational Corporations), 293
undemocratic states, 407–408
Underhill, Geoffrey, 78
Understanding on Rules and Procedures Governing the Settlement of Disputes (WTO Agreement), 312
UNDP (United Nations Development Programme), 321–322, 404, 410
unemployment, 63, 107
See also workers
unilateralism
of Bush Administration, 10, 373, 375, 380, 420, 425–426
multilateralism vs., 14
of U.S., 20, 328, 329, 348–349
unions, 287, 359
See also International Confederation of Free Trade Unions
unitary state actors, 406
United Kingdom
banking agreement with U.S., 176
financial liberalization, advantages from, 233
GDP growth, 63
international financial regulatory organizations, control of, 179
standards, corporate approach to, 66
as trading empire, 278
See also Britain
United Nations
Bretton Woods institutions as competition to, 185–186
Center on Transnational Corporations (UNCTC), 293
Code of Conduct for Transnational Corporations, 301–302, 403–404
Conference on the Human Environment, 347, 348
CONFERENCE ON TRADE AND DEVELOPMENT (UNCTAD)
creation of, 293
on developing countries' manufacturing exports, 271
developing countries' preference for, 58
first, 133
influence of, 301
on intra-firm sales, 275
on multinational corporation output, 24
on world trade, TNC domination of, 311
Corporate Charter, 186

Development Programme (UNDP), 321–322, 404, 410
Economic and Social Council, 186
GATT, relations with, 308
General Assembly, 291
globalization, attitude toward, 43–44
Monterrey Finance for Development gathering, 186
venue shifting away from, 308
United States
FINANCIAL AND ECONOMIC AFFAIRS
antidumping actions, 311
Asian economic zone, actions on, 413
banking agreement with UK, 176
bilateral trade agreements, 297, 298–300
companies' overseas investments, 279
crony capitalism, 222
Cuba, cancellation of debt of, 408
domestic differences, 110–111
Europe, manufacturing investments in, 280
external debt, size of, 397
foreign direct investments, patterns of, 280–281
FOREIGN RELATIONS
Argentina, abandonment of, 380–381
coalition building, post–September 11, 389
foreign attitudes toward, 325–326, 407
Marshall Plan, 114–116, 252, 292
world opinion, isolation from, 397
INFLUENCE, 2
on accounting standards, setting of, 180
on Bank for International Settlements, 172
on Basle Committee, 177
Bretton Woods system, cause of end of, 119
on capital controls, 110–111
on East Asian financial crisis, 239–240
on GATT, 303, 304–305
global, 417
on globalization, 42, 57
on GSEGIs, 55
on IMF, 108, 210–211, 217–218
on intellectual property protections, 268
on international financial regulatory organizations, 179
on international trade regime, 289–290
laws, extraterritorial application of, 169
leadership, exercise of, 13–14
on service sector agreements, 306
on trade agenda, 269
on World Bank, 193–194
on WTO, 268, 305, 307

United States (*continued*)

INTERNAL FINANCE
consumer debt, growth in, 64
current account deficit, 64, 233, 427
defense spending, 2
economic health, 62–64
economic subsidization, 24
economy, problems of, 427–428
economy, size of, 2
foreign reserves, 256
GDP growth, 63
IMF, returns from, 205
inflation, cause of, 119–120
per capita income growth, 62–64
savings and loan crisis, 228, 229, 247
tariff rates, early twentieth century, 291
LABOR ISSUES
services, employment in, 294
skilled labor in, 285
unions in, 360
legal system, 317, 371
POLICIES
agricultural, 308, 326–327
AIDS, military planners' views on, 44–45
benefits from, 120–121, 233, 256
on capital, 110, 222
on competition, 317
on criminal funds, tracking of, 378
on deregulation, 226
on environment, 342
on Europe, during Cold War, 292
on financial crises, 389
on greenhouse gas emissions, 350–351
on human rights, 368–369
on IMF, 204
influences on, 290
on intellectual property rights, 160–161, 325
on international economic policy problems, 70
on investment regime, 315
on Iraq, 299–300
on ITO, 294
on labor rights, 365, 368–369
on liberalization, 25, 233, 235, 301
on neoliberal international governance regime, 99
on offshore investment funds, 249
preemptive war, effects of, 398
on property rights, 319–322, 411
on protectionism, 290–291
during Reagan era, 265, 287
security oriented nature of, 28
self-interest strategies, 103

on service sector liberalization, 294
on special drawing rights, 396, 397
on trade, 279, 300, 312, 315, 328–329
unilateralism of, 348–349, 420, 425–426
against United Nations system, 308
WTO, disregard for rules of, 328
POWER
dominance, 2, 8, 10
extraterritoriality, exercise of, 329–330
as hegemon, 18–21, 57, 115
legitimization of, 8
military power, 420
self-view on, lack of, 53
sovereignty, perceived loss of, 316
unilateralism, 7
success, reasons for, 19–20
United States government
Central Intelligence Agency, 292
Commerce Department, International Trade Administration, 305
Comptroller of the Currency, 123, 223
Congress, 113, 138, 291, 296, 329
executive branch, 316
Justice Department, 359, 400
Park Service, 322
Patent Office, 323
President's Advisory Committee for Trade Policy Negotiations, 305, 306
President's Working Group on Financial Markets, 249
Senate, 354
State Department, 116, 346
Trade Representative, 298, 310, 328
Treasury Department, 173, 224
United States v. Lee, 169
Unocal company, 357, 359
unskilled workers, 286
Uruguay GATT Round, 290, 307, 315, 325, 330
U.S. Business Roundtable, 306, 325, 354
U.S.-Chile Free Trade Agreement, 299
U.S. Steel, 282
USSR. *See* Soviet Union
utility maximization, 85–86

Van Apeldoorn, Bastiaan, 128
verification, of environmental projects, 351–352
Vernon, Raymond, 73, 259
VERs (Voluntary Export Restraints), 307, 310
vertical trade, 263
VHS video format, 274
video recording, 274

videodiscs, 322–323
Vietnam, 194
Viner, Jacob, 107
Vines, David, 200
Vivendi company, 282, 288
VOC (Dutch East India Company), 47,
    170, 277
volatility of floating exchange rates, 383, 384
Voluntary Export Restraints (VERs), 307, 310
vulture funds, 232

Wade, Robert, 214–215
Wæver, Ole, 71, 429
wages, 281, 284–285, 286, 335, 360
Wal-Mart, 268
Wall Street Journal
    on exchange rate management, 113
    on IMF, 205
Waltz, Kenneth, 73–74
want, freedom from, 107
Wapenhans Report, 200
war on poverty, 195
war on terrorism
    effects of, 7, 393, 426, 429
    free trade deals as tool in, 426
    funding, tracking of, 227
    GSEGI policy shifts and, 218
    international cooperation on, 28
    international discontent over, 9
    See also September 11 terrorist attacks
Washington Consensus. *See* neoliberalism
Watt, James, 160
weak states. *See* developing countries
wealth, 39, 86–87
    See also income distribution
wealthy, influence, 31
Webb, Michael, 20–21
Weingast, Barry, 85
welfare, 333
welfare states, 112
Wendt, Alexander, 43
West Africa, 326–327
West Bank (Israel), 53
Western economists, on foreign invest-
    ment, 325
Western Europe, market policy, 272
Western interests, 167, 181
Western trade, early history of, 277
Westphalia, Treaty of, 150–151, 152
Westphalian order, 43–44, 51, 150–153
Westphalian states, 152
White, Harry Dexter, 33
Wilcox, Clair, 296
Williamson, John, 186, 187

Williamson, Oliver, 74, 87
Wilshire 5000 Index, 63
Wilson, Harold, 118
Wilson, Woodrow, 152
Witteveen, Johannes, 123
Wolf, Martin, 62–63, 409, 420
Wolfensohn, James D., 186, 199, 201,
    422–423
Woods, Ngaire, 35
work hours, 63
workers
    bargaining power, 360
    globalization's effects on, 284
    industrial, 267
    international economy, shielding from, 36
    restrictions on, 368
    unionized, 285
    unskilled, 286
World Bank (*earlier* International Bank for
    Reconstruction and Development)
    ACTIVITIES
        convention of 1985, 134
        debt recycling, 410
        failures, lack of reporting of, 199–200
        financial crises, identification of, 228
        loans from, 195, 199–200, 393
        reforms, attempts at, 422
        renewable energy projects, 355–356
        Structural Adjustment Loans, 197
    annual reports, 196, 221
    IMF, relationship to, 198–199, 202, 203
    Marshall Plan, comparison with, 114
    ORGANIZATIONAL ISSUES
        accountability, 193
        criticisms of, 198–199, 201–202
        decision-making structure, 193
        growth of, 195
        as legal institution, 193
        U.S. influence on, 193–194, 210–211
        Wolfensohn's criticisms of, 186, 199, 201
    POLICIES
        emphasis, shift in, 195
        environmental priorities, criticisms of,
            345–346
        ideology, influences on, 192
        rule of law, support for, 198
        strategic orientation, 195–203
        structural adjustment programs, insis-
            tence on, 195–197, 200
    U.S. acceptance of, 113
    VIEWS
        on national governments, coercion of,
            148
        on social policy, 361

World Bank (*continued*)
　　on structural adjustments, problems of,
　　　197
　　on workers, international economy's
　　　effects on, 36
　　Wapenhans Report, 200
　　See also International Monetary Fund
World Bank Group, 191–194
World Business Council for Sustainable
　　Development, 354
World Court, 301
World Development Movement, 129
World Economic Forum, 305
world economy, 47, 112
World Health Organization, 345
world political economy. *See* international
　　political economy, academic study of
　　(IPE)
World summit for Social Development, 361
World Summit on Sustainable Develop-
　　ment, 397
World Trade Organization (WTO), 308–312
　　Americans' view on, 315–316
　　MEETINGS
　　　Cancún meeting, 326–328
　　　Doha meeting, 422
　　　Fourth Ministerial Conference, 412
　　　Seattle meeting, 333
　　OPERATIONS AND ACTIVITIES
　　　Advisory Committee on Trade and Pol-
　　　　icy Negotiations, 162
　　　civil society members, 305
　　　competitiveness laws, jurisdiction over,
　　　　317
　　　dispute settlement, 167, 312–314, 339,
　　　　342–356
　　　global trade regime stability, promotion
　　　　of, 397–398
　　　legal powers, precedents for, 302–303
　　　method of functioning, 87–88
　　　operating methods, 290
　　　role, as sheriff, 329

　　unfunded mandates, 338
　　ORGANIZATIONAL ISSUES
　　　concentric club characteristics, 306–
　　　　307
　　　context for creation of, 87
　　　focus of, 304
　　　future of, 326–328
　　　influences of and on, 4
　　　objections to, 305, 330
　　　political economy of, 313–314
　　　uniqueness, 325
　　　U.S. influence on, 268–269, 305, 307
　　POLICIES
　　　on antidumping duties, 311
　　　businesses' legal standing with, 67
　　　environmental costs, disregard for, 333
　　　favoring advanced economies, 309
　　　free market bias, 282–283
　　　on free trade, 318
　　　investment as core of, 315
　　　on labor rights, 364, 365
　　　neoliberalism, advocacy of, 290
　　　TNCs, support for, 311
　　　U.S. views, incorporation of, 319
　　　trade regime and, 339–340
　　World Trade Organization (WTO) Agree-
　　　ment, 339, 343
　　World Wide Fund for Nature, 355
　　WorldCom, 427
　　Worth Global Style Network, 23
　　Wriston, Walter, 223
　　WTO. *See* World Trade Organization
　　Wyplosz, Charles, 209

　　Yellowstone Park, 322

　　Zacher, Mark, 295
　　Zaire, 199
　　Zambia, 411
　　Zaring, David, 180
　　Zevin, Robert, 48
　　Zoellick, Robert, 7, 299, 327